# WINNING AT ALL COSTS

JOHN FOOT is Reader in Modern Italian History in the Italian Department, University College London. His previous books include *Milan since the Miracle: City, Culture and Identity* (2001) and *Modern Italy* (2003). He writes for the *Guardian,* the *London Review of Books* and the *TLS*. He lives in London and Milan.

# WINNING AT ALL COSTS

## A Scandalous History of Italian Soccer

## JOHN FOOT

NATION BOOKS · *New York*
www.nationbooks.org

Published by Nation Books
A Member of the Perseus Books Group
116 East 16th Street, 8th Floor
New York, NY 10003

Nation Books is a co-publishing venture of the Nation
Institute and the Perseus Books Group

First published in Great Britain in 2006 by Fourth Estate as
*Calcio: A History of Italian Football*. This edition first
published in 2007 by Nation books.

Books published by Nation Books are available at special
discounts for bulk purchases in the United States by
corporations, institutions, and other organizations. For more
information, please contact the Special Markets Department
at the Perseus Books Group, 2300 Chestnut Street, Suite 200,
Philadelphia, PA 19103, or call (800) 255–1514, or e-mail
special.markets@perseusbooks.com.

Library of Congress Cataloging-in-Publication
Data is available

ISBN–10: 1–56858–368–0
ISBN–13: 978–1–56858–368–6

10 9 8 7 6 5 4 3 2 1

*For my dad, who loved football,*
*and my son, who hates it*

# CONTENTS

Roberto Maestri (Sampdoria), Gabriele Maggio (Inter), Stefano Boeri (Inter), Stephen Allen (Everton), Jonathan Morris (Southampton/ Milan) and Pierpaolo Antonello (Juventus). Massimo Condolo (Torino) took me round the whole of Turin to various footballing sites. I have also enjoyed conversations about football with numerous other people in taxis, on trains and at grounds.

My wife Marina Arienti (Inter) has always been sceptical about this book, blocking my attempts to install Sky-Italia for more than a year and scoffing at my attempts to describe watching football as 'work'. Her non-fandom has been a healthy corrective to any signs of obsessive behaviour.

Thanks also to Alan Sedunary from Reading for some additional details, and to Massimo Gramellini, Pierre Lanfranchi, Gianfranco Petrillo, Massimiliano Boschi and Nick Dines, to Fiora Gandolfi Herrera, who sent me a lot of material on her late husband, Helenio Herrera, Nicholas Bonner and Dan Gordon (for talking to me about their superb film on the 1966 World Cup), Enrico Deaglio, Pietro Cheli, Dave Hesmondhalgh, Francesco Caremani, Davide Rota, Roberto Carnero, Rogan Taylor, John Williams, Anna Locatelli, Jo Glanville, Brian Glanville and Piera Tacchino, who gave me a precious copy of Piero Sollier's autobiography,

# ACKNOWLEDGEMENTS

Many people have helped with the writing and editing of this book. I would particularly like to thank Matthew Hamilton (a Spurs fan), who was involved at the start of the project and provided expert and informed editing in its later stages. My agent Georgina Capel got the book off the ground and followed it right through to publication day, while Nicholas Pearson was an attentive editor at Fourth Estate. John Dickie (Stoke City) provided expert, tireless and critical readings of much of the book, helping me to stamp out a tendency to drift into cliché. Many thanks also go to Robert Gordon (Arsenal), Ken Clarke (Manchester United) and Ben Ginsborg (Napoli) for their comments on certain chapters. My brothers, Matt (Plymouth Argyle) and Tom (Arsenal), have provided a lot of support and were always ready to crush any signs of pomposity in my discussions of the book. Clare and Kate Fermont (both Arsenal) invited me to their home to watch innumerable games, thereby aiding my research. Michael Foot (Plymouth Argyle) – a true football fanatic – told me some stories about the game in the 1930s in his inimitable style. Monica Foot compiled the index. Rose Foot helped me out with some obscure information on one of the characters in the book.

Others who have helped me simply by being friends and fans, and may find themselves turning up at various times in this book, have been Julian Ferraro (Juventus), Helen Castor, Sergio Maggio (Inter), Graham 'Heckle' Stone (Arsenal), Daniele Arpini (Milan), Chicca Belloni (Milan), Martino Maggio (Inter), Tobias Jones (Everton),

# LIST OF PHOTOS AND ILLUSTRATIONS

*Figure 1.* Map of Italy indicating places cited in the book (map drawn by Lorenzo Sartori).

## Chapter 1
1 James Richardson Spensley in goal for Genoa, 1898.
2 Herbert Kilpin, 1899.
3 The Italian national team before the game against Belgium, 21 May 1922.
4 Genoa fans are proud of their English roots. This huge banner also underlines the fans' belief that their club represent the real heart of their city, as opposed to hated rivals Sampdoria. Genoa–Liverpool. UEFA cup, 4 March 1992.
5 Mussolini (in the white suit) receives the victorious World Cup team, 29 June 1938. Manager Vittorio Pozzo is second to the left of Mussolini, Silvio Piola third to the left.

## Chapter 2
6 *Akkiappa L'Arbitro*. The game.
7 Byron Moreno. He was blamed by Italians for their defeat at the hands of South Korea in the 2002 World Cup finals. A whole series of similar photos appeared on the web in the wake of the tournament.
8 Concetto Lo Bello. Immaculately turned out as ever, before the Milan derby, 18 February 1968.

## Afterword

## Author's Note

Readers are advised to consult the glossary at the back of the book.


Note for the United States edition:
Soccer is referred to as football throughout this book, apart from in the title.

# PREFACE

'Football is always late in making history'
GIOVANNI ARPINO and ALFIO CARUSO

I've never really forgiven Italian football, and Juventus, for buying my favourite player in 1980. Liam Brady was my hero and a footballing genius. I saw him from the North Bank as he scored against Manchester United in 1978. Later, I watched with awe as he destroyed Tottenham at White Hart Lane with one of the greatest goals ever seen on UK TV. Brady's last act for Arsenal was to miss a penalty in the ill-fated shoot-out which decided the Cup Winners Cup final with Valencia in 1980. I followed Brady's career in Italy religiously, waiting for signs that the prodigal son would return home. After two championships in two seasons with Juventus (the second of which was decided by Brady's ice-cool penalty on the last day) Liam was sacked in favour of Michel Platini. Surely, now, he would return to Highbury. But Italian football continued to employ him for another five years: at Sampdoria, Inter and finally even Ascoli. When Brady finally came back to England he was a shadow of the player he had been, managing one more season with West Ham (where he scored a beautiful goal against Arsenal) before retiring and finally coming back to Highbury as youth coach.

Italian football, then, stole my hero. Later, this interest in *calcio* (the Italian word for football) began to blossom when I moved to Milan in 1989 – ostensibly to study the origins of fascism in that ex-industrial city. My Italian was picked up largely through watching TV, and trying to follow the innumerable matches screened at that time. I started to buy the pink Italian sports daily – *La Gazzetta dello Sport*. My first vocabulary was football-linked: *calcio di rigore* – penalty; *penalty* – also penalty; *rimessa laterale* – throw in; *calcio di punzione* – free kick; *ammonizione* – booking; *calcio d'angolo* – corner; *corner* – also corner; *il mister* – the manager. Many of the terms seemed to be simply English words, although sometimes they had slightly different meanings. Other phrases were more difficult – *gamba tesa* – going into a tackle with your leg straight out; *espulsione* – sending off; *melina* – passing the ball around uselessly amongst the back four. I started to take the tram to one of the most stunning football stadiums in the world – the San Siro - at that time being refurbished for the upcoming 1990 world cup.

In my first year in Milan, Inter easily won the championship under record-breaking manager Giovanni Trapattoni. I had found my team. Surely, they would go onto success after success. Moreover, they were the club supported by my future Milanese wife (and, perhaps even more crucially, my future mother-in-law). The good omen of Arsenal's last-gasp championship victory in the same season sealed my decision. It was the wrong one. Inter would not win another championship for 17 years, and even then in the most bizarre circumstances imaginable. In the intervening years they specialised in farcical failure. In the early 1990s, however, AC Milan were the team to watch. Under the innova- tive tactical regime of manager Arrigo Sacchi, the city's other team played the most scintillating form of attacking football imaginable. *Catenaccio* (a defensive style of football, made popular in Italy) was rejected in favour of a fast-moving, aggressive game. Plus, Milan had the players to match this style of play. A Dutch trio dominated the early 1990s – dreadlocked Ruud Gullit (who flew back on the same plane as me to London on one occasion, and was followed around town by huge crowds of fans) provided pace, flair and explosive attacking skills. Frank Rijkaard was the midfield general (I also bumped into him at air- port – Milan is a small city) whilst up front prowled the most complete striker of his generation – Marco Van Basten. All this was supported from the back by two of the greatest defenders in football history – Franco Baresi and Paolo Maldini. Teams still played with sweepers when I arrived but Milan's success was to herald the death of that tradition. This was football from heaven. I also noticed that the team's President was a short, balding, charismatic businessman who smiled a lot and interfered with great frequency in his team's affairs. I was to see a lot more of this man through the 1990s. I even ended up studying him. His name? Silvio Berlusconi.

In 1989 AC Milan reached the European Cup Final for the first time in twenty years. They destroyed Steaua Bucharest in the final (4-0). I watched the game on the colour TV in my room. Foolishly, I decided to get a bus across town after the match. The bus arrived, and then stopped after about 100 yards amidst a mass of delirious fans. The driver finally gave up all hope when people began climbing on the roof. The celebrations went on for days. In 1990, Milan won the European Cup again – and on the way to the final they took apart Real Madrid - 5-0 - with a stunning display of authority, skill and power. There was no doubt that Milan were the greatest team in the world at that time, and Van Basten and Gullit dominated the European Footballer of the Year award throughout the early 1990s.

At San Siro, the atmosphere was electric, and vastly different to my experiences following Arsenal and Plymouth Argyle in England. Orchestrated singing was organised by 'head' fans with megaphones, who spent their time watching their fellow fans, and not the game. Fireworks and flares greeted the arrival of the teams. From San Siro's towering terraces, you could see the whole pitch as if it was a chessboard. In anger, Italian fans did not just boo, or whistle. They went crazy. Cushions and more dangerous missiles were routinely hurled onto the pitch. Violence was common, just as the shock of Hillsborough was finally cleaning up the English game. I noticed with pleasure that there were very few racist chants at Italian matches. This was soon to change, and for the worse.

And then there were the rivalries – not so much the local Milan derby - but regional differences appeared to provide the opportunity for violence and conflict. Naples and their star-player Maradona were particular hate-figures in the north. During the opening match of the 1990 world cup, Maradona was booed by the huge crowd during Argentina's warm up in the San Siro. Cameroon were the choice for the Italians and they duly won, 1-0. Maradona was to get his revenge in spectacular fashion in his adopted Naples, three weeks later, as his penalty knocked the hosts out of the tournament. Milan and Roma also had a long-running rivalry going. At an Italian cup semi-final, attended by 80,000 passionate fans in the San Siro, the tension was palpable. When Milan missed a last-minute penalty and lost, fights broke out. I left the stadium and walked towards the station. Suddenly, a stone flew past my head. I looked up; in front of me stood a line of riot police, complete with helmets, batons and, in some cases, guns. Behind me, I noticed a number of youths (Milan fans, not happy with the result) with handkerchiefs covering their faces. They were hurling rocks and sticks. What to do? Go back towards the fans, or forwards towards the police line? I decided on the latter option. For a second, the line parted to let me through, and then closed again. This whole semi-riot, which lasted some hours, was barely reported in the Italian press.

Media coverage of football was total, and impossible to ignore. Goals were analysed way into the night, from every possible angle, but so were offside decisions, and even lip-read words. This was normal. Referees were lambasted for errors of judgement, and routinely accused of corruption and favouritism. Players were denigrated for one bad performance, managers sacked after a couple of bad results, teams said to be 'in crisis, officially' after a couple of draws. Whole programmes consisted entirely of men shouting at each other about football, for hours. One such programme – *Il processo del lunedì* (Monday's Trial) – had been running since 1980. Local TV stations were also dominated by such low-budget programmes, concentrating largely on the Milan teams in my area, whose every game, training session and transfer was picked over in minute detail. I began to have conversations about football, quickly realising that English football was simply not taken seriously in Italy. For Italians, English teams still played the long ball game, and the back four consisted of lanky defenders who would never get a game in Italy. When people asked me who I supported and I told them, many replied, irritatingly, 'Aston Villa?' When I tried to explain who Arsenal were, I used Brady – but very few had heard of my club.

In addition, since the 1985 Heysel disaster, *all* English fans had been lumped together under the collective title of 'hooligans'. This was to prove a reputation that was very difficult to shake off. There were hardly any English players in the Italian league, and even fewer were a success. Milan's experiences with British players had been a near-complete disaster, with the honourable exceptions of Ray Wilkins and the much-loved Joe Jordan. Luther Blissett's move to Italy had assumed near-mythical qualities. Blissett became famous for being bad; symbolizing what was seen as the low technical level in the English game.

Italians invariably assumed that their league was the best in the world. There is no doubt that Serie A was and is the *hardest* league to play in. The defenders and goalkeepers are simply the best on the planet, and the tactics are a combination of subtlety and brutality. Winning or losing is all-important in Italy, so if an attacker gets past you, he must be brought down. The 'tactical foul' is a way of life for Italian defenders – and not to be confused with the 'useless foul' from which your team takes no advantage. To be top scorer in Italy was truly a formidable task. To make things even more difficult, own goals were deemed until recently as any goal where a defender has merely touched, or brushed the ball. Ian Rush, prolific in the English league for more than a decade, managed only seven goals in his single season with Juve. With the advent of the pressing game, there was less and less space for the *fantasisti* – those with great skill who created goals through genius and poetry. Hence the virtual exile of a whole series of discarded *fantasisti,* who became heroes abroad – Gianfranco Zola, Benito Carbone, Paolo di Canio. Even the genius of Roberto Baggio struggled to find space with a top club after his departure from Juventus in 1995. He later preferred to weave his magic in the provinces – with Bologna and Brescia. So many skilful players were produced by the Italian system, but very few were given a chance in the big teams. Winning – at all costs – was too important to allow for the luxury of inconsistency, or skill for skill's sake.

And then there was the pressure – from the media, the president and above all the fans, organised in groups known as *ultrà* since the 1970s and liable to turn nasty if things started to go wrong on the pitch. Inter sacked four managers in the 1998-9 season alone, largely thanks to *ultrà* campaigns. In 2001, enraged Inter fans petrol-bombed the team coach – with the players inside. In 2003 angry Naples fans stoned their captain's car as he drove down the motorway. In the same year two games in Serie A alone were called off early due to fan rioting.

In 2007 football grounds were closed all over Italy after a policeman was killed as fans clashed during and after a Catania-Palermo derby. Fans frequently go on strike, refusing to support their team or even turn up – they also display slogans attacking specific players, other fans, presidents and managers. Thousands turn up to training sessions, millions tune in to games. This is a country where the most-read daily is still the pink *La Gazzetta dello Sport* (which is flanked by two other sports dailies dealing largely in football as well as numerous monthlies and specialist publications) and where, until recently, millions of Italians did their version of the pools every week, spending billions of lire and then Euros in the process. *Calcio* is no longer a game. It is sometimes difficult to define it as a sport. It is certainly very big business. A better way to see *calcio* is as a kind of fanatical civic religion – where loyalty is total and obsession the norm. Fair play seemed to me to be a concept absent from Italian football discourse. Diving was common and not particularly frowned upon – as long as it worked. In fact, commentators often praised the 'craftiness' of non-sportsmanship. There was no moral code here. Winners were always 'right', losers always wrong.

As the 1990s wore on, I quickly began to realize that football in Italy was not only a massive sporting phenomenon, but also something that reflected on, and affected, political, cultural and social trends. I started to understand that it was almost impossible to comprehend Italy without understanding football, and vice versa. This conviction crystallized in 1994, when Silvio Berlusconi made a dramatic entrance into political life with an organization – *Forza Italia!* – whose very name was taken from a football chant, and whose language was dominated by footballing terminology. Berlusconi, in his own words, had 'taken the field', he had 'formed a team' and he used his footballing success to bolster his political consensus. Football and Italian politics were not only linked, they were symbiotic, and it was unclear where the division between the two lay, if such a division existed at all. This alone would be a good reason to study and recount the history of Italian football. When you add the sheer beauty of the game, the passion and the debate it provokes, every day, amongst millions of people, the temptation to write this history became overwhelming. In 2006, Italians were transfixed by the biggest scandal in the history of sport – which became known as *Calciopoli* or *Moggiopoli* after its main protagonist, football fixer Luciano Moggi. Weeks later, their national team won its fourth World Cup. No writer could have dared to hope for such an extraordinary combination of success and squalor, skill and sleaze.

Sometimes, during the work on this book, I have felt like Malcolm McDowell in *The Clockwork Orange*. I have been forced to watch things that, in the end, have made me sick. I did not think it would be possible but, by the end, I had almost fallen out of love with football. After innumerable chat shows, post-match interviews, clichés, violence, racism, hysterical protests, dives and fake injuries, biased referees and corrupt Presidents, I had almost had enough. But all this was never quite enough to stop me watching altogether. I kept going back, and, occasionally, the whole thing felt worthwhile. When Roberto Baggio scored his 200th goal for example, or Cristiano Lucarelli crashed in a left-foot shot, or Lillian Thuram, for the thousandth time in his career, trapped the ball, looked up, and passed it elegantly onto a midfielder. These moments, and many others, once made football the beautiful game. It cannot be described as beautiful any longer, especially in Italy, but all is not lost.

As with this opening chapter, the rest of *Winning at All Costs* will be organized around the themes which have dominated the thoughts of fans, players and football journalists: referees, teams and cities, managers and tactics, scandals, the media, foreigners, fans, violence, politics the national team and money.

*Figure 1*. Map of Italy indicates places cited in the book
(map drawn by Lorenzo Sartori).

## CHAPTER 1

# *Calcio* and Football.
# Origins and Early History:
# 1880–1929

## The first kicks

In the beginning there were the English. The first games on Italian soil of what we would recognize as football took place in the port towns of Livorno, Genoa, Palermo and Naples. Very little evidence exists of these impromptu games, apart from hearsay. Often they would simply be kickabouts amongst British sailors, perhaps even on the dockside, with some locals roped in to make up the numbers. Italy was on the way to and from India, and many British ships stopped off there. The opening of the Suez Canal in 1869 led to a boom in English communities on shipping routes. No records of actual football clubs exist until the 1880s and 1890s, and the official birth of *Italian* football is usually traced back to the employee of a British textile company, one Edoardo Bosio, who formed the first club in Turin in the late 1880s, using footballs he brought back with him from England.

Like everything about Italian football, even *these* origins are contested, controversial and politicized. This controversy begins with the very name used for football in Italy (and the title of this book). The nascent Italian football authorities gave the game an Italian name – *calcio* – in 1909. Previously, the organization which ran the game had been known as *Federazione Italiana Football*. This change was a politically inspired one. Nationalist ideals had already permeated those who ran the game in Italy, and there was hostility to foreign players. Hence the decision not to use an English term as was the norm elsewhere. The Germans had translated football into *Fussball*, whilst the French left the word as it was. But the choice of *calcio* was also historical. *Calcio Fiorentino* was a game, with a ball, and a pitch, which had been played in Florence during the Renaissance. The choice of *calcio* was an attempt by Italians to claim the game for their own. *They had really invented what was now called football many hundreds of years earlier.*

Under Benito Mussolini's fascist regime (1922–1943) this nationaliz-ation of football was taken much further. *Calcio Fiorentino* was not only identified as the precursor of modern football, but was reintroduced in Florence itself, amid much pomp and ceremony. The games were moved from the proletarian Piazza Santa Croce – where some original *calcio* tournaments had taken place – to the bourgeois Piazza della Signoria, and guidebooks made an explicit link between *Calcio Fioren-tino* and football. Even some experts tended to buy this version of events. The great Italian football journalist, Gianni Brera, wrote in his monumental history of *calcio* that the English had merely 'reinvented' the game.[1] Not all went along with this flagrant rewriting of history, however. One journalist refused to use the new term, arguing that he would still write 'football', and that the use of *calcio* offended the traditions linked to the ancient game played in Florence. Over time, despite this small rebellion, *calcio* did become the official word for Italian football.

There was one small problem here. *Calcio Fiorentino* bore very little resemblance to modern football. Ball games had been played for centuries in Italy and the church authorities in Pisa, in 1300 or thereabouts, had banned such games on their cathedral steps. In its original form, *calcio* had been played first by noblemen, and then increasingly by the plebs, in Florentine public squares, in the fourteenth and fifteenth centuries. Games tended to take place around important court events. The rules were lax, when they existed at all. In the version of the game that has survived there were two teams (of 27 players each, vaguely set up in a kind of 9–9–9 formation), a measured pitch, and six referees who stood in a small stand on the side of the pitch. Much else was left to the players themselves. The ball was moved by hand or by foot, but could not be thrown, apart from by the three 'goalkeepers' at the back, and points were scored by getting the ball across the opponent's end line, *or* into a kind of goal. Most forms of violence were permitted.

Pictures of *Calcio Fiorentino* show two teams massed together in the centre of a field or piazza, with a few spectators looking on. The players are wearing hats, and some lie injured on the ground. Musicians beat drums in the background. Later, re-inventions of the game codified a whole series of elaborate rules, but *Calcio Fiorentino* itself had been banned because of the increasing violence during and around matches. Ancient signs forbidding ball games can still be seen in some Florentine squares.

A version of *Calcio Fiorentino* is still played in Florence, with games taking place in the spring and summer and attracting significant numbers of tourists and locals. The tournament is now played in its original setting in Santa Croce. To watch a game is a bit like witnessing a combination of pub brawl, rugby match and medieval re-enactment. 'Players' spend much of the time wrestling with an opponent in complete isolation from the ball or the game itself. The 2005 tournament was suspended after the violence became so bad that one team simply walked off. In its 1930s reincarnation, and its current touristy form, *calcio* has been adapted to *appear more like football*. Games now last for 50 minutes and have various levels of officialdom. Team captains are given the task of stopping fights and calming down their own players and winning teams are rewarded with a purebred cow. So modern is the *Calcio Fiorentino* of today that it has its own, highly elaborate, set of anti-doping rules, downloadable from the internet. *Calcio Fiorentino* players can now be banned for more than two years for taking a series of banned substances, including marijuana.

*Calcio Fiorentino*, therefore, tells us little or nothing about the history of Italian soccer. Fascism had re-invented a tradition. To return to the real history of soccer in Italy, we need to go back to the English, and to those with links to England.

## Pioneers

Edoardo Bosio was born in Turin in 1864. He worked for the textile firm Thomas Adams (based in Nottingham), and had travelled widely in the UK and elsewhere. He took a liking to football in England, where it was already a highly popular and professional sport, and decided to import the game to Turin. In 1891 he formed the first soccer team in Italy from players drawn from his workplace. The club was called International Football Club. One problem for Bosio was that his team had nobody to play against. There were no football federations, no written rules, no referees, no pitches. Games were similar to park kickabouts. In 1891 another English player – Herbert Kilpin – reported on a match he had witnessed in Turin. 'I noticed two curious things: first, there was no sign of a referee. Second, as the game continued, our opponents' team got bigger and bigger. Every so often someone from the crowd came on to the pitch, with great enthusiasm. Soon we found ourselves playing against a team of at least twenty players.'

Quickly other pioneers took up Bosio's lead and formed clubs in Turin and elsewhere. In September 1893 (a date which is still, for many, the real birth date of *calcio*) the Genoa Cricket and Football Club was set up by British consular officials. No Italians could be members. A year later, another club was formed in Turin, the Football Club Torinese. These were small clubs, who rarely travelled beyond their own city borders. For a short time, even cricket was more popular than football.

## James Richardson Spensley

In 1897, an English maritime doctor, James Spensley, arrived in Genoa to look after the sailors on passing coal ships. A polyglot, philanthropist and scouting enthusiast, born in London's Stoke Newington, thirty years earlier, he was also a football devotee who organized the first real game in Italy. This pioneering match was between Genoa and Football Club Torinese in 1898, with a certain Reverend Richard Douglas offici-ating. In the meantime Genoa had changed their rules, on Spensley's insistence, to allow Italians to play and be members. A quota system was introduced to protect the English. Italians would not be allowed to make up more than half of the total membership of the club.

Numerous details survive from that historic first game: Genoa–Football Club Torinese, 6 January 1898. We know that 154 tickets were sold at the full price of one lira and 23 at half-price and that 84 people

James Richardson Spensley in goal for Genoa, 1898.

paid extra for numbered seats and that the whole event made a profit of over 100 lire. The police were present and drinks were available. The referee's whistle cost 2.5 lire while the doorkeeper was paid a mere one lira for a day's work. The Turin team took home a victory, and it appears that at the return match a decision was made to form an Italian football federation. This nascent body then set about preparing the first Italian championship, for May of the same year. Genoa retains its name to this day – despite being pressured to Italianize, along with all clubs with foreign titles – under fascism. Spensley is remembered with affection in the city and in the 1970s a plaque was unveiled in his honour, on the wall of his house.[2] There is still a Genoa club Spensley amongst the many supporters' clubs linked to the oldest team in Italy.

## The first championship

In May 1898, Italy's first football championship took place in Turin, in one day. Official records date from here. Genoa's victory in 1898 thus *counts as a championship success*, with the same statistical weight as that of 2004. The three-month-old Italian football federation brought together four teams for the tournament, three of whom were from Turin, along with Genoa.

For many years, championships were not fought out in a modern, league-type system but through 'challenges' similar to short cup competitions. All three matches in 1898 were played in a field on the edge of Turin, which bore little resemblance to the industrial city that was to sprawl across the Piedmont plains in the twentieth century. Players from all four teams took trams to the pitch and the first championship game was a derby, between two Turin-based clubs. Played at nine in the morning on 8 May, it finished 1–0 to Internazionale di Torino with John (Jim) Savage, who was a marquis and the team captain, scoring the winner.[3] Genoa (in white shirts) won their semi-final against Ginnastica di Torino 2–1 and the final, against Internazionale (at three in the afternoon, after a sandwich lunch), by the same score, after extra-time. Spensley was in goal for Genoa. The team contained three other British players and at least five foreigners. Genoa took home a cup – donated by the Duke of the Abruzzi – and each player was given a gold medal.

Italy's first football champions were therefore a club with an English name, Genoa. There were only around 50 spectators for the semi-finals and little over 100 for the final. As well as a referee (whose name remains unknown) there were two seated 'line-judges' whose job it was to adjudicate if the ball had crossed the goal line, or not, as there were no goal nets. According to football historian Antonio Ghirelli, the crowd cheered their teams and even fought briefly amongst themselves. They also booed the referee, 'a habit which would continue', he dryly notes.[4] The total takings were 197 lire. Football was way down the list of popular sports in Italy at the turn of the century, coming something like seventh in the reporting hierarchies in the newborn sports press. Cycling, riding, motor sports and hunting were all far more popular pastimes.

The small crowd was understandable. Many people had other things on their minds. May 1898 was not a particularly happy time for Italian society as a whole. As Genoa celebrated its first championship in Turin, Milan was in chaos. Bread riots had led to barricades going up across the city. The government decided to repress the protests and the army was sent in. To this day, nobody knows how many protestors (and bystanders) were killed, but modest estimates put the number at 400.

Martial law was declared, soldiers camped in Milan's central Piazza del Duomo and mass arrests were carried out, including priests and moderate reformists. King Umberto I rewarded General Bava Beccaris, at the head of the military operation, with a special medal.[5] All eyes were on Milan, as Italian society tore itself apart, and little attention was given to three ninety-minute games on the dusty periphery of Turin.

## Paleo-calcio. Rules, Managers, Foreigners, Sundays

The early game in Italy – which we might call *paleo-calcio* – was poles apart from the sport you witness if you turn on your satellite TV station today, or even pop round to your local football pitch. There were no managers of any sort (although people similar to managers began to emerge quite quickly, in some accounts as early as 1901), no training beyond a few shots with the ball, and the players were all, to a man, amateurs. There were no stadiums, no real tactics, the ball was heavy and goalkeepers didn't even attempt to catch it. Punching or kicking out were much preferred. Kit was made up of long-sleeved shirts, often with buttons. Many essential items were imported from England – balls, shirts, boots. Shorts were long, and trousers were often worn, as were caps. There were no changing rooms, so players usually turned up, and went home, already changed.

Many rules in place at the birth of *calcio* were dissimilar to those that govern today's game. A player was offside if, when the ball was played, there were fewer than three players between him and the goal and until 1907, the offside rule applied to the whole pitch. After that date, you could not be offside in your own half. For many years, a draw usually led to a replay, not extra-time. Disciplinary rules were rudimentary. Pitch invasions led to replays, not sanctions (thereby encouraging more pitch invasions). There were no shirt numbers until the 1939–40 season and no substitutes at all until 1968. Early Italian football history was also dominated by foreign players, presidents, clubs, entrepreneurs, referees and words, and above all by the English, the Swiss, the Germans and the French.

From the start, matches were often played on Sundays, despite the fact that Italy was a Catholic country. The reason for this anomaly was simple. Most people worked on Saturdays, and the battle for an 'English Saturday' – one without work – was one of the historic demands of Italy's nascent trade union movement in the early twentieth century. Later, the Church was to complain about this tradition (which is also true of Catholic Spain). Until the 1990s, when Pay-TV destroyed the rites and rhythms of the great Italian football Sunday, the Sunday afternoon match formed a central part of Italian culture. Some fans went to games, partaking in the physical act of watching their team. Others hung around outside stadiums, trying to get in free or just lapping up the atmosphere. Many others simply waited for news, or visited bars. Once radio became widespread, the little transistor became a key element of the classic Sunday family outing, pressed as it often was to the ear of the father, or listened to through a primitive plastic earpiece. With the advent of TV, the afternoon outing had to be cut short in order to get back in time for *Ninetieth minute*, a programme with short reports on all games, transmitted at about 18.30.

## Spensley and the Reign of Genoa, 1898–1904

James Richardson Spensley's Genoa team went on to dominate early Italian football history, winning the title in 1899, 1900, 1902, 1903 and 1904. The doctor played in goal in all of these finals apart from 1899, when he moved to left back to allow one of only two Italians in that particular team to take over between the posts. Spensley, the first name on the first team sheet of the first official game in Italy, retired as a player in 1906. He then became one of the earliest referees in the Italian game and a key member of the embryonic football associations. It is not clear what kind of managerial role Spensley played, if any. Did he select the team? Did the team train at all? Nobody really knows. But, being captain, we can assume that some kind of leadership was provided by the doctor and some Italian histories even list Spensley as a kind of modern coach of Genoa. This detail is an example of the temptation to read back football history, imposing the structure of the modern game onto that of the past. When war broke out in 1914 – although Italy did not join until May 1915 – Spensley signed up as a military doctor. He died in agony in a hospital in Germany, from injuries sustained, it is said, whilst tending to an enemy soldier.

In the photos that survive of James Spensley, the doctor-goalie is wearing a white shirt (not what we would think of as a football top – but a real *shirt*) and his sleeves are rolled up. His shorts reach down to below his knees. He is not particularly tall and his boots appear to be normal boots, without laces. He has no gloves and sports an impressive beard and moustache. The goal, behind him, has no net. In England, by this time, the game had taken on many aspects of modern football. Italy was still in the dark ages, in footballing terms, as the twentieth century began.

## The big teams are born. Juventus, Milan, Internazionale, Torino

Slowly, but inexorably, *calcio* grew in influence and importance. The second championship lasted three days, the third in 1900 twenty days. Other cities became football centres – above all Milan, traditional rival to Turin as Italy's football capital. The infrastructures associated with the modern game began to take shape. Clubs formed all over the country, including in the south, and the business possibilities of the game also became evident.

In November 1897 a group of school students from the prestigious Massimo D'Azeglio school in the centre of Turin – a school attended over the years by such Turin luminaries as FIAT magnate Gianni Agnelli and Primo Levi – met to organize the foundation of a new Turin sports club. They settled on a Latin name – Juventus – 'youth'. What was to be the biggest club in the history of Italian football became a *calcio* team in 1899 – Juventus Football Club. The famous black-and-white shirts came to Turin – allegedly – via an English referee called Harry Goodley.[6] Given the task of buying some football kit in England, he sent back Notts County's, which thus became the black-and-white of the Turin team.[7] Juventus won their first championship in 1905, by one point from Genoa. It was about this time that shirts and other items of kit began to be produced in Italy, and not simply imported from England. In 1907 Juventus pulled out of the playoff final in protest against a change of venue. They were not to win the title again until 1926.

The early history of Turinese football was extremely complicated but began to take shape in 1906 with the formation of a second, unified, Turin club to rival Juventus. Torino Football Club was set up in a beer hall by 'twenty or so Swiss men with bowler hats and a lot of good will' (Marco Cassardo).[8] Torino's first ever official game was a derby victory in 1907, although the club's fans would have to wait until 1928 for their first championship success. Since then, Torino's history has been intimately linked to that of its hated, rich and envied cousins. Torino's colours were claret red – leading to one of the club's nicknames (along with *Toro*, the bull, their symbol) – the *granata*. Many of *calcio*'s greatest, most controversial and most tragic moments were to be associated with the extraordinary history of Torino.

Herbert Kilpin, 1899

In 1899 a group of Milanese industrialists and English and Swiss footballers in alliance with the local *Mediolanum* gymnastic society created the Milan Cricket and Football Club. Milan had rapid success, winning their first championship in May 1901. The team's most influential early player was Herbert Kilpin. Like Bosio in Turin and Spensley in Genoa, Kilpin played a pioneering role in the development of Milanese *calcio*. In his native Nottingham he had played in a team named after the Italian nationalist leader Giuseppe Garibaldi, complete with red shirts. A minor player in England, he became a legend in Italy – perhaps the first real football star – underlining the huge gap in the level of play in that early period.

As a utility player, Kilpin popped up in defence, midfield and in attack, and was captain of Milan for ten years. His nickname was 'Il Lord'. Legend also relates that he chose the team's red-and-black shirts. There is some controversy over the team's 'Devils' nickname, however. Relatives of Kilpin argue that it was his Protestantism, in a Catholic country, which led to the epithet.[9] Kilpin is supposed to have said that 'our shirts must be red because we are devils. Let's put in some black to give everyone a fright.' Kilpin's Milan team won three championships, and might well have claimed a fourth if it were not for a split in the football federation (over the question of foreign players) in 1908.[10] Another oft-repeated story (first spread by Kilpin himself, and then rewritten with poetic licence by Gianni Brera) is that he abandoned his own marriage party to play a game in Genoa, whereupon he broke his nose. The most famous of all early footballers, he played up to the age of 43, and then became a referee. According to legendary Italian national manager Vittorio Pozzo, Kilpin liked a drink, and used to keep a bottle of 'Black and White' whisky in a hole behind the goal. Kilpin, again according to Pozzo, claimed that the only way to forget a conceded goal was to drink a sip of the hard stuff. When he died in 1916 the sports press was moved to hyperbole: '[Kilpin] . . . a magic name, which moved the first passionate crowds to sporting delirium . . . a name which encapsulates the history of our football'.[11]

Just how very different the early game was from today can also be seen by looking at Kilpin's official record for Milan. He played a mere seventeen championship games (with seven goals) between 1899 and 1906, for which he was awarded three titles. Early photographs show Kilpin running for the ball in a wide field with scattered fans looking on and some half-built houses in the background. In another famous photo Kilpin is decked out in full Milan kit, including long white trousers, long black socks, long-sleeved Milan shirt with buttons and Milan cap.

Kilpin left a very rare series of anecdotes about the early game, written just before his death in 1916. He relates that 500 fans turned

up in 1900 in the pouring rain for Milan's first ever match, and tells
the tale of a remarkable game in something called the Negrotto Cup.
In Kilpin's version (the only one we have) Milan's goalkeeper had
brought a chair onto the pitch with him as he had nothing to do all
game. There he sat, cross-legged, smoking a series of cigarettes and
sporting a straw hat, as the goals went in at the other end. 'In the
closing stages', relates Kilpin, 'he was bored to death. He asked me,
"Can't I play a bit as well?" I let him leave the goal, he went up front
and scored . . . the twentieth goal.' Milan duly won the match, 20–0.

Too old for the regular army, Kilpin remained in Italy after the
outbreak of World War One and died in mysterious circumstances in
1916. It was only in 1928 that he was given a proper burial, thanks to an
anonymous donor. His tomb was unmarked, and its location unknown,
until the 1990s when a dedicated Milan fan decided to find his club's
founder. After scouring the Protestant and non-Catholic sectors of
sixteen sites across Italy he finally discovered Kilpin in the city's vast,
flat, municipal cemetery. AC Milan paid for a proper tombstone, and
Kilpin was re-buried in the city's beautiful monumental graveyard.

In 1908, a split from Milan led to the formation of a new Milanese
team, Internazionale Football Club. An artist, Giorgio Muggiani, along
with 42 other rebels, organized the historic meeting in a city-centre
restaurant called The Clock.[12] Fanatical Inter fan Giuseppe Prisco –
who was the team's lawyer in the 1960s – later joked that 'everyone
knows that we were born from a split with Milan: well, we really came
from nowhere'. It appears that the motives behind the split were many,
but were dominated by a discussion over the role of foreigners (after the
end of the Kilpin era) and personal tensions. Inter's vaguely communist
name hinted at the squad's non-nationalist intentions, confirmed by
their first team, which contained eight Swiss players.

On the field, Internazionale enjoyed almost immediate success. In
1910, in their first title-winning year, Inter crushed their 'cousins' twice
in the derby; 5–0 and 5–1. Inter had won their first championship
just two years after their formation, amid great controversy over the
preponderance of foreign players in their side. According to the history
books, Internazionale introduced a new playing style, based upon short
passing and stylish touches. Their play was certainly attacking, as their
goals tally shows (they scored 55 goals against the 46 of second-placed

Pro Vercelli). Inter took the field in the Arena, an impressive amphi-theatre built by Napoleon in the early nineteenth century.

A photo of the Inter team of 1909 shows ten men in striped shirts, one with a large badge on his left chest (with a cross) – the captain. All the players sport moustaches and there appear to be two goalkeepers dressed in white. Another team member boasts an impressive potbelly. The championship portrait of 1910 is far more professional. Only the team are in the photo, Virgilio Fossati, the captain, is in the middle with a ball under his arm (and he has the physical shape of a modern player), whilst the others stand in formation around him. The eccentric goalkeeper – Piero Campelli, only sixteen at the time – the first player in his position to 'catch' the ball, instead of simply hoofing or punching it away – stands behind with his hands up holding a ball. The other star of that team is absent from this particular photo. Ermanno Aebi was a Swiss-Italian (born in Milan, his mother was Italian, his father Swiss), who learnt the game at school in Switzerland. He became a skilful attacking midfielder, scoring 100 goals in ten seasons with Inter, and winning two championships. Aebi was perhaps the first of a long line of stylish midfielders in the Italian game, who were to be at the centre of criticism, time and again, for their lack of application and grinta – 'grit'. Aebi was known, in fact, by the nickname of signorina – 'miss' or 'little lady'. Inter's second championship was not to come until 1920, after a series of mediocre seasons. The birth of Inter began the tradition of one of the world's great derbies – Milan–Inter.

In 1928, Internazionale merged with another Milanese club to form Ambrosiana. Usually interpreted as acquiescence to fascist diktat (against all foreign names and words) this fusion was probably more of a financial move. After the war, Inter returned to their original name and colours and they continued to play at the Arena, right in the centre of Milan, until 1947. AC Milan, after 1926, had their home in the newly constructed San Siro stadium, on the northern edge of the metropolis. Since 1947–1948, the two clubs have shared the magnifi-cent San Siro, which is sometimes compared to the city's most famous cultural arena of all – as La Scala of football.

## *L'Italia.* The National Team and the Reading Tour

Italy's national team began playing internationals in 1910, and the enthusiasm that surrounded them from the start was symptomatic of, and contributed to, the rapid growth of *calcio* after World War One. Yet, the early Italian teams were extremely weak in comparison with the major footballing nations of the time. Despite thrashing France and edging past Belgium, Italy were much less strong than Austria and Hungary. In the 1912 Olympics Italy lost to Finland and were crushed by Austria 5–1, although they managed to beat Sweden. With England, whom they did not meet at an international level until 1933, there was simply no comparison. Reading FC, a relatively minor club, toured Italy in May 1913. At the time, Reading had just finished eighth in the Southern League Division One.[13]

Reading took nearly two days to reach Genoa, where they thrashed the local team, 4–2. The next day it was the turn of Milan, who were dispatched 5–0, after Reading were four up within half an hour. Casale, who were to win the championship the following year, actually beat Reading, 2–1, but their pitch was so small that its width was close to that of a modern penalty area. On 15 May – their fourth match in five days – Reading bounced back. They destroyed Pro Vercelli – champions of Italy, and unbeaten for eighteen months – 6–0. On the following Sunday, in Turin, a match was organized between Italy and Reading. The English team won, 2–0, in front of 15,000 spectators. This was no scratch Italian team, but one with eight Vercelli players. Italy would take time to become a force on the world stage, but some talented players were emerging. Attilio Fresia of Genoa so impressed Reading that they signed him the following season, making him the first Italian to take part in professional football in England. He was not a success and moved on – to Clapham Common, for ten pounds – without ever making a first-team appearance. Reading's Italian tour made an eighteen-pound profit.

Despite its low technical level the Italian team, almost from the start, attracted large crowds and provoked widespread interest in the game. *Calcio* as a mass game was created in part through the efforts and the popularity of the national team. Rapid progress was also made in coaching and training systems after World War One so that, by the

The Italian national team before the game against Belgium, 21 May 1922.

1920s, Italy was able to challenge for major honours on the world stage.

## *Calcio* and World War One

Italy entered the war in 1915 following a series of violent pro-war demonstrations by a radical nationalist minority. The majority of Italians were opposed to the war and millions of peasants were forced to fight in terrible conditions under officers who spoke a language – Italian – that very few of them understood. Most Italians still conversed in local dialects. Thanks largely to the collapse of the Austro-Hungarian Empire, Italy was able to force a victorious armistice in November 1918. In return for relatively tiny tracts of new land, 571,000 Italians had died and over 450,000 had been seriously wounded. War lacerated Italian society, creating divisions that were to lead to near-civil war and the destruction of her fragile democracy in the 1920s.

Instead of signalling the start of games on 23 May 1915, referees all over the country announced the suspension of the tournament. A day later, war was declared against Austria-Hungary.[14] The conflict took a

terrible toll on young Italian players who were called up. Virgilio
Fossati, captain of Inter and the Italian national team, was killed on
Christmas Day, at the age of 25. In all 26 players and staff from Inter
lost their lives in the war, making their 1920 championship victory
appear something of a miracle.[15] Only two players played in both the
1910 and 1920 Internazionale championship teams.

During the war, Italian nationalists attempted to mobilize sport
behind the war effort. Soldiers were anxious to read about sport and
special sports papers were produced for them to browse through.
Soldiers also played football at the front and appeals were made for
footballs to be sent out to them. *Sports Illustrated* produced a war issue
that compared the conflict to a vast game 'in which there are no laws
and the spectators are also actors'. With time, this paper became less
and less about sport and more and more about war propaganda.
Fascism's use of sport as a potent propaganda weapon in the 1930s
was prefigured in this period of international conflict.

Although the official championship had been called off at the start
of the war, competitive football continued through a series of cup
competitions. All the big teams were involved, although crowds were
small, judging by the photos. Players were still being paid, much to
the chagrin of the sports press, who complained that 'nasty professionalism has still not disappeared'. There were even outbreaks of crowd
trouble, 'the usual fights'. In the reports of these games, *calcio* appears
to be far more modern than during the 'heroic' phase of its growth.
The players have the physical shape of modern footballers, the kit is
smaller and less baggy and includes knee bandages, headbands and
goalkeeping gloves. Football photographers were also improving. In
the early photos, the ball was a rare sight – and papers would use
crude photo montages to show 'goals'. Now they had begun to capture
goals, saves, tackles and even fights between players. Another modern
development was advertising around the stadium. Football had become
a business.

In 1919 the football championship began again in earnest and the
sport went through a period of considerable expansion. After the war
the foreign dominance on the field began to wane, although foreign
players continued to arrive, whilst the technical side of the game began
to be controlled by non-Italian coaches and managers. Foreign man-

agers were brought in by most of the big clubs after the war and many enjoyed immediate success. Symbols became important as *calcio* invented its own history made up of a mix of tradition and myth. From the 1923–24 season onwards, the championship-winning team had a *scudetto* (shield) symbol – with the colours of the national flag – sewn onto their shirts. The shield-patch remained there for the whole following season, and the word *scudetto* began to rival that of *titolo* or *campionato*.

## Running the Game. The Italian Football Federations. Splits and Reunions

We have seen that the first Italian football federation had been formed in 1898 and had organized the first championships, which slowly expanded from the minor one-day tournament of that year. In 1909 the federation changed its name to the FIGC (*Federazione Italiana del Giuoco del Calcio*) making *calcio* the official Italian term for football. That year also saw the adoption of a rule book and federal statutes. Referees were also brought under the auspices of a special commission. For the first time, relegation and promotion were introduced.

Almost from the beginning of the history of *calcio*, the 'problem' of foreign players produced heated debate. The early championships saw teams with English, Belgian, Swiss and German players in key positions. Genoa and Inter were often criticized for their preponderance of foreign players. In part, this was simply jealousy, but politics was also important. Italian nationalists argued that the domestic game should be reserved for Italians.

In 1908, the football federation took a radical step – all teams with foreign players would be excluded from the main championship and a special competition would be reserved for them. In protest, a series of big teams pulled out altogether, including Milan, Torino and Genoa. The foreigner ban was seen by the Milanese clubs as a crude attempt to take their power away, on and off the field. Milan were particularly angry as their chance of winning the special Spensley Cup, awarded for three successive championship victories, had been removed by diktat.

Under pressure again, after the farcical failure of the Italian-only championship, the federation re-admitted foreigners the following year, but the issue continued to provoke bitter debate. A gesture was made towards Milan, who were awarded the Spensley Cup without having actually won it. In 1910, Inter's championship victory was marked by controversy over the role of Aebi, an elegant Swiss-Italian player whose citizenship was called into question. These battles were also over territory (the head offices of the football federation kept shifting from city to city, and in particular between Milan and Turin) and about control over what was becoming big business. The world of *calcio* was, right from the start, riven by splits, controversies, rivalries and acrimonious debate. It was rare for a championship to go by without insubordination by one club or another and the federation struggled to impose its authority.

## Violence and Fans. The early years

Violence was part of *calcio* from the very beginning. Fights in the crowd were reported during the first ever championship tournament, the one-day affair in Turin in 1898, and violence began to afflict the game almost from the start. Football historian Ghirelli writes of pitch invasions during a match between Genoa and Juventus in 1905, which led to an immediate replay, and of stone-throwing during other early games.[16]

Between 1911 and 1914, a number of incidents marred games. Stones were hurled at a referee in 1912 in a match between Genovese team Andrea Doria and Inter. In December 1913 another referee was forced to run away from angry supporters in a match at Novara. A photo survives of this incident, depicting a number of men with straw hats milling around on the pitch, and a bemused goalkeeper-onlooker. Casale and Inter fans fought each other on the pitch in June 1914. Some of this violence was linked to actual games, some to local rivalries, and some to gambling, which was already widespread. Pitch invasions became commonplace, such as in a match between two Rome teams in June 1914 and in a Tuscan match in January of the same year, when shots were fired and stones thrown during a Livorno–Pisa derby.

In the brutal atmosphere of post-war Italy, football violence exploded on and off the field. For Ghirelli, there was a series of episodes that 'veered between farce and the time of the Wild West'.[17] Rinaldo

Barlassina, one of the most prominent Italian referees at the time, was the victim of stone-throwing during a match at Casale. After refusing to give a penalty, Barlassina used an umbrella to protect himself and he emerged unhurt. Ghirelli comments that 'it is unclear if this was thanks to his stoicism or to the fact that the stones had run out'.[18] Another referee was attacked by angry fans on his way home after a game at Modena.

In February 1920, a pitch invasion interrupted Pro Vercelli–Genoa and Guido Ara, a Vercelli midfielder, was hit by an angry fan. A rare photo survives of this incident, with supporters running towards the referee whilst the players flee. In the background, a number of fans have clambered up trees in order to see the match. In 1921 Pro Vercelli were again involved, this time against Inter, in Milan. In the first half, an Inter player was seriously injured. The home crowd blamed Vercelli's players. In the second half the atmosphere was 'electric' but Vercelli continued their 'dirty play', according to press reports. Finally, Vercelli's captain was sent off. Another injury followed – this time a broken leg – and the players squared up to each other. After a pitch invasion the referee took refuge in the dressing room. The Vercelli player blamed for the incidents was banned for six months and the match was never replayed.

Footballers also became directly involved in the political violence which tormented Italy after the war. Aldo Milano, 24, was the third of four brothers who all played for Pro Vercelli before and after the war. Milano the Third, as he was known, was also a militant fascist. One night, in January 1921, a group of Vercelli fascists decided to visit another nearby town to carry out a mission – the removal of a plaque that was seen as insulting to the war dead. Symbols were important in post-war Italy, and could get you killed. Socialists cried 'down with the war-mongers' and attacked those seen as responsible for the conflict, whilst national-ists and fascists flew the Italian flag and exalted the 'heroes' from the trenches. That fateful night, Milano the Third was helping the others remove the plaque in question when a local government doorkeeper shot him. Here, as ever, versions differ. Some claim that he was taken to hospital, but nothing could be done; others that his body was left on the street all night.

Aldo Milano had played just over twenty games for Pro Vercelli, who threatened to abandon the championship altogether before deciding to continue. Local fascists were quick to exploit the death of Milano, making him into the latest of a series of 'fascist martyrs', and the local fascist branch was immediately renamed in his honour. As on other occasions, the fascists 'organized commemorations . . . through which they tried to wipe out the memory of the socialist dead, whose numbers were far greater'.[19] This time, the setting for these commemorations was a football pitch.

The most violent *calcio*-related moment of the whole post-war period was *connected* to football, but was not really *about* football. Viareggio's 'red days' of 1920 reflected the spirit of the times. In this dramatic case, football was more of an excuse for, and not the cause of, the violence.

## Revolution. Viareggio's 'red days' of 1920

'Revolution, well before it is a "thing", is an emotion' – *Avanti!*
(Socialist Party newspaper) comment on the
'Viareggio days', May 1920

Viareggio is a sleepy, elegant seaside town in Tuscany, famed for its long beaches, its February carnival, its liberty architecture and its *bagni*; institutionalized strips of beach where the rich and the semi-famous can bathe in relative privacy. The town has twice in its history had an impact on the history of *calcio*. In 1926, the new 'fascist' football federation constitution – known as the Viareggio Charter – was drawn up there and in the post-war period a celebrated young players' tournament was organized (and still takes place) in the town. In 1920, however, at the height of the *biennio rosso* – Italy's 'two red years' – a football match in Viareggio was enough to spark a kind of local revolution.

The story begins in Lucca, the beautiful walled city just inland of Viareggio, where the local team took the field against Sporting Club Viareggio in April 1920. According to reports, the away fans were greeted with 'hostility and violence'. They vowed to get their revenge in the return match, planned for May. Worried about possible trouble, the authorities and the club advised all Lucca fans to stay at home. Only a tiny number made the trip to Viareggio. The referee was from Lucca, and he 'failed to appear impartial', according to press reports, during the game. As if to balance things up, a war hero called Augusto Morganti, from Viareggio, ran the line. Lucca came back from 2–0 down to draw level towards the end of the game, and this result was 'blamed' by the local fans on the referee. With the match drawing to a close, an argument erupted between the linesman and a Lucca player. The referee decided to end the game early, but Morganti was not of the same opinion. Both sets of players took the opportunity to settle some scores, laying into each other. This was the signal for a mass pitch invasion, and an 'enormous fight'. The few *carabinieri* (military police) who were present managed to rescue the Lucca players from the hostile crowd, and pushed the Viareggio fans back outside into the street.

News reached the nearby *carabinieri* barracks, and more men were dispatched to the scene. They arrived to find the crowd attempting to re-enter the stadium, and were greeted with whistles and threats. At this point, the facts are unclear. One policeman, it appears, lost his head (he claimed he was threatened) and shot Morganti – the locally-born linesman – at close range in the neck, killing him immediately. This tragedy enraged the crowd, and the *carabinieri* were chased away. Meanwhile, Lucca's players and their fans slipped out of a back door, and left town – they were forced to walk for twenty kilometres to the next station. In Viareggio the crowd turned its attention to more serious matters.

Arms were seized (including at least 100 rifles) and the railway lines blocked. The crowd surrounded the barracks and tried to get hold of the man who had shot the linesman. Barricades went up and telephone and electricity lines were cut. Viareggio was isolated, and in the hands of local subversives. Anarchists from local towns arrived on the scene: it felt and looked like a revolution. Three military columns were soon dispatched to quell the protests, some by sea. With some difficulty, and only after a couple of days, 200 soldiers took control. The taking of the town by local subversives entered into local mythology as Viareggio's 'red days'.

Football tried to draw a veil over the events of 1920. In 1921 a 'Peace Match' was organized in Viareggio and passed off without incident. However, in the 1921–22 season, violence was again on the agenda. Viareggio won the first derby, but the Lucca fans attributed their defeat to the intimidating atmosphere in the stadium which revived unhappy memories of 1920's riots. The return match, in the claustrophobic city of Lucca, was extremely tense. Viareggio's fans were escorted by the police, and after losing 2–0 they proceeded to smash up (according to the version provided by Lucca fans) anything they could find. Here politics, local rivalries (the Tuscan derbies, and in particular Pisa–Livorno, are perhaps the most emotional of all Italian derbies) and the social upheavals of the time, allied to protests against match officials, combined to produced an explosive situation.

## Early Games. Ropes, Nets and Fields

What were early games like? Much football writing extrapolates back from contemporary soccer, assuming that matches were similar to those we see today. Yet, apart from some of the rules, the pitch, the numbers of players and the goals, very little of what was called *calcio* or *foot-ball* resembled today's game. The players were not athletes, they rarely trained and they were, at least for the first 20–25 years, nearly all amateurs. It was only in the 1920s that the professional game, and the idea of football as a business – as a full-time occupation – really began to take root. Skill and tactics were rare, play was slow and often violent.

Games took place on impromptu fields, which were not designed specifically for football and were hardly conducive to skilful ball play. Neither was the mud that was far more common than grass in the rainy north of Italy. For some time crowds just gathered around the sidelines, or a simple rope held them back from the pitch itself. For the first ten or so years, football matches failed to attract significant crowd numbers. It was only with the birth of the national team in 1910 that the masses began to turn up to games. Four thousand people – a big crowd – attended the first ever Italian game in Milan in that year. In 1911 Italy's first football stadium was opened, in the Marassi zone on the edge of Genoa. The stadium had a capacity of 25,000 and was bordered on one side by a large stand with seats. Genoa's stadium was designed with dressing rooms and even a special room for the referee.

Genoa's ground was one of the first to give a team 'home advantage'. Just next door was the more intimate ground used by their city rivals, Andrea Doria (who would later become a part of Sampdoria). Here the crowd was so close to the pitch that a claustrophobic atmosphere was created. This ground was dubbed *La Caienna*, after a French prison camp. Other stadiums, usually consisting of one stand and some terracing, were constructed by Milan and other clubs before and during World War One while Venezia built a stadium on an island in 1916.

In the years before World War One, fan numbers multiplied. Away fans began to turn up to games, and groups of supporters awaited their team's return. By the 1920s, the strongest teams had groups of organized followers, and special trains were commissioned for away games. A 1923 photograph shows a group of Genoa away fans on a station platform. They have flags, banners (*viva Genoa Club*) and have scrawled graffiti on the train itself – including *Fan Carriage* and the rather poetic and self-deprecatory phrase: *Foot-ball, acute mania*. These were the first groups of obsessive, faithful fans, the grandfathers (and they are all men, in the photo) of the fanatical *ultrà* of the 1970s and 1980s.

Were there any tactics? According to some books, early teams tended to line up in a kind of inverted pyramid formation – a sort of 2–3–5 – with emphasis on attack and on kick and rush. It was only with the professional-style training methods of the first and second decades of the twentieth century and the modern coaching of foreign managers that the game began to resemble what we see today on our screens. The various alterations to the offside rules were also important in imposing change, and players did adopt specific positions on the field, right from the beginning (although tactical discipline was slow to take root). The birth and growth of the sports press, sports writers and football correspondents boosted understanding of *calcio*. Certain clubs began to be associated with specific styles of play, and with particular attitudes to the game, as with the aggressive reputation of Pro Vercelli, or Inter's association with elegance.

## Amateurs and Professionals

Early Italian football, as with the game in England, was strictly an amateur sport, played for honour, fun and physical well-being, but never for money. Payment of any kind was frowned upon. Most players had other jobs – as doctors, artists, businessmen, dockers, students. Amateurism was written into the statutes and rules of clubs and players caught taking money were banned. By the 1920s, this system had become unworkable. Money was beginning to flow into the game – through gate receipts, advertising, newspapers and journalists, and prizes. Working outside of the rules the bigger clubs began to employ coaches and pay players, using a series of tricks, such as calling managers 'consultants'. Sometimes they were caught, sometimes they weren't. Italy was slowly catching up with England, where there were already more than 4,000 registered professional footballers by 1914.[20]

From 1913–1914, Genoa's star player Renzo De Vecchi, who was known as the 'Son of God' because of his precocious talent, was handsomely paid for his 'work' as a clerk for a Genoa bank.[21] Other sectors of De Vecchi's pay (and transfer fee) were hidden as 'travel expenses'. Thanks to this new job, De Vecchi's transfer from Milan to Genoa was allowed to go ahead. In general, however, before World War One, the federation dealt harshly with those found guilty of professionalism.

When Genoa poached two players from local rivals Andrea Doria in 1913, they were caught breaking the rules.[22] Offered 1,000 lire each as a signing-on fee, the players accepted, but they had the bad luck to cash their joint cheque with a bank teller who was also a disgruntled Doria fan. Upset at the loss of two excellent players, the bank clerk copied the cheque and informed the football authorities. At first, the players were banned for life, a ban that was reduced to two years on appeal and then cut further by an amnesty. Both players proved to be excellent signings, going on to win three championships with Genoa and play for Italy.

The rationale behind the amateur ideal was ideological. Sport should not be played for money, which sullied the concepts of fair play and healthy physical activity. It was a leisure activity, not a job. These lofty ideals quickly collapsed in the face of the economic needs of clubs, presidents, players and the demands of fans for success. In the 1920s a number of very high-profile big-money transfers led to bitter public discussion and in the 1926 Viareggio Charter, professionalism was officially recognized for the first time. From that point on, players' wages (as players, not bank clerks or lawyers) were subject to negotiation and the big clubs began to buy up the best talent. And it was not just players who were on the market. The best-paid football employees never took to the pitch themselves, but selected and trained their teams: the managers.

## The first manager. The odyssey of William Garbutt

Foreigners had been largely responsible for setting up the game in Italy, and had been amongst the best early players. In 1912, Genoa became the first Italian club to appoint a professional manager. He was an Englishman, from Stockport, and was only 29 years old. William Garbutt had been a fine player with Reading and Woolwich Arsenal, before suffering a terrible injury while playing for Blackburn Rovers during a match witnessed, according to his own memoirs, by future Italian national coach Vittorio Pozzo. Garbutt's salaried employment as Genoa manager was outside of the rules, so he was paid through a series of semi-legal means until the onset of professionalism in the second half of the 1920s.

As with most Italian versions of early football history, the origins of Garbutt's employment by Genoa are unclear. What is certain is that he took up the reins of power at the club in 1912, and went on to have a quite remarkable career in Italy. Although not a manager by trade, Garbutt introduced some of the modern training techniques he had experienced as a player in England. He planted poles in the ground for dribbling practice, and supervised jumping exercises, abolishing the desultory kickabouts that had previously passed for training at most clubs. In 1913 Genoa finished second in the northern championship and they went one better in 1915 in the controversial war-suspended tournament.[23] It is said that the English manager also introduced a crucial aspect of post-match material culture to the Italian game – hot showers in the dressing room.

Genoa, which already had the best stadium in Italy, invested in the market, tempting players (illegally) from local rivals Doria and buying Renzo De Vecchi from Milan in 1913. Garbutt also used his contacts to bring over various English players. When war broke out, Garbutt returned to England before rejoining Genoa after the conflict, tempted by a wage increase to 8,000 lire a year. Genoa won the *scudetto* in both 1923 and 1924, and came close to a third successive championship in 1925.

Garbutt moved on to manage Roma in 1928, and then to Naples, where the team finished third twice in six seasons – their best-ever showing up to that point. Whilst in Naples he adopted a young orphan girl, Concettina Ciletti, an act of charity that endeared him to sentimental locals. The local press also accused him of hitting the bottle.[24] Garbutt then took control at Athletic Club Bilbao, where he won a title just as the Spanish civil war broke out. In 1938 he began his third spell with Genoa.[25] It is often said that the name given to managers in Italy – *Il Mister* – became popular thanks to the influence of Garbutt and other English managers in the 1930s. Even today players will refer to their managers as *il mister* in cliché-ridden post-match interviews: 'who will play next week?' – '*decide il mister*'; 'That's up to the *mister*'.[26]

When Italy entered World War Two in June 1940, Garbutt was advised to leave Italy but was tempted to stay on as his team had reached the Italian Cup final. He finally left the city on the eve of the final – which Genoa lost – and went into hiding in the Ligurian countryside with his wife, leaving his adopted Italian daughter behind. On 26 June, a warrant was issued for his arrest. Garbutt was too famous to be able to hide for long near Genoa, and in mid-July the couple were picked up. According to the arrest report, which was full of praise for the manager's reputation, Garbutt had remained in Italy 'thanks to his great sympathy for fascism'. After being held in a small and crowded cell for some time, Garbutt's health and that of his Irish wife Anna began to deteriorate.

Two weeks of negotiations between the authorities and the club followed. The Garbutts were spared the indignities of an internment camp, and instead sent into exile in the south of Italy, near Salerno. Garbutt was a familiar figure in the south, after his time with Napoli. The family ended up in a tiny village in the mountains, where they lived off their savings and, when those ran out, on a small state income.

In February 1941 an order came through to move the Garbutt family to an internment camp in the poverty-stricken Abruzzo region. There they were held for more than a year, until a palace coup removed Mussolini from power in July 1943. German troops poured into Italy and the Garbutts were terrified that they would be deported. In the chaos that ensued, the family used false documents and fled north. They were helped in their escape by a local politician, and ended up in a refugee camp in Imola in central Italy. In May 1944, Garbutt's 55-year-old wife Anna decided to go to the local church. The city was bombed by the Allies and the church was hit, killing Anna and many others. After Imola was liberated by Allied troops in April 1945, Garbutt returned south where he stayed with his adopted daughter's family.

This long and tragic odyssey was only completed with Garbutt's return to Genoa, nearly five years after his first arrest. A crowd formed when the news broke that *Il Mister* had come back to the city. After a brief spell in England, Garbutt was re-employed by Genoa in 1946, after being persuaded to return once again by Edoardo Pasteur, one of the club's original founders. He stayed in the job right up to 1948 – his sixteenth season with the club, thirty-five years on from his first spell in charge. He then worked as a scout for the port-city team until 1951, when he finally returned to the UK. Garbutt died in Leamington Spa in 1964, after moving to a small house there on retirement, still cared for by his faithful Neapolitan daughter.[27] This quiet death was met with indifference at home, but obituaries appeared in all the Italian papers. As Pierre Lanfranchi has written, 'the contrast between how he [Garbutt] is remembered in England and in Italy is astonishing. Forgotten in England, he is an historic figure in Italy, celebrated as the first real football manager and one of the major actors in the development of professional football in the peninsula.'[28] His biography is a perfect example of the ways that football history and Italian history simply cannot be separated.

## Fans and History

Italians fans have a deep sense of history. In the 1990s, in a derby game, Genoa fans produced an enormous banner – which stretched across the whole end – *We are Genoa*. The message here was twofold, referring to the English origins of the club, and underlining the belief that Genoa represents both real football history (as the oldest club in Italy) and the core of Genoa itself (as the oldest club in the *city* – rivals Sampdoria were only formed after a fusion between two other Genoa teams in 1946). The same appeal to a stronger historical identification with the city is often made by Roma fans (against 'provincial' Lazio followers) and Torino fans (against Juventus).

Genoa fans have always been proud of their English origins. Elegant, older and supposedly well-informed fans at the Genoa stadium were always known as 'the English'. Genoa fans are also renowned for their aplomb and irony. Forced to drop their English name in the 1920s (although recent historical work has argued that club authorities did so more out of zeal than under pressure from fascism) and call themselves *Genova*, the fans demanded a return to the English *Genoa* after the war. There are still supporters' organizations in the city that are known as 'Garbutt's clubs'.

Most serious Italian fans are well aware of the date of foundation of their club, its record, its founders and its historic players, managers and even the various stadiums where the club has played. All these historic features are a strong part of a civic religion – adherence to which is a crucial aspect of fan-identity. Founding myths, legends and stories permeate this self-styled football history, as tales are handed down from generation to generation. These stories are a key part of every fan's collective identity, and are reinforced by the presence of a series of institutional and footballing enemies. Many stories are linked to scandals, 'thefts' and injustices which teams have suffered in the past, and whose legacy can last for decades.

Genoa fans are proud of their English roots. This huge banner also underlines the fans' belief that their club represent the real heart of their city, as opposed to hated rivals Sampdoria. Genoa–Liverpool. UEFA cup, 4 March 1992.

## From Lions to bankruptcy. The rise and fall of Pro Vercelli

Vercelli is (and was) a sleepy, rice-growing town on the Piedmont plains, between Turin and Milan. Yet, between 1908 and 1913, and then again from 1921–1923, the town's football team – Pro Vercelli – was more or less unbeatable. Pro Vercelli lost just one championship in the five years between 1908 and 1913 – and even that was in extremely controversial circumstances. The club's rapid rise has been attributed largely to their modern training methods and tactics, and to the extraordinary fitness of their players.

This small-town team, with players who were not only all Italians but almost entirely from Vercelli itself, demonstrated that early football success was not so much about talent, but also about determination, preparation and teamwork. One of Vercelli's most celebrated players – the midfielder Guido Ara – allegedly coined the Italian cliché 'football is not a game for little girls'. Vercelli was the first modern Italian club, on and off the pitch, and the lessons of its victories were to become part of the DNA of *calcio* from that moment on. Corners and free-kicks were practised in training and the team controlled possession instead of simply booting the ball upfield. They were also very young – the average age of the 1908 squad was just twenty. In Genoa's 1906 team, Spensley was nearly 40 and Pasteur, another key early player, was 30. Pro Vercelli often dominated the last fifteen minutes of games, relying on their exceptional strength. The club was perhaps the first to have a serious youth policy which paid off handsomely. A series of legendary players came through the ranks. Giuseppe Milano was their formidable captain before the war and his brother Felice won five championships at Vercelli, before dying in the trenches in 1915, at the age of 24.

Pro Vercelli played in white shirts with starched collars and cuffs and were one of the first teams to inspire loyalty and almost religious fervour among their fans. Pro Vercelli were also given a rhetorical nickname – *The Lions* – which tied in neatly with the nationalist rhetoric emerging in Italy at that time. As an all-Italian, provincial and local team, Pro Vercelli represented national pride against the foreigner-dominated clubs from the cosmopolitan cities of Milan and Turin. It was no accident that in the first national team game in 1910 Italy's shirts were white, in homage to Pro Vercelli.[29] So dominant was the Vercelli squad in this period that they provided nine of the eleven players who played for Italy against Belgium in May 1913.[30] A staggering eight of these nine players were from the little town of Vercelli itself.

In 1910, Inter and Pro Vercelli finished level on points at the end of the season. The title playoff was to be played in Vercelli because of their superior goal difference. However, on the date chosen by the federation a number of Pro Vercelli players were committed to a military tournament. The club asked for the date to be put back but the federation (and Inter) refused. In protest, Vercelli played their *fourth* team (made up of 10–15-year-olds). Not surprisingly, Inter won easily, 10–3. Pro Vercelli were furious, and were banned until the end of the year for their impudence. An amnesty relaxed the ban in October and Pro Vercelli swept to the title in 1911, 1912 and 1913. The team was famous enough to gain a prestigious invitation to tour South America in the period before the war. After winning two more championships in the 1920s Pro Vercelli began a long decline. As a poor, small-town club, they were unable to hold on to their star players in an increasingly professional game.[31]

In decline, however, Pro Vercelli's youth team managed to produce a striker who turned out to be perhaps the most extraordinary player of his generation. Born in a small town near Pavia in 1913, Silvio Piola moved to Vercelli as a little boy and went on to a career that no other player has come close to matching. After making his debut in 1930 Piola played five seasons for Pro Vercelli, scoring 51 goals and he remained close to his old squad even after Lazio signed him for a record fee in 1934. Pro Vercelli's president had once stated 'we will never sell Piola, not even for all the gold in the world. Once we sell him, the decline of Pro Vercelli will begin.' He was right. His side finished bottom of Serie A with only fifteen points in that year and, once relegated, they were never to return to add to their seven championship titles. Piola went on to greatness and in 21 war-interrupted seasons stretching from 1930 to 1954 he scored 290 goals in 566 games in Serie A.

Pro Vercelli languished in the lower levels of the semi-professional game for a time, before rising slowly up to Serie C again by the end of the 1990s. However, by 2003, like so many other clubs, they were in financial crisis. In December of that year, bankruptcy proceedings began after the club failed to pay player wages. The company which owned the club – whose name was Spare Time – had debts of over £600,000. Pro Vercelli's players were forced to have a whip round to pay for their transport to an away match. A Committee to Save Pro was set up and began looking desperately for a buyer. Today, Pro Vercelli struggle on in one of Italy's third divisions, backed by a small group of loyal fans.

## The First Scandal. The Rosetta Case

In a society racked with scandal, suspicion, accusation and counter-accusation, and where the rule of law has always been something of an option, Italian football was caught up in controversy almost from the very beginning. Many early championships were marked by intense debate, as the football federation struggled to impose any kind of authority over the game. In 1906 Juventus refused to play in the title playoff against Milan after a change of venue and 1910 saw the Pro Vercelli 'baby-players' protest. The post-World War One period was marked by splits, debates and arguments amongst the various clubs and federations.

Italian football's first real scandal became known as the 'Rosetta case'. Virginio Rosetta was one of the most admired and prized defenders of the heroic early phase of *calcio* history. Born in Vercelli in 1902, he is usually recognized as Italy's first professional footballer and was the subject of the first big transfer fee. Rosetta's move was also the spark, for the first, but certainly not for the last time, of protests by one set of fans against the transfer of a player. An accountant by trade, Rosetta was idolized in Vercelli. As he approached his second championship victory with the club in three years (in 1922–23) rumours began to spread of an offer from Juventus. Rosetta had, it appeared, been tapped up. At that time Luigi Bozino, criminal lawyer and Pro Vercelli's president, was also president of the FIGC, so the case took on football-wide proportions.

A lot of money was involved. A cheque for at least 50,000 lire went directly to Bozino and Rosetta's new highly-paid accountancy post in Turin was underwritten by Juventus (and therefore by their owners FIAT). The Rosetta scandal led to the resignation of a number of leading members of the various football federations, and threatened to split the world of *calcio* wide open. Moreover for the first time the *amount* of money paid for a footballer led to scandal *in itself*. It was seen as immoral to spend so much cash on what was essentially just a game. The scandal dragged on. Rosetta moved to Juventus, but after just three games of the 1923–24 season, the federation ruled that the transfer had been irregular. Juventus were docked points for the three games Rosetta had played for them. Without this penalization, Juventus would have won the northern league. The scandal had effectively cost them the championship. Furious at this decision, Juventus's management threatened to pull their team out altogether. This is a unique scandal in Italian football history – with Juventus as the *victims* of an injustice. The trend since then has been for the FIAT club to be the benefactors of scandal and favouritism.

The controversial transfer was finally completed the following season, and Rosetta proved to be well worth the money. Pro Vercelli's fans were still angry at Rosetta's 'betrayal' when he came back in 1929 for a game against their team. He went on to win six championships with Juve as well as the 1934 World Cup. Rosetta's move also highlighted the increasing power of the big clubs, and the beginning of the long decline of the strong provincial sides who had taken *calcio* by storm in the early part of the century. Some writers even trace the deep hatred of many Italian fans towards Juventus to the 'Rosetta case'.

## Fascism and Football

Italian fascism had been created in 1919 from a ragbag group of nationalists, ex-socialists and futurist artists. By 1922 the violent anti-socialism of the fascists had destroyed the nation's powerful socialist and trade union movement through the use of systematic violence, with the support of many ordinary middle-class citizens and the backing of big business. Their next prize was the state itself. In October 1922 fascist leader Benito Mussolini led a 'March on Rome'. The idea was to frighten the fragile liberal elites, and the King, into submission. It worked. Meekly, in the face of the threat of an illegal armed insurrection, the King made the head of that insurrection prime minister. Mussolini was to remain in power for the next 21 years. By 1926, all vestiges of democracy had been wiped out through repressive laws and brutal violence. A dictatorship was in place. Opposition parties were dissolved, their leaders arrested or forced into exile, or murdered.

Football went on, regardless. Fascism was to see Italy become, officially, the greatest football team in the world, and the national league reach levels of popularity that challenged all other sports and pastimes. Under Mussolini, *calcio* became Italy's national sport, new stadiums were built in most Italian cities and the national league became a reality. During the Duce's reign, Italy won two world cups and an Olympic gold medal. Fascism was good for Italian football, and football was good for fascism. Individual fascists also made their mark on the game, as with the infamous events which closed the 1925 championship.

Mussolini (in the white suit in the middle) receives the victorious World Cup team, 29 June 1938. Manager Vittorio Pozzo is second to the left of Mussolini, Silvio Piola third to the left.

## The first 'theft'. Bologna, Genoa and the 1925 playoff final

In 1925, as Italy teetered on the brink of absolute dictatorship, fascism made its first, direct intervention into the football world. Leandro Arpinati had been the local leader of the fascist squads who roamed the Bolognese countryside and city in the post-war period. Using batons, guns and castor oil, these gangs wrought havoc as they 'brought order' to a socialist region. With the ascent of the fascists to power and the progressive move towards dictatorship the violence was toned down. It was no longer needed. Most people were too scared to protest, or had fled.

The 1924–25 season witnessed a titanic struggle between Bologna – Arpinati's team – and Genoa. There were no penalty shoot-outs, so drawn games were simply replayed. Five playoffs were needed to decide the fate of the championship. The third game in this series – played in Milan on 7 June 1925 – proved to be the most dramatic and controversial match in the short history of *calcio*. A massive crowd of some 20,000 fans turned up, including Arpinati himself, and many threatened to spill onto the pitch. Giovanni Mauro, lawyer and ex-player for both Inter and Milan, was the referee. One of the most authoritative figures in the game, he had been an influential member of various committees for over ten years, whilst continuing to officiate in important matches.

William Garbutt's Genoa were 2–0 up by half-time and the title seemed theirs. Midway through the second half, Bologna were on the attack when a close-range shot came in towards the Genoa goal. The goalkeeper spread himself, and Mauro gave a corner to Bologna. At that point, there was a pitch invasion, led by a group of black-shirted fascists. Arpinati stayed in the stands. The referee was surrounded for at least fifteen minutes. In the end – scared, it is said – he changed his decision and gave a goal. Bologna then 'equalized' with eight minutes left, but Genoa refused to accept the draw and play extra-time. Under federation rules, after the pitch invasion the game (and therefore the championship) should have been awarded to Genoa. However, Mauro, under pressure from Arpinati, wrote a bland report which mentioned the pitch invasion, but assigned no blame for it. The federation ordered yet another playoff.

The fourth final was played in Turin on 5 July, and ended in another draw. Genoa and Bologna fans clashed at the city's Porta Nuova station after the game, and gunshots were fired from the Bologna train. Most reports mention either two or four shots, but some put the number as high as twenty, and the fascist daily paper at the time wrote of 'quite a few revolver rounds'. At least two Genoa fans were injured, and one was taken to hospital. Bologna received a small fine, but the incidents caused national outrage, a long inquiry by the federation and a debate in Parliament. The federation decided on yet another game in Turin – this time with no crowd. However, the city's authorities refused to give permission for the match to take place.[32] Football had become a public-order problem.

The drama came to an end in August with a game behind closed doors on the outskirts of Milan at 7.30 in the morning. More than a month had passed since the violent events of Turin, and more than two months since the bizarre 'no-goal' game in Milan. Most of the Genoa team were called back from their holidays to play. The press was ordered to keep the location of the game secret, or to pretend it was in Turin. In the 'crowd' there were a few journalists, some club officials and assorted locals. The whole pitch was surrounded by *carabinieri* on horseback. Bologna won, 2–0, despite having one man sent off just four minutes into the second half, and another towards the end for 'insulting his opponents after a goal'.

Bologna's all-Italian team duly won their first championship, the national playoff with the southern champions being the usual formality, but in Genoa and elsewhere this success would always be known as 'the great theft'. As film-maker Giuliano Montaldo wrote in the 1990s, 'It is hard to believe now but before the war this was the main talking point at the Marassi [Genoa's ground]. The wound has only been healed in the last twenty years. Before that, when we said "Bologna" we meant "the thieves".' The sense of injustice was exacerbated by the rest of the club's history as Genoa were never to win another *scudetto*. The team was thus denied its tenth championship, an honour that gives clubs the right to sew a special star on their shirts. Inter and Milan currently have one star and Juventus have two.[33] Genoa have never got close to their star again and have been stuck on nine championships for eighty years. As is to be expected, Bologna's version of events is rather different. Fan websites hint at a 'hole in the goal net' which would explain the events of that day and leave us in doubt as to whether their team had actually scored, whilst Mauro's report is glossed over and the pitch invasion is blamed on both sets of fans. This version remains limited to one category of people – Bologna supporters.

In 1925, Bologna's powerful backers decided which version of events was made public. In 1926 Arpinati was appointed as the new *podestà* – unelected Mayor – of the city and in the same year he became president of the Italian football federation, a job he would hold until 1933. He reigned supreme over football, his club and his city until financial scandal brought him down in 1934.[34]

## The referees' strike of 1925 and the first 'suspicions'

Referees in the Italian leagues were increasingly unhappy with the pressure they were under by the mid-1920s. Giovanni Mauro, president of the referees' association (the AIA), called time and again for more protection for his members and less control over their activities. His organization was vehemently opposed to a blacklist of referees that had been compiled – in secret – by certain powerful clubs. In 1925 Mauro wrote in his magazine, *The Referee*, that there was a need to re-establish 'minimal levels of deference and respect towards referees whose current position is no longer like that of a judge, but more like that of a clown'. In 1926 a match between Casale and Torino was declared null and void because the referee had not officiated with 'the correct serenity of spirit'. This was code (and remains so, even today) for clearly biased refereeing. This besmirching of their reputation pushed the referees into strike action. Almost everyone in Italy had gone on strike in the wake of World War One. There was even a priests' strike. However, referees had never withdrawn their labour. In the mid-1920s this taboo was broken.

The action was moderate. The men in black simply refused to go to matches. Someone as conservative as Mauro, who had often linked his job to a lofty patriotic ideal, was hardly likely to organize picket lines and burning braziers outside grounds. In any case, the very threat of such a strike gave fascism a perfect opportunity to impose its will on Italian football. A commission was set up to draw up plans for sweeping reforms that would bring an end to the chaos in the game. In 1926, this led to the Viareggio Charter, the most important set of rules since 1909 and the basis for *calcio*'s re-organization under the regime.[35]

## The Viareggio Charter. *Calcio*'s constitution

In 1926, the tortuous history of the Italian football federation, with its splits, rivalries and scandals, led to the imposition of unity from above. The Viareggio Charter was drawn up by three self-styled experts in the elegant seaside town that had seen the 'football riot' of 1920. Viareggio's new rules revolutionized the game. First, professionalism was legalized.

This had been made inevitable by the increasing numbers of working-class footballers, who found it difficult to work *and* play professionally.[36] It was one thing being an accountant *and* a professional footballer – like Fulvio Bernardini of Roma. It was quite another trying to combine other, more humble professions with the demands of a full-time national championship.

Moreover, the charter clarified the role of foreign players: *they were banned*. The boom in players from the new frontiers of *calcio* – above all Hungary and Austria – was brought to a swift halt by these new rules. There were more than 80 such players in the Italian championship in the 1925–6 season. These foreigners were all forced to find work elsewhere, or as something else. Some became managers, like the Hungarian Arpad Veisz, who won the first Serie A national championship as coach of Inter in 1929–30 and two other titles in charge of Bologna in the 1930s.

Like many Italian laws and rules, however, the charter's procedures contained a big loophole. Who was Italian, and who was a foreigner? Banned from buying Hungarians and Austrians, the top Italian clubs began to look for 'Italians' amongst the millions of their fellow citizens who had left the country to find fortune elsewhere in the world. The hybrid category of the Italian *oriundo* (a person of Italian *extraction*) became part of footballing parlance. *Oriundi* were Italians who had been brought up or born in other countries, but were of Italian origin (an Italian grandparent was usually enough). For a long time after 1926, the history of foreigners in the Italian game – right up until the end of the 1940s, and in various phases after that – was synonymous with that of the *oriundi*.

Thanks to the charter, a unified national league was made inevitable by further rationalization of the championship, leading directly to a national Serie A and Serie B in 1929–30. As if to underline the central role of fascist leader Leandro Arpinati the offices of the football federation were moved to Bologna, away from the traditional centres of football power – Turin and Milan. These offices followed Arpinati to Rome in 1929, when he became undersecretary in the Interior Ministry. Finally, the Viareggio Charter abolished the referees' association, reducing their autonomy, but increasing their prestige. A special committee was given the power to select referees for specific games. Referees remained amateurs. Giovanni Mauro, Arpinati's ally in the 1925 Bologna 'theft', took control of this new body until well into the 1930s. His decisions in that 1925 final had done his career no harm at all.

## The inauguration which changed Italy

For Italy, 1926 was a key year, as Benito Mussolini was anxious to move the country further towards a fascist dictatorship. The spark which led to the final destruction of the country's fragile democracy was linked to football. Arpinati had ordered the construction of a spanking new stadium in Bologna in 1924 and by the end of October 1926 the ground was ready for an official inauguration, to coincide with the fourth anniversary of the March on Rome. Mussolini came to Bologna for the occasion, and entered the stadium on a white horse to huge applause. After making a speech and opening a fascist foundation, Mussolini was driven to the station by Arpinati himself, in an open limo known as a 'torpedo'. As the dictator passed through the crowds, a gunshot was fired into the car, missing everyone and, allegedly, passing through Mussolini's scarf. In the chaos that ensued, a fifteen-year-old boy was beaten to death by the crowd and identified as the potential assassin. The boy, Anteo Zamboni, was the son of a well-known local ex-anarchist. The whole Zamboni family was sent into internal exile for having organized the supposed attempt on the Duce's life. Years later, a plaque was unveiled where Zamboni had been killed.[37]

There are strong doubts about the role of Zamboni, and many historians claim that the shot was the work of dissident fascists or even the Italian secret services.[38] Arpinati, to his credit, pressed for an amnesty for the family – he was a friend of the boy's father. Meanwhile, the consequences for Italy of Mussolini's trip to Bologna for the new stadium were dramatic. In November 1926 new laws were passed re-introducing the death penalty that had been abolished in 1888. All political parties apart from the Fascist Party were banned along with their newspapers and a special fascist secret police service was set up. The last vestiges of free speech and democracy had been removed.

## *Calcio* and Italian capitalism

From the very beginning, Italy's business leaders were interested in *calcio*. One of the founders of AC Milan was Piero Pirelli, industrialist and part of the huge Pirelli rubber business set up in the city in 1872. Pirelli ran Milan from 1908 to 1929 and was responsible for the construction of the San Siro stadium in 1926. Senatore Borletti, another Milanese industrialist with various interests in the city (alarm clocks, bullets, watches, department stores, basketball), was president of Inter from 1926 to 1929. Most important of all, however, was the role of FIAT. Formed in 1899 in Turin, by the end of World War One FIAT had become one of Italy's biggest companies. By the 1920s, FIAT was producing 90 per cent of Italy's cars and the Agnelli family controlled 70 per cent of the company. In 1923, Edoardo Agnelli (who was just over 30 at the time) took control of Juventus and remained president until 1935, overseeing a series of astonishing victories in the 1930s. Edoardo was the son of Giovanni Agnelli, founder of the company. FIAT have been linked to Juventus ever since. Edoardo used to take his son Gianni with him to the stadium, and Gianni Agnelli was part of Juve's history until his death in 2003.[39]

In a way that is unique, Italy's biggest company has run Italy's biggest football club, and this alliance has created love, hate, loyalty and jealousy in equal measure. FIAT's wealth, and its business ethics, made Juve into the greatest producer of victories in Italian football, with a fan-base that spread across the whole country and dwarfed that of the other clubs. FIAT used Juventus to make money, but also to create consensus and popularity, with Turin workers but above all among ordinary Italians across the peninsula. Every victory was identified with the car company that paid the players' wages. By the 1930s Juventus could count on a fan-base bigger than that of all the other clubs put together.

## From *calcio* to football. A mass sport is born

By the end of the 1920s, *calcio* had become football. Italy had a professional game, with a national league. The history of *calcio* since 1929 is synonymous with the history of Serie A and Serie B. Italy also had a national team that was on the verge of making its mark as a world footballing power. There were stadiums all over the country, and many people – men and women – now saw themselves as fans. A series of spectacular scandals had rocked the game, including a playoff behind closed doors and cases of bribery and corruption. Shots had been fired between rival fans, and referees had gone on strike. Politics had intermeshed itself deeply into the organization, running and structure of the game, and of individual clubs. Money was also being made from football, and footballers could now live by the game alone. In just three decades, Italian football had moved on from a few tubby Englishmen kicking a heavy ball around on the dockside to a mass sport, which attracted millions of followers. Italian football had come a long way, in a short time, and it was never to look back.

# CHAPTER 2

# The Referee

'Rules exist, but they are not easy to interpret'

PAUL GINSBORG

'Perhaps the history of football would be best understood as a history of referees, and not through the histories of federations, national teams, big tournaments, managers, bosses'

GIAN PAOLO ORMEZZANO

'In Italy the referee question is more important than the southern question'          FABIO BALDAS (former referee)

## Hunt the Ref! *Akkiappa L'Arbitro!*

In 2003 Enrico Preziosi, games entrepreneur and football chairman, launched a new board game onto the lucrative Italian market. The game was part of a series. It was called *Akkiappa L'Arbitro* – which loosely translates as 'Hunt the Referee' (a dog-catcher is an *acchiappa-cane*). The 'Ks' instead of the 'Cs' are an extra insult, common in Italy but very hard to explain to foreigners.[1] The winner, the box says, is the player 'who hunts down the highest number of characters'. Two large salivating fans are depicted on the front of the game box, cheering. On the back there is a referee, running away. It is a simple game: you are provided with a small plastic football pitch upon which are attached a number of equally big-headed plastic referees, with light-buttons on

*Akkiappa L'Arbitro.* The game.

their tops. Some are completely bald, like Pierluigi Collina, Italy's most famous match official. Two padded gloves are also included. The object of the game? Hit (*akkiappa!*) the referee that lights up, in the quickest time possible. That's it. Hit as many referees, on the head, before your opponent does so, with a padded glove whilst the score is kept, automatically. As a game, *Akkiappa L'Arbitro* leaves something to be desired. As a metaphor for the relationship between Italians and referees, it is perfect. Not surprisingly, the referees' association complained about *Akkiappa*. Preziosi, who had spent the entire 2002–3 season moaning that his then team – Como – had been harshly treated by referees, apologized and said that he would withdraw the game from the shops. In 2004 it was still available. I purchased one in Milan (for £35) in January of that year.

All this might be seen as comic if it were not for the inflammatory consequences of Preziosi's frequent outbursts. In that same season, when Como were quite clearly not good enough for Serie A, a small group of their fans went crazy after a referee gave three penalties against them in a home match with Udinese. They decided to *akkiappare l'arbitro* in real life. After a semi-riot, the game was abandoned. It is not difficult to link Preziosi's conspiracy theories with this violence, and such attitudes rarely bring results. On the contrary, they give the players a great excuse for not trying very hard. It is all the referee's fault, so why bother running around too much? *Akkiappa* identified the guilty party in the chaos of Italian football as the referee. *He* was responsible for all the game's ills, and as such deserved to be hunted down, beaten up, punished.

A book published in 2004 (and to be found in the 'comedy' section of bookstores) was simply a list of incidents involving referees from right across Italy, in minor games of all kinds.[2] Here are some examples, from all parts of the peninsula and its islands:

> Mortara (Lombardy): 'after a player was sent off his son came onto the pitch without permission screaming: "referee, you are murdering my players". Asked to leave by the official, he first struck the ball violently towards the referee, and then kicked him in the leg, causing a strong bruise to emerge; the game had to be abandoned.'

> Vercelli (Piedmont), January 1995: 'The referee of Pro Vercelli–Olbia (Serie C2) gave a penalty to Olbia in injury time at the end of the game. They scored, and the referee blew the final whistle. At this point, he was chased by some Pro Vercelli players to the dressing room, where he remained "barricaded in" for half an hour or so, until the police came to his rescue.'

> Carini (Sicily): 'A player was banned for five years after headbutting the referee, breaking his nose and a tooth. The game was called off.'

> Montecchio (Emilia): 'After the game had finished, a supporter chased the referee on his motorbike for fifteen km, unsettling his driving.'

> Calabria: 'After a player was booked, the same player punched the referee in the face, who was then surrounded by the whole team, spat on, struck and kicked. The group included the stand-in linesman (who was from the same team) who hit the referee with his flag. The game was called off, but the same group of players tried to force the referee to continue and followed him to the dressing room.'

There are 202 pages of stories like this, chosen from official reports, and this is only a small selection of what has become a violent epidemic in Italian sport: *Hunt the ref!*

## Referees as a 'virtuous minority'

In 1993, a group of left-wing intellectuals met to discuss the tumultuous changes in Italian society. In the space of a few months, all the major political parties had been caught up in a massive corruption scandal, and the whole system seemed on the verge of collapse. The intellectuals argued that Italian civil society was marked by a series of 'virtuous minorities'. These people – judges, teachers, voluntary workers, nurses – fought daily, heroic and unheralded battles against the ills which had dogged the Italian state since its birth – clientelism (the exchange of all kinds of resources), corruption, organized crime, illegality. Referees were not mentioned by the intellectuals, but perhaps they should have been. In no sector of society were the virtuous minorities so isolated, so hated and so vulnerable as on the football pitches which, every week, play host to hundreds of thousands of matches. In no sector of society was the battle between respect for legality and violence so clear, and so difficult. Were Italy's *arbitri* her ultimate 'virtuous minority'?[3]

Every week, referees all over Italy went off, on their own, to nondescript small towns to officiate in minor matches. They were almost always unpaid – and might just get their petrol money back, if they were lucky. Yet, they still turned up, on time, on dusty pitches and always in front of small, usually hostile crowds where every insult or complaint could be heard loud and clear. Nobody was there to protect these people – by now men *and* women – from humiliation, intimidation, violence or the threat of violence.

Why *does* somebody become a referee in Italy? Nobody knows. Nobody has ever bothered to study this eccentric group of people, the only representatives of the state in the wilderness of Italy's complicated, weird and angry football world. The chances of fame and fortune, for a referee, were even fewer than for young players. So why do it, at all? Italian football journalists have usually gone for pop-psychological explanations – referees are failures of some kind (as footballers, or simply as people) who like to exercise power. For Gianni Brera, Italy's most influential football journalist, referees were generally people 'who had failed as players, or were so badly injured and so old as to be able merely to run after the others, and no longer after the ball'.[4] They were, he continued, probably 'sado-masochists' who enjoyed ordering people around. A football referee, whilst on the pitch, is one of the few institutional figures in the world to exercise complete power. Before TV replays, referees were 'the only judge, the judge without appeal' (Gian Paolo Ormezzano). Many therefore argued that a psycho-analyst was needed to understand referees. Sociology might also help us in our quest.

If we look at the jobs held down by the 36 referees who officiated in Serie A in the year 2000, we can get some tentative answers. Of course, for a modern referee, it helps to have a flexible job. Three of the referees listed their jobs as 'free professionals', two as 'financial consultants', three as bankers, four as shopkeepers or salesmen, and four as 'insurers'. Others were listed, generically, as 'businessmen'. Only one was a teacher, another was a policeman. Many came from small towns. The old cliché of the accountant from Peterborough (which is what most referees in the UK in the 1970s seemed to be) appears to be reinforced by this group of top officials. Referees are self-employed, petty bourgeois, conservatives, self-made men. However, there were some exceptions. One referee was a diet consultant, another was an expert in Chinese, one was a wine dealer, and another was a politician.

*Where* the referee is from is one final, key area, which matters immensely in Italy. Referees are usually listed with their place of birth (Ceccarini 'from Livorno', etc.) and one of the key federation rules states that no referee can officiate in a match in which his home-town is involved. This rule is now extended to the whole province where a referee lives. Regional identity is seen as a source of bias, *per se*, but is also extremely localized, and it also works both ways. A referee from Pisa would not be allowed to officiate in a match involving Pisa *or* their hated rivals, Livorno, for example. Referees are always under suspicion, by definition.

Italian referees can be compared to sheriffs in the Wild West (although referees are armed only with a whistle): trying to impose the increasingly flimsy authority of law and order in the face of mistrust, hostility and violence. Perhaps they should be seen as the real heroes of our time – taking legality courageously out to the killing fields and challenging, time and again, with dignity and respect, the disdain for the law so widespread in Italian society. Are referees like anti-mafia judges in Sicily, anti-corruption magistrates in Milan, honest journalists in Rome?

Very few Italians share this view. Brera wrote this about referees. 'In almost every case, we are dealing with either a frustrated person, someone who has need of transfer [a psychological term] in order to pretend to themselves that they exist and have free will; or a bully . . . who insists that the law be respected even at the cost of upsetting others.'[5] Brera's judgement is shared by most of his compatriots. The referee is *always* a bastard, a *cornuto*. This literally means 'cuckold' – or 'horned' – and is often accompanied by a hand gesture where the little and forefingers are raised. *Cornuto* is also used as an insult to imply that a referee should be at home with his wife rather than refereeing. Other common insults imply that referees are *venduti* (sold, corrupt, crooks). Bizarrely, whenever Italian teams are playing in Europe, or the national team is in action, Italian commentators usually claim that their officials 'are the best in the world'. In comparison with others, Italian referees are praised to the skies. At home, they are always *cornuti*.

## Rules, Laws and the Italian Referee

'Every game is under the control of a referee, who has all the authority necessary in order to make sure that the Rules of the Game are respected in the game in which he officiates'
*Italian football federation Rule Book, Rule 5*

Referees interpret a set of rules, in a context in which everyone has their own opinion on every single moment of every game. They have to make an instant decision, one way or the other, based purely on what they have seen. As if that was not difficult enough, many of the 22 players on the pitch (as well as managers and fans) often try and pretend that something different has happened, or simply hide reality from the referee's probing eyes. Players dive, appeal for throw-ins after

clearly kicking the ball out, crash to the ground screaming with pain
when they have not been touched, try sneaky handballs. They also
complain, constantly, about everything. Football games, like prison
riots, are 'essentially contested concepts'.[6] Agreement is not only hard
to come by, it is impossible.

All of this is much more difficult in Italy, for precise political and
historical reasons. As historian Paul Ginsborg has written, 'the referee's
authority is perforce uncertain, but it is made much more so in Italy
by the almost universal climate of suspicion, if not derision, that
accompanies his decisions'. In the relationship between the Italian
football fan and the referee, Ginsborg continues, 'it is not difficult to
discern . . . a series of emotions – suspicion, contempt, cynicism, even
hatred – that characterize the relationship between Italians and the
state'.[7] This relationship, moreover, is not confined to *Italian* referees
alone – although it is most pervasive with regard to the national
championship. Foreign referees are also accused of the same 'crimes',
and have been blamed for the failures of various Italian teams during
various World Cups. Occasionally a simple solution to the 'referee
question' in Italy has been proposed: import non-Italian officials. An
experiment of this type was tried in the second half of the 1950s –
with little success – and was unearthed again as a possible solution in
the twenty-first century, for key championship games.

Football rules have to be interpreted. Although the written rules
remain the same, the *application* of those rules differs across football
cultures, and the official representatives of these cultures are the referees. Thus, many tackles that are fouls in Italy are not fouls in the
British game. In Italy there is a special phrase for our more liberal
style of officiating: 'refereeing, English style' *(un arbitraggio all'inglese)*.
Moreover, the Italians are very clear that a straight-legged tackle – what
they call *gamba tesa* – is *always* a foul, even if you get the ball. In
England we sometimes call this 'foot up', but it is by no means always
a foul, especially if the tackler wins the ball. In Italy the idea is that
this kind of tackle is dangerous, *per se*, and therefore a foul. Once
again, the written rules are the same, their application is not, although
the globalization of football has led to more consistency across different
championships.

## Corruption, Suspicion, Legitimation

'The referee's decisions on the field are not subject to appeal. A referee can change his mind only if he believes that he has made a mistake or, as he wishes, after a signal from the referee's assistant, as long as play has not been re-started'

*Italian football federation Rule Book, 2002, Rule 5*

After Juventus lost the 1997 Champions League final to Borussia Dortmund, Roberto Bettega, former player and by then high up in the Italian club's management hierarchy, claimed that his team had been 'beaten by a stronger federation than ours'. In 2002, in the wake of Italy's dramatic defeat at the hands of South Korea at the World Cup, the Italian press was full of phrases like these: 'we do not have enough power at international level' and 'Italy does not count in the football federation'. When the team returned after a disastrous campaign (one victory in four games) most of the blame was aimed not at the players, nor even at the manager, but at Franco Carraro – a career football bureaucrat with a charisma bypass and Italy's man at the International Football Federation (FIFA). Carraro, the press claimed, had not fought hard enough to ensure fair treatment and 'good' referees for the Italian team. In a similar vein were the words muttered to me by a disgruntled Inter fan in 2003. 'Next year, I think *they* will let us win.'[8]

What does all this mean, for Italian football and for Italy in general? Quite simply, for the Italian football fan, the referee is *always* corrupt, unless proven otherwise. What remains to be discovered is *how* he is or has been corrupt, in favour of whom, and why. It is this thesis that dominates most discussions of Italian football. Conspiracy theories abound – are hegemonic, in fact. Who will be *allowed to win* next year, next week, tomorrow, and why? In Italy, there is the strong conviction that the state, its rules and regulations are flexible entities, besmirched with corruption and therefore ready to be flouted and challenged. This conviction has a strong historical basis. In Italy, as the writer and football critic Giovanni Arpino put it, 'those who hold power, even for ninety minutes, are never looked upon in a good light'.[9]

It is sometimes said in Italy that only an idiot adheres to the law.[10] This is also true on the football pitch. All institutions require considerable levels of *legitimation* if they are not to govern mainly through the use of or threat of force. A political system 'requires an input of mass loyalty that is as diffuse as possible'.[11] Citizens must have certain levels of faith in the right of the state to govern, collect taxes, enforce law and order, fight wars and educate their children in order for these institutions to work with any efficiency. The Italian state has found legitimation extremely difficult to obtain since the country was unified in 1861. In fact the Italian state has been in the throes of a *legitimation crisis* ever since its inception. The basic 'rules of the game' have never been accepted by most Italians. They have been partly replaced by unwritten 'rules' that have institutionalized inefficiency and privileged informal forms of behaviour and exchange. All of this can also be applied to the relationship between fans, footballers and pundits and the representatives of legality in the world of football, the referees. Referees are invested with enormous power to determine matches, championships and World Cups. They are, according to Italians, both eminently manoeuvrable and highly effective in their cheating. As with the state, Italians have both contempt *and* great respect for referees. This respect is for the authority they wield and the institutional position they hold. As individuals they are despised.

Most Italians who know anything about football history (and many know an awfully large amount) will claim that at least five or six World Cups have been decided by refereeing decisions. Thus, it is common knowledge in Italy that English referee Ken Aston kicked Italy out of the 1962 World Cup with his 'biased' display in the infamous Italy–Chile match, which soon became known as the 'Battle of Santiago'. Moreover, *all* Italians believe that England fixed the 1966 World Cup. Finally the embarrassing exit of Italy in the 2002 tournament was blamed squarely on an eccentric Ecuadorian referee, Byron Moreno. Whole websites are dedicated to ridiculing Moreno.[12] Even in earlier rounds, when Italy had three goals wrongly disallowed, the rising hysteria over the officials began to dominate all other ways of understanding Italy's weak performance on the pitch.

However, there is a contradiction here. If *all* referees are corrupt, then why should anyone be *blamed* for being corrupt? Somewhere there must be the possibility of a referee *not being corrupt*. Corrupt referees are often criticized for being weak-willed in the face of pressure,

which implies that a strong official might resist. In any case, in order
to win, you need the referee on your side *or* the say-so of the authorities.
Some external guarantee of 'fairness' is required. Italians believe that
this guarantee was missing in 1962 (for them) and in 2002. It was
certainly there when they won the cup in 1982, when the chair of the

Byron Moreno. He was blamed by Italians for their defeat at the
hands of South Korea in the 2002 World Cup finals. A whole series
of similar photos appeared on the web in the wake of the tournament.

international referees' panel was an Italian – Artemio Franchi. Italy
were even awarded a rather dubious penalty in the first half of that
year's World Cup final, which they managed to miss. What remains
strange is the *moral* revolt. If winning football matches, or tournaments, is simply a matter of getting the right referee in the right place
at the right time, then morality has no place in the argument. The real
game is played out elsewhere, not on the pitch.

## 'Psychological slavery'. Big and small clubs

One referee-related adage has been constant, in Italian domestic football. Rich clubs are always privileged over poorer clubs. They win more
penalties, have fewer people booked, have more goals against them
disallowed. On one level this is not very surprising. Rich teams are
usually better than poor teams, and thus tend to attack more, leading
to more fouls against them in the opposition penalty area, more shots
on goal and more corners. Yet, this technical explanation is not enough
to explain such a long-term trend in bias. In Italy, the big clubs have
also enjoyed 'favours' because they are run by powerful and influential
people. FIAT was Italy's most important company throughout the
twentieth century. The Agnelli family who founded and managed the
huge Turin-based car business were also the owners of Juventus. Money
and status are not necessary to oil the workings of favouritism, but
they help.

Croneyism, however, has largely been a state of mind. A key phrase
here is 'psychological slavery'. It was referee administrator[13] Giorgio
Bertotto, a Venetian optician in his other life, who first argued – after
a 1967 game between Venezia and Inter – that 'psychological slavery
towards the big teams' was rife amongst Italian referees. It is this
'institutional bias' which leads to a widespread cynicism over the outcomes of championships. Hence phrases of the type 'next year they
may let us win'. However, this scepticism does not prevent moral
outrage at the ways in which referees favour the big clubs. Often fans
will taunt Juventus with the chant *sapete solo rubare* – 'you only know
how to rob'.

Obviously, one factor enslaving officials is ambition mixed with
self-preservation. A referee is unlikely to have a long and glorious
career if he gives a series of penalties against Juventus. Journalists will
often write, after a particularly cringe-making performance by a referee
in favour of a bigger club, that an official will *fare carriera* – 'he will
have a good career'. Tradition is also important. This is how things
have always been done. Minor clubs have always argued that referees
tend to 'liquidate' them – especially in matches against the richer
teams. In the 2002–3 season the president of tiny Como spent the
whole season making this very point – even claiming that he would

withdraw his team in protest. In 2003–4 the mantle of the persecuted was taken up by Perugia, whose president threatened first to go to court, and then to withdraw his team from the last four matches of the season in order to make his case.

'Favouritism' has shifted in interesting ways over time. When big teams play other big teams, things become more complicated. Rich teams have also become poor. Genoa was a big team for a long time – they are now a relatively minor club. The same can be said of Torino, Fiorentina, Napoli and Bologna. Smaller teams have also developed into more powerful concerns after heavy investment, as with Parma in the 1990s. Three clubs have always been big in recent times – Juventus, Inter and Milan.[14] Amongst these perennially powerful clubs, the shift of 'bias' has moved with the times – depending on politics, money, and the close-knit nature of the refereeing body. Sometimes, luck or even footballing prowess has come into the picture. Any fan who spent any period of time in Italy came to accept this state of affairs as sad, but inevitable.

In the 1960s, many fans claimed that Inter were preferred over Milan and even over Juventus. The 'Great Inter' team of the 1960s went 100 league games without conceding a penalty. During the 1970s Milan fans complained constantly of harsh treatment at the hands of a series of referees. The 1980s saw grumbling and objections from Fiorentina and Roma and in the 1990s Inter felt that they had been robbed. The 2002–2003 season was notable for a series of violent arguments concerning the *arbitraggio* – the 'refereeing' – of Roma matches that began on the first day of the championship and continued right through until June. Many Italians are convinced that Juventus – the biggest and most powerful club of all – have been the most 'helped' of all. This includes Juventus fans themselves, who will shrug their shoulders and grin at the latest refereeing 'error' in their favour. One Juventus fan even published a pamphlet entitled *Eulogy to theft* detailing the pleasure he had taken in various biased decisions over the years.[15] Favouritism amongst the big clubs, it is widely believed, tends to balance out over time. Hence, many fans will claim that Lazio's last-day defeat in the 1998–1999 championship was 'balanced out' by *their* controversial last-day victory the following year. Similarly, Juventus were 'repaid' after losing a championship in the rain at Perugia in 2000 with an easy ride two seasons later. Injustices were righted by further injustices. What goes around, in Italian football, comes around.

This type of reasoning has become a science in Italy, and is known as *dietrologia* – 'behindology'. It is a science of all-encompassing conspiracy theories, where every event is explained with reference to the machinations of powerful, unseen forces. *Dietrologia* is commonly employed in footballing discourse just as it applies to the mafia or to the shady role of the Italian secret services in the 1960s and 1970s. By definition, these explanations are rarely proved to be right or wrong and here lies the source of their power. 'Behind-the-scenes-ology' has become a footballing commonplace. Most fans routinely see the game through this mindset.[16]

Within this broad picture, each fan has his or her own cross to bear – a particular decision, match or 'refereeage' (*arbritraggio*) which decided a championship or 'stole' a key match. Classic examples of this focus on individual decisions include the 1925 championship won by Bologna against Genoa;[17] Maurizio Turone's disallowed 'goal' for Roma against Juventus in 1981; Fiorentina's loss in the 1982 championship; Inter and Ronaldo's lost penalty, again against Juve, in 1998. Some of these controversies relate to normal refereeing decisions *during* games – penalties given and not given, offsides, sendings-off, 'ghost-goals'. Others are more complicated – decisions to play on in bad weather, replayed games, disciplinary questions.[18] For a long time, some games were decided by committees (*al tavolino* – literally 'at the table'), leading in turn to manipulation of *these* rules. Many of these decisions have led to incessant debates, and endless rancour. Legends are easy to create. Whole championships have been registered in the popular imagination as 'thefts'.

Not all referees are 'psychologically conditioned' in the same way. Some officials are viewed as pro or (much more rarely) anti-Juventus, others as more 'objective', others as simply erratic, some as just bad. Huge debate thus concentrates in Italy on *which* referees officiate in *which* matches, and *how* they are chosen for particular games. These procedures have changed with bewildering speed and frequency over the years.

## Choosing Referees. 'Designators', Draws, Secrets

The mechanisms (often referred to as the draw, or *sorteggio*) for the selection of referees – fiendishly complicated, and ever in flux – are the object of almost constant debate amongst fans, managers, presidents and players. It is interesting to contrast this interest with the complete lack of curiosity about similar instruments in the English game. Do any fans in England even know how and why certain referees are chosen for certain games, or do they care? In Italy, by 2004, even the linesmen were becoming the object of calls for them to be chosen by ballot, every week.

In 1926 the Viareggio Charter (football's constitution – the set of rules by which the game was governed) created a committee with responsibility for referee selection. Throughout the 1930s, 1940s and 1950s, officials for particular games were never announced beforehand, but only over the loudspeaker as the teams themselves were read out. The logic behind this system was to avoid the possibility of direct corruption. If nobody knew who the referee was, they couldn't try and bribe him. If you wanted to slip a referee a backhander, you needed access to this 'secret' information. The Catania corruption case of the 1950s was tied up with the passing-on of the valuable secret – by a referee's cousin – concerning which matches would be refereed by which officials.[19] Secrecy bred gossip, and word would often get out concerning referee selection. By the late 1950s, this system had become unworkable.

In 1958, a list of referees for games was issued in advance to the clubs and the press. From 1958 to 1960, this list was only given out on Saturday morning. Later, the list was available by Wednesday. Yet, the choice of referees was subject to the influence of the bigger clubs which tried to ban certain referees from their games. Juventus attempted to bar top referee Concetto Lo Bello in the early 1960s, but after a court case and a threatened referees' strike the club was forced to back down. 'Uncomfortable' referees were marginalized. In the early 1980s, under pressure after the 'thefts' of 1981–1982 – when Juventus won back-to-back controversial championships against Roma and Fiorentina – a much better system was introduced: the ballot. Referees' names were put into a (metaphorical) hat, and then drawn out for each game. This took place in public, to avoid corruption.[20] On the face of it, this was the fairest system of all. And, as it turned out, in one of the rare seasons when a free draw was used, a small club, Verona, surprisingly won the *scudetto*. Many commentators have drawn a link between these two facts. The 'psychological power' of the big clubs was reduced by the free draw. Referees would not be punished if their decisions cost the big teams, and particular referees could not be directed to specific games.

The free ballot was soon abolished, as the big clubs hated it. A technical committee chose referees until the late 1990s when it was replaced with a new kind of ballot – the 'piloted draw'. Here, referees were divided into two groups – international and non-international officials. The big games were drawn from the first group, the smaller games from the second. Yet, this system was still subject to other factors. Referees who made serious mistakes, highlighted by the press and by club officials, were disciplined, and sent to the 'hell' of Serie B.[21]

Key figures in both the ballot and non-ballot systems were the so-called 'designators' – ex-referees who did, or organized, the choosing. Under Paolo Casarin in the 1990s, there was a serious attempt to break away from the old murky methods and move towards fairer and more open systems. Casarin argued that 'all referees should referee all teams', thus breaking with the veto power of the bigger clubs. In a non-ballot system, the designators were all-powerful, but they were still important in a ballot system and were usually blamed if and when things went wrong. Currently referees are chosen by a weighted ballot system with names announced on Fridays. In the 2004–5 season, the 'directed ballot' was heavily criticized from all sides. In July 2005 the old 'designating' system was reintroduced, with only one designator – an ex-referee called Maurizio Mattei.

Pierluigi Pairetto held the post of 'co-designator' up until 2005. An international referee in his youth (he refereed the final of Euro '96, giving the Czech Republic a dubious penalty) and full-time vet, Pairetto has the most difficult job in the Italian football world. The youngest referee to officiate in Serie A, he was only 29 when he took control of his first game in 1981. Pairetto, when he was still refereeing matches, took his job extremely seriously. He trained every day, re-viewed previous games, and was in bed by ten every night. His mother ironed his kit for him. In 2000 he was at the centre of an embarrassing incident.

## Watchgate

In January 2000, a strange item of news started to break in the press and sports media. The president of Roma, Franco Sensi, had given the two most important and powerful figures in the referees' association – the designators – a nice Christmas present. Each had received a gold Rolex. Sensi's defence was that he had 'only spent' 120 million lire (about £40,000). Moreover, he had 'always' (at least over the last five or six years) given presents to the 'designators'. The year before, it had been champagne – six bottles at £70 a bottle. 'It was an act of courtesy,' he continued, 'Roma wants nothing from the referees. If they want to give the presents back, that is their problem. They are free to receive presents if they want. All the costs were declared and are included in Roma's budget. Everything has taken place in the open.'

After the storm broke, it turned out that a total of 41 Rolexes had been passed to many of the top referees, who were ordered to give them back. Only two of these were solid gold – worth £8,000 each on the street – whilst the lesser models were valued at a mere £1,800 each. Other presents turned up: Inter had given 36 electro-stimulators worth £700 each, while 74 linesmen had received Phillips watches worth £180 each. Some of the Rolexes could not be recovered. One referee had already sold his on. Nobody resigned. A judicial inquiry was opened, and closed, and the tax police also became interested for a while. Meanwhile, unlike the lowly referees, the 'designators' kept their gold Rolexes. The justification? 'If we had given the gifts back it would have led to more embarrassment and debate.' 'Watchgate' only underlined the contempt with which most Italians regard their referees. Nobody was particularly surprised, or even outraged. The case merely confirmed their suspicions.

## Bribing Referees. Cheques and more watches

'Only the referee can send a player off'.
*Football federation Rule Book, 2002–2003*

Given the widespread view that all referees are corrupt, unless proven otherwise, you would expect the history of Italian football to be packed with cases of corruption involving match officials. In fact, quite the opposite is the case. There have been many more cases of corruption, match-fixing and illegal betting involving players, managers and presidents than there have been involving referees. In 120 years of *calcio* history, very few referees have been caught in the act of taking bribes or fixing games. In a corrupt world, Italian referees have been paragons of legality. This could be seen as proof, if more proof were needed, of their heroic, virtuous minority status. The average Italian fan has an easy reply to this point. *You do not need to bribe referees*. They naturally favour certain teams at certain times. They are simply pawns in much wider power games. They become successful by helping the powerful, and following orders.

Nonetheless, there have been cases of referee corruption in the Italian game. In the early 1950s a group of referees were banned for life after it was revealed that they had been fixing results over a number of years. Later, one of the best-documented scandals involved referee Ugo Scaramella and Catania football club, at that time (1955 – a terrible year for the game in Italy, with at least three scandals) fighting against relegation to Serie B. This was not a simple story of corruption, and doubts remain about the real motives of the people involved. The whistle was blown by a journalist – Giulio Sterlini – who had also worked for the club in the past. According to Sterlini, he had personally given three cheques to Scaramella on three separate occasions, and had also bribed the referee's cousin to find out which games he would be officiating. Some claimed that Sterlini was trying to blackmail Catania with this information. The club filled the papers with dirt on the journalist – he had, for example, been banned from every school in Italy when he was a student – and argued that the stories were revenge for his sacking by Catania. Yet, Sterlini's story checked out – especially the money part. The club was sent down to Serie B; Scaramella received a life ban.

Other scandals have arisen which have placed referees in a good light – such as in 1974 when controversial referee Gino Menicucci was offered a watch (by a Foggia official) in his dressing room before a game with Milan. The watch was refused, and Menicucci mentioned the 'bribe' to the Milan president. After a 0–0 draw (which sent Foggia down), the gift was put on the table once more, and turned down again. Since Foggia were already down, they were punished with a deduction of six points in Serie B while Menicucci emerged with his reputation intact. In more than one hundred years of football history, in a country where scandals have been the norm, not the exception, the number of cases involving referees could be counted on the fingers of one hand. This had not helped their reputation. *Venduto!* – crook – was still the most common insult hurled at the men and women in black every Sunday afternoon.

## At the sharp end. Violence against referees

In the early 1990s, I went to a boys' football game near Florence with my ex-professor. His son was playing in goal. The vehemence and anger of the parents and relatives – the only real 'crowd' – were shocking. Some spent *the whole game* insulting the referee, and even threatening him. Others were happy merely to attack their own team, with particular focus on their own children. What was particularly disturbing was that the referee was also a boy, a little bit older than the players. The position of referees at the sharp end of the fragile legality of the Italian game has often led to violence against them. There are thousands of documented cases of attacks on referees in the minor leagues, week in, week out. In these lower leagues, and in the amateur game, referees receive little protection. Acts of violence against officials are so common as to be commonplace.

'Spitting, slapping and punching the referee are the eternal reality of football in the provinces,' wrote *La Repubblica* in 1993.[22] Things came to a head in that year after two events in February. In Naples a mother, Lella Buonaurio – ran onto the field after her son was sent off. She then handbagged the referee. Much further north, in Novara, a group of fathers – again after a sending-off – also attacked the referee. More worryingly, the protagonists of this violence did not appear to be particularly sorry. The Neapolitan mother was unrepentant: 'I'd do it again ... he seemed arrogant, he had sent off two players from our team. I just lost it.' 'Intrusive parents syndrome', which has been identified amongst sports-mad Americans but which seems a perfect diagnosis for Italy, appeared to have become an epidemic. Over the following decade, young players and even some clubs received long bans and big fines were handed out after yet more violence against referees, but very little changed.

Incidents of this type in the professional game have been much rarer, probably because of the very serious consequences for those involved. Nonetheless, referees have sometimes had to run for their lives, even in Italy's top league, Serie A.

## Legnano–Bologna, February 1952

In 1952 Legnano, a team from a small industrial town just outside Milan, were enjoying a rare spell in Serie A. The 'Lilacs' were at home to Bologna and desperately needed a win on an icy pitch. The referee was Bruno Tassini, from Verona. It was a dramatic game. Tassini first failed to send off a Bologna player after he had punched an opponent. He then refused to give two 'clear' penalties to Legnano before awarding a spot kick to Bologna, in the eighty-seventh minute, with the score at 2–2. The home crowd were incensed. Snowballs and cushions rained down from the terraces, and there was a minor pitch invasion. Tassini's reaction was to call the game off – according to the press he simply ran off the pitch – making it inevitable that Bologna would be awarded a 2–0 win under federation rules. Newspaper reports blamed Legnano's 'defeat' fairly and squarely on the referee. For the *Corriere Lombardo* Tassini had not respected the rules of the game and had 'falsified the result'. The paper hoped that it had been Tassini's 'last match' in charge. *La Gazzetta dello Sport* led with the headline 'Tassini defeats Legnano'.

After the game, some fans wanted more. The referee was a marked man. First, he was attacked in a bar in Legnano, where he claimed that his dentures were damaged. He then made his way to Milan for dinner with various officials. As he walked towards the Central Station to catch a train home, two cars drew up and six or seven young men jumped out. They announced that they were Legnano fans and set upon Tassini, who was saved by his linesmen. The referee was hospitalized and 'lost some teeth' (although it is unclear what had happened to his earlier broken dentures). The youths were arrested and charged whilst the majority of Legnano's supporters were still furious about the game itself. They travelled to Milan for a demonstration the next day, holding banners which read 'Forty years of passionate support betrayed' and 'Sport is dead in Legnano'. Many were factory workers in their blue overalls.

These protests were in vain. The league threw the book at Legnano, banning them from playing at home for *eleven months* (for the rest of 1952). The official report claimed that 'from the start' the local fans had been 'hostile' to the referee, and that objects had been thrown at, and had hit, Tassini. The referee had also been struck and kicked on his way off the field and in the bar. Finally, there was the attack near the station, at 11.30 p.m. Legnano were held responsible for the whole affair and finished bottom of Serie A, with a mere seventeen points. They came up the next season, and then promptly went down, and have never again played in the top division. Tassini, meanwhile, went on to be a very important figure in the referees' association in the 1960s.

## The Prince of Referees. Concetto Lo Bello

Concetto Lo Bello, 'The Prince', was the most famous Italian referee of all time. Authoritarian, controversial, brave, narcissistic, he presided, or ruled, over an unrivalled 328 games in Serie A between 1954 and 1974. Lo Bello was also a physical icon. A tall man, he looked extremely distinguished and was always immaculately turned out, with perfectly ironed white shirt collars and a manicured moustache. Lo Bello managed, over the years, to annoy all the big clubs, which would seem to imply that he was as fair as one could be in the difficult world of Italian football. At one point, Juventus even tried to exclude him from their games. Lo Bello's reaction was to force a grovelling reply from no less a personality than Umberto Agnelli, who was president of Juventus and, for a time, of the football federation, as well as part of the FIAT dynasty.

Lo Bello was at the centre of a series of memorable public arguments with Milan midfield star Gianni Rivera and manager Nereo Rocco. In

1973, after yet another clash with Lo Bello, who had sent him off, not for the first time, Rocco was interviewed by the press. He analysed Lo Bello's style: 'the personality has destroyed the referee', he argued, 'he does not referee games, he uses them as a stage on which to show off his show-off behaviour'. Rivera blamed Lo Bello and other referees for Milan's failure to win three championships in the 1970s (they finished second three times in a row) and they once had this exchange on the field. Rivera: 'I'm being slaughtered here. I can't believe you can't see anything.' Lo Bello replied with, 'I give you my word of honour that I can't see these fouls.' Rivera came back with, 'I don't trust your word of honour.' He received a four-game ban for his 'insulting' riposte.

Concetto Lo Bello. Immaculately turned out as ever,
before the Milan derby, 18 February 1968.

The most frequent criticism of Lo Bello's style was that it made *him* the star, and not the players or the game. He made his decisions crystal-clear by aggressive use of hand signals, so much so that on at least three occasions players were inadvertently knocked down as he thrust his arms up to signal a free-kick or a sending-off. There is no doubt that Lo Bello *was* a celebrity on and off the pitch, and he was the first referee to enter the world of politics, becoming a Christian

Democrat parliamentary deputy in 1972 (when he was still a referee) and briefly Mayor of Syracuse, his Sicilian home-town, in 1986. Lo Bello's son, Rosario, also became a leading referee, largely thanks to the reputation of his father. Not surprisingly, given his refereeing style, Concetto Lo Bello was at the centre of a number of startling incidents during his long and controversial career.

## Duce, Duce! Fiorentina–Cagliari. Serie A. 12 October 1969

Fiorentina were reigning champions, and began the 1969–1970 season in sparkling form, extending their unbeaten run to 29 games. Cagliari, surprisingly, were one of the main challengers for the *scudetto* that year and the clash before a packed crowd in Florence in October 1969 was between the top two teams in the championship. Cagliari won the game with a controversial penalty, 1–0, after Lo Bello turned down two penalty appeals for Fiorentina, and disallowed an equalizing goal three minutes from the end of the match for a marginal offside. He also sent off Florence star Amarildo and a Cagliari player for fighting. It was his 261st game in charge in Serie A.

The Florence public did not take kindly to these decisions. Towards the end of the game a familiar, rhythmical chant rang around the stadium, directed at the referee. The meaning of the slogan harked back to the fascist era: *Du-ce, Du-ce*. Lo Bello was a dictator, an authoritarian referee, a fascist. Bottles were thrown onto the field, a fight broke out in the tunnel and Lo Bello was trapped inside the changing rooms for a couple of hours. The referee and linesmen were escorted from the ground in a police van and the Cagliari bus was stoned. The post-match reports had little to do with the game itself. Instead, they concentrated on one man. 'Lo Bello has "written" the championship table', screamed the *Corriere della Sera*. Leading sports journalist Gino Palumbo wrote that the game had been 'a show, with only one star'. The story of the game was 'the story of how a referee, when he so desires, can become the master of a match and conduct it as he sees fit, challenging the rules, regulations, the players and the fans', he continued. 'This is not a report on Fiorentina–Cagliari, this is a report on the one-man show which Concetto Lo Bello performed on Florence's ground.' However, Palumbo also praised Lo Bello's 'courage' on the pitch.

Fiorentina paid heavily for the incidents during and after the match. They had to play their subsequent home games elsewhere and lost their next away fixture 5–1. The club was also fined for the 'Duce' chants – which were described as 'derisive comments'.[23] It could be argued that the whole fiasco cost Fiorentina a second successive championship, while the Sardinian club went on to win the *scudetto*. On his return to Florence the following week – for a referees' meeting – Lo Bello was given a two-man guard at the city station. As with many Italian footballing controversies, the Lo Bello 'case' also crossed over into Parliament. A Christian Democrat deputy argued in the debating chamber that the 'power' of referees should be limited. Florence fans took refuge in conspiracy theories – '*they* won't let us win two championships in a row' – and threatened a fans' strike. Journalists and football commentators complained about the 'excessive influence' exercised by Lo Bello over the outcome of games, and wondered for how long this trend could continue.

None of this had any effect on Lo Bello's style. In his next Serie A game, at Vicenza, he 'identified' a spectator who had insulted him 'repeatedly' from behind the goal, and had his name taken by a plain-clothes policeman. The spectator, Walter Giuliani, a 56-year-old lorry-driver, denied the charge, but Lo Bello sued him for defamation. The referee added that Giuliani was 'not a football fan, but someone who wanted simply to attack me'. Lo Bello's style led to a number of incidents similar to the Florence 'riot' through his long career. In 1948 he was forced to hide in the dressing room after a minor league game. Struck by a stone on the head, he carried on refereeing a game in 1957, and in 1971 he was saved by police in Turin, and chased in his car later, after sending off two Torino defenders. 'The Prince' left his mark on every game, and no referee since has dominated discussion or divided Italians in quite the same way. His authoritarian style was linked by some fans to the fascist era. Once again, the referee was associated – unfavourably – with aspects of the Italian state and its administrators.

## White Riot! Naples 1955; Livorno 1967

In the 1950s and 1960s the most dangerous stadium of all for referees was that of Napoli, first in the old Vomero ground and later at the new San Paolo stadium. On three separate occasions (1955, 1956, 1963) there were mass pitch invasions, and referees were forced to flee. In November 1955, Napoli's opponents were Bologna. The referee was Mario Maurelli, and Napoli were cruising to victory at 3–0 up with fifteen minutes left. Bologna made a great comeback, however, and snatched a draw with a last-minute penalty. Straight after the penalty was taken, Maurelli blew the final whistle. At that point, the crowd invaded, chasing the referee, who locked himself in the dressing room. Later, the Bologna players were also besieged inside their hotel. Bologna's team doctor was beaten up, and then arrested, before being released. At one point he had been seen brandishing a soda-water siphon on the pitch. He claimed that his actions had been in self-defence.

Napoli's punishment was relatively light – a two-game home ban. Achille Lauro – ship-building billionaire, Mayor of Naples and honorary president of Napoli football club – backed his own supporters. In a dramatic press conference in Milan, Lauro complained about Bologna's penalty and waxed lyrical about his city, justifying the riot. 'Neapolitans are a good and generous people who tend to rise up against injustice and arrogance.' After a brief survey of Neapolitan history, Lauro also called for professional and/or foreign referees. It later turned out that the Mayor had seen little of this with his own eyes, as he had left fifteen minutes from the end, with Napoli 3–0 up. For this politician, businessman and football entrepreneur – a real Berlusconi before his time – the violence of his fans was entirely the fault of the referee. It was hardly surprising that in Napoli's next home game – just after serving their ban – similar incidents exploded which led to yet another ban.

Livorno started the 1967 Serie B season with a bang. It looked like their long-suffering supporters might, at last, see them promoted back to the top flight, where they had not played since the 1940s. Then, in November, came a home game with Monza. A similar pattern emerged to that of other violent incidents elsewhere. First, referee Antonio Sbardella ignored Livorno penalty appeals. Then, with Monza 2–1 down, he awarded a free-kick to Monza from the edge of the area. After a first attempt hit the wall, Sbardella ordered it to be re-taken and Monza scored. Monza's manager then turned to the Livorno crowd and 'made a significant gesture', presumably involving an umbrella. The 'gesture of the umbrella' is the Italian equivalent of a V-sign, and involves hitting your right arm just below the elbow with the palm of your left hand, which is aimed at someone and thrust into the air. The gesture is often accompanied by an exclamation such as 'teh!'.[24]

Soon afterwards, a lone Livorno fan jumped over the fence, ran towards the referee and hit him in the face. Sbardella replied in kind, knocking the fan down. This led to a mass pitch invasion. Monza's goalkeeper was attacked, as were their reserve keeper and manager. The pitch looked like a 'scene from a western'. Things seemed to be under control when word spread that a commentator had 'insulted' Livorno's fans. Some tried to attack the broadcaster in question, others set fire to a radio van. Large parts of the stadium were smashed up, as the fans tried to storm the dressing room, where the referee was holed up with his linesmen.

After breaking through a set of outside gates, a group of angry fans arrived at the dressing-room door. The referees' group escaped to the Monza dressing room, which was still full of players. There, they were joined by the city's police chief and Livorno's Mayor. At 8.15 p.m., the referee was finally able to leave (without his luggage) and was driven to a nearby train station. As he left he 'noted the complete destruction of his dressing room' (football federation report). He was later stopped for speeding. 'Clearly he was in a hurry to return to Rome', wrote La Gazzetta dello Sport. Nobody was arrested.

Much comment followed in the press, some of it concentrating on the supposed rebellious nature of Livorno, with its port, its dockers and its left-wing subversive traditions. The next day, 4,000 Livorno fans demonstrated in their town centre, blocking traffic. The derby with Pisa was coming up and there were fears that things might get out of hand again. About 5,000 Livorno fans travelled to Pisa, but things passed off fairly peacefully. Then the verdict came in from the federation's disciplinary commission. Livorno would have to play their home games somewhere else for six weeks. In the end, the team stayed in B, and did not reach Serie A again until 2004, 37 years later.

Players have occasionally taken it on themselves to attack referees and linesmen. It is normal in Italy, in any case, for players to surround, push and shove and rush up to the referee. Moreover, such actions do not usually lead to a booking or a sending-off. The Italian press was highly amused by the long ban imposed on Paolo Di Canio in 1998 for pushing over portly English official Paul Alcock. You are far more likely to be booked or sent off for 'sarcastic applause' or 'offensive language' in the Italian league than for shoving the referee. Sometimes, however, things have gone beyond the limits of these self-imposed 'macho' boundaries. In the 1942–3 season a linesman was kicked in the stomach during a cup game. Roma hero Amedeo Amadei was banned for life for the incident and then pardoned by an amnesty. Sweeper Ivano Blason was banned for six months for hitting a referee in 1946. In December 1967 future World Cup star Roberto Boninsegna tried to punch a referee during a game. He was given a nine-match ban. More recently, in a Turin derby in November 1991, Pasquale Bruno tried repeatedly to attack the referee after being sent off in the first half. He was held back with difficulty by a team-mate, and eventually persuaded to leave the pitch. Later, Bruno, known as 'the Animal', was banned for five matches.

## Trial by Slow-Motion. Italian Referees and the *Moviola*

'A key instrument in mass culture, the ultimate but in the last analysis deeply useless authority'

PAUL GINSBORG on the slow-motion replay

Fan paranoia over the corrupt or inept nature of the refereeing in Italy is fuelled by interminable television debates where accusations fly back and forth. Episodes in games – penalties, fouls, goals – are replayed endlessly and conspiracy theories compete with different conspiracy theories. One particular programme – *Il processo del lunedì* (*Monday's Trial*) – sums up this whole mindset. As its name suggests, the show is loosely modelled on a criminal trial. Numerous characters appear and assume various roles; an ex-referee defends all refereeing decisions, a Fiorentina fan (sometimes the fiery film and opera director Franco

Zeffirelli) attacks Juventus; a Juventus manager defends his team. Another man stands up and begins to shout almost immediately, and doesn't stop for two hours. Calls are made for the sacking of managers (teams are said to be officially 'in crisis' after just one or two defeats), or the disciplining of referees. Journalists fuel rumours of transfers, player unrest and indiscipline. Millions of Italians watch this type of programme every week – their lives filled with stories of intrigue, bile and hope – waiting for the next match. No detailed studies have been done, but at least half of every episode is devoted to refereeing.

This kind of trial by television has been a long time coming, and has been driven by technology. In Italy, the *moviola* refers explicitly to football, and to slow-motion replays of controversial decisions. Since the 1960s, when technology first allowed replays of moments from matches, the *moviola* has become a key component of debates over football. Discussion today concentrates more on *moviola* incidents than on the game itself, and various variations on the classic *moviola* have been introduced over time. *Il processo del lunedì* now uses what it calls the 'super-*moviola*' with lifesize computer images which recreate incidents from the week's matches.

At first, the *moviola* was extremely primitive. Technicians at the RAI – the State TV service which ran a monopoly from 1954 to 1976 – invented a small camera which could film the match in slow-motion from a small TV screen. In 1967 the *moviola* was first used on the popular sports show, *Sporting Sunday*. It was an immediate hit. Sports journalists became *moviola* specialists – known as *moviolisti*. The pioneers were Heron Vitaletti and, above all, Carlo Sassi, who stayed in the job for over 30 years. The first *moviola* incident was a 'ghost goal' – a goal that was given but wasn't actually valid – in a Milan derby, by Gianni Rivera. Sassi and Vitaletti proved that the ball had not crossed the line. In 1969, the *moviola* became a key part of sports programmes and slowly became *the* central aspect of all discussion, replacing questions of tactics, performances and skill. Later experts emerged from the new private TV networks in the 1970s and 1980s.

Everything, even beyond football, began to be seen in terms of the *moviola*. In the popular film comedy *Romanzo Popolare* (1974) Ugo Tognazzi reviews his past errors through use of a hypothetical *moviola*. Every so often, the film stops, and Tognazzi turns to the camera and says – '*Moviola*'. He then comments on where his life has gone wrong. The word *moviola* became part of both football language and language in general. An *episodio da moviola* is a controversial incident that is guaranteed to be analysed time and time again. Footballers, when interviewed, would often say '*Vedremo stasera alla moviola*': 'We'll check that on the replay this evening'. Nowadays, they are asked to comment immediately on replays, as soon as they have showered. There is no more need to wait for the evening. During matches in Italy, a football commentator is assigned to the bench area, commentating in detail on the activities of the managers and substitutes. He will often pass on information concerning controversial incidents to the bench. *Moviola* replay judgements are thus 'seen' in real time, by those involved in games, whilst the game is still in progress.

Replays are generally seen as having the last word, as containing an absolute truth that could not be sorted out by the referee on the field. *La moviola ci dirà se . . .* 'the *moviola* will let us know if . . .'. Televisual truth is everything. Real-time action, even for those who played in the game, is always in doubt. *Only TV can tell us what has really happened.* Replays have changed the spectator's relationship with sport, forever, and the game is now 'told' to us by others. We need – we demand – a televisual version of something we have already seen, in order to understand it. In Italy, the *moviola* has taken on a particular power thanks to the enormous lack of confidence in the ability, or willingness, of referees to objectively officiate matches. In a society where bias is assumed, the *moviola* has become the only judge whose verdict is worthy of trust.[25]

The beauty of football is that few incidents are uncontroversial. There is rarely a correct answer or one single version. Clarity is the exception, even with the *moviola*. Hence, the years and years of debate about the 1966 World Cup final, or the impossibility of deciding if Liverpool's goal against Chelsea in the 2005 Champions League had crossed the line, or not. The *moviola* rarely puts an end to debate and usually provokes further discussion. Often, an incident will be replayed umpteen times, and various pundits in the studio will provide an entirely different interpretation of what they have just seen. The other beautiful but frustrating iron rule of *calcio* is that the referee's word is final, on the pitch. We cannot go back in time and 'allow' a disallowed goal, or award a penalty that was not given. Nonetheless, the authority of referees has been progressively undermined by the replay culture. The mystery and aura surrounding officials began to decline with the first *moviola* punditry, and took a massive blow with the brave decision by Concetto Lo Bello to admit a mistake in 1972.[26] As guest of *La Domenica Sportiva* Lo Bello patiently watched a 'penalty' incident. He then accepted that he had made a mistake calmly and with a smile, adding that he had not had 'the advantage of the *moviola*'. Many players and managers now argue for *moviola* replays during games, a move which would begin to replace referees altogether.

For referees, the *moviola* was long seen as an enemy. Many officials hated it, and there were calls for it to be taken off the air on various occasions. After the death of a Lazio fan in 1979, before a Rome derby, the chief referee Giulio Campanati asked for the *moviola* to be abolished. He argued that slow-motion replays were provoking violence among fans. There is no doubt that the excessive use of *moviola* 'evidence' – now much more sophisticated than in the 1960s – does excite fans and lead to increased hostility towards referees. This is especially true of programmes based almost entirely on the *moviola*, such as *Il processo del lunedì*. On one occasion the Italian referees' association even took the presenter Aldo Biscardi to court. With time, however, referees came to accept – and embrace – the *moviola*, and many sports programmes now use distinguished ex-referees to comment on replays.

## The Great Robberies. Penalties, Disallowed Goals, Sendings-off

Over the years, specific refereeing decisions have entered football mythology as examples of 'thievery'. Many of these examples came from the television age, when the *moviola* was able to show supposed injustices to the fans sitting at home. The three 'great thefts' of the 1980s and 1990s all involved Juventus.

Roman Turone's 'goal' against Juventus, 10 May 1981. The text reads 'with this disallowed goal Rome saw their second championship stolen from them' and 'in the 74th minute Turone's goal was disallowed for a non-existent offside'. Design courtesy of an anti-Juventus website.

## Maurizio Turone's disallowed 'goal'. Juventus versus Roma. Turin, 10 May 1981

Juventus and Roma had fought out the championship all season. By May, Juventus were only one point ahead. Then came the key clash, at home to Roma. Fifteen thousand fans travelled up from the capital for the game. In the seventy-fourth minute, with the game still goalless, a cross came in from the right, a Roma forward flicked it on and Maurizio Turone, their Ligurian sweeper, dived forward to score. The referee immediately disallowed the goal after the linesman signalled for offside. He was wrong, just: Turone had moved forward from an *onside* position. Photos show Turone wheeling away, arms up in triumph, whilst Dino Zoff moves his finger from side to side to say 'no'. A whole championship had been decided 'by centimetres'. *Sport*, a football newspaper, led with a celebrated front page headline: 'The goal was good. A linesman saved Juventus: THE *MOVIOLA* ACCUSES'.

Diego Perissinotto, now deceased, was the linesman in question while the referee was Paolo Bergamo, who would later become a powerful 'designator'. Many Roma fans never forgot that moment. After all,

they had only ever won one championship in their history. Massimo
D'Alema, former Italian prime minister, president of the left-reformist
party, the DS, and a Roma fan, wrote that he had never got over what
he called 'the complex of Turone's goal'. It was alleged that D'Alema
ended his friendship with Bergamo – a fellow member of the then
Communist Party – over the incident. Much later, journalist Gabriele
Romagnoli made a strong case in a brilliant 'what if' article that the
whole history of Italy had been changed by that disallowed goal.[27]
Roma–Juve matches have been lively affairs ever since.

## Fiorentina and Juventus. Last day of the championship. 16 May 1982

After an emotional season, Fiorentina and Juventus went into the last
game level on points. Fiorentina had not won the *scudetto* since 1969
while Juventus were the title-holders. Most commentators believed that
the championship would go to a playoff for only the second time in
its history – and a stadium was already lined up for the one-off match.[28]
Fiorentina fans had celebrated long into the night after drawing level
in the penultimate game. Yet, their team had the most difficult task,
away to Cagliari, who needed points to avoid relegation. Lowly Catanzaro, a Calabrian team from the deep south of Italy, who were to play
Juve at home, were safe.

Juventus were greeted by 30,000 hostile fans on their arrival in
Catanzaro. The home-town ground's total capacity was only 25,500.
Paolo Rossi, the great centre-forward who had just completed a ban
after becoming involved in a betting scam in 1980, was pushed around
to shouts of 'crook, crook' and 'prison trash'. Only a tiny number of
Juve fans made the 28-hour journey from Turin while Fiorentina
booked five charter flights to Sardinia, and at least 1,000 fans, including
the Mayor, made the long round trip.

The first controversial incident took place after 35 minutes, with
both games deadlocked at 0–0. A Catanzaro forward appeared to be
brought down by a Juve defender. Referee Pieri gave nothing. With
fifteen minutes to go, a playoff seemed inevitable. Nobody had scored
in either game. Then, Pieri did give a penalty, this time to Juventus,
for handball. Liam Brady stepped up to take it, knowing that he had
already been sold by the club to make way for Michel Platini. Brady,

destroy Perugia after a series of costly legal battles with the federation.

Gaucci was, as usual, over-the-top in his shrill protests, using conspiracy theories as a convenient excuse for his failure to build a team
strong enough to stay up. In late 2003, Gaucci even threatened to take
the football authorities into the civil courts, and have them charged
with 'sporting fraud'. He prepared a dossier of the decisions that had
supposedly gone against Perugia and a video which was to be used in
evidence. Such a move was unprecedented in footballing history, and
Gaucci pulled back from an immediate confrontation, promising that
the case would be brought at the end of the season.[31] The case was
never filed. Gaucci knew that his team risked massive points deductions
and even automatic relegation if they went to the courts.

Amazingly it is also possible that Gaucci was not entirely wrong.
His arrogant court campaigns over the summer of 2003 had annoyed
many influential people in the game. Gaucci's shrill claims were *also* a
kind of self-fulfilling prophecy. By arguing that there was a conspiracy
against Perugia, he helped to create a conspiracy against Perugia. A
'war with the *palazzo*' (code in Italy for a 'battle against the powers
that be') could only damage his club. This happened with Gianni
Rivera and Milan in the 1970s, when the great midfielder was banned
for weeks after making this statement: 'they don't want us to win the
championship, it's the third time in a row that the referees have stolen
it from us'. History repeated itself with Roma in the 2002–2003 season.
Roma president Franco Sensi spent the whole season complaining
about conspiracies and bad decisions. The result? A series of bad
decisions and a terrible season for Roma. None of this can be proved,
of course, but the trend was for referees and their peers to punish
those who 'protested too much'. The history of Italian football has
shown, time and time again, that those who complain about plots
against them only reinforce a kind of corporate hostility.

Perugia were not exactly setting standards in other areas. In January
2004, they were at home to Roma. In the second half, with Roma 1–0
up, Bothroyd burst into the penalty area between two Roma central
defenders, one of whom clearly held him across the chest. Bothroyd
tried to stay on his feet but he was unbalanced and his shot was weak.
No penalty was given. Manager Serse Cosmi went crazy near the bench,
not for the first time. Strangely, the target of his ranting was not the

referee, but Bothroyd. 'Go down, go down, why didn't you go down,' he screamed. Later, Cosmi repeated his comments, and added that 'Bothroyd should have gone to ground. Then the referee would have given a penalty.' Was Cosmi therefore angry with the 'fair' Englishman because he hadn't dived? The reality was more complex. Bothroyd should have 'allowed himself to fall' so as to 'make the referee's decision inevitable'. His 'not falling' had led the referee to make an error. Cosmi was bitter about the praise for Bothroyd's desire not to sprawl in the area. 'I expect they will build a monument to him,' he quipped, bitterly, and added that only the 'professional moralists' had criticized his stance. Cosmi had spoken to Bothroyd afterwards, telling him that a player should 'stay on his feet' in such cases 'only if he is sure that he will score. He should have gone down. It was a clear penalty.' Cosmi went further, in a post-match interview. Bothroyd had been 'naïve' to not go down in the area. 'A normal player, not a diver, falls down in that kind of situation. There are lots of campaigns against divers, let's have one against heroes as well.' No wonder the task of referees was so difficult in Italy, if such things were said openly, and almost with pride, by some of the leading figures in the game.

## Breaking the Mould? Pierluigi Collina

'The bourgeoisie sees its historical development like a sporting competition, with its own referee and its own rules which need to be followed'                    ANTONIO GRAMSCI

'It is very sad to think that referees are seen as puppets whose strings are pulled by someone . . .'                    PIERLUIGI COLLINA

In the 1990s a referee emerged from within the Italian game to become one of the most famous figures in the world of sport. Pierluigi Collina set new trends in many ways. He was the first referee to become a superstar, instantly recognizable, in part because of his shiny bald head, a result of the nervous disease alopecia which he has suffered from since his twenties. Collina was also much in demand for lucrative advertising contracts and the author of a best-selling and much-translated autobiography.[32] Few referees in Italian football's short history have become famous in their own right, or at least, not for respectable reasons. Concetto Lo Bello was famous, but only in Italy, and he was both loved and hated in equal measure. Sergio Gonella refereed a World Cup final in 1978 but he is a forgotten figure today. It is often said that referees should not be famous, *they should not stand out.* Collina is different, and he argues that 'the best referee is not the one who is not noticed . . . the referee is a protagonist . . . it's difficult not to be noticed if you take important decisions'.[33] You notice him, and he is very good – refereeing, almost without incident, a World Cup final and numerous international matches. Teams, whole nations even, demanded that their games be given to Collina, to ensure a 'fair' match.

Pierluigi Collina. The player is Franco Baresi of Milan, 1993.

Collina did things which no other referee had ever done, on the pitch. In 1997 he apologized to a manager, during a game, for a decision he had changed after consulting a linesman. Collina gave a goal and then disallowed it, before running over to the bench to explain his decision to the Inter manager, Roy Hodgson. The referee and the manager then shook hands. Times had changed. In 1981, Paolo Casarin, one of the most interesting referees of the 1970s and 1980s, spoke to both managers after a game (in private) to explain a decision. He was severely reprimanded by the referees' association. On another occasion Collina stopped a game until the authorities had removed an offensive fan banner. Collina also ordered two teams to change ends to protect a goalkeeper from hostile missiles from the crowd.

Domestically, Collina was a remarkable rarity – a referee who would not bow to the power of the big clubs, an official who adhered only to the rules. Such an attitude represented something of a revolution in the Italian game. On the last day of the 1999–2000 season, Juventus needed just a draw, away to Perugia, to clinch a championship playoff. The ground was covered in water after a biblical downpour during half-time, with the score at 0–0. Juve called for the game to be called off, but Collina refused to budge. On a number of occasions, he went out onto the field, bouncing a ball to see if the match could continue. In the end, 71 minutes later, the game re-started. Perugia won 1–0 and Lazio were champions. The referee was given top marks in the newspapers for his decision: 'I was pleased', he later wrote, 'that all the "neutrals" who were there shared my decision to wait and see'.[34] Since then, Collina has been viewed with some suspicion by Juventus – who have rarely done well when he has been officiating. It *was* possible, in exceptional circumstances, to simply apply the rules of the game, without recourse to political calculation, plotting and conspiracy theories. In this simple way, Pierluigi Collina was a pioneer, a hero of his time, a paragon of truth in a world of lies. His only weak spot was his most famous feature – his hair, or lack of it. After a TV joke about alopecia he once stormed out of a studio. He advised young referees to 'work hard, be courageous and always "decide"'.[35]

But Collina was, without doubt, an exception. He was 'protected' by his own fame, and his own reputation. When Collina was in charge, the rules were applied in an even-handed way. He had created for himself the power and the space to be able to referee fairly. Most other top referees do not have this leeway, and are forced into difficult balancing acts *between* the top clubs, whilst adhering to the traditional 'psychological slavery' that has always penalized smaller teams. Outside of the professional game, life for the rest of Italy's 26,000 referees was very different, light years away from the glamour, the wealth and above all the respect enjoyed by The Greatest, Pierluigi Collina.[36]

**CHAPTER 3**

# Teams and Cities: Turin

## The Old Lady. Juventus

'The team has followed the evolution of the nation'

UMBERTO AGNELLI

'Juventus is a team which unites everyone: from intellectuals to workers ... it is a universal team, a footballing Esperanto ... and then there are the fans, the real fans, from Sicily to the Aosta Valley. There are eleven million of us. Eleven million'

DARWIN PASTORIN[1]

In Florence you can buy stickers which read: *zona anti-gobbizzata* – 'hunchback-free zone'. Many shops and even houses carry these stickers, which state that their properties have been 'de-hunchbacked'. For many of the millions of tourists who pass through the city every year, these stickers must be difficult to interpret. Do the Florentines hate hunchbacks? Have hunchbacks been banned from the historic capital of the Renaissance? The answer to these questions is no, the stickers in question are linked to one of the great modern footballing rivalries. Hunchbacks are seen as lucky in Italy, and Juventus are referred to in this way because, according to Fiorentina fans, they have been extremely lucky over the years. Thus, Juventus followers and the team itself are *gobbi*. When Florence has signed Juventus players, they have sometimes been symbolically 'de-hunchbacked' by their own fans in a

strange ceremony. But Florence and, to a lesser extent, Rome are exceptions in Italy's footballing map, as relatively Juve-free zones. Very few
parts of the peninsula have been 'de-hunchbacked' and *Juventini* (Juve
fans) are everywhere in Italy. These contrasting passions have created
many other nicknames for the club, beyond that of *i gobbi*. Journalists
often call the club the old lady – *la vecchia signora* – as a sign of respect.
Other nicknames are less complimentary – *the thieves* being another
favourite.

As you travel across southern Italy, it is entirely normal to see
entire teams of young players decked out in Juve shirts in kickabouts,
hundreds of miles from Turin. Juventus have far more fans outside
Turin than in their home-town. When they play in Sicily, or Calabria,
or Milan, or Sardinia, they attract – and have always attracted – sell-out
crowds. For the industrialist and long-time owner of the club, Gianni
Agnelli, 'in the south people dreamed of going to see Juventus'. The
reasons for this extraordinary fan-base are both simple, and complicated. Success breeds support: Juve have won the Serie A championship
28 times, nearly twice as often as their closest rivals Milan and Inter.
Moreover, Juventus were extremely successful as *calcio* became a
national sport. In the early 1930s, coinciding with the 1934 World Cup
victory at home, they won five successive championships.[2] This was
also a time when radio and the sports press began to 'nationalize'
Italian sport coverage. In the early 1960s, a spectacular new Juventus
team fused perfectly with a new generation of post-war fans.

Between 1951 and 1967, Turin's population rose from 719,300 to
1,124,714. Many of these *terroni* immigrants – a racist term used by
northerners towards southerners – were already, or soon came to be,
Juventus fans. Goffredo Fofi, who wrote the best study of southern
immigration to Turin in the 1960s, noted that 'during a Juventus–
Palermo match, there were many enthusiastic immigrant Sicilian fans
whose sons, by now, like every respectable FIAT worker, backed the
home team'.[3] When the immigrants returned home, for holidays, wed-
dings or funerals, they took their footballing 'faith' with them. Turin
was New York for these emigrants, and its myths (wealth, success,
modernity) were transferred – including *la Juve* – to those aspirant
migrants still at home. As one immigrant has since said: 'all of us
became *Juventini*'.[4] Darwin Pastorin, one of Italy's most brilliant foot-

ball writers, has described the Juventus of the 1970s as 'proletarian'.[5] Southern migrants were particularly proud of the southern players in their team – defender Antonio Cuccureddu from Sardinia, winger Franco Causio from Apulia and above all Sicilian striker Pietro Anastasi – who was known as the 'white Pelé' but also as *u turcu*: 'the dark one'.[6] Marxist writers have interpreted the fandom of FIAT's southern workers more negatively, as a collective safety valve for the frustration and anger produced on the production line. As Gerhard Vinnai – student of Adorno and Marcuse – wrote in the 1970s, 'the goals on a football field are the own-goals of the dominated'.[7]

In the 1970s and 1980s yet another generation of *Juventini* were born – the children of these immigrants – who identified with the glamour and the style of the team's victories. Juventus's achievement also coincided with Italian success. The 1982 World Cup winning team contained seven Juve players. The Juventus name also helped. For Gianni Agnelli 'not having the name of a city has brought us great popularity. It makes us national.' Juve never went through a slump long enough to lose them fans. Only three times have they seemed about to lose their primacy: in the second half of the 1940s, to Torino, in the first half of the 1960s, to Inter, and in the first half of the 1990s, to Milan. Each time, they have come back, stronger than ever, to reaffirm their pre-eminence and power.

Juventus stamped their authority on Italian football in the 1930s, winning five consecutive championships with a team made up of South American stars with Italian citizenship and many local players. Juve used their money and influence to buy in the best players and coaches, becoming *the* national team. After suffering the humiliation of Torino dominance in the 1940s, Juventus struggled to rebuild in the 1950s. It was only with the arrival of another two foreign stars – Omar Sivori and John Charles – in the latter part of the decade that Juve began to dictate things again. After a period when Milan was the capital of world football – throughout the 1960s – Juventus built another 'cycle' of dominance in the 1970s and 1980s. Under Giovanni Trapattoni – a pragmatic Milanese coach and brilliant man-manager – Juve dominated for more than a decade. An impregnable defence with Dino Zoff in goal and Gentile, Scirea and Cabrini – was complemented by superb ball-winners such as Beppe Furino (who won a record eight titles between 1972 and 1984) and Marco Tardelli in midfield. Up front, these teams were blessed with skilful ball players and deadly strikers, from Paolo Rossi to 'the baron', Franco Causio. Juve also bought the best foreigners – Liam Brady, Zibi Boniek and above all Michel Platini. They rarely went wrong in the transfer market, or in their choice of manager.

A final 'cycle' of victories was built up by Paul Newman lookalike Marcello Lippi, who added another column to the Juve pantheon, again with a combination of stern defence, ball-winners and skill in midfield, including Zinedine Zidane at his peak, and free-scorers up front, from Roberto Baggio and Fabrizio Ravanelli to Gianluca Vialli and Alessandro Del Piero. Lippi took control of the team in two separate spells, winning five titles in seven years, as well as the Intercontinental Cup, dramatically snatched by fan idol Del Piero in 1996.

Only one trophy consistently eluded Juventus, so much so that it has come to be seen as cursed by fans and players at the club. For a team with 28 championships, more than half of them since the setting-up of the European Cup, Juventus's record of just two victories is a desperately poor showing. In seven finals, Juventus have lost five times. In 1973, they were outclassed by Johan Cruyff's Ajax. Ten years later, after going through the whole tournament unbeaten, they fell to an outrageous long-shot from Hamburg midfielder Felix Magath. Anti-Juve fans partied into the night and *Grazie Magath!* graffiti appeared everywhere. In 1985 the Heysel disaster took place before the final won by Juventus. Many people do not recognize the trophy awarded that year. Juve were back in the final in 1996, and this time they won – at last – beating Ajax on penalties. Lippi's team reached the final twice more in the next two years, losing to Borussia Dortmund and Real Madrid respectively. More graffiti appeared: *Grazie Real! Grazie Borussia!* In 2003 Lippi and Juventus were back for more, losing again, on penalties, to Milan. Seven finals, one victory; a terrible record that has divided Italy.

Well-timed (and continual) success was not the only explanation for Juventus's huge fan-base. FIAT were – and are – Italy's biggest company, producing millions of cars and providing millions of jobs. FIAT, for 100 years, *was* Italian capitalism, and FIAT signified power, influence, a way of life. Many claimed that Italy was really controlled by

FIAT – *FIATALY*. Southern immigrants yearned for a job in Mirafiori – the huge factory constructed on the edge of Turin in 1939. When it was opened the plant covered six per cent of the entire area of Turin and the workers' café could hold 10,000 people. Production lines ran for 40 km. Hundreds of thousands of peasants took the 'train of the sun' – especially in the 1950s and 1960s – to cold, foggy Turin to pursue the dream of a job with FIAT. In the north, they faced racism and hardship, but many also found a steady job and the ability to create a future for their families. Umberto Agnelli – of the Agnelli family who have always controlled FIAT – even claimed that 'one of the reasons which led migrants to choose Turin during the great migrations of the 1950s and 1960s was the possibility of going to see Juventus play'.

FIAT built schools, sent the children of its workers on holidays, constructed housing and provided pensions. The company made vast profits, some of which trickled back to its workforce across Italy. Juve was FIAT's team, and not just symbolically. The Agnelli family loved football, running the club as a family affair – just as they ran *their* company. The Agnellis went to games, spoke to players, sacked and employed managers, commented on tactics and gave interviews to the (usually fawning) sporting press.

Juve's victories were personally associated with the Agnelli family, who were loved and hated in equal measure. Gianni Agnelli, the tall, dapper, witty industrialist, was particularly important for post-war Juventus. He was a master of the pithy soundbite, giving players nicknames which stuck, and was also extremely canny with his transfer deals. The players were in awe of him, as were many fans. When he died in 2003, thousands of Turinese queued all night to pay respects to his body, on the futuristic race-track roof of the Lingotto ex-car factory in Turin. Many stories are told about 'The Lawyer', as Agnelli was known thanks to his degree in law. He dubbed Zibi Boniek 'beautiful at night' because of his great performances in European games. As usual, the nickname contained a hint of criticism. Boniek would often disappear on Sunday afternoons, in mundane league matches. Alessandro Del Piero was called Pinturicchio, after the Renaissance artist.[8] Again, the nickname was double-edged. Del Piero was a genius, but he was also a bit inconsistent and a touch lightweight. Only Platini really got the better of Agnelli. On one occasion, The Lawyer went down to the dressing room before a match, only to catch Platini puffing on a cigarette. 'That worries me,' Agnelli said to Platini. Instantly, a riposte came back. 'You only need to worry if *he* starts smoking,' said Platini, pointing at Beppe Furino, the tireless midfield ball-winner in that Juventus team.

Whilst Gianni Agnelli was the public face of Juve, his brother Umberto was a superb football administrator, with an eye for the right player at the right time, who did the necessary dirty work for the club within the power-bases of the football and sports federations. The Agnelli family constructed a powerful myth known as the 'Juventus Style'. Unlike other Italian clubs, it was argued, Juve accepted defeat with dignity. The epitome of this style was Giampiero Boniperti, who moved smoothly from star player to all-conquering president, presiding over a prodigious series of victories in the 1970s and 1980s.[9] Players, officials and managers were all expected to adhere to the rigours of the Juve style.

Juve, unlike many Italian clubs, has always been run as a business. Its books have usually been balanced – again unlike most other clubs – and it has tended not to splash out huge sums on players. When the price has been right big stars have been off-loaded: Juventus sold Christian Vieri *and* Thierry Henry in the 1990s. At certain times, crises at FIAT were reflected in the way Juve was run. In May 1978, FIAT offered much less for star striker Paolo Rossi than Vicenza, a minor club. At the time, the car company was going through a bad period. It simply could not be seen to be spending massive amounts on one football player when its workers were being laid off.

Of course, many people hated FIAT, and loathed the Agnellis. Juventus were widely reviled, and not always for purely footballing reasons. In the late 1960s a wave of wildcat strikes hit the company in what became known as the 'hot autumn'. For a time, the company's factories in Turin were occupied as FIAT lost authority over many of its employees. Demonstrators marched through the city behind banners that read 'We Want Everything!' (*Vogliamo Tutto!*). Italy's 'Long May' – violent, revolutionary, fascinating – lasted at least until 1980 and its capital was Turin. Later, FIAT managers were kidnapped, beaten up and even killed by fringe 'red' terrorist groups. In this context, football might have appeared irrelevant, but of course it wasn't. Many of the strikers were also Juve fans, and continued to support the team of the company with which they were virtually at war. This contradiction underlined – once again – the fundamental truth that you cannot choose or change your football team for political reasons.

FIAT have always attracted fans from all sides of the political spectrum. Palmiro Togliatti, leader of the Italian Communist Party from 1927 to 1964, was a *Juventino*. So was Giorgio Almirante, leader of the neo-fascist Italian Social Movement in the 1960s and 1970s. Other Juve fans have included Walter Veltroni, left-wing Mayor of Rome, Luciano Lama, leader of the communist-linked trade union federation in the 1970s, and Henry Kissinger.

Juventus are a team of contradictions. A club with something like eleven million fans in Italy, they rarely fill their home stadium, often playing before paltry crowds in Turin. They are the most loved of all teams, and the most hated. Millions rejoice when they win, different millions exult when they lose. Being a Juve player or manager carries massive pressure. A championship is just another victory, when you have already won 28 times. Twice, managers have been sacked after coming second.[10] Dino Zoff was dismissed as manager after winning the Italian Cup and the UEFA Cup in the same season. And then there are the conspiracy theories, petty jealousies, power-games and scandals. Juve can never win 'normally', they never triumph simply because they are better than everyone else. There is always something around which suspicion can be constructed – and examples of 'favouritism' or 'psychological slavery' are not hard to find in *calcio*'s long and controversial history. Juve fans are doomed to be insulted and derided whatever happens on the pitch. Still, they can always look on the bright side. Whenever Juve fans feel slightly down, they can take comfort in the long decline of their bitter rivals.

Torino, the other Turinese team, have had a history of triumph *and* tragedy. Theirs is a story of a small club that became unbeatable, and then vanished in a disaster that transformed Italy. Torino's history can only be written with reference to one date. Everything revolves around that moment: *before*, and *after*.

## Calamity. Superga. 4 May 1949

'This morning the Italian group left by plane to return home.
They should be in Turin at about 5 p.m.'
                                  *Corriere Lombardo*, 4–5 May 1949

The great Torino team which flew to Lisbon for a friendly on 1 May
1949 had all but clinched their fifth championship in a row. With
four games left, they were four points in front, had gone their last
eighteen games unbeaten, and had not lost at home for 93 games –
since 1943. Captain Valentino Mazzola nearly missed the plane with a
fever, and some newspapers reported that he had actually remained
at home. Other rumours claimed that the team's captain had got off
at Barcelona. Both, unfortunately, turned out to be false. After the
game in Lisbon, 31 passengers and crew flew back from Portugal on
4 May.

The weather was terrible that afternoon. Heavy rain lashed down onto
the city and dark clouds hung over the hills and mountains that
surround Turin, down on the Po river plain. Visibility was poor. It was
as if night had fallen early.

That afternoon there were very few people on the hill up at Superga,
where an eighteenth-century basilica stood, high above Turin. A peasant saw a plane fly past just above his head, another heard the same
aircraft circling in the mist and fog.

At 17.12 p.m. on 4 May a car screeched to a halt near to the restaurant
which stood on the small square next to the basilica. The driver said
he needed to use the phone, urgently. The journalist he spoke to at the
national press agency refused to believe his story.

Soon firemen and police vans began to arrive. A FIAT G-212 plane
had smashed into a wall at the back of the church. The wood around
the building was on fire, despite the driving rain. Nothing could be
done for the 31 victims and there were no survivors.[11] Bodies, luggage
and wreckage were strewn over a wide area. As news spread, thousands

Superga. The site after the crash. 4 May 1949.

of fans began to make their way up the hill, in the pouring rain, in a spontaneous and silent procession.

The horrific task of identifying the victims fell to Vittorio Pozzo, journalist and ex-manager of Italy. It was not easy – many of the bodies were burnt beyond recognition. Pozzo walked around the crash site for four hours but some victims were only identified from documents found in their pockets or rings on their fingers. Pozzo, who wrote for *La Stampa*, the Turin daily, filed his copy that same evening: 'The Torino team is no more,' he wrote, 'it has disappeared, it is burnt, it has exploded . . . the team died in action, like a group of shock troops, in the war, who left their trenches and never came back.' This article was later used in Turin schools as an example of the use of rhetoric. Pozzo knew many of the players well. He had picked a record ten members of the squad for the Italian national team in 1947.

In Turin's local *L'Unità* offices (the communist daily) the news came through at 17.30. A few journalists there jumped into a car and drove up the hill, passing hundreds of other people on foot and many other vehicles. At the top, they were told that 'everyone was dead'. Chaos reigned. Two huge wheels were strewn fifty metres apart. People stood around in shock; most were crying.

Special late editions of newspapers were printed, and people crowded around to read reports right across Italy. Work stopped at FIAT for one minute's silence, and shops closed all over the city. Trams going into the town centre were packed with people desperate for more news. A paper in Milan led with this headline: 'Italy cries for its champions: Champions forever'.[12] A 38-year-old woman in Bologna committed suicide on hearing the news. The tragedy united left and right, at the height of the cold war. *L'Unità* wrote that 'the whole of Italy' was 'alongside the burnt bodies' of the team. In Rome, Parliament suspended its sitting once the news had come through. The tragedy also involved Juventus, albeit marginally. Leslie Lievesley, a Berkshire-born former Crystal Palace player who had gone on to coach the Dutch national team, had worked with Torino since 1947. In 1949, he was set to become the coach of the other Turin team. The news of his appointment broke three weeks before the disaster, in April 1949.

The Torino of the 1940s were not known as *Il Grande Torino* for nothing. After winning the 1942–3 championship by just one point from Livorno, Torino again finished a mere point clear of Juventus in a truncated tournament in 1945–6. After that, the domination began in earnest. In 1946–7, Torino scored 104 goals in 38 games, conceding just 35. They ended up ten points ahead of Juventus. The following year was astonishing: 125 goals in 40 games, with only 33 conceded, and nineteen out of twenty games won at home. Torino massacred other teams, beating Alessandria 10–0, Lucchese 6–0 and Salernitana 7–1. One of the team's most powerful performances was away to Roma, in April 1946. After nineteen minutes, Torino were 6–0 up. At half-time – still on 6–0 – the manager told the team that there was no need to humiliate their opponents. The game ended 7–0, with the Roma crowd applauding the Torino team off the pitch. In their five winning seasons, Torino notched up 483 goals and conceded just 165.[13] Nobody, apart from Juventus in the 1930s and Milan in the 1990s, has ever come close to such a record.

The *Grande Torino* team, May 1948.

At least half a million people attended the funerals of the players, journalists and Torino staff on 6 May. The city's streets were packed with mourners, on another grey, rainy day. The funeral ceremony was transmitted live on national radio, and the coffins were transported through the town on huge lorries with flags and the names of the victims written on black cloth. At the funeral, the president of the football federation, Ottorino Barassi, read out the names of the dead players, beginning with Captain Valentino. There was no need to use his surname – Mazzola – everybody knew him by his first name. Barassi ended his speech with 'this is the fifth cup, Torino's cup, look how big it is, it is filled with the hearts of the world'. Thirty thousand people walked up to Superga to pay their respects and leave flowers that very day.

Why had the crash happened? The plane's pilot, Pierluigi Meroni, was an expert – an ace, even – who had won two silver and three gold medals in the war and knew the area well. The plane was new, although it didn't have radar. Three separate inquiries were held into the disaster: military, civil and judicial. All came to the same conclusion – the crash had been a chance event – a *fatalità* – not due to any malfunctioning of the plane but to human error caused in turn by the terrible weather conditions that day. Pilots often used the basilica as a reference point for their descent, but usually gave it a wide leeway. Meroni had probably only seen the building at the last minute. Rumours continued to spread concerning possible mechanical or human error – did the altimeter fail and thus did Meroni think he was much higher than he was? Other rumours were mere conspiracy theories: why had the plane not gone to Milan's much better airport? Were the players trying to avoid customs? Some witnesses said that the plane had been circling, presumably as the pilot attempted to find the right route. He was obviously confused, as he had confirmed that everything was fine minutes before the crash, and had asked ground staff to prepare him a coffee.

The club sued the airline company for the damage they had sustained, arguing that the players were worth more than 'simple' victims, because of their value as players. After various court cases, this claim was denied. The High Court decided that compensation should be paid only for damage to people and property, and not any extra for the 'sporting value' of the players (which was, obviously, enormous).[14]

Torino were awarded the championship, but decided to fulfil their last four games using youth team players, and their opponents did the same. The next home game was an emotional affair. Torino's fans were in a state of shock, and the match began in complete silence. Soon, however, the cry of *Toro, Toro* rang out around the Filadelfia stadium. Torino beat Genoa 4–0, maintaining the team's unbeaten home record, which would only fall the following season.

Superga left Italian football in tatters. The national squad was not to perform decently at a World Cup until 1970 – going out in the first round in 1950, 1954, 1962 and 1966, and not even qualifying for the tournament in 1958. Some argue that the long-term effects of Superga put the game in Italy back thirty years. 'Superga Psychosis' led to the national team – under the control of Torino president Novo – booking a boat to Brazil instead of a plane for the 1950 World Cup. The journey took two weeks, and many of the players were seasick for much of the time. Bored and unable to train properly, they arrived unfit for a top competition. After one game, they were out – having lost to Sweden.[15]

The second game – a victory against Paraguay – was irrelevant. The team were allowed to return by plane – a 35-hour journey.

## Superga. Football tragedy as a shrine, or as a tourist attraction? 1949–2004

'The fate of this team is already the stuff of legend'

VITTORIO POZZO (4 May 1950)

Before some Turin derby games in the 1970s, 1980s and 1990s (the so-called 'Derby of the Mole' after the symbol of the city – the *Mole Antonelliana* tower), while the Torino team was being read out by the stadium announcer, a number of Juventus fans would pretend to be planes. Swaying from side to side, with their hands stretched out, they hummed as if in flight . . . downwards. *Nnneeeeeoouuu*. As the announcer finished the team and came to the trainer – the humming ended: '*Boom! Superga!*' After the Heysel stadium disaster in 1985 in which over 30 Juventus fans died, the extreme wing of Torino's hard-core fans had something to fight back with. 'Another Heysel', they jeered, or '*Grazie* Liverpool'. There was also a song: *trentanove sotto-terra, viva viva l'Inghilterra* – 'Thirty-nine under the ground, long live England'. Genoa fans, allied with those of Torino, put up a big banner in the 1990s with these words, during a game against Juve: 'You gained pleasure from the deaths of the *Grande Torino* until that shitty wall fell down' (another reference to the Heysel disaster). Roma, allied with neither team, managed to offend both with 'Roma hopes for a black-and-white Superga'. Juventus play, of course, in black-and-white. The vast majority of fans of both teams did not indulge in such sick taunting, but many laughed along.

Football rivalry goes very deep in Italy, especially when there is a history of bitter derby games and recriminations, and above all in the cities of Rome and Turin.[16] Given their lowly position and lack of finances, Torino fans have tended to resort to irony, their only weapon left in Turin derbies. This banner was exhibited in a derby in 2001–2: 'You are uglier than the Multipla', and referred to a strange new FIAT car. Another Torino banner was about Antonio Conte, Juventus mid-fielder and captain, who appeared to be going bald and then turned up with a new head of hair. Torino fans accused their rivals of being 'like Conte's hair: fake' (Torino–Juve, 2001–2). Juventus replied with 'Romero. The city wants to know. Who exactly is your hairdresser?' Attilio Romero was Torino's president at the time, complete with an extraordinary hairstyle. On other occasions, the message has been clearer. When Aldo Serena left Torino for Juventus in 1985/6 Torino fans responded with *Serena puttana, l'hai fatto per la grana* – 'Serena, you whore, you did it for the money'.

Pain, hatred, reverence, shame: all these emotions are linked to Superga and to the disaster which took place there in May 1949. To get to the basilica (pronounced *Sue-pear-ga* with the accent on the *pear*) you take the number fifteen tram from the front of Turin's beautiful art deco station – Porta Nuova. The tram winds its way through the elegant centre of Turin before crossing the Po. The penultimate stop is called Sassi. From there, a cable car heads straight up the hill to Superga, 675 metres above the city; it takes twenty minutes.

Apart from the stunning view,[17] with the Alps in the background seemingly suspended in the air on a foggy day, there are two reasons to go to Superga. One is to visit the cathedral – which, for a long time, was the official chapel to the Savoy royal family.[18] Designed by the Messina-born architect Filippo Juvara the basilica is constructed in stunning yellow brick. It can be seen from most parts of the city below and is famous for its cupola. In front of the basilica, today, you find a rather squalid car park, two souvenir vans and a temporary bar. In the middle of the car park stands a strange eagle – a memorial to King Umberto I, killed by an anarchist in Monza in 1900.

Nowadays, the cathedral is rarely used for religious services and has fallen into decline as a royal space since the abolition of the Italian monarchy by referendum in 1946 (and their subsequent exile). To the casual visitor, it seems in urgent need of repair, and was occupied only by a beggar and a bored custodian when I visited in 2003. Recently two vandals tried to set fire to the doors of the basilica. The walls inside the church are covered in mindless graffiti, another sign of decline.[19] Most people come on weekends and, traditionally, the Turinese walk up the hill for their classic Easter Day trip, to picnic in the woods around the basilica.

Many other Turinese who 'go up to Superga' don't even visit the basilica. This is where the dream of the *Grande Torino* ended. It was here that the Fiat G212 plane crashed – into the top of the hill below the back of the buildings behind the church – killing all 31 passengers and changing the meaning of 'Superga' for ever. Since that fateful 4 May 1949 the church has also become a shrine, a museum and a place of homage to the *Grande Torino* team and, occasionally, a site for fan protests or celebrations. In June 2005, some fans made a 'pilgrimage' to the site to mark their team's return to Serie A. It is also a tourist attraction because of that disaster. Even the public toilets are draped in a Torino flag and a photo of the 1949 squad. The very visibility of the church from the city below has been a constant reminder to the Turinese of the tragedy.

In the tourist literature concerning Superga the crash is usually described as a *sciagura*, a calamity. On both sides of the basilica there is a sign indicating the way to the 'Plaque to the fallen of the Superga'. When you see the site of the crash, it is immediately clear that the pilot did not make a small error of judgement – he was a long way from clearing the basilica. On the wall there is a simple plaque, with the names of those who died (*I Campioni d'Italia*: 'The champions of Italy') and the following inscription:

> *Torino Football Club*
> *In Memory*
> *of its comrades*
> *– the glory of Italian sport –*
> *and those who died with them*
> *in a tragic air disaster*
>
> *4 May 1949*

The names of the dead are listed below.[20]

Superga is a place of memory, and now this memory has found expression in a new museum, close to the royal tombs – the Museum of Claret Red History (Torino play in claret red, or *granata* in Italian). Most of the collection held here was donated by amateur enthusiasts and fans, and many items were saved when the historic Filadelfia

stadium was demolished in 1997. On the way into the museum there
are photos of those who died. Inside, there is an assortment of miscel-
lanea; a wheel from the plane; shirts and wooden boxes containing kit
and medical items. Other exhibits are more famous. The museum has
managed to get hold of the original *Trumpet of Filadelfia*, which Oreste
Bolmida, railway worker and fanatical Torino fan, used to blow when
Torino needed to score. His call signalled the beginning of the 'Claret
red quarter of an hour': the fifteen minutes when the Great Torino
would usually crush their opponents. As he sounded the trumpet he
would run from one end of the pitch to the other. Legend has it that
at that point in the game, Valentino Mazzola would pull up his sleeves
(literally, and metaphorically), shout 'go', and Torino would go on
to win.

Superga is most animated on 4 May when, as on every 4 May since
1949, the team, family members linked to the victims and fans climb
the hill to the basilica. There, an annual mass is held to remember the
tragedy of the *Grande Torino* team and the current Torino captain
reads out the names of the victims. Wreaths are then placed near the
plaque.

A year after Superga, a large crowd, including Mazzola's sons Sandro
and Ferruccio, gathered to pay their respects at the site of the crash,
and unveil the plaque. On the tenth anniversary in 1959, Pozzo wrote
a bitter article, complaining about the 'empty words' that had surrounded the tragedy, which had become 'a springboard for literary
ambitions'. A minute's silence was observed before all matches in the
professional leagues. In 1999, on the fiftieth anniversary of the crash,
a special church service was organized with past players and dignitaries
from the city. Later there were friendly matches with ex-Torino players
wearing original *granata* shirts. The whole city took part in the commemorations and the press dedicated a series of articles to the memory
of the tragedy. Exhibitions and plays were mounted and the vast bibliography on the *Grande Torino* was further enriched.[21] Near the abandoned Filadelfia stadium old fans reminisced about the 1949 team as
if the players were still alive.

Remembering Superga is not always simple, or uncontroversial. The
former Torino financier/owner, Francesco Cimminelli, caused outrage

when he described the fans that visit Superga every 4 May as 'idiots' (the term in Italian was stronger – *coglione chi va a Superga*). He has never been allowed to forget that remark. Superga is a sacred place for Torino fans and it marked the inevitable climax of the 50,000-strong 'March of Torino Pride' in 2003, organized spontaneously after the worst season in the club's history.

However, Superga is also a place of kitsch, of bad taste and of fun for some Juventus fans. In the small souvenir shops near the basilica, a number of bizarre items are on sale – a thermometer in wood with a picture of the *Grande Torino*, a keyholder with the same photo, Torino egg cups and whisky glasses. Juventus scarves are also on sale, along with other Torino memorabilia. The postcards are even weirder. One reads *Saluti da Superga* – 'Hello from Superga' – and displays photos of the wooden Madonna, the church and . . . the Torino team. Another photo-montage card depicts a side shot of the basilica, with an enormous passenger aeroplane in the act of crashing into the *luogo della sciagura* – the site of the disaster. This is an official card, it seems, but the picture is so absurd that it could also be a Juventus creation – a joke. In the museum itself, another official card shows the 'Plaque to the glorious champions of Torino who fell at Superga on the 4 May 1949'. Yet in the corner of the postcard, there is another photomontage of an oversized passenger plane.

## The Myth

'*That* Torino team never died'          GIOVANNI ARPINO

After Superga the victims of the disaster, already close to perfection and nigh-on unbeatable on the pitch, entered into the realms of myth.[22] As time passed, devotion to the ex-*Grande Torino* developed into a kind of civic religion. Trips to Superga were described as 'pilgrimages'. People left flowers, cried or prayed by the plaque on the hill. One handwritten note left in 2003 ended with 'our claret red heart will never stop beating'. Photos of the dead stars were displayed all over the city, in people's homes, in their cars and in bars, clubs and restaurants. The trophy room at the Torino ground was known as the *sacrestia* (the sacristy) and the *Grande Torino* players became known

Superga. A postcard on sale at the site depicting the plaque to the victims
with a photo-montage of a large aircraft crashing into the wall above.

as *caduti* – the fallen, like angels, or war dead – and not simply victims.
All were young, and the players remained youthful in the photos that
were associated with the crash, which were similar to religious icons,
or *santini* (little saints, distributed in Italian churches).[23]

All the darker aspects of the past were forgotten or written out of
history – such as Mazzola's divorce from his first wife and the scandal
that had ensued. Relics were preserved – wheels and parts from the
plane, shirts, shoes, shoelaces. Enormous quantities of books, films
and poems were and still are dedicated to the *Grande Torino* players,
and not just in Turin.[24] Even romance could flourish in the ruins of
Superga. At one ceremony, the daughter and son of victims Giuseppe
Grezar and Romeo Menti met at the plaque behind Superga. A love
story was born which produced a child and a separation. Torino fans
were not just fans – they were different, they had a faith that had been
reinforced by tragedy and martyrdom, they were *devoted*. Massimo
Gramellini, Torino fan and journalist, invented a term for the generation of fans who had lived through the tragedy of 1949 – *uomo superga*;
Supergaman.

This devotion was strengthened, over the years, by a number of factors. For one thing, no Torino team was anywhere near as good as the *Grande Torino*. As a matter of fact, lots of Torino teams have been bad, and some have been very bad indeed. Over time, it appeared increasingly unlikely that Torino would ever be *Grande* again. Moreover, the rise and rise of Juventus led Torino followers into an increasingly melancholic nostalgia for the 1940s. This nostalgia was reinforced by the ritual humiliation of seeing Juventus win, time and time again. Finally, the team and the club suffered a series of other tragedies that reinforced the sense of bad luck, of a kind of curse.[25] Torino heroes Gigi Meroni and midfielder Giorgio Ferrini died young. On the pitch the team managed to hit the woodwork three times in the 1993 UEFA Cup final, which they lost on away goals. Torino even finished second behind Juventus in the 1976–77 championship, despite losing just one game all season.

Later Torino teams, in particular, never really came close to reproducing the form of the 1940s squad. Even the excellent 1970s team was only able to win one championship – the only *scudetto* won by Torino post-Superga. Torino contrived to lose the Italian Cup final *four times* in the 1970s and early 1980s – three times in a row and twice on penalties to the same team, Roma.[26] In 1993, when Torino appeared to be on the verge of a renaissance with a vibrant young team, it soon became clear that the club's finances were in disarray. The city of Turin could barely support one team – let alone two – as its population declined by 300,000 in twenty years. Even Juventus rarely filled their stadium and by 2003 were planning to reconstruct the hated Delle Alpi stadium (built for the 1990 World Cup) and *reduce* its capacity to 40,000.

Meanwhile Torino – whose fan-base was local, ageing and, some claimed, on the verge of extinction – slipped in and out of Serie A. The club sold off its best players and dismantled the most impressive youth programme in Italy. Christian Vieri, for example, who had come through the famed *granata* youth team, was discarded for next to nothing. With the team itself barely competitive in Serie B, Torino fans were left clinging on to their glorious past, with its tragedies, victories and epic derby games. Humiliation was piled on humiliation, and the club even ended up being owned by a card-carrying Juventus fan, but

Torino pride remained intact. Yet this pride and history also weighed down the current players – the particular demands of being a Torino player were too much for many youngsters, who often buckled under the pressure.[27] In 2005, the team managed to scrape back into Serie A at the end of a playoff that attracted more than 50,000 faithful fans. Soon afterwards, the club was declared officially bankrupt when huge tax debts were exposed by fake banking guarantees. Cimminelli left in disgrace, along with President Romero. This new club was given a new name – Torino Football Club and Cricket (*sic*). Thanks to a special agreement, Torino were re-admitted to Serie B, 'as a club which expresses a sporting tradition and has deep roots in the local community'. Without a training ground, a ticket office or even a kit, Torino 'celebrated' its 99th anniversary as a year zero – the lowest point in its long history.

## The Filadelfia Story. From Fortress to Ruin

INTERVIEWER: 'What do the other kids at school say when you tell them you support Torino?'
SMALL BOY: 'They think I'm mad.' (TV interview, 2005)

If you take the number fourteen tram in Turin, or just ask a taxi to leave you at the 'old stadium' in Via Filadelfia, not far from the city centre, you find yourself in front of a ruin. It is easy to get in through a hole in the red fence, next to the remains of some ticket offices. What you next see are the vestiges of one of the most loved and famous football stadiums in the world – the 'Filadelfia', home to the *Grande Torino* team. In 1948 Torino played nineteen home games here, winning eighteen of them. The pitch is still there, and there is even a goal with a broken crossbar. Beyond that, all that is left are a few strange pieces of stand – sticking up out of the grass like bizarre Roman monuments. Here and there you can see traces of the old stadium – signs, steps, barriers. Outside, the Torino fans have hung up a defiant sign – the *Casa del Popolo Granata* (Claret red home of the people) and a protest banner calling for *No Housing on the Filadelfia*.

Everything else, apart from one tower and a sparkling Torino emblem in stone on the front, has been demolished. Nonetheless, this

The Filadelfia Stadium, Turin. The pitch, 2003

is still a magical place that transmits a strong sense of history and tragedy. To walk on the field where Valentino Mazzola commanded play, rolling up his sleeves before ordering another attack, is to touch the very stuff of football legend. Torino fans can often be seen talking outside the ex-ground, or gathering in the Torino bars nearby. When journalist Massimo Gramellini organized a 'March of Claret Red Pride' in 2003, the starting point was at what he called 'the ruins of the Filadelfia'. The old stadium, however, is also a source of shame – the 'shame of all Turin' as one fan's website put it.

In 1926 the stadium opened with a 4–0 victory over Roma, in the presence of Prince Umberto (heir to the throne) and 15,000 spectators. It had an English-style design, with long stands and barriers. The spectators were extremely close to the pitch. Financed by the then Turin president Conte Enrico Marone di Cinzano the stadium stood on what was at that time the edge of the city, close to the FIAT factories which provided the bedrock of Torino support. Torino won their first championship here in 1928.

Torino's great 1940s sides – *Il Grande Torino* – did not just beat teams, they destroyed them. Playing with the 'method' system made popular in England, Torino attacked – scoring goals almost at will, especially from midfield, and rarely conceding at the back. They were also fitter than other teams – often scoring late-on. President Novo took physical preparation very seriously, and employed an expert English coach – Leslie Lievesley – to deal with this side of the game in the late 1940s. In addition, Torino were a remarkable unit, friends on and off the field, a team who had lived through the trials and tribulations of the war. Torino could also count on the intimidating atmosphere of the Filadelfia stadium that no visiting team could cope with.

After Superga, Torino continued to play in the crumbling venue until 1963, when they began to share the nearby Comunale stadium with Juventus.[28] Built in 1932–33, the Comunale was designed as a simple concrete bowl. It held almost 60,000 fans but lacked the intensity of the Filadelfia. The ex-'Benito Mussolini stadium' (renamed in 1945) was renowned for its enormous concrete tower, covered in lights – the *Torre Maratona* – with its huge sign saying *STADIO*. Torino played in the Comunale for 27 years, winning the championship there in 1975. The Comunale stood empty after 1990 – although Juventus continue to train there – while hundreds of turnstiles and ticket booths slowly rusted away.[29]

In 1990 both Turin clubs moved to yet another stadium, the Stadio delle Alpi, an impressive structure built for the World Cup of that year. However, it lies right on the edge of town – unlike the Comunale and the Filadelfia – and its athletics track (rarely used) and architecture make it hard to see the game properly from inside. Torino fans have had a dream for forty years – to return to regular games at a rebuilt Filadelfia. Many promises have been made over the years, and all of them have been broken.

\*      \*      \*

## The Filadelfia Story. Reconstruction, Promises, Ruins

'At the "Fila" we must start to make "Toro"'

MASSIMO GRAMELLINI

'A physical and moral black hole in Turin, a levelled ground
of ruins'                                      *La Repubblica*, 10.3.1999

Torino continued to train in the Filadelfia until the 1980s. For coach
Emilio Mondonico the secret of the magic of the Filadelfia was that
'people live in symbiosis with the players . . . it was a home, a monument, a den'. An added touch was the visibility of the ground afforded
to many residents in surrounding houses. Young fans mingled with
older fans and the players at training sessions, held in front of the one
remaining, long stand. In 1990 things began to move, at last, or so it
seemed. The stadium was handed over to the club and a project was
drawn up for a new 30,000-capacity ground. For the then president,
'the plan to go back to the Filadelfia' was 'above all an ideological
issue'. In 1994, the inevitable happened, after years of neglect. The
stadium was closed with the club claiming it was now too dangerous
to allow people in to watch the team train. Sessions were moved to a
FIAT field on the outskirts of town. Whereas 1,000 fans would still
turn up at the Filadelfia, only 200 fanatics bothered to travel out to
the new venue.

The Filadelfia site began a long decline. Later in the same year a
group of punks occupied the site and played football on the overgrown
pitch and drug-users began to frequent the abandoned field at night
as it emerged that Torino had debts of fifty thousand billion lire. Most
of the team was sold off as President Calleri became known as '*lo
smantellatore* – the dismantler. Yet, Calleri remained hopeful about a
return to the Filadelfia, a place, he said, where 'rhetoric and reality
coincide perfectly'.

In 1994 a Pro-Filadelfia Foundation was set up by Torino fan and
ex-city-Mayor Diego Novelli (a life-long communist). More promises
were made. 'The project is OK, we now need to find the money', said
Novelli. The 'new stadium' would be very small (just 15,000 seats) and

would be accompanied by a museum and a library. In 1995, fans were asked to 'buy a brick' for the new Filadelfia (for about thirty pounds each); wisely, only 400 fans did so. A new plan now provided for an even smaller stadium (down to 12,000 seats) that would only be used for training. The building site would open in 'one year's time'. In the same year Torino's fans unveiled this banner: 'The tragedy is not dying, but forgetting: save the Filadelfia'. Work was scheduled to start in 1996 and would be completed, Novelli claimed, well in time for the fiftieth anniversary of Superga.

In November 1998, the council declared that work on the new stadium would start 'very soon'. Time went by. No building work began. Meanwhile one of Torino's many ex-presidents, Gianmauro Borsano, who had taken the club to the brink of bankruptcy, was arrested. It emerged that he had more or less stolen fourteen thousand million lire from Torino. Another year passed but the site remained unchanged, if sadder and more overgrown. The club was sold – again – to Massimo Vidulich in March 1997 – a frontman for a mysterious group of Genovese financiers. 'We are very interested in the rebirth of the Filadelfia,' Vidulich told the fans, 'we will never leave there, at any cost.'

Discussions already seemed to be pointing in another direction, with plans to move Torino back to the Comunale. In July 1997, in what was both a good and a bad sign, more of the old stadium was demolished, preparing the way, it was hoped, for a new project. Many old players and staff were close to tears and Franco Ossola, son of a Superga victim (his namesake), said, 'I only had this field where I could feel that my father was alive, they are taking everything away from us.' Part of the monument to Superga was removed, leaving an empty plinth. Cynicism soon set in. Torino fan and journalist Massimo Gramellini wrote that 'the Egyptians took less time to complete the Pyramid of Cheops'. Meanwhile, as the team got worse and worse, Torino's long-suffering fans unveiled a banner – directed at the players – which read: 'Even in the last few games, you have been unworthy of this shirt'. Torino's followers occupied themselves mainly with songs about the past – chanting about heroes from the 1940s, 1950s, 1960s and 1970s.

In 1998 the council announced that work would begin 'soon' on

The Filadelfia Stadium, Turin. Ruins of the stands, 2003.

the new stadium which would be ready 'in a little while'. The fans, tired of endless lack of action, were suspicious. 'Politicians, Hands off the Filadelfia', they scrawled on the ruins of the stadium. In October 1998, *La Repubblica* wrote that the Turin council 'has obtained the necessary funds' to build a stadium on the historic Filadelfia site. May 1999 – the emotional fiftieth anniversary of Superga – came and went, amidst some farcical scenes. That day was supposed to see the laying of the foundation stone of the 'new' stadium. But the building site had still not been authorized and no ceremony took place. Fans screamed 'We want our Filadelfia back' at the city Mayor, Torino fan Valentino Castellani. He replied, 'So do I.' Christian Vieri, who had played his youth football at the Filadelfia, said, 'How sad it is to see it like this.' A warped fan even built a 'shrine' to the Madonna of the Filadelfia on the site.

In 2000 Torino appointed its seventh president since Pianelli (the last president to win a championship with the club) resigned in 1982. The team was now the property of plastics manufacturer and notorious Juventus fan, Francesco Cimminelli. By then, most Torino fans had given up hope of a new Filadelfia. Logistical problems (the size of the site, its residential location), speculation and financial poverty had combined to kill off what seemed increasingly like a project built on romanticism. What was to happen to the historic site was open to question. It looked like it would probably be turned over to housing or shops, something which journalist Gramellini has disparagingly called a *Supergamarket*.

As if to torture the club's loyal followers, yet another new project emerged in 2004, and was approved by the local council. Part of the old Filadelfia would now be made into a tiny new stadium, with just 2,200 seats. This 'stadium of memory' would be used for youth matches and friendlies, as well as first-team training. Torino followers were not impressed. Someone quipped that the minuscule stadium was an attempt to pass off a previous plastic model for the real thing. After all the past promises, false starts and plans, Torino fans were taking nothing for granted.

## CHAPTER 4

# Teams and Cities:
# Milan, Rome, Genoa, Florence, Naples

## Milan. Moral Capital and Football Capital

For the whole of the 1960s, the world's football capital was Milan. AC Milan and Internazionale had each won two European Cups in that decade, whilst Inter also lost another final. Domestically, the two Milanese clubs dominated the championship. Inter won three *scudetti*, and came second four times in ten years, Milan came first twice, and second twice. The 'moral capital' was also the key city in Italy in the 1960s. As the nation went through an unprecedented period of development and growth – the 'economic miracle' – Milan was the powerhouse of the 'great transformation'. Hundreds of thousands of Italian immigrants flooded into the city, finding work in the vast factories on the urban fringe – Alfa Romeo, Innocenti (who made the Lambretta scooter), Pirelli, Zanussi.

Despite the many stories in circulation, we still have no clear idea as to the reasons behind support for Milan or Inter, who have played in the same stadium since the 1940s.[1] Legend has it that Inter fans were originally more well-to-do, whilst Milan fans were drawn from the city's large industrial working class. There is no evidence to support this claim, and research on the contemporary fan-bases of the two clubs has found little social difference between them. Politics is also not a dividing characteristic – Inter have a hard-core of right-wing fans, but many left-wing supporters. Milan's *curva* has never ceded to the right, whilst their president and owner, Silvio Berlusconi, is certainly not on the left. There are no Inter and Milan zones in the city. Support was more a question of the family into which you were born – and *when* you were born. Inter became very popular during the period of the Great Inter in the 1950s and 1960s, Milan recruited millions of new fans during its triumphal 1990s.

## Internazionale

Inter's successes over the 100 or so years of Italian football can be concentrated into three 'cycles' of victories. After sporadic success in the early part of the twentieth century legendary striker Giuseppe Meazza inspired the team to two championships in three years in the late 1930s. A further two championships followed under the defensive management of Alfredo Foni in the early 1950s. However, the myth of Inter – its *national* fan-base, rivalled only by Milan and Juventus – was born in the 1960s, with the hyperbolic management of Helenio Herrera and thanks to the largesse of president Angelo Moratti. Herrera was a personality so bizarre, strong and successful that he was to dominate the game, and the sports media, for nearly ten years. This was the Great Inter, a team 'touched by the hand of God'.[2]

## Great Inter (*Grande Inter*)

In Nanni Moretti's hilarious coming-of-age satire, *Ecce Bombo* (1978), a group of students mope around Rome looking for a meaning in life. They try group therapy and politics, they experiment with alternative lifestyles. Nothing works. They stay up all night to watch the sunrise, only to find that their car is facing the wrong way. At one point in the film, some of the students study half-heartedly for a university exam. They are attempting to learn the names of the presidents of the Italian Republic since 1946. The list starts out correctly: 'De Nicola', but then the three students all repeat a different set of names, like a mantra: Burgnich, Facchetti, Bedin, Guarnieri, Picchi, Jair, Mazzola, Domenghini, Suarez, Corso: The Great Inter.

Inter's teams of the 1960s were built around an unlikely alliance between a self-made oil billionaire from a small town near Varese in Lombardy – Moratti – and an Argentinian-born Spanish-Moroccan manager who had made his name with Barcelona – Herrera. Together, and not without furious arguments, these two constructed a formidable side. They also revolutionized *calcio* in other ways, institutionalizing rigid, almost militaristic training regimes, organizing fans into travelling armies and bringing in a style of play that combined *catenaccio* defence with rapid and beautiful counter-attacking. All this was achieved with the luxury of a mercurial and lazy genius in midfield – Mario Corso. Herrera was the first modern manager, a superstar whose pay matched his fame. Since his departure in 1967, Inter have won just three championships in 37 years: a disaster for a club of their standing. No wonder that nostalgia about that glorious period of success is so strong amongst the generation of fans who grew up with that team.

## Not so Great Inter. *You Never Win!* The psychodrama of the *Interisti* since 1989

*4.5.2002. Sto ancora godendo*, '4.5.2002. I'm still enjoying it'
Juventus banner, Juventus–Inter, 2004

Inter's meagre haul of trophies since the 1960s would, in itself, be cause for pain, heartbreak and anger, but even worse than the losing has been the manner of their defeats. Inter have not just become celebrated because they 'never win' but also thanks to their ability, time and time again, to crumble under pressure. Successive Inter teams have made collapse into an art form, specializing in tantalizing their long-suffering fans with a taste of glory, before crushing their hopes with an inevitable self-inflicted debacle. The club has even been called 'the coitus interruptus of Italian football'.[3] An industry now exists around this collective psychodrama. In 2002–2003 alone, in the wake of Inter's latest and most spectacular flop, as they threw away yet another championship, a series of best-selling books was published around this very theme. A game was even put on sale: *Perdentopoli* (Loseopoly), based on Monopoly. Journalist and Inter fan Beppe Severgnini published two volumes entitled *Interismi* and *More Interismi*.[4] Another popular title depicted an Inter fan on a psychiatrist's couch, and *MiminoMoratti* was dedicated to the errors of Inter's generous president, Massimo Moratti, son of Angelo.[5] Moratti was often blamed for everything that had gone wrong with Inter. One well-known fan went as far as to say that if the Inter president had been Mayor of Milan, the city would have 'looked like Berlin in 1945'.[6] Other tomes were aimed at those Milan and Juventus fans who enjoy winding up their *Interisti* friends (and in Italy, everybody has an *Interista* friend). One of these titles was a small book full of jokes. Its title? *Non vincete mai*. 'You lot never win'.[7] A sample joke: Christ is on the cross when Moratti walks by. 'Help, help me,' says Christ, 'please pull out the nails from my hand.' Moratti, generous as ever, goes up to Christ and pulls one nail out. Christ thanks him. 'Please, the other one, the other one.' Moratti obliges. Immediately, Christ claps his hands together and laughs. *Non vincete mai*, he sings, joyously.

In 2005 another joke did the rounds, in the wake of Pope John Paul II's death. Inter would beat Milan, it was said, because they only win 'every time a Pope dies', an Italian phrase for 'very rarely indeed'. Inter, of course, lost both games to Milan.

The *non vincete mai* chant cuts deep as it is based upon the Inter *curva's* favourite chant – *non mollare mai*[8] – 'never give up'. Moreover, since 1989, Inter's rivals have never stopped winning. During Inter's drought, Milan have won six championships and three European Cups. The wind-up is strengthened every time a trophy is added to Berlusconi's already bulging cabinet.

This history of failure has reinforced a certain kind of *interista* psychology, marked by bursts of anger (above all directed at Inter's players, managers and presidents), black humour, fatalism, cynicism (conspiracy theories, especially after the 'great theft' of 2001, when the referee refused an obvious penalty against Juventus) and impatience. Players have found it hard to play for Inter over the years. The whole team is hounded by debate, rancour and bad behaviour – *nervosismo*. Young players don't last long. One bad performance, or perhaps just a misplaced pass, and you are mercilessly whistled. Occasionally, this anger transforms itself into violence. After a home European defeat the Inter fans caused a riot. Following a 6–0 rout away to Parma, the Inter team bus was petrol-bombed by its own fans. Restaurants part-owned by top players have been attacked. And there was more as bad behaviour became synonymous with Inter's hard-core *curva*. In 2001 Inter fans managed to smuggle a motorbike into the second tier of the stadium. It had a Bergamo number plate – Inter were playing

Atalanta. A group of fans then proceeded to destroy the motorbike before pushing it over the edge of the guard-rail, whence it crashed onto the emptied terraces below.

Inter's fans have had enough. In 2004, the whole *curva* left the stadium seven minutes from the end of Inter–Empoli (0–0 at the time), after promising that they would 'get their clubs out' and accusing their players of playing 'only for money'. Empoli won the game, in extra-time. A group of 500 fans then besieged the players' exit, only dispersing after a delegation of players had come out to speak to them. Inter's vast economic power has not been able to buy the club many trophies. Despite their undoubted position as one of the big three of Italian football, Inter have been forced to sit back and watch as Juventus, Milan and even the Rome clubs have shared championships amongst themselves. Losing to Milan twice in the Champions League in three years was the last straw. In April 2005 flares and fireworks rained down from the Inter *curva* with some seventeen minutes of the tie still to play. The game was called off, and Inter fans were banned from the next four European games. The psychodrama had become an international issue.

In the dark 1990s, Inter transformed a series of supposed stars into nonentities. Some of these were just bad buys, but others went on to do well elsewhere, proving that the problem lay with Inter, and not with the players themselves. Many of these players have become cult figures, after their departure. Serbian striker Darko 'the Cobra' Pancev was signed in 1992 after winning the European Cup with Red Star Belgrade. He went on to play just nineteen games in four years, scoring a miserable three goals. Dennis Bergkamp came from Ajax in 1993 amidst much fanfare. He lasted two years, 52 games and eleven goals. His second season was particularly poor, with just three goals. Bergkamp went on to become an Arsenal legend. Clarence Seedorf fell into the same category – a talented player who failed with Inter and, horror of horrors, went on to become a Milan player (where he has won everything there is to be won). Roberto Baggio was hardly given a chance by manager Marcello Lippi, who often left him on the bench. Most Inter fans never forgave English manager Roy Hodgson for selling on a young Roberto Carlos after just 34 games for the club. Perhaps most infamously, Inter purchased a Brazilian defender called Gilberto da Silva Mello in 1999. He was, allegedly, very good at five-a-side football and had been recommended by Ronaldo. He appeared just once in Serie A, and once in the Italian Cup, both times as a substitute, before returning to Brazil. Again, the problem was Inter's, as Gilberto went on to play for the national team on a number of occasions.

Why have Inter been so short on victories? It has certainly not been a question of money. Moratti has poured considerable quantities of his personal fortune into the team since taking over in 1995. However, his forays into the transfer market have often been less than successful and Inter has a long history of buying poor foreign players. A second explanation is, simply, an astonishing run of bad luck. Ronaldo injured himself twice, very seriously, whilst with Inter and ended up playing just a handful of games in three years after a fantastic first season. Moratti has not been particularly fortunate with his managers, and has tended to chop and change when immediate victory has not arrived. Defeat after defeat has led to a siege mentality amongst players and staff, and each year the pressure gets worse.

Inter's long-term decline – as a big club without the ability to win trophies – was masked for a long time by the disasters which befell Milan. For the first six years of the 1980s, Inter fans gloried in Milan's fate – which included a relegation to Serie B after a betting scandal, a president on the run from justice, and another relegation, this time after a terrible season. Inter lorded it over their rivals throughout this period. For a time, the butt of all the jokes were the red-and-blacks, not Inter. And then Berlusconi came along.

## Milan. From humiliation to domination

The modern history of Milan can now be written only with reference to a key moment: 20 February 1986. Milan had just spent their second season in four years in Serie B. The team had been rocked by financial and on-the-pitch scandals, and was up for sale. In stepped a short, balding, grinning multi-millionaire, who had made his name and his fortune in the building trade, and then as Italy's first private television mogul. Silvio Berlusconi had been born in Milan in 1936, and many claim that he was an Inter fan in his youth. He denies this (of course) but doubts remain. In any case, under Berlusconi, Milan's success story has been dramatic: twenty years, seven *scudetti* and, above all, four European Cups. In that time, Inter have won one championship and two UEFA Cups. There is no comparison.

Milan had had great teams before Berlusconi. The 1950s saw the club win four championships in ten years, with the legendary Swedish threesome – Gren, Nordahl and Liedholm – and a defence built around Paolo Maldini's father, Cesare. Later the goalscoring prowess of José Altafini was allied to the silky skills of Uruguayan midfielder Schiaffino. By 1960–1961, manager Nereo Rocco had taken over. Under Rocco, with Gianni Rivera in midfield, Milan won two championships and two European Cups in the 1960s.

The 1970s were a time of frustration as three second-place finishes led to innumerable arguments with the referees. A memorable last-day collapse at Verona handed a title to Juventus. Ten years without a *scudetto* was an eternity for Milan, and they finally won their first gold star – awarded for ten championships – in 1979, Rivera's last season. By that time, the team was transformed again and Franco Baresi was developing into a young star at the back. Yet disaster was soon to befall the club as betting and financial scandals and bad management led to two humiliating years in Serie B. A long period of mid-table obscurity followed, as the team rebuilt, slowly. Then, in 1986, Berlusconi arrived. Within a year he had bought the best three foreigners to play in Italy – together – in modern times – Gullit, Van Basten and Rijkaard. A number of brilliant young stars came through the ranks – with Paolo Maldini as the pick of the bunch. Milan were unstoppable for the next ten years, only dipping with the natural decline of that squad in the late 1990s. Berlusconi's media and political power developed Milan into a world-famous business, and the influence of TV reinforced an oligarchy that excluded smaller teams. Some commentators have seen this northern big-city supremacy as something entirely new, although the Milanese and Turinese clubs have (almost) always dominated modern Italian football, apart from some brief and short-lived provincial or southern victories in the 1970s and 1980s.

Most Milan fans adored Berlusconi, yet some experienced the success story of their politician-president in a schizophrenic fashion, unable to separate their hatred for the politician from their admiration for the football president. Sometimes, hard-core fans claimed that he was neglecting his footballing commitments for political reasons, but Berlusconi always made sure he turned up at the stadium, and often interfered in tactical and transfer decisions. He was well aware of the power that AC Milan gave him on the national stage, and the ways in which the club's triumphs naturally helped his personal fortunes in other spheres. With three national channels under his control, the product called 'Milan' was given hours and hours of free advertising and promotion, creating legions of new, young Milan fans ready to invest time and money in their support for their club and, often, for that club's president in his many other careers. The club and its president were – as he had hoped – almost symbiotic. Of course, this could work both ways, and Berlusconi was furious when his team lost key matches. Football, when it came to Milan in the 1990s and beyond, was far more than just a game.

## Rome. Occasional football capital

Roma: 'Look up to the skies. Only the sky is bigger than you.'
Lazio (reply): 'You're right. It's blue and white.' (Lazio's colours)
(Fan banners, circa 2001)

Unlike Milan or Turin, Rome's two clubs do not have huge followings outside of their city, or its immediate province. Lazio fans are seen as largely hailing from the province of Rome or the towns around the capital, whilst Roma fans are from the city itself. Unlike in Milan or Turin, being a fan in the capital is thus a territorial question. Certain zones in the city are Roma zones – Testaccio (where the Roma stadium once was), San Lorenzo, Garbatella. When Roma won their third championship in 2003, these areas were festooned with yellow-and-red flags, graffiti and murals, many of which can still be seen.

AS Roma was formed in 1927 after pressure from the Fascist Party led to the fusion of three Rome clubs into one (the three teams were L'Alba, La Roman and La Fortitudo). The only team that resisted the call was Lazio, who have a much longer history than their hated city rivals. This manoeuvre also led to a historic imbalance in the fan-bases of the two clubs. Roma have always had far more fans than Lazio.

Neither club has ever really challenged the sustained dominance of the northern cities' clubs. Despite their financial clout, star players and passionate following, Lazio and Roma have only won five championships between them. Lazio triumphed in the early 1970s and again in 2000. Roma won in 1943, 1983 and 2001.

Lazio became an important club, for the first time, in the 1930s – although they had challenged for early championships in 1913 and 1914. Star striker Silvio Piola arrived at the club in 1934 and helped the team towards a series of good finishes in that decade. Benito Mussolini, it is often said, was a Lazio fan but it is not clear whether the tendency of the club's followers towards the politics of the extreme right began under the regime itself. After the war, Lazio veered between Serie A and Serie B, and only made a serious challenge for the *scudetto* in 1972–1974, when they won one championship and finished second and third. That crazy team – with its scandals, violence and madcap behaviour – broke up quickly amid recrimination (as top scorer Giorgio Chinaglia left for the US league) and tragedy (the deaths of the manager Tommaso Maestrelli from cancer and midfielder Luciano Re Cecconi in a ridiculous accident).

Disaster struck in 1980, with the club relegated following the involvement of a group of Lazio players in the worst betting scandal in Italian football history. A series of other scandals, relegations and promotions followed until 1992, when wheeler-dealer businessman Sergio Cragnotti took over. Through massive investment and financial trickery – Lazio were the first Italian club to be floated on the stock exchange – the new president built a team able to win a *scudetto*, with a host of foreign stars and manager Sven Goran Eriksson. Yet, this success was ephemeral. Cragnotti went bankrupt and was arrested on charges of fraud and false accounting. The team was forced to sell off most of its well-known players and teetered on the edge of collapse. Only creative accounting saved the club from ruin in 2005. Lazio's fans, meanwhile, strengthened their reputation as the most racist and right-wing group of supporters in Serie A. Fascist symbols, slogans and even swastikas were a common sight amongst Lazio's hard-core support, who revelled in their extreme reputation.

\*          \*          \*

Roma's first manager was legendary Englishman William Garbutt, who soon moved on to Napoli. For years (1929–1940) the club played in a local, neighbourhood stadium – at Testaccio – where the atmosphere was extremely intimidating. The strong team of the 1930s and 1940s – with Fulvio Bernardini at the heart of the side and the 'eighth King of Rome', Amedeo Amadei, up front – only won the wartime championship. For years rumours circulated about the role of the fascist government in that Rome triumph (especially after the ref- ereeing of a hard-fought derby) but no real evidence of wrongdoing has ever emerged.[9] Roma's victory meant that, for the first time, the *scudetto* had gone to a team south of Bologna. After that 1942 victory the team languished in mid-table for much of the post-war period and even suffered the indignity of Serie B. Despite their financial power, a series of well-known players, famous managers and the new Olympic stadium, Roma never came close to the *scudetto* again until the late 1970s. Instead, the team specialized in winning the little-loved Italian Cup. This all changed as innovative manager Nils Liedholm built an exciting team around Italian stars Agostino Di Bartolomei, Bruno Conti and Roberto Pruzzo and the genius of Roberto Falção, the Brazilian playmaker. Roma were pipped to the championship by Juve in 1980 but they finally won a post-war title in 1983. The partying went on for days, complete with hit records by Roma fan and long- haired crooner Antonello Venditti. The titles of his songs were not over-imaginative: *Grazie Roma* being followed by *Roma, Roma*.

Roma came very close to winning the European Cup in 1984, only losing to Liverpool on penalties. They then threw the *scudetto* away (under Eriksson) in 1986. In the 1990s, a powerful new team was built around young genius Francesco Totti and Argentinian imports Gabriel Batistuta and Walter Samuel. Under Fabio Capello, Roma won their third championship in 2001, after being forced to watch Lazio triumph the year before. Yet, as with Lazio, the club's eyes had been bigger than its stomach. President Franco Sensi struggled to pay his players' wages and the club's debts reached unheard-of levels. To get out of financial trouble – like Lazio – Sensi sold off a series of stars and, in 2004, Capello left. The brief challenge of the Rome clubs to the Milan–Turin hegemony appeared to be over – it was simply too expensive to keep up with the big three.

*       *       *

The Rome derby is perhaps the most passionate, talked-about and violent fixture in Italy. Many fans from both teams will say that they prefer to win that game than the *scudetto*, and some actually believe what they are saying. Victories and defeats have become the stuff of legend, and a good performance in a Rome derby can make a player's career. Lazio fans celebrated for weeks after beating Roma away in 1932. Paolo Di Canio became a Lazio hero after a goal as a teenager in a 1989 derby, and Paul Gascoigne did the same with a late headed equalizer against Roma in 1993. When Di Canio returned to Lazio in 2004 (the fans had been asking presidents for years to 'give us back Di Canio') he was greeted by thousands of *Laziali*, on a sweltering August day, who cheered his every touch during training. Di Canio was given a microphone to talk to the fans. In tears, he finished off his 'speech' with a rousing rendition of *chi non salta della Roma è* ('anyone does not jump is a Roma fan') at which point the whole team, technical and management staff as well as all the fans, began to jump up and down. Di Canio's first derby in his new spell with the club was preceded by a week of traded insults in the press with Roma's most popular player, Francesco Totti. In the game itself, Di Canio scored a superb goal as Lazio won 3–1, and was then punished by a huge fine after he was photographed giving a fascist salute to his adoring fans.[10]

Rome derbies have often been marred by violence and racism. Whilst the hard-core Lazio fans – traditionally from the right and far right of the political spectrum – indulged in anti-Semitism and other forms of racism directed at the Roma 'end', Roma's fans tended to be on the left. Some were on the far left in the 1970s, even comparing the Brazilian midfielder Falção with Chairman Mao, in part because the two words rhymed well. In the 1990s, this began to change. *Both* sets of fans moved to the right whilst continuing to fight each other inside and outside the stadium. There were occasions, however, when Lazio and Roma supporters allied against their common enemy – the police. All this culminated in the shocking events of March 2004, when the derby was suspended after false rumours began to spread amongst the fans that a young boy had been killed after clashes with the *carabinieri* outside the ground. It later appeared as if the whole event had been set up to allow fans to attack the police.

Nowhere in Italy was football as important as it was in Rome, with its numerous fan clubs, football-dedicated radio stations, interminable phone-ins and *ultrà* bars. This fanaticism could be seen most clearly after the two championship victories – for Lazio, and then for Roma – in 2000 and 2001. The celebrations paralysed Rome for days, and left traces all over the city and its hinterland – through murals, graffiti, flags and street parties.

## Genoa. On the Margins

Since 1924, when Genoa won the last of their nine championships, the port city has only won the league title once, with Sampdoria in 1991. Genoa's best showing in all that time was fourth place in that same year, and they have spent much of their time in Serie B. Sampdoria – only formed from a fusion of two city clubs in 1946 (Andrea Doria and Sampierdarenese) – had their moment of glory in the late 1980s and early 1990s, with a team which relied heavily on the exceptional striking partnership of Roberto Mancini and Gianluca Vialli, and the wily transfer-market dealings of president Paolo Mantovani. Their manager was the hilarious Yugoslav, Vujadin Boskov, celebrated for his surreal comments in basic Italian. When asked about a controversial spot kick, he would invariably reply that: 'it is a penalty when the referee blows' (*Rigore è quando arbitro fischia*) or 'the team which makes fewer mistakes, wins . . . we made more mistakes. We lost'. There are now whole books full of Boskovisms. That side came within inches of winning the European Cup in 1992 at Wembley, as Vialli's misses allowed Barcelona to win with a late goal. Sampdoria also won the Italian Cup four times between 1985 and 1994 as well as the Cup-Winners Cup in 1989. All this success was built on unbreakable squad unity. Seven of the championship team used to hang out together, calling themselves the seven dwarves. Once the championship was secured, the whole team peroxided their hair for the final game.

Once Vialli left, and Mantovani died (in 1993), the team went into a slow decline – although they finished third and won the Italian Cup under the stewardship of Sven Goran Eriksson. In 1998 they ended up in Serie B and only returned to a dignified, mid-table Serie A finish in 2004. Both Vialli and Mancini became successful managers, confirming the analyses that had seen them as 'on-pitch' managers in the 1980s and 1990s.

Genoa's post-war history has been far less glorious. Like Torino, they have never lived up to a past that is now so far away as to be almost completely forgotten. William Garbutt came back for a time after the war but the club hovered between A and B, and never made a serious challenge for the *scudetto*. Winger Gigi Meroni briefly became a hero for the team in the early 1960s but the team was dogged by doping and corruption scandals. From 1965 to 1972 the club remained out of Serie A altogether and in 1970 they even ended up in Serie C, before tasting the top division briefly thanks to three promotions and the same number of relegations in the 1970s and 1980s. Genoa fans went though hell and humiliation as Sampdoria became a world-class team, and the derby 'of the Lantern' was rarely played while Genoa languished in B. Financial problems also hit the club in the 1990s. The only high point in the whole decade was a UEFA Cup-tie victory at Anfield in 1992. Otherwise, Genoa seemed destined to repeat the fate of a number of other ex-big clubs, scrapping for points in Serie B (with sides like Napoli and Torino) and living on distant past glories. Their only real hope lay with an ambitious and rich president, a dream that seemed to have come true with the arrival of toy billionaire Enrico Preziosi in 2004. Yet, once again, the loyalty of Genoa's fans was tested to the limit as a corruption scandal robbed them of a return to Serie A in 2005.

## Florence. Purple Pride

There is no derby in Florence. Only one team plays there – Fiorentina, a side whose dramatic recent history has overshadowed its glorious past, made up of victories which at times threatened to break the dominance of the big Milan–Turin axis. Fiorentina won the championship in 1956 and reached the European Cup final a year later, losing only to Real Madrid. They then finished second four times in a row, but always by fairly large margins. This was a team constructed by Fulvio Bernardini, one of the most talented and original characters in the history of Italian football. Player, journalist, intellectual, coach, manager, Bernardini remained at the top of the game for two generations and took two provincial clubs – Bologna and Fiorentina – to rare *scudetto* victories. Bernardini's record with Fiorentina was exceptional – one championship, three second-place finishes and one fifth place. The second Fiorentina *scudetto* was the work of ex-Napoli-star-turned-coach Bruno Pesaola, who kept the fiery Brazilian Amarildo under control just long enough to hold off the challenge of Cagliari in 1969.

Fiorentina were never to win another *scudetto*, but they came very close in the late 1970s and early 1980s with a team built around a stylish, loyal and unlucky midfielder: Giancarlo Antognoni, who suffered a series of horrific injuries. Only some extremely questionable refereeing denied the *viola* (the purple one) the championship in 1982, and an intense rivalry with Juventus was born. Fiorentina produced a series of superb young players in the 1980s and 1990s, none more so than fan idol Roberto Baggio, whose sale to Juventus in 1990 provoked a riot. Fiorentina replaced Baggio with Gabriel Batistuta, another hero who was loyal enough to play a season in Serie B for the club. With Giovanni Trapattoni on the bench, Fiorentina finished a creditable third in 1998–99. Then, total collapse. Club president and film producer Mario Cecchi Gori died in 1993, and was replaced by his fake-tanned son, Vittorio, who had political ambitions and an empty wallet.

In 2002 Fiorentina went bust, and were sent down to Serie C as punishment after finishing bottom of Serie A. Cecchi Gori was arrested on various charges, including drug use. The team suffered the intense humiliation of losing its name and original symbol – they became Florentia Viola for a year. New owner Diego Della Valle, who had made his money from a fashion company called Tod's, was forced to buy back the Viola symbol and name at an auction. After rebuilding with a young team, the squad was 're-called' to Serie B in 2003. The sense of injustice felt by Fiorentina fans and players was heightened by the huge debts declared by other big clubs, who were *not* relegated as a consequence.

## The Provinces. Bologna, Cagliari, Verona

Only three provincial teams have won championships since 1945. Bologna, under Fulvio Bernardini and with midfielder Giacomo Bulgarelli as their charismatic star, won a controversial playoff with Inter in 1964. Since then the club has been through ups and downs, including going bust and being sent down to Serie C in 1993. After that humiliating moment, the club worked its way back up to Serie A, where it settled into mid-table respectability, before slipping back to Serie B in 2005.

Cagliari's period of glory was in the late 1960s and early 1970s, and was based around the unique talent of Gigi Riva, who led the whole island into days of wild celebration after the 1969–70 championship. Provincial Verona, finally, won an unexpected *scudetto* in 1985, with a team lacking in stars apart from the Danish striker Preban Elkaer. Most commentators attribute that victory to the subtle management skills of a coach born in the working-class Milanese neighbourhood of Bovisa, Osvaldo Bagnoli.

Since Sampdoria's victory in 1991, it has been increasingly difficult for smaller teams to mount a serious challenge. Money talks in the age of pay-per-view and the Champions League, and just four clubs have shared the championship in the last fourteen years – Juventus (6), Milan (6), Roma (1) and Lazio (1). The massive financial difficulties of the Rome clubs by 2004 seemed to point to a three-horse race from here on in: *Juvemilaninter.* Inter were the odd team out in this equation, a big, rich club who kept failing to win anything at all.[11] Nobody else could get a look in. The unpredictability of the championship, which occasionally threw up romantic stories of loyalty, team spirit and shock results, had been killed off by the corporate nature of the contemporary game. Two football analysts have argued that this trend is part of a general shift towards something they call 'neo-football'. In contrast to the game that became popular in the 1930s and boomed again in the 1950s and 1960s, neo-football is above all a TV and business phenomenon. It is also detached from space and territory and increasingly globalized. The domination of the same big clubs – which are now brands marketed across the world, largely through internet and digital technology – guarantees a world-wide audience and also contributes to the decline of the national teams. In the neo-football world, only two or three teams are ever able to challenge for the championship, money talks and the rest are just bit-part players on a globalized world stage, where Milan players are household names in China and Japan and football is played 365 days a year.[12]

## Naples. The Longest Wait

As the fourth-best-supported club in Italy, Napoli have been starved of success ever since their formation in 1926. After some good seasons under William Garbutt in the 1930s they briefly threatened to win the *scudetto* in the 1950s, when ship-builder Achille Lauro pumped money into the team, and then occasionally in the 1960s and 1970s. Napoli's fans have always had a soft spot for charismatic foreign stars. The team's heroes over the years have usually been forwards – the flamboyant Paraguayan Attila Sallustro in the 1920s and 1930s, the Brazilian Luis Vincio in the 1950s, Omar Sivori and José Altafini in the 1960s. Nobody, however, has ever come close to the adulation received by the greatest player ever to play for Napoli, and the only man to bring a championship trophy to the city: Diego Armando Maradona.

## The King. Maradona and Napoli. 1984–1991

In the still desperately poor Spanish Quarters of Naples, groups of small boys drive motorbikes at high speeds through the tiny streets. Here, you can still see damage from the 1980 earthquake and the population density is amongst the highest in Western Europe. On one wall, towards the top of the *quartieri*, there is a huge mural. It depicts a man with black curly hair and a blue Napoli shirt. The mural is so large that an (illegal) window only takes up part of the face. It is peppered with bullet holes – local criminals used it for target practice, it appears.[13] The man is instantly recognizable, and not just to locals: Diego Armando Maradona – the King of Naples. Maradona played for Napoli between 1984 and 1991. In that time the team, which had won only two Italian Cups in its entire history, triumphed twice in the Italian championship (and finished second twice), as well as winning an Italian Cup, a UEFA Cup and an Italian supercup. In the same period, Maradona won the World Cup with Argentina and pushed his team to a second successive final, beating Italy, in 1990, in Naples of all places, on penalties. Since Maradona's departure, Napoli have returned to their previous ways, winning nothing. In 2005 they were to be found way down in Serie C after having gone bankrupt. For a team with a fan-base which rivals that of the big three Serie A clubs, this was an astonishing decline.

*       *       *

The story of Maradona's time at Napoli, when he was probably the best player in the best league in the world (a league with Platini and Mattheus and Van Basten and Zico), was one of poetry, histrionics, scandal, suspicion and doping. It was also the story of the greatest series of celebrations ever seen in domestic football history.

Between 70,000 and 90,000 people turned up, paying 1,000 lire each, to watch Maradona kick a ball around in the San Paolo stadium after he had been signed in June 1984, eclipsing the 20,000 who saw Omar Sivori train twenty years earlier. Tortuous negotiations with Barcelona had ended with the 23-year-old arriving at the end of the season, for fourteen thousand million lire, a record fee at the time. Napoli had a history of buying big, but their free-spending had brought them very little in the way of success. There were 253 journalists present as well as 78 photographers. This media circus was never really to calm down, and, in the end, would drive Maradona out of the city after six years of triumph and controversy. Maradona's signing paid off at the box-office. Eighty-six per cent of Napoli's spectators were season-ticket holders whilst the Argentinian played for them, and a San Paolo ticket was a hot one throughout the second half of the 1980s.

## Napoli's success and DAMM

The Napoli team of the 1980s was not just about Maradona, but it was Maradona-dependent. Built on a solid defensive foundation, with Ciro Ferrara at centre-back, the team could also depend on the tireless running of Fernando De Napoli and Salvatore Bagni in midfield and on excellent strikers such as Andrea Carnevale, Bruno Giordano and the Brazilian Careca. This whole unruly bunch was kept in check by managers Ottavio Bianchi (for the first championship) and Alberto Bigon for the second.

Maradona and the team took time to settle in. In his first season Diego scored fourteen goals and the team finished eighth, in his second year he scored eleven times and Napoli ended up third. From 1987 to 1990, however, Maradona played sublime football, scoring 50 goals in four seasons. Statistics tell us little about little Diego. Maradona's genius can only really be understood through images – his goals were, like those of Roberto Baggio, rarely dull or ugly – chips from outside the box, perfect free-kicks, mazy dribbles, goals whilst lying on the ground. Maradona was also able to provide numerous passes for others, and he never gave up, even when defenders took lumps out of his stocky legs. The 1990 *scudetto* team also saw the emergence of a sparkling young talent, who had been plucked from obscurity in Sardinia. His first nickname was MaraZola, but Gianfranco Zola, who played eighteen games that year, would soon be famous in his own right.

## The Party. 1987

On 10 May 1987, Napoli needed just a draw at home to Fiorentina to win their first *scudetto*. Carnevale scored for Napoli, and Roberto Baggio struck his first-ever goal in Serie A to equalize in the first half. No further goals were added. During the game, apart from the cheers after Napoli's goal, the city was as quiet as a grave. Italian anthropologist Amalia Signorelli went for a walk (it was a beautiful day). 'The world had changed,' she wrote, 'the noisiest, most crowded and most chaotic city in Europe was deserted.'[14]

As the final whistle blew, Neapolitans poured onto the streets all over the city, and in cities all over the world. 'By 7.30 along the sea front ... there was a single wave of Napoli flags, a long singing, dancing, jumping blue snake.'[15] Hundreds of buses were blocked in the crowd, with fans dancing on their roofs. Motorbike riders did wheelies all over town. Many revellers were dressed as Maradona, with curly black wigs. An enormous replica trophy was stuck on to a Dante statue. Blue cakes between six and ten metres long were displayed, and then eaten. The omens had been good. Number 43 had come up in the lottery for the Naples wheel (each city has a daily lottery); 43 stands for 'the god of players' – Maradona, in other words. A week later, 43 came up again, along with 61 (the number of years it had taken Napoli to win the championship). During the celebrations, Napoli's fans displayed all the classic traits of what has become known as the Neapolitan 'character': irony, parody and a sense of the macabre, obscenity, blasphemy. They also put on a show, and did so knowingly. Already, during the celebrations, illegal VHS cassettes of the same celebrations were being sold on the streets. This was theatre. Neapolitans were being

Neapolitan kids with a photo of Maradona.

filmed and then buying videos showing themselves celebrating the victory of Napoli.

Bunting was hung across the claustrophobic streets – the *vicoli* – of the city centre, and cars were draped in Napoli colours as they honked their way through town. Impromptu street parties went on for days, with pasta and seafood being prepared for all and sundry on massive long tables. Anybody could sit down for a meal. Citizens 'taxed themselves' to pay for all this. Fireworks exploded at frequent intervals. Nobody went to work the next day. Famously, someone wrote this graffito on the walls of the city graveyard: 'You don't know what you are missing!' – *Guagliu! E che ve sit pers!*. Pretend funerals were held for Juventus, complete with coffins and black-lined printed 'death notices'. Napoli's victory was also the chance of revenge after years of being seen as a poor city full of thieves. 'May 1987, the other Italy has been defeated, a new empire is born.' Urban myths circulated concerning the power of Maradona. It was said that 20,000 local government voters had written 'Viva Maradona' on their ballot papers, making their votes uncountable. Another improbable myth was that 100 donkeys had been imported from Sardinia for the post-*scudetto* celebrations. Floats were prepared with Maradona on a throne and Platini or Rummenigge prone at his feet.

During Maradona's time in the city, thousands of babies were named 'Diego', or even Diega. In one central parish 25 per cent of newly born sons were named Diego. Streets and whole neighbourhoods were given his name and murals sprang up comparing him to the city's much-loved patron saint, San Gennaro. In one such mural Maradona is depicted in the arms of San Gennaro himself. Many of these murals are now painted over or in a poor state of repair. One of the most interesting and important 'social centres' (alternative city spaces) in

Mural depicting Maradona in the Spanish Quarters, Naples.

Naples is called DAMM: *Diego Armando Maradona Montesanto*.[16] The cult of Diego was (and is) a real cult, combining idolatry, superstition and love. On one website dedicated to Maradona, there is a photo of his baptism. Many writers have stressed the ways in which Maradona was accepted by Neapolitans as one of them – in part because of his humble background, and in part because of his 'rebellious' nature. Maradona, according to Spanish writer Manuel Vazquez Montalbán, 'encapsulated the myth of lumpenproletarian emancipation'. Short, scruffy, ugly and ungainly, Maradona even *looked* like a grown-up street kid (which is what he was, after all) and the Neapolitans loved him for it. Northern journalist Gianni Brera played on the contradiction between Diego's physical appearance and his grace on the field, dubbing him 'the divine abortion'.

By 1987, after just three years in the city, Maradona had won the World Cup (and there was much celebrating in Napoli after Argentina's victory) and taken a much-loved team to its first *scudetto* in sixty-one years of Italian football. He was at the peak of his career. Sadly, from that moment on, self-destruction set in. He won a few more trophies with Napoli – including a controversial second championship – and took a weak Argentinian team close to another World Cup in 1990, but after 1987, Maradona would be in the headlines more for his private life than his performances on the field. His long slide into addiction and obesity was aided and abetted by nasty hangers-on, some unwisely chosen by Maradona himself, and by a sense that he was above any discipline and management. Diego's relationship with Corrado Ferlaino, Napoli's president since 1969, was always stormy and it is said that the club paid for private detectives to monitor his every move. These costs were even declared in the club's official budget. However, the club 'managed' Diego by basically allowing him to do what he liked, as long as he turned up for matches, and this indiscipline soon spread to the rest of the team.

## Drugs, scandals and the end of the Maradona fable

Although Napoli had triumphed in 1987, the tensions between manager Bianchi and certain senior players were soon to explode. The last game of the season was a dead match at Ascoli and Napoli played as if they had been celebrating for a week, which they had been. Towards the end of the match, with the score at 1–1, manager Ottavio Bianchi left the bench and the stadium. Songs from inside the dressing room seemed to call for his resignation ('when will you leave?') and the manager even offered to resign. Bianchi stayed, but the character clashes with a number of senior players were to resurface with a vengeance at the end of the following season.

The 1987 victory was popular across Italy, but things soon began to change. Mystery still surrounds Napoli's collapse in the 1988 run-in, when they managed only one point in their last four games, and Milan swept to victory. For years, rumours have circulated concerning the role of illegal betting rings, although no formal inquiry has ever been opened. After 1988, four players were sacked after writing an open letter of protest against their manager. Diego took no blame for the team's sudden decline. This was his best season on the field – as he scored fifteen goals and linked up superbly with Careca. In 1989, Maradona refused to return for the new season, claiming that the Napoli president had promised him a transfer to Marseille. After a long war of words, Diego came back after four games had already been played and led Napoli to a second championship.

Meanwhile, Maradona became a hate figure across Italy. In 1989 the rivalry with Inter had been violent and the 1989 and 1990 championships saw a bitter struggle with Milan. All this should be put in the context of the re-awakening of north–south tensions, provoked in part by a new and highly successful political movement in the north – the *Leagues* – whose propaganda drew upon anti-southern prejudice. As sport historians Papa and Panico put it, matches with northern teams 'took on all the significance of a cultural and ethnic challenge'.[17] All this was exacerbated by events during the 1990 World Cup where Naples, the south, Maradona and Argentina were all grouped together by Italy's fans, especially those in the north. Hatred of Diego reached a peak after his key role in the explosion of Italy's dreams in the tournament. The booing of the Argentinian national anthem before the final in Rome was the most public display of this antipathy. Enzo Bearzot, Italy's manager in 1982, later wrote that he was ashamed of the whole affair.

Maradona's time in Naples was coloured by controversy from the very beginning, and the tale of the various scandals with which he was linked in that period is expertly told by Jimmy Burns in his *Hand of God*.[18] Diego fell in with some unsavoury characters during his time in Naples. He was photographed in a jacuzzi with members of the Giuliano family, at that time 'Kings of Forcella', a run-down, central neighbourhood controlled by the Neapolitan version of the mafia, the *Camorra*. Maradona's coke habit flourished here, in the spruced-up fortresses of local bosses, during the frequent parties he attended.

On 17 March 1991, in his first season after knocking Italy out of the World Cup, Maradona's long decline was confirmed. He was found positive for cocaine after a match with Bari and given a massive fifteen-month ban. The Argentinian fled home with various judges hard on his heels. Many commentators, as well as Diego himself, have constructed elaborate conspiracy theories around this whole affair. It certainly was strange that Maradona was only found positive after the World Cup, as he had been taking cocaine on a regular basis for years. After the draconian ban, Maradona defended himself with wild talk of plots. It was all part of a complicated vendetta against him for daring to knock out Italy in 1990. Certainly, the god-like immunity that Diego had benefited from in the city was on the wane, but the breaking of the spell had begun well before the World Cup. In 1989, the old but damaging photos showing Maradona partying with *Camorra* bosses in the jacuzzi had been published in a city newspaper. Maradona also argued, this time with more justification, that cocaine was not exactly a performance-enhancing drug. The report of his contribution to the incriminating game wrote that he had 'turned up only to sunbathe'.

Drugs had been a part of Diego's life since his time at Barcelona, and remained so throughout his time at Napoli. Later, club president Ferlaino said that everyone knew about Diego's 'problem', but that he was adept enough to stay clean in the days before matches. Otherwise, Ferlaino admitted, the urine samples would be switched so as to fake any tests that were carried out. In any case, he was not the player he had been. All of his six goals that season came from the penalty spot.

Much later, Maradona was forced to contribute to the upkeep of a child he had fathered (in 1986) after DNA tests were carried out. The boy was named Diego Armando. This scandal dragged on during Maradona's time in Naples. Maradona did not meet the boy until May 2003, on a golf course. Little Diego has now become a minor star in his own right, turning up on a popular reality TV show to play for a media-created team called Cervia.

Later, Diego Senior was sent to trial (in his absence) and charged with drug dealing and pimping. He did a deal with the judges, who gave him a conditional sentence of eighteen months. The tax authorities also investigated his private affairs. Many of these accusations were the work of one man, Diego's ex-driver, Pietro Pugliese, who had turned state's evidence. According to Pugliese, Maradona had slept with 8,000 women during his time in Naples, many of whom were 'found' through his driver. Pugliese also dragged up the old story of the 'throwing' of the 1988 championship after pressure from the *Camorra*, which ran the illegal betting rings in the city. Maradona never played for Napoli again. At club level, his career was more or less over, at the age of 30, and his international career ended in ignominy with another positive drugs test in 1994.

## After Maradona. The long decline of Napoli

In 1990–91, with Maradona frequently injured, late and overweight, the team slumped to eighth. In 1991–2, with Maradona gone for good, Zola began to blossom, scoring twelve times as Napoli finished fourth under Claudio Ranieri, who was, however, sacked after just nine games of the following season. The team then oscillated between mid-table and relegation until the disastrous 1997–8 season, when they finished last. Although they were promoted in 2000, they were soon relegated again, and only just avoided the shame of Serie C in 2002–2003, before bankruptcy led to demotion in 2004.

Napoli's fans remain amongst the most obsessive (and numerous) in Italy, but their team has gone into financial and on-the-pitch free-fall since the late 1990s. Still, for key matches, the stadium is often a sell-out and local TV stations devote hours and hours of coverage to their local team. The city can still rally around when times are hard. In 2003 some 70,000 turned out for a Serie B relegation battle and the same number attended a Serie C playoff in 2005. Nonetheless, frustration with the side's recent poor showing has often descended into violence. Players have been physically attacked or threatened on numerous occasions in recent times, most seriously when Napoli defender Francesco Baldini was beaten with iron bars after being followed home by masked fans on motorbikes in November 2002. In February 2004 midfielder Renato Olive was surrounded by five young men who threatened him with a knife and told him that 'If you don't win against Messina, we'll come and look for you again'. After serious flooding damaged the crumbling and dangerous San Paolo in September 2001, opening up huge holes in the concrete, Napoli were forced to play their home games in smaller stadiums all over the south.

Diego, meanwhile, often appears on Italian TV these days, where he is something of a figure of fun: fat, tattooed, a friend of Fidel Castro. A TV comic does quite a good impression of him, but the real thing is much more tragic. Napoli fans always ask him when he is coming back, but only a madman, and Maradona is not mad, would take on Napoli in its present crisis.

## Disintegration

'Inside every fat man, they say, there is a thin man trying to get out. In the case of Maradona, it seems, there is an even fatter man trying to get in'                    MARTIN AMIS[19]

The early part of the twenty-first century saw Maradona's fortunes take another dip. Separated from his wife, he roamed around the world, staying for a time in Cuba, where he tried to break his drugs habit once again. His fortune, it appeared, was all gone. Maradona blamed his ex-agent, Guillermo Coppola. Others claimed that *all* of his entourage had wanted a piece of him. Grotesquely fat, he went along with a series of humiliating requests in Argentina, such as the opening of supermarkets. He took up a regular spot on the popular if squalid Italian TV football-argument show, *Monday's Trial*, and had an enormous likeness of Che Guevara tattooed on his upper arm. From Cuba, he attacked George Bush and the 'war on terrorism'. The 'Cuban Cure', however, did not seem to have done the trick.

In April 2004 Maradona was taken to hospital in Argentina with serious heart failure. He had played golf at night and then fallen asleep, and vomit had ended up in his lungs. Traces of cocaine – enough 'to kill a man' – were found in his blood. His heart, the doctors said, was only half-working. Diego was put on a respirator. The Italian press drew comparisons with the sad demise of 34-year-old cyclist Marco Pantani, who had been found dead in a Rimini hotel room only weeks earlier. Pantani was also a cocaine addict and, in the end, the drug had killed him. At the age of 43, Maradona was fighting for his life. Fans and well-wishers gathered outside the hospital whilst Argentinian TV showed his goals again and again. Diego was described as 'a little less than a god'. In Naples, shopkeepers set up message boards with photos of Diego; fans left notes stuck on the wall: 'we will never forget you'; 'Diego forever'; 'come back and help us dream'. A makeshift altar was assembled, with a *scudetto* sign, kitsch fake pillars, Napoli colours and a photo of a young, thinner Maradona. Fans touched the picture, crossed themselves, and prayed. Italian journalists wrote that it was 'a miracle' that Maradona was still alive and that he had 'the heart of an eighty-year-old'. Maradona survived, but only just, and the headlong drive towards self-destruction of this footballing genius, the King of Naples, continued apace, watched over by a voracious media machine. Just when he seemed to be finished, however, Maradona recovered, for the umpteenth time. He had an operation to lose weight, visited Napoli for an emotional testimonial match for his friend Ciro Ferrara, and even returned to the world of football, taking over as vice-president of Boca Juniors in 2005. The media would have to wait for the next twist in the Maradona saga.

## CHAPTER 5

# At the Back. Defenders and Defensive Football in Italy

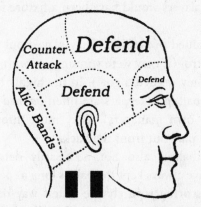

The Italian defensive mentality (spoof drawing, 2004).

## The Defensive Mentality

My sports teacher at school was called Mr Campbell. He was a good teacher, enthusiastic and tireless (although I shall never forgive him for putting me in goal at the age of nine), but he was hardly at the cutting-edge of modern football tactics. The first thing he told us in training was that we should remember this phrase: 'If in doubt, kick it out'. That was the motto our defence was to live by. Get rid of the ball. Kick it as high and far away from your goal as you can, and quickly. If it goes out, it doesn't matter – all the better. Now when Italian teams have been accused, ever since the 1950s, of being defensive, this accusation has usually been a false one. Italian teams have not been defensive. They have, quite simply, *been much better at defending* than other European teams. Italian defenders can all trap the ball, dribble and pass. They anticipate where the ball is going to go and they look up before deciding where to put it. If they are in doubt, they do not 'kick it out'. Kicking it out is their last option, not their first. Bad clearances are usually whistled by Italian crowds, as are skied passes – known as bell towers, or *campanili*. Italian defenders are also, usually, faster and more tactically aware than defenders in other countries. Most central defenders in the Italian lower divisions would not be out of place in Premiership teams. Added to these qualities has been the extremely high technical proficiency of Italian goalkeepers. In the 1990s Italian football produced a number of world-class keepers.[1] Any one of these players would have been a fixture for England in the same period.

Italian teams valued possession. They played out of defence, either with care and control (if they were winning) or with devastating speed and accuracy (if they needed a goal). In the highly technical world of Italian youth football, goalkeepers are often *banned* from kicking the ball out (by their own managers). They must throw or pass it to a nearby player and play out from the back.

Possession football is also not necessarily defensive. The great Brazilian teams have always kept the ball as long as possible. The fastest way towards goalscoring is rarely the fastest way of moving the ball towards the opposite goal – the long ball. Italian teams used the long ball – but usually with accurate passes out to the wings, and rarely through punts down the centre of the pitch. The flick-on was not seen as a key offensive weapon in Italy. Italians attacked less, but they attacked far more effectively – and in greater numbers. There is nothing more beautiful in football than a swift, clinical counter-attack. Arsene Wenger's Arsenal teams of the 1990s – widely praised for their attacking style – were counter-attackers who revelled in any space given to them by the opposition.

Defensive football is not just about technical ability or tactics, or even attitude to the game; it is also about the way football is understood. Ever since football began, followers of the game have sorted themselves into those who are interested in good play, and those who want to win at all costs. Journalist Gianni Brera often argued that the perfect football game would end 0–0. This way of reading the game was light years away from many of his colleagues, and anathema to those who watched or played in the English league. Nobody has ever argued in England that the perfect game would end 0–0. It is perhaps not surprising, therefore, that one of the key defensive tactics introduced in world football first took root in Italy in the 1940s and was later given an Italian name.

## *Catenaccio.* Football, Italian style

'*Catenaccio* was not invented by Gianni Brera. If it was part of the Italian character, as is probable, it could not be invented. In the same way as the slums around Rome were not invented by those who put them in neo-realist films. They were already there'                                        PIER PAOLO PASOLINI

*Catenaccio!* Even today the very word strikes fear into the hearts of football fans all over the world. This Italian word – it is generally thought to mean 'padlock'[2] – has come to symbolize all that is bad about football; defensive play, aggressive fouling, cynicism. Nobody knows for sure when the Italian word was used for the first time as a footballing term, but by the 1950s, it was commonplace. Internationally, Italian football first became stigmatized in this way in the 1960s, when Italian clubs had huge success in Europe. This is also a word whose meaning has changed over time – from the description of a tactical system to the simple labels of boring and defensive.

The history of *catenaccio* can be divided into three distinct parts. First, there is *catenaccio* as a *specific tactical system*, whose history can be traced from Switzerland in the 1930s through to Salerno in the south of Italy in the 1940s and on to Trieste and Padua (in the north) in the same decade before moving to Milan and the two Milanese teams in the 1960s and to Turin and Juventus in the 1970s. Using this interpretation, we can talk about formations, actual players and team-sheets. We might call this *real catenaccio* (as in 'real socialism') or *primitive catenaccio*.

A second way of thinking about *catenaccio*, however, sees it above all as a *state of mind*, a way-of-being on and off the football field, quite apart from the actual set-up of any one team. The idea that the priority was not to give away goals, and then try and score, is still widespread in the Italian league, especially away from home and in the lower divisions. This mentality can be summed up very simply by this phrase: *prima non prenderle*: 'our first priority is a clean sheet'. Very few teams actually play, nowadays, with an out-and-out sweeper or mark man-to-man. So *catenaccio*-type football is also a way of playing quite separate from 1950s-style tactics in the rigid sense of the word. This much looser definition of what *catenaccio* is applies to the way most smaller teams play in the Italian championship. They defend in depth, break up the play, and try to score on the break. If all goes well, the game ends 0–0. If all goes incredibly well, they win, scoring early and then using the space that opens up.

Not all minor teams approach games in this way, and in recent years some have even tried attacking from the start. In the lower divisions, however, *nearly all* teams play like this all the time, away from home. Just a glance at the goals scored and the number of draws in Serie B tells its own story, despite three points for a win. When American journalist Joe McGinniss followed lowly southern team Castel di Sangro for a season in Serie B, he found that, away from home, they invariably played with just one man up front. Sometimes, they sneaked a win, on other occasions they ground out a 0–0. Most of the time, they lost, and these tactics did not change over the whole season.[3] We might call this kind of football 'defensivist', the word that Brera preferred to *catenaccio*. Brera's defensivism was supported by strange evolutionary theories. The journalist was adamant that Italians were *physically* inferior to people from other countries, and therefore couldn't play an all-out aggressive game.

Finally, *catenaccio* is also applied to other aspects of the game – to a kind of cynicism which is often seen as particularly Italian: psychological tussles amongst coaches, fouling, play-acting, complaining to the referee, gamesmanship of all kinds, systematic 'tactical' fouling. These 'tactics' are not part of the official canon, but are nonetheless a crucial part of winning the battle on the pitch, and have come to be seen as part of a *catenaccio*-type way of playing the game. Italians have a word for everything that surrounds the game off the pitch, before matches begin. They call these aspects of a game 'pre-tactics' – team selection, false injuries, rumours about formations. In Italian football, much of the battle is won off the pitch.

## Real *catenaccio*. From Switzerland to Italy

Real *catenaccio* began in Switzerland, in the 1930s, with a coach called Karl Rappan. The original idea was a simple one: add a defender and take away an attacker. His system became known as *verrou* – padlock – which in Italian became *catenaccio*. Since most teams played with three centre-forwards at that time, and used man-to-man marking, once a striker had beaten the defence, he was usually clean through on goal. Rappan decided to try to put a stop to this. He removed a forward, and added a defender, who played behind the existing backs and did not have someone specific to mark. This was revolutionary. For the first time, a defender was asked to mark space, and not a particular player. This defender would 'sweep up' behind the others – hence the name given to this defender, sweeper or, in Italian, *libero* (the free one).

*Catenaccio* 'overturned the traditional dualism between the marker and the marked, and gave teams a strong defensive pattern'.[4] If someone beat the centre-backs, they had the sweeper to deal with, who would often simply clear the ball. Sweepers had to be strong but clean in the tackle (as they were often in the area, a foul would mean a penalty), intelligent (they had to predict what would happen next) and, although this was not essential, be good long passers of the ball. Rappan's new model brought immediate success, especially at the 1938 World Cup where Switzerland beat both Germany and Austria.

## Real *catenaccio* in Italy. Gipo Viani and beyond

In Italy the first sweeper was crafted by Gipo Viani, one of the game's great characters. Viani tried his hand at everything football had to offer: he was a player, trainer, manager and administrator at a number of clubs. After World War Two he took charge of Salernitana. A small club, Salernitana could not compete with the Juventuses and Milans of this world. Thus, they decided to defend a bit more. Like Rappan, Viani asked one of his attackers to track back in defence, marking the opposition's number nine.[5] This freed up one of his central defenders to act as sweeper. That was it. Put so simply, this doesn't appear to be a revolution, but it was. The extra man in defence seemed to make a difference, frustrating the opposition and bringing them further forward, and freeing space for rapid counter-attacking on the break.

It was typical of Viani that he should invent a poetic story to explain the genesis of *catenaccio*. Sitting on the dock of the bay in Salerno, after yet another sleepless night worrying about Salernitana's failures on the pitch, Viani allegedly observed the fishing fleet at work. He noticed that a reserve net was used as a back-up for the main series of nets. This, he later claimed, gave him the idea for the sweeper. It is a nice story, but almost certainly untrue.

Salernitana's tactical innovation provoked much comment. Viani was so personally identified with the new system that it was given his name – *Vianema*. Salernitana, however, were much less successful than the teams associated with the other great proponent of *catenaccio*, Nereo Rocco. In their only season in Serie A (1947–8) playing with *Vianema*, Salernitana's away record was appalling: they failed to win a single game. *Vianema* was *catenaccio* without counter-attacks, the worst kind of defensive football and, in its early form, it didn't really work. Viani also claimed that he personally passed on the system to Rocco in 1961. Rocco applied *catenaccio* with some success as manager of Trieste in 1947–50 and then at Padova, whom he took to an unprecedented third place in 1957–8.

Suddenly, sweepers and *catenaccio* were all the rage, even at big clubs, but this did not mean that they were popular. Big clubs were supposed to score freely and destroy the opposition, even in Italy. The first big club to play with a sweeper was Inter in the first half of the 1950s.[6] Alfredo Foni, manager of Inter, chose Ivano Blason as the club's *libero*. Blason was a slow and clumsy full-back, but he developed into an excellent sweeper with the ability to zip long passes forward. His main duty, however, was to block any player who threatened to move past him. Legend has it that Blason would scratch out a line on the pitch before kick-off, and then inform the opposition strikers that under no circumstances would they be allowed past that mark. Up front, Inter had speedy and skilful forwards and the ability to break that was a key component of successful *catenaccio*. Statistics from the 1951–2 season tell something of the story of *catenaccio* in action. Inter scored nearly 30 fewer goals than second-placed Juventus, but they conceded less than a goal a game. Their defence had won them the championship. Nobody could unlock the Inter padlock.

Foni's tactics caused something of a scandal, despite the *scudetto*. Torino, after all, had scored 125 goals in winning the 1947–8 championship, using an attacking system without a sweeper.[7] Inter were killing the game, it was argued, and driving away spectators. Foni's system was also a mentality, a way of understanding the game. Backed by Brera, Foni was condemned by many other journalists. Brera left us with this account of the way Foni's Inter played. After defending for long periods of the game, 'suddenly, Blason fired off a mortar shot: seventy metres away there were not many players around and a lot of empty space which Inter's individual players could exploit'.

## Sweepers Old and New. The Great Inter and beyond

When football histories are written, one team is closely associated with the successful application of *catenaccio*: Helenio Herrera's all conquering Great Inter side of the 1960s. Herrera, characteristically, claimed to have devised *catenaccio*, calling it 'a tactical system which I invented', but he also tried unsuccessfully to change its name, calling his method 'the cement'. Herrera's version of events – like that of Viani – should be treated with caution. It is often said that it was club president Angelo Moratti who convinced Herrera to adopt more defensive tactics, and Brera argues that Herrera was 'converted' to *catenaccio* in desperation after a poor start by Inter in the early 1960s.[8] There is no doubt that the exuberant Argentinian manager introduced important modifications to the simple 'extra defender' system, adapting *catenaccio* to the players he brought into the team.

The Inter defender who revolutionized football was a statuesque, blond 'giant' called Giacinto Facchetti. After coming through Inter's youth team, Facchetti played one of his first games for Inter in extraordinary circumstances. In protest against a league decision Herrera sent out a team of youngsters to play the mighty Juventus.[9] They lost

9–1 (a record) with Omar Sivori scoring six (another record). Facchetti became an Inter regular in 1962 and was a fixture in the team for eighteen years, as well as playing 94 times for Italy. Herrera moved Facchetti from centre-back to left-back, and gave him a licence to attack, thirty years before the advent of overlapping full-backs in the 1990s. Facchetti's gallops down the wing turned defence into attack and his physique and technical ability made him perfectly suited to his new role of a 'fluid' full-back. He soon became one of the first 'total footballers' – able to defend, stride forward and score goals. Facchetti was good enough up front to score ten times in a Serie A season, a better haul than most forwards. Born in the local Lombard town of Treviglio, Facchetti was idolized by Gianni Brera amongst others, being compared to a mythical god. Inter through-and-through, Facchetti remained within the club after retirement, becoming club president in 2004.

Were Inter a defensive side? The bare figures of Herrera's Inter teams tell something of the story. Herrera's more attacking teams failed to win the *scudetto* in his first two seasons in charge. In his third season – 1962–3 – the defence was watertight, and Inter took the championship in a low-scoring season. Inter soon developed into a team with a superb back five, an excellent goalkeeper and an attack that veered from the good to the prolific. Herrera's defensive reputation is not proven, and he almost always selected a team (usually against his will) which contained at least one player – Mario Corso – who spent much of the game strolling around, when he was not actually motionless. The worldwide unpopularity of Inter's 'style' of football had its roots in their long and successful European campaigns. Inter's will to win and cynical tactics created the legend of Herrera as the king of *catenaccio*, a legend Herrera was happy to play up to. Of course, tactics in themselves are neutral. Herrera's teams could be boring, but they were often spectacular, and, above all, they were winners.

Within the Great Inter's impregnable defensive system, the sweeper was all-important. By the 1960s, the role of the *libero* had changed. Early sweepers would invariably boot the ball as far away as possible, into space for attackers to run onto. Soon the sweeper became a player who could construct play, passing the ball out to the wings or straight to the 'director' in midfield. This role for Inter was filled, until 1967, by Armando Picchi, a Livornese-born, bony-faced defender who had previously been a right-back.[10] The last of the great defensive sweepers – he scored just one goal in Serie A for Inter, in 1960 – Picchi was the linchpin of Herrera's defence. Nothing got past him, and he was able to set up attacks. Brera called him a 'defensive director . . . his passes were never random, his vision was superb'.[11]

Captain Picchi was also one of the first on-the-field managers, able to adapt the team's tactics without reference to the bench. On one occasion, manager Helenio Herrera was trying desperately to get some instructions through to his team. In the end, he called over another player and told him to pass on the information to Picchi. After a while, the player came back over to the bench. 'What did he say?' asked Herrera. 'Up yours and up yours to Herrera as well,' came the reply as Inter went on to win the game. Picchi's nickname was 'White Feather' – because of his streak of grey hair, but also as a tribute to his elegance.[12] He only played twelve times for Italy, farcically being left out of the 1966 World Cup team after a debate over 'defensive' tactics.

As one of the few players to openly challenge the dictatorial authority of Herrera, Picchi was forced out in 1967, and consigned to a minor club – Varese. After a successful period there, Picchi became one of the youngest and most innovative managers in Italy, taking over Juventus at the age of only 35. Tragedy struck soon afterwards in 1971, when he was diagnosed with back cancer.[13] He died within months. Later, Livorno's stadium – his home town – was named after him. Picchi's career had effectively ended after a terrible injury whilst playing for Italy in 1968 (he broke his pubic bone), after which he bravely played on. The rest of the impregnable Inter defence was made up by 'The Rock', Tarciso Burgnich, an indomitable man-marker who rarely left space to an attacker, and Aristide Guarnieri, who began as right-back but then moved across into central defence.

The use of the word *libero* – the 'free one' – in Italy refers to the fact that he was 'free' of marking responsibilities. However, the sweeper, for many years, was the least 'free' of all the players on the pitch. Old-style *liberi* were not, despite their name, 'free' to move away from their area, and many rarely crossed the halfway line. Modern sweepers have specialized in coming forward, unexpectedly, causing panic in opposing defences. Franco Baresi did this occasionally for Milan, whose fans identified his thrilling runs forward with an American term taken from basketball: *coast-to-coast*. Baresi was one of the last breed of classic *liberi*, able to re-adapt his game as his role disappeared in the 1990s.

When I first saw Milan play in 1989, Baresi would build up play from *behind* his defence. By the early 1990s his team had adopted a flat back four, and Baresi had become a 'normal' centre-half. There was nothing normal about Franco Baresi, however. A quiet man, with rock-like features, Baresi was an outstanding captain for both Milan and Italy who won eighteen trophies with Milan in twenty years with the club. On the pitch, he ran with great grace, his shirt flapping outside his shorts, and would often dribble out of defence and move swiftly into attack. His tireless performance in the 1994 World Cup final, just weeks after a knee operation at the age of 34, was over-shadowed by his penalty miss in the shoot-out, and the tears that followed. It was his last act for the national team. Milan withdrew his number six shirt when he retired.

In the modern game, the sweeper rarely sits right behind the defence and goalkeepers play far further up the field, where *liberi* used to be. Yet, there *are* sweepers today. The brief fashion for three centre-backs allowed for one central defender to play slightly behind the others – Tony Adams at Arsenal in the 1980s and 1990s, Laurent Blanc for France – and when there are only two centre-backs, one tends to play more of a 'sweeping' role – Alessandro Nesta as opposed to Paolo Maldini with today's Milan, for example. The best teams still rely on classy defenders who can play the ball, and not just clear it. They are no longer known as *liberi*, but they are still essential to any good side.

## Stoppers. Man-Marking

Man-markers in the defensive systems of the post-war period were often known by another, more straightforward name – *stopper*. That was what they were there to do – stop their opponents getting the ball, or, failing that, stop them going anywhere with it. Italian defenders have always tried to anticipate forwards, unlike English-style defenders, and stay on their feet, not dive in. If the anticipation went wrong, then a well-placed and well-timed foul was always a key part of the stopper's armoury. In Italy this became known as the 'tactical foul' in the 1990s, and was taught to defenders as part of the game. They all knew when to foul and when not to, and how to foul without picking up a booking. Often, Italian football commentators will praise a defender for a foul, sometimes adding that 'maybe it isn't fair play, but . . .' Allied to this concept of the useful or tactical foul is the idea of the *useless* foul. Hence the parallel notion that being sent off for a useless offence is stupid, and unprofessional, whilst being called up for a *useful*, tactical foul is not only good practice, but deserving of praise as it represents – if the player has been booked or sent off – an individual sacrifice for the greater good of the whole team.

If Inter's defence dominated much of the 1960s, there were also great defenders elsewhere – Cesare Maldini, Paolo's father, at Milan, was another ex-right-back who moved into the centre. Maldini senior was so assured in his technical ability and skill on the ball that he would some-times make hideous errors, born of over-confidence. These (rare) mis-takes became known as *maldinate*. Maldini's pin-up son Paolo began playing for Milan in the 1985–6 season, after an entire childhood spent watching his father play and train. Paolo grew up with the Milan team. Tall, elegant and very good-looking, he made the left-back position his own in the very next season, and throughout the next three decades, both for Milan and for Italy. Thanks to his clean-living lifestyle (he refused to play the debauchery game, unlike many other Italian stars in Milan in the 1980s and 1990s) Maldini junior prolonged his career and played over 100 times for Italy. He also kept his boyish good looks and fitness. Rather than the dance floor, Maldini preferred to spin records, sometimes taking over as DJ in the absurdly glamorous and expensive Milanese night-club which he part-owned – Hollywood.

Maldini junior's success on the field was immense: more than twenty seasons, four European Cups, seven championships. He had the unique honour of lifting the Champions League trophy as captain in 2003, in England, just as his father had done at Wembley, forty years earlier. Maldini remained the idol of San Siro, so good on the ball that he would occasionally solicit a standing ovation from his adoring fans after a pass, a saving tackle or a dash down the wing. By moving into the centre of defence he was able to extend his career still further, at a time when most players of his age had long since retired. There were only occasional lapses in Maldini's impeccable record – a few sendings-off, some important mistakes, complete identification with the powerful and sometimes murky world of Silvio Berlusconi PLC.

In the 1970s, another defence was built which was to rival the power and fame of that of Herrera's Inter. This time, it was Juventus that constructed a back four which was amongst the greatest of all time. The sweeper in that side was Gaetano Scirea, the most elegant defender of the 1970s and 1980s. Scirea was neither physically strong nor particularly quick, yet his ability to read the game and anticipate play enabled him to move out of defence with the ball, or simply to shepherd forwards into the wrong positions. Scirea's technical ability and balance allowed him to win the ball cleanly, and he rarely committed fouls. He was the opposite of the stereotypical, brutal, physical Italian defender. Journalist and Juventus fan Darwin Pastorin called him a 'gentleman sweeper' and wrote that he played with 'the sound of silence'. Devoted to Juventus, Scirea joined the club as a scout on retirement in the 1980s. He died in a horrific car crash on a scouting mission in rural Poland in 1989 at the age of 35.[14]

The other key components of the Juventus defence were Antonio Cabrini, Sergio Brio, Claudio Gentile and Antonello Cuccureddu, a fine right-back from Sardinia. Gentile was born in Libya, thereby earning his implausible nickname 'Gaddafi', a label he played up to with his bushy haircut and alarming moustache. An uncompromising man-marker, he became the symbol of violent Italian defending in the 1980s, especially after marking Maradona out of a game during the 1982 World Cup. Gianni Brera wrote that Gentile wound up Maradona by rubbing his genitals against the Argentinian in the first half.

In reality, Gentile was rarely sent off, and was never dismissed in 71 games for Italy. Even Maradona later acknowledged the correctness of his play in that particular game. An old-fashioned defender, his job was to stop goals being scored, not score them. He hit the net just once for Italy and a mere nine times in eleven seasons with Juventus, where he won six championships. Later, he confirmed the thoughtful side of his game by becoming an excellent manager of the under-21 side, whom he took to Italy's first Olympic football medal in 68 years in Athens in 2004.

Sergio Brio was born in Lecce in the deep south of Italy. Extremely tall (his mother had taken him to the doctor when he was young to try and restrict his growth), Brio was not known for his ball-playing ability. Like Gentile and Inter's Burgnich, he used his physique to intimidate, hold back and, quite simply, stop opposing forwards. Faithful to Juventus, he never got a call-up for Italy, and on retiring from the Turin club in 1990 he went on to a minor management career in Italy and Belgium. Unlike Gentile, he sometimes scored (24 goals in eleven years; but only sixteen in Serie A). The great Juve defence of the 1970s and 1980s was built on a perfect combination of pure uncompromising defenders and more 'fluid' players. The most fluid of all was one of only two northerners to appear in that unit, Antonio Cabrini from Cremona.

Cabrini – *il bello*; the good-looking one (or *Italy's boy-friend*) – provided numerous, swinging crosses for various Juventus forwards over the years. It was his perfect cross that gave Paolo Rossi a simple chance and paved the way for the 1982 World Cup defeat of Brazil. All Rossi had to do was nod his head, and the ball was in the net. From 1976 to 1989, Cabrini – like his defensive partners – won everything that could be won – including the 1982 World Cup, despite missing a penalty in the final. In a way that was similar to Facchetti's style, he often scored – hitting the net 30 times in nearly 300 games for Juventus. In the 1990s, an equally good-looking attacking left-back seemed to provide an heir to Cabrini – at last – Gianluca Zambrotta.

In the 1990s, Italy once again produced more great defenders to rival those of the past. The national team was lucky to be able to rely on a rock-hard central defensive pairing throughout that decade, and Italy's near-triumph in the 2000 European Championships was almost entirely down to a defence which was difficult, if not impossible, to breach. Alessandro Nesta first hit the headlines as a promising youth player for Lazio in the mid-1990s. It was his tackle that broke Paul Gascoigne's leg in training, leaving both players in tears. Despite the fact that everyone, including Gazza, blamed the Englishman for what happened, Nesta was booed by his own fans for weeks afterwards. Soon, however, the statuesque Nesta developed into an outstanding centre-back. Strong, quick and assured on the ball, he was seen by some as a kind of modern sweeper, able to marshal the whole defence. With Lazio, he won a championship and much else besides, and his highly expensive and controversial move to Milan in 2002 led to more triumphs. Nesta's centre-back partner for Italy was heart-throb Fabio Cannavaro, who had been born in Naples in 1973, where he played for his local club before moving to Parma, where he struck up an excellent alliance with French World Cup winner Lilian Thuram. Nesta and Cannavaro were magnificent in Italy's march towards the 2000 European Championships final, where they held out for over 90 minutes before France equalized with a lucky Sylvain Wiltord goal, and went on to win in extra-time. Cannavaro's brief decline during his time with Inter was the latest in a long line of cases of 'the Inter disease', and he immediately returned to form with Juventus in 2004. Nobody filled this role in the 1980s and 1990s with as much dignity and professionalism as Ciro Ferrara, the most durable of all centre-backs. In a twenty-year career Ferrara won a record eight championships with Napoli and Juventus whilst playing in over 500 games.

## The Defender who Survived. Sauro Tomà

Sauro Tomà was born in Rebocco outside La Spezia in 1925, near to the beautiful Cinque Terre region in Liguria in northern Italy. As a young man he worked in the naval shipyards in La Spezia, one of the Allies' key bombing targets in World War Two. After playing for his local side at right-back and sweeper Tomà was transferred to Torino in July 1947. A great friend of Torino captain Valentino Mazzola, Tomà fitted well into the Torino system – attending training sessions by tram. Yet after an impressive first year, when Tomà played 24 games in yet another championship-winning season, he was seriously injured on the first day of the 1948–9 season after a clash with his keeper Bacigalupo. Keeping his knee injury hidden, Tomà played on for another week. Then it became so swollen that he collapsed and was taken to hospital. He was never to play with the *Grande Torino* squad again.

Tomà only began training again in Spring 1949, just before Superga. He was not fit enough to travel to Lisbon with the squad. On his way home on 4 May he noticed a small crowd outside his door. As he moved closer, he saw that many of the people there, including his wife, were crying. One of his friends blurted out the terrible news – 'they are all dead'. Immediately, Tomà rushed up to Superga, where he wandered around in shock.

At Superga, he was spotted by the crowd walking near to the plane just after the crash. Quickly, a rumour began to spread – *Tomà is alive! Tomà has been saved!* Another Superga myth was born – that of the *miracolati*, the saved – including Tomà, the president Novo (who was ill) and the celebrated radio journalist Niccolò Carosio, who didn't travel to Lisbon as he had to attend his son's confirmation. Tomà is remembered today as the 'only player to survive' from the *Grande Torino* team.[15] He later said that 'my youth remained amongst the ruins of that aeroplane . . . everything finished with Superga'. Another injury, and Tomà's career fizzled out in loan spells with Brescia, Carrara and then Bari. In his beautiful book *Me Grand Turin* he writes: 'My life has been dedicated to running after Torino, to that legend. I now live a few metres from the Filadelfia stadium, the field that is no more. I can just see the ruins. Every so often I meet some old fans, and we talk about the *Grande Torino* . . . to tell and remember, and tell again – this is the destiny of those who survived.'[16]

## The own-goal specialist. Comunardo Niccolai

Cagliari central defender Comunardo Niccolai became celebrated for his ability to score bizarre own goals in the 1960s, so much so that self-inflicted problems in general are often referred to as 'Niccolai-like'. Niccolai didn't score more own goals than anyone else, nor were they particularly important ones, but they were spectacular and surreal. He beat his own keepers with long shots, diving headers and even once on purpose after he had misheard a whistle. Maybe these goals were a sign of some odd illness – a kind of footballing 'Tourette's syndrome' – or a secret desire to make history. Niccolai's fame in this area remains intact, obscuring the fact that he was a fine player, good enough to win a championship with Cagliari and to play for Italy (briefly) in the 1970 World Cup finals. His name was also memorable, a sign that his parents were on the left of the political spectrum; *Comunardo* being a invocation of the Paris Commune of 1871. Cagliari's eccentric goalkeeper Ricky Albertosi became terrified of Niccolai on the pitch, unable to predict where the next potential own goal was to come from. Despite this, Albertosi and Niccolai were great friends, and were often to be found playing poker and drinking whisky together. Niccolai is still held

in great affection by many Cagliari fans, unlike a series of defenders
whose errors have cost their teams games, finals or even championships, and who have been demonized down the years. Most recently,
Inter's Vratislav Gresko took up this mantle. On the final day of the
2002 season, his terrible mistake cost his team a vital goal, and probably
the *scudetto* itself. That was his last game for the club.

This journey amongst some of the best, the worst, and the most
important home-grown players who have graced Italian football will
continue to move through the positions adopted by players on the
pitch. We are now amongst the battlers and ball-winners in the centre
of the park.

## Water carriers and 'destroyers of the play'

*Una vita da mediano/nato senzi i piedi buoni* – 'The life of a
*mediano*/born without skill', Luciano Ligabue, rock singer

Romeo Benetti played for Milan, Juventus and many other clubs in the
1970s. His appearance alone was terrifying. A huge muscle-built man,
with a big face, he sported a large red moustache. Rarely did he come
away from a challenge without the ball. His job in every team he played
for was a simple one – win tackles, and then give the ball to the
appropriate playmaker. Benetti was the epitome of the *mediano* –
defensive midfield ball-winners who were – and are – a key component
of every successful football team. Sometimes, Benetti would be given
the task of man-marking the opposing team's playmaker. On those
occasions, he would follow his victim around like an aggressive shadow.
Nobody enjoyed being marked by Benetti. You never had a moment's
peace, or a yard of space, and you came off the field feeling as if you
had been at war, not in a football match. Players like Benetti were the
water carriers or, to use one of my favourite Italian football phrases,
*distruggitori di gioco* – destroyers of play. Over the years, Italian football
made *destruction of play* into an art form.

In order for the skilful players to have the space with which to work,
somebody had to get the ball, and give it to them. The playmakers
couldn't be expected to do the running that was needed, the dirty

work, the pressing. Every team had at least two players of this type, if not three. Italian managers were occasionally tempted to fill their midfield with *mediani*, dispensing altogether with the ephemeral skill of playmakers and wingers. Milan playmaker Gianni Rivera was accompanied by a whole series of *mediani* – most faithfully by Giovanni Lodetti, who was known as his 'third lung'. For Lodetti 'it was worth doing the running' for a player like Rivera. Political writer and commentator Edmondo Berselli wrote this about Lodetti and Mario Corso's *mediano* for Inter, Gianfranco Bedin: 'Lodetti would ... run until he dropped ... and if he won the ball, he would pass it immediately to Rivera, the man with the extra touch, who would invent something ... Bedin was supposed merely to give the ball to Corso in the middle of the field and *que sera sera*.'[17]

Romeo Benetti playing for Juventus in 1976.

Giovanni Trapattoni was one of the greatest *mediani* of all, and a powerful series of myths and stories have emerged concerning his ability to *stop* other players from getting the ball. The most enduring Trapattoni myth concerns the greatest player of all time – Pelé. It is often said that Trapattoni 'did not let Pelé near the ball' when they played against each other in May 1963, and that he 'cancelled out' Pelé from the game.[18] The truth is rather different. In the friendly match in question, Pelé was injured, and only played the first 26 minutes. Pelé scored twice the next time the players came up against each other. Nonetheless, the fact that a player was feted for his negative-defensive abilities is indicative of the worth placed on this kind of activity in the world of Italian football. The Trapattoni type of player was also known as a *francobollatore* – someone who stuck as close *as a postage stamp* to their opponent. Players like Trapattoni rarely worried about such luxuries as a through pass or goalscoring. Trap scored just three goals in 274 games for Milan in the 1960s and 1970s.

Juventus specialized in *mediani*, and the greatest of all was Beppe Furino in the 1970s and 1980s. Little Furino, from Palermo in Sicily, ran himself into the ground in order to get the ball to a succession of playmakers such as Franco Causio, Liam Brady and Michel Platini. Yet Furino was not a one-dimensional player. Team-mate Marco Tardelli called him 'the most tactically intelligent player I have ever seen. He was always close to the ball.' For the Inter of the 1980s, and Italy, Gabriele Oriali did the same job. Inter fan Luciano Ligabue's hit song *Una vita da mediano* was dedicated to his hero Oriali. In the modern game, Milan's Rino 'Ringhio' Gattuso fills this role. Gattuso went to Rangers to learn his trade as an eighteen-year-old, and was full of praise for the fair play of the British game.

The life of a *mediano* was thus a melancholic one. They were always destined to be the supporting act, straight men, water carriers. They could never be stars and would remain forever in the shadow of their more skilful colleagues. Furino won a record eight titles with Juventus in the 1970s and 1980s, but is rarely mentioned in accounts of those years. Bit-part midfielders like Chicco Evani do not spring to mind when the Milan teams of the 1980s and 1990s are evoked. Nonetheless, *without* these players, no team could compete in any game.

# CHAPTER 6

# Players. Directors and *Fantasisti*

## Midfield Directors

Let us now move into the very centre of the park, where the 'director' – the *regista* – once reigned supreme.[1]

For a long period after the war, all teams played with a central 'director', a skilful playmaker who would distribute passes to the wings and to the forwards, but was not expected to do much running or tackling back. By the 1980s, this position was beginning to disappear – at least in its purest form. *All* players had to press and tackle back, and the 'fixed director' became a rarity. Teams still put skilful players in midfield, but their position was more fluid and one player could no longer be the centre of each move. The increased speed of the modern game also gave potential directors far less space in which to move. The golden age of the director was the 1950s and 1960s, but great directors still enriched the game after that, most notably the Brazilian Roberto Falção with Roma in the early 1980s.

The greatest director of all was Gianni Rivera, who graced Serie A over 21 seasons, the last twenty for Milan. Rivera was the epitome of the number ten – the centre of all play, the fulcrum of any side. In 1998, Rivera was voted the best Italian footballer of the twentieth century by an international panel.

## Gianni Rivera. Golden Boy, *Abatino*, Genius? (1943–)

*Career:* Serie A: Alessandria; 1959–1960 – 26 games, six goals;
AC Milan; 1960–1979 – 501 games, 123 goals. *Italy:* 1962–1974
– 60 games, fourteen goals. *Honours:* three championships, four
Italian Cups, two European Cups, one Intercontinental Cup, two
Cup-Winners Cups, one European Championship.

'My negative hero'                            GIANNI BRERA

'Rivera, Rivera, Rivera, Rivera'
                            ALF RAMSEY when asked to name the
                            four strongest Italian players in 1970

The European Cup final: 28 May 1969. Milan were playing the soon-to-
be-great Ajax team of Cruyff and Neeskens – at the Bernabeu in
Madrid. With fifteen minutes to go, and Milan already 3–1 up, Gianni
Rivera played a one-two on the halfway line and broke clear towards
the Ajax goal. He pushed the ball past the onrushing goalkeeper but
out wide to the by-line. Then, in the black and white film, the game
appeared to stop. Rivera, like all great players – Maradona, Platini,
Zidane – seemed to be playing in a kind of time capsule. He looked
up, waited, changed his mind, moved the ball to his right foot and
floated it across to the far post where, seconds earlier, there was just
space. Out of nowhere, an attacker rushed forward to meet the ball
perfectly with his head. Pierino Prati, the Milan number nine, had
begun his run seconds earlier, from 40 yards out. It is difficult to define
genius, but Rivera's pass – and his ability to wait – came close. It was
a pass to compare with Pelé's to Carlos Alberto in the 1970 World Cup
final.

Born to an unprivileged family during World War Two, Rivera's first
games were in the courtyards and streets of the small Piedmontese
town of Alessandria, and then in the playground of his neighbourhood
church. His father, a railway mechanic, organized a trial for the local
team when he was thirteen. At the trial, Rivera began to trap and pass
the ball, and a small crowd gathered to watch. Three days later a letter
arrived: *Mr Gianni Rivera is accepted as a young player with our club.*

Rivera's fame spread quickly. It is said that even the great Silvio Piola came to Alessandria to watch him play. Rivera's exceptional career began with a Serie A game for Alessandria at the age of fifteen – the second-youngest debut ever in the top division. In 1959 he was spotted by Milan's manager/director Gipo Viani, who recommended that AC sign him at all costs. They paid 90 million lire for the young star. The young Rivera was thin, almost skeletal, with a characteristic shock of hair. He was always a player of great grace, and early film shows him scoring goals with a delicate touch – lifting the ball over defenders and lobbing goalkeepers with precision.

At the age of seventeen, he was already a star with Milan, at first on the right wing, and then in the centre, behind the forwards. For almost every other Milan player the rule was simple – pass to Rivera, give *him* the ball. That year, Milan finished second. The following season, they won the championship – with Rivera providing the passes for José Altafini, Jimmy Greaves and Paolo Barison up front. By that time, the Milan manager was Nereo Rocco, with whom Rivera had a long and fruitful alliance. Over the next twenty years he was to play over 500 games for the *rossoneri*, scoring more than a hundred goals. We have no record of his assists, but Rivera's speciality was the final ball, the most difficult and delicate art in football. Over the years, successive generations of Milan (and Italian) forwards feasted on Rivera's vision.

Yet Rivera was also one of the most controversial players to have ever pulled on a football shirt. He was never universally loved, and was the object of one of the most sustained critical journalistic campaigns in sporting history. The journalist involved was the most powerful, controversial and brilliant football writer of his generation – Gianni Brera. He invented a term for Rivera (as with so many other players) that was to dog the player for his whole career – *abatino*. Literally, this word signifies 'young priest'. In Brera's strange linguistic world, the word took on a new meaning. Rivera was weak, he didn't fight, he wouldn't tackle. Players *like* Rivera – the *abatini* – were a luxury that teams simply could not afford. *Abatini* were half-men, people who didn't really count, losers, luxuries. The occasional moment of skill or genius could not justify the hole in midfield left by the *abatini*, with their aversion to physical effort. It was true that Rivera did little

Gianni Rivera playing for Milan.

running or tackling. A whole series of players were employed just to do his 'water-carrying'. As Brera wrote, 'If you have Rivera, you have to build the team around him.' The journalist declared that he had been subjected to years of insults from fans and colleagues for his stance on Rivera. The player claimed that he didn't read Brera's numerous articles, but the argument must have hit home. It was impossible to ignore Brera. His campaign began in the mid-1960s and reached a peak during the 1970 World Cup, when Italy split into pro- and anti-Riveraians.

In 1963, Milan won the European Cup at Wembley. Both assists – both for Altafini – in the 2–1 win were from Rivera. At that point, however, Milan's cycle of victories slowed down. Nereo Rocco left to manage Torino and Brera began to write about *abatini*. After Milan threw away the championship in 1964–5 (to Inter) Rivera was dubbed a loser. Rocco returned in 1967, with a different team. A new squad was built around the 'Golden Boy', which was one of Rivera's many nicknames and was used by Italians in English. That season saw another championship for Milan, with eleven goals for Rivera, along with the Cup-Winners Cup. A new cycle had begun, crowned by the European Cup in 1969 and the Intercontinental Cup the following year. The 'loser' label was dropped. Rivera was now an international star, being awarded the European Footballer of the Year award – the first home-grown Italian to win the *pallone d'oro* after the Italo-Argentinian Omar Sivori in 1969.

If Rivera's status with Milan was assured, everything was far more complicated with the national team. Rivera first played for Italy in 1962, at the age of eighteen. In that year's World Cup in Chile, he only took part in Italy's first match, a dull 0–0 draw with Germany. In 1966, things went from bad to worse, despite a manager who had made him the centre of his team. Rivera played well but Italy suffered a shock defeat against North Korea. For Rivera that game set Italian football back 'ten years'.

Rivera believed in a different kind of football, criticizing the *catenaccio* system which dominated the Italian game in the 1960s. For many journalists, this translated itself into a debate on the role of the defence, which Rivera argued should be more mobile. The use of a sweeper led to one man less in the midfield. Many interpreted Rivera's polemic as criticism of Inter – masters of the *catenaccio* system. Manager Edmondo Fabbri left out Inter's great sweeper – Armando Picchi – for the 1966 World Cup. Again, this was interpreted as going along with Rivera's ideas. Many thus attributed the Korea disaster to Rivera. Needless to say, Brera was a huge admirer of Picchi and lost no opportunity to underline the folly of the tactics in 1966, blaming Rivera in essence for Italy's exit, not for his play, but for his influence on the *way* Italy played.

Rivera and Brera had a love–hate relationship. They needed each other. Their fame was in part thanks to the arguments they provoked, but Rivera was sometimes vicious in his attacks on Brera, accusing him openly of being a drunk in his book *One more touch* (1966).[2] However, in the same book Rivera denied that Brera was his 'personal enemy . . .' He was more like 'his personal critic'.[3] Strangely, Rivera's greatest man-ager, Nereo Rocco, was one of the pioneers of *catenaccio*, whilst Rivera was painted as the arch-enemy of that system.

The 1970 World Cup was Rivera's triumph, and his nemesis. First, the Golden Boy argued with the national squad's managerial team and made his opinions public at a press conference. He threatened to go home and was only dissuaded by Rocco, who was flown to Mexico to calm the waters. For a time, it even seemed as if Rivera would be dispatched back to Italy. Then, Giovanni Lodetti, a midfielder who was known as Rivera's 'third lung' at Milan – *was* sent home from the squad as surplus to requirements. For the European Footballer of the Year, all this was humiliating. Yet, the squad (and especially Gigi Riva) always played better with Rivera on the pitch. The hyper-famous semi-final touched on all the elements of the *abatino* debate. Rivera's inability to clear the ball off the line for the Germans' third goal was the epitome of *abatinismo*, his side-footed winning goal a perfect combination of timing, intelligence and elegance.

Rivera's greatest footballing rivalry was with Sandro Mazzola, the equally gifted Inter midfielder who was also one of Brera's *abatini*. Rivera was captain of Milan, Mazzola often captain of Inter. But it was with the national team that the Rivera–Mazzola dualism most enthused public debate, particularly with manager Ferruccio Valcareggi's invention of the 'relay' – one half for each player – in the 1970 World Cup. By using the relay, Valcareggi was, without admitting it, adhering to Brera's *abatino* theory. Neither Mazzola nor Rivera, he believed, could play 90 minutes in the Mexico heat. Neither could be left out completely. So it was to be one half each. Two *abatini* were only as good as one 'normal' player.

This compromise worked well until the final, when Valcareggi broke his own rules, giving Rivera a token six minutes (and leaving Mazzola on) with Italy already 3–1 down. Yet, that humiliation pitted, in the minds of many Italian fans, Rivera against the rest of the squad, and against the managerial team. Hence the hostile reception in Rome for a team which had reached the final, with banners which read *Viva Rivera*. Rivera's own comment was typically caustic – 'maybe the manager didn't realize that there were only six minutes left'. Valcareggi dismissed the choice as a 'technical' one. The great Italian football journalist and historian Antonio Ghirelli called the six minutes 'in bad taste'.[4] In the end, Rivera played 60 times for Italy, scoring fourteen goals, and, apart from 1970, his World Cup record (he played in four tournaments) was modest. In 1974, once again, Rivera was left out of the key game – against Poland – which saw the *azzurri* knocked out. His difficult relationship with the national team management is revealed by the number of times he was made captain – on just four occasions in twelve years.

After the dramatic events in Mexico, Milan seemed a refuge for Rivera, but the final results just wouldn't come. For three years running, Milan finished second. Rocco left again and Rivera began a long-running feud with domestic referees, who were accused of being 'psychologically' in favour of Inter and Juventus. In 1975, the managerial team at Milan tried unsuccessfully to push Rivera out. Finally, in 1978–1979, Milan won their tenth championship, which earned them a gold star on their shirts. It was Rivera's last season in the game.[5]

Rivera's hair was also a symbol of his style – and when he adopted a parting there were weeks of debate in the press. In early photos it is always immaculate, but long for the early 1960s. Good-looking, intelligent and rich, Rivera was a constant presence in the gossip magazines that were and are so popular in Italy. He cultivated an almost English style. On the cover of a popular interview-book written with journalist Oreste del Buono in the 1960s he was depicted wearing a bowler hat. In the 1970s the Golden Boy was involved in a sex scandal that set tongues wagging across the country. After an affair with a young actress, she fell pregnant. Rivera left her, and her career suffered. Brera wrote caustically that 'he had many women who were not greatly loved and a daughter who is dear to him (she lives with her mother in San Remo)'.

With his playing career at an end, most pundits assumed Rivera would go into football management. He became part of the Milan machine, but this was a bad time for the *rossoneri* and Rivera was unable to prevent the financial and betting scandals of the late 1970s, which sent Milan twice into Serie B. Inter fans exulted – their proud slogan 'we've never been in B' was a slap in the face to their rivals. When millionaire and media magnate Silvio Berlusconi bought the club in 1986, the contrasts between the two men soon became insurmountable. Rivera was forced out, one of the few leading football figures to stand up to the future prime minister. Berlusconi even tried to write Rivera out of Milan's history, ordering supporters' clubs not to use his name. Rivera was no longer issued with free tickets to games.

His next port of call was politics. He was a moderate Catholic and stood for the Christian Democrats and then the centre-left Popular Party in various elections after 1987. As senator, he was appointed as an under-secretary in the Defence Ministry in 1996, but was defeated in the 2001 elections. By all accounts he had been an excellent minister. Nowadays, his name often pops up when calls come to 'clean up' football and he has been mentioned as a possible future Mayor of Milan. His sixtieth birthday in 2003 led to blanket coverage in the press, testimony to his lasting fame and still-boyish good looks.

## Tragedy of a Director. Agostino Di Bartolomei (1955–1994)

On 30 May 1994, a thirty-nine-year-old ex-footballer walked barefoot out onto the balcony of his villa in the south of Italy. It was 10.50 a.m. He then shot himself once in the heart with a .38 Smith & Wesson pistol which he had just cleaned. His stepson heard the shot and tried the kiss of life but his efforts were in vain.

Ten years earlier Agostino Di Bartolomei was captain of a Roma team which had just won its first championship in more than 40 years, and only the second in its history. The following year, Roma reached the European Cup final, in Rome, against Liverpool. After a 1–1 draw, Liverpool won on penalties. The date of that game was significant: 30 May 1984.

Nobody could understand why Di Bartolomei had decided to do what he did, least of all his wife and relatives. Some recent financial deals had gone wrong, but this did not seem enough to justify suicide. Then they found a note (torn into 32 pieces) in his pocket, and everything became much clearer. In seventeen lines, Di Bartolomei tried to explain his decision. He had been refused a loan, money was tight, and he made some bad investments. 'I can't see any way out', he concluded. It became clear that Agostino had not found space in the 'world of football', despite constant attempts to do so. He had opened a football school, but was having problems finding the financial backing to keep the project going. Some accused Roma of abandoning Di Bartolomei. Many ex-friends and players turned up at the funeral, including most of the 1980s Roma team. The fans also remembered 'Ago', as he was known, unveiling a banner which read: 'No words . . . only a place in the bottom of our hearts: Goodbye Ago'.

Di Bartolomei was one of the most elegant 'directors' of the 1980s. Tall and skilful, he also possessed a strong shot. Throughout his career, he was tormented by the criticism that he was 'too slow' (something which has stuck to almost all directors). He had been born and brought up in one of the poor peripheral zones of the capital city – still known as *borgate* in the 1950s – areas immortalized in the novels and films of Pier Paolo Pasolini.[6] Rome had seen vast migration throughout the twentieth century and public housing had not been able to keep up with demand. Many poor Romans and immigrants ended up in flimsy self-built housing without real roads or public services, where work was scarce. These slums were only really eliminated with the mass construction of ugly public and private homes in the 1970s and 1980s.

At fourteen Di Bartolomei was signed by Roma. He made his debut in 1973 after winning the youth championship with Roma and became first-choice the following season. In 1974 he suffered a serious knee injury so painful it kept him awake for eight nights. A year later, he was loaned out to Vicenza to 'build up his bones' in Serie B. Bruno Conti, another future Roma star, was dispatched to Genoa for the same reason. Slowly, Roma built a winning team – and Conti and Di Bartolomei returned. In 1979 a new president arrived; Dino Viola, an engineer from the small town of Aulla on the Tuscan/Ligurian border. With the Brazilian Falção in the midfield, and Di Bartolomei in front of the defence, this was a team with two outstanding 'directors'. Roma began to win, at last. Agostino was made captain and when he argued with referees, he always did so in an educated manner, with his hands behind his back. The fans – with whom he had a difficult relationship for years – began to sing his name: 'Ooooh, Agostino . . . Ago, Ago, Ago, Agostino *gol*!'

In 1982, Swedish manager Nils Liedholm moved Agostino back to protect the defence, despite his goalscoring prowess. From that position, Di Bartolomei hit long, precise passes to the wings for Conti or onto the head of striker Roberto Pruzzo. Liedholm said of him that 'he never moved on the pitch without a reason. His passes were long, and perfect. He always ran with great elegance, with his head up.'

Agostino played a key role in the memorable championship win, making 28 appearances and scoring seven goals. A huge party followed, lasting for days. The European Cup final defeat on penalties was one of Di Bartolomei's last games for Roma, who shouldn't have been in the final at all after Dino Viola had tried to bribe the referee in the semi-final against Dundee United. The attempted corruption was only unearthed well after the final had been played.[7]

After fifteen years with Roma, the arrival of Sven Goran Eriksson signalled the departure of Agostino. He moved on to Milan, who were in a re-building phase, where he played with Ray Wilkins and Mark Hateley. It was a bitter transfer, and Agostino gave a number of interviews in which he made his position clear: 'Why am I leaving? I don't know.' He had played 308 games for Rome, scoring 66 goals and captaining the team 146 times. Strangely, he was never called up for the national team. When Roma played Milan in Rome in 1985 the game ended in a fight, and Roma forward Ciccio Graziani struck Di Bartolomei. Bruno Conti said afterwards that 'it is not true that I am his friend . . . in Milan he still plays as he did for us . . . he never comes off the field in a sweat'. Later, this argument was patched up, at least between Conti and Agostino. The rumours of another dispute – over penalties – with Falção the night of the Liverpool game have always been strong. Di Bartolomei took, and scored, Roma's first penalty. Many urban myths relate that Falção refused to take a spot kick.

When Arrigo Sacchi arrived in Milan in 1987, Di Bartolomei moved on again. His career fizzled out with a series of provincial clubs, and he finally retired in 1990. Roma offered him nothing, and his business plans stuttered. The date he chose to take his life could not have been a coincidence. He could have been the player – the captain – who had lifted the European Cup, in his own city, if things had gone differently. Perhaps he simply couldn't deal with life off the pitch, forgotten by his former clubs. Football certainly played a part in Ago's tragic suicide. In 1984, he had said that the final was 'the game of his life'.

## Attacking midfielders. The Mazzola dynasty

## Valentino Mazzola (1919–1949)

*Career:* Serie A: Venezia and Torino; 1940–1949 – 231 games, 109 goals. *Italy:* 1942–1949 – twelve games, four goals. *Honours:* five Italian championships, two Italian Cups.

'Captain Valentino . . . inspired, eccentric, spoilt, talkative, surly'
                                                    NINO NUTRIZIA

Valentino Mazzola is often referred to as the greatest Italian player of all time, despite his relatively poor record with the national team. After growing up in a run-down neighbourhood in the small riverside town of Cassano d'Adda in Lombardy, Mazzola moved to Milan in the 1930s. In Italy's industrial capital he found work in the huge Alfa-Romeo factory on the edge of the city. It was in the Alfa team that Mazzola first played proper football, before being spotted by Venezia in 1939. There, Mazzola teamed up with Ezio Loik, who would play with him in Turin and die with him at Superga. Venezia won the Italian Cup and finished third in the league with Mazzola in the team. In 1942, in the middle of the war, Torino's president Ferruccio Novo paid 1.2 million lire for Mazzola and a legend was born. In five seasons with Torino Mazzola was to win five championships and score 102 goals.

Valentino was an attacking midfielder, not a pure centre-forward, with prodigious ability in the air and a strong shot. He scored an astonishing 29 goals from that position in 1946–7, eight more than the next-placed player, within Torino's attacking 'method' formation. In that season, Mazzola played in every game. Valentino's power with Torino was also as a captain. 'Captain Valentino' was the leader of the *Grande Torino* side, always pulling them through in their (rare) moments of difficulty. Others looked to him for inspiration. When he rolled his sleeves up, it was a sign for the whole team to attack. His whole life – including the way he played – is swathed in myth.

As one of the first modern football stars, Mazzola knew his own worth. He frequently asked for more money, refusing to play on certain occasions until it was forthcoming. President Novo, not surprisingly,

Valentino Mazzola in action for Italy against Hungary, 11 May 1947.

would not let him go. Mazzola argued with managers and fellow players, as well as with the national coach. He was one of the first players – after Meazza and Piola – to attract advertising and even sponsored a football – the *Mazzola*. Of all the iconic figures of the 1940s, Valentino Mazzola's blond curly hair, strong-running, muscular upper body and his smile symbolized the rebirth of Italy after the horrors and privations of the war.

The Mazzola football dynasty did not end with Valentino. Both Valentino's sons played professional football, and one – Sandro – went on to be as good a player as his father.

## Little Sandro. Sandro Mazzola (1942–)

*Career:* Serie A: Inter; 1961–1977 – 418 games, 116 goals. *Italy:* 1963–1974 – 70 games, 22 goals. *Honours:* four champion-ships, two European Cups, two Intercontinental Cups, one European Championship.

After his father's death, Sandro (who was six in May 1949) went back to live with his mother and brother in their home-town. Life at Cassano

Ferruccio Mazzola (on the left) and Sandro Mazzola with a photo
of their father.

was hard and Sandro's mother Emilia was forced to go back to work
as a teacher. The family's lives were hounded by gossip and groundless
jealousies, made worse by the suffocating atmosphere of 1950s Italy,
where divorce was illegal. Everyone knew that Mazzola had abandoned
Emilia for a younger woman, and that there had been a series of
complicated custody trials which dragged on even after Valentino's
death.[8] Sandro Mazzola's childhood was also dogged by the innumerable events held to commemorate Superga. He remembers being the
centre of attention at early anniversaries – and is in the middle of the
photos of the commemorations – where everybody referred to him as
'poor little Sandro'. At some point, when he could make his own
mind up, Sandro decided to stop going to these commemorations. But
everyone then wondered why, and began to ask questions. For the
twenty-fifth anniversary of the disaster, Mazzola wrote a short piece
for *La Stampa* explaining his absence: 'it is very difficult for me to
talk about my father, because I hardly knew him . . . I don't like
commemorations . . . I prefer to suffer alone'.

Sandro Mazzola was a gifted and natural sportsman – even as a boy
– and was particularly good at basketball. However, thanks to the

generosity of a prominent Inter player (Benito Lorenzi) who had been friendly with his father, Sandro and his brother Ferruccio were given football trials by Inter. Both were good enough to be taken on. Sandro made his Inter debut in the infamous 1–9 defeat at the hands of Juventus in 1961, when Herrera sent out his youth team in protest against a league ruling. Mazzola scored Inter's only goal, a penalty, which he coolly slotted into the top corner.

Sandro was fast, tricky and sharp in front of goal. Much debate centred on his best position on the field – centre-forward, central midfield, on the wing? – but Herrera understood him better than anyone else, and pushed him up front. Many of his goals were from close range, or after tricky dribbles. From that position, Mazzola won everything there was to win with Inter, scoring two goals in the 1964 European Cup final – the first from the outside of the area, the second with the outside of his boot after a mazy run – against Real Madrid. Some of his goals have become the stuff of legend – a derby strike after just thirteen seconds in 1962, and another amazing goal after juggling the ball seven times on the edge of the box.

Modest and loyal to Inter, Mazzola never reached the star status of Rivera or Riva, and a dislike for the high life kept him out of the gossip magazines. He wrote two excellent autobiographies and took part in the formation of the first players' association – with Rivera and others – in 1968. His career after retiring as a player was more chequered, especially within the management team at Inter, where the fans blamed him for some of the failures of the 1980s and 1990s. He now appears most often as a football pundit, writing for the local press and turning up on any number of Milanese local TV stations. Ferruccio, Sandro's brother, was much less gifted. He played only once for Inter (in two separate spells with the club) and spent the best part of his career at Lazio in the late 1960s, before playing for Fiorentina and Lazio.[9]

As Sandro began to make his name as a player – despite those who claimed that he was only being given a chance because of his surname[10] – he was never able to rebuild his relationship with Torino. On his first return to the city as a player nobody came to greet him from within the club. When Italy played in Turin in June 1966 Sandro was booed by the crowd and substituted with the local favourite, Gigi Meroni, who then scored. As Sandro became a great and successful player, none of these wounds were healed. At the fiftieth anniversary of Superga in 1999, the Mazzola family was, once again, absent.

The reconciliation appeared to be complete when Mazzola was employed by Torino as their sporting director in 2000. However, disastrous results on the field led to his sacking soon afterwards, and local journalists were not easy on him. It says something about the paranoia of Torino fans that some saw the appointment of former Torino heroes – or those with links to Torino's history, such as Mazzola – as a Machiavellian move aimed at deflecting criticism from shortcomings on and off the pitch and keeping the nostalgic hard-core of fans happy.

## Dribbling, skill, vision. The *Fantasisti*

Directors and attacking midfielders were complemented, at least until the 1980s, by tricky wingers or skilful midfielders, who could unlock defences with their dribbling or passing. These players were known as *fantasisti* – those with fantasy or imagination on the pitch.[11]

## The one-legged player. Mario Corso (1941–)

*Career:* Serie A: Inter; 1958–1973 – 414 games, 75 goals; Genoa; 1973–1975 – 23 games, three goals. *Italy:* 23 games, four goals. *Honours:* Four championships, two European Cups, two Intercontinental Cups.

Mario Corso, another key member of the *Grande Inter* team, was known as 'God's left foot'.[12] Whole books have been written about that foot, including one of the most fascinating studies of the relationship between football and the Italians, *Il più mancino dei tiri* (The leftest of all shots) by Edmondo Berselli.[13] Small, with a shock of black hair and, in the 1970s, enormous side-burns, Mario Corso did not look like much of an athlete. Lazy and often unfocused, with 'little desire to run' (Brera), Corso would drift for whole games, not touching the ball for long periods. Some claimed that this tendency was particularly marked when it was raining. Another urban myth is that he would always stand in the shady part of the pitch. It was said that he could 'hide himself in the grass' (Alberto Crespi). Then Corso would do something completely out of the ordinary – a long pass, a chipped shot, a free-kick, a dribble – which would often decide a game – all with that divine left foot.

Brera called his right foot 'a crutch'; others said that he only used it 'to get on the tram'. Corso's 'falling leaves' free-kicks were celebrated. They seemed to float over the wall and then dropped softly into the net, deceiving countless goalkeepers. A famous photo captured one of his free-kicks on its way in, against Liverpool in the 1964–65 European Cup. Goalkeeper Tommy Lawrence is watching the ball, transfixed. 'If Corso was on form, we always won,' said team-mate Carlo Tagnin.

Herrera 'detested him' (Brera) and would always try and sell him at the end of each season, but president Moratti would not oblige. No national team manager really understood how to use Corso, and he never made a World Cup squad. In May 1962, after a brilliant chipped goal for Italy at San Siro, he let himself go with an 'umbrella gesture' towards the stands.[14]

Corso was either terrible or brilliant, never average. He *looked* slow, but he wasn't. The journalist and cultural commentator Edmondo Berselli has argued that Corso was the last player from 'another epoch'. When Corso played 'football was still more or less a democratic endeavour, at which more or less all human beings could take part. Ability was still more important than athleticism. As long as they could play football, even dwarves, hunchbacks and fatties could make the first team.' When Corso had the ball 'the stadium went quiet'. Very few players in the history of football have had this ability, and the speed of today's game had made players like Corso an extravagance.

## Football's James Dean. Gigi Meroni (1943–1967)

*Career:* Serie A: Genoa; 1962–64 – 42 games, 7 goals; Torino; 1964–1967 – 103 games, 22 goals. *Italy:* 1966 – six games, two goals. *Honours:* one Italian Cup.

'More than anything else I love my freedom . . . painting is my real work'                                           GIGI MERONI

'Who was Meroni?'                 newspaper headline, October 1967

Gigi Meroni was born in sleepy, conventional Como, on the banks of the lake with the same name, in 1943 (the same year as Gianni Rivera, and a year before Gigi Riva). His early football was played in a tiny local courtyard (just 60 square metres) where he first learnt to chip and dribble the ball. Gigi's father died in 1945 and his mother was left to bring up three children on her own. Meroni was thin, fast but not particularly tall, with bandy legs. He soon burst into the local Como team and in 1962 was transferred to Genoa, a once-great club in long-term decline.

The way he played was anarchic, and poetic. He scored beautiful, impossible goals and his spindly legs drove defenders to distraction. At Genoa Meroni soon became the idol of the fans, with his stylish dribbling, non-stop running and occasional brilliant goals. He was also involved in an embarrassing doping case in 1963, after failing to attend a drugs test following the last game of the season. He claimed he had 'forgotten' to go to the hotel to take the test. The three players who *were* tested were found to have taken amphetamines. Meroni received a five-game ban at the start of the following season.

Transferred to Torino in 1964, Meroni came to a team emerging slowly from years of under-achievement to challenge for the title. The ghost of Superga was finally being laid to rest. Torino's manager was the arch-disciplinarian, Nereo Rocco. Meroni usually played on the right wing but was also able to drift inside and his dribbling and speed often took him into the penalty area. His play was not all style and no substance. His celebrated chipped goal at San Siro in March 1967 helped defeat an Inter team that had not lost at home for more than three years. His graceful running earned him the name of the 'purple butterfly', and his socks were always down around his ankles. Although he took terrible punishment from opposing defenders, he always got up and carried on. His idol was the equally anarchic Juventus forward Omar Sivori, and another one of Meroni's nicknames was 'the Italian Sivori'.

Meroni annoyed a lot of people – particularly in the conservative atmosphere which still prevailed in the Italy of the 1960s, a country on the edge of an extraordinary cultural and social revolution which would transform a generation of young people. One obvious sign of Meroni's rebellion was his hair – long (but not by today's standards) and often accompanied by a beard – a 'revolutionary symbol' in the age of Fidel Castro and Che Guevara. Meroni's hair became a national obsession. In 1963, after being selected for the Italian B team, the manager, Edmondo Fabbri, asked him to cut it. Meroni obliged, but the incident annoyed him. The next time Fabbri asked him – this time on the eve of a World Cup qualifying match in Poland in 1965 – Meroni refused, and justified his decision in a press conference: 'I hope I might play well even with long hair'. After the 1966 World Cup, the right-wing press adopted Meroni as the scapegoat for the disaster, despite the fact that he played in just one game. *Il Tempo* called Meroni a 'squalid personality' and wrote that 'the blue shirt [of the national team] had been devalued' by his selection.

Meroni's hair led to some of his many nicknames – gypsy, Calimero (a sort of small bird popular in Italian TV advertising at the time[15]), tramp, hidalgo. Opposing fans would shout at Meroni to cut his hair, and the length of his fringe fixated the sporting press. But it was not just the hair. Meroni dressed bizarrely – outlandishly even – and drove flashy cars. On trips with the national team he would get off the plane with his big dark glasses down on his nose, strange hats and loud suits. In Turin he began to design his own clothes, which became more and more over the top.

And as if this was not enough, there was Meroni's 'immoral' private life. Whilst playing for Genoa in 1962, Gigi had met a beautiful blonde woman in a bar near the port. The eighteen-year-old Polish-Italian – Cristiana Uderstadt – was a stallholder at the Milan funfair. Their relationship lasted until Meroni's death in 1967, despite Cristiana's decision to marry an assistant director after appearing in a brief scene of a Vittorio De Sica short in 1962.[16] Meroni even went along to the marriage in Rome. For some, he was hoping to stop the ceremony altogether, for others, just hoping she would say no. She didn't; but the marriage lasted only a few weeks, and the couple were soon back together. Meroni tried to hide Cristiana's identity at first – presenting her as 'his sister' to manager Rocco to avoid trouble.

Italian football in the 1960s was still dominated by iron discipline. Players were very much seen as the property of their clubs. Even the best-known stars were expected to lead lifestyles similar to monks, forced to eat controlled diets and with their private affairs spied upon.

A dapper Gigi Meroni with characteristic dark glasses in his sports car.

Before games, or after heavy defeats, players would be forced to go *in ritiro* – in retreat. This meant that the whole team would go to a hotel, or the training camp, for days. Here they would not be allowed to go out unsupervised, or see their wives or girlfriends. The system of *ritiri* was one reason why so few English players were able to hack it in Italy – being used to the much freer atmosphere of the English club system. Meroni hated the *ritiri*, and invented a number of excuses to allow him to see Cristiana (especially when she was in Milan in the mid-1960s).

Meroni was also a kind of situationist, organizing 'happenings' which shocked Italy, and especially the conservatism of his home-town, Como. One stunt has become legendary (and is often transferred to Turin in the re-telling). After a number of critical articles had appeared in the local Como press, Meroni decided to give people something else to talk about. With his friend Poletti, Meroni drew up in the town's main square in his smart Aprilia car. He had a chicken with him, on a lead. Meroni and Poletti walked around the square a few times with the chicken before going to the lakeside where Meroni tried, unsuccessfully, to dress the animal in a bathing costume.

*     *     *

In the summer of 1967 Juventus made a big bid for Meroni (750 million lire), which Pianelli, Torino president, accepted. Once this news broke in the city, the Torino fans took to the streets. There were demonstrations outside the Agnelli mansion and Pianelli's house. The fury was such that the transfer was withdrawn. Some fans even claim that FIAT would have gone on strike – many workers being Torino fans – if Meroni had gone. Torino began the next season with Meroni in his familiar position on the wing, socks rolled down, flying past defenders.

In October 1967, Meroni and his Torino colleague and friend Fabrizio Poletti were out on the town, celebrating a 4–2 home win over Sampdoria in the fourth game of the season. The two young men were in the centre of the city, looking for their girlfriends. It was around 9 p.m. Meroni had left the keys to his new flat, in Corso Re Umberto, 53, with his partner, Cristiana. He tried to call, but failed to find her. After parking their car, the two players decided to cross the road, and wait in the Bar Zambon on the other side of the wide Corso. Meroni was in a good mood – his girlfriend had just heard that her marriage had been annulled. *They* could now get married.

Ignoring the zebra crossing and traffic lights, Meroni and Poletti reached the centre of the wide boulevard, where two lanes took traffic in both directions. Suddenly, Meroni stepped back to avoid a fast car from the right. He did so just as another vehicle – a 124 FIAT Coupé – travelling the other way, was overtaking at some speed. The car braked, but could not stop in time. Poletti was hit and slightly injured, but Meroni was struck on the left leg. Poletti said that 'When I looked up Gigi was gone'. He was thrown into the air and across to the other side of the road, where an onrushing Aprilia hit him full on as he lay on the ground, dragging him along the asphalt for over 50 metres. The 124 came to a halt on the tram lines, further up the road.

The driver of the first car was Attilio Romero, nineteen, student and fanatical Torino fan (where he had a season ticket) and son of an important doctor. He had just passed his driving test. His favourite player? Gigi Meroni. Romero had a poster of Meroni in his room alongside a huge Torino flag. Some stories even claim that he had a small picture of his idol in the car itself. There is no doubt that he had been at the game earlier that day. Romero went along to the police station in the evening, and was released later that night. His address was (and still is) thirteen numbers down from Meroni's: Corso Re Umberto, 66. Romero even wore his hair like Meroni, and had once – some claim – been mistaken for the player by a group of Juventus fans who had taunted him with the classic anti-Meroni chant 'go and get your hair cut'.

The police interrogated both drivers soon afterwards. However, the fact that the two footballers had decided to cross the road well away from the zebra crossing, in the dark, led to the case being closed. Controversy continued over the details of the accident. Romero claimed that Meroni had stepped back from the centre of the road just as he was passing. Poletti denied that the 'step back' had ever taken place. Neither car was travelling particularly fast.

After Meroni was hit, another driver – Giuseppe Messina – took the two men to a nearby hospital as the ambulance failed to arrive in time, but there was little the doctors could do. Poletti was only slightly injured. One doctor claimed that 'Gigi will never play again, but he might survive', but all efforts proved useless. Meroni died at 10.40 p.m. from a collapsed chest. Both his legs and his pelvis were broken, as well as his cranium. He was 24 years old. A crowd gathered outside the hospital. Later, a newspaper wrote that 'all Turin cried'. Brera, no fan of maverick players like Meroni, wrote that Gigi had been a symbol of 'freedom in a country of conformists'. Some prisoners got together in Turin's Le Nuove prison to send a wreath.

Meroni's funeral (which was attended by 20,000 people, and is often compared to that for Superga) was celebrated by 'Torino's priest', Don Francesco Ferraudo, who told the crowd that Gigi 'was not just body, muscles, nerves . . . but also genius, kindness, courage, understanding, generosity'. In an interview in Nando Dalla Chiesa's beautiful book about Meroni the priest recalled how much criticism he had received for that funeral, in church, for a 'public sinner'. *La Stampa* and other publications even called for the priest to be disciplined by the religious authorities. Moralist letters flooded into the paper.

*       *       *

The events on the Sunday after Meroni's death are well known, and have become part of football legend. It was the Turin derby, and the Torino players were still in shock. A small plane dropped some flowers on the pitch before the game, and they were placed on the right wing where Meroni used to play. The match itself was just as dramatic, and for a long time the crowd stood in silence. Nestor Combin, a strong and skilful Argentinian forward, was a close friend of Meroni's, and had been suffering from a fever in the days before the match. After

The photo of Gigi Meroni near the spot where he died,
Torino, Corso Re Umberto, 2003.

just three minutes Combin scored with a stunning free-kick. He ran to the Torino fans in the *Curva Maratona*, who sang 'Gigi, Gigi'. Combin added a second four minutes later, with a shot from even further out, and completed his hat trick fifteen minutes into the second half. To conclude the victory, the player wearing Meroni's number seven shirt scored in the second half. At 4–0, the game remains Torino's biggest ever derby victory. Meroni had played in seven derbies without ever finishing on the winning side. Flowers were sent to the ground by Attilio Romero. Two weeks later – although this run was not to last –

Torino went top of Serie A for the first time since Superga. It was to take them nearly ten years to win the championship.

Meroni's death also set an important legal precedent. After Superga, the club had sued the airline for the costs borne by them for the loss of players who were assets as well as people. In the 1950s, after a long legal battle, this claim was rejected by the Italian courts. However, after the Meroni tragedy, Torino tried again, and this time their insurance claim was successful, with a final judgement in 1971. This decision marked an important shift in the understanding of the law and responsibilities towards victims and their former employees.

As with all Torino stories, there was to be a final, weird, twist to this tale. In 2000 Torino appointed a new president. He was a life-long Torino fan and had worked as a spokesman for FIAT. His name? Attilio Romero. The same Attilio 'Tilli' Romero who had run over his idol – Gigi Meroni – in 1967. The club was now run by a man who had killed one of its most famous players, albeit by accident. This bizarre fact did not pass without comment. Some fans, unhappy at the performance of the team, took to shouting 'murderer' at Romero.

In 2003, Cristiana returned to Italy after 22 years in Costa Rica, where she had worked in the hotel business. Immediately, she gave an interview to the Turin-based sports paper, *Tuttosport*. Whilst much of the piece was taken up with references to her love affair with Gigi Meroni (he used to give her a red rose, every day) there was also more than a hint of bitterness towards Romero. According to Cristiana, Torino had always sent a wreath to Meroni's grave in Como on his birthday. After Romero took over, Cristiana claimed, this tradition came to a sudden halt. Moreover, Romero, in 36 years, had never got in touch with her or with Meroni's family. 'I am not surprised', concluded Cristiana, 'that Gigi has remained in the hearts of the Turin fans. I am shocked that Romero is president of Torino.' Romero wrote a letter to *Tuttosport* that glossed over the question of the flowers. However, he then made an official visit to Como in 2003 (on the sixtieth anniversary of Meroni's birth) and the club placed a wreath in Corso Re Umberto near the photo of Gigi.[17]

*All* of these tales need to be looked at with care. This whole story is full (as with Superga) of urban myths – the tale that Cristiana leaves seven red roses (seven as in Meroni's shirt number) every year on the Como grave is, I am told, untrue. When Meroni's gravestone in Como was attacked, the culprit turned out to be someone who could not accept that the footballer was actually dead. The Meroni myth lives on. His photo stands on the side of the road where he was hit by the car – near to a tram stop – and is often visited by fans and onlookers, who leave messages and flowers. When Torino won the 1975 championship, over 400 fans gathered near the photo. During the 50,000 strong 'March of Purple Pride' in 2003, the demonstrators stopped at the Meroni photo on their way to Superga.

There is now a website entirely dedicated to the life of Gigi Meroni and one of the best-selling and best-written books on Italian football tells the story of the Torino winger's career.[18] Meroni's life and death have inspired poems, songs, plays, paintings, exhibitions, essays, and countless newspaper articles. Torino fans still sing Meroni's name at games – *Gi-Gi Mer-oni* – more than 35 years after his death.

## Roberto Baggio. God has a Ponytail. (1967–)

*Career:* Fiorentina; 1985–1990 – 94 games, 39 goals; Juventus; 1990–1995 – 141 games, 78 goals; Milan; 1995–1997 – 51 games, twelve goals; Bologna; 1997–1998 – 30 games, 22 goals; Inter; 1998–2000 – 41 games, nine goals; Brescia; 2000–2004 – 95 games, 45 goals (total: 452 games; 205 goals). *Italy:* 1988–2004 – 56 games, 27 goals. *Honours:* two championships, one UEFA Cup, one Italian Cup. Penalty kicks: (all competitions including national team) 122 taken, 106 scored.[19]

'The angels sing, in his legs'                    ALDO AGROPPI

In 1989 Napoli – Italian champions – were playing Fiorentina at home. A young, thin, tiny-looking player called Roberto Baggio with a shock of long curly black hair picked up the ball in his own half. He then seemed to move with it in a strange diagonal direction. As one defender came towards him, he shifted straight towards goal, and with a little skip over another defender's leg, breached the entire defence. Almost without needing to dribble, thanks to a remarkable sense of the space of the pitch, he was through on goal. There, as usual, he was cool enough to dribble past the goalie, get the ball caught up in his legs and still have time to slide it into an empty net. In his career, Baggio scored dozens of goals as good as this one, some of them just as good as Maradona's second goal against England in the 1986 World Cup. Baggio has also been the most prolific penalty-taker in Italian football history, converting 86 per cent of his kicks. How odd, then, that he should be remembered above all for a penalty he missed, in the searing heat of the Pasadena stadium: the miss that decided the 1994 World Cup final.

Like many great players, Roberto Baggio has an unprepossessing physique; you would not notice him in a crowd. Yet, that anonymous build masks an elegance of touch and movement rarely seen on a football field. When Baggio scored his two-hundredth league goal in 2004 – after a trademark dribble and perfect side-foot – TV stations showed many of his past efforts. A very high percentage of his goals were items of sheer beauty – chips, dribbles, free-kicks, volleys. In the 1990 World Cup he scored the goal of the tournament against Czechoslovakia after a run and delicate chip. Moreover, Baggio scored all these goals from a position that was not that of a pure forward – very few were tap-ins or headers – and often for minor clubs – Brescia, Bologna, Fiorentina.

Roberto Baggio was born to a well-to-do family in the Veneto rural town of Caldogno in February 1967. His first games were with Vicenza, the best local team, and it was there that he suffered the first of a series of terrible knee injuries that have plagued his career. Turning sharply (in May 1985) he twisted the cruciate ligaments in his right knee. Baggio did not play again properly for nearly two years, after re-injuring the same knee nine months later. In the meantime he had been signed by Fiorentina. In Florence, he quickly became a hero, striking up a formidable partnership with striker Stefano Borgonovo.[20] With Baggio, and Eriksson on the bench, Fiorentina qualified for Europe and got to the UEFA Cup final in 1990. Baggio started to unveil his whole repertoire of goals for the *viola* fans – the perfect free-kicks, the tight dribbles, the ability to stay cool under pressure. Against Milan, in the San Siro, he again took on the whole opposition defence, and scored. As a penalty-taker, Baggio often waited for the goalkeeper to move. He missed very few, fewer in fact than any other player in the history of Serie A.

In 1990 news started to spread in the Renaissance town that Baggio had been signed by arch-rivals Juventus. Fiorentina had just lost the UEFA Cup final to Juve after two violent games. Fans rioted, and the police were called, but it was too late. Baggio had gone, never to return. Baggio chose Juve at the wrong time. The team had just been re-founded under the 'modern' leadership of manager Gigi Maifredi, who had taken Bologna from Serie C to Serie A. Although 'the divine ponytail' scored regularly, the team did very badly, finishing a disastrous seventh. Nor did Baggio endear himself to the Juventus faithful by his loyalty to Fiorentina. In the Fiorentina–Juve match in April 1991, Juve won a penalty. Baggio refused to take it, and it was missed. He was then substituted, and on his way to the bench picked up and put on a Fiorentina scarf. Weeks of argument followed.

At the end of the season, Maifredi was sacked, and Juve returned to old favourite Trapattoni. Baggio continued to score hatfuls of goals, winning the UEFA Cup in 1993 and being made European Footballer of the Year. He became *the* key player for the national team, taking the team almost single-handedly to the 1994 final. But domestic honours eluded him. When Trapattoni was replaced by Marcello Lippi in 1995, Juve went on to win the championship, but the relationship between Baggio and his new manager disintegrated. He played a mere seventeen games in that championship-winning season (with eight goals), and moved to Milan the following year. Baggio's fame led to frequent arguments with many of the managers he played under, and he always railed against tactical instructions.

Milan's fans (as with all Baggio's teams, apart perhaps from the *Juventini*) loved Baggio, but once again he was marginalized by a succession of managers. He only turned out 51 times in two years for Milan, winning another championship. Desperate to get back into the national team, Baggio decided to move to a smaller club, Bologna. His best season followed: 22 goals and a call-up for the 1998 World Cup 'by popular demand'. In France, manager Cesare Maldini absurdly left him out of the key matches, although he was a hair's breadth from knocking out the eventual champions and hosts with a golden goal attempt. Back in Milan, this time with Inter, the old problems with Lippi re-emerged. Left on the bench, his talent seemed to be going to waste. By the end of the season, his relationship with Lippi had deteriorated so much that the two hardly spoke. He left his mark in his final game for Inter, a playoff for a Champions League place, where he scored two classic goals to give Inter victory. Baggio later criticized Lippi in the first of two highly successful autobiographies, writing that 'he is not my enemy. I simply have no respect for him, just as he has no respect for me.' For a time it seemed as if Lippi would even sue Baggio over this and other comments.[21]

Once again, his career seemed over, but was revived by a small provincial club – Brescia. With Baggio in the team, Brescia reached the heights of seventh place and competed in Europe. In 2002, yet another knee injury seemed to have put paid to Baggio's romantic hopes of one last World Cup with Italy. A miraculous recovery, just 76 days after the injury (and with two goals in his comeback match), put pressure on Trapattoni to pick him, but the miracle did not happen, despite special websites and phone lines dedicated to the campaign: *Baggio in nazionale!* During the 2003–4 season, as he scored his two-hundredth league goal (and he had already reached 300 career goals), Baggio announced his retirement at the end of the season. As one of the very few players to transcend club loyalties, Baggio even has a club dedicated to him, which attracts fans from all kinds of teams. As a tribute to his popularity Trapattoni picked Baggio for one last friendly match for Italy, where a sell-out crowd applauded his every touch.

Apart from his genius on the pitch, Baggio was different to so many of his fellow stars of the 1980s and 1990s. A shy, reflective family-man, he shunned the high living of stars like Vieri and Totti, with their model-and-media girlfriends and expensive night-club and yachting lifestyles. Baggio was a Buddhist in a Catholic country, and rarely displayed the histrionics so common at all levels of Serie A. He knew what he wanted, but he could also express emotions that seemed to have no place in the modern, cash-dominated game. When fellow Brescia player Vittorio Mero died in a car crash in January 2002, Baggio was instrumental in getting a game called off as a result (the players had heard of the accident just before kick-off). He later dedicated goals to Mero and continued to remind fans and players of the tragedy throughout the following season. His decision to play out his final seasons with lowly Brescia allowed him the space and security that he had rarely had in the rest of his career, and he created yet another set of loyal, almost fanatical Baggio-followers. Despite his vast talent, Baggio played only 56 times for Italy, scoring 27 goals (the fourth best, behind Piola, Meazza and Riva). His international career was cruelly restricted by his outspokenness and his resistance to rigid tactics. Had he played 100 times, as he surely should have done, he would have easily beaten Riva's goalscoring record for the national team.

## Francesco Totti. King of Rome (1976–)

*Career:* AS Roma; 1993–2005 – 308 games, 110 goals.[22] *Italy:* 46 games, eight goals. *Honours:* one championship.

When he first appeared for the club he had supported since he was a boy, Francesco Totti was already a precocious talent. He made his debut at the age of sixteen, and was a fixture in the side well before he entered his twenties. Totti's skills are limitless. He can do anything with the ball: from ferocious free-kicks to audacious flicks. The King of Rome's finest season saw Roma win only their third ever championship, in 2001. This was after he had become an international star with his stunning performances in the 2000 European Championships. A mixture of super-cool and hot-headed, Totti has often suffered from a touch of over-confidence. With the national team he showed his cocky side – and his fearlessness – with a chipped penalty 'spoon' shot in the shoot-out that took Italy to the final. Under pressure, Totti would simply stop and look up (like Rivera) or let the ball roll past the goalkeeper before scoring.

There was a less endearing side to Totti. He liked to wind up opposing fans, especially those of hated rivals Lazio. After scoring in one derby he exhibited a T-shirt underneath his shirt that read *vi ho purgato ancora*: 'I have purged you again'. This insult led to sophisticated replies from Lazio fans, who plastered websites with photos of Totti sitting on the toilet. Opposing defenders soon woke up to the fact that Totti was not in control of his temper, and set out to provoke him. He took terrible punishment from man-markers, and often lashed out himself.

As a result, his disciplinary record was dreadful. Martin Keown used similar tactics in a Champions League match at Highbury in 2003, and Totti duly fell into the trap, elbowing Keown and receiving his marching orders.

In Rome, Totti became bigger than the team itself. He argued at length with Fabio Capello, both before and after the manager left Roma, and it was said that he set a bad example for some of the wilder elements in the team. Totti also liked the high life, and after a succession of high-profile affairs, he shacked up with TV dancer Ilary Blasi. SkyItalia transmitted all four and a half hours of their marriage live in 2005. One PR masterstroke endeared Totti to the general public. For some time, jokes had been circulating in Italy that played on the fact that Totti did not appear to be over-intelligent when interviewed. In what was to be a masterpiece of public relations, Totti collected together the jokes and published them himself, donating the proceeds to charity. *Jokes about Totti told by Totti* became a runaway best-seller, and even spawned a follow-up volume. Totti did not come cheap. In his last lucrative contract with Roma it was said that his personal trainer's entire wages were included amongst his expenses.

## Gianfranco Zola. From Sardinia to Sardinia (1966–)

'He will be better than me'       DIEGO MARADONA[23]

*Career:* Serie A: Napoli; 1989–1993 – 105 games, 32 goals; Parma; 1993–1996 – 102 games, 49 goals; Cagliari; 2004–5 – 31 games, nine goals. Chelsea; 1996–2003. All competitions – 312 games, 80 goals. *Italy:* 35 games, nine goals. *Honours:* one UEFA Cup, one Cup-Winners Cup, two FA Cups.

Gianfranco Zola's father ran a bar – Bar Sport – in the small town of Oliena in the mountains above Nuoro in central Sardinia. He also ran the local football team – 'as a kind of president', according to his son. Zola made his debut for his father's team at the age of sixteen and his size was already eliciting comment. He was 'tiny' and nobody really believed that he could make it in the game. At that age, he was only 150 cm tall. At eighteen he was signed by a local club, Nuorese, who played in a lower league of Serie C, and from there he moved to yet another team from the island. Despite his talent, it looked like he would never make it out of Sardinia. At the age of 24, he was spotted by arch-fixer Luciano Moggi, then with Napoli, and signed for the southern club soon afterwards.

When Maradona saw him for the first time, he commented that 'finally we've got someone who is smaller than me'. For two years, Zola trained with and watched the maestro at work. The story of his apprenticeship with Maradona is so often repeated when Zola's career is recounted that he himself became tired of the comparison. 'I already knew how to play a bit', he later said. Nonetheless, when Maradona gave him his number ten shirt just a month before his positive drugs test in 1991, the handover seemed complete. Gianfranco Zola was finally able to escape from the shadow of Maradona. After winning a *scudetto* with Napoli, and a fourth-place finish without Maradona in the team, Zola made his name with Parma – a small club on the verge of great things. Brilliant on the ball, Zola specialized in free-kicks and corners, scoring a series of goals that gained him fame in Italy and, thanks to Channel 4's coverage in the 1990s, in the UK. After Carlo Ancelotti dropped Zola from the Parma team in 1996, he was picked up by Ruud Gullit for Chelsea.

In London, Zola became a legend, but suffered from the prejudices of a succession of Italian national team managers, who refused to pick players based abroad. As a result, he only played 36 games for the national side, scoring just eight goals. His luck was usually out with Italy. In the 1994 World Cup he was absurdly sent off for a foul just twelve minutes after coming on as a substitute and he was blamed for Italy's early exit from the 1996 European Championships after missing a crucial penalty. His finest moment was the winning goal against England at Wembley in a 1997 World Cup qualifier, but Cesare Maldini didn't even pick him for the subsequent tournament.

In 2003 the 37-year-old Zola signed for Cagliari in Serie B. He had turned down huge sums of Russian cash to return to his home-island and to play a marathon 46-game season in an expanded lower division. After an extraordinary year filled with his usual repertoire of free-kicks, dribbles, perfect through passes and hard-running, Cagliari were promoted. Zola's noble and poetic gesture – 24 years after the retirement of Gigi Riva – added another layer to the Cagliari myth. For their last match, the whole team died their hair in Cagliari's colours and painted the symbol of the island on their faces (not easy: it is made up of two faces). This romantic story did not end there. Zola went on to play beautifully in Serie A, and even scored a towering header to equalize against the mighty Juventus in the last minute of a Cagliari home match. The sheer pleasure of watching Gianfranco Zola play football in this way after a slightly disappointing career with the national team was a refreshing antidote to the mercenary attitudes displayed by most top players. In June 2005, Zola announced his retirement in typically modest fashion, saying that he wanted to dedicate himself to 'too many things he had ignored for too long'.

# CHAPTER 7

# Goalscorers

We are now up front, with the goalscorers – always the most famous and most controversial of all positions. Italians have some fantastic words for centre-forwards: from the descriptive – *centravanti*; to the evocative – *goleador*; to the explosive – *cannoniere* (gunner) and *bomber*. Italian strikers have come in all shapes and sizes, from big, British-style target men to skilful, wily and clinical players.

## The Greatest? Giuseppe Meazza (1910–1979)

*Career:* Serie A: 1927–1946; Inter 1927–1940; Milan 1940–1942; Juventus 1942–3; Atalanta 1945–6; Inter 1946--7. 367 games, 216 goals. *Top scorer:* 1929; 1935; 1937. *Italy:* 1930–39 – 53 games, 33 goals. *Honours:* two World Cups, two championships, one Italian Cup.

'To have him in your team meant to start 1–0 up'

VITTORIO POZZO

'He was football'

GUIDO NASCIMBENE

For twenty seasons, the 'perfect' ball skills of Giuseppe Meazza graced the Italian league, and the international stage. After playing for Inter, Milan and Juventus, Meazza retired with two championships, one Italian Cup and two World Cups to his name. Meazza was the most famous player of his generation, a legend, the first Italian footballing superstar. After his first game for Inter *La Gazzetta* wrote that 'a star is born'.

Milanese, Meazza was born in 1910 in the Porta Vittoria area of the city, where the fruit and vegetable market once stood. His father died during World War One – when Giuseppe was just seven – and his mother ran a vegetable stall. Young Giuseppe's lungs were weak and he was sent to the 'open-air school' in Milan – in the Trotter park where some of the first football games in the city had been played – with its vast outdoor swimming pool and mini-zoo.

Meazza was blessed with extraordinary technical skills, at a time when such skills were the exception, not the norm. Equally good with both feet, he was also an excellent passer of the ball. His technical ability allowed him to drop back into a deeper role in support of rival-ally Silvio Piola in the 1938 World Cup. Faced with a goalkeeper, Meazza would draw him out of the goal, and then slide the ball past him, like the great modern forwards. Brera compared him to a bullfighter and described goalkeepers as 'the disoriented victims' of Meazza's clinical finishing.[1] On other occasions, he would dribble past the keeper and walk the ball into the net.

Giuseppe Meazza scores another goal for Inter.

This final act was often preceded by a mazy dribble through the defence, although when playing for Italy Meazza also thrived on the through passes of Fulvio Bernardini. It was said that Meazza did not kick the ball, he *caressed* it. A popular song of the time claimed that 'he scored to the rhythm of the foxtrot'.[2] Meazza was also a fine athlete, renowned for his bicycle-kicks.

At Inter, where he made his debut in 1927 at the age of seventeen, Meazza was god-like. He scored two goals in his first game, and in his second season racked up 33 goals in 29 games. This was followed by 33 in 31 games in 1928–9 and 31 in 33 the year after, when Inter won the first national Serie A championship. The sense of betrayal when he played briefly for Milan during the war ran deep amongst the Inter fans. Meazza even scored for Milan in a derby, but he later returned to Inter and remained part of the club until his death.

Meazza's international career was intimately linked with Vittorio Pozzo, who presided over the national team for nineteen consecutive years. Pozzo's second game in charge (in February 1930) was Meazza's first and the forward's last appearance was not to be until 1939. During that time Italy won three international trophies, and Meazza played a key part in two of them. Only three months on from his debut, Meazza exploded onto the world stage as Italy showed they were a force to be reckoned with. He scored a hat-trick as Italy beat Hungary for the first time, 5–0, in May 1930.

Controversy surrounded the 1934 World Cup victory, and Meazza was at the centre of the storm. Spain's players complained about a foul committed by the striker in the quarter-final and similar complaints were made by Austria after the semi-final. Meazza's performances, and his crucial winner against Spain, were central to the victory. Meazza's fame reached unheard-of levels with his two goals in four minutes against England in the famous 'Battle of Highbury' game just after the 1934 World Cup. He would later say that the failure of a team-mate to pass to him near the end was the greatest regret of his life. Meazza was again at the centre of the 1938 World Cup victory when he was made captain. Piola scored four times in the tournament and Meazza only once but he provided a number of assists from his new deeper role.

As with all legendary figures, accounts of Meazza's career are built around a series of myths. One of the most enduring concerns a game in Napoli when Meazza was supposedly selected for Italy in place of a local favourite. The fans allegedly booed Meazza from the off, making his mother – who had come down from Milan – cry in the stands. Then

Meazza silenced his critics with two goals. Another story surrounds the penalty he took – to win the game – in the 1938 World Cup semi-final. It is said that the elastic in Meazza's shorts had gone. Rather than change them, it is claimed, he trotted up to take the kick with one hand holding them up. The goalie went one way, he slotted the penalty the other. Italy won, 2–1. Another version of the elastic story is that his shorts began to fall down as Meazza ran up. Instead of stopping, he simply carried on and scored. On the film we have of the penalty, it certainly seems as if he is holding up his shorts. Yet, the goalkeeper did not dive the wrong way, remaining immobile as the penalty went into the corner.

Meazza feats were the stuff of dreams. On 27 April 1930, against Roma, he scored three goals in the first three minutes of the game. According to legend the Roma goalkeeper, Ballante, came out of goal for the first three chances, and was consistently beaten by the clinical Meazza. When he was through on goal for a fourth time, Ballante refused to come out. Meazza scored anyway. As he was trotting back to the halfway line, Ballante ran up to him and performed what Italians call 'the gesture of the umbrella'. Meazza then said 'it went in, you know', whereupon Ballante replied 'yes, but I didn't come out!' Another of his famous goals – against Austria for Italy at Milan – was similar to that scored by Puskas at Wembley in 1953. A dragback saw two Austrian defenders on the ground. Meazza then dribbled past the goalie and scored.

A further story is told by Brera: Meazza, it is said, awoke one Sunday afternoon in a bed which was 'not his own' and with a woman on each side of him. The game was about to start. In his pyjamas, he took a taxi to the Arena stadium in the centre of town, arriving just in time 'for the fascist salute', and had to score twice for his team-mates to forgive him. There are various other versions of this – probably apocryphal – story. It is often said that Meazza rarely trained, and was more or less free to do what he wanted in what Brera called 'generous and easy-going Milan'.

We need to be very careful with these stories, based as they are largely on journalistic hearsay. Meazza was a hero in an epoch when sport was a key fascist propaganda weapon. The stories told about him fit perfectly into useful narratives of nation-building (as with the

Milanese player accepted by the Neapolitans after helping the national team win) and heroic status – the fragility and bravery of the shorts story, the sexual potency and rapscallion edge to the brothel tale. Meazza was originally given the nickname *Balilla* because of his boyish looks and youth. The *Balilla*[3] were military youth groups organized by Mussolini. This nickname did link Meazza to fascism – and it is difficult to separate the career of the striker from the ways in which the regime exploited the success of the national team in the 1930s.

In those years, Meazza's face was everywhere, in cartoon strips, in adverts and in the sports papers. As the first football superstar, Meazza's image was much in demand. He advertised bathroom products when still a teenager: toothpaste and, obviously, brilliantine for his famous ·hair. Some journalists wrote of a 'cult of personality' around Meazza, something which fascism tried to boost. Most Italians 'saw' Meazza through the enthusiastic radio commentary of Niccolò Carosio, who exalted the Milanese striker with his fiery rhetoric. Mussolini told Meazza in 1938 that he had done more for Italy than any of its ambassadors.

Meazza's career, as with so many great players, was seriously disrupted by the war. He also suffered a terrible injury, at the age of just 29, whilst playing for Italy. A blood clot – Meazza was given appalling treatment by opposing defenders – led to his left leg 'going cold'. It was a year before he could play again, and he was never the same. During the war, Meazza played for Milan, Juventus and even Varese, scoring goals, but never at the same rate as during the 1930s. After the war, he spent a season in Bergamo with Atalanta before a last cameo with Inter – in a poor season for the blue-and-blacks in 1946–7 (seventeen games, two goals). Meazza's reputation was such that two defenders would often be assigned to mark him, leaving more space for the others to score.

Meazza became exceedingly wealthy: 'he bought a car and spent a lot of time in daytime and night-time bars. He earned hundreds of thousand-lire notes. His family . . . lived happily on his back' (Brera).[4] He would often slip into Milanese dialect and was deeply rooted in his native city. After he became a star, he bought a flat in the central Piazza Cairoli, very close to the Arena stadium where Inter played until after World War Two. A self-made man – in the richest and most modern Italian city – he epitomized the American dream.

On retirement, Meazza was still a star. He played himself in the film *Milano miliardaria* (Milan billionaire) (1951). In the movie a Milanese photographer and Inter fan stakes his wife in a football bet with a Neapolitan barber. A year later a popular documentary about the national team – *The eleven musketeers* – was released and both Meazza and Silvio Piola took part. Meazza's career as a manager was a respectable one and he even trained the national team in the early 1950s. Yet his record in charge of Italy was very poor – a 'disaster' according to Brera – eight games, two wins, one draw and five defeats.

Meazza's greatest post-career achievement was the nurturing of a fine group of youth players at Inter, some of whom would become footballing legends. Star midfielder Sandro Mazzola and defender Giacinto Facchetti both played in Inter's youth team under Meazza and spoke warmly of his kindness and technical help. Mazzola tells one story about Meazza's technical skill, even in the 1950s. A film crew had come to the Inter training ground to shoot some penalties for an advert; the director ordered the goalkeeper to dive one way whilst Meazza would shoot into the other corner. The goalie complained and Meazza told him to try and save the penalties. After ten goals in which the keeper dived the wrong way, he gave up. In the 1970s, Meazza was unhappy to lose his national goalscoring record to Gigi Riva: 'Well done Riva,' he said, 'he scored a lot against Cyprus and Turkey. My goals were more important.'

Meazza's private life, as the first real star of Italian football, was of great fascination to the general public and journalists. He was short and stocky but good-looking, and he was also rich, successful and talented. Married twice, Meazza is generally remembered as a ladies' man and he was often compared to screen heart-throb Rudolph Valentino – and he hung out with another similar character – Giuseppe 'Gipo' Viani – the future manager of Milan. Newspapers spoke of the 'hundreds and hundreds of perfumed letters . . . intercepted by his mother'. One of his team-mates, Pietro Rava, later wrote that he 'adored women and we had to be careful that he didn't run away from training camp . . . it's difficult to tell if he had won over more girls than the goals he scored.'

Wherever he went, people would crowd round him, desperate to shake his hand. This expansive side of his character – the women, the night-clubs, the flashy car, the 60 cigarettes a day – grates somewhat with the frequent descriptions of Meazza as reserved and modest, but he was not particularly fond of his fame. When he was dying, he convinced his family to keep things secret and hold a tiny, private funeral. He also insisted that he be buried without a tombstone. Most sports books still claim that he died in his holiday home at Rapallo, in Liguria. In fact he passed away much closer to his native Milan, in Monza.

His immortality was confirmed when the most beautiful and atmospheric stadium in Italy – San Siro – was re-named after him in 1980. The stadium is now referred to either by its old name or simply as 'The Meazza'. For once, Inter and Milan fans – who share the stadium – agreed on something. Nobody else was worthy of such an honour.[5]

## The quiet goal machine. Silvio Piola (1913–1996)

*Career:* Serie A: 1929–1954; Pro Vercelli; 1929–1934; Lazio; 1934–1943; Juventus; 1945–1947; Novara; 1948–1954. 566 games, 290 goals. *Top scorer:* 1937 and 1942. *Italy:* 1935–52 – 34 games, 30 goals. *Honours:* one World Cup.

'A Stakhanovite of the shot, a proletarian of the goal'

GIANNI MURA

Meazza's striking partner in the 1938 World Cup victory was also his most prominent rival, ally and team-mate: Silvio Piola. Only five players in the history of Serie A have scored more than 200 goals and only three of these have been Italian: Meazza (216), Roberto Baggio (206) and Silvio Piola – unreachable, way out in front – with 290 goals in 566 games in Serie A. Some have calculated that with his goals in all competitions Piola scored more than 500 times in his long career. As journalist Gianni Mura wrote, 'goals and Piola were equivalent in Italy'. He was a goal machine, perhaps the only real player of that type and quality Italy has ever produced. Whilst Meazza liked to run on to through balls and Paolo Rossi thrived on crosses, Piola scored both from close range and distance. He could shoot with both feet and was also good in the air. His astonishing goal record was despite three years 'lost' in the chaos of the war and one season where his 27 goals for Torino (in 23 games) did not count, as the championship was disrupted by the conflict. His record with Italy – again interrupted by the war for five years – was 30 goals in 34 games. Italy only lost twice when he played for them – over a period that covered seventeen years.

Whilst playing for his first club, Pro Vercelli, a local football expert described Piola as 'afraid of nothing . . . his head is always half a metre above everyone else and his legs take him everywhere on the pitch ahead of the others'. Tall ('but he seemed taller than he was', said

Silvio Piola playing for Italy.

Brera), gangly, with a small head and sticky-out ears, Piola did not look like much of a footballer. Yet, in action, he was 'a force of nature' with a perfect grasp of when to arrive in the area, which some described as a kind of 'sixth sense'. Journalists compared him to a 'catapult' and wrote that he ran with 'long strides which appear to take possession of the ground he has covered'.[6] He was one of the pioneers of the volleyed goal, the scissors kick and the bicycle-kick. Less technically proficient than Meazza, they were perfect partners. Piola's proposed move to Inter in 1934 was supposedly blocked from on high. A team with Meazza *and* Piola would have been too strong for the rest. At the last minute, Piola was shifted to Lazio (for the huge sum, at the time, of 250,000 lire) – Mussolini's team and the club of the football federation president, General Giorgio Vaccaro. Piola later said that 'at that time, a player couldn't say no'.

At times, he couldn't stop scoring. He hit six goals against Fiorentina in 1933 and four away from home (in forty minutes) at Alessandria in 1931.[7] After he left the game, every new striker was compared to him. As Gian Paolo Ormezzano later wrote: 'For a long time it was impossible to talk about a centre-forward in positive terms without someone saying: "You are only saying that because you didn't see Piola play"'.[8]

Unlike Meazza, Piola was a humble country boy who led a quiet, almost reclusive life, and liked to go hunting with his three dogs. If Meazza was a star, Piola was the epitome of the *antidivo*.[9] He neither drank, nor smoked nor womanized and he disliked doing adverts. The supposed rivalry between Meazza and Piola is seldom mentioned, and was hushed up under fascism. Gianni Brera, as usual, was franker than most, claiming that Piola's late debut for the national team was down to resistance amongst the old guard and that Meazza 'considered him a second-rate usurper' even in 1938, after the World Cup triumph in France.

Piola became a national hero (and world-famous) after the 1938 World Cup. Fascism made much of that victory – away from home. The relationship between Piola and fascism was not direct, or personal, but nonetheless the striker went along with all that was required of him by the regime, and remained proud of his meeting with Mussolini after the victory. 'In those days,' he later wrote, 'the love for one's country was strong, not like today ... this had nothing to do with fascism. It was an emotional moment to be received by the Prime Minister [Mussolini] and to be told, "well done ... Italy is proud of you".' Piola's physical power was also glorified. The centre-forward was held up as a kind of new Italian superman who 'gave the lie to the classic characteristics of our race with his spectacular physique: tall, robust, well balanced'.[10]

Despite his success with the national team – two goals on his debut as Italy beat Austria for the first time and two goals in the 1938 World Cup final – Piola never won a championship. This lack of domestic honours was without doubt down to his 'choice' of club. With Inter, he certainly would have won a few *scudetti*. Nonetheless, Piola was a hero with Lazio for his goals and his bravery, coming back on to the field twice with a badly cut forehead to win a derby in 1941. One goal was a header, after which his wound started to bleed heavily again. His nickname in Rome was simple, but effective: Piola-*gol*.

Piola's career was curtailed by the war. In 1943, he was on a visit to his home-town of Vercelli when Italy was split in two by the dramatic events of 8 September. By pulling out of the war, Italy made itself into a battlefield for a wider conflict. Nazi troops poured into the country from the north, whilst the Allies fought their way up the peninsula from Sicily. Half of Italy was under Allied control, as the King of Italy with his government fled to the south, and the other half was run by the Nazis. Piola couldn't make it back to Rome to play for Lazio. Such a journey was more or less impossible. Communications also broke down between the 'two Italies'. A newspaper in the capital led with the false headline, 'Piola Killed after Bombing'. There are even stories of mourning rites being celebrated in Rome. Meanwhile, Italy's most famous player 'found a club' in the north – Torino – where he played in a championship which did not count, and which was eventually won by a team made up of firemen from La Spezia, on the Ligurian coast. Today, Turin is only 50 minutes away on the direct train route from Vercelli, yet Italy's transport links were in a disastrous state in 1943–4. It used to take Piola *six hours*, standing up 'and squashed like a sardine', to even get to Turin.

After the war he played briefly for Juventus (26 goals in two seasons) before moving to Novara in Serie B. Most people assumed his career was over, but he managed to play for seven more seasons as Novara were promoted immediately. Piola was to score another 70 goals in Serie A, including eighteen in one season at the age of 38. He scored his last goal at the age of forty. Piola's quiet lifestyle helped him play for longer than almost any of his contemporaries despite the violent treatment he received from clogging defenders.

Despite his quiet reputation, Piola's long career was not without its moments of controversy. Two incidents are particularly noteworthy. In 1937 the Rome derby in February ended in violence, with *carabinieri* on the pitch to separate fighting players. Journalists accused a Roma defender of kicking Silvio Piola in the back. Later, however, a different

Roma full-back took responsibility for the kick through a letter to the press.[11] Piola, as Lazio captain, was given a one-game ban as punishment for his 'moral responsibility' in failing to control his fellow players.

The second incident was Piola's 'handball' goal against England in 1939, which remained something of a black mark on Piola's gentlemanly image. According to the striker, the goal was born of instinct, not design. With the score at 1–1, Piola tried an overhead kick, which failed. As he fell, he claimed that 'I brought my hand up towards my head and the ball just flew in'. The referee was unsighted and gave the goal, but the English protests were taken up by the British press. In the end, the game finished 2–2. Gianni Brera later wrote that both the newspapers and Piola had covered up the incident of the 'manina santa' (the little, holy hand) for years.

Piola's last game for the national team came as late as 1952, against England with Meazza on the bench as coach. At 38 years old, Piola's call-up created huge interest in the press, especially as it was his first game for the national team since 1947. Many critics argued that he was too slow for a game of such importance. Just before the big match, Gianni Brera wrote a beautiful open letter to Piola 'to explain my attitude towards you'. First, he appealed to their common Pavese roots ('our land') but the letter went on to describe the 'infinite sadness' in Piola's eyes and his fear of decline. 'The man on the street', he continued, 'looks upon you as an example to be followed.' But 'physical strength does not allow for dreams'. Brera attacked the management for calling Piola up, and thereby forcing the journalist into such a difficult task – that of the harsh critic. 'I cannot lie . . . you must not close a great career such as yours with a pitiful memory . . . you must remain, for us, what you have always been . . . a superman, an idol.'

Piola was unsure whether he should play, and this insecurity reached the press. One headline read 'Silvio is tired' and he arrived late for training sessions in the weeks before the big game. After a national team practice game, he was 'doubled up' with pain. With Novara, he hardly trained towards the end of his career, and was unused to such activity. Another journalist, Ettore Brera, likened him to a 'retired tenor who tries to make a comeback'. The management team persuaded him to play, and promised him special, light training. In the end, bravely, he accepted.

In Florence, Piola was given a great reception from a packed crowd of 95,000 people. Many had arrived the night before and cinemas were opened for those without hotel rooms to sleep in. The gates were open at 10 a.m. for a game beginning at 4 p.m. – the ground was already full by midday – and police were called in from as far away as Sicily to control the situation. The game finished 1–1, and Piola came close to scoring with a deflected shot. Brera wrote afterwards that he had been 'by no means the worst' player on the pitch and praised Piola for his 'fighting spirit and courage'. The international and English press, including a young Brian Glanville, were less generous: Piola was 'in decline'.

He finally retired in 1953–4, at the age of 41, after 24 years of top-flight football (and a record 21 seasons). For some time after that, Piola remained within the football world as a manager and coach. Every morning he would read the sports press and check on his various clubs – Pro Vercelli, Lazio, Juventus, Torino and Novara. According to his daughter, he was always in bed by 11.30 p.m. After finally leaving the professional game, 'he lived like a ghost',[12] quietly, near Vercelli until his death in 1996 after a sad period of Alzheimer's.[13]

## Other strikers. Target men and tricky forwards

Italian centre-forwards can be seen as essentially falling into two groups, divided loosely into the styles adopted by Meazza and Piola. On the one hand, there were those strikers who used physical force and a sense of timing to arrive in the right place at the right time: strikers *di sfondamento* (break-through strikers) as they were called in Italy. On the other there were those centre-forwards who used their technical skill and guile to score. Here are some examples of both types of goalscorer.

# Thunder. Gigi Riva (1944–)

*Career:* Serie A: Cagliari; 1964–1976 – 315 games, 164 goals. *Top scorer:* 1967; 1969; 1970. *Italy:* 42 games, 35 goals (top scorer of all time). *Honours:* one European Championship, one championship.

'Riva is eternal for Sardinia, he is a mythical ... almost a religious figure'                            VITO BIOLCHINI

'Riva: some of my literary colleagues have ticked me off because I gave Riva a 9+ mark for the game against Atlético ... I baptise him *Rombo di tuono* [thunder-clap] ... one of the most extraordinary athletes ever produced by Italian football'
                                                          GIANNI BRERA

'Riva plays poetic football. He is a realistic poet'
                                            PIER PAOLO PASOLINI

Before Gigi Riva joined them, Cagliari were a provincial club who had won nothing, and had spent most of their time in Serie B. With Gigi Riva in the team, Cagliari won a historic championship – in 1969–1970 – and also finished second and fourth in the same period. With that victory, a big new stadium was built putting Cagliari briefly on the football map. After Riva left, in 1976, Cagliari returned to the anonymity of the 1950s. Riva *was* Cagliari for more than ten years – one Sardinian fan of Gigi remembers seeing a game at a roadside in the island where all 22 players wore Riva's number eleven shirt, and his myth lives on in Sardinia.

A great player at a small club, Riva was not linked to Sardinia by family or regional ties. He was born into a poor family in the lakeside town of Leggiuno,[14] near the Swiss border in northern Lombardy, during the last winter of World War Two. 'My father', Riva later said, 'had survived three wars, was a hairdresser and a tailor ... at the end of the war he found a job in a local factory ... a piece of metal flew out of a machine and hit him in the stomach. They took him to hospital, but there was nothing they could do for him. I was nine. My mother had to go to work ... I was sent to a religious school, away from home.' The school (known as a *collegio* in Italian) was sadistically strict. Many Italian children ended up in these places, especially around wartime. Gigi hated it. 'They forced us to pray and only then they would give us bread ... they humiliated us because we were poor. I ran away more than once.'

After three years in the horrible *collegio*, Riva found a job in a lift-factory – and continued to play football. In 1960 he signed up for a local side, and in 1962 he was spotted by Legnano, a much bigger team who had had spells in Serie A but were by then languishing in Serie C. In 1963 Cagliari paid 37 million lire for him, a big fee for a nineteen-year-old. At that time he was unconvinced about Sardinia: 'It seemed like Africa to me: the island where they sent people in order to punish them!'

Tall, strong and (later) powerfully built, Riva was a physical icon in the 1960s and 1970s. He was also good-looking, *the* pin-up of the 1970s. Bars and bedrooms were plastered with photos of Riva, and not just in Sardinia. Numerous statues of the centre-forward were sold and placed in bars all over the island. One can still be seen in the Bar Marius in Cagliari – where fans gather. This wax statue is life-size, and Riva was a tall man. Local journalists worked full-time on Riva, following him everywhere. Gianni Brera gave Riva the perfect nickname: *Rombo di tuono*, 'Thunder', which only added to the myth.[15] The legend of his strength led to a series of stories. In October 1970 a nine-year-old boy, Danilo Piroddi, was standing behind the net during a training session in Rome when a Riva shot broke his arm. His shot was timed at 120 km an hour. Cagliari's goalkeeper would often skip training to avoid parrying hundreds of powerful shots, leaving this unenviable task to the reserve keeper. Much has been written about Riva's left foot. One of the best books about the Cagliari side of 1969–1970 is called *A left-foot shot*. At elementary school, his teachers had hit Riva on the hand to stop him writing with his left. Later, at religious college, he had to 're-learn' to write.

He was a superman, but a very fragile one. Riva's style, and his bravery, led to so many injuries that in one of the many books about him, his doctor is interviewed. Reams and reams of newsprint were spent analysing Riva's injuries in gory detail. He first broke his leg in

March 1967 against Portugal, after a clash with the goalkeeper, and was out for the rest of that season. He then went on to score 31 goals in two seasons, and became the first-choice number nine for Italy.

Meanwhile, at Cagliari, a team was being built which – against all the odds – would be ready to challenge for the title. Apart from Riva, Cagliari signed Italy's goalkeeper – Ricky Albertosi – as well as the excellent Domenghini on the right, and the silky Brazilian Nené. At the back the stars were Niccolai, a strong central defender with a penchant for spectacular own goals, and Cera, who played as a kind

Gigi Riva salutes the Cagliari *curva* after the championship
victory, 1970. Note the spectators sitting on the advertising
hoardings at the back of the crowd.

of modern sweeper – in front of the defence rather than behind it. The team played a form of 'total football' and was run by 'The Philosopher', Manlio Scopigno, a witty and intelligent coach from the Friuli region of north-east Italy. In the 1969–70 championship season, Riva scored 21 goals in 30 games, whilst Cagliari only let in a miserly eleven goals – a record. Many players claimed – as with Napoli in 1987 – that one championship with Cagliari was worth ten elsewhere.

Riva was a spectacular player. His goals came from powerful long shots, overhead kicks and crashing headers. One goal for Italy against

East Germany in 1969 was shown countless times on Italian TV, and became part of the credits sequence of the most popular sports programme, *Sporting Sunday*. A cross came in from the left and Riva launched himself at the ball, reaching it with a diving header when his body was completely horizontal. The ball flew into the net. In the photo that caught the moment, Riva has his eyes open, watching the ball. The goalkeeper's dive began only as the ball entered the goal. Riva's battles with a series of central defenders were nothing short of epic, such as those with Inter's Tarcisio Burgnich – who was known as 'The Rock'. In one game, Riva broke one of Burgnich's teeth, and the Inter player spent the rest of the game looking for revenge. At the end of the game, Riva recalls: 'We embraced. He still asks me where that tooth is, whenever we meet.'

For Italy, Riva was a key – if controversial – player for nearly a decade. Left out of the 1966 World Cup[16] – he was 'taken along' for the experience, but was not in the playing squad – Riva led Italy to the 1968 European Championships, scoring in the final. In the 1970 World Cup he scored three times as Italy again reached the final, although more was expected of him after Cagliari's extraordinary season. Heavily criticized in the press, his private life was placed under great scrutiny[17] and only with the semi-final goal against West Germany in extra-time did he fulfil his potential. Journalist Mario Gismondi later called that goal 'the best goal of the best game of the best sport in the world'.[18] In the final itself, he was exhausted, and also missed a good chance in the first half. By 1974, his career was more or less over, and his performance in the finals that year was poor. He even suffered the indignity of being booed by Italian fans in Germany.

Riva sacrificed his career for the national team – twice. In 1967 he was badly hurt against Portugal and in October 1970 (after a nasty foul by the Austrian defender Ronald Hof) his career was shortened by another terrible injury during a game in Vienna. Hof's own career was tormented by that foul in the years that followed: 'every time I came to Italy on holiday people would ask me about the incident . . . I don't want to talk about it any more.' In 1989, before a game with Austria, an Italian journalist interviewed Hof. The piece was entitled: 'The man who broke [Riva's] leg. He left football and now makes ice-creams'. Without Riva's 1970 injury, Cagliari might well have won a second championship. Hof died of cancer in 1995.

The story of Gigi Riva's career can only be told with reference to Sardinia in 1969–1970, an island which was still desperately poor even in the late 1960s and where people were forced to emigrate to find work. Bandits controlled parts of the island and kidnappings became common in an economy reliant upon ancient traditions of pastoral farming. Yet, the late 1960s was also a time of modernization. Mass tourism was starting to ruin the stunning eastern coastline after the Aga Khan bought up huge tracts of land in the early 1960s. State money was also poured into the island in a vain attempt to develop a petrol industry that turned out to be a mirage. Stefano Boldrini, in his beautiful book about Gigi Riva, argues that the striker's fame modernized Sardinia. He 'forced shepherds to buy transistor radios so that they could follow Cagliari . . . women in black – the Italian *chador* – fell in love with him'.[19] In 1970 Riva gave Sardinia its only football championship, leading to a party which went on for days, and numerous books, films and documentaries.[20] In Olbia in the north three Juventus fans were forced to wear Cagliari shirts, and hundreds of 'false funerals' for Cagliari's rivals were organized. Four huge banners were put up in the city which all read: 'Welcome to the capital of football'. *L'Unione Sarda* sold 125,000 copies – an unprecedented number – the day after the championship was won. Riva never left Cagliari, despite offers from all the big clubs – especially Juventus to whom he was 'sold' in 1973 (he refused to go) – and this loyalty endeared him still further to his adoring fans.[21] Juve – it was said – had offered six players in a swap deal for Riva.

It is often said that if everyone who claims that they had seen the match which clinched the championship against Bari in Cagliari on 12 April 1970 had actually been in the stadium, there would have been a quarter of a million people in the ground (in that season the stadium was normally packed by eleven in the morning).[22] Two fugitives from justice were arrested in the stadium but were allowed to watch the rest of the game in handcuffs. The victory was historic, the first and last time that a side from Italy's islands won a championship. As Gianni Brera wrote, 'Cagliari's championship signifies the entrance of Sardinia in Italy'. For writer Nanni Boi, Riva achieved 'the miracle of the unification of Sardinia'[23] – an island which had always been divided from city to city and region to region. This success was reflected in the national team. For the 1970 World Cup, six players were called up to the squad, and four were in the side as Italy reached the final: Domenghini, Cera, Albertosi and Riva.

Controversy dogged the end of Riva's career. His business interests were raked over when he sacked some workers employed in his car showrooms in Sardinia, and he was asked to cut his own wages to help the club. By the mid-1970s, however, the injuries had taken their toll. Riva rarely played, and was unable to turn out for Italy again. In January 1976 he scored his last goal. Then he picked up yet another injury, this time at San Siro. 'It is all over,' he told a journalist in the dressing room. Meanwhile, Cagliari were relegated. Riva finally announced his retirement in April 1977. He then went on to become part of the national team staff. When Roberto Baggio missed that famous penalty in the 1994 World Cup final, Riva's was the shoulder upon which he cried.[24]

## Paolo Rossi. 'I made Brazil cry' (1956–)

*Career:* Serie A: Como; 1975–6 – six games; Vicenza; 1978–9 – 58 games, 39 goals; Perugia; 1979–80 – 28 games, thirteen goals; Juventus; 1981–1985 – 83 games, 24 goals; Milan; 1985–6 – twenty games, two goals; Verona; 1986–7 – twenty games, four goals. *Top scorer:* 1978. Italy; 1977–1986 – 48 games, twenty goals. Top scorer in the 1982 World Cup. *Honours:* one World Cup, two championships, one Italian Cup, one European Cup, one Cup-Winners Cup.

'Paolo Rossi was not a player, but a novel . . . he was loved and hated . . . he experienced success and failure . . . he was glorified and forgotten . . . his playing life could fill the pages of *War and Peace*'                                    DARWIN PASTORIN

Nobody gave Italy much of a chance in the World Cup group match against Brazil played on 14 June 1982, in the sweltering heat of Barcelona in northern Spain. Italy had to win to qualify, a draw was enough for their opponents – one of the finest Brazilian teams of all time – with Falção, Socrates, Cerezo, Junior and Zico. Paolo Rossi's hat-trick – a header, a run and shot, a flick on the turn – knocked out Brazil and made a nation despair. No wonder that Rossi's autobiography is called *I made Brazil cry*.[25] It was that moment which turned Pablito from a misfit whose reputation had been badly besmirched by scandal into a national hero, a status which was strengthened as Italy went on to win the cup thanks to his goals in the semi-final and final. A slow decline set in soon afterwards, however. Rossi would never be as good again, and his career was cut very short by a series of terrible knee injuries. He retired in 1987 at the age of just 31.

Two goals, both of them headers, sum up Paolo Rossi. The first came in a European Cup game for Juventus at Villa Park in 1983. After a brilliant move involving Bettega and Cabrini, a cross came in from the left. While the defenders stood and watched, Paolo darted in, beating all of them, to nod the ball home. Less than 60 seconds had passed since the kick off and, in Italy, commercial TV missed the goal as the ads overran. On the replay, it looks as if the defenders are frozen in time. The other goal is the first in that Brazil match. Again, a Cabrini cross came in from the left. Again, Rossi arrived at the far post, his timing perfect, to knock the ball in.

Little Paolo – with his curly black hair, slight build and impish good looks – was born in 1956 in Prato near Florence (whose town's local team would later spot another, very different striker, Christian Vieri). He was spotted whilst playing for an amateur team in Florence and snapped up for Juventus for twelve million lire, but his knees were fragile even then. Like Roberto Baggio, his career almost ended before it had begun. He underwent three operations before he was eighteen, and Juve got rid of him, first on loan to Como and then to Vicenza in Serie B, with Juventus keeping 'half' of his 'property'.[26] Vicenza moved Paolo up front, and his career took off. His strengths lay in his remarkable sense of position, and an ability to lose his marker almost at will, which saw him ghost into the box on numerous occasions at just the right time. His 21 goals led to promotion, and 24 goals the following season made him top scorer and took provincial Vicenza to an unprecedented second place.

Enzo Bearzot selected the young Rossi for the 1978 World Cup, where he played well in a superb team performance. On his return, his fate was decided by a 'game of the envelopes'. This is the destiny of players owned by two clubs. If both teams want the player, his destination is decided by 'secret' bidding. Both clubs put a figure in an envelope, and the biggest figure wins. To everyone's surprise – and the event caused weeks if not months of comment in the press – Vicenza's president Giuseppe Farina (who would later go on the run from illegal bankruptcy charges whilst in charge at Milan) bid far more than Juventus. Yet, Farina had overstretched himself. Vicenza went down, and Rossi moved to another minor club – Perugia. It was there that he became involved as a bit-part player in a huge betting scandal – a controversial affair which cost him a two-year ban. Juventus – six years after buying him for the first time – finally got Rossi back and the ban ended just in time for Paolo to play three end-of-season games under Trapattoni (winning a championship).

Bearzot took Rossi to the 1982 World Cup against the advice of the whole press corps. The media seemed to have been right in the early games. Rossi was appalling. He couldn't trap the ball, he looked slow and his passes invariably went astray. He later wrote that he had 'never played so badly'. Everything changed with the hat-trick against Brazil. International fame and fortune followed and Rossi was voted European Footballer of the Year in 1983. The world was at his feet.

Yet, despite some occasional brilliant performances for Juventus in a star-studded and winning team, Paolo never reached the heights of Spain again, or even the form he had shown with Vicenza. Many fans started to believe that he was being kept in the side purely because he was so famous. Manager Trapattoni lost patience and kept substituting Paolo. It was as if the magic had left him, and he scampered around the pitch, desperately looking for an opening. Juventus sold him on to Milan the eve of the European Cup final in 1985 and his last 'game' for them was a tragic one – at Heysel. He had scored just 23 goals in three league seasons with Juve, and he managed a mere two in a whole season with Milan.[27] With Italy, he never repeated the form of 1982 and the team failed to qualify for the 1984 European Championships. Bearzot took Rossi to the 1986 World Cup, but he did not even make the bench. In all, he played just 215 games in Serie A, ending his career after a poor season with Verona in 1987. Just five years had passed since the triumphs of Barcelona and Madrid.

Rossi's fame had reached way beyond Italy's shores. His 1982 heroics led to a lucrative contract with an American advertising company, and everywhere he went, people recognized him. This fame made his rapid decline even more melancholic. He was living on past glories, and his scoring touch had deserted him, not temporarily, but forever. His exploits in 1982 had led to vast wealth but also jealousy and over-expectation. The fans and the journalists were quick to turn on Rossi when he did not live up to these expectations, and his frail body could not stand up to the stress of regular football. It was perhaps no coincidence that the 1982 triumph came after more or less two seasons out of the game through suspension. In retirement, Rossi continued to turn up on chat shows and nostalgic re-evocations, living off his 1982 reputation. For the Italians, he would always be *paolorossi*, the man who had won the World Cup. None of the rest really mattered. He had come good at just the right time, and in such an unexpected way, that history would soon forget the tragic waste of his talent after his greatest triumph.

## Other Strikers since the 1970s. Paolino Pulici, Roberto Pruzzo, Gianluca Vialli, Christian Vieri, Giuseppe Signori, Alessandro Del Piero

Alongside Paolo Rossi, Italy continued to produce powerful and skilful strikers and generally they fell into one of the two types symbolized by the greats of the past – Meazza and Piola. Paolino Pulici was some-where between these two prototypes of centre-forward. Powerful, but very skilful, he formed a lethal partnership with Ciccio Graziani in the mid-1970s, taking Torino to an emotional *scudetto*, their first and only championship since Superga. Pulici – nicknamed *Puliciclone* by Brera – scored goals inside the area, but also from far out, sometimes with outrageous chips. He was idolized by the long-suffering Torino faithful in the same way as Riva at Cagliari. Top scorer three times in Serie A – 1973, 1975, 1976 – his best seasons were with Torino, where he scored 134 times in the championship at a rate of a goal every three games. When he came back to Torino with Udinese towards the end of his career the home crowd booed their own defender when he fouled their 'ex'-hero. The championship success in 1975 was celebrated with huge photos of Pulici, whose goal sealed the *scudetto*. Torino fans still sing his name today, seventeen years after his last game for the club. At the fiftieth anniversary of Superga, Pulici waited until everyone had left the basilica before paying his own, silent tribute to the *Grande Torino*.

Roberto Pruzzo was undoubtedly in the Piola mould. The idol of the Roma *curva*, he was top scorer in Serie A on three occasions and brilliant in the air. Pruzzo had a difficult relationship with the national team and Bearzot's decision to leave him out of the 1982 World Cup squad was heavily criticized at the time, but hardly mentioned after Italy won the tournament. Other strikers who played in a similar style to Pruzzo were Pierino Prati – for Milan and Roma – and Ciccio Graziani – for Torino, Fiorentina and Roma. Roberto Boninsegna – *Bonimba* for Brera – was another player similar in style to Riva. In fact, the two had played together with Cagliari for a year before Boninsegna was sold on to Inter. In Milan, Inter won a title with *Bonimba* as Serie A top scorer; he then moved on to Juventus, who won two more *scudetti* with Boninsegna up front. He also scored nineteen penalties in a row, a record. Strong in the air, and with an instinctive shot, Boninsegna only became part of the national set-up when Juventus forward Pietro Anastasi was injured on the eve of the 1970 World Cup. His performances in that tournament were stunning, including a brilliant goal and the run and cross that set up the winner in the semi-final against West Germany. Unusually for a striker, Alessandro Altobelli held the national team together throughout the second half of the 1980s, and became an idol at Inter. Tall but extremely skilful – his nickname was *spillo*, needle – he is best remembered for his cool finish which gave Italy an unassailable 3–0 lead in the 1982 World Cup final.

Modern forwards tended to combine technical skill with power. Gianluca Vialli was born into a rich family in the farming zone of Cremona in Lombardy in 1964, the same year as Roberto Mancini, his striking partner and close friend. He developed into an all-action, muscular striker, who won everything that it was possible to win with Sampdoria and Juventus. Fast, strong and with a lightning shot, Vialli was similar to Riva in style, scoring with spectacular headers and overhead kicks. He was at the centre of Sampdoria's exhilarating 1991 *scudetto* victory and almost took the Genoese team to an unlikely European Cup victory in 1992, missing key chances in their unlucky final defeat at Wembley against Barcelona. With Juve, he became even more of a star, forming partnerships with Baggio and Fabrizio Ravanelli, and winning yet more trophies. However, Vialli never fulfilled his potential with the national team, after a stunning start. He underperformed in the 1986 World Cup and his behaviour caused uproar during the 1990 tournament when his thunder was stolen by Salvatore Schillaci. After being left out by Sacchi for the 1994 competition, he controversially claimed to have backed Brazil against Italy in the final. Vialli ended his career with Chelsea, where he went on to be a young and brilliant manager, winning a series of trophies before he was unfairly sacked. Intelligent and erudite, Vialli became Skysport's representative in Italy in 2003.

Footballing nomad Christian 'Bobo' Vieri was born in Bologna in 1973. He moved to Australia when he was just four as his father Bob Vieri – a player with Sampdoria and Juventus – emigrated on retirement. As a boy Christian preferred cricket to football, and he grew up with a broad Aussie accent that he retains to this day. In Sydney he played with the Italian Marconi team. Solid and very strong, but surprisingly quick over the turf, Vieri was picked up by Torino's once-celebrated youth programme. It is said that Vieri would stuff himself with hamburgers during his lunch breaks and preferred to talk to the young Nigerian players at the club in English rather than converse in Italian. Torino rarely allowed him the opportunity to play and he was sold for a scandalously low price to Pisa before moving to Bergamo with Atalanta. He has often been accused of being the ultimate footballing mercenary, moving from club to club and accepting the highest wages on offer. Very few footballers in the sport's history have cost so much, and moved so often.

After Atalanta came Christian's big break: Juventus, in 1996. There he fought with manager Marcello Lippi in the dressing room, but also inspired his club to a championship victory which included a 6–1 thrashing of Milan in the San Siro stadium. By now, Vieri was the complete centre-forward, with a powerful shot to add to his stunning aerial power. Vieri was soon on his way to Atlético for a huge transfer fee, just after Juventus fixer Luciano Moggi told the press that he was 'unsaleable'. He had spent just one season with Juve. Since then, nobody has ever trusted Moggi's word. In Spain, Vieri indulged in a playboy lifestyle. It was said that he pinned up the underwear of his conquests on his bedroom wall. On the pitch, he became a star. His 24 goals that season included four in one match and a rare chipped goal from close to the corner flag. Vieri had become the most sought-after player in the world, and Sergio Cragnotti, president of Lazio, broke the bank to bring him back to Italy in 1999. Under Eriksson, Vieri very nearly inspired Lazio to the championship. He wept profusely on the pitch as the club lost out, by one point, on the last day, to Milan.

Yet the next season saw Christian on the move again, this time to Inter for a record transfer fee close to £30,000,000. He became known as 'Mister Ninety Billion Lire'. Vieri paid back that investment with interest in his first four seasons with Inter, taking the club to second place and scoring nearly 80 league goals. Only a series of shocking injuries to Ronaldo hindered the creation of a potent striking partnership. Inter's fans adored Vieri, ignoring his love for night-clubs and beautiful young women. Christian had a very public affair with TV dancer Elizabetta Canalis, and opened his own club and restaurant in a fashionable zone of Milan. In 2003, however, things started to go wrong. Injuries began to take their toll on the striker's huge frame, and he fell out with the more hard-core sectors of Inter's frequently angry fans.

In October 2003, Vieri smashed in a late penalty equalizer against Brescia, but refused to celebrate the goal. Manager Hector Cuper was promptly sacked; leading to suspicions that Vieri himself had demanded a new boss. The rest of the season saw Vieri and the fans in open contempt for each other. Vieri kept *not* celebrating his goals, the fans demanded his dismissal. Christian was said to be demanding a transfer, but very few clubs could afford his massive wages. His national career was in steep decline, and he performed poorly in the 2004 European Championships. Slowly, the relationship with the *ultrà* was patched up. Vieri began to score again and even to celebrate his goals. He became a fan favourite once again, and remained Inter's most prolific goalscorer of the post-war era. Then, at the end of the 2004–5 season, he moved yet again, to Inter's hated rivals Milan. A drunken

Inter fan took out his frustrations on Vieri's posh Milanese restaurant, throwing a brick through the window in protest.

Alongside these power forwards, there have always been the more mobile, tricky frontmen who have graced the Italian league – the heirs of Meazza. Roberto Bettega was famed for his shock of white hair, his backheels and his tremendous heading power. Many Juve fans still recall his trademark flicked goal against Milan in the San Siro in 1971 while English fans remember him best for a diving header which knocked England out of the 1978 World Cup qualifiers. Bettega also had a nasty streak, once almost ending David O'Leary's career with a terrible tackle at Highbury in 1980. Turin-born, Bettega was the linch-pin in attack of the great Juve teams of the 1970s and 1980s – winning seven *scudetti*. His career was interrupted numerous times by illness and injury, which cost him a place in the 1982 World Cup after a brilliant tournament in 1978.

Lazio fans were so in love with Giuseppe Signori that they rioted to prevent his sale in 1997. Small, fast and with a ferocious shot, he dominated the top-scorer lists for much of the 1990s. Czech manager Zdenek Zeman discovered him with Foggia but it was at Lazio that he really shone. His lack of charisma led to his exclusion from the national team, for whom he played just 28 times. Signori briefly became a national hero with his hard-running performance in a World Cup match in the 1994 finals, when he ran the Norwegian defence ragged in the searing heat with Italy down to ten men. His swansong was with Bologna where, as with all his clubs, the fans adored him, forcing out a manager who would not play their hero.

Alessandro Del Piero was the most modern centre-forward to grace Serie A in the 1990s. Small and, at first, very lightweight, he possessed a deadly right foot and tight dribbling skills. He also preferred to drift out left rather than stay in the middle as a target man. In his early seasons he perfected a curling shot into the top corner of the net – scoring like this so often that it became known as a 'Del Piero' shot. After emerging as a youngster in the Vialli and Ravanelli era, Del Piero really came into his own once those two strikers had left, winning numerous titles and scoring a series of beautiful goals, including the winner in the Intercontinental Cup in 1996 when he turned and shot in one movement ten minutes from the end. Highly paid, Del Piero stayed out of the limelight, provoking rumours about his private life despite his 'official' girlfriend. Like Vialli, Alex had a very difficult relationship with the national team. He performed poorly in his first European Championship (1996) and in two World Cups (1998, 2002). In the 2000 European Championship final he missed two clear-cut chances to seal the game when Italy were 1–0 up. France equalized and then won the game, and Del Piero was blamed by many for the defeat.

A series of injuries late on in his career slowed him down, reducing his effectiveness both for Juventus and for Italy. He linked beautifully with Zidane and Trezeguet, but fell out with Pippo Inzaghi, who specialized in 'stealing' goals from him, including tapping in a series of Del Piero shots that were on their way over the line. When Gianni Agnelli died in 2003, Del Piero scored a stunning volleyed backheel in the very next game, before pointing to the sky to dedicate the goal to his ex-patron. Juve's fans were loyal to Del Piero, but his managers had less and less faith in him. When Fabio Capello took over the side in 2004 he decided to ration Del Piero's performances, substituting him 29 times. Del Piero took all this with great dignity and refused to speak out in public, and his performances helped Juventus win their twenty-eighth *scudetto*. He also shunned stardom, getting married in secret in June 2005 with a few guests, in stark contrast with Francesco Totti's star-studded marriage in the same month that was shown live on Sky-Italia. In a footballing world packed with cheats, divers and hysterical complainers, Del Piero was something of an exception. He rarely complained about decisions, was seldom booked and got up when he was fouled. In the modern game, Del Piero was closer to the tradition of John Charles than any other Italian striker, a paragon of fair play in a world of rule-breakers.

# CHAPTER 8

# Managers, Tactics, Fixers

'If he wins he is a combination of Einstein, Leonardo, Saint Francis, Plato and Dante. If he loses he is a sewer-rat'

GIAN PAOLO ORMEZZANO

'Ancelotti is a pig'

(Juventus fan banner, 1998; Carlo Ancelotti was their manager at the time)

'The Italian league is the tactical league'    JOSÉ MOURINHO

Italian football managers live on the edge. One defeat and their 'bench starts to shake' (*trema la panchina*), two defeats and 'they won't eat Christmas cake' (they won't last until Christmas), three defeats and the dreaded sack (*esonero*) is almost inevitable. Managers have been sacked even before the season has begun. Some have been dismissed before their team has played. Very often, managers are given an ultimatum: win the next game, or you are out. At top clubs, the pressure is even greater. A number of managers have gone after draws, not defeats, or after finishing second, or winning 'just' an Italian Cup and/ or a minor European trophy. Occasionally, player-power has led to manager departure. When Milan president Silvio Berlusconi was forced to choose between Marco Van Basten and manager Arrigo Sacchi in the late 1980s, he went for the Dutch forward. Sacchi was replaced with Fabio Capello; Van Basten stayed on.

A top manager is expected to be a combination of soothsayer, psychologist, financial wizard, fortune teller, propagandist and press officer. His every word and gesture is analysed in minute detail. His every decision, or non-decision, is picked over endlessly by pundits and fans. Blame is rarely laid – after a defeat – at the feet of the players. It is the manager who is responsible, and it is he (or she[1]) who must pay the price if things go wrong.[2]

Italian managers are also team players. In fact, they are not known as managers but as *tecnici* – technicians. Italian clubs have – in the modern era – been run by a triumvirate. First there is the president, who is usually also the man with the money, and is the real boss.[3] Then comes the CT (*Commissario Tecnico*, for the national team only) or *tecnico*, who chooses the team and, in theory, decides tactics. Finally we have the sporting director (DS), who does everything else. Unlike in the British game, managers do not decide on transfers. This power is held by the DS, who makes his decisions in consultation with the president/owner (who must bankroll all operations) and the CT. The post-war game has been run by a series of powerful sporting directors, who work behind the scenes but have increasingly come to public prominence. In the modern era, the most important sporting directors have been Umberto Agnelli with Juve in the late 1950s and early 1960s; Giuseppe Viani with Milan in the 1960s; Italo Allodi (with the *Grande Inter*, Napoli, Juventus and then the national team in the 1960s and 1970s); 'Lucky' Luciano Moggi with Roma, Lazio, Torino, Napoli and Juventus in the 1980s and 1990s; and Adriano Galliani, Berlusconi's right-hand man with Milan in the 1990s and beyond. This tendency towards a kind of managerial panel was also used for the national team, where groups of managers and trainers were responsible for various aspects of the squad at various times before and after World War Two. Memorable domestic double-acts included Rocco and Viani with Milan in the 1960s, whose relationship was, to say the least, stormy.

One other key figure was one of the first agents, who specialized in the transfer of British players to Italy, Gigi Peronace. A short, dapper man from the deep south of Italy, Peronace masterminded the highly successful John Charles move to Juventus in the late 1950s and the far less successful transfers of Jimmy Greaves, Joe Baker and Denis Law in the early 1960s. Greaves wrote that 'his knowledge of football and, in particular, footballers, was profound and matched by his financial acumen'.[4] From the splendours of his house in the Vale of Health in Hampstead, Peronace's elegant wheeler-dealing was legendary and he was also sporting director of various Italian clubs for a time.

As the richest and hardest league in European football, Serie A has attracted or produced some of the best managers to grace the modern game. Many of these were foreigners, especially in the early period of the game, and many helped to write the history of football itself, and not just in Italy.

## Managing the *Grande Torino*. The tragedy of Egri Erbstein

Perhaps the most remarkable manager of all was Ernesto Egri Erbstein, a Hungarian of Jewish origins, who was technical director of Torino in 1938–39 and 1946–49. The dates here are important, as we shall see, and not just because of the huge success Torino enjoyed in his second phase in charge.

Erbstein was born in Budapest in 1898 and began his career with a team called Bak, where he was good enough to get a call-up for the national team. As an amateur, Erbstein made his living as a stockbroker until he emigrated to the USA in 1924. After playing for Brooklyn Wanderers, Erbstein moved to Italy. He turned out for a team from Fiume (now Rijeka in Croatia) – the small city which symbolized Italy's nationalist aspirations after World War One – and then for Vicenza before beginning a coaching career with Bari in the south. As manager, Erbstein took Lucchese – from Lucca – right up to Serie A from Serie C in only five years. In 1938, his reputation was confirmed with a prestigious job with Torino, but the timing was disastrous. That year, Mussolini decided to follow Nazi Germany down the shameful and murderous road of legalized anti-Semitism. A series of measures was passed which excluded Italian Jews from economic and social life, including banning all Jewish children from Italian schools. All first and second generation Jews had to register with the authorities and many lost their jobs and property. Now the Erbsteins and their children had been christened as Catholics, but the anti-Semitic laws applied to anyone of 'Jewish origin', a wide definition that also included Torino's manager.[5] At first, Erbstein tried to flee to Holland, but was refused passage through Nazi Germany and decided to return home, to Budapest. Unable to work in the world of football, Erbstein became an importer of Italian textiles, and continued to visit Turin to help his old team. It is said that the signings of future superstars Mazzola and Loik were made on his recommendation.

In March 1944 the Nazis invaded Budapest. Erbstein was taken to a labour camp, whilst his daughters and wife went into hiding. Later, the manager was able to escape and join his family, and they found sanctuary in the Swedish embassy. With the liberation of Hungary, Erbstein was re-employed by Torino. A series of remarkable successes followed, as the Hungarian created an unbeatable team – the *Grande Torino*.

Thanks to his studies in physical education in Hungary, Erbstein was one of the first managers in Italy to adopt modern training methods, more advanced than those Garbutt had used at Genoa. He forced his players to work for hours with repetitive exercises, which they hated, but which led to excellent results. Tactically, he revolutionized positional play, asking the team to use all the space available on the pitch. Like Helenio Herrera in the 1960s, Erbstein inspired his team with slogans and psychology, using the work of a Dutch philosopher called Johan Huizinga. Yet, once again, Erbstein found himself in the wrong place at the wrong time, this time on the FIAT G212 that crashed at Superga in 1949. His daughter Susanna still lives in Torino, where she is a well-known choreographer and ballet teacher.

## The Wizard (*Il mago*). Helenio Herrera

'He was born on a white island in the Rio de la Plata or on the Tigre, nobody is quite sure when ... the world was his country: he chose to be a foreigner, different, everywhere ... he spoke a strange mixture of idioms, French, Spanish, English and Arabic.'[6]

*Pensa veloce, agisci veloce, gioca veloce* (Think quickly, act quickly, play quickly)          HELENIO HERRERA

The dominant personality in the Italian football world of the 1960s was a coach of uncertain origins, who took Inter to glory and provoked debate, love and hatred in the same measure. The son of a Spanish anarchist trade-unionist, he was born in Argentina, brought up in poverty in Casablanca, and became a professional footballer in France. He spoke a bizarre mixture of Italian and Spanish full of colourful phrases. Gianni Brera, who had a love-hate relationship with Herrera, described him as 'a clown and a genius, vulgar and ascetic, voracious and a good father, sultan and believer ... boorish and competent, megalomaniac and health-freak ... he is all this and more ...'[7]

Helenio Herrera was an authoritarian man-manager, a dictator, a man who could not abide dissent, and who tried to control the private lives of his players. If they did not conform to his view of the world, they were out (with a few notable exceptions). Juan Antonio Valentin Angelillo, the brilliant Argentinian forward, scored 33 goals in as many games for Inter in 1958–9, a figure which is still a record for Serie A. His scandalous (for the times) private life did not endear him to Herrera, and he was sold on. Armando Picchi was the captain of the Great Inter, a battling sweeper who could also pass the ball. Picchi paid the price for daring to argue with Herrera. At the height of his career, he was transferred to lowly Varese. One of the few players to survive Herrera's wrath was Mario Corso, he of 'God's left foot', a lazy, meandering left-winger capable of touches of genius. Corso was the favourite son of Inter president Angelo Moratti, who refused to sell him despite Herrera's constant pleas. Corso played more than 400 times for Inter, secure in his protection from on high.

Herrera took charge of Inter in 1960 after success with Atlético and Barcelona – and at a time of crisis for the great Milanese club. After two championships in the early 1950s, Inter had been unable to win another *scudetto*, and had only those two trophies to satisfy their many fans since 1939. Moratti, an oil baron with unlimited resources (the Abramovich of his day), had become president of Inter in 1955, and in the five years since he had employed numerous managers.[8] In seven years in charge, Herrera was to win three championships (including the 'star' *scudetto* – the tenth championship), two European Cups and two Inter-Contintental Cups (an important trophy for Italians). In addition, Inter finished third once, second twice – losing only in a playoff in 1964 and on the last day in 1966–7 – as well as reaching the European Cup final again in the same year, where they lost to

Celtic. This was the Great Inter, and Inter were never to be as great again.

Psychology was a key part of Herrera's strategy. His teams, he boasted, would 'win without getting out of the bus' and he preached something called 'deep concentration' during games. Herrera's ideas were elaborated in bizarre notes written in black, blue and red ink, samples of which were reproduced in the small book *Tacalabala*, published by his third wife Fiora Gandolfi after his death. These slogans were vital to Herrera's psychological preparation of his players. Some were written on the dressing room walls, others were repeated mantra-like by him or by the players. Much of this was laughed at, at the time, or dismissed as 'Mussolini-like' (Ghirelli), but it seemed to work. The *Grande Inter* were a team like no other, a unit that played with unheard-of unity. Cynics argued that the massive win bonuses negotiated with the players also helped.

Helenio Herrera points to one of his famous slogans in the Inter dressing room. It reads 'Class + preparation. Athleticism + intelligence = the championship'. The other slogan reads 'Defence no more than 30 goals, Attack, more than 100 goals'.

*Taca la bala* – Attack the ball[9] – this was a motto that epitomized Herrera's ideas about pressing and the use of space on the field. You did not wait for your opponents to come to you, but tried to anticipate their movements. Still, today, this kind of play is characteristic of the difference between Italian and English defenders, for example. Far from what is usually seen as *catenaccio*, many of Herrera's theories about the use of space were similar to those used by 'total football' gurus in the 1970s. 'Create empty spaces. In football as in life, in painting, in music, empty spaces and silences are as important as those that are filled' was another of Herrera's slogans. His teams relied on rock-solid defenders, but also utilized – for the first time – defenders who could attack. This foundation was complemented by fast, skilful wingers and attacking midfielders – the Spanish genius Luisito Suarez, Sandro Mazzola, the Brazilian Jair. Herrera's enduring reputation as the 'controversial missionary of *catenaccio*'[10] is built more on what was seen as the cynical will-to-win of his teams – their *attitude* – than on the way they actually played football.

*Lottare o giocare? Lottare e giocare!* (Fight or play? Fight and play!). Herrera would embrace all his players before every match. Years later, this technique was adopted by another – much less successful – Argentinian manager at Inter, Hector Cuper. During his meetings with players, in one-to-one talks which became known as confessions, Herrera would try and convince them of their worth. Famously, he once told the pedestrian winger Bicicli that he was 'better than Garrincha', the celebrated Brazilian star.

He also anticipated modern methods with his attention to diet – at that time many Italian players still smoked and drank what they call 'super-alcolici' – whisky and grappa. Herrera changed all this. It is also said that he invented the *ritiro* – military-style pre-game get-togethers where the player's behaviour was strictly controlled. English forward Gerry Hitchens famously said that leaving Herrera's Inter was like 'coming out of the bloody army'. Herrera believed strongly in the importance of crowd support for his team, especially in away matches, and helped to set up an extensive network of clubs and associations. Thirty thousand Inter fans travelled to Vienna for the European Cup final in 1964, and the extensive fan-base of the club today, right across Italy, dates from the 1960s domination. It could be said that he invented the *ultrà*.

Herrera had a long, striking face and slicked-back black hair which many said was dyed. Journalist Camilla Cederna wrote that his hair 'was a bit too black'. Like an ageing film-star nobody really knew how old Herrera was. His wife later said that he had changed his documents by making the 0 (from 1910) into a 6, giving him six years more 'life' at a stroke. It was also claimed that his own father had falsified his son's birth documents in order to avoid a fine for late registration of a birth. After a Yoga session every morning Herrera would pronounce this sentence: 'I am strong, calm, I fear nothing, I am beautiful'. His philosophy of life was built around a bizarre combination of sergeant major and Buddha.

In 1969 Herrera suffered a heart attack during his second spell with Inter. Typically, he said, 'How lucky I have been . . . think what would have happened if the heart attack had taken place in the mountains, and not in Milan where there are good doctors.' Later, another miracle occurred. After crashing his car in the 1970s, he fractured his spinal cord. His response was typically bullish: *I'm alive.* He claimed to have his own, personal, fan-base, and that these fans had changed team – from Inter to Roma – when he left Milan in 1967. He argued that he had invented many aspects of the modern game, and would often say: 'What would football be without me?'

Controversy dogged Herrera's career. In a famous gesture in 1961, he put out Inter's youth team against Juventus in protest against a federation ruling that had cost Inter the championship. The youngsters lost, 9–1, but the point had been made. Inter received far better treatment from the football authorities after that game. He was frequently criticized for his over-the-top training methods and what Brian Glanville called his 'hooded authoritarianisms'. The double defeats at the end of the 1967 championship – which cost Herrera his job and Inter a *scudetto* and a European Cup – are usually attributed to the exhaustion of the players. In Herrera's first two seasons in charge, Inter fizzled out after stunning starts. Doping and 'vitamin' rumours dogged the performances of the Great Inter sides. Mystery also surrounds the death of young striker Giuliano Taccola in a dressing room in Cagliari in March 1969, when Herrera was in charge of Rome.[11] He also often fell out with big stars – Angelillo, Kubala in Spain, Corso, Picchi. In Herrera's teams, *he* was the real star. He was the first super-manager of the modern age, and the first to command wages and bonuses that rivalled those of his players.

The Great Inter of Herrera and Moratti was intimately related to the economic miracle of the late 1950s and 1960s, which propelled Italy from the ravages of the war into a major industrial power. The capital of this miracle was – without doubt – Milan, and hundreds of thousands of Italians poured into the city from all over the peninsula to look for, and find, work. This multitude of ex-peasants manned the assembly lines of the factories that covered the city's flat, grey and foggy urban fringe. Herrera and Moratti – a self-made man and a self-made immigrant – were the architects of the Great Inter team. 'Inter', Brera wrote, 'is the symbol of hardworking, rich and flashy Milan.'[12] The double collapse of the team in 1967 and the departure of Herrera were sure signs that the miracle was over.

Herrera was unable to win much with Roma, where he took over after leaving Inter the first time. Herrera had his own theories about the lack of success in the capital: 'It was very strange. We lost matches in incredible ways. My players committed strange handballs in the area without reason, we let in some strange goals. It was science-fiction. At the end of games I would ask myself: why did we lose?'

He hinted that some of the players in that team were being bribed to lose matches and were in thrall to betting rings. Much later, in 1980, a full-scale betting scandal exploded with its epicentre in Rome. After the demise of the *Grande Inter*, Herrera's career fizzled out. With Roma he only managed to win one Italian Cup, and his return to Inter in 1973 ended in farce as the old guard refused to bow to the methods of old.

He never properly retired and was tempted back by lowly Rimini in 1975 to save them from relegation, and again by Barcelona in the early 1980s. Later he became a TV pundit and, rather sadly, a figure of fun on the satirical-trash programme, *Striscia la notizia*. He spent his semi-retirement in Venice, at first on an island and later in a house near the Rialto. Herrera's death in 1997 was almost as unusual as his life. Four of his seven children from his three marriages came to the funeral, where former Inter defender Facchetti made a speech.

Herrera had wanted a non-religious ceremony, not an easy thing to obtain in Italy, even nowadays. After an embarrassing interlude when his ashes lay behind an unmarked little stone, he was finally given a proper space after – it was said – the British royal family, who controlled some of the spaces in the non-Catholic part of Venice's beautiful island cemetery, had intervened on his behalf. His tomb now displays his controversial 'date of birth' and all his clubs, as well as an urn in the shape of the European Cup.

Helenio Herrera's gravestone, in the form of the
European Cup, Venice Cemetery.

## Nereo Rocco. The God of Catenaccio

JOURNALIST: May the best team win.
NEREO ROCCO: I hope not.[13]

'In Nereo Rocco there is half of the history of Italian football'
GIOVANNI ARPINO and ALFIO CARUSO[14]

If Helenio Herrera was the missionary of *catenaccio*, Nereo Rocco was its god. Born in Trieste in 1912, Rocco was a fine, combative midfielder with a ferocious shot, good enough to play just once for Italy in 1934.[15] Like Herrera, he was not from a rich background, and had worked in his grandfather's butcher's shop before becoming a footballer. Rocco was the first Italian manager to adopt *catenaccio* wholesale, and used the system with great success with a series of provincial teams in the

1940s and 1950s. He took lowly Triestina to an historic second place in the 1947–8 championship,[16] and then led even lowlier Padova to a series of fantastic results. They finished third, seventh, fifth and sixth with minimal resources between 1957 and 1960, and no team enjoyed playing against them. In 1961, at last, a big club called him up. Milan's sporting director at the time was Giuseppe 'Gipo' Viani, the pioneer of Italian *catenaccio* – known then as *Vianema* – with Salernitana in the 1940s. Viani had led Milan to a title as manager but then suffered a serious heart attack and was forced to take a back seat. He decided to put his trust in Rocco. The gamble paid off. Rocco won the championship in his first season and the European Cup in his second. After leaving for Torino to keep a promise he had made to that club's president, Rocco returned to Milan in 1967 to win both the championship and European Cup again, as well as the Intercontinental Cup, football's club world championship. *Catenaccio* had conquered the globe.

*El Paròn* – the boss – was an extraordinary personality. Physically, he was memorable, with his square face, his largish belly and tiny legs, and the trademark tracksuit (on the training ground) and trilby (on the bench). But Rocco was also a born comedian, a bully, a brilliant man-motivator and an astute reader of the game. Stories and myths abound concerning things Rocco was reported to have said, or done. Many of these stories are recounted in the best and funniest book about Rocco's life, Garanzini's *La leggenda del Paròn*.[17]

Trieste was Rocco's home-town, and his favourite stamping-ground, and he returned there whenever he could – usually on Mondays during the season, by car, from Milan. He was even elected as a Christian Democrat councillor in the city in 1948. Rocco's language was peppered with Triestian dialect and terms and he only spoke 'pure' Italian on television. He liked a drink – often in company with Gianni Brera in Milan – and one of the causes of his death was cirrhosis of the liver. In each city where he managed the local team, he would set up his unofficial office in a central restaurant, where he would hold court, surrounding himself with friends, journalists and players.

Although Rocco became associated with *catenaccio*, he played attacking football when given the chance and always filled his teams with highly technical players. At Padova he used the brilliant Kurt Hamrin up front and with Milan Rocco often played an out-and-out striker – José Altafini – and an attacking midfielder – Gianni Rivera. Milan scored 83 goals (22 more than any other team) in the 1961–2 season, and the destruction of Ajax in the 1969 European Cup final, inspired by Rivera, was a devastating display of attacking football. *All* his players were asked to run, press and track back, however, and Rocco had some memorable run-ins with those who refused to do so – Altafini and Jimmy Greaves for example (whom he sold after ten games, and nine goals). Rocco, when he had both players in his team, told the press that 'those two need to understand that during a football game you get kicked, and not just well-paid'. Only Rivera, whom Rocco nurtured and who became a friend and his talisman, was exempt from this rule. Rocco always picked a tackling midfielder alongside Rivera whose job – purely and simply – was to give the Golden Boy the ball.

Nereo Rocco closes the padlock (or *catenaccio*).

Yet there is no doubt that Rocco's teams often set out to blunt the opposition. One of Rocco's most famous 'sayings' (it is unclear if he ever actually said most of the things attributed to him) was this advice to his players: *kick everything that moves, if it is the ball, all the better.*[18] On another occasion he told one of his defenders to mark an opposition midfielder 'from the dressing room to the toilet'.

Bullying was one way in which Rocco created a strong group of players. Full-Metal-Jacket style, he liked to set up young victims for his jokes and anger, and rarely criticized the older, established stars. He was also obsessive about the private lives of his players, following them in his car and checking up on their relationships. Gigi Meroni had to pretend that his girlfriend was his sister when Rocco was his manager at Torino.

During games, Rocco became highly agitated. He was sent off on numerous occasions and had a particularly volatile relationship with referee Concetto Lo Bello. He would scream at his players throughout the game, a habit later picked up by Giovanni Trapattoni, one of Rocco's many disciples. Stories abound about his behaviour on the bench and his dialogue with the crowd. Rocco hated the ball being lost in midfield, and, as his eyesight went, he would ask his assistant who had been the culprit. 'Giovanni' was often the reply, which was a cop-out. Rocco's later Milan teams had three Giovannis.

At the back, Rocco's mainstays were strong, intelligent, rock-like defenders – Ivano Blason, one of the first sweepers, who followed Rocco around Italy for much of his management career, or Cesare Maldini (who was also from Trieste) and who later became a Rocco-like manager of the Italian under-21 and national teams, or Karl-Heinz Schnellinger, the tall German who played for Milan for nine years. Enzo Bearzot, who played for Torino under Rocco, and was also from the north-east of Italy, took many of the lessons of Rocco-type management into the international arena with Italy between 1978 and 1982.

Rocco was apt to go crazy during training or in the dressing room. On one occasion he took out his anger on a bag that he thought was full of shirts. It turned out to be a tool kit. None of the players laughed, as they were terrified of Rocco's reaction as he hobbled off. Whilst with Torino, Rocco would often drop into the bar at the Filadelfia training ground for a drink, or two. He would then take a nap, choosing to sleep on top of the lockers in the training room. The players were under strict instructions never to wake him. Another story relates to a Milan game. Milan needed a draw in order to qualify for a bonus of a million lire each. Rocco spent the whole match shouting at midfielder Morini to get back in defence. During the second half, he had a further go at Morini: 'Get back, or we'll lose the million'. One player had to be substituted he was laughing so much. Many of the other stories rotate around the use of a Triestian swear word/insult – *Mona*. Garanzini has compared Rocco to Italy's most popular and brilliant comedian, Totò.

Rocco was never called up to manage the national team, beyond his double-act with Gipo Viani for the 1960 Olympics. The exciting and successful young team prepared for that tournament – with Rivera, Burgnich and Trapattoni – showed that Rocco would probably have succeeded if he had been given the chance to manage Italy full-time. The Olympic team was extremely unlucky to lose out on the final and a possible gold medal to Yugoslavia after the toss of a coin following a 1–1 draw decided the semi-final.

Brera and Rocco were great friends and allies. They were both convinced northerners, they both loved good food and wine, and they both supported 'Italian-style' defensive football. A documentary film made about them in the 1970s shows them chatting, arguing and joking for what seems like hours in an open-air restaurant as the wine bottles pile up beside them. They only really disagreed over Rivera – Rocco's favourite son but Brera's *bête noire*. Brera called the Rivera issue 'our Stalingrad'. After the triumphs of 1969, Rocco's career went into slow decline. Milan were extremely unlucky to come second three times in a row in the early 1970s, but the lack of trophies led to another divorce and Rocco moved on to Fiorentina, where he had little success. Soon after his retirement, he died, at the age of 69, in 1979.

## Total Football

'Full-backs and centre-backs would turn into attackers, surging forward with the ball, to be replaced by attackers who would effortlessly become defenders. The narrow, limited, specialized footballer would be no more' BRIAN GLANVILLE[19]

Johan Cruyff, although he never played in Italy, had an enormous impact on the Italian game. Ajax's three European Cup victories in the 1970s revealed a new type of football to the world – 'total football' – based on movement, flexibility and a swift, short-passing game. As David Winner has written, 'total football was built on a new theory of flexible space'. In attack, teams 'aimed to make the pitch as large as possible', in defence, they collapsed space.[20] This was supposedly the complete opposite of *catenaccio*, which was based around rigid man-marking, discipline and a mixture of long passing and counter-attacks. Two of Ajax's victories were at the expense of Italian teams – Inter in 1972, Juventus in 1973 – and these defeats inspired some Italian coaches and presidents to attempt to abandon, or at least modify, *catenaccio*. The game against Inter in particular was seen as something of a watershed. Inter had ground out a semi-final victory over Celtic on penalties after two 0–0 draws. Cruyff's two goals won the final for Ajax, in a clash of styles which Brian Glanville summarized thus: 'Total Football had totally eclipsed *catenaccio*'.[21]

Total football was not easily accepted by Italian teams, fans or players. The defensive mentality remained entrenched and Brera, not surprisingly, remained a firm supporter of 'Italian defensivism' and a harsh critic of 'presumptuous total football'. Yet although there was a gulf between total football and *catenaccio*, especially in the fluidity of positional play and the use of short passing, there were also continuities between the two supposedly contradictory systems. Herrera's teams, for example, contained elements of the total football played by the top Dutch teams. In the *Grande Inter*, attackers came back, defenders moved forward and the space on the pitch was compressed. *Taca la bala* – attack the ball – was Herrera's most-repeated catch-slogan and pressing was a key part of the successful Milan teams of the 1960s.

In the same decade, manager Paulo Amaral at Juventus played with a mixed system, a 'kind of total football which was years ahead of the Dutch phenomenon'.[22] Paraguayan manager Heriberto Herrera – no relation of Helenio despite the same surname and initials – won a *scudetto* in 1967 with another kind of pre-total football. Herrera the Second (as Brera dubbed him) preached *movimiento* (movement) in order to create space, but his system penalized flair players, especially Juventus hero Omar Sivori. For Heriberto Herrera 'the individual must help the team, and not serve his own ambitions'. Sivori and Herrera fell out, and the Argentinian went to Napoli. Total football in its Dutch version exalted the vision of its players, but when it was employed as a dogma – as it sometimes was in the 1970s, 1980s and 1990s – it exalted tactics above all else. The players were all the same, all they had to do was to follow the correct tactical model, and everything else would fall into place.

With the successes of Ajax and the Dutch national team, as total football became a kind of mantra, some of the big teams experimented with a new breed of managers, who followed the Dutch way of playing. Milan tried Giuseppe Marchioro, who was summarily sacked after two wins in fifteen games in 1976–77, and briefly replaced by the king of *catenaccio*, Nereo Rocco. In the 1990s, Juventus (with Gigi Maifredi) and Inter (with Corrado Orrico) both tried to revolutionize their teams with supposedly spectacular systems of play. Both experiments ended in disaster. Italians were finding it difficult to break with entrenched defensive styles. It was to take a manager who had never played the professional game to revolutionize the game.

## Arrigo Sacchi and the rise of the zone, Italian-style

'All my players have to learn how to play in defence and up front, and they must attack space'     ARRIGO SACCHI

For years, man-to-man marking – with the obligatory sweeper – had been an unchangeable feature of all Italian teams. The classic *catenaccio* defence was rarely altered. No manager dared to make a complete break with the five-at-the-back philosophy. In the mid-to-late 1970s, things began to change. Luis Vincio used zone-type defences with Napoli in 1974–75, but the 'Italian road to the zone' was only really laid out by Swede Nils Liedholm – who had been a masterful player with Milan in the 1950s. Liedholm, with Roma, lined up his four defenders without a sweeper behind them and used playmakers in front of the defence.[23] Later, other managers experimented with an alien – for Italy – attacking philosophy. Czech manager Zdenek Zeman encouraged his players to always play as if the game was still at 0–0. His teams were spectacular, but they won nothing beyond many plaudits.

When Milan president Silvio Berlusconi plucked a young, balding manager with huge glasses and even bigger sunglasses (which he 'also wore at night'[24]) from second division Parma in 1986, few commentators could have predicted the successes that would come to a club who had not won a championship since 1979, and had twice been in Serie B in the meantime. Arrigo Sacchi had not been a good player (a rarity amongst managers) and his professorial style seemed out of place in the hysterical, macho world of Italian football. He preached a zone-based pressing game, similar to the total football of the 1970s, and was a fanatical supporter of 'his module', arguing that *any* player could fit into his system and do as well as the next. Critics argued that *anyone* would have won with *that* team and *those* players.

Nonetheless, despite this dogma, Sacchi's success was built around a group of truly great stars – the Dutch trio of Ruud Gullit, Frank Rijkaard and Marco Van Basten, and the all-Italian defence of Baresi, Maldini, Costacurta and Tassotti. Given this foundation, Sacchi was able to nurture relatively average players who did the dirty work with Carlo Ancelotti as the anchor in midfield. Sacchi's system was attacking, lightning fast and spectacular, when it worked. Every player had a specific pressing task to fulfil, from Van Basten up front to Sebastiano Rossi, the goalkeeper.

After years of success with Milan, Sacchi took control of the national team in 1992. Soon, he became a hate-figure for millions of Italians, who derided his obsession with his 'module' and his fixation with tactics over individuals. The country was divided into 'Sacchisti' and 'Non-Sacchisti'. Despite relatively good results – reaching the 1994 World Cup final was the highlight – Sacchi's teams rarely played well and his selection policy verged on the ridiculous. He used an implausible 77 players in 53 games (including 55 debutants) and never picked the same team twice.

Sacchi's tactics led to the death of the old-style *libero*, who was never to be resuscitated. When I saw Milan play in 1990, they still had Franco Baresi (the last great sweeper) playing *behind* the defence. The pressing game demanded offside, a flat back four and two or three central defenders. What players did *without* the ball was just as important as the way they played with it. The real sweeper became the goalkeeper, who was expected to be able to play with his feet for the first time and not just boot the ball away. Play was crushed into midfield, and became faster and faster. When good players were on the pitch, this could be thrilling. When the players were simply compressing space, the game became a dull series of tackles and fouls.

By the 1990s, few teams used man-to-man marking, and most clubs advocated a pressing game. Yet, this tactical revolution had not led to more attacking football. Most teams still played with just one out-and-out striker, and the speed of the game had forced out many of the skill and flair players. Football had become an overwhelmingly athletic sport, dominated by hard running, physical power and huge squads, with little space reserved for guile, invention or reflection. The demise of *catenaccio* had not improved the spectacular qualities of *calcio* and many older fans yearned for the game that they had watched as children. Despite the speed of the game, and the undoubted skill and physical power of many players, matches were often more boring to watch than they had been in the 1950s, 1960s and 1970s.

Sacchi never repeated his success with Milan after leaving in 1991. He had disastrous spells with Atlético Madrid, with Milan again and briefly with Parma, where he resigned complaining of stress. In 2005, he became sporting director of the biggest club in the world, Real Madrid.[25] His disciple, Carlo Ancelotti (who had played for his best Milan teams), took over Milan in 2002 and constructed a fine team, able to win yet another European Cup and a championship with a pleasing possession game.

## The Old Breed I. Rocco's Heir, Trapattoni

At club level, the most successful manager of the 1970s and 1980s was a Rocco devotee, who had played with his mentor at Milan in the 1960s and 1970s, Giovanni Trapattoni, *Il Trap*. Hailing from the model, middle-class garden city of Cusano Milanino, on the edge of Milan, Trapattoni was a loyal defensive midfielder for AC (he played twelve seasons for the reds-and-blacks).[26] His ferocious man-marking nullified Johan Cruyff in the 1969 European Cup final. After a long and successful playing career, Trap went into management with Milan as Rocco's number two, in 1972, and took over the full squad a couple of times in the 1970s, finishing third in 1976.

Yet, it was with arch-rivals Juventus that Trapattoni would go from triumph to triumph. He won the *scudetto* in his first season there (1977) with 51 out of 60 points, and the UEFA Cup. Between 1977 and 1986 Trap's Juve won everything there was to win, and more – six championships and a complete set of European trophies (if we count Heysel). His all-Italian squads, later augmented by a few top foreign stars in the early 1980s, were often unbeatable. Although Trapattoni was associated with a modern form of *catenaccio*, his teams – as with Rocco's – were usually easy on the eye and played some beautiful football. Trap liked to protect his skill players with hard-tackling midfielders and he built the greatest defensive unit in the history of the Italian game. His instincts were defensive; when in trouble, he would almost always take off a striker and put on a defender.

On the bench, Trap was irrepressible. He shouted, screamed and whistled throughout the game, although little of what he said could be heard on the pitch. In a Cup match at Aston Villa he jumped up so violently that he smashed his head on an iron bar above the bench. A huge bruise grew on his forehead – cartoon-style – as the second half wore on. After moving to Inter, Trap won another championship there before returning to Juve where he finished second twice. In Germany, with Bayern Munich for a second spell in 1996, Trapattoni became a cult figure after a surreal press conference held in a mixture of pidgin-German and Milanese dialect where he attacked his own players, smashing his hand into the table for emphasis. The outburst is still available on the web, and made Trap into a household name in Germany.[27] Trap was already legendary for his incomprehensible interviews on TV, which were mercilessly lampooned (complete with subtitles) by the satirical sports programme, *Mai dire gol* (*Never Say Goal*).

On his return to Italy Trap's career went into a slow decline. He failed with Cagliari but did well with a strong Fiorentina side. He finally got the call-up to the national team in 2000, at a time when his style of football management belonged decisively to the past. The results were disastrous. Italy scraped through to the 2002 World Cup, where they won just one match, blaming the referees for their ignominious exit against South Korea. Trapattoni's antics had become embarrassing by then, augmented by a small bottle of 'holy water' (Trap's sister is a nun) that the trainer would drip on the ground at opportune moments. Trap's decision to replace a forward with a defensive midfield player with Italy 1–0 up was lambasted by critics and fans at home. Nonetheless, he was retained for the 2004 European Championships, where his misplaced faith in the old guard led to a first-round exit and an immediate sacking. Trap had not given up, however, and at the age of 65 was taken on by Benfica, whom he took to yet another title, before moving on to Stuttgart in 2005.

# The Old Breed II. Bagnoli and Boskov

Italy continued to attract and produce world-class football managers throughout the 1980s and 1990s. In part this is down to the superb technical training which managers are obliged to go through, in courses held at the country's state-of-the-art training centre, at Coverciano near Florence. Another reason for this success is the system whereby great managers have groomed their successors, over time, using them as their assistants after they have retired from the game and, in some cases, even when they are still playing.

Osvaldo Bagnoli was born in the working-class inner suburb of Bovisa in Milan in 1935. His mother lived in the neighbourhood until her death in the 1990s. He first kicked a ball – barefoot – on the factory pitch of the Ceretti and Tanfani cable-car factory, which has since been converted into the lecture rooms and offices of the Architecture Faculty of Milan's world-famous Politecnico. We have no record of his political beliefs but one story about Bagnoli is that Silvio Berlusconi refused to take him on with Milan because he was convinced that he was a 'communist'.

Bagnoli was a hard-tackling midfielder who played for Milan, Verona and Udinese in the 1950s and 1960s. He then went into management, and was able to engineer one of the more remarkable upsets of the last twenty years, Verona's one and only championship victory in 1985–6. Using a mixture of exceptional foreigners – the Danish forward Elkjaer and the German defender Briegel – and a set of undervalued Italians welded into an unshakeable unit, Bagnoli produced a defensive team which played devastating counter-attacking football. Verona were and still are a small provincial club with merely local support, and Bagnoli's achievement was all the more striking for the opposition – above all the Juventus of Platini. Bagnoli took Verona all the way from Serie B to the Serie A championship, and they were good enough to challenge Juve in the European Cup the following year, only losing after a highly controversial series of refereeing decisions. Verona's *scudetto* remains the only championship won by a club from the Veneto region of Italy, desperately poor until the 1960s, but now one of the wealthiest areas in Europe, thanks to an industrial revolution built around small, quality businesses: Diesel, Benetton, Police and Luxottica are all to be found in the Veneto.

Bagnoli was a modest man, who liked to appeal to his working-class and Milanese roots, and often talked to his players in local dialect. Dennis Bergkamp couldn't understand a word he was saying when he expressed himself this way as manager of Inter in the early 1990s. His philosophical tendencies earned him the unlikely nickname of Schopenhauer from Gianni Brera. Moreover, Bagnoli was seen as a communist, or at the very least as someone on the left. He retired after a dignified second place with Inter in 1993, at the age of 57, saying that the modern game was 'not his own' any more.

The late 1980s and early 1990s saw a number of provincial teams emerge from the shadow of big-club domination. One of these was Sampdoria, Genoa's 'second' team who had only been set up in 1946. As with the Verona of Bagnoli, Sampdoria challenged for the title and for trophies in Europe. Although the team was a heady mix of talent, power and skill, above all with the world-class strike pair Roberto Mancini and Gianluca Vialli, the whole squad was welded together by a diminutive Yugoslav of few words, Vujadin Boskov. The sayings of Boskov have become part of football legend. The master of the under-statement, Boskov's laconic acceptance of refereeing decisions – 'the game ends when the referee blows his whistle' – was almost surreal in the hysterical world of Italian football, when every verdict was con-tested. His other sayings were in similar vein, all with a thick Yugo-slavian accent: 'the team that wins the championship is the one with the most points' or 'it is better to lose 3–0 once than 1–0 three times'.

## The New Breed. Lippi and Capello

The real titans of Italian football management in the 1990s were two ex-players with similar, rock-hard reputations, Marcello Lippi and Fabio Capello. Lippi had been an above-average sweeper for Sampdoria who was good enough to play – once – for the Italian B squad. Very good-looking – many have compared him to Paul Newman – it was said that he was 'too beautiful to be good at football'. Lippi's manage-ment career took some time to get going. After running a series of minor clubs (and being sacked twice) he did fairly well at some biggish clubs – Napoli and Atalanta – before moving to Juventus in 1994. In Turin, he built a solid and sometimes spectacular team around a spine of motivated older players – above all Gianluca Vialli – and an exciting set of youngsters such as Del Piero. His purchases were inspired – Zidane, Paulo Sousa, Nedved. In his first spell he won three championships and one European Cup (at last, for long-suffering Juve fans in Europe). The only black marks were a tendency to lose big finals (two European Cups in a row) and the public breakdown of his relationship with a footballing genius, Roberto Baggio.

Lippi was unable to win elsewhere, however. After resigning to take on a new challenge, at Inter, he failed to turn the Milanese club around and was back at Juve after just two seasons away. The final straw with Inter was a press conference he gave after the first game of the 2000 season (a defeat away to Reggina) where he said that the players needed a 'kick up the backside'. This was after Inter had embarrassingly lost in the qualifying rounds of the Champions League to the Swedish part-timers of Helsingborg. Lippi had lost the dressing room by then and Moratti had little option but to sack him. Once again, his difficult relationship with Roberto Baggio (who had moved to Inter to escape Lippi) was a factor.

Back at Juve, the victories began again. Two more championships and another European Cup final defeat followed, this time with a different set of players. Third place in 2003–4 led to another resignation, this time accompanied by a 'long goodbye' complete with laps of honour and love-ins with the fans. His next task was to turn around an ailing enterprise: the national team.

Fabio Capello was a fine midfielder with Roma and Juventus, where he played like a 'policeman directing the traffic' (Gian Paolo Ormezzano). In 1973 he had the honour of scoring the goal that saw Italy beat England at Wembley for the first time. Like Bearzot and Zoff, Capello hailed from the Friuli region of northern Italy and spent most of his post-playing career with Milan, where he seemed destined 'for a desk job in the Berlusconian empire'.[28] He was groomed as a manager with the youth team, where he coached a young Paolo Maldini, but his chance with the first team was limited to just five games in 1987. In 1991 he had the unenviable task of taking on the triumphant Milan team of the late 1980s, which he inherited from Arrigo Sacchi. The results were unprecedented. Capello took Milan to three championships in a row, which included a record run of 58 games without defeat and, especially in the early years, his teams played attacking football of a kind rarely seen before or since in Serie A. In the 1992–3 season Milan won 5–3 against Gazza's Lazio at home, 7–3 in Florence and smashed Napoli and Samp 5–0 and 5–1 respectively. This phase ended with serious injury to Marco Van Basten – whose career ended at the age of only twenty-nine in 1995 after two years when he rarely played. Capello was forced to shift tactics, falling back on the best defence in the world game (Baresi, Costacurta, Maldini, Tassotti and later Desailly). After winning the championship in 1992–3 with some ease Milan achieved a hat-trick of *scudetto* victories by conceding just fifteen goals in 34 games in 1993–4, whilst scoring a mere 36. The same team also won yet another European Cup and lost twice more in the final. That year signalled the beginning of the end of Capello's cycle of success. One more *scudetto* was to follow – in 1995–6 – with Baggio, Di Canio and George Weah in the team, as well as a young Patrick Vieira, who played just twice.

After moving to Spain, where he won a title with Real Madrid, he made the first real error of his coaching career, returning to Milan in 1997 to a team that had run out of ideas. Capello was sacked (and even booed by the home crowd) as Milan finished tenth. After a year's rest, big Fabio turned up at Roma, where he confirmed his place as one of the best managers in the game by taking the capital-based team to only their third *scudetto*, and to two second-place finishes. A strong manager – he was known as Don Fabio – Capello was also able to deal with some of the more difficult characters in the game. He got the best out of Totti and young rebel Cassano, who fell out with every other manager they played under. Juventus pulled off a coup in the 2003–4 close season by tempting him to Turin. In his first season there he won yet another *scudetto*, with a squad which everyone acknowledged was weaker than their nearest rivals, AC Milan. By 2005, Capello had won seven championships with four different teams, in both Italy and Spain.

Soon, a new, young breed of highly innovative Italian football managers emerged from within the Italian system. This generation was best represented by Roberto Mancini. A genius on the pitch with Sampdoria, Lazio and, very briefly, Leicester City, Mancini had shown leadership whilst he was still playing, and had taken his coaching course very seriously, writing a thesis on the role of the playmaker in the modern game. After shadowing Sven Goran Eriksson as a player in Genoa and with Lazio, Mancini took over as manager of Fiorentina just after retiring from the game and won an Italian Cup there before the club went into financial nosedive. After moving to Lazio, he found himself, once again, at the centre of another financial crisis not of his own making. With a depleted squad, Mancini's Lazio played the best football of the 2003–4 season and won the Italian Cup against Juventus. Mancini was snapped up by Inter, where he faced the most stressful job in world football. His cool head on the bench (in marked contrast with his often hysterical displays as a player) made it possible that he would bring the Milan club success after years of playing the also-rans. His first season was promising, and third place plus the Italian Cup in 2005 were just enough to quell the anger of the club's long-suffering fans.

Two experienced managers from Serie A made an impact on the British game in the 1990s. Claudio Ranieri had a fairly successful career in Italy, taking Cagliari from Serie C to Serie A and then Napoli to an excellent fourth place – with Zola in the team – in the 1992–3 season. After lasting just nine games the following season, he moved to Fiorentina where he again won promotion to Serie A and then won an Italian Cup, before a spell in Spain with Valencia, and then in England with Chelsea, where he achieved a popularity never afforded to him in his home country. Sven Goran Eriksson, meanwhile, took nearly twenty years to shake off the label of 'loser'. After arriving at Roma from Gothenborg in the mid-1980s, he took the team agonizingly close to the second championship in their history, only for his team to throw it all away with an implausible home defeat against already relegated Lecce, who had failed to win away all season. At Fiorentina, he had the pleasure of managing a young Baggio before moving back to Benfica and then on to Sampdoria, where his teams always played well but had only an Italian Cup to show for it. Finally, with Lazio, the championship came in 2000, after a heart-stopping last-day head-to-head race with Juventus. Loser no longer, Eriksson moved on to manage England. Always respected, but never loved, the stress of football management in Italy was to be as nothing for Sven when compared to the microscopic examination of his private life that he was to suffer from in the UK. At least in Italy the criticism was confined to how his teams performed on the pitch.[29]

# CHAPTER 9

# Scandals

'In Italy we have never heard of fair play'   GIANNI BRERA[1]

'Eighty per cent of the games in Italy are fixed'
LUCIANO GAUCCI

## Fixing Matches I. Settling for a draw

It is not easy to fix a football match. After all, games are public events, played in front of crowds, and on television, with at least three match officials, twenty-two players and two managers. But there are various ways to get around these obstacles. Both sides often come to a tacit agreement over a result. This 'agreement' can be made before kick-off, for example when players 'decide' that a point is enough, or during a game. Draws of this type are common in the lower divisions or between relegation candidates in Serie A, especially towards the end of the season. Strictly, this kind of agreement is not *match-fixing* at all, but a natural part of the game.

'Settling for a draw' is usually accepted with a kind of cynical disdain in Italy. Occasionally, the sports papers will draw attention to such games by refusing to give the players involved a mark. There have been times where everyone on both sides has been awarded a *senza voti* – no mark – which is usually reserved for those who have only come on for a few minutes and therefore cannot be judged. Moreover, since no formal agreement has been made, nothing can ever be proved.

Nonetheless, betting is still routinely suspended on games 'at risk' of this kind of result. Fans are well aware of the danger of settling for a draw. In 1993 supporters at an end-of-season Serie B match displayed a banner that read 'We reckon this will be a draw'. The final score was indeed 0–0.

End-of-season match-fixing can also take on another form, which has been the object of constant discussion and outrage over the years. The typical scenario is the following. A big team, with nothing left to play for, is playing a small team in relegation trouble. Over the years, the small teams have often won these games, leading to frequent accusations of agreements between players or clubs. The reality is more simple, and perhaps more shocking. Quite simply, nobody in Italy expects the big team to try *too hard* in these cases. No agreement is needed: it comes naturally. In fact in Italy it is often seen as scandalous, as outside of Italian canons of 'fair play', to put in too much effort in games of this kind. It is rare for someone to play for pride alone. Useless effort is frowned upon.

It is not hard to dig out examples. In May 1999 Bologna had nothing to play for in an end-of-season game against Sampdoria (who were desperate for points). In goal for Bologna was ex-Sampdoria hero Gianluca Pagliuca. The game ended 2–2 and Sampdoria went down. In the following season, Sampdoria were drawn at home to Bologna in the Italian Cup. Their fans went mad, reserving their hatred for Pagliuca, and the game was called off after metal taps torn from the stadium toilets were thrown at the goalkeeper. Such anger can explode after games where teams 'try too hard' when they have nothing concrete to play for. Another recent example, which left a long legacy of bitterness, came on the final day of the 1999–2000 season. Juventus needed a point for the championship while Perugia had nothing to play for. Yet Gaucci, the Perugia president, threatened his players with the sack if they didn't play their hearts out. On a rain-soaked pitch, Perugia won 1–0 and Eriksson's Lazio took the title. Accusations flew back and forth throughout the next season, and the Perugia–Juventus fixture has been especially lively ever since. At the back in the rain for Perugia was Marco Materazzi (ex-Everton), who later moved to Inter.

One last example of alleged 'extra' effort involved Materazzi again. Once again, it was the last game of the season, this time in 2002. Inter

were playing Lazio in Rome and needed just a victory to win their first
*scudetto* in fifteen years. Typically, they collapsed, losing 4–2. At one
point in the second half Materazzi was captured on camera, close to
tears, as he remonstrated with some Lazio players. 'Up yours!' he
said. 'I helped you win a championship!' The reference was to the
aforementioned Juventus–Perugia game in 2000. Massimo Moratti,
the Inter president, complained that the Lazio team – poor for most
of the season – had played as if they were 'in a final of the Champions
League'. The inference was simple – *why had they tried so hard?* What
was in it for them? These games, where teams played normally, were the
exceptions that proved the rule. In a culture that prioritised winning
above all considerations of fair play, trying hard was only justified when
it brought concrete rewards. Lazio had played well *when playing well
was pointless.* In Italian football, this was something out of the ordinary,
something damaging and inexplicable. A perfect illustration of this
mindset came at the end of the 2004–5 season, when Torino officials
were accused (by Genoa) of having encouraged Venezia to 'play well'
against Genoa in an end-of-season fixture. In Italy, players sometimes
had to be bribed simply to do their job – try and win a game of
football.

## Fixing Matches II. Agreeing on a result

A much more serious kind of match-fixing occurs where some sort of
verbal agreement is made between players, or when non-players –
businessmen, betting-fixers, club staff, fans – become involved. This
type of corruption does not always involve money. Both teams could
just settle for a point. The two captains might exchange brief words
before a game, or just a nod, or word might spread in the dressing
room. If the result is to be a draw, things are usually clearer. Victories
are more complicated to organize. Exact scores (useful for betting
scams) are quite tricky. If the agreement is to benefit both teams the
justification is at least linked to football. If money is involved, the
moral high ground (the excuse that 'we did it for the good of the club',
for example) begins to crumble.

Nowadays, players have to be careful what they say on the pitch or
on the bench, on their mobile phones and even in the dressing room

as they can be heard, lip-read or interpreted by the tens of TV cameras and microphones that surround games. The authorities have also decided in recent times to bug the offices of football personalities and tap their phones. In 2001 a scandal seemed to emerge when Torino defender Fabio Galante was lip-read apparently telling a fellow defender to '. . . let them score'. Eighteen seconds later his team conceded a goal from a corner with a mistake by the same defender, who appeared to stop playing. Galante claimed that his words had been misread – he had really said 'Don't let them score'. It was not until 2004 that this particular case was dropped by magistrates. During football betting scandal investigations in 2004, some players on the bench were lip-read as they discussed results. Some top managers took to covering their mouths with their hands when speaking to other players or the referee during or after games.

In May 2005 both Rome's teams were in relegation trouble, and both were happy to take a point from the derby. The players appeared to try in the early part of the game, but then a few conversations took place, as noted by the journalists present in the stadium. Nothing else happened and there were few attempts on goal. Both teams managed a total of six shots in ninety minutes. *La Gazzetta dello Sport* refused to award the players individual marks for their performances, although they gave everyone a six for the purposes of their popular fantasy football competition. 'There was no game', they wrote. With eight minutes to go, that rarest of all events occurred: Roma and Lazio fans began to sing together. 'Clowns, Clowns' they cried and 'Suspend the Game' followed by 'Why did we bother to come?' Why indeed? The players crept off to a chorus of boos and whistles, although Paolo Di Canio threw his shirt into the crowd to 'show that it was wet with sweat'.

Match-fixing can go wrong when some players are not in on the scam, or refuse to toe the line, or are simply not on the payroll. The 1980 *Totonero* betting scandal was exposed precisely because two small-time businessmen lost a lot of money trying to fix results which did not turn out as they expected. Players can score by mistake, or let in goals in error, or even win penalties they don't want. Ex-player Carlo Petrini's controversial book *Down in the mud with the football god* includes some hilarious examples of match-fixing going disastrously wrong. One alleged recent example of this phenomenon is worth recounting.[2]

In January 1999 Venezia were playing Bari at home. With thirteen minutes left, the score was 1–1 and both sets of players gave every impression of having 'settled for a draw'. Then on came a Venezia striker, the Brazilian Moacir Bastos Tuta – tall, new to Italy and not yet *au fait* with the language. In the ninetieth minute, and in thick fog, Tuta scored. His fellow players did not seem overjoyed, fights broke out in the tunnel and no one rushed to congratulate him.

Tuta later said that he had been abused and threatened by both sets of players as he left the pitch, and that fellow striker Maniero had been particularly upset. When Tuta had come on, he added, 'Maniero told me that I shouldn't score because it was better if the game ended up at 1–1'. An investigation was opened but there was little evidence of any wrongdoing, and the Venezia players blamed Tuta's poor Italian for what they called a 'misunderstanding'. Tuta was soon transferred back to Brazil (he played just eighteen games in his only season). This seemed, however, like a clear-cut case of a fix gone wrong. Tuta had misunderstood the agreement made between the players, or he had ignored it. The players closed ranks, Tuta was ostracized, and the video of the game was not enough to build any sort of indictment. At the end of February the case was closed, despite what the judge called 'strong doubts' about what had happened.[3]

Yet how many times has match-fixing worked and not been noticed? How many times has everybody involved simply got away with it? We will never know. It is precisely the fact that low-level match-fixing fits perfectly with Italian attitudes towards sport which makes it so difficult to prove or even detect. Italians can always turn these questions around, and who is to blame them for doing so? Why should a team try as hard if it has nothing to play for? *Why not* settle for a draw if both teams need a draw? Why risk injury when the season is effectively over? In the second type of match-fixing – where there is an explicit agreement – proof is still hard to come by, relying on testimony, or the breaking of ranks. It has only been where money has been involved that a crackdown has been possible. Money leaves traces – betting slips, unusual betting patterns, cheques, bank accounts; tacit agreements create no possible proof. Different writers and experts have voiced various opinions on the importance of the weak kind of match-fixing. If we believe Carlo Petrini's version of events, then match-fixing was common practice in the 1960s and 1970s – and presumably remains so today. Others have reduced the incidence of scandal to a few isolated games. The vast majority of players and managers deny that there is even a problem.

One further consequence of the 'don't try too hard' mentality is a widespread culture of suspicion, and all-encompassing conspiracy theories – developed by fans, commentators and presidents. These suspicions have been fed by the ways in which rich and ruthless businessmen have been allowed to build up enormous football empires in recent years, often involving three, four or even five clubs (although never in the same division) and the financial and political alliances between various big and small clubs which have existed over time. At the end of the 2001 season, in a story told by Tim Parks in one of the best books about Italian football – his incisive *A Season with Verona* – Parks comments that his team's triumph was seen by some onlookers as suspicious because Verona's president 'had worked for many years' at Parma. Parks reflected on that match, which he saw: 'If you knew a game was fixed, you would hardly want to watch it, would you? But the suspicion that it *might* be fixed only makes it more fascinating.'[4]

The culture of exchange, of patronage and clientelism, is so deep-rooted in Italian society that results are often seen as *strategic*, and not as simply the outcome of footballing prowess. A strong sense of history pervades these conspiracy theories, as exchange implies that the payment of favours or anti-favours must be linked to similar payments in the past. All of this is complicated by the role of the football authorities (because yes, they can also be involved in various forms of match-fixing). The football establishment is widely seen as having fixed whole championships over the years, usually in favour of the bigger clubs, above all through the ways in which the disciplinary and doping rules have been applied and the influence over and selection of referees.

In his fine account of a season in Serie B with a tiny team – Castel di Sangro – Joe McGinniss is scandalized by the apparent throwing of an end-of-season game by the team he has followed all year. Yet, such shock could only come from someone not in tune with the cultural rules that govern Italy. As we have seen in this chapter, results and performances of this kind are far from rare events and tend to lead more to the shaking of heads or the shrugging of shoulders than to outrage. Italian football is a cynical world, where fair play is rare and often actually frowned upon, and where effort without tangible rewards is seen as an idiotic waste of time. This is not the fault of the current crop of players, managers or presidents, but the historical and cultural product of a world-view that permeates Italian institutions of all kinds. One other area where such attitudes are easily understood is that of cheating on the field – diving, feigning injury and handball-goals.

I have a strong memory of a televised game in the 1990s. A famous international was playing up front. At one point, he found himself near the corner flag, surrounded by two defenders. He fell to the floor, clutching his leg, and a free-kick was given. At first sight, it seemed like a clear foul. Then, the replay was shown; he had dived; nobody had touched him. He had cheated. What was more interesting, however, was the reaction of the commentators. Laughing, they commented that the player had been 'crafty' (*furbo*). His dive was commented upon as a *positive action*, which had won his team valuable time and space. His cheating had been an act of craftiness, which had helped his team's pursuit of victory. Cheating was OK, as long as it got results.

This is more or less the attitude that prevails in the world of *calcio* today, with some interesting variants. Diving and feigning injury and other forms of cheating are *officially* frowned upon, and there have been a number of (failed) attempts to punish these acts over the years (such as the use of slow-motion replays to ban divers and feigners). Particularly obvious dives or acts of cheating are met with outrage. But this outrage is usually directed at the referee who has 'bought' the dive, and not at the protagonists of the cheating. Gianluca Zambrotta was heavily criticized after he admitted diving to win a penalty for Juventus in the 2004–5 season: but for the *admission*, not for the dive. Cheating *is* frowned upon (by the victims, and by some 'neutrals'), when it works – but only because it has led to a wrong decision by the eternal magnet for all blame – the referee – and not for any moral reason.

Cheating is thus not seen as morally wrong, just as pushing into a queue in a post office or failing to pay your taxes are not seen as morally wrong. This world-view, of course, does not apply to *all* players and all commentators, and there are those who have led long campaigns against divers and feigners. There are also players who are known for their 'loyalty', for the fact that they never dive, but they are a clear minority. The *norm* is elsewhere, as it was in the political world of the 1980s and 1990s where the few politicians known for *not* taking bribes were given the nickname of 'honest' to mark them out from the grey mass. In support of this argument, it is interesting to note the reactions of Italian players in the Premiership in the 1990s, almost all of whom, to a man, commented on the fact that 'in England you don't dive' and that fair play was the norm. Paolo Di Canio's image transformation from a flashy dribbler, known to go down rather easily in the area, to a paragon of fair play was perhaps the most dramatic example of all.

## The exaltation of cheating

Serie B: January 2004; a mid-season match of some importance. Top of the table Atalanta from Bergamo were playing Avellino, away, in the deep south of Italy. The teams were level, 1–1, with ten minutes to go when the referee gave a penalty to Avellino. Massive protests followed, as usual, with the referee surrounded by angry players. Meanwhile, Atalanta player Carmine Gautieri had an idea – in itself it was a touch of genius, taking cheating to a new level. Not content with simply digging a hole under the penalty spot, as some had done in the past in order that the kick would fly over the bar,[5] Gautieri *eliminated the penalty spot altogether*. Whilst his team protested, and the referee wasn't looking, Gautieri proceeded to wipe out the spot with his boot.

It took six minutes to find paint and a painter in order to redo the spot. Finally, an Avellino player ran up to take the long-awaited kick. He scored, but the referee ordered the penalty to be retaken because the player had interrupted his run-up. The second kick was missed. This event, in itself quite funny and probably unique in the history of football, was made more interesting by the way in which Gautieri recounted his deed. Far from being sorry for his blatant cheating (and no disciplinary proceedings were begun against him) he was unrepentant. 'It's not the first time,' he said, 'I dug a hole under the ball in the match against Genoa and they missed the penalty . . . I was thinking, if they score we will lose the game. So I tried to hassle the penalty-taker. While nobody was looking, the idea came to me – *rub out the spot* – we can waste time and create a bit of confusion. And in fact we lost a lot of time when the ref couldn't find the spot.'

Gautieri was in a very good mood for his newspaper interview the next day. When he was asked about fair play, he reacted aggressively. 'Let's not be moralistic. You know what football is like? It's the use of instinct, craftiness, being able to react to different situations. It's not the first time that these things have happened and it won't be the last. This is football, and anyone who thinks otherwise has never been on a football field. Would somebody have accused me of cheating if, last year, during the relegation playoff with Reggina, I had dived in the penalty area and won a penalty which kept us in Serie A? The truth is that in a football game you are always trying to fool the referee or your opponents, you try a lot of little tricks all the time. Anyone who says otherwise is talking rubbish, or is a hypocrite.' Gautieri thought of himself, therefore, as a kind of hero. Cheating was not just laudable, but *essential*, it was a key part of the game. It was only after he admitted to the cheating that an investigation was begun into the incident. As with Zambrotta, making cheating public was seen as worse than the cheating itself. Scandal is thus an everyday affair in the world of Italian football, but scandals have only become public, judicial and serious when they have involved bribery and money.

Over 100 years, footballing scandals have led to one championship being revoked, a number of relegations and numerous points deductions, as well as innumerable bans for players, managers and administrators.

## The Mother of all Scandals. Torino and the 'missing championship', 1926–1927

'There is something rotten in Denmark'
                    *Il Tifone* (Rome newspaper, 1927)

Only once in Italian football history has a championship been taken away from a team who won it on the pitch. The 'victors' were Torino and the scandal involved their bitter rivals, Juventus. Even now, there are still calls for the 1927 *scudetto* to be 'given back' to Torino; the scandal remains an open wound. It is also a classic Italian mystery: the evidence was thin and unreliable and no account has emerged as the true version.

The facts: Torino won the key game, on 5 June 1927. Juventus had defender Luigi Allemandi in their team. Weeks after that match, with Torino already champions, word started to filter through to the press of a possible scandal. *Lo Sport*, a Milanese paper, hinted at something and *Il Tifone*, a fascist Rome-based publication, then published the whole story.

A secret federation inquiry followed which found that Allemandi had been bribed by a Torino official before the derby. The sum mentioned was a hefty 50,000 lire. The official was known only as Dr N. Now everyone agrees that Allemandi played well in the match, and, not surprisingly, the mysterious Dr N. refused to pay him. Dr N., it is said, confessed to everything, after being 'overheard' remonstrating with Allemandi in a hotel room. Another piece of evidence included a ripped-up note allegedly written by Allemandi.

The punishment was harsh. Torino's championship, their first, was taken away, while Dr N. (who was later unveiled as someone called Dr Nani) and Allemandi were both given life bans, along with the whole committee which ran Torino. Allemandi denied everything. Dr Nani had apparently been over-zealous in his desire to please his president, who was not directly implicated in the scandal. No team won the championship that year, probably because Bologna had finished second and if they had been awarded the *scudetto*, suspicion would have pointed straight at the federation secretary, leading fascist and Bologna fan Leandro Arpinati (who had carried out the inquiry).

Allemandi's 'life' ban did not last long. An amnesty associated with the King's wedding in 1928, which was also applied to football 'crimes' after Italy's third place in the 1928 Olympics, let him off the hook. He returned to win a championship with Inter and the World Cup with Italy in 1934 as well as captaining the national team. Torino triumphed the next year, but the 1927 championship remains forever blank in the official statistics.

## The Golden Fix

One of the most talked-about corruption scandals in Italian football history was dubbed by Brian Glanville the *Golden Fix*. This was a scandal that never really became a scandal. Nobody was banned, no team was found guilty of anything, no serious inquiry was held. Suspicions remain, but the story is probably more one of an international cover-up than of anything else.

When it broke, the Golden Fix scandal was front-page news, at least in England. Brian Glanville, *Sunday Times* journalist and Italian football expert, had found a referee who had refused to be bribed, he claimed, and had 'blown the whistle' on a corruption scam aimed at helping the Great Inter team of the 1960s in the European Cup and Juventus in the same competition in 1973. In April 1974 the *Sunday Times* led with the story on its front page. The headline? 'The $5000 fix that didn't work'. All of this is in the open, and has been for many years. Yet when Glanville repeated his accusations in the *Sunday Times* in 2003, the outrage was widespread. Former players accused him of being 'a drunk' and of 'mud-slinging' in the direction of the dead (above all former Inter president Angelo Moratti). There was talk of suing Glanville for libel.

The whole cover-up is described in detail by Glanville in at least three of his books.[6] It is a great story, elegantly recounted and backed by real indignation. It is a tale of attempted corruption, and of a Portuguese referee called Francesco Marques Lobo who refused to bow to the pressure of certain big clubs. If Glanville's accusations were true, then many of the big European competitions of the 1960s, 1970s and 1980s were fixed. What remains important is that the Italian clubs – Inter, Juve, Milan and later Roma – all, it seems, got away with it. At that time, Italy's footballing power at an international level was immense – financially and politically – and they were able to cover up any scandals that threatened to slip out. Otherwise, the meekness of the Italian press was also interesting.

Usually, when any scandals had touched the national squad, the press had shut up shop. The Golden Fix had one key villain – football wheeler-dealer Italo Allodi – and in the 1970s Allodi was part of the national team management. But that was not enough to explain the mass closing of ranks. Perhaps the scandal was simply too big. The fact that the accusations were coming from a foreigner grated somewhat, even from a foreigner with such intimate knowledge of Italian football as Glanville (who had, after all, written for the *Corriere dello Sport* since the 1950s). Whatever the explanation – and the very popularity of the Great Inter teams of the 1960s is another possible reason – the potential scandal was brushed aside, and is hardly mentioned in accounts of the glorious years of the 1960s and 1970s. Some of Glanville's evidence relates to an infamous Inter–Liverpool game in 1964. The game finished 3–0 to Inter, and Liverpool complained bitterly that two of the goals should have been disallowed. Looking at the game again today, the goals appear legitimate.

In any case, if the Italians did fix – or try to fix – some matches, they could not buy the European Cup *finals*. Juventus kept losing theirs and Inter lost as many finals as they won (to Celtic in 1967 and to Ajax in 1972). And when the Italians did win in the final, they did so fair and square, on the field, by playing the better football – as with Inter's two 1960s victories and Milan's equally impressive two 1960s cups.

## Betting in Italy. *Totocalcio*, *Totonero* and the iron hand of the state

Italians have always liked a bet – the state lottery is incredibly popular – but illegality in this sphere has been encouraged by strict state gambling rules. At the time of writing, *all* legal gambling in Italy was still under state control. Until the partial liberalization of betting in the late 1990s, moreover, *all* legal football betting was based around a single system called *Totocalcio* (which was extremely hard, if not impossible, to fix). From 1946 onwards in newsagents or bars all over Italy, punters filled out a form (the *schedina*) with twelve games on it (from Serie A and Serie B). Gamblers simply had to predict if each game would be a draw, a home win or an away win – 1, X or 2. Gamblers could also hedge their bets by betting on two or even three possible outcomes. Obviously, these doubles and triples cost more than singles.

The total takings from the whole of Italy were then added up (minus tax) and shared out to those who had got eleven or twelve results right. In 1946 45 per cent of the takings went to winnings, 16 per cent to tax, 7 per cent to the Olympic federation, 5 per cent to the football

A *Totocalcio schedina.*

federation, 7 per cent to the shops that took the bets and 20 per cent to the betting organization, a para-state body. In 1951 the number of games was raised to thirteen. In the early years, the *schedine* were counted by hand and mechanization did not come in until the early 1980s. Big winners became famous, such as a Sardinian miner who was the first punter to win a six-figure sum in 1950. From 1948 to 1998 50 billion *schedine* were filled out by Italians.

Like the British pools, certain combinations of results could produce huge payouts for a few lucky gamblers, or 'democratic', small winnings for many. *Totocalcio* was hugely popular, producing a whole new language (*ho fatto 13!*) and a related industry of magazines and 'systems'. Millions of Italian men, out for Sunday walks or on the beach with their families, could be seen with tiny transistor radios glued to one ear and their betting slip – the *schedina* – in their other hand. *Tutto il calcio minuto per minuto*, the programme the RAI dedicated to Sunday afternoon football, became a national tradition. The beauty of *Totocal-*

*cio* is that anybody can win, and that player and punter interest was kept going for the full 90 minutes.

*Totocalcio* filled the coffers of the state and the sporting authorities right up until the 1990s, when Pay TV (which took the most important games away from Sunday afternoon) and the increasing importance of Europe began to erode its popularity. Alternatives were introduced to keep interest going such as *Totogol* (which relied on a prediction of the number of goals scored in various matches) and *Totocalcio schedine*, dedicated to half- and full-time scores, European matches and World Cups.

However, many Italians also wanted to bet on individual games, on scorers, on the results of championships. They could not do so, legally, so they resorted to vast illegal betting operations known generically as the *Totonero* (*black* betting, as in the illegal black economy in Italy, which covers some 20 per cent of the nation's GDP). Controlled largely by organized crime, with its heartland in Naples (where the camorra became rich importing heroin and through the *Totonero* in the 1970s and 1980s), illegal betting also encouraged the corruption of players, clubs and presidents. It has been estimated that illegal betting activities bring in nearly two thirds of the sums spent on legal gambling every year. By the end of the 1970s, the *Totonero* had become a parallel business, run more or less openly. In some betting shops illegal odds were displayed alongside official ones. Illegal bookmakers would 'set up shop' behind little tables *inside* state betting shops, and collect money. The ability to bet on individual matches was particularly popular.

The 1980 *Totonero* scandal had its origins in the attempt to fix individual results by paying off groups of players and laying off huge bets. There are still doubts about the end of the 1988 championship, when Naples threw away a seemingly unassailable lead. Many fans and commentators believe – without any hard evidence – that certain Naples players threw the *scudetto* at the behest of the Neapolitan *Camorra*. These fans and commentators pointed to the fact that Maradona had been seen socialising with *Camorra* bosses and drew their own unsubstantiated conclusions.

Partly in response to the illegal sector, and in order to offset the decline of *Totocalcio*, the state-controlled betting system was liberalized in the late 1990s. In official betting shops, you could now bet on individual games, scores, and groups of games. Odds were set centrally and state officials kept a watchful eye open for 'unusual' amounts of money suddenly being directed towards certain games and results. In some cases, betting was suspended and investigated. In 2000, a number of players from Atalanta and Pistoiese were found guilty of match fixing – and received bans which varied from six months to one year – after strange betting patterns on a cup match. All of the players were absolved on appeal due to the lack of proof of an agreement. Nobody had confessed. If the match had been fixed, everyone involved had got away with it.

## The Mother and Father of all Scandals?
### *Calcioscommesse* and *Totonero*. 1980[7]

'And what is so new about all this? That football is fake, corrupt. We knew that already, even if some people pretended
they didn't know, or didn't want to know because they have
economic interests, or simply because they are fans . . . do you
really think that the people who run football want to blow
things wide open. I don't . . . they'll find a couple of players
near the end of their careers, and football will emerge stronger
than ever' MAURIZIO MONTESI, Lazio midfielder, 4.3.1980

Between December 1979 and February 1980, two Rome-based businessmen were to be found in the stands of a number of Serie A and
Serie B matches across Italy. They visited Palermo and Avellino in the
south, and Bologna in central Italy. The men *were* football fans, but
they were not at the games out of a sense of fun. In fact, they thought
they knew something that virtually no other spectator of those games
knew – the final result. *The games were fixed . . . and they had fixed
them* – or at least tried to. It must have been extremely strange for
these two men to be watching those matches, knowing as they did that
a number of players, and sometimes managers and even club presidents, had agreed on a certain result. Strange, and also very stressful,
as a lot of money was riding on the ability of those players to fix things
correctly. The two men's names were Massimo Cruciani, 32, and Alvaro

Trinca, 45. This scandal was given a number of different titles, such as *calcioscommesse*, but is best known by the name *Totonero*.

*Totonero* was (and is) the term given to illegal football betting systems in Italy – where *Totocalcio* is the legal, state-run betting game. Illegal punters could bet far more extensively than legal ones, but they trusted their money to people without scruples, who were often at the very least on the fringes of organized crime syndicates. It goes without saying that no tax was paid on any of this betting, and that the potential for quick lire was immense – a temptation that our two businessmen, and a number of players, found hard to resist. This is a complicated story, so let us begin with our two potential fixers, Cruciani and Trinca.

The game-fixers and whistle-blowers were two minor players in a corrupt system: Alvaro Trinca, restaurant-owner and snappy dresser, and Massimo Cruciani, fruit and vegetable trader and fanatical Roma fan. Both lived in Rome and were friendly with a lot of professional footballers. A group of Lazio players used to eat regularly in Trinca's restaurant in Rome – *La Lampara* (where he was famous for making 'frozen fish seem fresh') – including Lionello Manfredonia, Bruno Giordano, Pino Wilson and Massimo Cacciatori. Lazio's president had become convinced that eating there brought his team good luck. Events were to prove him wrong. It was here that the plot was hatched. Certain players would receive sums of money to fix games, which Cruciani, and his friends, would bet on, illegally. Between 1979 and 1980, this form of football betting became rife. Footballer Carlo Petrini, who was in on some of the fixing, also claims that it was not so much the money involved (which had to be divided amongst a lot of people) as the sense of power that attracted some of the players. They really felt that they were above the law. Working together, Cruciani and Trinca tried to fix the results of at least eight games in twelve weeks in 1979–80.

The two men's first fixing attempts failed to bring any reward. A friendly game between Lazio and Palermo 'did not count', as the Lazio players missed the plane for Sicily. Then, a bet on Taranto–Palermo was lost, as the game – fixed as a draw – ended up as an away win.

The two sorry fixers went down from Rome to see the game. The player who had guaranteed the draw promised he would make things up to them after they angrily confronted him in an airport lounge, and even offered them his win bonus. Trinca said that the player kept trying to give penalties away in the second half, to no avail. At their third attempt – Avellino–Perugia – their bribes finally worked. That fix was mediated through an acquaintance of Cruciani's, a former Roma player who played for Avellino.

At this point, despite their previous losses, the two fixers were about £3,000 up. As time went on, the sums involved became bigger and bigger, and word began to spread about the fixing. Some illegal bookmakers started to refuse to take their bets but they went on regardless. For a Milan–Lazio game Cruciani was informed that Lazio player Montesi 'was not in agreement' with the fixing. By then, Cruciani was fixing two matches at once, but his efforts were hit and miss. Cruciani and Trinca lost 200 million lire on one match and they began to suspect that they were being taken for a ride: 'From that moment on', Cruciani said, 'we stopped dealing with the Lazio players.'

The last game the two men tried to fix was Bologna–Avellino in February 1980. By then, they were desperate. Cruciani went to the game, and told the players that if things went wrong 'he would be completely ruined'. Everything seemed to be going well. At one point the players simply passed the ball around at the back amongst themselves – *melina*. But Bologna forward Giuseppe Savoldi scored a winner for Bologna fifteen minutes from the end. Carlo Petrini – who was in on the fix – later called Savoldi 'an idiot' for scoring that goal. The fix had failed, yet again. Cruciani didn't even win on a Bologna–Juventus draw (which he said he did not fix, because it was already agreed upon independently) because he had played a double with another game, whose result didn't turn out as expected.

Not only did Cruciani and Trinca not have enough resources to fix games properly, but they were also defrauding a group of ruthless men – the illegal bookmakers. Moreover, they did nothing to cover their tracks, talking openly about their plans to a whole series of people and writing innumerable cheques in their own names. The whole enterprise was bound to end in disaster, and they would not go down alone.

Rumours began to spread. The scandal – which broke in March 1980 – was a long time coming, and had been brewing in the press for some weeks. In January 1980 the left-wing daily *Paese Sera* claimed that profits from the illegal *Totonero* system were close to those of the official, state-run *Totocalcio*. This was a huge and embarrassing claim. There was also a brave whistle-blower amongst the players. Lazio midfielder Maurizio Montesi was on the political left in a very right-wing side. His unprecedented interview with journalist Oliviero Beha caused a storm. After attacking the 'generalized' system of illegal betting, Montesi concluded that 'corruption exists everywhere' in Italy, and the world of football was no exception. There is no doubt that Montesi's career suffered as a result of his outspokenness.

Following revelations and gossip in the press, a tentative sporting inquiry was opened by magistrate Corrado De Biase on behalf of the football federation in January 1980. Days later, De Biase – a conservative magistrate close to retirement, who had run the football federation's investigative body for years – turned up in Rome. He wanted to speak to some Lazio players – including Montesi. All denied either betting or taking bribes, but all confirmed the existence of illegal betting rings. Suspicion surrounded Montesi's absence from a particularly 'suspicious' game with Milan, when he had 'been injured in the warm-up'.

Two days later, Milan's veteran goalkeeper and former national hero Enrico 'Ricky' Albertosi gave an interview to Milanese newspaper *Il Giorno*. Albertosi admitted that he 'liked a bet' and had indeed backed – illegally – his own squad in the past. Questioned by De Biase, Albertosi adjusted his story, claiming that he had only had a few bets with his friends. After talking to Montesi again, De Biase was ready to close the case. There wasn't enough hard evidence to go any further. Once again, it was a journalist who pushed things on, this time in *L'Europeo*, a photo-investigative magazine similar to *Life*. An anonymous football bookmaker was quoted as saying that players would regularly bet on their own team to lose. This was a kind of 'insurance policy'. If they won, they got a win bonus. If they lost, they picked up their winnings (tax-free). De Biase decided to continue his investigations.

The ability to make money from illegal gambling made match-fixing very attractive to players. Without the opportunity to bet, the fixing of matches (for *footballing*, not financial gain) could only be done through straightforward bribery – much more expensive, and risky, and therefore very rare – or through the exchange of *footballing* favours – especially where a draw suited both teams. *Totonero* offered far greater opportunities for fixers, and was especially appealing to seasoned professionals, eager to make their last tax-free cash sums before retirement. *Totonero* also meant that players could bet on those games that had *already* been fixed for 'footballing' reasons. Many players and journalists knew perfectly well what was happening, but few were willing to make their knowledge public. As ex-player and whistle-blower Petrini later wrote, 'those who tell the truth about *calcio* are treated like the supergrasses from the mafia'.

As they lost more and more money, Cruciani and Trinca began to bet on credit – and when the players failed to deliver, again, they ended up in debt. Unfortunately for them, the people they owed money to not only were unwilling to wait for their cash, but they were also furious that *they* had been duped, and threatened to get nasty. Cruciani's father, Ferruccio, was extremely worried, and tried to get back some of the uncashed cheques which his son had handed out to various players. In the meantime, the family began to receive threats and one of their vegetable lorries was burnt.

At this point, Ferruccio Cruciani went to the authorities. He had taped some of his phone calls with players and had copies of cheques. Meanwhile, Trinca and Cruciani hired a lawyer, Goffredo Giorgi (who apparently knew 'nothing' about football), and told him their story. Giorgi placed an article in the Rome paper *Il Messaggero*, which led to frantic phone calls from various players to Cruciani. Giorgi then met with football federation president Artemio Franchi, whom Brian Glanville later described as 'a man who prefers to be honest'. Giorgi told Franchi that his clients – Trinca and Cruciani – had lost a billion lire 'thanks to certain players'. If something was not done to put things right, they would go to the police. Franchi said he would do his best to sort things out.

However, no money was forthcoming. The blackmail and veiled threats had not worked. At that point, a national scandal was inevitable

– all attempts at a cover-up and a deal having failed. On 1 March, Cruciani and Trinca drove up to the Rome law courts in a black Renault. Later, they went to the offices of the Rome sports daily, the *Corriere dello Sport*. The paper sat on their scoop until Monday. Under the 1948 Italian constitution, magistrates are obliged to investigate any crime about which they are informed, so a case had to be opened, once Cruciani and Trinca had pressed charges. Their statements were detailed, and they named names, but they kept some information back. There was quite a lot of proof to back up their claims – photocopies of cheques, bank records and phone taps.

The legal situation was not so straightfoward, however. Cruciani and Trinca had tried to defraud a series of (illegal) bookmakers and had themselves in turn been ripped off by a number of (dishonest) players. This was clearly a massive scandal – but only because *other people* had also been defrauded – fans, 'normal' punters, journalists, other teams – *not* Cruciani and Trinca. The chances of a successful prosecution were slim. What kind of court would see Cruciani and Trinca as victims of fraud? The very idea was slightly ridiculous. Moreover, the crime of 'illicit sporting activity' or cheating in sport did not exist at that time on the statute book (it was only added in 1989), so match-fixing was not, in itself, against Italian law.

After going to the police, Cruciani and Trinca fled Rome for a few days, but on 7 March, the restaurant owner was arrested. Five days later, Cruciani gave himself up. Both now told the police almost everything they knew. Cruciani was particularly detailed, so much so that his interrogator dubbed him 'the clock' for his precision. Soon, news began to trickle out – first on television and then in the press. In Italy it is common for the details of judicial investigations – including phone tap transcriptions – to be leaked. The story was huge international news. Some players panicked, calling Cruciani (whose phone was now under police control) or producing absurd stories to justify cheques they had received from the vegetable man. Meanwhile, the tax police prepared themselves for match day.

The police operation was perfectly timed – and stretched across six Italian cities. The idea was to prevent the players from agreeing their story. One thing you can be sure of with professional footballers – they will be in a certain place at a certain time, during the season. On Sunday 23 March 1980, at half-time, the eleven players and other officials due to be arrested were all on the pitch, or in their respective dressing rooms, or in the stands. At the agreed time, the police, tax police (a militarized body in Italy) and *carabinieri* stepped in. Milan were losing 2–0 to Torino at home when the entrance to their dressing room was blocked. Two players – Ricky Albertosi (40 years old by then, goalkeeper and World Cup finalist with Italy in 1970), and Giorgio Morini (who was arrested in the changing room after being substituted) – were picked up, as well as club president Felice Colombo. All were placed under arrest and driven away.

At Palermo injured club captain Guido Magherini was arrested in the stands, and 'handcuffed like a criminal'. At Pescara, Avellino player Stefano Pellegrini left the field after somebody told him what was going on. When he reached the dressing room, he found a colonel and a deputy-police-chief waiting for him. At the end of the game in Rome, it was the turn of Italian nationals Bruno Giordano and Pino Wilson, who were allowed to shower first, whilst the injured Lionello Man-fredonia was identified in the stands. All of the arrestees were taken to Rome's crumbling Regina Coeli prison. A number of other players were 'asked to appear' in front of investigating magistrates. The shock news was the presence on the list of centre-forward Paolo Rossi, the Golden Boy of Italian football and the linchpin of the national team's attack. Special editions of sports programmes reported from all the grounds. The news made all the front pages the next day.

Soon, the players started to confess, at least in part. Morini admitted that he had taken money to Cruciani, but said that his role was limited to that of a 'postman'. Milan's president Felice Colombo came clean: 'Albertosi offered me a deal before a game with Lazio. I said no, but after we had won I agreed to pay Cruciani twenty million lire'. This account convinced nobody. The *Gazzetta dello Sport* led with the head-line: 'Colombo confesses: Milan are in deep trouble'. Albertosi admitted that he had asked Colombo about the payments, and added that the money had been given to Morini to take to Rome. Massimo Cacciatori – Lazio's goalkeeper – also confessed that he had received a cheque for fifteen million lire from his captain, Pino Wilson.

In prison, the newspapers claimed, Wilson and Giordano were given 'special cells with toilets' (this turned out to be untrue) and spent their time playing football, reading the papers and preparing their defence. Other prisoners joked with them after Lazio won the following Sunday: 'They don't need you any more'. The players and Colombo were all released together, eleven days later, on bail. As they emerged, blinking, from the prison gates they were met by hundreds of photographers, camera-operators, journalists and onlookers. Cruciani was also in the same prison, and at one point was threatened by a group of prisoner-fans. On the following Sunday, Giordano and Manfredonia – who had been suspended from playing, like all the arrested players – went to watch Lazio from the stands. They were virtually ignored by the fans. At Genoa, goalkeeper Girardi was applauded.

The role of the Golden Boy was a controversial one. Cruciani claimed that he had given Paolo Rossi a minuscule two million lire. The striker, allegedly, was happy to agree on a draw (the game was Avellino–Perugia) but wanted to score, so 0–0 was no good. The game finished 2–2, Rossi scored twice and he has always denied all charges, saying that he had only briefly met Cruciani – for 'two minutes'. The evidence in the Rossi case was certainly weaker than that against many of the other players, and some have later claimed – including Rossi himself – that his name was used to scare off the others.[8]

On 24 April, a month after the arrests, Rome's chief prosecutor charged 38 people (33 of whom were players), including the two failed fixers, Trinca and Cruciani. The accusation was the same for everyone – aggravated fraud. The same day, the charges also came in from the 'sporting judge', De Biase. Twenty-one people were accused of various sporting crimes, as well as all the clubs. Milan were in most trouble, given the role of their president, whilst all the other nine teams faced a lesser charge of 'objective responsibility'. A week later, De Biase dropped a bombshell – charging both Bologna and Juventus.

Sporting justice was far harsher than the criminal courts. The sporting sentences, confirmed on appeal, were swingeing. Lazio and Milan were sent down to Serie B. Fifty years of bans were applied and 25 points removed from various clubs. President Colombo received a life ban and Albertosi got four years (stubbornly, he later came back to play in Serie C at the age of 44). The whistle-blower Montesi also received a short ban, for failing to inform the authorities of the match-fixing plan. He was ostracized by his colleagues and his career petered out in the provinces. For most of the players banned, the sentences effectively ended their careers – only Bruno Giordano, Paolo Rossi and Lionello Manfredonia played on with any sort of success. Some of these sentences were later modified in time for the 1982 World Cup, especially that of Rossi – who was thus able to take part in that tournament, and played a key part in Italy's victory.

Meanwhile, the state trial started in June in Rome (with Rossi and Giordano both excluded from the national team in the European Championships, held that year in Italy). In December, all of the accused were acquitted, despite that fact that the public prosecutor had asked for a total of 42 years in prison, with a maximum of 30 months for Cruciani, Trinca and Magherini. In 1980, as we have seen, Italian law did not provide for 'sporting fraud', a crime only introduced to the statute book in 1986 and modified in 1989. Thus, it seemed, no crime had been committed.

The affair seemed closed, but of course, it wasn't. Many questions were left unanswered, and many players continued, and continue, to protest their innocence. In 2004, when yet another betting scandal emerged, Giordano said that 'nobody has ever apologized to me for what happened in 1980'. Only Petrini and, to a lesser extent, Wilson have shown any remorse for what happened.

One game was mysteriously excluded from the *Totonero* sentences – both sporting and criminal. It has been claimed that this 'exclusion' was due to the influence of the most powerful of all Italian clubs. Carlo Petrini played in the game in question, which saw Bologna at home against Juventus. The date was 13 January 1980, two months before the arrests across Italy. Petrini claims that well before the game, the sporting director of Bologna called the team into the dressing room and told them that they had 'agreed on a draw'. Nobody said anything. Again, according to Petrini (who has never received a libel writ), once the sporting director had left, a club official suggested that they bet on the match. Everyone chipped in and the illegal bet was placed. Petrini alleges that the agreement was confirmed in the players' tunnel.

Now, Petrini was something of an expert in fixed games. According to his book, an agreed draw would normally end 0–0. But, on the pitch, things go wrong – you can score by mistake, for example. To avoid such 'mistakes', Petrini wrote that in a fixed game as a forward he would usually 'shoot from long range', or try 'impossible tricks'. In this game, nobody really tried to score, and the first half passed without incident. After just ten minutes of the second half, however, disaster struck. An innocuous shot by Juventus forward Causio slipped under the Bologna keeper's grasp. Nobody celebrated. Now Bologna would have to score. For a time, it appeared as if the agreement had 'been broken' mid-match, and arguments broke out on the field. Then Brio scored in his own net, and everybody calmed down again. According to Petrini, Cruciani was paid off by Juventus, who thereby managed to avoid punishment. Bologna were caught up in other fixed matches, and docked five points, and Petrini was banned for three years. Juventus slipped out of the investigation.

One thing which everybody agreed on was this. *Such things should never be allowed to happen again.* But this optimism was misplaced. The Italian league was rocked by another gambling scandal in 1986,[9] and a series of other similar – if less serious – scandals throughout the 1990s, culminating in a further investigation in 2004. Even the mass arrests and bans of 1980 had not worked. Illegal betting and match-fixing were endemic in the Italian game. What was really frightening was this. *How many times had they got away with it?* How many games had been fixed without charges being brought? How rotten was *calcio*, and how far back did the disease stretch? 1980 was not a watershed. It was the first – and perhaps the only – serious attempt to deal with the dark heart of Italian football. *Calcio* was not cleaned up. Scandals of all kinds continued to plague the game.

## Lightgate. Marseille–Milan, 1991

Milan's great teams of the 1980s and 1990s were not used to losing. In 1991, after two European Cups in a row, the *rossoneri* came up against a strong Marseille team in the quarter-final. After a 1–1 draw at San Siro, Chris Waddle gave Marseille a 1–0 lead in France with a minute to play, and they looked to be cruising to victory. At that point, one of the four floodlights in the stadium went out. The referee stopped the game to await repairs with three minutes of injury time still to be played. After seven minutes, half of the offending floodlight had come on again. It was not perfect, but certainly not pitch black. All Milan's players, apart from their captain, Franco Baresi, came back on. Suddenly, down on the pitch, there appeared the vast, bald figure of Adriano Galliani, Berlusconi's right-hand man since the 1970s, ex-TV-aerial expert and high up in the Milan hierarchy.

Galliani grabbed Baresi, who then told the referee that 'it was too dark' to play. Ruud Gullit followed his example as Galliani ordered his players to leave the pitch. Marseille came on again, this time without Milan. The referee had no choice but to call the game off. In the press conference which followed, Galliani issued this statement: 'Tomorrow I will place a claim with UEFA concerning the low visibility and the double pitch invasion [by photographers and some ball boys, not by Marseille fans] ... When some of the lights came on again, we were asked to continue, but I didn't think there was enough light, and the players told me that they didn't feel in the right spirit to begin playing again.'

This appeal was never sent to UEFA and Milan president Silvio Berlusconi soon apologized in the papers for the whole farcical event. At the Milan derby the following week, Inter's fans sang: 'The fans of Milan/have a dream in their heart/put out the light, put out the light.'

Milan were banned for a year from all European competitions whilst Gullit and Baresi escaped punishment. Galliani received a two-year ban. In 36 years of European competition a team had never abandoned a game. The match itself was awarded to Marseille.

## Sexygate. Lucky Luciano

Luciano Moggi is one of the most powerful and obscure figures in Italian football. Born in the small Sienese town of Monticiano in 1936 – as was Carlo Petrini, later Italian football's biggest whistle-blower – he was a car-salesman before becoming a scout for Juventus. In 1976 he joined Roma as sporting director, before spells at Lazio, Torino and Napoli, where he shared in the triumphs of the Maradona era. Italian football's most important wheeler-dealer is now DS at Juventus, the biggest club in the country.

In the early 1990s, however, whilst working for Juve's rivals, Torino, 'Lucky' Luciano Moggi was involved in a major scandal. The key players were a referee, Moggi and three Italian prostitutes. Three UEFA Cup matches in 1991–1992 provided the background to the unfolding events. This is Monica Marini's story: 'We went to a hotel near the station. I knocked on the door and a foreigner opened it. We had sex. I only found out later that he was a referee.' Torino won all three games and the three women received two million lire each. Moggi had apparently asked for some 'interpreters' – and this was his defence later on – but he admitted giving presents to referees, saying that this was 'normal practice'. After an investigation by the Turin courts under anti-prostitution laws the charges were dropped, 'largely for technical reasons'. These isolated occasions were not 'constant' enough to constitute regular exploitation of prostitution, and there was no clear evidence to link the women with Moggi or Torino.

The court concluded that 'there was clearly an attempt to sweeten the severity of the referees, in favour of Torino of whom they were guests, and render them less free in their judgements.' Despite this, UEFA did nothing. No case could be made against the three officials, as the whole thing had been organized with great subtlety. Arriving in their rooms, they found the women sitting on their beds. Men of the world, they took this as a good sign, and one thing led to another ('They didn't think I was a thief!' one woman said). Cheating appeared to have taken place, but nobody could prove just who had ordered the cheating. 'Lucky' Luciano remains one of the most important figures in the Italian game, often appearing on TV as the official voice of Juventus.

## The Horse, the Referee and the President. Perugia, 1993 and beyond

'I went to that town for a relaxing walk, in the land of my ancestors'                                           LUCIANO GAUCCI

Five personalities dominate this tale. One was called Senzacqua, another Gaucci, the third Veyer, the fourth Hatith and the fifth Fericov.

One of these characters was a referee; a second was the president of a football club. The third, fourth and fifth names were those of three racehorses (now deceased). This is the story of how these horses relegated a football team.

June 1993: Perugia were challenging for promotion from Serie C1 to Serie B.[10] Their president was the passionate racehorse entrepreneur Luciano Gaucci, a man with many opinions and many chins, a very

Luciano Gaucci during a Roma–Perugia game.

loud if squeaky voice and a big interest in horse-trading. In fact, Gaucci had won the Arc de Triomphe in 1988 with the celebrated nag Tony Bin. Moreover, Gaucci was a former Christian Democrat politician and personal friend of Giulio Andreotti, seven-times prime minister and still one of the most influential men in Italy.

Emanuele Senzacqua was very interested in buying horses. He obtained his first horse from Gaucci's stables in 1992 and later a second animal was traded. However, Senzacqua was also a referee who worked in Serie C1 – the division where Perugia played. In 1993, Senzacqua and Gaucci had lunch in the referee's home-town. They talked – they said – 'only about horses'. At that lunch, a further deal was agreed – the sale of a horse called Hatith – for fifteen million lire. Yet, this lunch took place just three days before a key game – Siracusa–Perugia – for which Senzacqua had already been appointed. The game finished 1–1 and Siracusa's fans were furious with what they called the 'biased' refereeing of the game. The press wrote that 'the biggest compliment that can be paid to the referee is that he was having a bad day'.

Perugia won the promotion playoff that season, and it seemed, after years of anonymity, that the team was finally on the way up. The *Corriere della Sera* screamed 'Perugia in paradise'. Yet, even as their fans were celebrating promotion, things were beginning to turn sour. The Italian football association opened an inquiry into a presumed case of corruption and the judiciary became involved. In 1989, after the *calcioscommesse* scandals of the 1980s, a new crime of 'cheating in sport' had been added to the statute books, with a possible prison sentence of between three months and two years.

The charge against Gaucci was simple; he had tried to gain an advantage by wooing the referee of a game in which his squad was involved. As the scandal broke, Senzacqua was interrogated by the *carabinieri*. Gaucci claimed that the whole horse sale had been perfectly legal. As a back-up, he took refuge in a time-honoured Italian defence. *Everybody was corrupt.* This defence is similar to that used by former Italian prime minister Bettino Craxi in the 1990s. In Italy everyone is corrupt, *so why are you picking on me?* Senzacqua was finished, and he had also 'forgotten' to declare a conflict of interests (his past dealings with Gaucci) at the start of the season. It did not help that he kept changing his story. Rather like his name, his story held no water.

The fans, not surprisingly, were incandescent with rage. Twelve thousand of them had made the long and costly journey to the playoff final in Foggia in the south, and had celebrated long into the night. Violence broke out all over town on 11–12 June, as news came back from Rome of the investigation and probable cancellation of the promotion. More than a thousand fans gathered, angry not only about the possible sentence but also because they had gone through the whole playoff process without any real hope of going up. As night fell, the fans blocked the highway for two hours, lit fires and smashed up road signs. Later, stones and bottles were hurled at the police, who fired tear gas, and reinforcements were called in from Bologna, Florence and Rome. For some unknown reason, a nearby school gym was burnt down. The school president toyed with the idea of asking Gaucci to pay the bill, given his 'incendiary' statements about the football authorities. A number of fans even tried to take over a live televised women's basketball match to make their case to the nation.

Perugia's fans were tired of scandal. In 1973–74 the club had been absolved after accusations of match-fixing, but five points had been deducted after the 1980 betting scam (they were duly relegated the following year) and the team had even suffered a double relegation (from B to C2) after the 1986 revelations, when it became clear that the club had been involved in yet more match-fixing. Meanwhile, Acireale's fans – whose team would go up in Perugia's place – were in party mood, although they could not celebrate fully until a charge of match-fixing against *their* team had been dropped.

Back in Perugia, protests continued right up to the hearing at the end of June. Local workers went on strike, for one minute, and parliamentarians of all persuasions waded in with questions about the case. Later, 20,000 people signed a petition of protest and Gaucci called the whole affair a 'conspiracy with a pre-defined sentence'. The poor horses fared even less well. Gaucci called them 'mediocre animals' for which Senzacqua had paid too much. He wasn't bluffing. Veyer died soon after the sale of an allergic reaction, while Hatith had to be put down due to a limp.

The punishment handed out was severe: Perugia's promotion was cancelled, Gaucci was banned for three years and the referee Senzacqua for life. One outcome of this case was something called 'clean whistles', set up by the referees' association. All referees were to undergo a strict series of 'honesty' tests. Salvatore Lombardo, at that time president of the referees' association, claimed that 'we want to show that we have nothing to hide'. The Senzacqua affair had 'destroyed years and years of work'.

Press predictions that Horsegate would ruin Luciano Gaucci have proved to be well short of the mark. While Senzacqua returned to his work as a car mechanic, Gaucci's football career took off. Far from retiring (as he had briefly threatened, or promised) he took Perugia up to Serie A in two straight seasons after 1993, where he became one of the most controversial characters in the bizarre world of Italian football. Gaucci became popular thanks to his frequent TV appearances, where he made accusations against all and sundry, and for his increasingly weird publicity stunts. He also continued to buy and sell teams, exploiting the rule which allowed Italians to own more than one club, as long as they were not in the same division. Another trait of Gaucci was his penchant for sacking managers. The first woman manager in Italy, Carolina Morace (a highly proficient coach who had been a great player), was dismissed after just three games in charge of one of Gaucci's other clubs, Viterbese.

Despite his more or less complete lack of knowledge about the game itself, Gaucci interfered continually with the work of his managers. He harboured a number of grudges after the events of 1993 and went on the attack after that, refusing to accept the 'sporting' justice handed out by the federation and increasingly referring cases to civil and criminal courts. But he was also a canny trader of players, just as he had been with horses. Armed with a library of over 1,000 videocassettes of players, Gaucci built teams with little-known foreigners, who were then sold on to bigger clubs for huge profits. The best known of these buys was Nakata, the Japanese star who went to Roma and then to Parma, but others included Ahn (a South Korean winger) or products of English youth schemes such as Jay Bothroyd. Gaucci also signed and got rid of players purely for publicity purposes. Perugia discovered a number of excellent Italian players in the lower divisions.

The most unexpected Gauccism of all was the signing of Colonel Gaddafi's son, Al-Saadi, in the 2003 close season.[11] Al-Saadi had never made any secret of his interest in football, and in fact held a sizeable minority stake (seven per cent of shares) in Juventus, who played the 2002 Italian Supercup final in Tripoli partly as a favour to him. However, although he had trained with Juve, nobody had ever imagined that the dictator's son was good enough to actually turn out in Serie A, except Gaucci. Despite Gaucci's best efforts, Perugia manager Serse Cosmi obstinately refused to play the 30-year-old Libyan. A number of excuses were invented – he was 'injured', it was the 'wrong game'. Gaucci pleaded publicly with Cosmi, asking if he could play Gaddafi 'for just one half . . . even if he is not very good'. Cosmi held firm. Gaddafi sat on the bench once without coming on. The case was resolved in a spectacular manner. On 5 October 2003 (after his first 'game' as non-playing substitute) Gaddafi's urine sample was found to contain traces of an illegal substance – Nandrolone. He was banned for three months, without ever having played for the first team. The Gaddafi saga was not over, however. Having served his ban, Al-Saadi finally came on, for fifteen minutes, in a key relegation game against Juventus in May as Perugia won, 1–0. A week later an attack of appendicitis put him out for the rest of the season.

Saad-Ali Gaddafi playing for his team, al-Ittihad, against Juventus in a pre-season tournament (the Aosta Valley trophy), 27 July 2002.

The most controversial chapter of Gaucci's war with the football authorities dominated the sporting press for the whole of the 2002 close-season. One of Gaucci's many teams, Catania, had been relegated from Serie B in the previous season. Yet Gaucci had discovered that in one game the opposing team had committed a minor irregularity. According to Gaucci, Catania should therefore have been awarded the game in question. The federation rejected this claim, but Gaucci refused to accept the verdict and, against all sporting tradition, went to the courts. Innumerable trials and hearings were held throughout the summer. One day Catania were up, then they were down. The press had a field day: *Catania in B*; *Catania in C.* The sporting authorities began to panic. How could they resolve this situation? If Catania stayed up, should someone else (in this case, a huge club such as Napoli) go down? They resisted, and resisted, but the final court decision was in favour of Gaucci. The federation was forced to reinstate Catania, but Gaucci's actions had opened up a Pandora's Box as a series of other clubs also went to the courts. Finally, the government decided to act – passing a special law to sort out the mess. Serie B would be expanded – for one season only – to 24 clubs.

Yet, Gaucci was still angry, despite this judicial vindication. As the next season began, his teams – in particular Perugia – began to do very badly. Gaucci blamed the referees, claiming that the federation 'did not want' Perugia in A any more, They were 'punishing' him for what had happened over the close-season. Perugia were still winless in mid-December and things reached a head in that month. After Lazio beat Perugia in a fiery match that saw both benches and a group of players involved in a punch-up, Gaucci announced a court case against the football authorities, accusing them of attempting to spoil his teams' chances. His evidence? A series of videocassettes of the games in question. When journalists pointed out that this would probably lead to the loss of points under the new rules, Gaucci replied with 'we cannot do worse than we are doing at the moment'. Once again, he was openly challenging the football authorities, and whipping up his various fanbases.

Things became more surreal towards the end of the season. After another controversial game involving Perugia, Gaucci announced that he would withdraw the team from the championship. Four games were left and Perugia had to win *all* of them – including games against Roma and Juventus – in order to be in with even a chance of staying up. For a whole week, Gaucci repeated his threat, before he backed down. Perugia duly won their last four games to get into a relegation playoff. In any normal season, they would have gone down anyway. *The only reason such a playoff was being held was thanks to Gaucci's actions in the close-season*, which had led to the increase in teams in both Serie A and Serie B. Moreover, suspicion surrounded three of Perugia's last four victories. One was against Roma, with whom Gaucci had very strong links. Another was against Juventus – where Juve shareholder Gaddafi played his one and only fifteen minutes. Finally, there was Ancona, who were run by Gaucci's former right-hand man. Clearly, this was all coincidence. Whatever the truth, the conspiracy-theorists had a field day. At this point Gaucci decided to sell Catania – the club that had caused all the trouble in the close-season. Perugia didn't make it anyway, losing to Fiorentina in the playoff. Gaucci's last bluff had – just – failed to work. After the defeat in Florence, Gaucci was back to his usual tricks. All the players would be sacked, he said, apart from two: Fabrizio Ravanelli and Gaddafi. Meanwhile, Perugia manager Cosmi moved to Genoa and, in June 2005, was appointed as coach of Udinese. His first signing was a player who was now 'out of contract': Al-Saadi Gaddafi.

## Doping

'Football today is more and more of an industry and less and less a game'          ZDENEK ZEMAN

'The use of banned substances with the aim of increasing psycho-physical energy and therefore helping your perform-ance on the field'
'Doping', *Dizionario internazionale illustrato del calcio*, 2004

On the face of it, Lou Gehrig and Gianluca Signorini did not have very much in common. One was a celebrated US baseball player in the 1920s and 1930s, the other a defender who had a distinguished foot-ball career with Parma and Roma and as captain of Genoa in the 1980s and 1990s. Yet, the two are connected, and in tragic fashion. Gehrig gave his name to a rare disease, which he died of in 1941, *Lou Gehrig Syndrome* or, in Italian, *Il Morbo di Gehrig*.[12] Now Lou Gehrig syndrome is a horrible wasting disease that leads to the slow, progress-ive and irreversible paralysis of muscles, the spinal cord and the heart. Gianluca Signorini began to show the symptoms of the syndrome in the late 1990s, and finally died, after a long period in a wheelchair, in 2002. Most sufferers die of suffocation. There is, at the moment, no cure. Nobody knows, for sure, what exactly causes Lou Gehrig syn-drome, but there are strong suspicions that it is linked to the taking of performance-enhancing substances or strong vitamin-substitutes. Some argue that excessive heading of the ball may also be part of the cause. There is no doubt that footballers are vastly over-represented amongst sufferers. There have been 36 known cases of Lou Gehrig syndrome amongst footballers, and thirteen deaths. The rate of this disease amongst the general public is something like one in 100,000, amongst players it is 100 times more common. Jeff Astle, of West Bromwich and England, also died in the same way.[13] Many of these deaths were to form the backdrop to an explosive doping inquiry launched by a Turin investigating magistrate in the late 1990s.

Doping has been an official part of the Italian football scene since testing began in the early 1960s. Suspicion first fell upon the *Grande Inter* team, after some minor players were found positive in 1962. In May 1963 five Genoa players were banned for a few games for doping – after three were found guilty of taking amphetamines and another two – including Gigi Meroni – of avoiding the test. For the 1964 season, it was decided that if any players were found positive the game would be awarded to the opposition. In that year, in part thanks to this new rule, the question of doping dominated the season through the Bologna saga, which led to near-riots, acres of newsprint and a lot of bitterness.

Many suspicious footballing fatalities have been linked to doping. Former Fiorentina midfielder Bruno Beatrice's death of leukaemia in 1987 at the age of 29 was blamed on the radioactive treatment he had as a player. His wife later accused the club of manslaughter. His case was reopened by magistrates in 2005. Questions have also been asked about the early deaths of Armando Picchi (back cancer, at the age of 35), Torino midfielder Giorgio Ferrini (of an aneurism at the age of 37) and Juventus defender Andrea Fortunato (leukaemia, aged 23, in 1995).[14]

Only one player actually died on the pitch itself. Renato Curi was a key part of the remarkable Perugia team which climbed up to Serie A in the 1970s. In October 1977 he collapsed in the rain in the centre circle of his home ground during a game with Juventus, with 40,000 people looking on. His heart had given way, at the age of 24, and long arguments followed about the role of various doctors in the tragedy, who had noted problems but had passed him fit to play. A series of court cases looked at the incident, and the players' association pressed for justice. The case ended with compensation being paid to Curi's young widow, who had been pregnant when he died. Later the local stadium was given his name. 'I think his death could have been avoided,' was the comment of ex-Perugia player Paolo Sollier, who was on the field at the time.[15]

Another controversial death was that of promising young striker Giuliano Taccola in the Roma dressing room at Cagliari in March 1969. Taccola had not even played in the match in question, and had been suffering from bouts of fever for months. It is said that he had been pressurised into playing, but had felt unwell in the dressing room and was unable to take to the field. The ambulance was caught in the post-game traffic, and he was pronounced dead on arrival. Taccola had even had his tonsils out in a fruitless attempt to solve his illness problems. Giuliana, his wife, fought a long, lonely battle for justice. The judicial investigations came to nothing and no case was ever brought to trial.

Carlo Petrini, one of the few ex-players to openly discuss drug-taking, portrays a whole world of doping in the 1960s and 1970s, where players were pressurized into taking pills given to them by club doctors, as well as going on drips with substances about which they knew very little. He was also frequently injected with drugs that he was told would 'help him play better'. After this treatment, he felt 'as strong as five men' and started foaming at the mouth. Petrini felt terrible when the effects wore off, and often found sleeping extremely difficult after a 'doped' match. Football commentator and ex-midfield player Marco Sandreani claimed that a bowl of pills was kept in the middle of the dressing room, and each player could take as many as they wanted before playing. Many of these drugs were heart stimulants.

## The Bologna case and the playoff. 1964

Only once has the Italian football championship been decided by a playoff, and only once has a doping case been central to the outcome of a Serie A season. Both of these events occurred in the highly dramatic 1963–4 season. The scandal broke first in the press. On 5 March 1964 the *Corriere d'Informazione* led with this headline: 'Drugs: five Bologna players are being investigated'. Bologna had just beaten Milan 2–1 at

San Siro and were playing superbly. If this story turned out to be true, Bologna would lose any points gained in the match in question, and fall behind in the championship race. The tests, it later appeared, had been done on 2 February after a game with Torino, which Bologna had won 4–1. Five players had been found positive[16] – including such stars as Pascutti and Fogli – and the football federation had no option but to award the match to Torino. As if that was not enough, all the tested players were banned, as was the manager (for eighteen months).

Instead of being level on points with Inter, Bologna were suddenly three points behind, and with half a team. Bologna's fans went wild in what writer Renzo Renzi called 'an insurrection'. Cars with Milanese number plates were attacked, road blocks were set up and a delegation was sent to Rome. For Brera 'a revolution almost broke out'. Milanese papers kept the tension high with provocative headlines: '*Bologna drogato*': 'Drugged Bologna'.

A series of conspiracies did the rounds. The urine samples had been tampered with, it was all a set-up, Inter wanted to 'steal' the championship. A number of Bolognese lawyers (the club itself could not go to the courts under federation rules) brought a case against the federation complaining about the ways in which the tests had been carried out. In the meantime the points deductions and suspensions were put on hold and the championship continued. Bernardini was forced to sit in the stands and used a two-way radio to transmit instructions to the bench. Bologna were due to play Inter in April and the press built up the game as a possible 'Easter of blood'. There was even talk of bringing in a foreign referee. In the end, Bologna's fans showed their sportsmanship by applauding off their opponents, who had outplayed them in a 3–1 victory.

In May, the final appeal verdict came through: Bologna were cleared. The correct procedures had not been followed, and there were some disturbing stories about the possible switching of samples. Bologna had their points back, and were now neck and neck with Inter. Fans partied on the streets of the Emilian city and many felt that their conspiracy theories had been vindicated.

More drama was to come as legendary self-made textile millionaire and Bologna president Renato Dall'Ara travelled to Milan in June for a federation meeting. Dall'Ara had taken his club to a series of titles in the 1930s but had a weak heart and had been told by a series of doctors to take things easy. In Milan he got into an argument with Inter president Angelo Moratti over player bonuses. Suddenly Dall'Ara collapsed. There was nothing to be done and he died almost in Moratti's arms. Vittorio Pozzo wrote with a typical rhetorical flourish that he had died 'like a soldier'.

Four days later on 7 June Serie A's only playoff was held in Rome in front of 60,000 fans, many of whom wore black armbands in memory of Dall'Ara. Bologna were clearly the better team in the searing heat and won through a Fogli goal and a second from the Dane Nielsen. It was said that Inter's players were exhausted after their triumph in the European Cup at the end of May, but they had had ten days to prepare for the playoff. At the end of the game Fulvio Bernardini made the 'umbrella gesture', although he later claimed that it was directed at a Roman supporter who had 'insulted him for the whole game' (Brera).[17] Bernardini – the Brian Clough of Italian football – had done it again, winning his second championship outside of the big cities after his triumph with Fiorentina in 1956.

The truth of the whole affair has never come out. Helenio Herrera wrote in 1982 that Bernardini had promised to reveal everything to him 'before he died'. Herrera was still angry about the whole affair, 24 years on. Bologna captain Giacomo Bulgarelli was of a different opinion. 'We were the best team,' he said; 'the level of the drugs which they had "found" was enough to kill a horse. Without the "doping" episode we would not have needed a play-off.'[18]

## Zemangate and the Guaraniello inquiry. Juventus on trial

*Agnelli spacciatore* – Roma banner: *Agnelli pusher*

Zdenek Zeman is not an attractive character, although his teams tend to play attractive football. Quietly spoken and a chain-smoker, he stands out even in the weird world of Italian football. As manager of Palermo's youth teams in the 1970s, he dismissed the mafia as a 'minor problem'. In 1998, Zeman shocked the world of football with a series of statements (published as an interview in the weekly magazine *L'Espresso*) that led to the most sensational doping investigation and trial in Italian football history. The interview followed a series of doping scandals in the world of cycling. 'Football must get out of the pharmacy,' Zeman said, 'there are too many drugs around.' One subject of Zeman's accusations was the most powerful club in the country – Juventus. He expressed surprise, for example, at the 'muscular explosion' of Alessandro Del Piero.[19] These statements led to angry denials from the Juve players. Gianluca Vialli called the Czech a 'terrorist', and manager Marcello Lippi demanded that the Czech be given a five-year ban. A series of libel cases were filed.

However, the outburst caught the eye of a well-known and meticulous Turinese investigating magistrate, Raffaele Guariniello, who had been one of the few people in Italy to stand up to FIAT. In the 1970s, Guariniello had unveiled the shocking fact that the huge car multi-national kept hundreds of thousands of illegal political and personal files on its employees. This time, he decided to open up another Pandora's Box. He interviewed Zeman, seized medical records and carried out an inquiry which lasted for two full years, and was widened to include some of football's many suspicious deaths. In the end, the evidence accumulated was enough to send Juventus to trial: for 'sporting fraud' and the 'illegal use of medicines'.[20] Guariniello claimed that the increasing physical stress and speed of the modern game had led to widespread use of sophisticated medical substances, especially at the higher levels of football.

In 2002 the trial for 'sporting fraud' opened in Turin, and it closed only in 2005. A procession of stars, trainers, doctors, agents and journalists were brought in to testify. Many players took refuge in a series of 'don't knows' and 'I can't remember' replies which so irritated the presiding judge that he took them to task on a number of occasions. Past and present Juventus stars only admitted to taking different kinds of 'vitamins' and 'pain-killers'. Three personalities were on trial: Juventus president Antonio Giraudo, the club doctor Riccardo Agricola and a Turinese pharmacist who provided most of the drugs. Zinedine Zidane later admitted to taking *creatina*, which was not on the list of banned substances.

Furious Juventus officials adopted a three-pronged defence. The substances they had given their players were *not* illegal, they had told the football authorities everything and, in any case, Guariniello was persecuting *them*. Why were the other clubs not on trial? The answer was historical. Only Guariniello had the courage to take on a big club in this way – and as he said, laconically, 'I work in Turin'. Other judges in other cities had simply ignored the issue. On this last argument, the club had a point, but the rest of the Juventus defence simply did not stand up. The magistrate produced a three-page document of unauthorized medicines used by Juve between 1994 and 1998 – with names ranging from Adalat to Zovirax.[21] Juventus and other clubs had also regularly broken the rule whereby they were supposed to inform the authorities of all medicines used. There were also strong suspicions that the anti-doping centre – based in Turin – had covered up or manipulated positive tests, and destroyed records. The damage to the club's reputation was immense, and revealed a formerly secret world where players spent as much time with doctors as they did on the pitch.

In November 2004, the sensational judgement came in. The Juventus doctor was guilty of supplying and administering illegal substances, including the banned substance EPO, although the club itself escaped direct punishment. This was a typical Italian compromise. The court had found that doping had taken place, involving Juventus, but they couldn't prove the club had *ordered* the drug use. Juventus appealed whilst Zeman felt that his earlier comments had been justified. There were calls for the trophies won by the club under Lippi (three championships) to be taken away. When Zeman's Lecce came to play Juve in Turin in April 2005, the Czech was subjected to sickening abuse from the home fans for the whole game. He commented that he had thought that Turin was a 'civil' city. Later in 2005 a shocking home video was leaked to the press which showed Fabio Cannavaro, then with Parma, injecting himself with something before a big game some years earlier. Cannavaro claimed that the substance had been 'vitamins'. In December 2005, however, the appeal verdict came in. Everybody at Juventus was absolved of the crime of 'sporting fraud'. The appeal court decided that the law at the time did not see what had happened as a crime, and that the EPO had not been used. Antonio Giraudo was joyous, claiming that 'justice has been done'.

For years, it was clear that the dope-testing system was fixed, or was easy to get around. One classic ruse was for players to hand over other people's urine. Napoli have since admitted to using this system to protect Maradona in the late 1980s, and Carlo Petrini also acknowledged that such practices were widespread. In the 1990s, it emerged that numerous records relating to anti-doping tests had been manipulated, or simply 'lost' from the anti-doping centre right next to Juventus's training ground in Turin and another centre in Rome.

In the 1990s a number of big-name players were found positive after dope tests. Maradona and Caniggia were both banned for cocaine use and Italian internationals Peruzzi and Carnevale of Roma were given long bans after traces of stimulants were found in their samples. In 2001, the steroid Nandrolone became the favourite drug: Jaap Stam, Edgar Davids, Fernando Couto and others were the guilty parties here, although their bans were much reduced from those given out in the past, amounting to as little as four months in the case of Davids. Colonel Gaddafi's son Al-Saadi was found positive in January 2004, despite never having played for his team, Perugia. All of these players angrily professed themselves totally innocent, but all served their bans without too much fuss. In 2004, blood tests were introduced in a supposed crackdown. Most fans had no faith in the system, and were firm believers that players were 'found positive' only as a result of power games and conspiracies. Napoli fans, for example, were convinced that Maradona's positive dope test in 1991 only came as his playing worth declined, and was a convenient way to get rid of him just as he was becoming an embarrassment. Maradona himself later admitted taking cocaine throughout his time with Napoli. It was difficult to have faith in a testing campaign where hundreds of records had gone missing, and where the truth had only begun to emerge thanks to someone from outside the world of football: investigating magistrate Raffaele Guariniello.

## Ci Risiamo – Here we go again. The latest betting scandal, 2003–2004 season

It was widely believed at the time that the huge *Totonero* scandal had killed off betting rings involving players, especially given the swingeing sentences handed out to important stars and the increasingly high wages earned in the game. Who in their right mind would risk fame, fortune and their reputation for a small bet, especially when they were all so rich anyway? This confidence was misplaced. It was not long before more betting scandals exploded. The problem was endemic, and cultural, not financial. In 1986, 1990 and then again towards the end of the 2003–4 season, betting scandals rocked the Italian football world.

In May 2004, a number of clubs and players were investigated for the organization of match-fixing and betting rings. A number of bets had been laid both legally and illegally after agreement on results across all of the divisions. *La Gazzetta dello Sport* led with a huge headline; 'Here we go again. The nightmare of the *calcioscommesse*'. The investigation began with anti-mafia magistrates in Naples and quickly spread to other cities, with the use of phone-taps, the analysis of betting patterns and videos of games, and even the lip-reading of players chatting on the bench. At least eight games were involved, and three Serie A clubs, and everything seemed to centre – once again – on Naples and the camorra. In the end, concrete proof of match-fixing did not emerge. A few minor players and small clubs were given a slap on the wrist – small fines, short bans, minor point deductions. The football authorities, terrified of another series of court cases, decided to wrap up the scandal as soon as possible. There was no repeat of the drama of 1980. Nonetheless, confidence in the world of football was reduced to an all-time low.

Then, in June 2005, came perhaps the most spectacular scandal of recent years. Enrico Preziosi, the games billionaire who had invented 'Hunt the Ref', had taken over Genoa in 2003. He proceeded to invest a small fortune in a creating a team good enough to return to Serie A, after ten years in the doldrums. Towards the end of the season, however, his side began to stutter. They were held to a draw at Piacenza in a game which ended in violence on and off the pitch, and needed to beat already-relegated Venezia at home in the last match of the season to secure promotion. The game itself was dramatic, as Venezia took the lead before Genoa finally won 3–2, sparking celebrations throughout the port city. Three days after the game, following a series of phone-taps by police, a Venezia manager – Giuseppe Pagliara – was stopped by *carabinieri* leaving one of Preziosi's factories. In his car were two yellow envelopes containing €250,000. Suspicion had been raised by the fact that fifteen Venezia players had called in sick or injured before the Genoa game, and had not made the trip, and that their goalkeeper – who was playing a blinder – had been substituted at half-time. Pagliara's defence was that the money was an illegal payment for a Venezia player. Venezia were bankrupt, and had been unable to even pay their staff towards the end of the season. Both the sporting authorities and the judiciary opened investigations. Phone-taps appeared to show that the game in question had been fixed. On 28 July, the sporting authorities found against Genoa, who not only saw their promotion revoked, but were sent down to Serie C1, with the added penalty of a three-point deduction. Enrico Preziosi was banned for five years from football, and resigned as president minutes after the sentence was issued.

For the fifth time in 24 years, betting, match-fixing and financial scandals had brought the Italian football championship into question. The system was rotten. A season which had begun in scandal had ended in scandal – and another summer of uncertainty, court cases and appeals beckoned. Very few teams were able to balance their books, and many risked exclusion or relegation for financial irregularities. Italian football was not just going through yet another temporary setback, but was in what Antonio Gramsci once called an *organic crisis*, from which there was little chance of a dignified or brief exit.[22]

## CHAPTER 10

# The Media

'Football is the most beautiful game in the world for all those who love it. Unfortunately, or fortunately, not all those who love football are able to understand it'   GIANNI BRERA

## The Press

Any account of the Italian sporting press should begin with 'the pink paper', *La Gazzetta dello Sport*, Italy's best-loved, most-read and most important sports daily. Founded in 1896, for a long time *La Gazzetta* concentrated on other sports to a far greater extent than *calcio* – above all cycling and hunting. In fact, the paper organized the *Giro d'Italia* – Italy's version of the *Tour de France* – in which the leader of the race wears a pink jersey, as in the colour of the *Gazzetta*'s newsprint. It was not until the 1930s that football started to challenge these sports in terms of national popularity. The *Gazzetta* was somewhat 'fascistised' in the 1930s, and came out accompanied by a supplement called *Fascist Sport*.

The pink paper is not the only Italian sports daily. On today's news-stands you can find two others – the *Corriere dello Sport*, born before the war, in 1924, and based in Rome, and *Tuttosport*, born after the war, in 1945, and based in Turin. In addition, there are the weeklies and monthlies – *Guerin Sportivo* (founded in 1912), the glossy *Calcio 2000* and many others, including numerous popular club magazines. In the past, one of the most popular genres of magazine in a pre-television age was the sport-photo magazine, most importantly *Sport Illustrato.*

Italian football journalism has a long and glorious literary and intellectual tradition, beginning with Bruno Roghi, who was known as the 'poet of sport' or the 'D'Annunzio of the 90 minutes'.[1] As editor of the pink paper from 1936 to 1943 and then again after the war, Roghi presided over the boom in Italian football and was the first sports journalist to become a household name. Roghi had spent time as a war reporter in Ethiopia in the 1930s and his prose was celebrated for its rhetoric, as in this phrase used to describe a goal for Italy against Germany in 1936: 'the crowd was hushed as if it had been hit with the point of a foil'.

Italian sports newspapers are still going strong. The *Corriere dello Sport-Stadio* sells 240,000 copies a day with an extra 80,000 on Mondays. *La Gazzetta dello Sport* shifts 362,000 copies and half a million on Mondays whilst *Tuttosport* (whose main focus remains the two Turin clubs) sells 130,000 copies which rises to 142,000 on Mondays. *Controcampo*, launched in 2002, is Silvio Berlusconi's recent response to *La Gazzetta*, and is heavily publicized for free on his three Mediaset national channels. In Italy, sports newspapers can always be found in bars, when they are read and re-folded by dozens of customers every day, so the gap between buyers and readers is particularly wide.

## Journalists. From Gianni Brera to Antonio Ghirelli[2]

> 'Brera was imitated, debated, loved. With him people learned how to write, how to eat well, how to drink better, how to live life'
>
> GIAN PAOLO ORMEZZANO[3]

Of all Italian sports journalists, only one figure has been revered and despised in equal measure. Gianni Brera invented a completely new language for talking about football. He has had books, plays and songs written *about* him and found time to translate three plays by Molière and write four novels. Brera was able to shape debates, rewrite whole tournaments and mould a series of myths around various footballing events and personalities. *Gioannbrerafucarlo* (he liked to sign his name this way – meaning *JohnBrerausedtobecalledCarlo*) was a 'writer pretending to be a journalist'.[4] His prose was beautiful – smooth, witty, educated, clear. He was a writer 'whose subject happens to be sport' (Brian Glanville).

Brera was born in 1919 in the small Pavese town of San Zenone Po, just south of Milan, on the rice fields of the flat Po plain. His father was a tailor and barber but Gianni Brera moved in other circles, graduating in political science in 1942 with a thesis on More's *Utopia* – before moving at a very young age into sports journalism. In 1944 he joined the anti-fascist partisans in the Val D'Ossola in Northern Piedmont where, in his words, he 'never fired a shot, but was fired upon many times'. In 1950, at the age of just 30, he became director (editor) of the *Gazzetta*. Brera's origins were important. He always thought of himself as 'Padanian', not Italian, and had bizarre ideas about the south of Italy and the 'races' who made up the peninsula. He was extremely attached to his home town and region and never really left it.

Gianni Brera playing football in the Arena stadium, 16 March 1960, Milan.

Working mainly in Milan – the capital of Italian football and of Italian journalism, then as now – Brera devised a brilliant ruse in order to escape from the Milan-or-Inter question, which would have put him irredeemably in one camp or the other in a divided football city. He claimed he was a Genoa fan. This lie – he later admitted – allowed him to write more freely without taking sides. It was not clear which team he really supported, although he had a soft spot for *both* Milanese clubs. Nonetheless, many Milan fans were fiercely opposed to Brera thanks to his frequent and savage criticisms of their favourite player – Gianni Rivera. This violent opposition did not prevent them buying newspapers purely to read Brera. Journalist and writer Oreste del Buono wrote that 'he made himself hated, as a real critic should be'. Over the years, Brera built up huge numbers of faithful readers through his many columns in *La Gazzetta*, the *Guerin Sportivo*, *Il Giorno* and *La Repubblica*.

It was the long and endless debate over tactics that really marked out Brera. A committed 'defensivist', he argued that a perfect game would end 0–0. His heroes were either defenders – Picchi, Burgnich, Facchetti – or strong, old-style forwards – Piola, Riva. He claimed that the 'natural' weakness of the Italian physique meant that Italian teams should play a counter-attacking, defensive game, preserving their energy. These rather eccentric, almost racial theories were backed by a tactical aversion to new systems of play, especially the attacking methods made popular by Arsenal in the 1930s and the *Grande Torino* side of the 1940s. Brera loved *catenaccio* – which he dubbed 'Holy'. His manager-heroes were the proponents of *catenaccio* – in particular Nereo Rocco, with whom he built up a close friendship, but also Enzo Bearzot and Giovanni Trapattoni. Brera's realist vision of football came from his plebeian roots, in the hardworking flat plains of the Po Valley. Success was about waiting for the right moment, physical strength and survival, and nothing to do with tricky Brazilian-beach wing-play or Dutch total football. Football was anthropology, and the anthropology of Brera's home town was light years away from that of Pelé, Garrincha and Johan Cruyff.

His polemics were often vicious, and he was not afraid to get personal. His monumental, one-sided and opinionated *Storia critica del calcio italiano* (which takes the story of Italian football up to the 1980s) is packed with gossip, overheard stories and (unsubstantiated) personal asides. Many of the myths about Italian football are taken from that book – which journalist Darwin Pastorin has called 'the *War and Peace* of Italian football'. It is not a work of history, although it is usually seen as such. Brera's *Storia*, like his journalism, is a mixture of auto-biography, poetry, pen-portraits, gossip and prejudice.

Most of all, Brera is celebrated for his invention of a new language. Over the years he made up words for players, moments in games and numerous other aspects of football.[5] Many of these phrases were so apt, and powerful, or funny, that they have become part of the Italian language, and not just football parlance. *Melina* – the word for passing the ball uselessly around at the back – is one of his inventions. Brera invented nicknames that stuck – *Thunder* for Riva, *Abatino* for Rivera – and even became part of the personality of the players involved. As such, Brera was a true original – someone who simply could not and cannot be copied. Whole dictionaries have been published of *Brerian* – the *calcio* language of Gianni Brera. Very few writers have added quite so many words to a spoken and written language, and nobody before or since has written with such style, panache and originality about what was once the 'beautiful game'.

Apart from sport (and Brera adored cycling as well as football) the other loves of Brera's life were mostly to be found at the dinner table – wine and conversation. He set up a woman-free 'Thursday club' (wives were allowed to come once a year) in a central Milanese restaurant that was attended by players, journalists and – usually – Rocco. The wine bottles would pile up as the evening went on. A common criticism of Brera was that he was a drunk – a comment made by both Herrera and Rivera. On one occasion, Rocco – then manager of Milan – wrote down the team for an impending derby on a tablecloth. Brera published the scoop, which went down badly with his fellow journalists, who claimed that Rocco was giving his friend preferential treatment. Small and very plump, with a pipe permanently hanging from his lips, Brera was certainly no athlete, although he had played football in his youth, as well as dabbling in boxing.

Although Brera's criticisms of Rivera and others were ferocious, he was (secretly) a great admirer of the Milan midfielder. He later claimed that his censure had been played-up in order to sell more copies: 'I pretend to criticize those I admire'. He certainly did shift a lot of papers, especially whilst working for the innovative broadsheet newspaper *Il Giorno*, founded in Milan by state-oil-magnate Enrico Mattei in 1954. *Il Giorno* used new graphical techniques – photos above all – to break with the conservatism of the Italian press. Brera was its star writer, and sales when he was writing increased noticeably.

Arguments with other journalists were also frequent and often violent. Brera notoriously had a punch-up with distinguished sports writer
Gino Palumbo in the stands in Brescia before a game. Palumbo was
a great Rivera supporter, and a proponent of attacking play, which
placed him in direct opposition with Brera's world-view of *calcio*. The
rivalry got personal (and almost racist) with Brera calling attention
to Palumbo's Neapolitan origins. Another journalist later wrote that
'Palumbo and Brera disagreed on everything. One was Neapolitan, one
was a Lombard; one was an editor-manager, the other was a columnist;
one was linked to attacking football and goals, the other to defensive
football, the counter-attack, the importance of winning above all else.'[6]
Brera had no respect for Palumbo, dismissing him with this phrase:
'he isn't a journalist because he doesn't know how to write'.[7] Another
public argument pitted Brera against the novelist and football critic
Giovanni Arpino, who called Brera's approach 'critical Stalinism'. The
two writer-journalists fell out in the 1970s, and 'insults flew' whenever
they met after that.[8]

Palumbo revolutionized the graphic design of the *Gazzetta* after
taking over in 1975. He got rid of boring, old-fashioned, small headlines and introduced big, dramatic print. *La Gazzetta* became a mass
paper, a sports tabloid – the only real tabloid in a print market dominated by quality or political newspapers, or total trash gossip. For a
time, in the 1980s, the *Gazzetta* outsold all the other papers, a further
sign of the footballization of Italian society. In reaction to this trend,
other papers dedicated more and more space to sport, and in particular
football. The quality centre-left daily *La Repubblica*, which at first (in
1976) had snobbishly excluded sport and crime altogether, was forced
into an abrupt about-turn and signed up Gianni Brera in the 1980s.
Brera could also be extremely nasty. After Brian Glanville exposed the
'golden fix' in the 1970s, Brera insulted the English journalist in his
weekly magazine column and the two fell out over the incident.

Sometimes, Brera's arrogance got the better of him. In 1966, before
Italy–Korea, he wrote that 'if we lose to Korea, I will change job: no
more writing about football'. He was to be reminded of this gaffe on
thousands of occasions in subsequent years, as Italy went down 1–0 in
probably the greatest shock in World Cup history. Brera was certainly
not a nationalist, and could be extremely cutting, and honest, in his

reports on Italian games. After the 1962 World Cup debacle, for example, he refused to blame the English referee, Ken Aston, and wrote that Italy had 'reaped what it had sown'. Four years earlier, after Italy had failed to make the 1958 World Cup finals, Brera wrote that 'we have already won too many cups, a long time ago'. He was also cynical about the Italians' relationship with the sport: 'fair play, in Italy we have never heard of it'.[9] It was unsurprising that Brera had fallen out of love with the money-dominated football championship by the 1980s, and he dedicated less and less time to the game which had made him famous.

Twice, in 1979 and 1983, Brera stood as a Socialist Party candidate in Pavia. The PSI had once been a revolutionary party but by the 1980s was pre-Blairite (moderate before its time) and extremely corrupt. Brera did not take his candidature too seriously. In one campaign speech he made three proposals: first, new sports stadiums across Europe; second, the re-opening of state brothels; third, the repatriation of southerners to the south. He was not elected. Later in the 1980s and 1990s, the regionalist Northern Leagues claimed Brera as one of their own. He did not have much time to confirm or deny this allegiance. In the early hours of the morning of 19 January 1992 a horrific car crash killed Brera near his home-town in the foggy province of Milan. Brera was not at the wheel at the time; one of his friends was driving. The car was a wreck and Brera's readers have been in mourning ever since.

Journalists since Brera have inevitably had to measure themselves against his myth. They even called themselves by a collective name: the *senzabrera* (the withoutBreras). Gianni Mura is the contemporary journalist closest to his friend Brera. A caustic, economical writer, Mura is an expert on cycling and football. Writing in *La Repubblica*, Mura invented a Sunday column – *Seven days of bad thoughts* – where he gave 'votes' to players, managers and other journalists. His marks were usually very harsh and he had little positive to say about the modern game. Like Brera, again, Mura was a gastronomic expert, writing regular restaurant columns and reporting on the meals he ate while covering the *Giro d'Italia*. Mura's style was non-Brerian; nobody could compete with the master. He recounts in one story how he had tried to reproduce Brera-type language as a young journalist, only for his editor to tear up the piece and throw it in the bin.

Antonio Ghirelli revolutionized sports writing in the 1950s by producing the first real history of the game. His *Storia del calcio* is based on serious historical research, although it is written in a journalistic and easy style.[10] Ghirelli was a man of the left and his political views are upfront in the *Storia del calcio*. All historians of football start with this book – it remains a constant reference point, thanks to its detail and its accuracy. As a Napoli fan, moreover, Ghirelli was very attentive to the development of the game in the south, in marked contrast with Brera's 'northernist' approach. In the 1980s, Ghirelli became chief press officer for the Socialist President of Italy, Sandro Pertini, and later for Prime Minister Bettino Craxi. During the 1962 World Cup, Ghirelli and a journalistic colleague were held personally responsible for the hostility of the locals towards the Italian team, after writing a series of articles criticizing the hosts Chile in the national press.

## Commentators. Radio and TV

Generations of Italian football fans grew up visualizing games through the voice of Niccolò Carosio, the first and most eminent radio commentator. From his first game in 1933, Carosio dominated the radio waves until an embarrassing incident – in 1970 – saw him shunted quickly into retirement. Carosio's bias and nationalist passion painted pictures that became part of football history, as in his commentary on the 'lions of Highbury' game between England and Italy in 1934. Paolo Ferretti wrote that 'he hated the English', but his mother *was* English. Something strange was going on here. Carosio's commentary on the 1966 World Cup final was massively pro-German, and his insinuations about the refereeing did much to create the widespread conviction that England 'bought' that World Cup. Much of the myth-making about Italy's glorious 1930s successes was also thanks to the power of Carosio's biased vision, in an age before TV and when literacy in Italy was an exception, not the norm.

Famous for his mistakes – the wrong player was often given as the goalscorer – Carosio had the difficult task of commentating live, in poor technological and meteorological conditions. For many years he did not have a TV monitor to check what had really happened. He usually kept a bottle of whisky with him to get him through the colder games and some critics hinted that his many errors might be down to one drop too many. One of Carosio's most celebrated traits was the use of the phrase 'nearly goal'. Many times, he would shout 'goal', driving millions of listeners into ecstasy or agony, before correcting his earlier claim into 'nearly goal'.

The 1970 incident that ended Carosio's seemingly interminable career took place during a World Cup game between Italy and Israel. Gigi Riva had a goal disallowed for offside, thanks to the indication of an Ethiopian linesman. Carosio lost his cool: 'What is that bloody blacky doing? He's disallowed the goal, he's mad, damned blacky.' Official protests came in from the Ethiopian embassy, and this was not a minor matter. Italy had invaded Ethiopia twice – once in the 1890s and again under fascism, using poison gas on the latter occasion to quell the rebellious locals. Carosio was told to come home. He refused to do so, but no more matches were assigned to him. He slipped into retirement.

The next commentator to dominate the TV football scene was Nando Martellini, a far more sober and laid-back personality who was more in touch with the televisual *spectator* as opposed to a radio *listener*. Usually laconic, Martellini was prone to memorable eruptions of joy and triumph. He became celebrated above all for his commentaries during the victorious 1982 World Cup in Spain, and especially for the way in which he closed the final: 'Champions of the World, Champions of the World, Champions of the World!' as the referee blew the final whistle and held the ball above his head. Martellini was also the commentator for the key games in the 1970 World Cup, and his simple but effective *Riva, Riva, Riiiivvvvaaaa* for the goal which made the game 3–2 has also entered into commentating history. His relaxed commentary on the final – dominated by Brazil – was a masterpiece of understatement. After Brazil's fourth goal, Martellini said only this, in a quiet voice: 'and now the Coppa Rimet is on its way to Rio de Janeiro'.

Meanwhile, radio commentary continued to be extremely popular right through the 1960s and 1970s. The most important programme was, not surprisingly, that on Sunday afternoons. *Tutto il calcio minuto per minuto* began transmission in 1960. Its format was simple: a series of correspondents went on air in order to report on goals and other incidents. They could interrupt – ask for 'the line' – if something important happened. Millions of tiny transistors were sold to allow Italians to keep up with results. People also began to take their radios with them to the match, so they could follow other games at the same time. *Tutto il calcio* was marked by the hilarious rivalry between two anchor-men; Sandro Ciotti – *the voice* – whose gravelly tones were perfect for radio – and Enrico Armeri. Often, the two would bicker on air, especially over the length of time given to certain reports by Armeri. On one famous occasion, the two traded insults, convinced they were off-air. Ciotti was also a successful songwriter and writer. Armeri covered over 1,600 games for state radio.

Until the 1980s, only the four most important games were covered by *Tutto* . . . After that all Serie A matches and some Serie B matches had live reporters at the grounds. Slowly, however, with the advent of pay TV and the end of the traditional football Sunday, radio began to lose its place in the hearts of Italian fans. Everything could now be watched, and re-watched, *ad nauseam*, or checked on the internet.

Bruno Pizzul took over the reins of TV commentary for the national team from Martellini in the 1980s, although he had been commentating since the late 1960s. Measured, but openly biased in key games, Pizzul was well prepared but entirely lacking in a sense of humour. In 1994 he had already put Italy out, verbally; 'We are leaving this World Cup without leaving a trace'; when Baggio equalized against Nigeria in the last minute, Italy then proceeded to go all the way to the final, much to Pizzul's embarrassment. Pizzul's most difficult night came in 1985, with the Heysel stadium disaster. He was heavily criticized for his commentary that evening. However, others claimed that Pizzul did a good journalistic job in terrible circumstances. After a long period as number-one commentator, Pizzul stepped down after the 2002 World Cup debacle (where his commentary bordered on the hysterical) and was replaced by a new generation of young, very able and much more relaxed commentators.

## Re-inventing football coverage and subverting the genre. From *Bar Sport* to *Mai Dire Gol*

'The first transmission in Italy to really take the piss out of the world of football'[11]

In 1983 a local, left-wing radio station in Milan, which had been set up as a militant, illegal pirate station in the 1970s, decided to cover a football game for the first time. This decision, in the words of radio journalist Sergio Ferrentino, broke 'the taboo on the left towards football'. After Juventus lost the 1983 European Cup final to Hamburg, the station opened up their phone lines and discovered a whole new type of listener: 'Thank you, Magath [the Hamburg goalscorer]', they cried, in delight, 'shitty hunchbacks', 'Viva Germany'. The two journalists – both Juventus fans – just had to sit there and take it. 'It was a hard night', one later wrote. After that, they had the idea of a football programme, on Sunday nights, 'but we needed to find another couple of idiots first'. They did, and *Bar Sport* was born. One of the first conscious decisions taken was to adopt the language of the fan, and not of the football expert. Luther Blissett, for example, was 'simply crap – and that was it'. The programme, as journalist and Inter fan Gad Lerner put it, helped people 'rediscover the fan-beast within themselves'. Maradona, for example, was usually referred to as 'the fat dwarf'.

In the early days the programme consisted simply of comments on what had happened that Sunday on the pitch and on the way it was being reported by the most popular sports programme of the time, *Sporting Sunday*. *Bar Sport* would also ring up people in Milan – fans and intellectuals – and then give out two prizes – *perbacco* (good!) *e devi morire* (you must die! bad) – for the best and the worst 'things' of the week. There was then was a kind of vote, where people phoned up and expressed preferences – for players, managers or TV commentators.

Another innovation of *Bar Sport* was that the people who phoned up would be treated extremely rudely, especially if they stated that they were 'first-time callers'. Usually, when someone did say this, they were immediately cut off. Commentary on the game – which rarely talked about the actual game – was interspersed by debates about entirely irrelevant issues, music, and random phone-ins. The 'commentators' were a mixture of fans and amateur experts, often saying that a pass was 'rubbish' or that a player was 'a wanker'.

With the Roma–Liverpool European Cup final of 1984, the team started to 'commentate' on real matches, inviting listeners to turn down the television volume, and turn up their radios. Some of these early experiments were even more surreal, because the fake commentators commentated on both the 'real' commentators *and* the match itself. In the end, this became too difficult, so the sound was turned down (at least in people's homes, not in the studio, where it was occasionally turned up).

So the central idea behind *Bar Sport* was both simple, and brilliant. Instead of commentating on the actual game, the 'commentators' would talk rubbish, or go off on long tangents, or talk about something else, or take a phone call, or just make a series of stupid jokes. The result was hilarious, and highly original. Over time, these commentators developed a new language, full of words they had invented to describe the 'game'. *Bar Sport* built up a cult following in the 1980s, at first in Milan but then across Italy. These commentators were not ignorant about *calcio*. Far from it: they were highly knowledgeable, but *Bar Sport* was a programme dedicated more to fans and fandom than to the game of football. It reproduced and translated the ironic way in which many people watch the game, at home or in the stadium. By turning down the sound on their TV sets, fans were also refusing to accept the usual boring, sober version of what they were seeing.

On the night of the Heysel tragedy, the programme mutated again into a forum for serious debate and journalism. Callers told *Bar Sport* that there had been deaths at the ground well before the news broke on national TV. A correspondent burst into tears on the phone, and people rang up through the night asking for news about their relatives who were at the game.

Many commentators passed through the *Bar Sport* studios over the years, and huge events were organized around the big international tournaments, complete with big screens and bars. The 1986 World Cup was dominated by a joke concerning the huge shadow on the pitch that the *Bar Sport* team called a *Gialappa* – after a brand of

Mexican laxative. After that tournament, two of *Bar Sport's* team left little *Radio Popolare* for Fininvest, at that time Berlusconi's television holding. There, they started a football-based programme that would change the way sports programming was conceived. The programme was – and is – called *Mai Dire Gol*.

*Mai Dire Gol* in its earlier years (the first transmission was in 1990) consisted of a series of sketches and skits dedicated to football. *Vai con liscio* was set to circus music, and showed footballers falling over, missing open goals or failing to trap the ball. *Le interviste possibili* tried to translate the incomprehensible interviews of Giovanni Trapattoni, or underlined the grammatical errors of football presenters. One of the most surreal items involved the obsession of Milanese comic Teo Teocoli with Wimbledon striker John Fashanu, whom he called *Fasharnooo*. Fashanu himself later appeared on the programme. *Mai Dire Gol* dissected the highly serious and self-important world of football media and football punditry, making it look as ridiculous as it really was. During big football tournaments, the three *Mai Dire Gol* presenters (Carlo Taranto, Marco Santin and Giorgio Gherarducci, whom the TV spectator never saw) went back to their *Bar Sport* roots with crazy commentaries on radio.

Later, tired of the football focus, the programme became a more general comedy-sketch 'container' show. *Mai Dire Gol* achieved massive ratings, and created a whole series of cult moments for its many fans. Romanian and future West Ham striker Florin Raducioiu, for example, became a cult hero on the programme, famed for his unfailing ability to blast the ball over the bar. The Gialappa's band were TV cannibals, living in the world of television but also outside of that world, and maintaining a critical distance from the official media. Numerous players and managers appeared on the programme over the years, happy to be set up as figures of fun by the Gialappas.[12]

## Quelli che il calcio . . .

Football coverage was revolutionized once again by another pioneering programme, created by innovative TV presenter Fabio Fazio – this time on state television – in 1993. Fazio concentrated on fans and

fandom at the cost of actual pictures of football. He took the *lack* of
live coverage available – thanks to the increasing cost of TV football
rights and Pay-TV stations – and made it into a virtue. You didn't
need to actually see the game to enjoy or talk about football. The
programme always began with a surreal song by Enzo Jannacci – and
a series of strange shots from grounds around the country – which
depicted fans eating sandwiches, linesmen pulling up their socks or
ballboys messing about.

Fazio constructed a simple studio – with seats for fan-guests, each
of whom had a TV monitor on which they could watch their own
team play. He then proceeded to create a 'group' of regular guests
drawn from everyday life and the world of celebrities. All were fans,
and were always presented as such. Other guests were sent to various
grounds to comment on games. A series of fanatical supporters became
famous in this way – the regulars. There was Idris, an erudite and
black Juventus fan; Suor Paola, a nun and Lazio follower, a university
professor who backed Fiorentina. Other regulars included the comedian and Milan fan Teo Teocoli, who did perfect impressions of
Adriano Galliani and Cesare Maldini. The whole programme was kept
in check by football experts, and by frequent updates on the scores via
the state radio station.

Some of the ideas introduced by the programme were the stuff of
genius. A financial journalist reported from grounds by simply describing what was happening, literally: 'A number of men are running
around a pitch after a white ball, some are dressed in red and some in
blue, there is another man in black who sometimes blows a whistle.'
The effect was very funny at first, although the gag quickly wore thin.
Other guests included an astrologer whose predictions always went
wrong. Fans would plead with the astrologer not to tip their team.

Sometimes, the light tone of the programme changed, in reaction
to events linked to football. When Genoa fan Claudio Spagnolo was
stabbed to death before a game with Milan in January 1995, Fabio
Fazio decided to abandon the show. The cameras kept running on an
empty studio and the effect was extremely powerful – more eloquent
than the rivers of empty words spent by the other sports programmes.
On the final day of the 1999–2000 season, when Juventus lost the
championship in Perugia after their game was delayed by rain for

71 minutes at half-time, Fazio's programme achieved huge viewing figures as it switched between Perugia and Rome, where Lazio players and fans were waiting anxiously for the result. Fazio also dug out forgotten players and commentators from the past, playing intelligently on the nostalgia which infects all real football fans.

After Fazio left the programme the format was taken over by presenter Simona Ventura, whose husband was also a Serie A footballer. The programme slowly lost its originality, becoming increasingly similar to the numerous – and terrible – 'variety' programmes which pollute Italian TV schedules. Some new ideas were – however – fascinating. In 2003–4 the programme hired some ex-players to recreate goals that had just been scored and then transmitted the 'replays'. The success of this idea was down to the choice of very high quality ex-players, whose goals were often more spectacular than the ones they were attempting to copy.

## Pure Satire. *Cuore Mundial*

Published sporting satire took on a new look with the appearance of *Cuore Mundial* during the 1990 World Cup. *Cuore* was a left-wing satirical weekly which had a brief moment of glory in the late 1980s and 1990s. The magazine drew on a group of highly talented journalists and cartoonists, and was always ready to challenge previous taboos. *Cuore Mundial* was a special edition produced for the World Cup – and became famous for its covers. One example was '*Giannini è una pippa!*' Giuseppe Giannini was Italy's central midfielder at the time; very skilful but quite slow. *Pippa* is a rude term often applied to inconclusive footballers. The piece continued, 'it takes him half an hour to tie his shoelaces. Either he plays in moccasins or he should be dropped.' Every daily edition after that was graced with 'the *pippa* of the day'. Other pieces combined political and football satire: *Schillaci resolves the southern question* was one example. Totò Schillaci was the Sicilian centre-forward who unexpectedly became a star during the tournament, the southern question was the name given to the territorial inequalities in Italy which had dogged the nation since unification in 1861. Other jokes were just childish: the World Cup symbol – a stick-man called '*Ciao*' – was depicted with huge genitals.

As Italy – through Schillaci's goals – marched towards the final, the satire became more and more silly. 'Totò! We desire you physically' was another headline. Before the semi-final against Argentina in Naples *Cuore Mundial* led with: 'In Naples against Maradona in a spirit of sporting friendship. Watch out boys, the dwarf is a cheat!' A grotesque photo-montage of Maradona was placed on the front page with an enormous head and tiny legs. Other comments were just stupid jokes: 'Klinsmann missed a goal which even Ironside would have scored'. Sadly, *Cuore* closed in the mid-1990s. The paper's founder, Michele Serra, claimed that in a country where Silvio Berlusconi was prime minister, satire was dead. Reality was far more surreal.

## Stickers. The Panini Phenomenon

Before the age of mass television, many Italian children became obsessed with a peculiar footballing product – the Panini sticker album. Brothers Benito and Giuseppe Panini were newsagents from Modena and in 1960 they hit upon the idea of a sticker album for football players. The first envelopes were filled by hand, and included a foot-ball that could be blown up. Panini albums were a huge success. In the first year alone, three million sets of stickers were sold. Doubles were swapped with other children and some stickers were extremely hard to find. One celebrated rarity was Pierluigi Pizzaballa, a substitute goalkeeper for Milan in the 1970s. In the 1990s, in a brilliant marketing operation that played largely on nostalgia, the editor of the left-wing daily *L'Unità*, Walter Veltroni, sold completed albums of stickers from the 1960s and 1970s. The slogan used to publicize the initiative was 'Have you got Pizziballa?' If you really couldn't find a player, you could buy it directly from the company. The Panini business grew into a huge concern, although it hit a crisis in the 1980s and ended up in the hands of Robert Maxwell. Even today, some children still complete the albums, although the cost of the stickers is now beyond most families and the album has expanded to include players from many of the lower divisions.

## Local Television. *Telelombardia* and Sports Coverage

The importance of *calcio* in Italy can be gauged by a simple examin-ation of the programming of one local TV station, based in Milan. *Telelombardia* covers, as the name might suggest, the whole of the Lombard region, one of the richest zones in the world with a popu-lation of some nine million people. Around half of the *total* programme time of *Telelombardia* is dedicated to football. However, *Telelombardia* has no rights to live games. Hence, half of all its time is dedicated to *talk* about *calcio*. Moreover, this talk is concentrated on the ups and downs of the two big Milan teams – AC Milan and Inter – with a significant chunk also dedicated to Italy's best supported team – Juventus – with its hundreds of thousands of fans in Lombardy.[13] Very little time is spent discussing the other Lombard teams. So, half of all programme time is dedicated to talk about two or three teams.

How does this work in practice, given that very little actual football is shown? *Telelombardia* football shows are all staged in the studio, with outside broadcasts from various stadiums, at San Siro and in the players' tunnel. This is cheap TV and the studio itself is decorated with shop-window mannequins wearing football shirts. Women appear rarely – although *Telelombardia* has a very good female sports presenter – when they are not 'showgirls'. Usually, a group of middle-aged men are seen sitting around a long curved table, whilst the anchor-man stands opposite them. *They* can see the games, but we can't. Behind the presenter is a kids' goal, but more about that later. At the back of the studio, in a kind of glass box, on a pedestal, sits a mini-skirted young woman, answering phone calls.

## Football Chat

A lot of football chat is not about specific matches. This type of discussion ranges far and wide, from tactics to scandals to referees, to the form of particular players and, above all, to the choices of managers and presidents – transfers, tactics, football gossip. Who's coming, who's going, who's unhappy, who's overweight, who's been out on the town, who's just bought a flat in Turin, and so on. Much of this is invented, especially when it deals with the transfer market. Whole summers have been spent discussing the next 'jewel' on the market – Giggs, Anelka, Owen, Beckham. *None* of these players ever arrived in Italy.

Then come the games themselves. This is *Telelombardia*'s speciality. Commentators are sent to the grounds and a small camera watches *them* as they commentate. The station can't film the game itself, but we often get snatches of what surrounds games – the crowd, crowd violence, the teams coming on and off. These commentators are not objective, they are fans – and fanatically so. Everybody knows which team they support. When their team scores, they go mad. When they lose, they despair – on camera; they beat their hands on the table, throw away their microphones, insult the players. This dynamic – in the studio there are a selection of various pundit-fans – reproduces the classic milieu of the bar-room discussion/argument. Many of these 'experts' are also ex-players.

Many fans prefer to 'watch' the game in this way than to see the actual players play football. *They prefer the chat to the calcio.* My mother-in-law would choose to watch *Telelombardia* even when the same game was on another channel, live. Added spice comes from the relationship between some of the personalities involved. Tiziano Crudeli, *Telelombardia*'s top pundit, is a small, unprepossessing Milan fan. Usually, during games, he will joust verbally with Enzo Corno, a long-suffering Inter specialist. When Milan score, Crudeli usually shouts out 'Cooorrrnnno', provoking his colleague. The theatricals are often completed with some counter-accusations of cheating/bribery/luck directed at Milan.

In order to explain what has happened out there, on the real pitch, *Telelombardia* has a magnetic blackboard, which the anchor-man (who is *not* an obvious Milan or Inter fan, in contrast with everyone else in the studio) uses to reproduce goals and other events using coloured pieces. Occasionally, a real ball will be used to mimic shots or saves in the kids' goal mentioned earlier. For big games, fans are invited into the studio to cheer or boo. Finally, there are the post-mortems. After games, the chat goes on, and on, and on, for hours (and days) with an obsessive unpicking of games, the referee's performance, and tactics accompanied by conspiracy theories and ritual calls for substitutions, resignations, changes, and sackings.

Why are these programmes so popular? One key reason is they reproduce discussions which all fans have in pubs, bars or living rooms. The 'experts' use the same language as ordinary fans. *Telelombardia's* most famous Milan fan – Crudeli – finished his commentary from the championship-winning 1999 season standing in the middle of the *curva* with a microphone, dancing up and down. Another reason for the success of these programmes is the pleasure gained from the art of humiliating your opponent, the joy in seeing your rivals depressed, angry and belittled.

Increasingly, in the 1990s, the *Telelombardia*/local TV model for covering football became the norm in the Italian media. Less and less actual football was shown, more and more time was taken up with chat, and that chat was almost exclusively about the three clubs who dominated Italian football financially and on the field – Milan, Juventus and Inter. The spread of Biscardism, named after Aldo Biscardi, presenter of the flagship and pioneering football chat programme, *Il processo del lunedì*, appeared to be inexorable. Even the coverage of matches was increasingly marked by chat and gossip, and less and less by comment on the match itself. A specialized 'commentator' was placed near the bench, and he 'commented' on the anger or joy of the various managers and players. More and more time was given over to short (but increasingly long) advertising breaks *during* matches. Football coverage became more and more obsessed with the medium itself, the opinions of commentators and pundits, and everything that surrounded the game.

Television critic Aldo Grasso tried to explain the success of these local programmes in an analysis published in 2004, and their high viewing figures even when the same game was being transmitted live on another channel. What was going on? mused Grasso. Did people 'watch' games with two televisions, or did they change frequently between the game and the 'comment' studio? Grasso's explanation was simple. Most people still watched the game on the national channels, but when an 'incident' took place – a goal, a foul, a penalty appeal – they used their zapper to get the comments from local channels: 'they popped (virtually) down to the bar, to the club, to check out their friends'. Local TV was far more human than national TV. Its presenters were 'from next door'. Globalization and the increasing power of the big clubs had intensified the need for a local alternative, without the glamour, razzmatazz and distance of the international arena.[14]

## Football and TV. The State (1954–1980)

For thirty years televised football in Italy was totally under the control of the state channels. Private TV did not start to make inroads into the market until the mid-1980s. The RAI used its monopoly to construct massive audiences for games and analysis programmes. Football was intimately linked to the history of Italian television. The first live game was transmitted only weeks after the birth of TV – Italy–Egypt in January 1954. At that time, only 90,000 TV licences had been issued (whereas four million Italians had radio licences) but this quickly rose to more than a million – many in bars and clubs – by 1956. Televised sport really took off with the Rome Olympics in 1960, but colour did not come in until 1977. In 1980 Berlusconi broke the public monopoly on football transmission although the RAI kept control of the main televised football rights throughout most of the 1990s. Berlusconi's private channels preferred to deal with the state channels for a share of the material available, and to concentrate on what it saw as the premier football competition – the Champions League (which his team Milan won in 1989, 1990, 1994 and 2003). Italian national games were almost always the property of the RAI, and remain so today. Televised football changed the viewing habits of Italians, and has led to some of the biggest audience figures in Italian television history. Seventeen million tuned into the 1970 semi-final with West Germany, and 32 million watched the 1982 World Cup final.

At first, viewers would crowd into bars to watch games, as very few people actually had their own sets, or would invade the homes of those who did. A second long phase followed where matches were watched at home – with the family. With the advent of Pay-TV in the 1980s and 1990s, more and more people returned to pubs and bars. Special rules were set out for these matches. Drinks had to be bought and often tickets were needed to reserve a place.

Television-watching also affected everyday life in more dramatic ways. In October 1963, many residents in a small mountain town called Longarone were in bars and clubs, watching a football match. At about

10.40 p.m., a huge landslide led to one of the worst disasters in Italian history, as fifty million cubic metres of water poured down into the valley from where it had been trapped inside a dam. The town was wiped out, and many of the victims were killed as they watched the match.

## Programmes. *Sporting Sunday* and *90th minute*

*Sporting Sunday*[15] – *La Domenica Sportiva* – is the oldest Italian sports programme. It has been running since the birth of national television in 1954. In the 1950s the games were shot on 16 mm film, and then taken by train to special production centres where the film was developed. This took about an hour, after which the clips were edited and sound was added in time for transmission at 10.30 p.m. However, the programme only took off in the mid-1960s, when it was given an hour slot for the first time. *Sporting Sunday* was not just a football programme, and in fact space was dedicated to other sports, above all motor racing and cycling.

In 1970, the technology was advanced enough for the RAI to introduce what is still its most watched sports TV show, *90th minute*. Beginning just after 6 p.m, *90th minute* relied on fast editing and required individual journalists to prepare their reports on games more or less as they were watching the match. The format of the programme was simple. First, the results would be read out. Then, as with *Tutto il calcio minuto per minuto*, each game would be given five minutes – where the journalist would show major incidents and goals and then give a brief comment on the match, live. Of course, a lot could go wrong – and it frequently did. Very often, the short highlights would not work, or the commentator would lose his place in the clips, or the link would break down. The success of *90th minute* (it had an audience of eight million viewers at its peak) depended on the skill of the main presenter. For thirty years this was cheery Paolo Valenti, who would often burst out laughing at crucial moments. Obscure regional sports reporters were made into household names – and household faces – through the success of the programme, although to many viewers it appeared as if they were almost all extraordinarily ugly.[16] *90th minute* began a long decline in the 1990s. The break-up of the Sunday afternoon schedule dealt the programme a fatal blow, as many of the big games were played on Saturday or Sunday night. The distance between attending the game itself and watching it filtered on television – a distance which had always been there – became an abyss.

## Fans, Spectators, Audiences and Crowd. The football-TV experience

At the stadium, we are spectators; we *see* the game, from one point of view. At home, we are part of an audience; we *look* at a television set, from a series of different points of view.[17] In the stadium, our whole attention is taken by the event in front of us; at home we make coffee, answer the phone, flick between channels, eat dinner and even tape the match to watch later. At home, the game is frequently interrupted by advertising. At first, this was a minor irritation – tiny slogans on the screen – sometimes accompanied by an annoying 'Bing!' The game was not interrupted. Nowadays, during any short break, whole adverts are shown. In the stadium, we can usually see the whole pitch, and the movement of players into space. TV concentrates on the ball. At the stadium, the fan or spectator could choose what to watch. On TV, it was the studio director who chose what the spectator would see. With satellite technology, innovations were introduced which allowed the spectator to pick certain angles, or even follow individual players, but research showed that the vast majority of viewers followed the traditional, director-led version of any one game.

Italian TV coverage did have some peculiarities of its own. Unlike in England, the crowd's volume was often 'turned down', giving games a surreal, theatrical quality. Moreover, Italian studio directors avoided the frequent close-ups of players that were so common on British TV. Time is also altered in the two physical spheres. At the stadium, time is real time; at home, time is altered and shifted through replays, slow-motion and other technological tricks. TV constructs football as a spectacle and drama. The mass media also have a tendency to consume any event or discipline that they transmit – so much so that sport exists *only* through the medium of television.

During the 1990s one innovative programme was very quickly dropped from the schedules. It was probably too dangerous. The most important incidents from all that week's games were shown without comment or commentary. The effect was illuminating. Commentators were superfluous – you did not need them to enjoy or understand the game. The best sporting programme of the last ten years is known simply as *Sfide* (challenges), and its theme tune is David Bowie's 'Heroes'. By utilizing the rich RAI archives, and telling uncomplicated stories from football's past, *Sfide* brought sports documentary-making into a new dimension. The most fascinating series of *Sfide* episodes was dedicated to a football team that had been set up in a Milanese prison. As the team went through the season (not surprisingly, they only played home games) the tension grew, and *Sfide* kept its viewers informed of their progress. The prison director had promised that the experiment would only continue if they won promotion. After winning their derby (against the prison officers) the team were promoted, although the release of some of their best players on parole was a bitter blow to their chances for the following season.

## Pirate TV. Berlusconi and Televised Football

Berlusconi made his dramatic entrance into the world of televised football by buying the rights (for nearly a million dollars) to an international football tournament in 1980. The tournament was in Uruguay – then a military dictatorship – and was known as the *Mundialito*. It grouped together all the countries who had won the World Cup. Later, Berlusconi's channels concentrated on the big European competitions, on slick chat shows and on the team owned by him – Milan. The constant success of Milan in the 1980s and 1990s was in part due to the promotion and power of Berlusconi's media empire, which brought in vast sums of money to reinforce the team. Of course, private television could not cut itself off entirely from all those fans who did not support Milan, but Berlusconi's team rarely came in for much criticism.

Mediaset used comedians, scantily-clad showgirls, actors and the usual diet of ex-players and ex-managers to spice up its football coverage, and its programmes always had a more modern look than the stale and old-fashioned – and long-winded – items produced by public TV. Bizarre personalities emerged from these new programmes, reinventing themselves as football critics. Giampiero Mughini had been a left-wing intellectual in the 1960s and editor of the far-left newspaper *Lotta Continua*. In the 1990s, complete with orange glasses and wavy grey hair, he popped up as an erudite football pundit and Juventus fan.

The 1990s saw football gossip become big business, as footballers became TV personalities, and were often seen in the company of actresses and dancers from the world of the mass media. One of Berlusconi's football programmes even began to include a special gossip item in its Sunday evening shows. Footballers had become stars in their own right, detached from their performances on the field of play. Berlusconi's world was one where football was all-important, in all spheres of his political and economic life. He called his new party *Forza Italia!* (Goforit Italy!, a football chant) and his government 'a team'. His party's local branches were known as 'clubs'. This was *Bar Sport Italia*, a country where sporting language had become hegemonic. Berlusconi was convinced that the success of Milan brought him consensus in other fields, as was Achille Lauro with Napoli in the 1950s and 1960s. Thus, he was, as he put it, 'forced to keep winning', to keep buying the best players, to keep interfering in the affairs and tactical decisions of 'his' team.

In 2000, after Italy had come within seconds of winning the European Championships, Berlusconi gave a press conference where he launched into a long critique of the tactics used by the Italian national manager, Dino Zoff. Zidane should have been man-marked, claimed Berlusconi, and he 'could not believe' that Zoff had not seen that this was necessary. Offended, Zoff resigned, and was replaced by Giovanni Trapattoni. In 2004, Berlusconi ordered his own team manager – Carlo Ancelotti – to play with two forwards for the rest of the season. Ancelotti obeyed, and Milan won the title. In the same year, Berlusconi continued to appear on sports programmes, even during the election campaign. Yet, perhaps this magic was beginning to wear thin. Despite Milan's triumph, Berlusconi lost those particular elections. Italy's *calciocracy* was, it seems, starting to crumble.

## Poets, film-makers, writers. Pier Paolo Pasolini and the poetry of Football

'The afternoons I spent playing football – we used to play for seven or eight hours without stopping – were *undoubtedly* the best of my life. It almost makes me want to cry, if I think about it'                    PIER PAOLO PASOLINI

Despite his formidable intellectual abilities – as film-maker, poet and novelist – Pier Paolo Pasolini's first love was football. When he was asked what he would have become without cinema and literature he replied 'a good footballer. After literature and Eros, football is one of my great pleasures.' As a cultural commentator and journalist, Pasolini often wrote about the game and dusty, interminable matches on the periphery of Rome also turn up in his novels.[18]

A passionate Bologna fan, Pasolini interviewed a group of Bologna players for his 1963 documentary about sexual mores in Italy, *Comizi d'amore* (Meetings of Love). They replied to his questions with mono-syllabic, embarrassed answers. He was particularly pleased to meet his idol, midfielder Giacomo Bulgarelli. His friend Sergio Citti later wrote that 'it was like he had met Jesus'. Later, Pasolini offered Bulgarelli a part in his raunchy version of the *Canterbury Tales*. The offer was refused.

Pasolini wrote in highly original terms about the analysis of foot-balling language. For Pasolini, dribbling was poetry, and the best drib-blers in the world – and therefore the best football poets – were the Brazilians. *Catenaccio*, on the other hand, was 'prose . . . based on synthesis and organization . . . its only poetic moment is the counter-attack'. In the 1970 World Cup final, Italy's prose had been beaten by Brazil's poetry. 'Football', he wrote, 'is a system of signs, a language . . . the last great rite of our time'. Football historians have pointed out that Pasolini's scrutiny of football 'created no interest' at the time.[19] Many people 'underlined his passion for football', but his analysis of the game was not taken seriously. It would be years before the proper study of football – through semiotics, sociology, history and cultural research – would be seen as an acceptable field for intellectual comment and academic activity.

Pasolini loved to run, and he played on the wing. He had first played seriously in the 1940s in Friuli and in 1966 he toured Italy with a line-up made up of actors, singers and film-makers. The team included two of his own protégés – who had been plucked from the Rome slums to star in his films – Ninetto Davoli and Franco Citti. In 1975 he directed his last film in central Italy, *Salò*, a dark, controversial and violently sexual fantasy. Just down the road, Bernardo Bertolucci – who began his directing career as assistant director on Pasolini's first film, *Accattone* – was directing a six-hour epic called *Novecento*. A

Pasolini playing football on the Rome periphery.

game was organized between the two film sets at Parma – and the teams were called *900* and *120* (as in the subtitle of Pasolini's film: *The 120 days of Sodom*). It turned out to be one of Pasolini's last games. A report appeared in the local press: 'Bertolucci beats Pasolini 5–2 thanks to their psychedelic shirts'. Pasolini's team – he was captain – wore Bologna shirts, whilst *Novecento* had special multi-coloured tops made which rendered the sight of the ball difficult. The evening ended with a huge meal on the banks of the Po. Some controversy remains over the game's conclusion, with some saying that Pasolini was annoyed because *Novecento* had called in a couple of ringers from Parma, at that time in Serie B.

On 1 November 1975 Pasolini was murdered – beaten to death on a dusty football pitch near Ostia, outside Rome. Mystery still surrounds his murder. A young man Pasolini had picked up near Rome's central station confessed to the crime. Many still argue that the official version – that the young man, acting alone, killed Pasolini – is highly implausible. Indirectly, a combination of football and Eros had led to Pasolini's downfall.

## Italian cinema and Italian football

Raf Vallone was one of the few professional footballers to make the transition to a successful acting career. After playing just 31 games in seven seasons in the 1930s and early 1940s for Torino and Novara, he went to work as an investigative and cultural journalist with the Communist Party paper *L'Unità*. A useful, skilful midfielder, his best season was with Torino in 1938–9, where he played fifteen times, scoring three goals. His film career took off, unexpectedly, with the neo-realist classic, *Riso Amaro* (*Bitter Rice*), where he played a heart-throb soon-to-be-discharged soldier alongside the stunning Silvana Mangano. The film was a melodrama based on the rice fields of northern Italy and was a huge international hit. After that, he made a series of films including one football-based movie, *Gli eroi della Domenica* (1952) (*Sunday's Heroes*).

Football has appeared in many Italian films, when it has not actually been the subject of movies. Sometimes, football was just background – as in the final scenes of *The Bicycle Thieves* (Vittorio De Sica, 1948). Other times, it was the subject of films. In the 1970s and 1980s a series of slapstick comedies was made around football. Milan fan Diego Abatantuono played three different fan caricatures in the popular comedy, *Ecceziunale . . . veramente* (1982). As in real life, the analysis of the game by film-makers gave way to a focus on fans, corruption and violence. Ricky Tognazzi's *Ultrà* (1990) attempted – with little success – to paint a realistic picture of the violent young people that followed football in the 1980s. Documentary film-maker Daniele Segre looked at the *Fighters* group of Juventus fans in his *Il potere dev'essere bian-conero* (The power must be black and white) (1978).

Alberto Sordi, Italy's most celebrated comic actor, played a club president in *The President of the Borgorosso Football Club* (1970). At first, Sordi is disgusted by the world of football he experiences after taking over his father's club. But soon, he becomes like the fans that follow his team – based loosely on Juventus – and buys Omar Sivori even though his money has run out. In *L'allenatore nel pallone* (1984), Lino Banfi plays a trainer so bad that he has been taken on so that his team will lose. As in *The Producers*, however, Banfi turns out to be a genius – almost by chance – and his team goes from strength to strength.

Some of the new breed of Italian film directors liked to cite football in their films. In Nanni Moretti's movies, there are frequent references to the game. In *Ecce Bombo* (1978) the students who are at the centre of the film are more likely to cite the formation of the *Grande Inter* than the list of Italy's presidents for a university exam. In *Sogni d'oro* (1981) he messes around in his room with a small ball and an even tinier goal whilst in *La Messa è finita* (1985) Moretti, who plays a priest, rushes onto a local pitch and ends up in a fight with some of the boys.

Gabriele Salvatores – Inter fan and film director – also loves to include football in his generational films. In *Marrakech Express* (1988) the forty-somethings who have met up after many years to help a friend in need in Morocco end up playing a football game in the desert to win back their travel money. The soundtrack to the game is left-wing singer-songwriter Francesco De Gregori's *La leva calcistica della classe 68*. In *Mediterraneo* (1991) a match amongst Italian soldiers on an isolated Greek island is interrupted by a rare visit from a plane, whose pilot brings the shock news that World War Two is over. The whole scene is completed with a sporting punch-line, as the pilot tells the soldiers that the spot kick they were arguing about 'was never a penalty'.

Italian songwriters have often turned to football. In the 1960s pop star Rita Pavone had a smash hit (*La partita di pallone*) with a song about a girl left alone on Sunday whilst her boyfriend, ostensibly, went to the football game. In 1999 rock-star, Inter fan and film director

Luciano Ligabue wrote a song dedicated to Inter midfielder Gabriele Oriali: *Una vita da mediano*. Roma have their own songwriter, Antonello Venditti, a piano-playing melodramatic crooner with a big hairstyle whose two 1980s songs, *Grazie Roma* and *Roma, Roma,* became anthems for the championship victory of 1983. After the 2001 championship, when Venditti played a concert at the huge party that followed at Circo Massimo in the centre of the city, some of the Roma fans became angry at what they saw as his exploitation of their victory.

Football has popped up from time to time in fiction and literature in Italy. Poet Umberto Saba from Trieste dedicated some of his work to football, as did Vittorio Sereni in Milan. Giovanni Arpino's work is perhaps the most celebrated, especially his highly entertaining novel about the 1974 World Cup, *Azzurro Tenebra*.[20] A country where a writer of the quality of Arpino was sports editor for a major daily paper is a country that treats its sports fans with great respect. As Brian Glanville wrote in 1995, 'Italian readers were and are treated as literate, while the English tabloids have seldom ceased to treat their readers as morons.'[21] Quite apart from the books and poems based around football, Italian sports writing in general has always been of a very high standard, although there has been a marked decline in the quality of the sports press in the 1990s.

However, the 1990s saw a massive boom in quality football writing in Italy. Much of this was thanks to the vision of a small publishing house based in Tuscany, Limina from Arezzo, who published a series of best-selling volumes – biographies, stories and tales of scandal – based on football. Nando Dalla Chiesa's two books stood out from the pack – a biography of Torino winger Gigi Meroni which went to four editions and the story of Inter defender Armando Picchi. The translation of *Fever Pitch* did extremely well in Italy, and inspired numerous local imitations, some more interesting than others.[22] The quality market was augmented by books aimed largely at specific fans – histories of small clubs, of which there are thousands – and comedy books which analyse the more grotesque or surreal features of the world of *calcio*, such as the inventive banners which are frequently displayed at grounds.[23] Finally, there is a large market for footballing-scandal books, looking at doping, financial corruption and match-fixing.[24] The mother and father of all football-scandal books was an astonishing autobiography published in 2000 by a Milanese publishing house, Kaos. The book was by a talented ex-centre-forward, Carlo Petrini, who had become involved in a series of corruption cases in the 1980s and 1990s. Petrini depicts the world of football as not just nasty, but rotten from top to bottom. Its title is an appropriate one: *Nel fango del dio pallone:*[25] *Down in the mud with the football god*, and was followed up by a second volume, *I Pallonari*, in 2003.[26]

The most flourishing aspect of football culture, however, now lies on the internet. There are thousands of sites dedicated to footballing history, nostalgia (especially the 1970s), bad players, the hatred of other clubs (with particular attention to the big clubs – above all Juventus – and local rivalries). Other sites look at particular events, scandals, the records of players, or statistics. Many players have their own sites – Baggio, Maldini, Shevchenko – but also Cristiano Lucarelli, the Livorno striker who made the news when he left Torino for his home-town club in 2003, taking a 50 per cent cut in his salary. A number of journalists maintain sites, as do all the football newspapers and clubs, although the official sites are usually the most disappointing of all. Finally, there are myriad fan sites – with sections often known simply as 'the wall' (*Il muro*)[27] – where fans vent their spleen against their own team, or referees, or other teams, or other fans. Many of these sites are terrifying for the ferocious and obsessive nature of the contributions. Many of the fan walls contain an uncensored series of insults and bitter accusations, backed by the threat of violence.

I gave a mild interview in 2004 to a small newspaper in Milan concerning the differences between football hooliganism in Italy and the UK. Later, I was surprised to discover not just that the interview had ended up on the web, but that I had also attracted a whole series of extremely violent replies including the delightful invitation to 'eliminate my own children'. If that was the reaction to a moderate series of opinions in an obscure Milanese daily, what would make these fans really angry? The experience was a sobering one.

# CHAPTER 11

# Fans, Supporters, *Ultrà*

*'Il tifo è il nostro mestiere'*, Being a fan is our job

Roma slogan, 1970s

## Sick! The Birth of a Word

In Italy, fans are known as *tifosi* and it seems that the words *tifo* and *tifosi* were first applied to football supporters in the 1920s. Football historians dispute the occasional Italian claim that the word had 'educated origins, from the Greek *typhus*: smoke, steam'.[1] They argue that the term had pre-World War One origins and was derived from a medical word (*tifico*). In 1920, the word was already being used in newspaper reports.[2] 'Sporting fans were linked to a kind of mental epidemic, which was contagious and produced forms of confusions, typical of the symptoms of this illness.'[3] Other symptoms of normal typhoid include the following – mental aberrations, fevers, ups and downs. Like football supporting, typhoid came and went in cycles. Far from being sane, sporting fans or 'English-style'[4] supporters, Italian followers of the game were sick, ill, and diseased. The roots of this collective madness were already present in the 1920s, but it did not really take hold of millions of Italians until the 1930s and 1940s. By 2001, out of a total population of 56,995,000 Italians, 26,177,000 declared themselves as football fans.

# A Civic Religion?

It is not difficult to find strong elements which link religious belief with football fandom. Fans and believers both partake in physical and ideological rites, in specific designated places, and dress in precise, often unchanging ways. These rites are also verbal, and involve the repetition of certain chants, often in the same set order, and under the control of appointed spiritual leaders, who are often charismatic. Fans refer to their support as 'a faith'.[5] It is something they cannot give up, even if they wanted to, and that will accompany them to the grave (and sometimes, as we shall see, even after that). Venezia fans displayed this banner as they were about to be relegated at the end of the 1990s: *La fede non retrocede*: 'our faith will not go down'. Moreover, the language of football is full of religious terms; *miracolo* (miracle), usually used for an inspired save by a goalkeeper; *la salvezza* (salvation), being saved from relegation; faith; belief; suffering. 'A football championship', as Piero Brunello has written, 'can be seen as something halfway between a liturgy and the heart of the Catholic Church.'[6]

For many fans, *these rites were more important to them than the game itself*. In the way they saw the world, history had been abolished, and had been replaced by a series of myths and self-referential ceremonies. Managers and clubs also indulged in pagan or religious rituals, blessing stadiums, dripping holy water on the field or sprinkling salt to ward off evil spirits. We could go even further, arguing that the Catholic Church has lost many battles with other 'lay' religions in contemporary Italian society: consumerism, hedonism, the media. Far from being parallel worlds, these other idols were competing for customers and, in Berlusconi's Italy, the Church had gone out in the first round.

There are, of course, many people in Italy who hate football (some 13,299,000 according to a recent survey) and most of them are women. There are also many who have no particular team, and only get excited about football when the national team is playing. Some revel in their distaste for the world of sport, seeing it as dominated by groups of boorish semi-morons. Many intellectuals have taken this stance in Italy, although there is a parallel and proud tradition of intellectual fandom.

## From the Armchair to the *Curva*

*Real* fans – those who follow a particular team – can be divided into various types. For *armchair fans*, their fan-identity is not linked with their physical presence at games. These fans are happy to watch and support their team from afar, to take part in tactical debates, to buy merchandise, argue about football in bars and read the sports press. A second group includes those who went through a phase of going to the stadium regularly, and then stopped. Others perhaps just go to the big games. Many stadium fans are not fanatics – the majority do *not* stand in the *curva* (the home fans' end), nor do they sing for the whole match. These fans have a love–hate relationship with the more hysterical behaviour of other supporters of their team. *All* fans follow results and 'suffer' with their teams. They also – and especially from the mid-1960s onwards – organize fan clubs and cultural societies. In the 1970s, groups of Italian fans began to set up entirely new forms of organization – and they gave themselves an evocative name: the *ultrà*.

## The *ultrà*. The fanatics get organized

The *ultrà* are the real fanatics – and they are proud of their fanaticism. *Ultrà* go regularly to the stadium, travel to away games and stand in the *curva*, the fan-heart of any stadium.[7] As a term, *ultrà* should not be confused with hooligan, although it is often translated that way. Italy's *ultrà* are more complicated than British hooligans – and violence is only a small part of their make-up. For British hooligans, violence is an end, for Italian *ultrà*, it is a *means*. Unlike hooligans the *ultrà* have adopted forms of self-organization similar to those found in political groups and amongst social movements.[8] The most important have offices, bars, meetings, 'membership' and their own merchandise as well as radio stations, fanzines and newspapers and even their own coach companies. Nonetheless, the differences should not be taken too far. Many Italian *ultrà* idolized British hooligans and when it came to the actual violence, they were often far more deadly.

The first modern *ultrà* organization was probably the *Fossa dei Leoni* (Lions' den) group formed by Milan fans in 1968, although many fan clubs and circles were set up in the 1930s and during later decades.[9]

Milan's *ultrà* had their base in a specific, numbered part of the *curva*.[10] Soon afterwards, Inter fans formed the *Inter Boys SAN* that, rather alarmingly, stands for Armed Black-and-Blue Squad.[11] Since the 1970s, Inter's hard-core support has tended to the right or far right, whilst Milan's fans have at least avoided extremism. The SAN title was apparently inspired by the SAM, a small group of fascists operating in the north of Italy after 1945. Although fascism collapsed in 1945, and those who still called themselves fascists were a tiny minority, far-right organizations still attracted significant numbers of young people in the post-war period. The use of 'Boys' betrayed the English inspiration of many of these groups – 'English' in the sense of their fandom (songs, scarves, standing up) and of the cult of violence and the hooligans. In 1971 Sampdoria fans formed a group named after a popular player from the 1950s and 1960s (Tito Cucchiaroni), and the same year saw the *Brigate gialloblu* (Verona) and a Florentine group take shape. Torino's younger fans set up the *Granata Corps* (now a very right-wing group) in 1973. Juventus's more lively fans were organized into the *Fighters* – which needs little explanation – and the *Drughi*, inspired by *A Clockwork Orange*.

The *ultrà* were mainly – but not only – young men, although their leaders were often older. Over time they gained control of the 'territory' made up by the *curva*, and ran things in that area – checking exactly who went in and out, what was sung and how people behaved. All this was organized, hierarchically, around groups of leaders known as the *capocurva*. During games one or two *capocurve* sit facing the crowd with a megaphone to lead the singing. *Ultrà* leaders – not elected, they 'emerge' – are close to the management of many clubs, and are issued with tickets and often free access to away transport. In part, this was to the advantage of the clubs, who thereby guaranteed support, but it was also a relationship based on threats and fear: *'either you give us free tickets, or else'*. *Ultrà* leaders decided whom to boo and whom to cheer and which banners and flags should be shown.

Violence was (and is) a key component of *ultrà* identity – within the stadium – through the throwing of objects or battles with police – and outside, with other fans or (again) the police. Rarely did *ultrà* try and 'take' opposing ends, unlike in the England of the 1970s, although they liked to steal banners and flags and display them as trophies.

*Ultrà* groups proliferated in the 1980s, and frequent battles took place amongst different (and often short-lived) organizations over the control of the stadium, or specific parts of the *curva*. It was in this period that the *ultrà* model took root across Italy, right down to tiny semi-professional teams playing in the lower leagues.[12] However, the proliferation of the *ultrà* signalled the end of the unified model of the 1970s, where single groups had been able to unite whole *curve*. The murder of a Genoa fan in 1995 was the sign of a deep crisis in the *ultrà* movement, and led to some surprising attempts to change direction and calls for a return to a – highly mythologized – *ultrà* purity.

These fans often acted outside the law, although they had their own private rules and regulations. Part of the stadium was *theirs*, and they could do what they liked there. Whilst normal fans were often meticulously searched on their way into the stadium (and metal detectors were briefly introduced in 1979 after the death of a Lazio fan) the *ultrà* were allowed to bring in flares, flags, huge banners and fireworks, as well as megaphones and speakers. Travelling fans were provided with special trains – which they used for free, intimidating anyone who asked them to provide a ticket. These trains were often smashed up, or used as bases from which to attack other fans.[13]

This trend towards a world apart was also extended to the economics of football. It was well known that Lazio football club do not engage in the normal production and sale of shirts and kit, as this lucrative business is controlled by their *ultrà*.[14] Dangerous alliances, built on a system of threats, blackmail and violence, were formed between *ultrà* groups, management and players. Deals would be done to avoid violence, or indeed to spark it off, if needed. By the 1990s, no player, no president, no manager could survive without the support of a restricted group of *capi-ultrà*, who were increasingly politicized. Yet, only a small minority of fans were *ultrà*. *Most* fans, even in the stadiums, were not *ultrà* members and not so violently obsessive about their football.

Violence was not directed at *all* opposition fans. In Italy, a system of club 'twinning' has developed which has no equal anywhere else in the world. *Ultrà* representatives decide on their friends, and their enemies. With their friends, 'fan twinning' takes place, and in games between the 'twinned' clubs the *ultrà* tend to fraternize. Sometimes these twinnings are based around reciprocal hatreds, other times they are political.[15] Brescia in 2003, for example, were twinned with Milan, Cesena, Salernitana, Mantova, Catanzaro and St Etienne. Twinnings were not permanent, and could be 'broken'. The collapse of old alliances and the formation of new ones could occur through misunderstandings, or perceived insults, or simply events on the pitch. Livorno and Genoa were sworn enemies purely because Genoa were twinned with Livorno's arch-rivals Pisa. When Genoa broke their twinning with Pisa, they duly linked up with Livorno. These twinnings are listed in guides and semi-official press releases announce changes to fan alliances.

Some – especially from within – saw the *ultrà* as a political or social movement or, rhetorically, a 'cultural world'.[16] Very few commentators or researchers took refuge in traditional social explanations of *ultrà* violence. All studies of the *ultrà* have shown that very few are particularly poor or underprivileged. The *ultrà* were part of a collective culture, not the result of money or the lack of it. Two of the *capi-ultrà* involved in the 2004 semi-riot at Roma's stadium turned out to be a cameraman and a financial consultant. The rituals and pleasures associated with *ultrà* behaviour were many, especially in a society where the political push from 1968 was on the wane and the cultural opportunities offered to young people were few and far between. The *ultrà* were clearly 'not only a public-order problem' (Edmondo Berselli) but something much more deep-rooted. They were a 'world apart, which constructed its own identity in an enclave of marginality' (Berselli).

All *ultrà* groups – left- and right-wing – organized themselves through strong hierarchies, and lived almost as military units, especially during the matches themselves. Their enemies were other fans and the police, who were often described as 'murderers'. A Cosenza banner summed up this philosophy: *Basta con la violenza. Via la polizia dagli stadi.* 'Let's stop violence. Get the police out of the stadiums'. Like all ritualized groups, *ultrà* had their trophies, heroic myths and martyrs. Stories – handed down by word-of-mouth or written up in fanzines or on websites – usually involved clashes with other fans. Given the military-type security used by police forces inside stadiums, many fights took place elsewhere – the streets, railway stations and above all motorway service stations, the true killing fields of the Italian football fan in the 1980s and 1990s. *Ultrà* myths exalted courage and stigmatized cowardice. Many *ultrà* songs accused other *ultrà* of running away from physical confrontation.

The *curva* is an extraordinary – if slightly scary – place to be on a Sunday. A community of 15–20,000 people, in the big stadiums, who move almost as one. Police very rarely move into the realm of the *ultrà* – and tend to react to any violence with liberal use of batons or tear gas, aimed merely at containing the fans in their territory.[17] To some extent, this strategy is successful, but it is also very expensive. By 2003 some 8,000 police and military police were being employed every week within and outside stadiums, at a cost of 31 million euros (which was paid by the state, not the clubs). Violence is pushed onto the streets. In the 2002–3 season, only 20 per cent of football-related violence took place inside stadiums, and two thirds of that violence was linked to the throwing of objects. Opposing fans rarely get to each other inside grounds, surrounded as they are by thousands of (armed) riot police.

Much else besides goes on during games. *Ultrà* fans openly smoke huge joints (many are just out for a good time), drink out of whisky bottles (the more hedonistic *ultrà* groups revelled in their supposed 'alcoholism') and fight with police more or less with the certainty that they might be beaten up, but they probably wouldn't be arrested.[18] New repressive laws have tried to deal with this 'problem', and closed-circuit TV is often used to identify culprits, but there are clearly unholy alliances between the police and *capi-ultrà*, the former using the latter to keep 'their' fans in check. Some fans were able to leave and enter stadiums almost at will. In May 2001 Inter fans even managed to bring a motor-scooter into the *curva* at San Siro halfway through the game (right up on the second tier). They then proceeded to smash up the vehicle in question before throwing it down onto the crowd below. Luckily, nobody was hurt, but the incident raised some alarming security issues.

It should be added that many Italian stadiums are unsafe, and that little has been learned in Italy from the disasters of Heysel (blamed exclusively on the British hooligans) or Hillsborough (ditto). *Ultrà* always stand in the *curva*, and every year there are cases of fans falling to death or serious injury from one level of the stadium to another. Fires are lit and fireworks and flares ritually fired across and even into stands, whilst items are thrown at players and down onto the heads of other fans. Most stadiums still have protective fences and ditches (and sometimes these are up to twenty metres high – the maximum height set by the Taylor Report after Hillsborough was 2.2 metres) and little stewarding has been introduced. Of the 122 professional stadiums in use in 2003, 69 (57 per cent) were *officially* unsafe and could only be used thanks to special permission given by local mayors on a weekly basis. The idea that crowd control was above all a public-order problem blinded the authorities to the real dangers present in these stadiums. Much lip-service is paid to the 'English model', but very few people take the trouble to study what actually happened after the Taylor Report. Italian fans express amazement at the lack of fences and trouble inside English stadiums, but hardly anyone bothers to ask why this is now possible, and the peace and quiet in England is often attributed to the supposed hard line imposed by Margaret Thatcher in the 1980s.[19]

## Racism and Italian football. North and South. Viva Etna!

Before the late 1980s, racism amongst Italian football fans was largely directed at other Italians. Apart from some vicious local rivalries – city derbies as well as long-running hostilities, such as those between Ascoli and Ancona, Pisa and Livorno or Varese and Como – this racism was especially evident in games involving northern and southern teams. Verona fans, (in)famous for their racism, started to up the stakes in the 1980s with the notorious '*Vesuvio facci sognare*' – 'Help us dream, Vesuvius' – banner in a Napoli–Verona match, a reference to the huge (dormant) volcano which overlooks the southern city. Similar sentiments were expressed by Milan fans in 1991, 'Give us a present: another Pompeii', and by Verona (again) away to Catania – *Forza Etna* (an allusion to another volcano which towers over the Sicilian city). Neapolitan fans responded with a legendary banner: 'Juliet is a slag!' (with reference to Romeo and Juliet, set in Verona).

With the rise of the regionalist *Lega Nord* in the 1980s, a party hostile to the south that frequently referred to southerners in racist terms, regionalist sentiments proliferated on the terraces. The *Lega* often called for Italy to be separated into northern and southern nations, and attacked the very basis of the nation-state. In 1993, Milan fans displayed a banner which read *Garibaldi infamone* (Garibaldi, who had united Italy, was a 'disgrace') and southerners were attacked for not being 'Italian'. Northern fans depicted the south as a hostile land, inhabited by thieves and mafiosi, which was not a worthy part of the Italian nation. Hence the 'Welcome to Italy' banner displayed by Verona's *curva* (at home to Napoli) in 1985, or references to dirty and smelly southerners, to 'Those with Cholera' or even 'Earthquakers'. Milan–Roma games were especially tense. Roma fans loved to sing, to the tune of *Il sole mio* – 'I have only one dream/Milan in flames'. Milan's fans replied with irony: 'Milan in flames? And where will you work?' Such sentiments could also be displayed *between* northern fans. Genoa fans were accused of 'stinking of fish' by their Milan rivals in a game in the mid-1990s in Milan.

## Other Racisms

Lazio fans were openly anti-Semitic, associating rivals Roma with the city's small Jewish population. There was no justification for this link, although Roma had been run by Jewish presidents in the past. In the 1980s, a huge banner was displayed across the Lazio end during a derby: '*Curva Sud* full, Synagogues empty'. Roma's fans stood in the *curva sud*. In 1994, when the general election was extended across two days in order to accommodate the Jewish New Year, another Lazio banner appeared – *Andatevene senza fretta, potete votare anche domani*; 'Don't hurry home, you can also vote tomorrow'. Later banners were more offensive: *Auschwitz la vostra casa*; 'Your home is Auschwitz', or *SQUADRA DE NEGRI, CURVA D'EBREI*; 'Team of blacks, curve of Jews'. Unfortunately, Roma's support was also slowly taken over by the far-right in the 1980s and began to display racist slogans and boo black players. A long struggle took place over the 'control' of Roma's *curva sud*, with a shift towards extremist far-right politics. It was not difficult to spot fascist symbols in both the Lazio and Roma *curve* on a Sunday – Celtic crosses, Mussolini banners, swastikas. Lazio fans would often sing the national anthem, complete with fascist salutes. New laws were

Racism. Lazio banner directed at Roma fans during a derby. 'Team of
blacks, *curva* of Jews', 29 April 2001.

introduced against banners in grounds after a notorious incident in
January 2000, when this *striscione* appeared in the Lazio *curva*: '*Onore
alla Tigre Arkan*'. The banner was dedicated to Serbian war criminal
'Tiger' Arkan as well as a homage to their idol, Serbian defender Sinisa
Mihajlovic.[20]

Other notoriously right-wing *curve* were those at Verona, Padova,
Inter and, in another shift from left to right, Fiorentina. When Lazio
played Arsenal in the Champions League in October 2000, Patrick
Vieira was racially abused, he alleged, by Lazio's Serbian central
defender Sinisa Mihajlovic. The crowd also booed many of Arsenal's
black players. Vieira went public with his accusations, and Mihajlovic
was forced into a humiliating climb-down by the club, having to read
out a mealy-mouthed statement before Lazio's next home game.[21]

Italy became a country of immigration for the first time in the 1980s
and 1990s – with the arrival of more than one and a half million
foreigners, mainly to work in the dirty end of the rich Italian economy.
These immigrants came from a whole series of countries, with the
most important groups originating in North Africa (Morocco, Senegal,

Egypt), the Philippines, China, the East (Albania, Romania) and South America (Ecuador, Peru). These arrivals were linked to various historical moments and events across the world, such as wars, economic change and the end of the Cold War. In many areas these immigrants were essential to the functioning of the economic system, especially as the 'Italian' population is ageing at an alarming rate. Nonetheless, it is clear that these immigrants are, to cite Aristide Zolberg, 'needed but not welcome ... there is a contradiction between their presence as economic actors and the undesirability of their social presence'. The increasing fear and tension linked to deindustrialization, rises in criminality and the spatial segregation of the major cities have created tensions that Italy appears to be unready and unwilling to confront.

It was around this time that racism became an open wound in society, and was reproduced at football grounds. When I watched AC Milan play in the late 1980s, I was surprised by the *lack* of racism, having been used to constant bu-buing at English grounds. Very soon, this all changed. Bu-bu chants, directed at black players whenever they touched the ball, were heard at San Siro (Gullit and later Desailly were victims) and at other stadiums. Gullit himself had become a symbol for the anti-racist movement in the city, dedicating his European Player of the Year award to Nelson Mandela and appearing in concert at the city's immigrant club, the Zimba. Other black players were subjected to constant racist abuse. The authorities were slow to react, but they finally introduced fines and even threatened more serious sanctions against clubs with racist fans. Verona were constantly fined, and flirted with the banning of their home ground in the 2000–2001 season, a story told in some detail by Tim Parks in *A Season with Verona*.[22] In the 2002–3 season Fiorentina fans displayed this banner in a local derby against Prato: '*Folza Plato*'. This racist banner made reference to the fact that Prato has a large Chinese community.

The contradictions of this kind of overt racism were exposed at Inter when the Milanese club signed the black English midfielder Paul Ince in 1994. Ince soon became a crowd favourite and the bu-bu chants disappeared. At a match between Cremona and Inter in 1995, Ince was involved in a clash with the home team goalkeeper. Soon, the whole stadium erupted in a chant of *negro-di-merda* (shitty blacky). Ince applauded the crowd, sarcastically, and was booked for his gesture.

This incident provoked outcry and led to a letter of apology from the Mayor of Cremona to Ince. There had been some ominous warning signs in the late 1980s and early 1990s. First, the signing of Israeli international Ronnie Rosenthal by Udinese was called off after an anti-Semitic campaign by local *ultrà*. When Dutch international Aron Winter signed for Lazio (another club with extreme right-wing connections), graffiti complaining about the signing of a 'black-jew' appeared in Rome.

Verona's fans revelled in their racist reputation. On one occasion, they displayed a large black doll hanging from a noose with this message attached: 'Give him the stadium to clean'. A few years later, Verona's president told the press that he would never be allowed to buy a black player because of the hostility of his own fans. Some of the contradictions of this kind of attitude were revealed when the hero of Lazio's title-winning season in 2000 was a black player (with a Che Guevara tattoo): Juan Sebastian Veron. Later, Lazio signed one of the best young Italian players – Fabio Liverani – whose mother was from Mogadiscio and had met her Roman husband in Italy in the 1960s. Inter's fans also indulged in racist chanting, and immigrants who ventured into the *curva*, even if they were just selling soft drinks, were in danger of being beaten up. Many traditionally left-wing *curve* moved to the right, and towards open racism, in the 1980s and 1990s. Fiorentina and Roma, as well as Torino and Juventus, were amongst the most important examples. In 2005 an Italian barman and *ultrà* was killed after he intervened to stop a fight between two Albanian immigrants. In the wake of the murder, *ultrà* from Varese and Milan descended on the small town that had hosted the tragedy. Fascist and anti-immigrant slogans were heard as skinhead fans from the *Blood and Honour* group linked to Varese paraded through the town, attacking an Albanian who happened to be passing by.

These incidents are not the whole story. Many black players also became fan idols, from the 1960s onwards. In the 1990s, courageous fans tried to oppose the racists, and an annual festival grouped together anti-racist supporters. The football authorities tried with some success to clamp down on the chanting. One bizarre case took place in Treviso, in the north-east of Italy, during the 2000–2001 Serie B season. As

Treviso teetered on the brink of relegation, some of the club's fans abused their own striker – the Nigerian Akeem Omolade. At the next home game, the whole Treviso team came on with their faces painted black in solidarity with their team-mate. Whilst this Black-and-White Minstrel protest might appear somewhat anachronistic, it was at least a sign of dissent. Much racism was politically motivated. Far-right groups such as the neo-fascist *Forza Nuova* organization easily took control of many *curve* in the 1990s and most of this racism came from within society. It was not invented by football fans, nor was it confined to football stadiums. Racism was everywhere in Italy, even amongst ministers and politicians. *Lega Nord* leader Umberto Bossi referred to immigrants as 'Bingo Bongo' whilst he was Minister for Reform and other members of his party went even further, calling for immigrants to be dropped from planes, without parachutes, or tattooed on their feet. Yet, it was also from within society that trends were emerging that were in direct opposition to this prejudice. More and more black Italians were being born, and becoming part of the professional game. By 2004, both Fabio Liverani and defender Matteo Ferrari (whose mother was Italian and father from Algeria) had played for the national team, while athlete Andrew Howe Besozzi – born in Los Angeles, brought up in Rieti – was part of the Italian Olympic squad, and spoke in a broad local Italian accent. Liverani played alongside Paolo Di Canio, who had this to say in his best-selling autobiography: 'If we're not careful, in ten years' time Italy could be a Muslim country. I have nothing against Muslims, but I don't want my Italian culture to disappear.'[23]

## Againstism. *Gufare!*

*Gufare*: 'To bring bad luck, to hope for the bad luck of another,
to snort, to hoot, to scoff, to *support against*'

There is a glorious tradition amongst Italian soccer fans of *againstism* – supporting whoever is playing against the team you hate. The Italian word for this is *gufare*. In many cases, this behaviour is linked to local rivalries. Lazio fans will party when Roma lose, and vice-versa, especially in big matches. Lazio fans supported Liverpool against Roma in the 1984 European Cup final, and celebrated when Roma lost on penalties. After the 1985 Heysel disaster pro-Liverpool slogans became much more sinister. Sick *Grazie Liverpool* graffiti appeared all over Italy. Later, in 2002, Lazio played Inter at home. Inter needed to win the game to win the *scudetto*, and, if they lost, Roma were still in with a chance of the championship. Lazio's message to their own squad was clear: *lose*. Peruzzi (their goalkeeper) was politely asked to 'lean on his post'. The squad disobeyed, winning 4–2.

However, some clubs are more 'supported against' than others, especially those with the most real fans – Juventus, Milan, Inter. Anti-Juventus feelings are particularly strong.[24] This is a team that has won too much, and inspires jealousy and bitterness in equal measure. Sometimes, this againstism is 'political'. Many who hate Berlusconi have loathed Milan ever since the businessman-turned-politician took over the club in 1986. After a big defeat, graffiti immediately appear (*Grazie* for the team which has beaten the team you want beaten) and text messages fly back and forth. Againstism is particularly controversial with the national team. Verona fans have been known to boo Italy, as have Fiorentina supporters. Gianluca Vialli famously admitted that he had backed Brazil against Italy in the 1994 World Cup final, so great was his dislike of manager Arrigo Sacchi. In 2003 Milan lost the Intercontinental Cup final against Boca Juniors from Argentina. Interviewed that evening, Fabio Cannavaro (then of Inter) admitted that he had *gufato* – supported against – Milan and was happy that they had lost. This was seen as rather inelegant, but Cannavaro was only being honest.

Victory in Italy is always an occasion to 'bury' your rivals. Fake funerals are often prepared after championship successes. Cagliari fans carried little coffins through the streets as they (rather optimistically) 'buried' Juventus in 1970 and Napoli fans did the same in 1987. In Naples thousands of black-edged fake death notices for Juventus were produced and stuck up all over the city. When Fiorentina went bankrupt, Pisa fans produced a huge banner with a massive white cross and the words: '1926 AC Fiorentina 2002. *Riposa in pace!*' (Rest in peace). Joy in victory is made doubly joyful by the humiliation of your rivals. Some of this tradition can also be found on the internet (as in the well-maintained www.antijuve.com site) and in the successful series of books with titles like *No Milan*, and *No Inter*. There is also a very funny anti-Milan site with Milan hero Rino Gattuso depicted as the missing link and other jokes at Berlusconi's expense. When Milan lost to Liverpool in the 2005 Champions League final, Inter fans were in ecstasy. One Inter wag went to the trouble of collecting together black and red balloons, which he then floated past the offices of Milan fans.

Againstism is very strong in the city of Florence, where numerous shops carry joke stickers which proclaim that they have been 'de-hunchbacked', in honour of a common Juventus nickname – *I gobbi*, the hunchbacks. When Enzo Maresca (once of West Brom) joined Fiorentina from Juventus for the start of the 2004 season, a strange rite was performed at the training ground. A group of Fiorentina fans armed with brushes and water proceeded to brush and wash Maresca's upper back. All this was done with his own consent, and amidst much laughter. Later, the meaning of the whole rite became clearer. Maresca himself had been symbolically 'de-hunchbacked'. In Genoa, Pietro Cheli has written that 'the relationship between the fans of the city's two teams [Genoa and Sampdoria] can only be understood by psycho-analysts. Is it more pleasurable if your team wins or the other team loses? Is it more important to win the championship or the derby?'[25]

A key component of 'everyday' fandom is the *sfottò* – taking the piss – jokes, insults, reference to past defeats, irony. At the stadium, the *sfottò* is often expressed through *striscioni* (banners) prepared by fans and displayed during games. In 2004 a best-selling book was brought out with some of the best examples from all over Italy (and without many of the nasty, racist or political banners which had plagued the game for years).[26]

These *striscioni* are the best expressions of the combination of wit, fatalism, protest and local rivalries that marked the most creative and loyal fans. Sometimes, banners led to collective 'replies' during the game itself (it is said that fans occasionally reveal the content of their banners to their rivals). Certain themes are obsessive, and go to the heart of fandom and fan history; Lazio fans being seen as provincial, Juventini as 'thieves'. *Striscioni* often refer to recent events or political and/or financial crises. They are also, frequently, directed at the fans' own teams, particular players or presidents. On other occasions, returning players are praised or insulted, or dead players remembered. Often, the banners were just good jokes.

Examples include *See you back at our place* – Ancona–Notts County, 1993; or *We are jealous of your view*. This Messina banner was displayed when they were playing Reggina from Reggio Calabria, which lies just across the Sicilian straits on the mainland. The best banners are self-deprecating. This Siena banner reverses the usual boastful slogan, making a joke out of their meagre away support. *One of us, a thousand of you* (2003). When tiny club Chievo Verona got close to European qualification in 2001, they displayed this slogan: *How do you spell Champions League?* A minor team, Fano, also used irony to exalt their 'minor' status. *We've never been in B* is a slogan often used by Inter against Milan fans. In Fano's case, it was also true, but because they had always been, more or less, in Serie D.

Of course, againstism has its dark side. Roma and Torino fans celebrated openly after 32 Juventus fans died in the Heysel disaster. Juventus fans have joked about Superga for years. Many rivalries stem from violent incidents, or have produced death and destruction, over the years. Florence became something of a militarized zone during its matches with Juve in the 1990s,[27] and Rome derbies are almost always accompanied by violence and have been tainted by tragedies. The dark side of againstism is that being in the wrong place at the wrong time, or having the wrong scarf, can lead to violence. Claudio Spagnolo was murdered because he was a Genoa supporter, and Antonio De Falchi died purely because he had a Roma scarf around his neck.

## Choreographies

One of the positive aspects of the rise of the *ultrà* is the atmosphere and spectacle in Italian stadiums. Supporting is almost a military operation – organized, stunning and exciting. Not surprisingly the Italians refer to this as *coreografia*. This supporting-as-theatre takes many forms. Huge flags are unfurled and rolled down the *curva* – sometimes covering one whole side of a stadium. Lazio's Eagles supporters produced a 56-metre-long banner in 1976. Fireworks are let off causing loud bangs and massive plumes of coloured smoke that can hold up the game for some time. Singing is rigorously coordinated and sometimes accompanied by music – drums, trumpets, bugles.[28] Even more ambitious displays have included the distribution of thousands of coloured cards to the whole Lazio *curva* in the 2000–2001 season. The outcome of this massive effort was somewhat prosaic: a massive slogan across the whole *curva* which read *Roma Merda* – but the whole thing was the object of enormous pride amongst the Lazio faithful.

Sometimes players adopt the behaviour of the *ultrà* – either in an attempt to win over their own fans and/or alienate others, or simply for the fun of it. Francesco Totti displayed a series of provocative T-shirts in the Rome derby that infuriated the Lazio fans. Paolo Di Canio was an ex-*ultrà* from the badlands of the Rome urban periphery who later played for the team he supported as a lad – Lazio. His attitude on the field was often in mimicry of the world he had known and loved, and he had never made any secret of his right-wing politics (shared by many Lazio fans) nor of his admiration for Benito Mussolini (right down to the *DUX* tattoo on his arm). In his best-selling autobiography Di Canio described Mussolini as 'basically a very principled, ethical individual'.[29] Brought back to the club at the end of his career in 2003, in his first league game he first helped win a penalty and then pushed away the designated penalty-taker in order to take the kick himself. After scoring, he played the *ultrà* game with ritualized badge-kissing and over-the-top celebrations.[30]

Striker Cristiano Lucarelli from Livorno continued to follow his team as an *ultrà* even whilst he was playing professional football with other clubs. His shirt number when he finally signed for his home-town club – 99 – was a homage to the most extreme of the Livornese *ultrà* groups, the *BAL*, formed in 1999. Ex-*ultrà* did not just become players. Some even developed into decision-makers. Right-wing politician Maurizio Gasparri had stood on the *curva sud* as a young man, when he had been a fanatical Roma supporter. Gasparri later became Communications Minister in the second Berlusconi government and drew up a law regulating Italian television.

As football and politics became ever more intertwined, it became more and more common to see politicians in stadiums, in the exclusive VIP stands. San Siro was home to the Berlusconi clan, and associated northern politicians. In Rome, everyone turned up: Francesco Rutelli,

Green Mayor of the capital in the 1990s and a Lazio fan, was a regular, as were Massimo D'Alema – centre-left Roma fan – and assorted right-wing politicians as well as starlets, wannabe celebrities, hangers-on and foreign dignitaries.

## Protest. Fans on strike

The organization of the hard-core fans was often directed, impressively and often quite terrifyingly, against their own players, managers and owners. Sometimes, this protest has taken a peaceful form. Fans will come in ten minutes late, or leave – *en masse* – ten minutes early. Often, however, these protests have slipped into violence – ranging from threats and insults to the throwing of missiles to the production of makeshift bombs. On some extreme occasions, fans have decided that they have had enough, and have put a stop to games through violence. This happened with Torino's long-suffering fans in February 2003, and at Como after three penalties were awarded against their team in December 2002. In the first case, the protest was directed at the Torino team, in the second it was aimed at the referee.[31]

The outcome was the same – the games were abandoned. Protests of this type are often accompanied by a clear message or a press release from the fans involved, or a banner. Inter fans left their *curva* empty in 2004 and on another similar occasion Milan fans went home early on the last day of the season, leaving a banner that read: 'After a season like the last one, you deserve this support'.[32] Many *ultrà* groups were bitterly opposed to the commercial trends in the modern game – higher ticket prices, the moving of matches away from Sundays and above all Pay-TV. One common banner seen at grounds during the 2003–4 season read *Questo calcio ci fa sky-fo*: 'This football disgusts us' (a play on the word for disgust – *schifo* – and Sky, which owned TV rights at the time). Fans complained about the way games were moved around. When a Fiorentina game in the 2000–2001 season was moved to a Monday local fans unfurled a banner which read: 'We are all hair-dressers'. In Italy barbers are closed on Mondays.

The *ultrà* hated journalists and the mass media, whom they blamed for their negative image and for the repression they felt they had suffered at the hands of the police. Journalists were frequently insulted

Inter's *ultrà* fans refuse to turn up for the start of the match, leaving only two banners which read '. . . have we missed anything???' and 'Apologies for the late arrival'. Inter–Chievo, 14 March 2004, Milan.

(purely as *journalists*) and even beaten up by *ultrà* at or outside grounds. In return, fans were marginalized by the televisual way of presenting football. In Italy fan sound would often be turned down or off so that it would not distract from our commentator-filtered view of the game.

*Ultrà* groups occasionally decide that a manager has to go, and do everything in their power to get rid of him. Carlo Ancelotti was *persona non grata* with hard-core Juventus fans from the very beginning of his term in charge in February 1999. Banners calling him 'pig-face' complete with a picture of a pig appeared even before he took over. Inter president Massimo Moratti resigned soon after a 'Moratti out' banner had appeared in the Inter *curva* in January 2004.[33] Once a player has become the object of the *curva*'s hatred, it is very difficult for them to continue, although fans tend to be fickle. The relationship between the *curva* and even their heroes can quickly degenerate. Christian Vieri was the idol of the Inter fans in 2001–2003, when he scored 46 goals in 48 games. This all changed very quickly in the following season, especially after Vieri was interpreted as having been part of a plot to get rid of manager Hector Cuper. Vieri stopped celebrating his goals, sending a clear message to the fans that he was not happy. Journalists began to focus more on the behaviour of Vieri than on his play. Groups of fans started to boo him – throughout the game – and he reacted with sarcastic applause. Finally, the Inter fans made their feelings crystal clear with yet another banner in April 2004: *Non sentiamo più ragioni, Bobo fuori dai coglioni*: 'We have had enough: Bobo [Vieri] out'. Hardcore fans usually prefer a mediocre player who tries hard to a good player who can't be bothered. *Go to work!* is a very frequent admonishment from the *curva*, as is *Never give up!*

In the 1990s and beyond, attacks on players became more and more common. In February 2004 Napoli player Renato Olive was threatened with a knife near his home by fans who ordered him to 'try harder'. Earlier that year an Avellino player was attacked in Cagliari's airport by a fan furious about a missed penalty. The most serious case of anti-player violence took place during a Serie C derby between Latina and Tivoli. Latina was one of the most right-wing cities in Italy, built (in 232 days) under fascism as a new town in the 1930s. The citizens elected an openly fascist Mayor (with 73 per cent of the vote) in 2002 who set about restoring many of the town's buildings, including one in the shape of an enormous M – for Mussolini. Here, the local team's *ultrà* fans revel in their fascism and call themselves after the original name of the city, Littoria. After a 3–2 home defeat in February 2004, a number of fans invaded the pitch and attacked certain players, chasing them to the dressing room.

The fickle player–*ultrà* relationship is often revealed when players return to their old clubs. Sometimes, they are cheered and presented with flowers and scarves, other times they are whistled at for the whole game. The line between these two 'receptions' is a fine one. Pavel Nedved received the 'good-ex-player' treatment when he returned to Lazio with Juventus, Alessandro Nesta was mercilessly booed when he went back to the same club with Milan.

## Local Stories. Venice, Mestre and *Veneziamestre*

Despite all the talk and moral panic about the *ultrà* movement, very little serious study was made of these people. In the late 1990s two Venetian historians, Filippo Benfante and Piero Brunello, decided to look in detail at the ways in which their local team was supported. Their methods were highly original. They went to the games, and commented on what they saw, heard and felt, as well as delving deep into the cultural identity of the people around them. They wrote that 'we realized that we could talk about a little world by beginning with a stadium'. The result was the most interesting and important book about football to appear in Italy. Not surprisingly, it was also a book that was almost completely ignored.[34]

AC Venezia had been formed in 1907, and adopted green-and-black shirts. In the 1920s a rich and powerful entrepreneur – Count Volpi – decided to make the Venice area an industrial port. He requisitioned vast swaths of the mainland across from historic Venice and enticed state-funded factories to settle there. The result was the city of Mestre, a working-class sprawl that would soon dwarf Venice itself and would pollute the city's waters over the following decades. Mestre founded its own football team, AC Mestre, in 1929 – they played in orange.

Neither team was particularly successful. Venezia won the Italian Cup in 1941, when they also finished third in Serie A, inspired by midfielders Valentino Mazzola and Ezio Loik, who would soon go on to stardom with the *Grande Torino* team. However, a long decline began in the late 1960s and Venezia spent most of the following decades in Serie C. AC Mestre were a smaller club, who spent one season in Serie B after the war but for the rest of the time languished in the lower divisions. Both clubs were affected by social change. Venezia itself haemorrhaged residents from the 1950s onwards as people were re-located to the mainland, becoming a kind of artistic Disneyland for US tourists. Mestre's huge and smelly chemical industries began to close in the 1980s, and it was later discovered that hundreds of workers had contracted cancer thanks to their dangerous working conditions.

In the 1980s, to the horror of both sets of fans, the teams merged into *Veneziamestre* (which became AC Venezia in 1990). The result was an identity crisis. Some fans simply refused to go to the stadium (which switched between Mestre and a Venetian island before finally fixing on the latter venue). Most *ultrà* tried to maintain their previous identity, right down to the old colours. All three colours were present in the club's shirts, although the supposed 'marginalization' of orange at the start of one season led to such protest that the shirts were redesigned. In Mestre's old stadium, the two sets of fans had one *curva* each. On the island, they divided up the *curva*. For a long time, fans from the same team came to blows, before some sort of peace was established as the team ended up in Serie A, before dropping down again.

Despite these divisions, Venezia's fans were also united in many ways: in their use of dialect; in their hatred of other Veneto teams; in their anti-racism. Some of the Venezia *ultrà* launched a campaign against the racist chanting which infected most Italian grounds in the late 1990s. This took the form of banners, leaflets and sarcasm. In one game against Verona – notorious for its racist hard-core support – Venezia's fans turned the racist bu-bu chants against Verona's white players, thereby rendering the whole concept of the chant absurd. The Venezia *curva* also supported the peace movement during various international wars, and sometimes revelled in a shared 'Venetian' identity. One favourite song is sung to the tune of 'God Save the Queen', and is called *Un giro in gondola*. The performance of the chant also involves the miming of the gondolier's actions and the whole *curva* swaying to and fro.

Much of the tension between the 'two' sets of fans is also political, or politically inspired. Since 1979 four referendums have been held by those who wish to separate the local governments of Mestre and Venezia – joined together under fascist *diktat* in 1926. All have been defeated (albeit narrowly). Mestre and Venezia fans are even divided over statistics and history. Who is the club's top scorer of all time? What should be put in the trophy cabinet? Should the two teams also have their history merged? Venice's beautiful (and rather dangerous) football stadium, reached by a small bridge and with views of the lagoon with ships passing by, is a 'place of divided memories'.[35]

## Conclusions. The *ultrà* and fanaticism

'We don't know how to insult you any more'
(Inter fan banner, directed at their own team, 2004)

By the start of the twenty-first century, the *ultrà* had surely taken fandom far too far. They were no longer simple *tifosi* but fanatics who lived their whole lives through football. But the game itself – on the pitch – was increasingly a sideshow. The spectators in *calcio*'s over-indulgent circus got far more excited about transfer deals, the night-time antics of their players, contractual negotiations or rumour and gossip than about the action on the field. They were also self-obsessed, more interested in their own activities than in those of their team. The football itself had been drained of meaning, and only made sense when filtered through complicated rivalries and disputes which had little to do with a game played by 22 men on a grass pitch with a round ball. Being a fan was very rarely fun, or even satisfying. It was usually frustrating, expensive, time-consuming, stressful and nerve-racking – and it was a life-sentence.[36]

**CHAPTER 12**

# Murder, Massacre, Normality: *Calcio* and Violence since 1945

Italian football – on its own soil – has never had a Bradford, an Ibrox or a Hillsborough. There has never been a major stadium disaster despite the hundreds of thousands of games at all levels since the beginning of the twentieth century. However, *calcio* has been marked by frequent and disturbing outbreaks of violence. A number of individuals have lost their lives inside and outside football stadiums. Guns have been fired, and riot police have often been sent in. Frequently, this has been ritualized violence – the 'violence of the saloon', as Gian Paolo Ormezzano has called it[1] – but it has often been more serious, and the potential for a football-linked disaster remains strong. Moreover, the very normality of violence, especially since the 1970s, has numbed journalists and commentators to the problem. Violence has become part of everyday footballing life, in the stands, outside the ground, during games, and even in the dressing room. Clashes with the police are a key part of the *ultrà* way of life; 'a powerful symbolic moment, which moves from a minimum (slogans such as *shitty job/ carabiniere*) to attacks, vandalism or open conflict using urban guerrilla war techniques'.[2] This normalization of violence remains one of the most worrying aspects of today's crisis-ridden system. This chapter will limit itself to some of the most serious incidents since 1945.

During Easter 1945, around the time of the final liberation of Italy from the Nazis by the armed anti-fascist partisans and Allied armies, Juventus and Torino played a friendly match in Turin. Ostensibly, the event was a commemoration for a Juventus director who had died after one of the numerous bombings of the city. After about half an hour of the second half, a fight between the players broke out after a hard challenge on Valentino Mazzola. As the tussle continued, someone fired a shot into the air from within the crowd. Soon, more guns appeared and most of the fans threw themselves to the ground. After an uneasy truce, another fight broke out on the pitch and further shots were fired amongst the fans, although nobody seems to have been hurt. For the record, Juventus won the game, 3–1.

Very few fans – in comparison with other countries – have died during games within Italian stadiums. One of the exceptions to this rule took place in Salerno on 28 April 1963. During a Serie C match between Salernitana and Potenza, some fans invaded the pitch. The police struggled to control the situation and shots were fired. During the clashes a spectator, Giuseppe Plaitano, died of a heart attack. His son, who was at the game with him, had no idea what was happening, and did not find out about his father's fate until much later that day.

## Murder. Vincenzo Paparelli. Rome. Olympic Stadium. 28.10.1979

Angelo Paparelli couldn't make the Rome derby on 28 October 1979. He lent his season ticket to his brother, Vincenzo, a car mechanic born in 1936, who went along to the game with his wife, Wanda.

In order to get a good view for the Rome derby, you need to get there early. Vincenzo arrived more than an hour before kick-off, and grabbed a bite to eat on the way in. Shortly after they had sat down in the packed *curva nord*, Vincenzo's wife heard a kind of *phhhfff* sound. She turned to her husband to see him slumped forward. Something was sticking out of his head and blood had splashed onto other spectators. Her immediate reaction was to pull the object out. It had penetrated his brain through his left eye, and smoke was still coming out of its tail. The item lodged in Vincenzo's skull was a nautical rocket and it had flown something like 160 metres over the whole pitch to embed itself in the head of the young father of two. A doctor who tried to save Paparelli later spoke of a 'war injury'. Vincenzo died on the way to hospital. The game continued, amidst violent scenes as the Lazio fans tried to invade the pitch. Rome declared a day of mourning and the whole Lazio team attended Paparelli's funeral.

The rocket had been 'smuggled' into the stadium and launched by an eighteen-year-old Roma fan, Giovanni Fiorillo. In 1993 Fiorillo died of a drugs overdose. After Paparelli's death, he had gone on the run for fourteen months, before returning to face trial. He was sentenced to six years and ten months in prison along with two accomplices who received lesser sentences. Later, it seems, a plaque dedicated to Paparelli 'disappeared' during work for the 1990 World Cup. Cruel Roma-inspired graffiti appeared all over the city: examples have included *1–10–100 Paparelli* and '28.10.79 a white and blue tomb was built'.

The Paparelli case led to a lot of talk and little action. Some referees blamed the media, calling for a ban on the *moviola*. Little was done to control dangerous items taken into the two *curva*, and still, today, all kinds of rockets are fired inside stadiums. More deaths have been caused by rockets since Paparelli in 1979 and at times even mini-bombs have been hurled onto the pitch. On a number of occasions, players have been hit or temporarily deafened by flares and fireworks. So ritualized is this that special fire teams, with buckets of sand, are on call during games in order to put out flares. They usually stand behind each goal. Many fans are searched on their way into the ground. Normal spectators routinely have rings and even keys taken away, and are forced to remove the tops of drink bottles.[3] *Ultrà* or fan-leaders are outside of these regulations, and are often (unofficially) allowed through with whole boxes of fireworks and flares. In 2005, after Inter fans threw a number of flares onto the pitch during a Champions League match, hitting Milan goalkeeper Dida on the shoulder, the government ordered that any game should be abandoned after the first flare. Unsurprisingly, this rule was not enforced.

# Massacre. Heysel. 29 May 1985

'Get those bodies back the full ten yards!
They're covering up the advertising boards!'

Chumbawamba, 'Heysel Stadium'

## Preamble. Memories of a Massacre

It was a game everybody was looking forward to – fans, neutrals, football aesthetes. The great Liverpool side of the 1970s and 1980s – Rush, Dalglish, Grobbelaar – against a great Juventus side – Platini, Boniek, Paolo Rossi, Scirea. The prize? The European Cup, which had brought so much bad luck to Juve over the years. For a team with over twenty league titles, they had a terrible record in the world's greatest club competition. Juve had only reached the final twice in eleven attempts, and had lost both times. This was the only international competition that Juventus had *never* won. Liverpool, meanwhile, were looking for their fifth European Cup.

This disaster – in which 39 people died (32 of them Italian) – has taken the name of a stadium that is no more – *Heysel*, in Brussels. The legal, political and cultural repercussions of Heysel were enormous, and are still being felt. British clubs were banned from European competitions for five years, and the massacre led, along with Hillsborough, to a first serious attempt to make football grounds safe in the UK. In Italy, Heysel cemented the images of the English fan as 'hooligan', and led to ferocious arguments over what happened that night. The story of Heysel is a story of incompetence, violence, cover-up, shame and lies. It is also a story of forgetting. Many people have an interest in not remembering what happened that night: the players, many fans, the Belgian politicians and police forces. These various groups have succeeded in obliterating the memory of the horror of that night. But most ordinary fans, who watched the game on TV, or who were there, can never forget.

In the town before the game, things were relatively calm. There were scuffles, and many of Liverpool's fans were drunk, but nothing serious appeared to take place. Some reports came in of a fight in which a Liverpool fan had been stabbed. A day later, it was reported that the fan in question had died. His name was given as Stephen Jackson.[4] Later, however, it appeared that this news was untrue. Fans even fraternized, exchanging scarves and flags. Simone Stenti, a Juventus fan from Milan, swapped his scarf. He had a ticket to Sector Z, the 'neutral' section of the ground.

Heysel stadium was constructed in 1930. Its last major football game as 'Heysel' was held on 29 May 1985 (although Milan played a European Cup match there in 1990). By the 1980s the stadium was crumbling and grass sprouted from the concrete terraces. Only flimsy wire-netting separated many of Liverpool's fans from Sector Z. The police were notable by their absence. Later reports stated that there were only eight policemen in that part of the stadium, and it later transpired that their walkie-talkies had no batteries. Many Juve fans had purchased expensive tickets for Sector Z through travel agencies. These were not the hard-core fans, who were at the other end of the ground, but middle-aged couples or fathers with their children, from all over Italy. Entry into Sector Z was through a tiny door, at which there was a solitary ticket collector. In amongst these Juve fans there was a smattering of French and Belgian spectators.

The Belgian police were worried about the thousands of counterfeit tickets which had been issued. They promised that 'the stewards will examine all tickets with great care'. However, fans reported that tickets were thrown back over the wall to let others in. The ground was built in a sunken pit, with the actual pitch well below street level. One Liverpool fan later claimed that the same ticket had been used four times. Other reports mentioned whole crates of beer being carried into the stadium by the Liverpool supporters.

About an hour before the game, the tension started to rise. Drunken Liverpool fans moved around freely on the terraces. At some point, it seems, they started to throw things at a group of Juve supporters. Then, at around 19.20, they charged, pulling down the inadequate wire fence with ease. The Juve fans and neutrals looked to escape and, in the near-absence of any police, were forced into a space far too small for the numbers there. At this point, the infamous 'small wall' collapsed. Some died under its bricks, many others were suffocated by the pressure of other bodies. In a few minutes – less than ten according to the Belgian authorities – 38 people were dead. It could have been far worse. Some argue that the collapse of the wall actually saved lives.

Desperate attempts were made to rescue dying fans. Bodies lay everywhere. Blankets were used as stretchers. The Belgian police truncheoned some of those who tried to escape onto the pitch. The policeman in charge of the operation had not supervised a football match before. He was later to express 'amazement' that trouble had occurred before the game. As Nick Hornby later wrote in *Fever Pitch*, 'a simple phone call to any metropolitan constabulary in England' would have helped him on this matter.

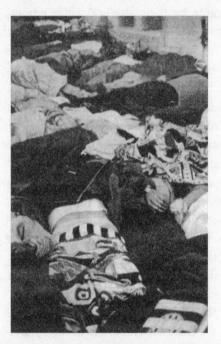

Heysel. Bodies covered in Juventus flags.

Slowly, the Belgian authorities gained some control of the situation. By now, understandably, the Juve fans at the other end were furious. One Juve fan was photographed firing a gun which turned out to be a starter pistol. The fan in question was one of six Italians arrested in Brussels. Fans moved freely in and out of the stadium, and some of those who had survived the carnage re-entered at the Juve end. Others fought with police, or looked for Liverpool fans to attack. Hundreds of police and gendarmes entered the stadium, in a ridiculous and tardy show of force.

Meanwhile, behind closed doors, a furious debate was going on about how to proceed. Should the game go ahead? Few of the players wanted to play. UEFA ruled that the match had to be played, purely for 'public order purposes', as corpses lay covered with sheets in the stadium car park.

Who were the Heysel dead? Thirty-two were Italian, four French, two Belgian and there was one Irishman. The youngest victim was eleven years old. At least 300 people were injured. Many uninjured fans had a narrow escape, and were left traumatized. Simone Stenti, the Juve fan who had swapped his scarf with a Liverpool supporter, only survived by climbing up onto the toilet at the back of the stand and jumping down to the street below through barbed wire.

The list of the victims reflected the national and international nature of Juve's mass support. Only two of the dead were from Turin itself. Full details are difficult to obtain, but of those who died, all but two were men. Rocco Acerra, 29, was a southern migrant (from Francavilla near Chieti in the Abruzzo) and worked for the post office; Francesco Galli, 25, from a place called Calcio near Bergamo, was the youngest of eleven children. He was a carpenter. Roberto Lorentini, 31, was a doctor from Arezzo in Tuscany. Roberto stopped to give the kiss of life to a boy, before being crushed by the crowd. He was later awarded a medal for his bravery. A thirty-ninth victim died after 66 days in a coma in a Brussels hospital. Patrick Radcliffe, 37, was from Northern Ireland. He was an archivist who worked for the European Commission in Brussels. Presumably, he had picked up a ticket for the game in Sector Z. The deaths had an enormous echo back in Italy; 7,000 people turned out for the funerals of the two victims from Bassano del Grappa.[5]

As injured and worried spectators were treated in the dressing room area, they mingled with the players, who already had their kit on. Many fans pleaded with the players not to go ahead. One of the great Heysel controversies is linked to how much the players knew about what had happened and why they decided to play on. Later, many would claim that they knew little or nothing about actual deaths, others that they were unsure what had happened. Kenny Dalglish maintains that he did not know that people had died before the game started: 'I had fallen asleep and I didn't know there had been any fatalities'. Phil Neal and Alan Hansen have different stories to tell. Hansen later wrote that Neal had come into the dressing room and said 'people have died out there'. Juve defender Cabrini, interviewed by the newspaper *Reporter*, said that 'we knew everything'.

In the twenty years since Heysel, different versions have been issued by the players who were there on the night. Paolo Rossi, in his autobiography, published in 2002, uses the word *ignari* – 'unaware, ignorant'. 'This is the only truth. The rest is mystification . . . when we took the field in that ugly, crumbling stadium, we only had a vague idea of what had really happened.' Rossi claims that the players 'did not know' about the deaths. They had heard talk of injuries and even deaths, but they 'were a thousand miles away from the cruel reality' of what had happened. As for the game, it had been 'real', as far as was possible, in the circumstances. And the celebrations? 'We acted out our parts right to the end . . . perhaps we were too cynical . . . looking at that lap of honour again, I am not proud.' It was Rossi's last game for Juventus.[6]

Antonio Cabrini, Rossi's old friend, gives us something of a different story in his own autobiography – *Io, Antonio* – which came out in 1988. Word had got through to the dressing room, and not just word. 'Fans started arriving in our dressing room, crying, screaming, their clothes in tatters . . . many were injured . . . we were shocked . . . "there are deaths" . . . "give us some shirts, shoes" . . . "a wall collapsed".' A UEFA official told them that the game was delayed: 'there are many dead and they are probably all Italian'. As for the celebrations: 'it was not a party . . . but simply a release of tension. For me that cup will always be covered in blood. The cup of death.'[7]

At 21.30, Phil Neal and Juve captain Gaetano Scirea stepped up to the loudspeaker. Neal, playing his last game for Liverpool, spoke to the crowd. Clearly shocked, he asked the public to calm down so that the players – who were 'sick and tired of waiting in the dressing room' – could 'get on with it' (an appeal met with cheers from the Liverpool fans). Scirea read out a prepared statement. 'We will play this game only to allow the forces of law and order to reorganize themselves. Do not respond to provocation. We will play for you.' Later reports, wrongly, claimed that both captains had said the same thing. This remains the official version, although it is enough to watch the film of the speeches to see that Neal did not read out the same statement as Scirea. Platini later claimed that there had been a debate amongst the players as to whether to play or not.

At around 21.40 the teams came on to the pitch from separate directions, in a funereal atmosphere, although both sets of fans soon began to 'support' their heroes. The next day, *La Gazzetta dello Sport* duly produced a report on the game itself, complete with votes for the players. The title of the piece was 'Juve win a cursed cup'. When the game started, the paper pointed out, it wasn't even clear if the game 'counted officially' or not. This was in any case a 'cup covered in blood'.

Newspaper reports were full of inaccuracies. *Il Manifesto*, a left-wing daily, led on 30 May with a headline that spoke of 60 dead, *La Gazzetta* mentioned 47 victims. Unfortunately, nobody took the decision to remove an advert carried by the *Gazzetta* the day after the tragedy, which announced special gold and silver coins 'to celebrate the victory in the European Cup'. Candido Cannavò, editorialist for the pink daily, called for the cup to be handed back. The final had been a 'macabre recital'. Cannavò attacked the 'grotesque moments of joy' which had occurred during and after the game.

Michel Platini's wild celebrations after the winning penalty were seen by all as in incredibly bad taste. Later, he said that 'when the referee blew for the start of the game, we only thought about football . . . the show must go on'. The spot kick had been wrongly awarded by the Swiss referee, Boniek was brought down well outside the area, and the official was later accused on Belgian radio of having 'allowed' Juve to win. But Platini was not alone: the whole bench leapt up as the penalty went in. Criticism was also made of the players' reactions during the game. Tacconi later said that Platini's face expressed 'pain' in the moments after he scored.

The cup was not awarded on the field, but handed over to Juve in the dressing room, in a wooden box ('as if it was in a coffin', goalkeeper

Heysel. The lap of honour.

Tacconi later said). After that some, but not all, of the Juve team –
including Platini – went back onto the pitch and did a highly inappro-
priate lap of honour, in a gesture which, years later, a father of one of the
victims would say had made him 'want to vomit'. Platini said that the lap
of honour 'was for the fans . . . we had to do it' and he justified the game;
'if we had not played, it would have been the end of football'. Paolo
Rossi added that 'we just wanted to thank our fans'. Yet many Juve
fans had pleaded with the players and Juve officials *not* to play. Francesco Rutelli, at the time a Radical Party Deputy – he would become
Mayor of Rome in 1993 – was highly critical: 'the behaviour of all
those involved in the football match was disgraceful'. Later reports
mentioned a small party amongst the Juve players in their hotel
although manager Trapattoni said that 'nobody celebrated'.

Further offence was caused when the cup was paraded on the team's
return, and by the celebrations in Italy. Anyone watching the game on
television knew full well that over 30 people had died that night, and
they still went out and rejoiced. In Turin, thousands of fans drove
around the city honking their car horns and champagne bottles were
opened. The 'party' went on for some hours. When some of the
survivors of the disaster arrived in Turin at four o'clock in the morning,

they found a city '*in festa*', with something like 50,000 fans on the streets. On the plane which took the fans back to the city, there had been a 'deathly silence' for the whole trip. Turin's Mayor, Giorgio Cardetti, criticized the celebrations: 'What kind of person can celebrate when there have been deaths?' In Milan there were also noisy festivities, and flag-sellers appeared in the town centre. Juve fans celebrated in most Italian cities. In the small town of Fiuggi, 48 fans were charged with 'seditious assembly and disturbing the peace'. Later, Turin's Mayor had posters put up around the city, as a day of mourning was declared. The poster's message finished in this way: 'Turin's local administration expresses its displeasure for the inopportune manifestations of joy which took place in the streets and squares of the city after the game had finished.'

Anti-Juventus fans soon began to exploit the tragedy. Sick graffiti appeared on the walls of Juve's ground soon after the tragedy, and in Rome, some Roma fans were photographed, smiling, with Liverpool scarves behind a banner which read 'Brussels teaches us this: Juventus fans must die: *Bruxelles insegna: i juventini devono morire*'. Torino fans got their revenge for years of sick Superga chants, and '*Grazie* Liverpool' graffiti appeared in many cities. In May 1995 (on the tenth anniversary of Heysel) some Torino fans put up this banner: 'One hundred more days like this: Thank you Heysel' during a home game and some others sang: *Alè Bruxelles, Forza Liverpool.*

Many commentators, journalists, politicians and ordinary fans argued, at the time, that Juventus should hand back the cup.[8] Many others claim that the game was 'an enormous lie' and, in the wake of the massacre, rumours circulated that UEFA had asked for a 0–0 draw to be played out. Other rumours mentioned an agreement that Juve would win the match. Juve president Boniperti's written statement, issued at half-time (when the score was still 0–0) seemed to accept that the match was not a 'normal' one, and that there were doubts that the game would be classified as official.[9] One wonders what would have happened had Liverpool won. All of these accusations were angrily denied by the referee, the players and UEFA, although no official inquiry was ever conducted. Juve have always refused to contemplate any handing back or declassification of the cup, claiming that the game had been 'real'. Later, the trophy was justified as a kind of memorial to the dead. Juve president Boniperti said that 'we have earned this cup with the blood of our fans'.

## The TV coverage[10]

At 20.10, nineteen million Italian viewers from all over the country, and millions of others in the 29 countries with live rights, tuned in expecting to see the players warming up. They were greeted with a vision of hell. Fans were crushed in all over the ground, police wandered around the pitch, other fans moved in and out of the terraces through smashed-up fences. Italian commentator Bruno Pizzul had the difficult task of describing the scene, live. He spoke of 'clashes' earlier on, and outside the ground, and criticized the 'complete inefficiency' of the Belgian police and authorities. Pizzul expressed 'strong doubts' that the game would go ahead. At this point, no mention was made of injuries. At 20.23 – eight minutes after the game had been due to start – fighting was still going on in some parts of the ground. The live cameras showed some doctors on the pitch, who then proceeded to carry away what was clearly a body, in a blanket. No comment at all came from Pizzul or from the studio in Rome. The next shot was of some Juve players – in their kit – who had left the dressing room to see things for themselves. They were shown talking with fans, some of whom were crying and angry, whilst others kissed their heroes. After five minutes, during which the players were completely surrounded, they jogged off. Pizzul read out some more news. 'There are some deaths, we don't know from which nationality or how many, yet.' This news was 'not official', however. A policeman was shown locking one of the gates to a Juve fan section, using a chain and a pair of handcuffs.

The impression, watching the film again, is that nobody at all was in control. Some fans were laughing and singing, others simply waited. At 20.34 the Belgian director suddenly cut – without warning – to some previous footage of the fights which led to the massacre. Pizzul took a couple of minutes to get his bearings, before confirming that this was not live footage. Meanwhile, thousands of relatives and friends all over Italy had no idea if their loved ones were dead, injured or safe. TV stations and newspapers were besieged with calls.

At around this time, all the banners were taken down in the Juve end, whilst the Liverpool end remained a sea of red and white banners as well as many stolen Juve flags. Pizzul stated, boldly, that 'the game is of no more importance'. Surreal shots showed children, and police standing around waiting for orders and mounted guards 'protecting' the pitch. At around 20.50, Pizzul gave the shocking news which, at the time, was very hard to believe. *Thirty-six people were dead.* No names or other details were available. Some younger Juve fans fought with the police and displayed a banner which said 'Reds: Animals'. It was unclear if this banner had been prepared after the trouble started, or beforehand.

At 21.30, Neal and Scirea spoke to the crowd. Soon afterwards, the game began. German television refused to show the match at all, and instead transmitted footage of the incidents before the game. Later, the RAI would come in for heavy criticism for the decision to broadcast the game. Thirty million Italians watched at least some of the long transmission. Once the match started, Pizzul's commentary was dignified. He followed the game without raising his voice and often repeated that the game was not a real game, but was being played only for 'reasons of public order'. Meanwhile, an appeal to relatives of Juventus fans to phone the Foreign Ministry ran along the bottom of the screen. Later, however, Pizzul became carried away. He finished his 'commentary' with the oft-criticized phrase: 'this is a glorious day for Italian sport'. In Parliament, neo-fascist deputy Ignazio La Russa defined Pizzul as 'an imbecile for whom we can only have pity'.

## Who was to Blame?

Certainly, the control over ticket sales was absurdly lax, and opposing fans ended up more or less side-by-side within the stadium. In Belgium, three police officers were sacked: a major, a captain and a colonel. The government collapsed in July when the Interior Minister refused to resign. In 1987 the secretary of the Belgium football federation (Albert Roosens) was charged with manslaughter and 'massacre'. Other accused also included the then president of UEFA, as well as the then Mayor of Brussels and two relatively minor police officers. In the same year 25 Liverpool fans were extradited to Belgium to stand trial, after

a year of legal wrangling and examination of video pictures. This was
the biggest extradition in British judicial history. The 25 were flown out
on military aircraft. Local newspapers greeted the men with headlines
such as 'Welcome in [sic] Belgium red animals'. After a five-month
trial, fourteen of the fans were found guilty of voluntary manslaughter
in April 1989. All of them were given conditional sentences. Moreover,
gendarme captain Johan Mahieu was given a six-month suspended
sentence as was Roosens. UEFA paid some compensation to the
families of the victims, after Secretary-General Hans Bangerter was
also found guilty of negligence.

Of course, the Liverpool fans who charged across the terraces were
the major protagonists of the tragedy, although it is difficult to prove
that some or any of them were out to *kill* opposing fans. Without their
drunken and violent behaviour, 39 people would still be alive today.
However, many commentators went further, blaming the English, as a
*race*, for Heysel. The Argentinian writer Osvaldo Soriano wrote of us
as 'conquerors of seas and football stands' and Gianni Agnelli described
us as a 'race of incorrigible hooligans'. Bobby Charlton said that he
was 'ashamed to be English'. The prevailing myth of *all* English supporters as 'hooligans' was born that night in Heysel.

## Roma 1984

Francesco Caremani, in his excellent book on Heysel, argues that there
were 'no incidents' during the Roma–Liverpool European Cup final in
Rome in 1984. He attributes this 'success' to the high numbers of
Italian police used that evening.[11] This judgement was true as far as
trouble *inside* the ground was concerned. However, many Liverpool
fans have a very different memory of the Roma match and its aftermath
in the city and around the stadium. There is no doubt that many
Liverpool fans were attacked, more or less indiscriminately, *outside* the
stadium after the final and in the city centre. Some were stabbed –
such as a 45-year-old fan, attacked from a passing scooter – others
were beaten or had missiles thrown at them, some had glass smashed
into their heads. Fan coaches had bricks thrown at them. Brian Glanville argues that the memory of that violence probably contributed to
what happened at Heysel – 'in the streets [after Rome 1984] the after-

math was savage, and would bear bitter fruit in Brussels'.[12] Violence also occurred at the Supercup final between Juve and Liverpool in Turin in January 1985. This should not be seen as an *excuse*, but it may well be helpful as part of an *explanation*.

Soon after the game, various attempts were made to unveil a plaque to the Heysel victims. Yet, three years after the tragedy, the name of the stadium was changed to The King Baudouin Stadium and an expensive renovation followed in the 1990s. The forgetting had begun. In 2000, during the European championships, a wreath was laid by the Italian team near to the plaque dedicated to the disaster. The plaque itself is somewhat short on explanation: it reads simply: *29.5.1985. In memory*. There are no names, no story; no memory. Italian newspapers reported that the area around the plaque was also a kind of rubbish dump. In Italy in 1986 an association was set up amongst the families of the victims.[13] The sorry state of affairs at the ex-Heysel stadium was finally rectified exactly twenty years after the tragedy, when an impressive monument to the victims of the tragedy – including all their names – was unveiled by the Belgian authorities at the ground.[14]

## The *smemorato* (loss-of-memory man) of Heysel

When all the bodies had been counted, and all the relatives contacted, one mystery remained. Marco Manfredi, 40, a medical driver from Moncalieri near Turin, was still missing, and he wasn't amongst the victims. A search was set up in Belgium and his wife Rosita flew to Brussels. His face was picked out on photos from the massacre. There was no news for eight days. Then, on 5 June, a man was seen wandering around in the centre of Turin, near to a hospital. The police picked him up. His clothes were ripped and dirty, and he had a beard. Soon, they recognized him as Manfredi. He remembered nothing of the match. In his pockets were two fines he had received on French trains for travelling without a ticket. Marco remembered being in Nantes and other French cities. He had lived off 'apples and cheese' until his money ran out and somehow, he had got back to Turin. The *smemorato* of Heysel was not the fortieth victim.

## Endgame

Tragically, the lessons of Heysel were not heeded by the authorities. It took a further disaster, with the victims this time being Liverpool fans, to change the way football was organized, at least in the UK. Yet, the shadow of Heysel lives on, and the lack of reform to Italy's fan system – with *ultrà* power untouched within dangerous stadiums – meant that a similar disaster could easily happen in Italy, sooner or later. Italians saw Heysel as a combination of Belgian incompetence and English brutality. This was a fair analysis, as far as that single event was concerned, but Heysel also had things to say to everyone in football about the organization of games, the power of fans and the safety of stadiums. None of these questions was even raised in Italy. Twenty years on, when Juventus were drawn against Liverpool in the Champions League quarter-final in 2005, Italian fans attacked their English counterparts, who were protected by the Italian police. *La Gazzetta dello Sport* referred to 'Italian hooligans' and there was much discussion of the 'English Model' for dealing with crowd violence and safety. Roles had certainly been reversed.[15]

Liverpool, Belgium and, to a far lesser extent, Juventus all have good reason to be ashamed of the events of 29 May 1985. Twenty years on, another Heysel is unlikely, but not impossible. In England, much has changed, but in Italy violent fans still hold the upper hand, domestically. And were not *all those who watched the game*, who *didn't turn off* their TV sets, in some way tainted with the show-must-go-on mentality which UEFA upheld that evening? It took the Hillsborough tragedy of 15 April 1989, when 96 Liverpool fans were crushed to death, for major reforms to occur in stadium safety and the organization of football in the UK. 'Heysel was an organic part of a culture that many of us . . . had contributed towards' (Nick Hornby).[16] It could be argued that this culture is now strongest in the country that was the victim of the Heysel tragedy: Italy.

## Attack. Brescia, 20.11.1994

Planned violence was in the air in the 1994–1995 season. Before the Brescia–Roma game in November, a number of telephone calls had warned that there would be trouble. These warnings turned out to be correct. The violence that day was planned with military precision. About 500 Roma fans arrived in the well-to-do industrial city of Brescia at about midday. Their first act was to destroy the local buses that took them from the station to the stadium. Later a policeman was stabbed and makeshift bombs were thrown. Some of the protagonists of the trouble were identified as part of a neo-fascist group calling itself *Opposta Fazione*. The violence continued outside the ground throughout the game. Some analysts argued that the violence was aimed at destabilizing Italy on a day of local elections. Journalist Enrico Curro wrote in *La Repubblica* that 'football is finished'.

## Murder. Claudio Spagnolo. Genoa, 29 January 1995

The three young men met, as usual, in a pizzeria – its name was 'The Smile' – on the north-west edge of Milan. There, on Thursday 26 January, they were given tickets to Sunday's match with Genoa by some older *ultrà*.[17] They were advised that their group would *not* take the official Milan train, but would travel at a different time without scarves or club colours. The group – the most violent part of the Milanese fan world – had been associated with a fringe *ultrà* sector known as *Il gruppo brasato*, and they had been linked to the murder of young Roma fan Antonio De Falchi outside San Siro in 1989. A smaller group within this loose 'organization' was known as the Barbour Gang, thanks to the posh English jackets worn by its 'members'. Simone Brasaglia, one of the Barbour Gang, was just eighteen. It later emerged that Brasaglia was not particularly interested in football, and had been a Juventus fan who had changed sides thanks to the influence of a few friends.

In the past season, a Genoa – Milan match, played at Naples for public-order reasons, had led to violent clashes. A Genoa fan was stabbed. Relations between Genoa and Milan *ultrà* had broken down in the early 1980s after clashes between fans during some delicate relegation struggles. Before that, the two sets of fans had been 'twinned'.

Vincenzo Claudio Spagnolo was a good-looking, robust young man, who had worked in tourism. He still lived at home and often went to a Genovese 'social centre', associated with the no-global movement. At his funeral, there were many clenched fists around his coffin. He was not an *ultrà*, but simply a fan, although after his death many were to claim *ultrà* status for him.

Having caught the 11.00 a.m. intercity from Milan to Genoa, Brasaglia 'seemed nervous' and 'walked up and down the train showing off his knife'. He told some other fans that he would later 'cut someone'. The group of about seventy Milan fans got off the train in the centre of Genoa at about 1.30 p.m. A further 850 Milan fans had already arrived with the official special train, guarded by police. The smaller group moved quietly, but as a group, towards the stadium, which stood about 1.5 km away, on foot. Once they were in the area around the ground, they attempted to provoke some Genoa fans, in part by moving towards the Genoa 'end' of the ground. Brasaglia had his knife in his hand. Bottles and stones were thrown, and fights broke out. The small group of Milan fans then ran off. Claudio 'Spagna' Spagnolo joined the Genoa group chasing after them. Suddenly the Milan group turned, some with knives out again.

It was at this point that Spagnolo ended up face-to-face with Simone Brasaglia. Spagnolo did not run away, but moved forward. The knife pierced his abdomen, close to his heart, and Claudio turned round and said 'they have got me'. Brasaglia put the knife in his underpants and ran off with the others, many dropping their own knives as they fled. Spagnolo lay on the pavement, dying. He was 24 years old. Meanwhile, the Milan fans – including Brasaglia – filed into the ground and the game began. Some Milan fans shouted out 'one less' to the Genoa fans. For the 924 Milan fans in that part of the ground, the nightmare had only just begun. Brasaglia, one of the 924, took out the knife and showed it to a fellow *ultrà*.

Brasaglia changed his coat, which was stained with blood. Video cameras captured him doing this – crucial proof for a future trial. The game was also transmitted live on Channel 4 in the UK: it began on time at 14.30. Spagnolo's death was announced on the radio 38 minutes into the first half; his name wasn't given and the journalist spoke of 'at least one Genoa fan' being killed. Word spread as the first half came to an end. Genoa's fans first called for the game to be stopped and when it wasn't, some went crazy while others simply left. Genoa's captain went over to the stands and asked what was happening. He held his head in his hands and then tried to convince the referee to call the game off. The referee consulted various people and then the city's Prefect came onto the pitch. The players walked off and applause broke out around the ground, which soon turned into more anger. At 15.55 Genoa's captain read out this short message over the loud-speakers, with Franco Baresi, Milan's captain, beside him: 'Genoa and Milan have decided to call off the game as a sign of mourning, in the hope that this gesture will help in the future to avoid the repetition of events which have nothing to do with football.'

For the first time, a game had been stopped in this way. But the suspension of the match had not placated the anger of the Genoa fans. A group tried time and again to get through to the Milan end and, outside the ground, a full-scale riot broke out. The riot did not start immediately. First, some fans tried to speak to the *carabinieri*, asking to be allowed through so that they could 'deal with' Claudio's murderer. Obviously, this request was rejected. At 16.30 the police charged, and then the riot began in earnest. Molotov cocktails were thrown. Inside the stadium, about 300 Genoa supporters tried to smash the plastic wall dividing the stadium. If the wall had given way, Genoa could have become another Hillsborough. Luckily, it held firm, and the police gained some sort of control. Tear gas was fired as the 300 were pushed out onto the streets below. It no longer being possible to get through to the Milan 'end', the Genoa fans began to indulge in violence 'for violence's sake', burning cars with Milanese number plates.

Barricades were set up, and the police even fired some shots. Only at 11 p.m., after seven hours, once things had calmed down outside, did the police feel that it was safe to move the Milan fans. Groups of Genoa supporters had lined up outside the station and along train lines leading to Milan, so the police packed the Milan faithful into city buses, and drove them off. It took four hours to get to the edge of

Milan. There, the fans were all photographed and identified. Brasaglia was arrested at home, as he rang his own doorbell. He confessed soon afterwards but pleaded self-defence.

Fabio Fazio, Savona-born and a Sampdoria fan, was presenting his popular football-variety programme *Quelli che il calcio* on one of the state channels that afternoon. As news came through of the murder, Fazio decided to abandon the programme altogether. Everybody left, but the cameras kept running. The images of the empty studio were an eloquent testimony to the disgust felt in the face of such a crime, linked to football.

## Reactions. Police and Fans

Spagnolo's murder left the world of Italian football in deep shock. In an unprecedented decision, *all* of the following Sunday's games were cancelled. This applied not just to professional games, but all games organized in some way through the federation, a total of 40,000 matches. Meanwhile, thousands of people visited the place where Spagnolo had been murdered, leaving flowers, scarves and messages. Not surprisingly, the area was also packed with media representatives of all types, who hassled Spagnolo's family at their home. Thirty-nine people were arrested in connection with the murder and the riots during and after the match, and 33 of these were sent for trial. In January 1996 Brasaglia was sentenced to eleven years and four months. On appeal, his sentence was increased to sixteen years because the murder had been 'for futile reasons'. Claudio Spagnolo's family were not satisfied with the outcome of the trial. They argued that Brasaglia and the others were simply the shock troops in the operation, and the real blame lay with the so-called *capi-ultrà* who had 'sent' the young men to Genoa.

In an unprecedented development, the murder of this young Genoa fan led to a kind of 'peace treaty' amongst *ultrà* groups. Meetings were held all over the country between rival fan organizations as well as the first ever 'national *ultrà* gathering' in Genoa on 5 February and a collective 'policy document' was released, part of which read as follows: 'On Sunday Claudio Spagnolo – a Genoa *ultrà* – died. This umpteenth absurd attack leads us to say: Enough! Enough of these people who are not *ultrà* who try and make the news by using the *ultrà* world to gain importance and by ignoring the evil of what they do. Enough with this trend of twenty against two or three and Molotovs or knives . . .

'*Ultrà* fans: once the championship starts again we will be faced with a difficult period. The police can now do what they like; the only people who will be blamed will be us, who have nothing to do with these cowards. If being an *ultrà* is truly a way of life, let's get tough [*tiriamo fuori le palle*]. On other occasions we ignored events, arguing that they were not our problem, now we must shout; *Enough!*

'What is the alternative? We find ourselves caught between policemen who would like us to disappear and these filthy scum who don't care about anything and will continue with their cowardly "attacks". Let us unite against those who want to destroy the world of the *ultrà*, a free and true world despite all its contradictions.'

Although some of the sentiments in the document – no more knives, no more mindless 'attacks' – were laudable, the rhetoric was somewhat overpowering (especially the absurd references to courage). There was an attempt to compare good, loyal *ultrà* with groups of violent mavericks: 'these are not *ultrà*'. Yet, despite these claims, it was clear that Spagnolo's killers came from within the *ultrà* world (and that Spagnolo was *not* an *ultrà* martyr – just a simple fan) and that many of those who lived within that world were attracted to and protagonists of violence. There was very little 'self-criticism' here, unfortunately. In any case, the document did seem to have an effect. There have been no football-related stabbing deaths in Italy in the ten years since Claudio's murder (whilst the number was on the rise in the years leading up to the murder). The 'Genoa mission' which began in that pizzeria on the edge of Milan turned out not to be the first of many such knife 'attacks', but – hopefully – one of the last.

Claudio Spagnolo's father later wrote an open letter to the *ultrà*. It began with this phrase: 'it is absurd to die for a football match'. Political reaction was also swift, with a new anti-violence decree that concentrated above all on repressing organized fans (whilst leaving their power more or less intact within the stadium). Outside the shared Genoa and Sampdoria stadium, there now stands a monument dedicated to the memory of Claudio Spagnolo.

Unfortunately, since 'Spagna''s murder, *ultrà* power has not diminished. Violence has become so everyday as to be commonplace, almost unworthy of notice in the mass media except when death or tragedy occurs, and death and tragedy have occurred on a regular basis throughout the 1990s.

## The Train of death. Piacenza–Salerno, 24 May 1999

The lack of rules and legality with regard to the *ultrà* was also to be seen in the so-called 'special trains', provided by the state with the connivance of the clubs, which transported fans to away games. These trains were often smashed up, and the life of drivers and cleaners was made impossible. Fans were still, in theory, meant to buy tickets for these trains. Nobody, in practice, did so. In 1999, the whole question of the 'special trains' became a national issue thanks to a tragedy that left four fans dead.

Salernitana (from Salerno, south of Naples) needed to win their last game at Piacenza – in the north of Italy near the Po River – in order to stay up in Serie A. After defeat, and relegation, a special train was provided for the 1,500 fans to return to the south. Angry at their defeat, the fans wrecked the train. At every stop, they tried to cause trouble, throwing stones at people waiting on station platforms as the train trundled through the night. As the train stopped for two hours in Naples, fights broke out on the station platforms. On at least five occasions, the fans pulled the emergency cord. After twelve hours, the train was finally nearing its destination. Following prolonged clashes with the twelve policemen assigned to the train (who were all from Piacenza – and half were young women), some fans decided to light a fire, in a thirteen-km-long tunnel, after first letting off all the remaining extinguishers (the rest had been thrown out of the windows). The idea was to create a diversion that would allow them to escape arrest on arrival in Salerno. They lit curtains and toilet paper mixed with rubbish but the fire got out of control, burning down a whole carriage. Some fans jumped out of train windows into the dark, but four didn't make it, their bodies so badly burnt as to be unrecognizable. Two of the dead were cousins – both just sixteen years old – and all of the victims were from poor neighbourhoods of Salerno. Only the bravery of the driver – who carried on driving the train out of the tunnel – prevented an even worse tragedy. It later emerged that the vast majority of the fans were drunk or stoned. In the wake of the Salerno disaster, there were calls for the special trains to be phased out. A series of trials took place with the police chief of Piacenza in the dock. The train, unsafe as it was, probably should never have been allowed to leave for the south.

This was not the first time that the special trains had been the centre of violence. In 1989 a train taking Bologna fans to Florence stopped just outside the city. At that point, a Molotov cocktail was thrown through a carriage window and exploded where Ivan Dall'Olio – a fourteen-year-old Bologna fan – was sitting. The bottle hit him in the face, leading to horrible burns. Seventy per cent of his body was affected. The three Fiorentina fans who threw the bomb served prison sentences.

## Assorted Violence: Refereeing Decisions, Sales of Players, Bombs

Controversial refereeing decisions have often led to violence. Sometimes, this violence has exploded well away from the actual games concerned with the controversy. After a perfectly good goal was disallowed during a Juventus–Parma game in May 2000, Lazio fans went on the rampage in Rome, accusing the football authorities of fixing the championship. Five hundred or so fans marched to the football federation offices, and later fought running battles with the police for more than three hours. Eggs, oranges and stones were thrown at the *carabinieri*, who replied with baton charges. Later, cars and rubbish bins were burnt, as fans and police fought it out right in the centre of the city, and even on the Spanish Steps. Fabrizio Piscitelli, 'leader' of the *Irriducibili* – one of Lazio's *ultrà* groups – announced that this was only the beginning: 'We have had enough. A fuse has been lit. We are going to create trouble right across Rome . . . the national team won't be able to play here any more.' The fans unveiled a huge banner which read: 'Juventus: history repeats itself. Lots of thefts, lots of victories'.

Fans have also often rioted in protests against the sales of players: in 1966, peaceful protests by Torino fans persuaded the club to go back on its decision to sell Gigi Meroni to Juventus; Fiorentina fans blocked the city centre after Roberto Baggio was sold to hated rivals in 1990; Torino fans besieged the head offices of their club after the transfer of Gigi Lentini to Milan for a huge sum in 1992; Lazio fans prevented the sale of Beppe Signori to Parma with their protests in 1996.

## Organized Chaos? The Mystery of the Rome derby 2004

The pictures, shot by Sky TV, were shown all over the world. Francesco Totti, Roma's most famous and popular player, and the idol of the *curva sud*, was standing near the crowd. He was with three men, all of them *capi-ultrà*, and an argument was taking place. One of the men assured Totti that a boy had just been killed, outside the ground, after clashes with the police. Another man – a minor official – argued that the story was untrue. Finally, one of the *capi-ultrà*, dressed in a leather jacket and woollen hat, told Totti to 'go and call off the game, please'. Totti returned to the pitch, where another debate was continuing.

There, referee Roberto Rossetti was on the phone with Adriano Galliani, president of the football federation. This phone call took place in the centre-circle of the Olympic stadium, packed to the rafters with fans, at a moment when play should have been taking place. Rossetti laid out the situation to Galliani, who gave him the go-ahead to abandon the game. Within seconds, Rossetti blew his whistle three times and the players jogged off. Meanwhile, the fans filed away. Outside, a night of violence left over 200 police injured.

The whole farce had begun just as the second half kicked off, with the score at 0–0. Strange movements amongst the fans began to alert onlookers that something was happening. Banners were put away and the fans stopped following the game. Chants began which were either directed at the police – 'murderers' – or were calls to end the game. Soon, it became clear that a rumour had spread: a boy had been killed during clashes with the police, outside the stadium, before the game. Nobody could confirm the reports. A loudspeaker announcement was made stating that *nobody* had been killed (or even hurt). This later turned out to be true, but the fans weren't having it.

Once the rumour reached the pitch, play was stopped. Rossetti tried to find out what was happening – and was also told that the story was false. Nobody had died. But the players were unconvinced. Twice, they refused to play on when told to do so and young Roma forward Antonio Cassano grabbed the ball from Rossetti. Then, Totti jogged over to the fans, and Rossetti made his phone call.

Acres of newsprint and hours of TV debate were dedicated to these bizarre events. Who had spread the false rumour about the boy? Why were the *capi-ultrà* allowed on the pitch? Why had the game been called off without consulting the police authorities?

The police later arrested – and released – all three *capi-ultrà*, and an investigation began. There were two hypotheses at work. One was that the rumour had been an accident, and had got out of hand. Another version, however, had far more sinister implications. The story had been spread on purpose. If this was what had happened, why would anyone do such a thing? Perhaps the fans just wanted to cause chaos, creating the possibility of a pitched battle with the police. Maybe they were showing everyone just how powerful they were – a warning to those in power not to mess with them again. This latter hypothesis linked the violence and false rumours with the disastrous financial positions of the two Roma clubs. Earlier in the year, Prime Minister Silvio Berlusconi had tried to push through a special decree which would have allowed crisis-ridden clubs to pay off their tax-debts over a very long period of time, effectively helping them to ride out their indebtedness. Berlusconi had justified the decree – which was never issued – by saying that if two or three big clubs were allowed to fail 'there would be a revolution'. Maybe this was an attempt to show he was right. One outcome of these events was that Roma played their next two home games at a neutral venue – Palermo. The club had been held responsible for the behaviour of their fans. The police investigation was ongoing in 2005.

## Violence on and off the Pitch. 2000–2004

An increasingly violent football world mirrored an increasingly intolerant society, where everyday frustrations and annoyances – driving incidents, work disputes, little mishaps – were left without mediation, leading directly to violence. In part, this violence also reflected the emotive power of conspiracy theories and the lack of legitimation enjoyed by authority and the law in the game of football. Violence was everywhere, on the pitch, on the terraces, in the players' tunnels – and its protagonists were not just fans, but players, substitutes and even managers.

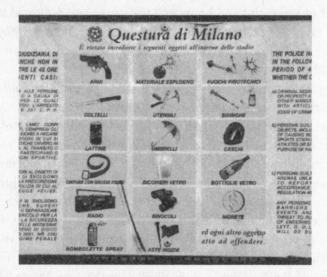

San Siro, 2005. List of items officially not permitted inside the ground, including knives, weapons, syringes, belts with big buckles, umbrellas, money, fireworks and tin cans.

In June 2001 a young Messina fan – Antonio Currò, 24 – was killed when a makeshift bomb thrown by a Catania fan struck him on the head. TV pictures showed fans cheering and jumping around after the missile reached the Messina supporters. Things got worse, if that was possible, in the 2003–2004 season, as violence exploded, time and again, on and off the pitch.

The season began in tragedy when a young Napoli fan was killed after rioting in a derby match at Avellino. Sergio Ercolano, twenty, was at his first ever away game, and fell ten metres to his death onto concrete after a plastic roof collapsed. He had been trying to escape in a panic after violence on the terraces spilled onto the pitch. In February 2004 Inter defender Marco Materazzi was in his suit, on the bench, watching his team play Siena; he was injured. At left-back for the visitors was Bruno Cirillo, who had previously been with Inter. According to Cirillo, Materazzi insulted him throughout the match, telling his team-mates to 'attack Cirillo, he's rubbish'. With the game over – Inter won 4–0 – Materazzi confronted Cirillo in the tunnel. Words were exchanged, and the Siena player ended up with a split lip. He immediately gave a blood-spattered live interview, saying that he wanted to show the world 'what kind of person Materazzi was'. Endless debate ensued and the Inter defender was banned for two months.

In a Serie B match towards the end of the season, in April 2004, Venice goalkeeper Salvatore Soviero completely lost his head. After a penalty, he sprinted towards the Messina bench, lashing out with kicks and punches, being subdued only with great difficulty. He received a five-month ban. In the same match, his colleague Rubens Maldonado was banned for a year for 'kicking and pushing the referee'.

Finally, in an end-of-season playoff to decide a promotion place in Serie B, Lumezzane were playing Cesena, at home. After an equalizing goal the Cesena manager – Fabrizio Castori, a short, rotund figure – ran onto the pitch and began to kick and punch various players. A mêlée ensued, involving about twenty players, and the police came onto the pitch to separate the two sides. One Cesena player – who had been sitting on the bench without his boots – repeatedly kicked a prone Lumezzane player in the head. Castori received a three-year ban, which he complained about, bitterly. Cesena won the game and were promoted.

An additional category of football violence involves attacks on players by their own fans. This type of violence is widespread in Italy and has become more and more serious in recent years. The frustration of Inter's fans in the 1990s was understandable. After all, they were one of the big three clubs in Italy, with a fan-base only surpassed by Juventus, and yet they had only won the UEFA Cup – three times – since 1989. This lack of achievement was attributed to bad management and to a supposed 'lack of effort' on the part of some players. A violent minority amongst the Inter fans decided to pass from words to action. The most serious incident took place in December 2000. Before an Italian Cup game with Parma at home – attended by only 1,000 fans in the 80,000 capacity stadium (Inter had lost the first leg: 6–1) – a Molotov cocktail was thrown towards the Inter team coach. It struck the side of the bus and parts of the coach floor caught fire. The players rushed off and somebody put out the flames with a fire extinguisher. The lone attacker was never found. A policemen later said that 'the petrol tank could have caught fire, and they would all have died'. 'We are lucky to be alive,' said manager Marco Tardelli.

The players were terrified, and shocked. But an opinion poll amongst Inter fans seemed to show that there was a fair amount of support for the attack. Thirty per cent of those questioned replied that the incident was 'due to exasperation'. In 2004 two restaurants part-owned by Inter players Fabio Cannavaro and Christian Vieri were fire-bombed, leading to minor damage.

Threats towards players are commonplace in Italian football, where the most extreme fans frequently turn up to training to praise their heroes, and insult their enemies. Cars are sometimes surrounded, and the invective flies back and forth. Some players lived in fear – trepidation which was clear on the faces of the Roma and Lazio players during the 2004 suspended derby. Sometimes this violence took place during actual games. In one case, a 29-year-old Cagliari fan ran onto the pitch in November 2002 and attacked the Messina goalkeeper, Emanuele Manitta. The goalkeeper left the pitch on a stretcher, and the game was suspended and awarded to Messina, 2–0. Meanwhile, the fan ran back into the crowd and escaped, only to be picked up a few days later. Manitta spent ten days in hospital.

## Violence amongst players. The story of Francesco Bertolotti

Blackburn-born Francesco Bertolotti was a midfielder for Modena in the 1990s. His football career ended on 19 November 2000. A game with Como had been marred by a fight between Bertolotti and Como's captain, Massimiliano Ferrigno, 27, who was sent off. An hour after the end of the game, Ferrigno struck Bertolotti on the head in the tunnel area. The Modena player fell to the floor and smashed his head. He went into a coma, and doctors carried out an emergency operation on his brain. Ferrigno claimed that he had acted in self-defence. After a worrying few days, Bertolotti survived, but he was never to play football again. His assailant was banned for three years, and came back to the first team in 2003. A case was also brought before the criminal courts, where Ferrigno was given a ten-month conditional sentence.

## Footballing Violence

Obviously, football could also be violent on the pitch. Usually, this consisted mainly of what journalists in England call 'handbags' – largely symbolic displays of aggression. However, on-pitch violence could take on more serious forms, and here the Italians were also victims. The most infamous violent match of all was that involving Milan and the Argentinian club Estudiantes, in the Inter-Continental Cup final of 22 October 1969.[18]

The game, played in the La Bombonera stadium in Buenos Aires, came after Milan had easily won the first leg of the final, 2–1. Milan's team included the black Argentinian-born French forward, Nestor Combin, as well as stars such as Gianni Rivera and Pierino Prati. On entering the field, hot coffee was poured over some of the Milan players: 'So began one of the most violent games in the history of football'.[19] Combin had scored in the first game, and some of the locals claimed that he was a deserter. This was an error: having left Argentina for France when he was nineteen, Combin had chosen, legally, to do his military service in the latter country. In any case, he was to be the object of the most violent assaults from the Argentinian players.

As Milan warmed up, the Estudiantes squad began to boot footballs towards them. Then the game began, if it can be called a game. Lodetti, Milan midfielder, remembered that 'when you had the ball, someone would arrive and hit you. The referee, a Chilean, did nothing (although he later sent off two Estudiantes players). A defender cut Prati down, and then the goalkeeper kicked him in the back. He had to go off.' It was said that one of the Argentinian players had a needle, which he used to jab his opponent. In the second half, with the score at 2–1 to Estudiantes, Suarez hit Combin, breaking his nose and cheekbone. Manager Rocco asked him to go back on but he fainted on the side of the pitch. As he was recovering in the dressing room, covered in blood, four policemen turned up and arrested him for 'desertion'. Frantic diplomatic efforts followed the game, as the players refused to leave without their team-mate. Finally, Combin was released after a night in the cells and Lodetti recalls that 'we all made the gesture of the umbrella towards Argentina' on the plane steps. Combin got off the flight in Milan with his face grotesquely swollen, holding the cup. After the game the Argentinian authorities cracked down on violence – arresting three players and banning one for life and two others for 30 and 20 games respectively. The *Gazzetta dello Sport*'s headline read 'Ninety minutes of a man-hunt' and produced a medical bulletin as if the game had been a war.

## Conclusion. The normality of violence

By 2004, violence pervaded all levels of Italian football – even 'hot' games in Serie B and Serie C required thousands of policemen just to keep order. Unlike England, Italy had never had a national problem with hooliganism; very few travelling fans followed the national team. Football violence was a local and domestic issue. None of the reforms applied in the UK after Hillsborough had been applied in Italy; the costs of keeping order were still collective, and not private, and stadiums were places where nobody in their right mind would take a child. Many fans stood up throughout the game, especially in the *curva*, and numbered tickets were meaningless in certain parts of stadiums. Fences, huge ditches and massive nets still hemmed in most fans. Young conscript police and *carabinieri* spent their Sunday afternoons avoiding missiles, or laying into fans, dressed in gear appropriate for a full-scale urban riot. The emphasis was on containment, and repression. The road towards peaceful and democratic stadiums would be a long and hard one, and it would entail taking on those hard-core fans whose territory was a *zona franca* – out of control of the clubs, the state and the law.

# CHAPTER 13

# Power and Politics

'*Vincere, E Vinceremo*'; 'Win, we will win'
BENITO MUSSOLINI, 1940; Inter banner, 2005[1]

'Falção is our Mao' – Roma slogan, 1970s

The idea that politics and sport should be kept apart is laughable in Italy. Politics is everywhere, from the choice of which bar you frequent to which team you support. The big teams have complicated political allegiances. Lazio fans are more right-wing than those of their rivals, Roma. Inter have a strong right-wing fan-base, along with many long-suffering left-wing supporters. Milan's *ultrà* fans have never ceded to the right, but their president Silvio Berlusconi is a hate-figure on the left. Juventus was always the team of FIAT, but was also backed by hundreds of thousands of car-workers. Beyond the hard-core of fans, football has always been a potent source of political capital. Fascism was the first regime to exploit the propaganda possibilities of the game, and intervened heavily in the running and organization of *calcio*.

Much of the fascist influence on sport – as in Italian everyday life – was symbolic. Players gave a stiff-arm fascist salute – known as a Roman Salute in Italy – before matches, black-shirted officials sat in the best seats, a small fascist symbol appeared on Italy's national team shirts, even Mussolini himself sometimes turned up. Leading fascists took over the football federations and influenced important areas of football organization and sanctioned individual transfers. Some clubs

Italianized their names in line with fascist *diktat*, others of their own free will; *Genoa* became *Genova*, *Internazionale* changed to *Ambrosiana*. A series of impressive stadiums was built in fascist style, and used for sporting events and showpiece meetings. Many of these stadiums survive, in modified form, to this day, in Bologna, Florence and Lucca, for example. None of this made football fascist, but it did make football *look* and *sound* fascist. All of the teams went back to their old names in the 1940s, and nobody gave a fascist salute after the fall of Mussolini – unless they were in the crowd or were Paolo Di Canio.

The more repressive aspects of fascism occasionally impacted upon the world of football. Jewish players and managers were hit by the anti-Semitic campaigns of the mid-1930s and the anti-Semitic laws of 1938 that removed Jews from public life in Italy. Hungarian manager Egri Erbstein arrived at Torino in 1938, but left soon after the anti-Semitic campaign began in earnest, only to return after the war. William Garbutt was interned and sent into internal exile after war was declared against Great Britain in 1940 – in his case for being English, not Jewish. Like everyone else under fascism, football players and fans were careful to hide any anti-fascist opinions they may have held, and known anti-fascists in the football world did their best to get by, whilst living in fear of the many spies who informed for the regime.

After 1945, a series of rich and politically ambitious figures used football to build local support: shipbuilder Achille Lauro in Naples and, most successfully, Silvio Berlusconi in Milan. Politics (and history) have also intersected at various times with the rich history of Italian football in other ways – touching on the unresolved issues left by a legacy of war, civil war and Cold War, problems over national identity and the unresolved southern question. This selective journey amongst the political aspects of football history in Italy begins in the extreme north-east of the country.

## Football and the Politics of the Frontier. Trieste

Nowhere in Italy were politics and sport so closely entwined as in Trieste.[2] A key city within the so-called 'unredeemed' lands after the unification of Italy in 1860, it hosted many different peoples, from Slovenes to Austrians to Slavs. The city was also the site of national and ethnic conflict. During World War One the Italians took Trieste in 1918 and the city became officially part of Italy after the post-war settlement. The 'Trieste question' was also a strategic one, symbolizing the shifting allegiances of a country torn (historically) between Austria, France and Germany.

How did football fit into this complicated pattern? Trieste formed a team in 1918 called the *Unione Sportiva Triestina*. After spells in the lower divisions, Triestina scraped into Serie A in 1929, and in 1933 the fascists built a 20,000 capacity stadium. Triestina were to remain in Serie A, against all the odds, until 1957. As a football team on the national stage, Trieste provided a number of key players in the 1920s and 1930s. The two most important figures from this time were Gino Colaussi and Pietro Pasinati. Colaussi – whose name had been Italianized under fascism from Colausich[3] – was born in Gorizia in 1914. A winger of great skill, he was celebrated for his *doppio passo* (stepover). 'He went forward, leaving the ball behind, thereby confusing defenders . . . when he was asked where he had learnt how to dribble like that he replied, "I don't know".'[4] Colaussi scored two of the goals that won the 1938 World Cup final against Hungary.[5]

Piero Pasinati was the other World Cup winner to emerge from the Trieste team of the 1930s. A tough, uncompromising wing-back, it was said that Giuseppe Meazza hated coming to Trieste as he knew he would be marked by Pasinati. After eleven years with Trieste (he played a record 344 games for the club) Pasinati made a big-money move to Milan in 1938.[6] A further key figure in the history of Triestina has a familiar name – Guglielmo Cudicini, father of Fabio (who played for Milan in the 1960s and 1970s) and grandfather of Carlo, who kept goal for Milan and Chelsea in the 1990s and early twenty-first century. One of the team's best players in the 1930s was a strong, square-faced, local lad with a fierce shot – Nereo Rocco. He was the first Triestino to play for Italy, even if his only appearance lasted a mere 45 minutes. Over the next twenty years or so, the history of Triestina would be intimately linked to the personal career of Rocco.

Trieste was occupied by the Nazis in September 1943. The city had one of the biggest Jewish communities in Italy, and was the only part of Italian soil to host a death-camp, set up in a warehouse close to the football stadium. Tito's victorious Yugoslav armies liberated the city in

April 1945, arriving ahead of the Allied troops. Tito repressed dissent in the city in brutal fashion as reprisals took place against fascists but also against those whose only crime was to be Italian. These atrocities, which have become known as the *Foibe* massacres thanks to the deep pits into which some of the bodies were thrown, remain an extremely controversial historical episode. The *Foibe* events were later used as Cold War propaganda, and the numbers of those killed was exaggerated to heighten their emotive value.[7] On the other side of the divide, the massacres were either ignored, or the victims dismissed as fascists or collaborators. Even in the early twenty-first century, this issue continued to divide Italians along political lines, revealing once again the dangers of the 'public use of history'.

After 1945, Trieste was a front-line state in the Cold War as the border region was divided into two zones similar to Berlin and Vienna in 1947. Zone A, which included Trieste, was governed by the USA and the UK, Zone B by Yugoslavia.[8] The right called for the city to be given entirely to Italy, and organized nationalist demonstrations within Trieste, some of which were suppressed by the Allies. The left prevaricated, although Italian communists pledged their support to Italy in the unlikely event of a Yugoslavian invasion. Meanwhile, the Slovenes demanded their own nation and Tito continued to claim Trieste as Yugoslavian territory. Tensions in 1953 reached such levels that war between Italy and Yugoslavia seemed possible. It was only with the 1954 treaty that the Trieste question was finally resolved, with the city (Zone A) being handed 'back' to Italy and other territories (Zone B) going to Yugoslavia. After the Yugoslavian civil war in the early 1990s Slovenia finally became an independent state, taking in the former Zone B of the 1940s and 1950s.

With a city run by the Allies, in a place that was 'nowhere',[9] football began to re-emerge from the ruins and the tensions of the world war, which – in Trieste – had also been a civil war. Trieste's unique symbolic role increased the power of football as a political weapon. At various times, substantial amounts of political and financial capital were invested in teams whose real sporting value was, usually, marginal.

The port area of Trieste had always had its own small team – Ponziana, formed in 1912 – who were backed by a passionate group of fans. In 1946, the history of Ponziana took on a strange twist, as the Yugoslavs decided to recruit the team into their own league, and were prepared to invest heavily in order to make their project work. In the poverty-stricken city of the post-war Allied administration, the offer of proper wages to play football in Yugoslavia was difficult to turn down. The Yugoslavian authorities had also approached the perfect team – Ponziana – with its communist and working-class fan-base, sympathetic to Tito. The team was given a new name – Amatori – and financed from Belgrade. Amatori would play in the Yugoslavian first division, and not in Italy. The 'schizophrenic' (Giuliano Sadar) city of Trieste now had two teams in two divisions in two different countries.

Problems soon emerged, as Yugoslavia had a strong league, and Amatori kept losing. More money was pumped in to bring in better players. Neither Amatori nor Triestina was allowed, at first, to play in Trieste itself. The Allied administration was afraid that ethnic and political tensions would be exacerbated by football. Meanwhile, the local press dedicated varying amounts of space to Ponziana's adventure. The right-wing, nationalist *Il Piccolo* newspaper hardly mentioned the team (and called the players traitors), whilst the Yugoslavian and Slovene press devoted 'wordy' articles to the fortunes of the team. Once the home ban had been dropped, big teams such as Red Star Belgrade came to Trieste, and Amatori attracted up to 12,000 fans. Away, after long journeys by train or coach, these minor players occasionally played in front of 50,000 people. In their first year, they finished tenth, avoiding relegation. In all, the experiment lasted three seasons. When Tito broke with Stalin in 1948, the propaganda advantages to be gained from a Trieste-based team were greatly diminished and Yugoslavia pulled the plug. Amatori became Ponziana again and went back to their local league. Meanwhile, hundreds of thousands of refugees poured into Italy from Yugoslavia, and were given shelter across the peninsula.

Triestina, meanwhile, were still in Serie A. In their very *first* match in the 1946 season, they risked making history by beating *Grande Torino* on their own Filadelfia ground, something no team achieved between 1943 and 1949. At 1–0 up with three minutes left and with Torino down to ten men, Trieste had a second goal disallowed after the referee (officiating in his first game in Serie A) gave it, and was then forcibly taken over to the linesman, who signalled offside. Whilst the Trieste players were still protesting, Torino took a quick free-kick and scored in an empty net. Incredibly, the referee allowed the goal. Ivano Blason, one of Italian football's first sweepers and Triestina's best player, lost his head, hitting the referee. At first he was given a life ban, which was later reduced to six months. Every player in the match was fined.

Without Blason, and with none of the players they had traditionally recruited from Istria, Triestina were in trouble. In addition, they were not allowed to play at home 'for public-order reasons'. At one point in the 1946–47 season the team lost eleven games in a row. Nonetheless, Triestina were cheered at every away game, and awarded a series of cups, trophies and bouquets in Italian colours. Trieste, in those years, 'was truly a city held dear by Italians'.[10] The rhetoric surrounding Trieste's season also had a slightly pompous, almost fascist edge to it. 'Long live Triestina', wrote *La Gazzetta dello Sport*, 'a team of proud youngsters' who were 'pilgrims of a sporting ideal who carry our nation's aspirations'. On many occasions 'games . . . took on a patriotic tone' and the national anthem was always sung.[11] Reports of games underlined the 'fraternization' of the players in the dressing room and the brave performances of plucky Triestina. *La Gazzetta* even set up a special Trieste edition, with lengthy reports on local games. Despite all this goodwill, Trieste finished last, with just eighteen points, after five wins and 25 defeats. They were going down to Serie B, for the first time since 1929.

Or were they? Frantic meetings were held in Rome, and pressure was put on the football authorities. A curious decision was taken. Trieste would be re-admitted to Serie A 'thanks to their sporting merit'. The league was expanded to 21 teams and the other two relegated teams accepted the decision without protest. In 1947, the question of Trieste was hotter than ever and the government decided to follow Tito's lead and invest in football as cash was transferred to the club's coffers from Rome. One player was even purchased from Ponziana although he had to serve a six months' suspension for having played 'abroad'. At the same time the inexperienced Nereo Rocco was appointed as manager, at the tender age of 36.

Rocco has gone down in Italian football history as one of the ideologues of *catenaccio* and in the 1947–8 season, he began using a sweeper. He also created a strong team spirit, and just fifteen players turned out for the club that season. The results were spectacular. From last place, Trieste climbed up to second, behind the unbeatable *Grande Torino* side. They were never to reach such heights again, but that second place was not a freak result. Rocco's Trieste came eighth in both 1948–49 and 1949–50. Yet, at that point, the team began to break up and Rocco left. In the meantime, the club's debts mounted and internal conflicts and jealousies began to dominate the running of the team. As results worsened still further, there were calls for Rocco to return.

In the end, Rocco did come back, but his days were numbered. Controversy surrounded his decision to recall ageing former star Guglielmo Trevisan (37 at the time) and to pay him 50,000 lire a match. Rumours spread, including claims that Rocco was taking backhanders every time Trevisan played. Meanwhile the cash-flow from the government's coffers in Rome was beginning to dry up. The Trevisan experiment came to an abrupt end in a match at San Siro as Milan thrashed Trieste, 6–0. Rocco left for good along with Trevisan while star defender Cesare Maldini was transferred to Milan to begin a long and glorious career. Triestina began a long decline.

As the city became Italian again in 1954, the propaganda value of the team waned. Trieste went up and down to Serie B, before a long and bumpy slide down to Serie D by the 1970s. In 1974, an amazing 20,000 fans turned out for the first Trieste–Ponziana derby since 1927, showing that the divisions in the city were still strong. Rocco went to Padova, where he created another great provincial team, before moving to Milan and international glory. Trieste's decline reached its nemesis with bankruptcy in the 1990s after the construction of a beautiful but costly stadium – the Stadio Rocco. The club was forced to work its way up from the amateur leagues. Unbelievably, in 2003, Triestina were one win away from Serie A.

The continuing ethnic and political tensions in the region were revealed by two incidents in 2002–2003. In September 2002, Italy played Slovenia in a friendly at Trieste. Crowd incidents marred the whole game, both national anthems were booed and a provocative banner was displayed by the Slovene fans: 'The IX Corpus is back'. In 1945, Tito's IX Corpus troops had occupied the city for 40 days, arresting 'fascists' and 'oppositionists', putting the clocks back to

Yugoslav time and painting this slogan on the stadium: 'Long Live Trieste: Autonomous city in a democratic and federal Yugoslavia'. Reports in the national press misread the reasons behind the violence, putting it down to a kind of generalized 'hooliganism'.

A second, different incident took place in the match between Livorno and Triestina in 2003, as the enduring emotive power of the *Foibe* events of 1943–5 exploded into the world of sport. During the first half, a small group of Livorno fans unveiled this banner: 'Tito taught us this: The *Foibe* is not a crime!'.

This provocative message was aimed directly at the more right-wing elements amongst the Trieste fans, but the banner also offended those related to the victims of the *Foibe* massacres. Livorno's fans are known as the most 'left-wing' in Italy. Widespread protests followed, including a fine for Livorno. The president of the Committee of the Martyrs of the Foibe called for their fans to be prosecuted. All this related to events that had occurred some 58 years earlier. This was yet more proof, if proof was needed, that history is explosive in Italy, and that Italians are still divided over how to interpret their past.

## Right-wingers in Football. The Commander. Achille Lauro and Napoli

'If Napoli win Lauro gains 50,000 votes'[12]

Silvio Berlusconi was certainly not the first big-businessman, politician and power-freak to control a major football club. In 1936 Achille Lauro, shipbuilding billionaire, took control of Napoli for the first time. The owner of over thirty ships was to dominate the history of one of the most important clubs in Italy until the 1960s. On taking over the team, legend has it that Lauro immediately moved all the offices of Napoli in with those of his shipping company. He was infamous for his impatience – one manager was sacked after just three weeks in charge – and for his huge investment in a team which had won nothing in its history, and won nothing with him either. Lauro was desperate to win a championship and he left the club in 1940, disillusioned by his lack of success. In 1952, he was back in charge, and soon afterwards he smashed the transfer record to buy Swedish star Hasse Jeppson (who cost 105 million lire and scored 52 goals in four seasons). A march through the city was held to celebrate the acquisition of the Swede. Later 'fan' rallies combined celebrations of footballing deeds with calls to 'vote for Lauro'.

Lauro had a tempestuous relationship with manager Eraldo Monzeglio (who had won the *scudetto* with Roma in 1941), who resigned on a number of occasions before being ritually re-employed. Lauro also interfered in all aspects of club policy: from tactics to transfers to team selection. Another legend claims that Lauro brought the Brazilian striker Cané (who would go on to play for ten years for Napoli) after seeing his photo and saying that 'he is black and ugly and he'll scare the opposition'. Later, another star was purchased to play alongside Jeppson, the Brazilian Vincio, who also became an idol for the fans. Moreover, Lauro had a huge new stadium built on the edge of the town centre – the San Paolo. All this money couldn't buy a *scudetto*: in Jeppson's four seasons with the club Napoli finished fourth, fifth, sixth and fourteenth.

Lauro was open in his use of his football team to serve his political ambitions. His slogan was: *Un grande Napoli per una grande Napoli* – 'A Great Naples for a Great Napoli' (or vice-versa, the team and the city have the same name). After breaking from the potent governing party, the Christian Democrats, Lauro led a maverick monarchist coalition that romped to power in local elections in the 1950s and 1960s. In 1952 he won an astonishing 117,000 preference votes, and in 1956 this figure was almost tripled. The Commander was well aware of the enormous power-base Napoli helped to give him, as well as his ability to preside over clientelist networks at a time of uncontrolled building speculation. This period is most vividly depicted by film director Francesco Rosi in his agitprop masterpiece *Hands over the City* (1963).

Always a controversial political figure, Lauro had made his first millions from the arms trade linked to fascism's colonial adventures, after he won the navy contracts for the African campaign in the 1930s. The 'vice-King' (another of his nicknames) missed no opportunity to attack central government and the north, thus reinforcing southern pride in their most powerful and well-supported team. The result was power and consensus on a remarkable scale – a system known as

*Laurism* at the centre of which was this charismatic and populist businessman. Lauro was Mayor of the city for most of the 1950s and 1960s (he was in office for more than 2,300 days), governing with massive majorities. The city was run as a kind of fiefdom, with little space for discussion, and this reign only came to an end when the Christian Democrats (DC) lost patience. They ditched Lauro through a highly unlikely anti-corruption drive which led to the dissolution of the local council in 1958 (just before the local elections). Before long, the DC were firmly in control of political power in Naples.[13]

On the pitch, the much-awaited *scudetto* would not come, and Napoli even went down to Serie B twice: in 1961 and in 1963. A huge crowd riot led to massive damage to the new stadium as Lauro's political fortunes also took a turn for the worse. He handed over the reins of power, although his family still held a large stake in the club, which his son (president for a time) used to exercise power over transfers and managerial decisions. Achille Lauro remained Honorary Life President. His legacy to the city and the club was a disastrous one: an urban landscape ravaged by illegal and poor housing, and vulnerable to earthquakes; and a team full of stars, who left the fans innumerable memories, but whose victories amounted to nothing. The trophy cabinet remained empty (apart from two Italian Cups) until the arrival of a small Argentinian genius in 1984. The story of Achille Lauro, and the deep connections he created between football and power in Italy, shows that it would be foolish to ignore the influence of the nation's most popular sport when trying to understand the vicissitudes of her complicated political system.

## Armed and Dangerous. The Lazio team of the 1970s

Lazio's unlikely success in the first half of the 1970s – which culminated with the club's first *scudetto* in 1973–4 – came with a team of bad boys, self-declared fascists and gun-toting parachute enthusiasts. Lazio were armed and dangerous. They fought opposing teams on and off the field – clashing with the Arsenal team and staff outside a Rome restaurant in 1970 and with Ipswich in the dressing room in 1973. This Lazio team also fought, frequently, amongst themselves. The players were so divided that they changed in two separate dressing rooms, and any infringement of the other clan's territory could end in violence. Weekly training games were so competitive that they would often go on into the night until one team won. Some first-team players wore shin-pads *only* in these training games, and not in Serie A. The manager – Tommaso Maestrelli – always tried to end these games in a draw. Some of these tensions even spilled out onto the pitch. Most famously, the explosive Welsh-Italian centre-forward Giorgio Chinaglia once ran after and kicked teammate D'Amico at San Siro – up the backside – after an on-field dispute.

So many of the team carried guns that on one occasion a pilot refused to take off with the players on board. They had to leave their weapons behind – to collect later. Usually, however, the captain would just put all the guns in a bag. One of the few team members *not* to carry a pistol around with him was the tall, blond, eager midfielder Luciano Re Cecconi. Goalkeeper Felice Pulici later said that 'we all carried guns, in holsters'. Before home games, the team would stay in a large hotel (L'Americana) situated in open countryside, seven km out of Rome. There, partly to ease the boredom, the team would shoot at things 'all the time' (Franco Nanni, left-midfield) – lampposts, birds, rubbish bins, each other and, notoriously, some Roma fans who had come to keep them awake before a derby. Sergio Petrelli (right-back) claims that he shot a light once because he couldn't be bothered to get up and turn it off. Another joke led to a shot being fired into a bed between another player's legs. Most of the protagonists now admit that they went too far but that, at the time, it had been great fun.

The 1973–4 championship was a one-off, a masterpiece constructed by a clever and subtle coach, Tommaso Maestrelli, who built a team in which the individuals hated each other, but were united once they had taken the field. Looking at the players he had, and the money he spent, Maestrelli's victory in 1973–4 was something of a miracle. If we add the fact that, as we now know, the team spent the whole season arguing amongst themselves, then the achievement appears even more unlikely. In Maestrelli's first year in Serie A with Lazio, the team came a surprising third, only one win away from champions Juventus. Lazio's home form was excellent (they were unbeaten in Rome) and their defence impregnable (they only conceded sixteen goals in 30 games). Giorgio Chinaglia was top scorer with ten goals. Maestrelli's Lazio played an Italian version of 'total football', based on constant running and 'dynamic' play.[14]

In 1973–4, the promise of the previous year was repeated. The team gained the same number of points, but this time their rivals fell away. At home, Lazio won twelve out of fifteen games and again their defence was the best in the league. Up front, Chinaglia exploded, finishing top scorer with 24 goals. The team was settled and Maestrelli only called on eighteen players all season, two of whom only played once.

One key story about the will to win within that 1974 team relates to a crucial home game against Verona. Losing 2–1 at half-time, as they returned to the dressing room, Giorgio Chinaglia was winding up for one of his furious rants. Then, Maestrelli simply said, 'back on the field' (in two other versions it is Chinaglia who led the return). The players trooped straight back on and took up their positions on the pitch. Soon, the crowd started to go mad. By the time Verona appeared, the Olympic stadium was a wall of sound. Lazio won: 4–2.

At the centre of the mad, bad and dangerous group was Giorgio Chinaglia (pronounced Kin-al-ya). A lot of words have been spent on Long John, including a biography in English, one in Italian and numerous articles. He was, in many ways, the dominant player in the Italian league in the early to mid-1970s, as much for his activities off the field as on it. He inspired love, almost exclusively from Lazio fans who elected him the greatest player in their history in 2000, and a lot of hate – from the left, from other Italian fans and from journalists. Chinaglia was another player with a whole series of nicknames. The self-evident Giorgione – big George – and Long John, after John Charles, with whom all English (and Welsh) centre-forwards were compared.

Chinaglia arrived at Lazio in 1969. His career had been a roundabout one, to say the least. He was born in the marble-mining town of Pontecimato near Carrara in Tuscany in 1947; Giorgio's father emigrated to Swansea, to work in a steel factory, leaving the young boy with his grandmother. In 1953, Giorgio followed his parents, alone (at the age of six) with his destination address sewn onto his jumper. Soon, his father opened 'Mario's Bamboo Restaurant' in Swansea; John

Charles was one of its clients. After a spell in the old Second Division with Swansea City, Giorgio was given a free transfer. 'He will never become a professional,' said Glen David, Swansea's president. They thought he wasn't going to make it – and he played only five games for Swansea, scoring once. Giorgio's endemic indiscipline had played a part in the decision. His early career is packed with stories of clashes with managers, fellow players and authority figures. Chinaglia, however, was convinced that he was good enough. He told his fellow Swansea players that they would one day 'beg him for his autograph'. When Chinaglia came to Wembley to play for Italy in 1973, the Welsh press was amazed by his progress.[15]

In 1966 Giorgio came back to Italy to do his military service and play for a small club close to his birthplace, Massese of Massa Carrara. He then moved to Napoli's now-defunct other team – Internapoli – for two seasons in Serie C, where he played with Pino Wilson, the Anglo-Italian who would be his constant companion with Lazio. Whilst in Naples, Chinaglia fell in love with the daughter of a NATO official. Her name was very Neapolitan – Connie Eruzione. After fourteen goals in his second season in Naples, Lazio snapped up Giorgio for 200 million lire, along with Wilson.

The first years were a mixture of highs (a winning goal against Milan) and lows (relegation in 1971). Chinaglia peaked in Lazio's championship year, finishing as top scorer and inspiring the whole team. His personal mark on the *scudetto* was sealed with the winning penalty in the penultimate game of the season. On the field, Chinaglia was spectacular. He harassed opposing teams, screamed at referees, attacked his own players for not passing to him, and provoked the crowd. He was also a great player, strong, fast and difficult to knock off the ball, with a uncanny sense of position. His shot was so powerful that it is said that he broke the crossbar during his first training session with Lazio. Weak in the air, his strength was in running at defenders. Chinaglia built up a very close relationship with Maestrelli after Argentinian coach Lorenzo was sacked in 1971. Giorgio would often stay in Maestrelli's house and would always run over to the bench and embrace his manager after scoring.

Outside the select circles of Lazio fans, Chinaglia became the detested symbol of an unpopular team. Part of this was down to politics. In 1972 Giorgio declared publicly that he would vote for the *Movimento Sociale Italiano*. The MSI in 1972 was a self-declared neo-fascist party, led by Giorgio Almirante, who had been responsible for anti-Semitic round-ups during Mussolini's ill-fated Republic of Salò in 1943–5. 'I liked Giorgio Almirante,' he would later declare, 'he wasn't a real politician, he was outside of the usual political games.'[16]

Chinaglia was probably not even a real fascist. It is tempting to think that he said these things just to wind people up (one of his favourite pastimes). Lazio fan David Grieco calls him 'a right-wing anarchist'. Nonetheless, for left intellectuals, Chinaglia became something of a symbol of right-wing boorishness and violence. Pasolini criticized him, as did novelist and football writer Giovanni Arpino, who called Chinaglia 'one of the most squalid and most negative personalities from the recent history of our game'.[17] Opposing fans often chanted *fascista* at Chinaglia (this happened at Florence and Perugia, for example). Paolo Sollier – the revolutionary footballer – called him *Khinaglia*. The left in the 1970s used a K instead of a C to signal reactionaries, as in *Kossiga* (an Italian politician – actually called Cossiga). It is said that Chinaglia gave a fascist salute after his last game for Lazio. Later, Chinaglia's politics appeared to become more moderate. He stood for the middle-of-the-road Christian Democrats in the 1990 regional elections, just missing out, and again for the centre-left Popular Party in 1999, losing again.

Roma's fans, of course, hated Chinaglia for footballing reasons, dubbing him 'the hunchback' for his stooping gait.[18] Not only did he take Lazio to success at a time when Roma were in transition (they finished eleventh and eighth in 1972–3 and 1973–4) but he also made a habit of scoring in the Rome derby. Whilst Lazio fans chanted: '*Giorgio Chinaglia è il grido di battaglia*: Giorgio Chinaglia is our battle cry', Roma's followers responded with this 'song':

'*O brutto gobbo/scava la fossa/sarai sommerso dalla furia giallorossa/ quando saremo vicino a te/noi ti daremo un altro duce un altro re: Piero gol!*'

'Ugly hunchback/dig your grave/you will be buried by red-and-yellow anger/when we come close to you/we will show you another duce another king: Piero gol [Piero Prati was Roma's forward at that time]!'

Life for Chinaglia in the capital city became impossible and it was difficult for him even to walk down the street. Roma fans attacked his new jeans shop in the city. 'I used to carry a pistol, a 44 magnum. It could have been useful. But I didn't buy it for self-defence. With Lazio we were nearly all armed. It was fun, a game.' Chinaglia's unpopularity was also intimately linked to the farcical events of the 1974 World Cup. Giorgio was blamed for Italy's failure and fans gave him a hard time wherever he played. Italian fans had quickly forgotten Chinaglia's greatest moment for the national team in November 1973 when his run and cross led to Italy defeating England for the first time at Wembley. The hostility towards him after 1974 was a key factor in his decision to leave Italian football altogether, just two years after winning the championship as top-scorer.

Giorgio had first been seriously tempted by a new football career in the United States in 1975. He even took out a full-page advert in the Roma sports daily *Il Corriere dello Sport* to explain his decision to the Lazio fans. His wife and kids had already moved to the US, but Lazio wouldn't let him go and, as with Giuseppe Signori twenty years later, the fans wouldn't allow it. Chinaglia stayed on, but Maestrelli was side-lined through illness and the new manager wouldn't tolerate Giorgio's bad behaviour. In April 1976, at the height of his fame in Italy, he finally packed his bags and took off to New York, to play with Pelé, Bobby Moore, Franz Beckenbauer and ... Steve Hunt. The timing, however, did not go down well at home. Lazio were on the brink of relegation and Giorgio abandoned them with three games left to play. He was never to return, as a player: after 122 goals in 246 games, Chinaglia's Italian career was over, at the age of 29. In the US he became a footballing pioneer. For a time, it looked as though soccer was going to really break through in the States and, during that golden age, Chinaglia was a big star – playing 222 games in a row, scoring 241 goals in 252 games for the New York Cosmos (including seven in one game) and appearing on the cover of *Sports Illustrated*. Chinaglia was top scorer in the North American Soccer League six times in eight years and was elected to the hall of fame in 2000.

In 1983, Chinaglia invested huge sums of his own money to buy Lazio, who had just come up from Serie B where they had been sent after the 1980 betting scandals. Football presidency, however, was not something Chinaglia was cut out for. He accused referees of corruption and received an eight-month ban after attacking Florentine referee Menicucci with an umbrella after a 2–2 home draw with Udinese – his first game in charge. Menicucci had given a disputed penalty and then seemed to block the wall at a free-kick from which Udinese scored. Chinaglia's Lazio just avoided relegation that year. In Giorgio's second year as president they amassed a mere fifteen points and finished last, winning only two games all season. In 1986, Chinaglia left and he was later charged with false accounting and fraudulent bankruptcy. Fourteen years later, Giorgio tried to run a club again, this time with Foggia, with equally disastrous results. Today, Giorgio is a far more acceptable character, making a living as a TV commentator and PR man.

Pino Wilson, the sweeper, was the least famous 'Anglo-Italian' in the Lazio team. His parents had met in Naples during the war but he was born in Darlington. Soon afterwards, his father took up a NATO post in Naples and Wilson never returned to County Durham. If Chinaglia was more Welsh than Italian, Wilson was much more Neapolitan than English. A rugged, even dirty defender, good enough to play for Italy, Wilson bestrode the two Lazio clans. He changed in one dressing room but was 'allied' with the Chinaglia group. Between 1971 and 1975 Wilson did not miss a single league match and as captain was the linchpin of the *scudetto* side. In 1978 he spent a season with the New York Cosmos alongside Chinaglia. After the betting scandals of 1980, he was estranged from Lazio – and has only been back twice to the stadium since.[19]

Politics were important in the Italy of the 1970s. Lazio had been Mussolini's team, and the club's fans revelled in their far-right reputation, especially in the 1970s when most hard-core supporters in Italy were firmly on the left. In 1972 a number of Lazio players openly declared their intention to vote for the neo-fascist *Movimento Sociale Italiano* (Chinaglia, Petrelli, Wilson and left-back Luigi Martini, who later became a right-wing parliamentarian, Alitalia pilot and part-time poet). 1972 was a tumultuous year for Italian politics and an open admission of support for the MSI – who did very well in the elections of that year – was enough to alienate large sectors of public opinion. Many on the left called for the MSI to be banned. Under the 1948 Italian constitution it was illegal to 're-form' a fascist party.

The combination of the guns, the right-wing sympathies and a predilection for militarism – some of the players were parachute enthusiasts – was a heady mix which to any left-wing person in the 1970s signified one thing: *fascists*. On Lazio's *curva nord*, this politics was reflected with symbols (the Celtic cross, for example) and frequent stiff-armed salutes, as well as violence that looked very much like that adopted by British hooligans. Like their volatile team, Lazio's fans – especially but not only away from home, where police controls were less severe – were dangerous, and frequently very angry.

Paolo Sollier – the self-styled football revolutionary who played for Perugia – wrote this in 1975. 'Perhaps it is incorrect to talk about "Lazio's fans". "The Lazio fascists" is better. They beat people up, attacked buses, slashed tyres.' Before a Lazio–Perugia match, Sollier had been interviewed by a Roman daily. The headline read: 'If we win, we will have beaten Mussolini's team'. During the game, Sollier was substituted. 'I had been whistled every time I touched the ball ... I walked off with *Sollier Boia* [Sollier executioner] being screamed out by those shitty people, their hands in the bastard form of a fascist salute. I went into the tunnel without doing anything. If I had given a clenched fist salute it would have merely drawn attention to their insults ... once I was inside I was afraid ... shivering ... I wanted a rifle to kill the whole *curva*.'

The Lazio team of the 1970s was often involved in violence, on and off the pitch. The most infamous incidents of all involved two English clubs – Arsenal and Ipswich – both of whom played against Lazio in Europe in the Fairs Cup, a forerunner of the UEFA Cup, in the 1970s. Arsenal were holders of the trophy when they drew Lazio in the first round of the 1970 competition. Two John Radford goals in Rome put the Gunners in control, but Chinaglia struck twice near the end to snatch a draw. The match had been dirty, but everything seemed to have been smoothed over at a luxurious dinner in a central Rome restaurant. The two teams sat at separate tables, apart from Chinaglia, who chatted amiably with his old Swansea team-mate, Arsenal's defender, John Roberts. Then, without warning, all hell broke loose.

There are different versions as to what sparked the fight. According to one, the trouble began when the Arsenal players complained about the 'effeminate' little bags they were given as presents by Lazio, and started throwing them about. Years later, Roberts would say, in a kind of sartorial *mea culpa*, 'looking back those leather purses were lovely ... in those days British men wouldn't have carried them around but now they would'. In any case, a Lazio player threw one of the purses into Bob McNab's face, and then grabbed his ear. Soon, 'the refined restaurant was transformed into a bar full of pirates fighting over their treasure'.[20] The players piled outside and laid into each other, egged on by the two managers, including Lorenzo, the Argentinian who had led his national team during the 1966 World Cup, and perhaps had a score or two to settle. Incredibly, Chinaglia stayed out of it. The return in London was a mild affair by comparison, but the Highbury crowd gave Lazio a torrid time. Arsenal won easily, 2–0. The Fairs Cup Committee gave both teams a warning, but took no further action. They were not to be so lenient two years later.

In November 1973 it was the turn of Bobby Robson's Ipswich team. In the Portman Road tie, Ipswich, who had beaten Real Madrid in the first round, no less, destroyed Lazio, 4–0, with Trevor Whymark scoring all four goals. Towards the end of the game, the Italians became violent and three Ipswich players were injured as the tackles flew in. Nobody gave Lazio a chance for the return leg in Rome, but within half an hour, they were 2–0 up. Ipswich held out until the seventy-fifth minute, when they gained a dubious penalty that killed off the tie. Pino Wilson later claimed that the game had been 'fixed' and that the referee 'was not in full possession of his mental faculties'.

At that point, the game turned very nasty. Objects were thrown onto the pitch, and then picked up by the Lazio players and hurled at their opponents. Lazio scored again, twice, before Ipswich broke away to make the final result 4–2. Frank Keating wrote at the time that 'The whole idea of a civilized football match went to blazes as the Lazio men swirled punches around the referee and lashed out with their boots at the nearest Ipswich player'. Four times, the Lazio players moved the ball from the penalty spot as the Ipswich penalty was about to be taken. After the goal, police had to come onto the pitch to separate the players. The 'Battle of Rome' had begun, and things were to get worse.

When the final whistle went, Ipswich's players ran to the dressing room and locked themselves in, but goalkeeper David Best was attacked by Lazio players before he could make it to safety. Outside, tear gas was fired into the crowd. Police guarded the dressing-room door and it was an hour before Ipswich felt safe enough to come out. Bobby Robson was furious: 'No Italian player can be excused. They acted like savages, animals. The only Lazio player who acted with any sort of restraint, and came to my men's assistance, was Chinaglia. If any one of my players had acted even fractionally like that they would never be allowed even to wear the shirt of Ipswich's youth team.' Once again, strangely, Chinaglia was the peace-maker (but Trevor Whymark later said that Chinaglia had gone 'berserk' on the pitch). The consequences for Lazio were much more serious than they could have feared. Banned from Europe for three years, this was reduced to one on appeal. But that one-year ban was crucial; it meant that they could not dispute the European Cup for the first and only time in their history. This only sank in, however, after the championship had been won in the spring.

After a good season in 1974–5, the following year was a disaster. Chinaglia was unsettled, Frustalupi (a key figure up front) was sold and there was little investment in the future. Injuries started to take their toll and the team slumped to fourth last, only being saved from relegation on goal difference. The impregnable Lazio defence was no more. That year, the team conceded 40 goals. Lazio's championship team was broken and the club would have to wait for more than ten years before it became competitive again.

In March 1975, less than a year after the *scudetto* triumph, Maestrelli discovered that he had terminal stomach cancer. The effect on the team was immediate: they lost their next game 5–1 at home. For a time, it seemed as if he would recover, but the cancer took its toll and Maestrelli died in October 1976. By that time, Chinaglia had already left for the USA but he came back to carry his mentor's coffin. Yet, for the 'dirty dozen' who made up the 1974 championship team, there were soon to be other colleagues to mourn.

Luciano Re Cecconi was born in the grey hinterland of Milan – in Nerviano – in 1948. His father was a worker and he found a job in his cousin's metal-beating workshop whilst playing for the local side. A battling, hard-running midfielder (he rarely scored, but when he did the goals were usually spectacular) Re Cecconi was tall, gangly and very blond. He started his career with Pro Patria – formerly a big club from the textile town of Busto Arsizio near Milan – and was then signed for Foggia in Serie B where he played under Maestrelli. He moved to Lazio in 1972 and won the *scudetto*, playing 23 games, in his second season. Re Cecconi was known as *Cecconetzer* – because of his blond hair and his similarity in appearance to the German midfielder Gunter Netzer. He was good enough to play twice for Italy and to go to the 1974 World Cup (where he remained a substitute) – and he could well have played more often. His non-stop, all-action running game was perfect for the 'total football' so in vogue in the early 1970s.[21]

Luciano Re Cecconi.

Re Cecconi admitted that he 'knew nothing' about politics, but people still dubbed him a fascist, in part because of his suspicious love of parachute-jumping – seen as a right-wing pastime in Italy – in part because of his team-mates. At Lazio, Re Cecconi fitted naturally into the group of 'northerners' separated 'in their own house' from Chinaglia and Wilson. His best friend in the team was Luigi Martini – who was also seen as a fascist. They were so close they were known as 'the twins'.

On 18 January 1977 at 19.30 Re Cecconi, Piero Ghedin (who also played for Lazio) and another friend went to take a look at a jeweller's shop not far from the centre of Rome. Cecconi decided it was a good moment for a joke. Keeping his hands in his pockets, he shouted out 'Stop, this is a robbery'. The shopkeeper, Bruno Tabocchini – who had his back to the three men, at first – pulled out a gun and pointed it at Ghedin, who put his hands up. He then turned his pistol on Re Cecconi, who didn't. The jeweller shot him, once, from close range. As he slumped to the ground Re Cecconi muttered, 'It's a joke, it's a joke.' They were his last words. He died half an hour later. He was 28 years old.

Later, the shopkeeper was arrested and charged with 'excessive use of self-defence'. In the trial held eighteen days later he was acquitted of using excessive force. It emerged at the trial that the blond midfielder had already tried a similar 'joke' in another shop in Rome, that the jeweller had already shot a potential thief in February 1976, and that the pistol he used (one of three he possessed) was armed with special coated bullets. As a non-football fan, he had not recognized the players, he claimed; not even the tall, blond, almost albino Re Cecconi. The concept of self-defence – outlined in Article 52 in the Italian penal code – was a controversial one. But the 1970s were the 'years of lead', when right- and left-wing terrorists were at their strongest and used armed robbery to finance their political activities. Murders were common, and shopkeepers and bank tellers were very jumpy. An even stronger form of self-defence was applied to the police in 1975, with the emergency 'Reale Law' (named after the politician who promoted it in Parliament). Thanks to this measure, something like 625 people were killed 'legally' by the Italian police, *carabinieri* and army between 1975 and 1989. Re Cecconi's absurd death was seen by many as the natural if tragic outcome of the jokey but violent atmosphere at the club in the 1970s.

Re Cecconi left a wife and two tiny kids. He died just 47 days after carrying the coffin of Maestrelli, who had transformed his career by bringing him from Foggia to Lazio. Cecconi's son later played in defence for the local team – Nervianese – in the stadium named after his father. His grave has this simple inscription, *Luciano Re Cecconi: Footballer, 1948–1977*, and in 2003 a street in Rome was named after him.

*      *      *

Something of a 'curse-myth' surrounds that 1970s Lazio team. Three of its protagonists are now dead – Maestrelli, Re Cecconi and Mario Frustalupi in a terrible car crash in 1990. Another three have had run-ins with justice or the authorities – footballing and 'civil'. After the 1980 betting scandals Lazio were relegated as punishment and team captain Giuseppe 'Pino' Wilson was banned for three years. Goalkeeper Pulici went on to work for Lazio and was involved in the scandal of Juan Sebastian Veron's false passport in the 1990s. Giorgio Chinaglia was charged with financial irregularities after running the club in the 1980s. Renzo Garlaschelli, Chinaglia's striking partner, was found by journalists living with his sister, and nearly penniless, in the 1980s. Very few – really only midfielder Vincenzo d'Amico – went on to long or successful careers in Italy.

## Silvio Berlusconi. Football takes power

Born in 1936 in a working-class district of Milan, Silvio Berlusconi rose from crooning on ocean liners to become the ultimate self-made man. By the 1980s not only was he the richest person in Italy, but he also controlled large sections of the nation's media, including three national television channels and Italy's biggest publishing house – Mondadori. Berlusconi was already very famous, but he was only to become a household name with his dramatic entry into the world of football. His success with Milan – which he purchased and became president of in 1986 – was to propel Berlusconi to super-stardom, and help to create further cultural hegemony in a city where his powerbase was already extensive.

It was, however, strange that Berlusconi chose to become president of *Milan*. He was, after all, allegedly, an Inter fan. For years, an urban myth to this effect was doing the rounds but the truth wasn't confirmed until 2004 by the sports daily *Tuttosport*. Berlusconi always denied the story, saying that 'I have never been an Inter fan, you can't change your religion'. But in 1980 he had even tried to buy Inter and, as many journalists have pointed out, only an Inter fan could possibly want to buy Inter.[22]

Berlusconi's political success was closely modelled on football. His supporters are just that – supporters or fans, personally, *of him, Berlus-*

*coni*. His party – *Forza Italia!* – formed *clubs* that were a 'combination of Lions clubs and *ultrà* organizations'. After long research, Berlusconi's advisers came to the conclusion that the only language that unites Italians was that to do with football. Half the total electorate are self-confessed fans, after all. In June 1994, just after taking control of his first government, he promised to 'make Italy like Milan', and he wasn't talking about the city. According to opinion polls, Berlusconi polled very well amongst Milan fans. Berlusconi also applied his business acumen to the world of football, not just in terms of marketing and advertising, but also through the buying-up of players purely so that other big teams would not get hold of them.

In 1986 Milan was a club with a glorious history and a huge fan-base that had been going through lean times. The previous president was on the run after a corruption scandal and Milan, twice winner of the European Cup in the 1960s, had spent two separate periods in Serie B in the late 1970s and early 1980s. Berlusconi set about re-building the team, playing a highly visible role in saving a club in crisis. The crucial television-football-politics link, spectacularized by his own Fininvest (now Mediaset) channels in the early 1980s, began to take on more shape. Berlusconi usually attended matches, he became friends with the players and advised his managers on tactics. The *tribuna d'onore* at San Siro became the place to be seen in Milan and Berlusconi became a favourite with the fans. In 1987, he appointed a little-known manager called Arrigo Sacchi. Within a year, and with the help of three brilliant Dutch players and two of the greatest defenders in the history of Italian football – Franco Baresi and Paolo Maldini – Milan had won their first championship under Berlusconi. The miracle-worker had done it again, in his own city. In 1989 and 1990 the club won the European Cup, and impromptu street parties paralysed the city. More than 20,000 Milan fans made the round trip to Barcelona for the 1989 final, using twenty-five charter planes, 450 coaches and a ship.[23]

It was not just the winning, but the style of it. Milan played a spectacular attacking game which bore no relation to the classic *catenaccio* tactics still used at the time by many Italian managers. Berlusconi was able to make football into family entertainment, not an activity for fanatical fans alone. AC Milan managed to sell 70,000 season tickets in the early 1990s, and the success continued throughout that decade, with five more championships and another European Cup.

Many studies have underlined the ways in which Berlusconi's language is both televisual and sport-based: he 'took the field'; his organization is a 'team'; he often explains political debates in tactical terms.[24] However, what has often been overlooked is both the territorial aspects of the link to Milan (as a *Milanese* team, but also one with a strong national following) and the symbiosis between control of the media – especially television – and the success of the club, combined with the political visibility of Berlusconi in the 1990s. In a country where the best-selling newspaper is entirely dedicated to sport, and mainly to football, and where refereeing decisions are discussed for years, and often lead to parliamentary debates, the control of one of the top three football teams in the richest league in the world, and the identification as president with that team's (frequent) victories, has been a crucial factor in Berlusconi's rise to political power at a national and local level. Berlusconi himself claimed that his intention was to 'Milanize Milan . . . to import into the company those business-type methods and initiatives which would make the team represent our city'.[25]

As prime minister, on a number of occasions Berlusconi made direct interventions into the world of football. As his government was voted into office in the Senate in 1994, his Milan team were – at the same time – wiping out Barcelona (4–0) in a quite devastating display of attacking football. Italian political life had been 'footballized'.[26] During his second term in office, Berlusconi often commented on footballing matters and even passed a decree allowing major clubs – including his own – to spread out their massive tax debts over a number of years. By 2004, there were no more dividing lines between Berlusconi-the-Prime Minister and Berlusconi-the-Football-President, although many still complained when Silvio used his football power to make political points on sports programmes in the middle of an election campaign. One very dark suspicion remained. Perhaps Italians were more interested in Berlusconi's footballing career than his politics and perhaps, even more worryingly, Silvio the football president exercised more ideological power over his subjects than he did as a politician.

## Left-wingers. Football and Civil War. The Partisan Footballer, Bruno Neri

Born in the central Italian town of Faenza in 1910, Bruno Neri played his first football with a local club.[27] He became a classy central midfielder and made his debut at the age of sixteen in Serie B. After being spotted by Fiorentina in 1929 he was signed for a modest fee and moved to the Tuscan city. In 1931 a new, sparkling stadium was built in Florence, and dedicated to a fascist 'martyr', Giuseppe Berta, who had been killed by a communist during the post-war violence that swept across Italy. Fiorentina went up to Serie A in the same year, and Neri was good enough to get a call-up for the national team. He then played for Lucchese and for Torino, the team finishing second under Hungarian coach Egri Erbstein. He retired from the game in 1940 after 356 games, including eleven for various national teams.

In the 1940s, Neri was won over to anti-fascism through his cousin Vittorio Neri, a notary in Milan. Later, during the war, Vittorio was arrested, tortured and deported to Mauthausen. He escaped from the train and managed to cross the border into Switzerland. After Bruno was called up to the Italian army in 1943, he was sent to Sicily. Amidst the chaos of 8 September, when Italy changed sides, mid-war, Bruno joined up with partisan groups and made his way north. As a well-known ex-footballer, he worked 'with extreme care' with the partisans, gathering information and attending secret meetings in the city. He even played football for a makeshift Faenza team for a time before, identified by the Germans, he was forced into hiding with partisan groups in the mountains.

On 10 July 1944, surprised by a German patrol near an isolated hermitage, 800 metres up in the Apennine mountains, Neri was shot and killed after a brief exchange of fire. His body was recovered by another group of partisans and buried in the local cemetery the next day. In September 1944, Faenza was liberated by troops from New Zealand. A monument now stands at the place where Neri was killed – placed there by a group of Torino fans in 1994 – close to the now abandoned and overgrown hermitage.

In the town of Faenza, above a bread shop, there is a small plaque.

It reads as follows: *Here was born/Bruno Neri, partisan leader/who fell on the field of battle, at Gamogna the 10 July 1944, after having had success as an athlete/as a clandestine anti-fascist during the war he showed magnificent virtues as a soldier and a leader/an example and a warning for future generations.* The plaque is signed by 'The Partisan and Patriotic Associations of Faenza' and dated: 1955.

Bruno Neri's path crossed briefly with other footballers who died during Italy's vicious civil war between 1943 and 1945. Dino Fiorini was a quick right-back with the powerful Bologna team of the 1930s and 1940s. In September 1943, just as Neri was making his choice to join up with the anti-fascist partisans, Fiorini signed up for Mussolini's National Republican Guard. Very few records survive of that period, and we know only that Fiorini was killed by partisans in September 1944.

Even less is known about the death of Cecilio Pisano, who played for teams in Liguria in the early 1940s. 'All we can say for sure is that he died in the city of Genoa.'[28] As the liberation drew closer the port city was the scene of street-to-street fighting between partisans and fascists. Pisano was amongst a group of fascists who took control of a newspaper office on 24 April, and appeared to be playing a dangerous double game, probably in an attempt to disorientate the partisan forces. A number of versions survive of Pisano's death, which probably took place on 25 or 26 April. Fascist historian Giorgio Pisanò (no relation) claims that he was 'thrown out of a window'. Others maintain that Pisano threw himself out, preferring suicide to capture. What is clear is that Pisano was one of many Italians who fell just as the war was coming to an end. As with all civil wars, revenge and gratuitous violence accompanied the conflict, and Italy was no exception. Each side had its martyrs to mourn, and each side had its plaques to put up. The reprisals which marked the end of the war continue to inspire debate and bitterness, 60 years on.

## 1968. Footballers get organized

1968 was not just the year of the barricades, of the French May and of the occupations of hundreds of Italian universities. In the same year a number of highly famous and rich young men formed a trade union.

Their business was football, and their trade had never seen anything of its like before. Before the formation of the *Sindacato Italiano Calciatori Professionisti*,[29] by such stars as Gianni Rivera, Sandro Mazzola and a young, intelligent ex-player (and lawyer) called Sergio Campana, players were effectively the property of their clubs. They could not refuse transfers, and their contracts were largely the business of their employers.

Bizarrely, these players were demanding basic workers' rights – insurance and pension payments, protection against injury – as well as the relaxation of restrictions imposed on their trade (or the obligation for them to move) by federation and club rules. These rich, young and world-famous footballers were asking, simply, to be considered – in legal terms – like any ordinary FIAT assembly-line worker. It was to take thirteen years for this demand to be satisfied through legislation.[30]

The battle was a long and difficult one. Footballers could hardly go on strike – too much money was linked to the certainty that they would take the field at a certain time on a certain day – but they could now negotiate and, through Campana, negotiate they did. They also had the law on their side. There was no reason why footballers should have been considered as different from other 'workers', despite their high wages. Once the association had managed to attract the poorer players from within the professional game – up to 3,000 members – their arguments also gained more moral power. The players demanded unemployment funds for those without contracts as well as – in the 1970s and 1980s – guarantees for those caught up in club bankruptcies.

Slowly, the out-dated aspects of players' contracts were modernized. Insurance was made obligatory for all footballers in 1972 and pension rights were conceded in 1973. Finally, after a further protest in April 1974, efforts were made to free players from the obligation to move to where their clubs told them to go. Up to then, they had had no choice at all. One Sunday, all Serie A teams came on ten minutes late in solidarity with Augusto Scala, a player who had refused to move from Bologna to Avellino and had been dropped as a result. All the captains involved in the protest were punished with a booking. The union also demanded reforms to the highly-corrupt transfer system – in 1978 the police turned up at the transfer market hotel-venue in Milan to check

on the legality of the proceedings – and more democracy. The players'
union wanted the right to vote on federation decisions, and to attend
meetings.

In the 1980s and 1990s, the union organized a series of increasingly
militant protests over various issues – violence against players (by fans
and, sometimes, by presidents), victimization, foreigners 'taking their
jobs' and the promised fund for unemployed players. The lack of
support for this fund led to an unprecedented event in March 1996:
the first Serie A footballers' strike, led by Gianluca Vialli and others.
The strike was solid as stadiums lay silent all over the country and the
players won their battle. Then Europe took centre-stage. Most of the
issues over which the union had been fighting for years were resolved
in a radical way by the 1995 Bosman ruling.

The increasing and often grotesque wealth of the top players – and
the top clubs – made the union's work much more difficult, as public
opinion began to show its disgust with the excesses of the world of
calcio. By 2004, the players were perhaps too powerful (along with
their many agents) and the union itself was in danger of becoming
irrelevant. It was also entirely lacking in any sense of renewal: Sergio
Campana had remained at the union's head since 1968, and showed
no signs of retiring.

## The Footballer as revolutionary. Paolo Sollier

'Playing football meant that I had a different life from all my
friends, being political distanced me from those who played
football'                                            PAOLO SOLLIER[31]

Italy's 'Long May' of student and worker protest after 1968 was the
longest, most creative and, in the end, most violent of its kind in
Europe. Large sectors of society were politicized and many joined
radical left-wing or right-wing parties. Millions of Italians occupied
schools, went on strike or simply protested. It was in the 1970s that
overdue civil and political rights were wrenched from a conservative
and corrupt political class – divorce, abortion, the right not to be
imprisoned for adultery, the right to name an illegitimate child, the
right not to be murdered by a jealous husband.

Football was not exempt from this general radicalization of society. Many footballers and managers openly declared their political affiliations, to the left and the right of the spectrum. Nonetheless, it was still unusual for a footballer to be a paid-up member of a revolutionary political party. Probably the most well-known politicized player from the 1970s was Paolo Sollier, a journeyman midfielder[32] who became 'part of the history of *calcio* more for his political militancy than for his talent'.[33]

Paolo Sollier whilst playing for Perugia, 1976. This photo was used for the cover of his book, *Kicks, Spits and Headers.*

Sollier wrote one of the best and most unusual books about *calcio* in the 1970s – whose title already tells us something about the content of the volume: *Kicks, Spits and Headers: Autobiography of an Accidental Footballer.*[34] The cover depicts Sollier in his most celebrated pose – red shirt, clenched fist raised high, beard, long straggly hair. Sollier used to celebrate his (few) goals in this way, with his fist clenched and defiant.

Sollier's actual career was a modest one. Born in a tiny village in the mountains 60 km from the edge of Turin in the middle of the post-war reconstruction he played for Pro Vercelli before moving to Perugia, where he made his name. The red-shirted team, under inspirational manager Ilario Castagner, were promoted to Serie A in 1975 and Sollier played for a year in the top division before moving on to a series of minor clubs. After retirement, he became an excellent trainer in a number of lesser clubs, and a cult figure for enthusiasts of the more intriguing aspects of football's history in Italy.

Perugia was a radical place in the 1970s (and remains solidly left-wing today), a town that still revelled in its anti-fascist traditions, carried down from the war. During his time with Perugia Sollier was a paid-up member of *Avanguardia Operaia*, one of the most important far-left groups to emerge from 1968. The 'miracle' team of the 1970s, whose peak was a second place in 1979, had the backing of the entire city.

The extraordinary feature of his autobiography/diary is the way in which this political militancy was combined with the discipline of life of a footballer. He recounts how he would move from a political meeting or a demonstration to regimented training and the prisoner-like life of the football star. Elsewhere, Sollier reflected on the banality of the discussions in the dressing room: 'everyone talks about women, all the time, and, when they don't, they talk about women'. He was dismissive of those obsessed with football, calling fandom a 'social illness' and arguing that football chat was a way of avoiding the examination of real issues. The book was also very open about areas that footballers had never discussed before – sex, the dressing room, masturbation, the fans.

Not surprisingly, Sollier was unpopular amongst some other players and with journalists (who are savaged in the book). He received frequent threats in the violent atmosphere of the time and fascist groups told him that they planned to kidnap him and beat him up. He also liked to provoke opposing fans. Sollier was a rebel amongst players, refusing to wear the club suit or to abide by the rules of the 'retreats' before games, and he often argued with managers. Autograph hunters were told unceremoniously to 'fuck off'. Sollier donated some of his wages to various political causes. At the time, he later stated, 'the world of football was closed, repressed and cowardly'.

Sollier today plays down the political nature of his rebellion: 'at the

time there were only a few people who said what they actually thought
... I was confused with a rebel only because I didn't hide who I really
was'. He is also tired of questions about the clenched fist salute. 'That
was a choice made by the publishing house [to publish the photo with
the clenched fist on the cover]. I didn't agree at the time.' Sollier's
playing career probably suffered as a result of his outspokenness, and
he played out the latter part of his time with Rimini, in Serie B and
Serie C. The book was never republished (the author opposed such a
move) but Sollier is often the subject of interviews and has even had
poems dedicated to him (one begins, 'As sad as a Factory Council'[35]).
The film director Gianni Amelio was tempted to make a movie of his
life. Sollier's story remains the exception, not the rule, in the conformist
world of Italian football. As football historians Papa and Panico have
put it, 'the wind of dissent, which in those years pushed many young
people towards extreme choices, blew very little in the stadiums of
Italy'.[36]

## The most left-wing fans in the world? Livorno

On 22 December 2002 a group of people at a sports event unveiled an
enormous banner. It depicted Joseph Stalin. Underneath, these words
appeared: *Eternal honour to you, Great Man. 21.12.1879.* It was the day
after Stalin's birthday and the fans were those of Livorno, Tuscan
port-town with a long and radical revolutionary tradition. As Livorno
hovered on the edge of promotion to Serie A – for the first time since
1949 – these fans were at the centre of national attention. In a sporting
world where most of the *curve* in Italy were controlled politically by
the far-right, if not by actual fascist and racist groups, Livorno represented a remarkable exception to the general rule.

The *ultrà* group known as the *Brigate autonome Livorno* (BAL),
whose symbol is a skull and crossbones, was set up in 1999. This group
immediately marked itself off from other Livorno fans by its tendency
towards violence and its expressly Stalinist politics. The group declared
that 'the struggle of our lives is that of the working class, of anti-fascism
and of anti-capitalism, and so it will be in eternity, wherever we go'.
During the triumphant 2003–4 season, many members of the BAL
were issued with banning orders that forbid them from attending

Livorno games. Some of these bans were for offensive banners (one depicted a right-wing female deputy impaled on an Italian flag) and some were for violence. In the 2003–4 season, more than 200 BAL members – a record in Italy – were banned from attending games. All these fans had to attend the local police station on match-days in order to make sure that they were following the order. The BAL's leader – Lenny Bottai – had received a record five bans, the latest one after having attacked 'on his own' (as the police report read) a coach full of Sampdoria fans. These bans – which the BAL dubbed 'repressive' – did not dim their fanaticism. On one occasion in that season, two coaches full of BAL members made the 2,000 km round trip to Sicily where Livorno were playing *just to hang up a BAL banner*. All of the fans knew that they could not get into the game itself.

The BAL's provocative enthusiasm for Stalin needs to be put in context. Italy's huge post-war Communist Party was extremely Stalinist, only really breaking with the Eastern Bloc in the 1980s. Moreover, on the far, non-communist left in 1968, support for Stalin was far from uncommon and far-left groups would often parade with large photos of Uncle Joe at demonstrations. Admiration for Stalin was also a sign of extremism and of opposition to what were seen as the sell-out policies of the social-democratic left.

Livorno itself has a long history of subversive politics. The Communist Party was formed in the town in 1921 and long strikes marked the period after World War One known as the *biennio rosso*. The town remains – proudly – the most left-wing city in Italy. A huge Che Guevara flag usually appears in front of the *curva nord* at Livorno, along with banners in Russian, red flags, Cuban flags, political and anti-fascist symbols. Livorno fans often sing the 'Red Flag' (*Bandiera Rossa*) and the anti-fascist song *Bella Ciao*.

Throughout the 2002 and 2003 seasons, Livorno's fans amused themselves with songs and slogans insulting the then Prime Minister of Italy, Silvio Berlusconi. On each occasion, the club was fined (technically, because Berlusconi is a signed-up member of the football association, and therefore insulting him is to be censured by the football authorities, *not* because he was prime minister). Their favourite song went like this: *Berlusconi: pezzo di merda* (Berlusconi: piece of shit). These fines were quite hefty, sometimes reaching the figure of 20,000

euros a time – about £15,000 but the usual 'cost' was much lower –
about £1,500 for 'rude chants'.

Paolo Di Canio salutes the Livorno fans,
Lazio–Livorno, Rome, 10 April 2005.

On 27 March 1997, Italy's under-21 side played a friendly in Livorno
against Moldova. In the team, up front, there was Cristiano Lucarelli
– a local lad and crazy Livorno fan, raised in the notorious popular-
housing project in the city known locally as Shanghai.[37] Constructed
in the 1930s under fascism, the Shanghai neighbourhood was poorly
built ('when you went to the toilet the whole building knew about
it') but created a strong community. Cristiano later said that he felt
'Shanghaiian'. Strong, tall and quick, Lucarelli finally managed to score,
in front of his home supporters (and family), in the second half. He
ripped off his shirt. Underneath, he had on another T-shirt. On the
front? Che Guevara. The Livorno fans went crazy but Lucarelli was
severely criticized in the press, and rarely played for Italy again, despite
his excellent under-21 record of ten goals in eleven games.

Cristiano Lucarelli's career went through a series of ups and downs after the Che incident. He did well for Lecce, and very well in his first year with Torino. Yet, his second season with the Turin club was a disaster and he was accused of 'not trying' and of 'being overweight' as Torino were relegated. During a 6–0 defeat against Milan at San Siro, Lucarelli was sent off for arguing. Torino's president told the press that Lucarelli was 'a cretin'. This, and other incidents, convinced the Livornese forward to seek a transfer. He decided to try and fulfil his boyhood dream – to play for Livorno and take them up to Serie A after 55 years in the lower leagues.

Negotiations dragged on, and his agent was highly sceptical of the move, but Lucarelli dug his heels in. In the end, he was loaned out to Livorno and took a huge pay-cut – a thousand million lire less than he previously earned. Lucarelli later said that 'some players buy themselves a Ferrari, or a yacht, for a billion lire, I bought myself a Livorno shirt'. Livorno had just got back into Serie B after more than twenty years in Serie C. Even when he was playing for other teams, all over Italy (from Lecce and Cosenza in the south to Padova and Torino in the north) Lucarelli would always try to get to Livorno away games.

Lucarelli's other dream was to strike up a partnership with Livorno legend Igor Protti, a seasoned and charismatic forward who scored goals with every club he played for in a long career. Just as he signed for Livorno Lucarelli discovered, to his horror, that Protti had decided to quit. Cristiano picked up the phone and started, in his own words, to 'torment' his friend. In the end, Protti was persuaded to delay his retirement.[38] Livorno gained a world-class striking partnership. The rest is history. Lucarelli demanded a shirt with 99 on it, identifying himself with the notorious *ultrà* group the BAL, founded in 1999, and he began to crack in the goals.[39] Livorno stormed through the second part of the season, with Protti and Lucarelli scoring a record 51 goals between them. Lucarelli was attacked by other fans for his open political beliefs and his response was often a defiant clenched fist salute. Not surprisingly, the Livorno fans worshipped his every move. Promotion to Serie A was won with two games to go and a huge party followed. Lucarelli's agent wrote a best-selling book about the whole saga, *You can keep your billion [lire]*,[40] but Lucarelli was still a Torino player. After long and tortuous negotiations, Livorno finally paid a transfer fee

(Lucarelli had said that he would rather stop playing than go back to Torino) and secured his contract.[41]

One game from the first day of the 2004–5 Serie A season stood out from all the others: Milan–Livorno. Silvio Berlusconi's team would host the most left-wing fans in Italy. Preparations for the away game began in earnest in August and an implausible 11,000 Livorno fans made the trip, joined by at least three thousand Livornese from Milan itself. Berlusconi himself had been in the news over the summer largely for his attire during his holiday with Tony Blair – above all a bandana that covered the effects of an attempted hair transplant. Livorno's fans had thousands of bandanas made with 'Silvio, we are on our way' printed on the front. During the game, a number of banners were displayed by the Livorno fans, including 'Under the Bandana, noth- ing'[42] and 'Right up until the last Bandana'. The fans sang the 'Red Flag' and, after eighteen minutes, launched into a highly predictable '*Ber-lus-coni, pe-zzo di mer-da*'. It was said that money had been raised through fan collections to pay the inevitable fine. One fan displayed a hammer and sickle with the taunt 'You don't like it, do you?' The game itself was dramatic as Lucarelli twice equalized for Livorno and was only denied a hat-trick by a controversial refereeing decision. The game ended 2–2. Lucarelli kept on scoring right through to the end of the season, finishing as top scorer in Serie A with 24 goals. He even scored four times in one game, and still finished on the losing side, in a match Livorno lost 6–4. Livorno finished the season safe in ninth place, ahead of Lazio and equal on points with Roma, and the Lucarelli fairy-tale was completed by a call-up to the national team at the age of 30, and a goal on his debut, in a friendly in the USA against Serbia. After ten years in the international wilderness, Lucarelli had finally been forgiven for the Che Guevara T-shirt.

Livorno fans have one other key obsession beyond that of politics – Pisa. Derbies with the team from the rival port-town – just a few kilometres up the motorway – are amongst the most heartfelt, violent and important in Italy. Weeks of preparation precede these Tuscan derbies, and thousands of police are usually needed to keep order. This hatred of Pisans is not confined to football. A well-known 'satirical'

Cristiano Lucarelli salutes his fans. Milan–Livorno, 10 September 2004.

newspaper published in Livorno – *Il vernacoliere* – is almost entirely
devoted to jokes at the expense of people from Pisa; a typical headline
read: 'Two turds discovered floating in the sea: Pisan couple saved'.
Livorno fans habitually accuse Pisans of being backward peasants. One
Livorno banner read: 'Pisan and peasant: your destiny is really terrible'
(*Pisano e contadino proprio brutto il tuo destino*: 1997). Another banner
read: 'You are Pisan, have you realized what that means?' When Pisa
were relegated from Serie A in the 1980s parties were organized in
Livorno and Luther Blissett's crucial (and rare) goal for Milan against
Pisa which sent them down in 1984 was marked by an (even rarer)
banner dedicated to the ex-Watford forward: 'Thank you Blissett'.
Before one derby in the 1990s something like 20,000 Livorno leaflets
were dropped over Pisa from a specially hired plane. Politics was
important to Livorno's followers, but it was not everything.

## CHAPTER 14

# Foreigners.
# The Good, the Bad and the
# Ugly. From Orsi to Gazza

## South Americans as Italians, Italians as South Americans

*Oriundo*: of . . . extraction (stock, origin, descent); Italian – of
Italian extraction

The Boca neighbourhood of Buenos Aires lies close to the sea in the
historic centre of the city. Houses there are painted in bright reds,
blues and yellows and carry characteristic tin roofs. Genoese dialect is
still the most-spoken language in the district. At the centre of the zone
lies a football ground, the mythical La Bombonera stadium. This is
home to Boca Juniors, a club set up by Italian emigrants in 1905. Boca
is still an Italian neighbourhood, with its roots in early emigration
from the north of Italy in the nineteenth and early twentieth centuries.
Millions of Italians took the boat to South America and the exodus
was biblical. By the 1870s the Italians in La Boca already had their own
church, newspaper and opera house and one third of the entire Buenos
Aires population in the 1920s and 1930s was made up of children of
Italian emigrants.[1] By 1911 there were something like two million
Italians in Argentina and 40 per cent of the 3.7 million Europeans who
migrated to Brazil were from Italy. Football spread like wildfire in this
continent, and Brazilian- and Argentinian-born players have formed
the vast majority of foreigners to play in Italy since the boom of the
1920s. Over the years, Boca Juniors nurtured a whole series of future

stars, none more so than one of the greatest players the world has ever seen: Diego Armando Maradona.[2]

The presence of foreign players in Italian football has always been in close relationship with the complicated and often-changing rules that have governed the game. After the Viareggio Charter of 1926, only *oriundi* (limited to two per squad) were permitted. This rule – which led to an exodus of English and central-European players – remained in place until 1949, when the category of *oriundi* was briefly abolished. In 1955 the *oriundi* were back, but from 1956 onwards only those who had played for the national team were permitted.[3] *Oriundi* were neither Italians, nor non-Italians. They had Italian 'blood', Italian surnames and Italian relatives, but they had often never been to Italy. They were a strange mix of foreigner, and non-foreigner. They often spoke local dialects, or Spanish, or Portuguese, but less often Italian. The very term *oriundo* was a misnomer. On paper, Italian-born emigrants or sons and daughters of emigrants were, quite simply, *Italians* with more or less the same rights as those living at 'home'. A more accurate term was *rimpatriati* (the repatriated), although the *oriundi* expression survives to the present day. In the 2004 European Championships Italy played an Argentinian-born winger, Mauro Camoranesi, who was often described as an *oriundo*.

Given the restrictions of the Viareggio Charter, and the boom in South American football, the big clubs soon began to seek out talent amongst the Italian communities of Buenos Aires and Montevideo. Juventus signed Raimundo Orsi and Luisito Monti in 1928 and 1931 respectively – and both played a key part in the success of the Turin club and that of the national team in the 1930s.[4]

Orsi was a talented left-winger who was spotted whilst playing in the 1928 Olympic tournament. His transfer was controversial, and the Argentinians accused the Italian fascist government of having paid his transfer fee. Orsi was unable to play for a whole year whilst Argentina denied him permission. Debate raged on about Orsi's identity: for the Argentines, he was a 'pure creole', for the Italians, he was a citizen of *their* country.[5] This was true – legally – but not so clear in other ways. For example, he spoke no Italian. Orsi went on to win five championships with Juventus and a World Cup with Italy, scoring in the 1934 final.

Why did all these South American players come to Italy? The reason was simple: money – and lots of it. Italian football was already rich enough by the end of the 1920s to buy up the stars of Argentina, Brazil and Uruguay, as long as they were *oriundi*. Another Argentinian-Italian striker, Renato Cesarini, was offered wages of 4,000 lire a month by Juventus in 1929, four times the average income of a doctor or a lawyer.[6] South American football was unable to match these figures, especially in the 1930s, when Argentina was in the throes of a deep economic crisis. Players in the Italian league also received numerous perks – bonuses, cars, free housing. Italy's success at an international level in the 1920s and 1930s would have been much more difficult without the *oriundi*. Because of the spending power of Italian football, the national team was able to draw on talent from three or four countries. This imbalance was criticized back in South America, where many promising young players were lost to the European game. The transfer of stars was seen in colonial terms, and the authorities did their best to block such moves.

Renato Cesarini, the son of a cobbler and a housewife, was raised in Argentina, where he became known as 'the magician' and 'the Italian' and made his debut for the national team at the age of sixteen. In 1929 he signed for Juventus where – like Orsi – he went on to win five successive championships. Eccentric, extrovert and intelligent, Cesarini rivalled Meazza and Piola as a footballing superstar. His life has become the stuff of legend: it is said that he would walk around town with a monkey on his shoulder, that he had a special suitcase for his ties and would only sleep on silk sheets, that he learnt his Italian from prostitutes, and that he smoked prodigious numbers of cigarettes. He later opened an unlikely tango bar in Turin complete with two orchestras. Another legend has it that he would arrive for training with his clothes over his (silk) pyjamas. But Cesarini was above all a great right-sided forward, who only played eleven times for Italy because – it is said – manager Vittorio Pozzo disliked his rebellious nature. However, in that short national career, Cesarini managed to give the Italian language a new phrase: the *zona cesarini*. Put very simply, the *zona cesarini* signifies the last few minutes of a game, but is now also applied to other spheres of life – from politics to culture. The phrase has precise origins: a winning goal Cesarini scored in the last minute of a game against

Hungary in 1931 in Turin after pushing a fellow Italian out of the way to get to the ball.[7] On retirement, Cesarini became a young manager and was one of the first coaches to apply total football in Argentina.[8]

The selection of *oriundi* for the Italian national team led to controversy. Some commentators criticized their use for the *azzurri*: why not play local talent? they argued. These debates led to distinctions between different 'types' of *oriundi*. Those born in Italy – like Cesarini (who left the seaside town of Senigallia in the Marche region for Argentina when he was just a year old) – were seen as more 'Italian' than those born in South America. Vittorio Pozzo drew a line between 'direct descendants' of Italians, and others – whatever that meant. 'For me', he later wrote, 'those players [the former] were Italian.'[9] Further debate surrounded the identity of Uruguay-born Michele Andreolo, whose parents had emigrated from the Cilento region near Salerno in the south of Italy. Andreolo played 26 times for Italy between 1936 and 1942, winning a World Cup in 1938. Pozzo admitted that Andreolo was 'not Italian'. The difference appeared to be that he was not born in Italy, but then neither was Orsi. However, Andreolo had fought for Italy during the war. There was no legal difference between these so-called *oriundi*. Distinctions were made with regard to symbolic factors – such as place of birth – but for the Italian state, *all* of these players were Italians, with dual nationality.[10] Andreolo, meanwhile, won four championships with Bologna, played throughout the war and continued his career until the late 1940s.

Fascism promoted the 'Italianness' of the *oriundi*, and exalted their role in the triumphs of the 1930s. Fascist ideals of an expansive, colonial 'great Italy', which included the Italian diaspora, linked in smoothly with this propagandist exploitation of the *oriundi*. However, there were ambiguities here. The fascist regime relied on the *oriundi* to win championships – but then discriminated against them after those victories. In 1934 the three *oriundi* in the World Cup winning team were refused the special medal given to the other players. Meanwhile, the South Americans accused the *oriundi* of treachery, and threatened them with exclusion from *their* national teams if they went to Italy.

\*     \*     \*

The whole category of the *oriundi* was thrown into crisis when the membership of a nation, or not, became a matter of life or death. During wartime, the 'grey zone' occupied by the *oriundi* was tested to the full. Enrique Guaita was born in Nogayà in Brazil to Italian parents in 1910. He played for Roma and won the World Cup with Italy in 1934, scoring a key goal in the semi-final before setting up the winner in the final. Guaita was therefore something of a national hero, as well as a local one in the capital city, where he hit 28 goals in 32 games for Roma in the 1935 season. In that same year, he was to find himself at the centre of an international diplomatic incident.

After a long propaganda campaign, fascist Italy invaded Ethiopia from its bases in Eritrea in October 1935. A rapid campaign saw quick victories and the symbolic 're-taking' of Adowa (where Italian troops had been defeated by local forces in 1896) and occupation of the capital, Addis Ababa, in May 1936. The war caused widespread international protest and sanctions were imposed against Italy, but the conquest was popular at home, coinciding with the peak of consensus achieved by the fascist regime. The campaign was accompanied by racist propaganda and brutality by the Italian troops, including the use of poison gas. As the war began, many young men were called up to fight, including a series of famous footballers – including Orsi from Juventus and Guaita from Rome.

Here, as with so many Italian mysteries, versions start to differ. What is clear is that Guaita, with his two fellow Roma *oriundi*, Alessandro Scopelli and Andrea Stagnaro, escaped to France in September 1935, after they had received call-up papers. Orsi, the hugely popular Juventus player (who had played 35 times, scoring thirteen goals, for Italy), soon joined them. The case caused a national scandal, and the fascist authorities accused the four of cowardice, theft and contraband. None of the players ever turned out for Italian teams or for the national team again. Pozzo later finessed the question through the use of classic conspiracy theories. Guaita, he wrote, 'was forced to run away'.[11] Blame was also laid at the door of ex-Roma president and banker Renato Sacerdoti, who had resigned five months earlier and who was later caught up in a financial scandal and interned by fascism. The fact that Sacerdoti was Jewish may also have had something to do with this treatment.[12] Brera, on the other hand, attributed the escape of the four

players to a lack of courage, and later cast aspersions on the commit-
ment of the players to their adopted country.[13] Guaita went on to play
for Racing Club in Argentina and later became a manager.[14]

Before World War Two thanks to the restrictive (Ghirelli calls them
'xenophobic') rules of the Viareggio Charter, very few foreigners turned
up in Italian football, and those who did were of a high standard. The
rules remained simple – only *oriundi* were allowed in. After the war,
things changed. The rules were tinkered with in line with political
whim, the performances of the national team, club pressure and European law. In 1965, all foreigners were banned and in the 1980s and
1990s, the key distinction became that between Europeans and non-
Europeans. Many more foreigners arrived and a lot of them were not
very good at all. Gian Paolo Ormezzano succinctly describes this trend
as 'lots of arrivals, lots of rubbish'.[15]

The nationality of the foreigners signed up by Italian clubs reflected
a complicated series of factors. Rules were crucial, setting geographical
limits for clubs looking for players. In addition, *geo-politics* were important: fascism looked to the emigration community, and favoured
*oriundi*. Mussolini's colonial policies also had an effect: a few Albania
players turned up after the invasion of Albania by Italy in 1939, and
some Yugoslavs were also signed up during the war itself. After 1945,
footballing fashions held sway – with preferences for Scandinavians,
Hungarians, English and Brazilians at various times. Cost was also a
factor. Young South Americans could often be picked up for less than
players from other countries, and this later applied to Africans. Key
results in international tournaments or games also led to groups of
players arriving. In 2004 a number of Greeks were signed after their
unexpected European Championship victory. The Bosman ruling (in
late 1995) led to a massive increase in the number of foreign players –
486 (40 per cent of the *total* number since 1929) arrived in the four
years after Bosman. Sometimes, players have been signed for publicity
reasons as well as their capacity to play football; Juventus brought in
two Russian players in 1988 as a kind of sop to *Glasnost* whilst Perugia
made huge amounts from advertising when they signed Japanese midfielder Nakata in 1998.[16]

# Stories. Foreign players in Italy since 1945. From Genius to Rubbish

## Antonio Valentin Angelillo: the 'angel with the dirty face' and the unbeatable goal record

'Angelillo was a good boy, he was a champion: a woman ruined him'                                                                HELENIO HERRERA

Three Argentinian stars arrived on the Italian scene in 1957, after helping their adopted country to win the Coppa America, where they thrashed Brazil 3–0 in the final. All were *oriundi*; Omar Sivori's family were from Liguria; Humberto Dionisio Maschio's from near Pavia; and Antonio Valentin Angelillo's forebears were from Basilicata in the south. They were immediately baptized 'the angels with dirty faces', partly for their looks, and partly because it was a good line. Sivori went to Juventus, Maschio to Bologna and Angelillo, who was just twenty, to Inter, for ninety million lire. For Danilo Sarugia – 'he came to Italy with a suitcase, a Charles Boyer [a film star of the 1940s] moustache and sparkling Brylcreemed hair'.[17] The thin tash was more Clark Gable, but the description is a good one. As he had not completed his military service, Angelillo was unable to return to Argentina until 1977, when an amnesty removed his classification as deserter. Arriving in June 1957 with his parents, he soon moved into an apartment at Lambrate, to the east of Milan. At weekends, the other Argentinian players would come to the city to partake of his mother's home cooking. After they returned home, Angelillo would only see his parents every summer in Uruguay, at World Cup winner Juan Alberto Schiaffino's home in Montevideo.[18] He was unable to attend their funerals in Argentina.

Angelillo was a highly skilful midfielder-forward with a heightened sense of when to make runs into the box. He tended to play in a modern free role, behind the strikers. His first touch was superb and the fans invented a story that he had paintbrushes instead of studs on the soles of his boots. In his first season (1957–8 with English manager Jesse Carver) he scored sixteen goals, but it is his second year that he is most remembered for. In 33 games, he scored 33 goals (with only four penalties) – a record that stands to this day. The Argentinian became the 'idol of San Siro',[19] scoring two goals in the last game of the season to claim the new record. Every so often, these days, somebody seems about to break the 33 barrier, but nobody has really come close. It is probably unbeatable. Yet, even with Angelillo, Inter still failed to win the championship, something that was becoming an obsession for president Angelo Moratti. In 1960 Helenio Herrera took charge of Inter.

Juan Valentin Angelillo in his Inter days.

Inter had made an extraordinary start to Herrera's first season in charge, with Angelillo a fixture in the team and club captain. They won their first game in the Fairs Cup 8–2 away and then went on a good run of results with Angelillo scoring seven goals. The Argentinian was also just starting to make his mark at international level, having made his debut for Italy. He was then, rather surprisingly, dropped by Inter – and not brought back until February – when he played five more games. *Why did Herrera drop him?* Most critics agreed that he was not on top form, but this was only relative.

Somewhere along the line, Angelillo was being made a scapegoat for Inter's frustrations over missing out on the championship. Moratti criticized his captain for lack of effort: 'Angelillo is an actor,' he complained, 'when he wants, he is the best actor of all, when he doesn't, he hides.' 'Nobody is indispensable,' he added, darkly. The relationship with Herrera broke down, and the Argentinian was summarily dropped (and stripped of the captaincy) for a home match with Juventus. This decision coincided with a move to a more defensive system after some narrow away defeats. The clash with Angelillo was front page news ('The Angelillo Problem' was a typical headline), and Herrera responded with the promise that 'he will play again when he is back on form'.

Many journalists put the striker's relative decline in form down to a highly-publicized affair with a singer, Ilya Lopez (who was from Brescia: her real name was Attilia Tironi), he met in the fancy Milan night-club *La Porta d'oro* (The Golden Door). Brera wrote that 'on the field, his performances were inversely proportional to his exploits with Jlia (sic)', adding that 'Angelillo's decline would be something of a mystery if we did not know that he is taken with non-sporting passions'.[20] Herrera made the same claim years after the event: 'he had no strength left'. An arch-disciplinarian, Herrera couldn't stand Angelillo – and it is not clear if the love affair counted as much as people say; many claim that it did, but others, including Angelillo himself, argue that the scandal was used as an excuse. Whatever the truth, Herrera asked Moratti to sell the Argentinian. Huge offers came in: 270 million lire from Roma, 200 million from Argentina. For Brera Angelillo had been 'a semi-god, now he is a mere mortal . . . Herrera has had enough courage to drop him'.[21]

Moratti often resisted Herrera's whims. Mario Corso stayed for years despite Herrera's dislike of his lazy style, but on this occasion the Spanish-Argentinian won the argument, despite Moratti's fondness for Angelillo ('I was like a son to him', he later said). The papers also hinted that the problem was really his private life: according to *Il Giorno* (a Milanese daily), the Argentinian forward had been asked to spend Christmas away from Ilya 'far from every temptation' but the paper also noted that the two had dined together at a top Milanese restaurant. In any case, the dropping of Angelillo did not work. Inter lost the championship by four points, after leading at the halfway stage.

Angelillo had an unlucky international career. During the early 1960s, he played twice for Italy, scoring once. However, the *oriundi* were excluded after the 1962 World Cup debacle, and Angelillo, by then, was unable to play for Argentina either. The Argentinian authorities had decided not to consider players plying their trade abroad. Like Brazilian-Italian striker José Altafini, he had made the wrong choice. Both were hugely talented players caught in international limbo, unable to play for either their home country or their adopted nation.

At the end of the season, Herrera allegedly (the claim is his own) told Moratti that Angelillo was 'finished'. Moratti didn't want to sell the Argentinian in Italy, to a potential rival, but he ended up taking the best offer – from Roma. A clause was inserted in his contract that prevented him from joining Juventus, Milan or Fiorentina for three years. According to Brera, girlfriend Ilya went as well, to a job in a top Rome club. After some average seasons in the capital Angelillo went to AC Milan where he played a few times in the 1967 championship team before a final year in Serie B with Genoa. Meanwhile, Moratti bought Luis Suarez, who was to be a cornerstone of the Great Inter team of the 1960s.

When Herrera died in 1997, Angelillo did not go to the funeral, saying that it would be hypocritical of him to do so. The bitterness was still there, more than forty years on. Herrera, the Argentinian claimed, had been jealous of his fame: 'in Milan there was the *madonnina* [the symbol of Milan – a small golden Madonna on top of the cathedral] and then came Angelillo'.[22] After his playing career was over, at the age of 32, Angelillo set out on a long and nomadic coaching career.[23] He had some success with minor teams in Serie A, and took Pescara from B to A, but his record was generally modest. Angelillo also became a scout in South America for Inter, recommending two of the better buys of recent years: Cordoba and Zanetti. He now lives in Arezzo in Tuscany, in relative obscurity. His name, however, remains one of the most cited in Italy, as the holder of that unique, unbeatable 33-goal record.

## Omar Sivori. Dribble-mad and out of control

'Sivori is a bad habit'                                    GIANNI AGNELLI

'He only has a left foot but he uses it like a big and delicate paint brush'                                    GIANNI BRERA

A whole generation of football fans were raised on the 'drunken' dribbling of Omar Sivori, one of the most extravagant personalities of post-war Italian soccer. Sivori had two nicknames: *el cabezon* – 'the big head' and *el gran zurdo* – 'the great left-footed one'. Small (he was only 1 m 70 cm), dark-haired and very fast, Sivori liked to humiliate defenders, driving them mad with his crazy movement and frequent nutmegs. His socks were invariably rolled down onto his ankles. In the pre-match warm-up he *always* smashed the ball into the opponent's empty net. On the pitch, Sivori was a winner, striking up an indissoluble partnership with John Charles – for whom he provided innumerable crosses – in the late 1950s and early 1960s. He was also something of a fiery personality, who liked to argue with referees, opponents and managers alike. He set records for sendings-off (ten) and 'days for which he was banned' (thirty-three). It is said that Charles once slapped him in the face to calm him down, on the pitch (another version of the same story relates that Charles carried Sivori off after he had been dismissed and was trying to attack the referee).

Born in Argentina in 1935, Sivori was signed by Juve in 1957. In 1959–60 he scored 27 goals in one season, and he took Juventus to two successive titles. In 1965, Sivori moved to Napoli, after a series of disputes with Juve manager Heriberto Herrera. At Naples, he was an immediate superstar. Twenty thousand people turned up to see him in training sessions, prompting cynical articles in the northern press about 'lazy' southerners with nothing better to do all day. He took his revenge on Herrera by doing up his shoes, very slowly, in front of him and thousands of laughing Neapolitan fans. After yet another hysterical argument on the field – which culminated in him crying and throwing himself to the ground – he was given a six-game ban and left Italy altogether. In all, he scored 147 goals in 278 championship games. A victim of the debates over the use of the *oriundi* in the national team, Sivori played only nine times for Italy, scoring eight goals.[24] He was also voted European Footballer of the Year in 1961. For years, all forwards were compared to him. Torino winger Gigi Meroni, who idolized the Argentinian, was known as 'the Italian Sivori'.

## The English, the Scottish, the Irish and the Welsh

Since 1929, and the birth of the national league, three Scottish players, two Welsh players, three Irish players and 23 English players have turned out for Serie A clubs.

## The Gentle Giant. John Charles

> Record: Juventus: 1957–1962 – 150 games, 93 goals; Roma: 1962–3 – 10 games, 4 goals

There is no real competition for the title of the greatest British player to play in the Italian league. John Charles was more than a footballer; he was (and is) a mythical figure, a legend who is still a household name amongst Juventus fans and soccer enthusiasts in Italy. Charles was a superstar, a hero, a role-model for millions of fans, players and

Omar Sivori, John Charles, Gianpiero Boniperti
(from left to right) in 1959 (Juventus).

even for those completely uninterested in the game. It was sad that his post-football life was marked by financial problems and illness, and that the aneurism which finally killed him struck in Milan in January

2003, as he was on his way to take part in a Sunday night football programme. After having part of his foot amputated, Charles recovered just enough to be taken back to England (accompanied by two Juventus doctors) where he died in February.

Charles wasn't unbelievably tall – he was 6 feet 2 – but he was big and strong – and he *looked* enormous, especially alongside the diminutive Sivori and Giampiero Boniperti. Not all of his goals were scored with his head, he was fast and had a strong shot, but he became renowned for his towering headers. He was never booked or sent off in Italy – in sharp contrast with the fiery Sivori. Signed from Leeds in 1957 for a British record fee (£65,000) through arch-broker Gigi Peronace, 'The King', as he was known at Elland Road, made an immediate impact.

Juventus had been going through one of the darkest periods in their history before the arrival of Charles. By 1957, they had gone six years without a championship victory and in that year they finished a humiliating ninth – for the second year in succession – alongside the provincial club of Spal (from Ferrara). Charles – with Sivori – transformed the club, and they went on to win three *scudetti* in four seasons. This potent strike partnership scored 50 goals in their first season together and 50 again two years later (when Juve hit 92 goals in one season). Despite Charles's description of Italian football as 'defensive', this was a spectacular team, with *three* goalscoring forwards – the Welshman, the Argentinian and Boniperti.

This winning system collapsed in 1961–2, with the rapid decline of Charles – after a long series of injuries and the retirement of Boniperti. Juve slumped to twelfth, briefly flirting with relegation. Charles was even moved back to centre-back on a few occasions, without great success (his later claim that playing there for Juve was 'the easiest job in football' was not entirely true).[25] At the end of that season, Charles went back to Leeds, but claimed that he couldn't hack the English game any longer. He had 'become Italian', he later wrote. Tempted back to Italy with Roma, Charles scored just four goals in ten games before finally settling back home, where he turned out for a series of minor clubs (Cardiff City, Hereford United, Merthyr Tydfil), playing right into his forties.

Hundreds of stories have survived around the Charles legend and many relate to his physical strength. It was said that, in training, he would lie on the ground, face-down, and Sivori would cross the ball time and time again onto his forehead. In England, everyone assumed that Charles was on huge money. Certainly, he earned well, but he made some terrible investments. His The King's Restaurant in the centre of Turin lost a lot of money, and he ended up in financial trouble.[26] Like ex-Charlton player Eddie Firmani before him, he complained about the cost of living in Italy. Charles was one of the best-paid players in Italy, but this was a different world from that of today's soccer billionaires. In his book *The Gentle Giant*, he wrote, prosaically, that 'butter, for instance, is a much more costly item in Italy than it is in Britain . . . vegetables and fruit are very popular' and 'the flat was centrally heated'.

John Charles remains the model against which *all* foreign players – and especially British players – have been measured – an exemplary figure on the field (through the stereotypes of fair play, bravery and naïve physical power) and off the field (where he was modest, generous and 'good', and he loved playing with his four sons). No other British player has come close to the Charles myth, and the contrast with the spoilt-child behaviour of Jimmy Greaves and others was marked. A whole generation of Juventus fans grew up with the Charles–Sivori double act, which coincided perfectly with Italy's economic miracle. A minute's silence was observed by both Roma and Juventus after his death in 2004, a rarity for a foreign player.[27]

### Greavsie in Italy. 1961

Record: AC Milan, 1961 – 10 games, 9 goals (4 penalties)

'I didn't know much about Italian football'

JIMMY GREAVES, *Greavsie. The Autobiography*[28]

'I can pinpoint the day, the hour, the minute, the second that I doomed myself to life as an alcoholic. It was the moment I signed my name on a contract that tied me head and foot to AC Milan . . . over a period of about a year, I was in a state of turmoil. Frightened, frustrated, bored, aggravated, depressed. All the classic ingredients that drive a man to drink' – Jimmy Greaves.

\*        \*        \*

Jimmy Greaves moved to AC Milan in 1961. He lasted a mere ten league games – three months, more or less – before coming back to England, to London and to Tottenham Hotspur. On the field, his performances were often good – he scored nine goals in Serie A and Milan won the championship that season – but the team as a whole had a poor start. Off the field Greaves was unhappy, disorientated and always in the Italian press. He couldn't hack the ultra-disciplined, military-style methods adopted by Italian clubs and the dictatorial attitudes of the team manager, Nereo Rocco.

Anyone with a modicum of know-how could have given Greaves the rundown on Milan, *calcio* and Rocco. Somebody should have advised Jimmy that players were expected to go to pre-game *ritiri* (getaways) where wives were forbidden and attendance was obligatory; or that he couldn't go out during the week, or be seen in city night-clubs. Jimmy didn't realize that he would be spat at, poked in the eyes and provoked on the pitch. Nobody bothered to pass on this information, and Greaves spent the whole time running for cover, becoming the most celebrated in a long line of short English stays in Italy.

So why did he go at all? In a word, money. Greaves was a huge star at the time, but the £20 maximum wage was still in place in England. Milan offered him £15,000 as a signing-on fee, and £130 a week plus bonuses through Gigi Peronace, of whom Greaves later wrote 'he could charm a bracelet' and 'when he removed his jacket he folded it like origami'. He was also given a free luxury flat. According to Jimmy, he immediately had second thoughts and tried to pull out. Neither club would let him, so he was off to Milan – probably the football capital of the world at that time. Hard-up Chelsea made £80,000 on the deal. Greaves was just 21 years old.

Greavsie's memory of his time in Italy is rather selective, when it is not downright weird. For one thing, he writes in *Greavsie*, his 2003 autobiography, that he arrived to hear that 'Giuseppe Viani [one of Milan's managers] ... had died of a heart attack'. Viani (also called *Vianni* in the same book) had indeed suffered a heart attack, but he was not to die until 1969, and was still close to Milan (he was sporting director of the club) in the period when Greaves was there. Greaves also fails to mention that he played up front not with Gianni Rivera, but with José Altafini. The Italo-Brazilian was the greatest striker in Italian football at the time, and ended up top scorer in the league that season. Greaves and Altafini were an attack that would have scared any team in the world. But Jimmy seems not to have noticed his fellow striker at all.

At first, Greaves was impressed by the stunning facilities at AC Milan – the stadium, the training pitch, the players' restaurant. But things started to go wrong almost from the start. Greaves missed his first flight to Milan after a boozy lunch at Heathrow in July, arriving just in time to score on his debut in a friendly. Meanwhile, Greavsie's wife Irene was heavily pregnant and when he insisted on attending the birth, he was fined (£50 for each day he was late). It was to be the first of many such punishments. At one point, Greaves would be paying his whole wage in fines. He arrived a day late for his first training session, and refused to play by the club's hyper-strict rules.

Milan's manager was the formidable Nereo (not Nero, as stated in *Greavsie*) Rocco. Some indication as to Jimmy's confusion can be found in the fact that he still is under the impression, forty years on, that Rocco 'was a Neapolitan who was suspicious of the Milanese' and 'loathed Tuscans, despised the French and hated the Spanish'. Rocco was, in fact, *very much* from Trieste. In fact, his *being-from-Triesteness* was one of the most central things about him. He was about as non-Neapolitan an Italian as you could find. Greaves had not only started off on the wrong foot, but was a touch misinformed about Italian customs and traditions.

It would be putting it mildly to say that the two did not get on. 'He made my life hell', writes Greaves in his autobiography. Rocco was a disciplinarian who liked to publicly humiliate his players, particularly the younger ones and the new arrivals. Greaves fitted the bill perfectly. He was undisciplined, off and on the pitch, young, new and English, and he liked a drink. Greaves claims that he only had the occasional beer in Milan – that alcohol was 'not a problem in my life at the time' – but Italian journalists wrote that he consumed 'rivers of whisky', 'wouldn't train' and, worst of all in their eyes, criticized Italy abroad.

The introduction to the world of *calcio* was one short, sharp culture-shock. On day one Greaves received a detailed list of his daily activities from the club, including his official bedtime. Training was led by Rocco, 'who constantly barked orders like some demented sergeant major'. Food was ordered for each player by Rocco; smoking and drinking were limited by Rocco. Stories soon began to make the Italian press and got back to England thanks to the bevy of hacks who had followed Jimmy to Milan. According to Greavsie, some Milan henchmen even nailed up the door to his balcony to prevent him drinking in public.

The Italian press was not tender with Greaves, criticizing his performances even when he had scored, and Rocco, interviewed almost daily, made his displeasure clear. Greaves was out of form, he would not get back and defend, he was too static up front. Greaves also began to pick up a dangerous reputation for laziness. He was, the press claimed,

Jimmy Greaves with his wife Irene and Jimmy Hill, Milan, 1961.

brilliant in friendlies (on Thursdays) but anonymous in Serie A games (on Sundays). Occasionally, journalists disagreed with Rocco, writing that Greaves should have been played as an out-and-out striker, but Rocco's system would not work with both Altafini and Greaves in the team. When the Brazilian played, Jimmy was invariably asked to track back, or pushed out on the left or on the right.

Nonetheless, Jimmy still scored, frequently. He notched one, as usual, on his debut in June and two at home against Udinese (including a penalty) on 13 September. However, after that game, Milan went on a terrible run, losing to Bologna and being knocked out of Europe. They slipped to seventh in the league, a position made worse by Inter's superb form. Rocco lashed out, publicly, attacking his strikers: 'Altafini, Greaves where are you?' In away games, Rocco claimed, his centre forwards didn't fight, they were too lightweight. Already, the relationship with Greaves was close to collapse. Rocco began to press for a substitute.

When Milan lost 3–2 to Sampdoria (Greaves two, one a penalty) at home, the 'crisis' became acute. Greaves recounts that Rocco screamed at him in the dressing room after his foul led to a free-kick which created Sampdoria's winning goal.[29] Greaves could not cope with the provocative tactics of Italian defenders. He claims that a Sampdoria player spat at him, so he kicked back. Rocco said this in a post-match interview: 'you can't put him on the wing because it's not his role, and not even as an inside forward, because if he has to track back he gets tired. You tell me, what should I do with him?'

At the end of September, after only five Serie A games with Milan, the Italian adventure appeared to be over. Greaves had been seen out on the town the night before a game, 'looking drunk'. Italian journalists even coined a new phrase for these adventures – the *jimmyfollie* – the 'jimmymadnesses'. He was fined a massive 500,000 lire. Jimmy Hill, football's trade-unionist who was campaigning for the end of the maximum wage, arrived from the UK to try and negotiate with the Milan management. The British press began to pick up on a big story. 'The whole of London is talking about us', one Italian journalist claimed. 'One thing is certain,' wrote the *Gazzetta dello Sport*, 'he will not play in the derby.'

Yet, Altafini was banned for the Inter game (Milan's next fixture) and Greaves *did* play. On his own up front Jimmy scored 'a stupendous goal' after eight minutes of the second half in front of 56,000 spectators, as well as hitting the bar with a free-kick. Milan won the derby, 3–1. But with Altafini back, the problems returned. The *rossoneri* lost away to Venezia, where Greaves was injured after two minutes and forced to hobble out on the wing (there were no substitutes then) for the rest of the game. Soon Jimmy Hill was back to smooth things over again. 'One thing is certain,' he told an Italian journalist, 'Greaves will spend next Christmas with Milan.'

Jimmy returned for a cup game against Modena that saw Milan

knocked out sensationally in the second round and he missed a sitter. His penultimate game with Milan was on 22 October at home to Roma. Once again, he scored (in the eighty-ninth minute, a tap in) in a 3–1 win. Jimmy turned out for the last time in Milan colours in a disastrous defeat away to Fiorentina. Milan lost 5–2. Greaves scored both Milan goals, but his team had been 3–0 down after only fifteen minutes. Jimmy's goals had not helped his team. Milan were languishing in seventh place, five points behind Inter. It was now clear that Milan would sell him, at the right price.

The arrival of Brazilian Dino Sani in Milan on a cold November night has become something close to legend for Milan fans. According to the myth, when Milan staff saw the thin, bald, slightly overweight 29-year-old step off the plane, they thought they had made a terrible mistake. He looked more like an accountant than a footballer. More or less immobile on the pitch, he was known as *il campione che cammina* – 'the walking champion'. Brera memorably wrote that 'he could no longer run, so he trotted'. Sani nonetheless was a fine passer of the ball and superb at organizing the midfield in front of his defence. He was certainly not a replacement for Greaves, but Rocco didn't want another striker.

Sani's debut on 12 November sanctioned the end of the Greaves experiment. Milan thrashed Juventus 5–1, with Altafini scoring four. Jimmy was left out, and his bags were packed. The papers talked about him in the past tense: 'San Siro is La Scala of *calcio*, and Greaves was announced as a new Callas'. 'Greaves is gone', they continued, 'and we would like to say "unfortunately" because he is a great player, but let's say "finally" because we are tired of his childish contradictions.' Milan fans joined in the criticism, letting down the tyres on Greaves's sparkling new Jaguar, which meant that he missed training again. For once, he had a proper excuse. Freed of his two-striker nightmare, Rocco didn't care any more and didn't even bother to impose the usually stringent fine.

Sani took over Greavsie's luxury apartment as Jimmy moved into a hotel and waited for the offers to come in. Both Chelsea and Spurs wanted him. After a bidding war, Tottenham finally got their man for a record £99,999. Bill Nicholson, famously, didn't want Greaves to be known as the 'first £100,000 player'. On 19 November Milan's president, Angelo Rizzoli, issued a press release: 'Greaves is no longer a Milan player'. After deciding to drive back to London, Greaves pretended to be leaving on good terms with the Milan club. There was even talk of an unlikely hug with Rocco. However, Jimmy had already negotiated an exclusive deal with *The People* for his story. His 'revelations', largely repeated 40 years on in his autobiography, were widely reported in Italy. Greaves claimed that he had been a virtual prisoner in Milan, he had been spied upon, his letters were opened, and his shopping habits had been checked out. He also attacked the defensive style of Italian football, and the brutal tactics of Italian defenders.

Meanwhile, Altafini continued to score, Sani controlled the midfield and young star Rivera – who took over Greaves's early nickname of 'Golden Boy' – exploded onto the football scene. Rocco had been wrong about Greaves the player, but right about the balance of his team. With Jimmy on the pitch, Milan lost three games (two at home). With him gone, they only lost one other game all season, winning all but one at home and scoring 83 goals in all, 24 more than Inter in second place. If this was *catenaccio*, it was *catenaccio* of a very strange kind. In the second half of the season Milan won 31 out of 34 available points. Altafini finished up with 22 goals.

Most Italian commentators and journalists – and Milan fans – attribute the championship that year to the switch between Greaves and Sani. Brera, who was a close friend of Rocco, recounts that the manager had been close to quitting and was unpopular with the Milan upper management for his rudeness, and demanded that Jimmy be sold. Greaves made his debut for Tottenham on 16 December, at home to Blackpool, netting a hat-trick. He went on to score 21 goals in the 22 league games that remained that season.

## From boom to crash. Denis Law and Joe Baker in Turin, 1961–62

Records: Torino; 1961–1962
Denis Law – 27 games, 10 goals; Joe Baker – 19 games, 7 goals

Torino splashed out on two Scottish stars for their 1961–1962 campaign. Joe Baker, born in England but raised in Scotland, had scored a record 42 goals for Hibernian in the previous season. A strong but skilful forward, Baker could score with spectacular diving headers or long shots, as well as classic penalty area goals. When he was refused a £5-a-week pay rise in Scotland, he was on his way out, for £75,000. Denis Law came from Manchester City. The combined cost of the two players was a Torino record – something like 300 million lire – and the deal was brokered by the club's omnipresent sporting director Gigi Peronace. Torino's fanatical fans were delirious. At last, they had players of class who would take them back to the top of the championship for the first time since Superga.

Joe Baker tries to show that he prefers tea, Turin, 1962.

After an explosive start, including the ultimate prize for a Torino player – a winning goal in a derby – Baker soon began to get frustrated with the disciplines of the Italian system. He became a target for the *paparazzi*, who feasted on the night-lives of these two young, good-looking men. Baker was photographed out on the town in Rome (in Via Veneto, heart of *La Dolce Vita*) in the autumn and disappeared after being selected for an Italian league team in November. Each time, the club responded with a heavy fine. On the pitch, Baker (like Greaves) could not cope with the provocative tactics of Italian defenders, and was sent off twice in sixteen games. Baker was given permission to go back to Scotland on a number of occasions, always with the promise that he would 'bring his mother back' with him on his return. The club believed that Baker's working-class mum would be a calming influence. Yet, Baker and Law invariably returned late, and there was no sign of either mother.

Baker's first game back after his second sending-off was in Venice, a city he 'had never seen'. Soon, Joe was in the news again. On 9 January 1962, the day before the Venezia match, Baker and Law decided to take a stroll around the city. They were followed by a pack of photographers. Baker made clear his aversion to more pictures, but a local *paparazzo*, 35-year-old Celio Scapin, continued snapping away. Joe lost his cool (later in his career he famously knocked down big Ron Yeats at Highbury) and attacked Scapin, punching him and shoving him against the barrier of a canal. Scapin's glasses fell in the water (although he was not actually pushed *into* the canal, as the legends about the incident maintain). Law separated the two, and the whole thing was, of course, captured on camera. It was big news. As punishment, Baker was dropped for the match and given a massive fine. Scapin, who had got himself a lawyer in the meantime, milked the incident for all it was worth and asked for three million lire in damages. The club, as with Milan and Greaves, had lost patience, and the manager sent Joe to the dressing room for lack of effort during training soon afterwards. Baker played just three more games for Torino (without scoring) before the dramatic events of early February.

On 7 February 1962, Joe Baker picked up his new car – a white Alfa Romeo Giulietta Sprint. Up to then, he had got around Turin in a humble Fiat 600 (still a luxury for many Italians in the early 1960s). Baker, Law, Denis's brother Joseph and Gigi Peronace decided to make a night of it. These unattached and well-off men first went for a dinner, accompanied by 'fine' Barolo wine, with some players and the team manager. The next step was Baker and Law's notorious hillside pad, where 'whisky and Coca Cola' was consumed and music listened to. Then it was on to at least two night-clubs. At 4.10 a.m., the group piled back into the Giulietta Sprint. Baker was at the wheel, with Denis Law next to him and Joseph behind. Driving at relatively high speed, and with alcohol in his blood (the Italian drink-driving laws, then as now, are notoriously lax) Baker attempted to take a corner without slowing down adequately. His car caught the edge of a wall below one of Turin's monuments to Italian hero Giuseppe Garibaldi (the papers joked that Baker had failed to 'dribble past Garibaldi'). The vehicle then flipped onto its back, spun again and crashed into a lamppost thirty metres down the road. Baker smashed his head against the steering wheel, breaking his palate, his nose, both his cheekbones and his jaw. His face was covered in bits of glass. Law was more or less unhurt and Law's brother escaped without a scratch. Baker was hysterical, and had to be sedated in order to take him to hospital. He was convinced that Law had been killed in the crash. Four operations were needed to fix Baker's face. The car was a write-off: it had 112 kilometres and 970 metres on the clock and still sported a temporary cardboard number plate.

The next day, Baker's humble working-class parents arrived from Motherwell, accompanied by his glamorous seventeen-year-old girlfriend, Sonia Haughie, a Glaswegian window-dresser of Italian descent. They were met at the airport by 30 photographers, who also managed to take pictures of Baker in his hospital bed and, amazingly, on the operating table. Baker managed a few words, which was just as well, as a second operation the next day meant that he would be unable to speak for some time, and could only take liquids (something the Italian papers joked that he was used to).

When Sonia (who the papers later claimed was just sixteen, and then eighteen, and then seventeen again) was asked whether she was jealous of Joe's notorious night-life, she replied that she would expect a man of 21 to be out on the town. *La Stampa* disagreed, arguing that 'it is extremely serious that two professional athletes should still be out at that time of night'. The transfer rumour mill got going again with a vengeance, as Baker was linked with various Italian and British clubs. Meanwhile, the papers continued to follow his recovery. One Peronace publicity stunt was to take the Torino team – including future World Cup winning manager Enzo Bearzot – to hospital where Baker, his swollen face encased in a grotesque Hannibal Lecter-type mask (something called a *ferule metalliche*), did some keepy-uppy for the cameras in the hospital ward. He even practised a header. As the season came to an end Baker was notified of a further club fine and attempts to have his contract rescinded. The club sent him to the mountains to recuperate. He turned up at a couple of home games and began training in April. Law's mind was elsewhere – with Manchester United, as the papers rightly claimed.

Baker never played for Torino again, and was transferred to Arsenal at the end of the season after nineteen games, seven goals and two sendings-off. He proceeded to score regularly for the rest of his career. Law, meanwhile, was briefly left out as punishment but played through to the end of the season. Bought by Manchester United for £110,000, he went on to become European Footballer of the Year in 1964 and won the European Cup in 1968. Torino fans see the loss of Law as a 'missed opportunity' and he received rave reviews for his performances on the pitch. A final legend – which is probably untrue – surrounds his departure at the end of the season. It is said that Gianni Agnelli wanted to sign Law for Juventus. Allegedly, a group of Torino fans went to Denis's house in the middle of the night and drove him to the airport, where they put him on a plane back to the UK – with a one-way ticket. Baker's angelic good looks didn't seem to have suffered much from the car crash, judging by his grin after being signed by Arsenal in 1962. He went on to score 100 goals in London in only 156 games. In 2001 he returned to Turin as a guest of the club during the celebrations for the return to Serie A, and was applauded by the Torino fans.[30]

## Luther Blissett. From *super-bidone* to *agent-saboteur*
Record: Milan, 1983–84 – 30 games, 5 goals

> 'Blissett, once he starts to score he won't stop. Take my word
> for it'                    ILARIO CASTAGNER, Milan Manager,
>                              *La Gazzetta dello Sport*, 18.9.1983

Some players are so bad they are hated. Some are so bad they are forgotten. And some are so bad that they are loved, talked about, treasured. Luther Blissett, who spent one lonely season with Milan in the 1980s, falls into the latter category. Blissett arrived at Milan on the back of being the top scorer not just in England, but across the whole of

Europe in the previous season. A series of myths and legends surround Blissett's time with the red-and-blacks. One commonly held belief, at the time, was that Luther's brother had been sent instead, playing somewhat on the racist stereotype that 'they all look alike'.

Luther became famous for his fantastic misses. When it came to *not* scoring, he was something of a genius. His first penalty at San Siro was not just sent into the crowd, it nearly went out of the ground (some reports state that it did actually leave the stadium, which is impossible). According to legend, San Siro then broke out in spontaneous applause. Most Milan fans were happy just to be back in Serie A, after a year in Serie B. In a derby Luther managed not to score from a yard out and the miss was immortalized by a series of photos in *La Gazzetta dello Sport*.

Some Milan fans looked (and look back) on Blissett with affection and 'went mad' when he got the ball. Their relationship with Luther was a bit like that between the Lazio *curva* and Gazza. English flags adorned the stadium when he played. However, this was not true for *all* Milan fans. Many booed Luther, and asked for him to be taken off. Milan were a bit lightweight up front that year: their top scorer, the veteran Damiani, scored just seven goals and Luther's five was a total also reached by a central defender, Battistini.

Luther also seemed to be improving towards the end of the season. After two terrible spells – he didn't score at all in the league between 30 October and 8 January, nor between that match and 29 April – Blissett's goals won games against Torino and Pisa away from home. Some compared him to another, famously bad, Milan forward: Egidio Calloni – calling him *Callonisset* (a nickname coined, of course, by Brera). Luther's Milan were not the club of the 1990s. They were recovering from a disastrous betting scandal and were run by a president, Giuseppe Farina, who would soon go bankrupt after selling the team to Berlusconi, and go on the run to South Africa.

One key lesson a new player must learn on arrival in Italy is this: don't promise too much. In July 1983, the *Gazzetta* screamed this headline: 'Platini scored the most goals last year with 18? Milan. I will score more.' Later in the same month another headline appeared: 'with his boxer's physique, how many teams will he knock out?' On 20 August, yet another headline (the sports papers struggle for material

A smiling Luther Blissett receives his golden boot as top scorer in Europe from Milan legend Gianni Rivera before a game in 1984.

in the summer months): *Blissett superstar!* For the pink sports daily, Blissett was better than Cerezo, Zico and Laudrup (all new to Serie A that year). Luther was following the pattern of all English players since Greaves – brilliant in pre-season friendlies (he had scored seven times). It was not a good sign.

Unfortunately, the season actually had to start some time. In September, however, Milan's coach Castagner already seemed to doubt his new player's scoring ability: 'The Blissett formula makes Castagner happy: "He tires out the defence, his team-mates score"'. The headlines got worse, and quickly. These ranged from the simple: 'Blissett, when will you score?' (6 September), to the terrifying: 'Blissett, listen to Jordan' (17 September).[31] In the same month Luther did finally score, against Joe Jordan's Verona. He talked of 'the end of a nightmare'. But the nightmare had only just begun. He managed one goal in October, by which time he had officially become a 'case' – a serious problem. Against Inter in the derby he 'used the ball to challenge the upright' (*La Gazzetta dello Sport*). By November there was talk of an imminent return to England, a minority of fans started to call for him to be substituted and the staff at Milan stopped defending their expensive purchase. Some of the affection for Blissett is clearly nostalgic. At the end of the season, Luther went back to Watford. In his various spells there, he scored 186 goals in 503 games for Elton John's club.

Within the increasingly popular genre of anti-fan-books, *Milano No* is one of the best. Tommaso Pellizzari, Inter fan, takes us through a series of anti-Milan moments, games and players. In his chapter entitled: 'Thank you lads. The ten *Milanisti* I have most loved', Luther comes in an impressive fourth, behind Calloni, Patrick Kluivert and Farina (Blissett's president). Pellizzari describes Blissett's departure as 'sad'. 'We would have liked him to stay much longer . . . for us he was an idol.'

Milan finished a lowly eighth that season, eleven points behind champions Juventus. The whole team scored a pathetic 37 goals in 30 games all season, finishing with a minus three goal difference. Blissett had thrived on Taylor's long-ball game at Watford, where his relative lack of technical skill was not a problem. In Serie A, he was cruelly exposed, forced to contribute to build-up play. Often the ball would simply bounce off him. But Luther was not alone. The other new foreigners in the league that year were by no means great successes: who remembers Ludo Coeck, Francesco Eloi, Donizete Luvanor, Luis Pedrinho, Alexander Trifunovic or Willem Kieft, for example? Was there something more sinister going on? Some journalists have mentioned xenophobia, but I have found no direct evidence of this.

In any case, despite that one, disastrous season, Blissett lived on in Italy, in a highly unusual way. Many people are aware that *Luther Blissett*, or to be more precise, his name, has had a second life after Luther's return to Watford. Adopted as a 'collective name' by a group of militants and writers in Bologna, Luther Blissett published a best-selling historical novel – *Q* – that came out in the UK in 2003. Before that, stranger events had taken place. In the early 1990s a story was doing the rounds that a group of people had refused to pay their fares on a Rome bus. They all later gave their names as *Luther Blissett*, and repeated that claim in court. Later it turned out that this *whole story* was invented.

In 1995 other members of this mysterious 'group' carried out a fantastic hoax on Italy's popular *Chi l'ha visto?* TV show – a missing-persons programme that has run for years on the third state channel.

*Luther Blissett* invented a lost person – a British artist called Harry Kipper – who had 'disappeared' whilst on his bike in northern Italy. The hoax nearly made it to the screen, but the programme-makers discovered they had been duped just before going on air (was it the fact that Harry's alleged route spelled out the word ART which had alerted them?). *Luther Blissett* issued a statement to the press: *'Chi l'ha visto* is a Nazi-pop expression of the need for control'.

What remains obscure is *why* these people chose Luther's name. Was it by chance? Was there something about Luther that drew them to him? One of the group – who now call themselves *Wu Ming* (no name) – has said that 'we needed the name of a person who had been stupidly underestimated and misunderstood'. Another compared Luther to cult film director Ed Wood (so bad he was good). One explanation may simply be a pun: *Q* is largely about Lutherans in Germany. A final answer may lie in this political analysis of Luther that I found on the Internet. It is worth citing in full:

## NEGATIVE HEROES. Luther Blissett and the refusal to work

*Comrade Luther was well aware that his daily life was both a means and an outcome of the struggle. Sold by the music and word merchant Elton John to a pre-Berlusconian Milan, he immediately assumed the role of a producer of immaterial symbolic power, overturning the sense of his every gesture and highlighting his rebellion against the system. Only the blindness of a young fan led me to hate him, then, for those badly-treated footballs, or for that misplaced trap against Roma, after a pass that had almost stopped in front of him. In reality, he was a saboteur, he revealed himself to 80,000 consumer-producers as a wooden wedge [used to stop assembly lines by militant workers in the 1970s], a sabot stuck into the production line by a worker: and he prefigured, at the same time, the later role of computer viruses within a society based on control and communication. Blissett refused to be integrated; he understood that capital is a parasite that sucks away our humanity. The game of football was made up of interaction, communication, intelligence and knowledge, and he understood that this system was part of a valorization of goods.*

*He decided, therefore, to refuse to be an interface in this system. He decided to stop communicating, to be a living short-circuit. So he started to move around the field at random, appearing to not care about the game. In reality, he was very careful to avoid all communication with his fellow players. He was also able to understand the future. He saw his colleagues as potential agents of capital: in fact, at that time, players like Baresi and Tassotti were emerging, who would be the backbone of that producer of triumphant images which Milan would soon become.*

*Moreover, he refused to trust the more progressive sectors of the dressing room; he refused to go along with the long kicks of the goalkeeper Terraneo, which tempted him into taking part in the game. Thus, at Milanello [Milan's training ground] he stopped talking altogether.*

*He became invisible, he could not be represented as part of a social system: he was a drifting mine ready to explode every Sunday in unexpected ways, with strange gestures which broke with the cold normality of the football-system. This true revolutionary aimed at complete self-valorization, creating a niche of liberty founded on the systematic removal of wealth from the cycle of added-values.*

*We don't know where he is any longer, but I like to imagine him in a place without time, a dynamic space situated somewhere between Brixton and the Caribbean where people are still able to construct networks of knowledge and relationships. Perhaps only the reggae rhythms of Jamaica will set the tempo of life in the interstice in which we lay down the bases of the revolution.*

*Luther, the black bomber, one of us.*

And thus the communication ends. Maybe we have underestimated Luther. Blissett himself remains perplexed: 'I am not pleased but what can you do', he is quoted as saying. In a later interview he was more forthcoming: 'Obviously I think it is weird . . . in fact it's rather funny . . . but it doesn't bother me at all . . . knowing some people use my name as a "multiple name" does not confuse me. When I look in the mirror, I do not see another Luther.'

## Mark Hateley, Attila the Hun and the Leap of God
Record: AC Milan: 1984–87 – 66 games, 17 goals

One key way to enter into the hearts, and the memories, of Italian fans is to score in the derby. A derby goal by Gazza helped Lazio fans forget a lot of indifferent performances and Mark Hateley's time with Milan is remembered chiefly for a goal he scored against Inter while, in general, his Italian adventure was not a huge success. He scored seventeen goals in 66 games and had terrible injury problems. Yet that goal was enough to write Mark Hateley into Milan history and its timing was crucial. Milan had just been through the darkest period in their existence – with two spells in Serie B (once thanks to betting scandals, once just with a bad team) and Inter fans had been enjoying a rare period of absolute dominance. Milan had not beaten them in the championship for six years. Then, the 1984 derby – 28 October: Hateley had been with Milan for a month after arriving from second division Portsmouth to replace Luther Blissett. Inter led through Altobelli before Di Bartolomei equalized. Then, Virdis crossed from the left for Milan. In the area, just in front of the penalty spot, Hateley was marked by World Cup-winning defender Fulvio Collovati (an ex-Milan player, well-known for his heading ability). Hateley rose high above Collovati and crashed a header into the right corner past Zenga's dive: 2–1.

According to Inter fan Tommaso Pellizzari, 'many Milan fans still have the celebrated photo of that goal . . . for them it represented the end of a nightmare, for us the end of happy days . . . an epoch-making goal'.[32] Italy's football *Dizionario* called it 'legendary'. The photo of the goal was sold on thousands of posters. Another Milan fan wrote this in 2003: 'for years I had a gigantic poster of that goal by my bed: for us that game meant a return to winning ways after years of purgatory'. The *Gazzetta* published the photo again and again, under headlines such as 'Mark Attila has struck again' and 'Hateley the man of the derby'. Comparisons were made with John Charles, inevitably, and Charles himself stated that 'Hateley will be better than me'.

Frequent references were made to Mark's physical power. His doorkeeper told a sports paper that Mark had unloaded his heavy luggage from England 'by hand, bare-chested'. 'He is a beast', he concluded. *La Gazzetta* wrote that: 'He is like Conan, the mythical, invincible barbarian, like a barbarian Hateley looks his opponents in the eye, like a barbarian he throws himself into the most furious battles, like a barbarian he celebrates when his rivals are destroyed.' He was 'as big and strong as a mountain', and 'you would need a fireman's ladder to climb up the skyscraper of Mark . . . or you could take a helicopter'. The omens were good, but the decline was quicker than anyone could have imagined.

Mark Hateley's winner in the Milan derby, 28 October 1984.
The defender is Fulvio Collovati.

Hateley suffered a serious knee injury in his very next game, and he never fully recovered. The peak of his Italian career was that derby victory and he only scored another two goals all season. For some cruel fans, Hateley was 'yet another example of a forgettable player made unforgettable by Inter'. Mark argued constantly with president Farina and, like John Charles, he found the cost-of-living rather high in Italy, writing in his book *Home and Away* that he 'had a steak last night that cost me £45 without the trimmings'.[33] Two seasons, and eight goals, later, new president Berlusconi sold Mark to Monaco (where he played under Arsene Wenger). 'Attila', as the Milan fans called him, was on his way.[34] Berlusconi already had a new striker on his books – Marco Van Basten. But the fans remembered Mark with some affection. When Hateley came back to the San Siro for Franco Baresi's farewell game, the cheers for him were surpassed only by those for Van Basten and Baresi himself.

## A Foreign Country. Ian Rush at Juventus, 1987–1988
Record: Juventus, 1987–1988 – 29 games, 7 goals

'Give them plenty of bullshit'
                    IAN RUSH's advice to future players in Italy

'This time it really is Arrivederci Italy – for good'
                    IAN RUSH, *My Italian Diary*[35]

For Liverpool, Ian Rush's record was astonishing: 346 goals in 658 matches. In the season before joining Juventus in 1987 he had managed 40 in 57 games. At 25, he was in his prime, and was going to Italy's top club. Yet his record with Juventus was terrible. One season. 29 games. Seven goals. Another British failure, then? The latest in a long line.

Famously, Rush had apparently said that being in Italy was like living 'in a foreign country' (he denies ever having done so).[36] But even this level of naïvety doesn't explain why such a great player did so badly – and then returned to the UK to score plenty of goals for a number of seasons. Signed in 1986, for £3.2 million, Juventus wanted to leave him at lowly Lazio for a year, to acclimatize, as they had done successfully with Michael Laudrup. Rush preferred to play on for Liverpool. He left only after the 1986–7 season was over. Seventeen days into his marriage to childhood sweetheart Tracey, Rushie was on his way to Turin. 'The Eagle', to cite the unfortunate nickname given to the Welsh striker with the distinguished nose, had landed. On arrival, Ian and Tracey moved into a massive hillside villa. The early entries in his diary are all enthusiastic, like a child on his first trip abroad. Rush arrived amidst great fan enthusiasm, and nobody mentioned Heysel, at first.

One reason for his subsequent failure *is* clear. It *is* much harder to score goals in Italy. The defenders are better, the goalkeepers are better, and the managers are more technically competent. And the game is dirtier; you will be fouled – systematically – to break up your game. If they find your weak spot, they will ruthlessly exploit it. Moreover, the rules on goal-*attribution* were very strict until recently. Goals which would routinely be given to strikers elsewhere were marked down as own goals in Italy. Even a slight deflection signified OG on the score-sheet. Rush claims this happened to him on at least two occasions, once with a tap-in that hit the defender on the way into the goal ('I thought I'd scored the first goal today', he wrote in his diary, 'but it was given as an own goal').

Moreover, John Charles was an impossible act to follow. The comparisons were obvious – they were both Welsh and both strikers – but Charles – as Brian Glanville points out – played alongside Boniperti and Sivori. Rush had Angelo Alessio (25 games, two goals), Massimo Mauro (25 games, no goals), Michael Laudrup (27 games, no goals) and Renato Buso (19 games, two goals) for support. There was also the Heysel problem. Juventus fans had certainly not forgotten that tragedy and Rush's transfer is sometimes seen as a way of building bridges between the two clubs after 1985. Rush claims that there were no problems with Heysel during his time in Turin, but some of the diffidence towards him may well have originated with the bitterness still there amongst many fans.

Above all, however, Rush was joining an exceptionally weak Juventus team whose winning cycle was coming to an end. This was a team built on a series of risky buys of young Italian players, most of whom failed in Turin. The replacement for Platini was a skilful, but slow, midfielder called Magrin who was known only for his precise free-kicks. And then there were the defensive tactics adopted by the manager, Marchesi, which had already been criticized by Platini. Juve scored a mere 35 goals in 30 games that season, and at least three regular midfield and front players ended up with no goals at all. Rush was isolated up front, and asked to track back. In this context, Rush's seven goals were something of a triumph (and he scored thirteen in all competitions, although some writers have later pointed out, sarcastically, that *seven* of these goals were against Pescara). Even Juve's famous defence was in trouble. The great sweeper Gaetano Scirea was in his last season (he played only six times) and Cabrini was nearing the end of his career. Juve finished the season seventh, and only a playoff saved them from the shame of not qualifying for Europe for the first time in 25 years.

Rushie's *Italian Diary*, ghosted by Ken Gorman, puts a gloss on this in the cover blurb: 'In 1987–88 he was the leading scorer with the glamorous league club', it gushes. Seven goals? Leading scorer? That fact alone tells more about Juve's season than any other.[37] Platini, who had dominated the previous five years, was gone while Michael Laudrup was young and unable to play a leadership role. His record in the 1987–88 season was eloquent. 27 games, no goals. 'A shocking season' (Brian Glanville). The 'diary' is a sad document, touching in its account of a poor season at a great club, and of the isolation of Rush in the dressing room ('Why weren't they talking to me? Where were my mates?'). Rush seemed much more interested in the rather dull details of the Welsh national team, and was always desperate to get back to England for any kind of friendly. He seems genuinely shocked by the Italian press, despite being warned by Souness and others who had been through the mincer in Italy. The cover authenticates the diary with some dated real 'pages' written in a childlike hand: 'the gardens here are luxurious enough for a castle with peach-trees, grape-vines, roses . . . all a bit different from downtown Flint where I was born'.

After scoring ten goals in pre-season friendlies, Rush picked up a series of annoying injuries at the start of the season. When he returned, against little Empoli (Juve lost, 1–0), he realized just how tough things were going to be: 'I didn't receive a single chance in the whole game'. After scoring twice at home against lowly Pescara, Rush was part of another defeat, away to Verona (Juve's away form all season was the stuff that relegation is made of: played fifteen, won one). Once again, Rush was given no service: 'I hardly had a kick'. In the defeat at Inter, the home fans greeted Rush with that cruellest of chants: *Blissett, Blissett* – in memory of Luther's disastrous season with Milan. The crisis deepened towards the end of the season, and by the end of March Rush had scored just a penalty in 1,500 minutes on the pitch: 'an eternity', wrote one Italian daily. Marchesi, who would be sacked at the end of the season, blamed his Welsh striker; 'he is not right', he told the media, 'for our football'.

Rush became paranoid, as Greaves had 25 years earlier in Milan. He was convinced that his phone was bugged ('just about everyone who calls tells me there's a strange buzz at my end of the line') and that his landlord was feeding stories to the papers. His poor Italian didn't help. Laudrup was supposed to translate for him, but didn't take his new job too seriously. Italian did not come easy to Rushie. He started with language cassettes. In his diary he confesses that 'I can hardly speak English that well, never mind a foreign language like Italian'. An endearing photo in the diary depicts him with enormous headphones and a *Buongiorno Italia!* book in his hands. After a year in Italy, his wife's grasp of Italian was no better, despite her claims that 'we had mastered the language'.

Juventus finished seventh, with the same number of points as Torino, and were knocked out in the second round of the UEFA Cup. They did manage to qualify for Europe through a playoff with Torino, thanks to a Rush penalty. Meanwhile, Rush increased his unpopularity by scoring the winning goal for Wales against Italy in Brescia in June, in a dirty game. Nonetheless, Juventus wanted to keep Rush for at least another season, and he expected to stay. Yet, after the 1988 European Championships, Gianni Agnelli fell in love with a USSR midfielder, Zavarov. The Russian was signed, increasing Juve's foreigners to four. Only three could play, and when Laudrup's move to Holland fell through, Rush was offered a move back to Liverpool. More triumphant seasons followed, whilst back in Italy, Rush's photo took up its place in the album of failed foreign stars.[38]

## Other British and Irish Players in Italy.
## Wilkins, Platt, Brady, Elliot, Rideout, Firmani, Hitchens, Cowans

English players in Italy can be divided into four categories. There were those who played just a few games, who soon found out that Serie A (or B) was not for them (and vice-versa). Former Nottingham Forest winger Franz Carr, who played six games for lowly Reggiana in the

1990s, falls squarely into this category, as does Lee Sharpe (three games – all defeats – with Sampdoria at the end of that decade). Irish striker Robbie Keane (just six appearances for Inter in 2000–2001). Then there were those who lasted a season or two, without making much impact: Aston Villa's Gordon Cowans and Paul Rideout played for Bari in the mid-1980s, Paul Elliot had an injury-hit two seasons with Pisa and Des Walker joined Sampdoria after the 1990 World Cup. Paul Ince had a couple of good years with Inter in the mid-1990s.[39] There have also been some more obscure figures, such as a player called Charles Adcock who played for three provincial teams after World War Two, or Anthony Marchi from Spurs, who turned out for Vicenza and Torino in the late 1950s.[40]

A third category can be dubbed relative successes: Trevor Francis at Sampdoria and Atalanta in the early 1980s mixed brilliant perform-ances with long periods out with injury. Ray Wilkins elegantly ran the Milan midfield in the same period, as did Graeme Souness with Sampdoria. David Platt had a good four years in the 1990s, especially with Sampdoria, but failed to break through at Juventus – where Trapattoni deployed him as a defensive midfielder. Finally, there were those who stuck it out, learning Italian and moving from club to club – winning trophies. Such players have been few and far between. In fact only four English-speaking players (or those who played their football in England) have been unqualified successes: John Charles, Gerry Hitchens, Eddie Firmani and Liam Brady.

Gerry Hitchens had the longest career of an Englishman in post-war Italy. He played for four different clubs over nine seasons, scoring goals wherever he went. In many ways, Hitchens was a similar player to John Charles – hardworking, unselfish, good in the air, rarely injured – perfect for a championship where heading ability was not top of the list for central defenders. After scoring two goals for England against Italy in May 1961, when Hitchens broke the goalkeeper's cheekbone, Inter president Angelo Moratti snapped him up from Aston Villa. His first season, with Herrera's Inter, was his best – sixteen goals as the team came second to Milan. But Herrera needed to play his other two foreigners in the following season, and Hitchens moved on, in November, to Torino as Inter won the championship. In Turin he scored 28 goals in three seasons. It was then lowly Atalanta for two seasons and up-and-coming Cagliari for another two. Gerry had made enough money to live a long and comfortable retirement. It was not to be. In April 1983, at the age of 49, he collapsed and died of a heart attack on a football field in Wales.

Hitchens famously compared his transfer away from the authoritarian leadership of Herrera as 'like coming out of the bloody army'. Brian Glanville recounts that Hitchens was once left behind on the training field after falling behind in a jog. He had to find his own way back to the town – six miles away. Hitchens' promising international career was cut short by his move to Italy. Alf Ramsey ignored him and after going to the 1962 World Cup (where he scored against Brazil) he faded from international recognition. Jimmy Greaves used to meet Hitchens for secret drinks in the bar of Milan's central station. According to Greavsie, Hitchens 'was forever looking over his shoulder'. In terms of staying power, however, Hitchens' only rival in that period was a striker from Charlton Athletic, Eddie Firmani.

Born in South Africa in 1933, with an Italian grandfather who had emigrated there from a small town on the Adriatic coast, Eddie Firmani became one of the most successful foreign imports of the early 1960s. In 1952 Eddie was spotted by Charlton's manager whilst in Cape Town and offered £7 a week to play in England. He was nineteen and he didn't make his league debut until 1954, against Derby County, at the Valley, in front of 45,000 fans. In the next season, he cracked in the goals. A huge offer came through from Sampdoria – £35,000 (a British record at the time) plus a £5,000 signing-on fee. For someone on £7 a week, this was too good to turn down. Firmani met with Gigi Peronace – who else? – in a London hotel. Firmani would also have a car, a flat and 'bonuses' if he played for the national team. Eddie didn't speak Italian, but was a quick learner.

Like all foreigners in Italy, Eddie was surprised at the rigid training regime, detailed in his autobiography.[41] He started poorly (like Ian Rush, he felt isolated up front: 'for two months I couldn't get in a *shot* at goal'). He also noticed the emphasis on style in Italy: 'they think about the *artistic* instead of the *effect*'. His first goal came in December, but things improved after that. Skilful and fast, he went on to score 100 goals in six seasons with Sampdoria and Inter. As an *oriundo* (he had dual nationality) Firmani was picked for the Italian team, scoring on his debut against Switzerland in 1956 with a thirty-yard shot. He was surprised to see a banner reading *Fuori gli oriundi* ('Out with the players of Italian origin') in the crowd (Firmani was one of only two *oriundi* in that particular game).

People were confused by his nationality, always asking him if he was 'South African, English or Italian?' He earned a negative nickname, despite all the goals, 'Cold Turkey', which referred to a supposed lack of effort on the pitch. This nickname was later to be applied by Inter fans to Dennis Bergkamp. After Inter, Firmani played another two seasons with Genoa before moving back to Charlton. He became manager of the London club in the late 1960s and then a successful football coach in the USA with the New York Cosmos. He remains the only man ever to have scored 100 league goals in both England and Italy.

Firmani's long spell in Italy led to fantastic stories about the money he was earning, stories he was anxious to play down in his slim autobiography, *Football with the Millionaires*, despite its title. One photo in the book carries this caption: 'the author goes shopping with his wife Patricia. They reckon they spend approximately £1 a day on meat'. Firmani was very open about his wages in the book. He claimed to earn £70 a month and even provided a monthly budget for his readers. It read as follows:

Rent of flat: £21
Telephone: 10 shillings
Maid: £11
Gas: £2, 12 shillings
Electricity: £4
Insurance: £4, 12 shillings
Garage for car: £7, 10 shillings

'You will notice that it leaves me about £20 to feed and clothe the family for a whole month', he concluded. He wrote that he missed 'custard powder . . . lean bacon . . . and even baby food' (which they had sent over especially from England). He relied, he wrote, on 'the careful housekeeping and budgeting' of his wife in order to save some money for the future.

The first and most successful foreign player to arrive in Italy after the fifteen-year foreigner ban, which lasted from 1965 to 1980, was Liam Brady, who joined Juventus from Arsenal after helping to knock the Turin club out of the Cup-Winners Cup the year before. Brady's silky skills fitted in perfectly into the trophy-machine that Juve had become in the late 1970s. He won two championships in two years, and is best remembered for the penalty that clinched the thrilling 1982 championship, slotted home close to the end of a crucial away game on the last day of the season. That penalty was made more dramatic by the fact that Brady was aware that he had already been discarded by Juve. Only two foreigners were allowed by each club at that time and Juventus had just brought Michel Platini. Brady cried when Giampiero Boniperti broke the news to him towards the end of the season. Undaunted, Brady went on to play another six seasons in Italy with Sampdoria, Inter and Ascoli but he was never able to reach the exceptional levels of those first two years.

## Gazza in Italy. King of the *Bidoni*?

*Career:* Lazio: 1992–1995 – 41 games, 6 goals

'This is Rome, right, but where's Lazio?'
                    PAUL GASCOIGNE, 1992, Lazio club shop

*Ubriacone con l'orecchino*
*Paul Gascoigne facci un bocchino*
Drunkard with an earring
Paul Gascoigne give us a blow-job     *Roma* chant, circa 1993

'Your daughter . . . big tits'
                    GAZZA to Lazio president SERGIO CRAGNOTTI[42]

In 2003 a video was issued for the Italian football market. Its title? *Bidoni*. Now a *bidone*, in Italian, is a rubbish bin, but *bidoni* in football parlance are rubbish players. We are not talking about normal rubbish here – this is rarefied badness – crap on a huge and costly scale. *Bidoni* are cult figures, so bad they have become popular (in retrospect). In recent times, *bidoni* have usually also been expensive foreigners. Roma brought two famous *bidoni* in the late 1980s. One, the Brazilian Andrade, lasted just nine games. His memory, however, lives on. He became known as *Er Moviola* – Mr Slow-motion-replay – for his pace. The other Roma *bidone* that year was Renato, a long-haired winger who dedicated himself with far more energy to Roma's pulsating night-life than he did to providing crosses on the field. Both have become cult figures.[43] Only one player, however, is portrayed on the front of the *bidoni* video. There, in pride of place, hands on hips, stands Paul 'Gazza' Gascoigne, in his Lazio shirt.

Gascoigne's time in Italy coincided perfectly with the boom of the Italian game in the UK and its popular Channel 4 coverage. Gazza's presence, in fact, was a key part of that success. Gascoigne was at the height of his fame then, in the wake of the 1990 World Cup, and he became a regular on the show, chatting away with wag presenter James Richardson and introducing his own special slots. Unfortunately for Gazza, and for Lazio, he spent more time on Channel 4 than he did on the football pitch. In three highly-paid years for Rome's less famous team, Gazza played just 41 league games, scoring six goals. He was substituted 30 times. Lazio won nothing in that time and it is difficult to describe his time in Rome as other than an unmitigated disaster.

Gazza had been 'signed' by Lazio from Spurs for eight million pounds in 1991 just three weeks before his infamous FA Cup final appearance against Nottingham Forest. After his mad, masochistic performance in that match, which led to his cruciate ligament injury, Lazio were forced to wait for his knee to heal. The deal did not go through for more than a year, and Spurs lost nearly half of the transfer fee in that time, during which Gazza managed to have two fights in two night-clubs and even broke the kneecap of the knee in question. His fee still represented a club and British record, however. When he finally turned up in Rome, in September 1992, Gazza appeared to have been on a crash diet that had drained him of all his energy. He had not played for fifteen months. Over-thin, in his first game he managed a few mazy dribbles on the halfway line before being substituted at half-time. Italy, of course, had been the scene of Gazza's greatest triumph, and of his ultra-famous blubbing, during the 1990 World Cup.

Ups and a lot of downs followed. Lazio's followers, however, loved Gazza. Over 1,000 fans greeted him on his arrival in Rome, causing absolute chaos, and his training sessions were mobbed. Some 30,000 turned out for his first friendly appearance in Rome, in the pouring rain. He was the idol of the *curva nord*, just as Paolo Di Canio had been in the late 1980s. His equalizing goal near the end of a Rome derby helped (what was amazing was that he was still on the pitch in the eighty-eighth minute) but it was Gazza *himself* they adored – his drinking, his obvious love of football, his craziness, his genius, his belly. The club claimed that the mere presence of Gascoigne usually meant an increased gate of 5,000–10,000 fans. Often, at home games, a Lazio fan would 'dress up' as Gazza by wearing a swim suit or Tottenham shirt and sit in a large dinghy. The dinghy was then lifted by other fans above their heads. Gazza is remembered with great affection at the club; his name appears in the 'unforgettable' section of the Lazio website alongside such heroes as Giuseppe Signori, Giorgio Chinaglia and Paolo Di Canio. True to form, Roma fans made Gazza their hate figure, although much of their abuse was tinged with a sense of fun. In one derby, they displayed an enormous fake wheelchair (Gazza was always injured) and during another they threw Mars Bars onto the pitch. Gazza, typically, picked one up, slowly unwrapped it, and gobbled it down. That was pure Gazza. In fact, in his own words, he spent a lot of time 'being Gazza instead of Paul Gascoigne' whilst he was in Italy.[44]

Soon after the derby in 1992, Gazza scored a quite brilliant solo goal, dribbling past three or four players and chipping the goalkeeper – admittedly against lowly Pescara. A series of minor injuries followed, and Gazza was dropped for the home game against Juventus. When asked about the decision by a female journalist he did something that he thought was funny, but the Italians didn't; he burped into her microphone.[45] Headlines followed: *La Stampa* dedicated an entire page to the incident. *Burpgate* had exploded. A right-wing deputy, Giulio Maceratini, called for an official inquiry: 'what disciplinary measures', the deputy asked, 'will be taken by the football federation towards the player and how will the category of journalists be defended?'. The burp *was* embarrassing, above all for Gazza, but it did not warrant more coverage than that usually devoted to a small war in the Third World.

Club president Sergio Cragnotti told him off, fined him and declared in a *Sun* interview that he would 'not buy any more English players'. Gazza, however, did not learn his lesson. A few weeks later he attempted a variation on the wind theme, 'noisily' farting this time in the general direction of a man whom Ian Hamilton described as a 'distinguished *Il Messaggero* journalist'.

On the pitch, usually against lesser teams, when given space, Gazza could still shine. When he performed his famous double shuffle in the (unloved) Italian Cup, the press went crazy. One journalist wrote that 'this unconstrained lunatic Gascoigne has exhumed an ancient and

Gazza celebrates his equalizer in the Rome derby, 29 November 1992.

musical movement which has the rare beauty of a valuable relic'. The 1992–3 season, his first, which yielded a modest 22 games and four goals, turned out to be Gazza's best for Lazio, who qualified for the UEFA Cup. Rumours that he was about to be sold dominated the following season, when he played seventeen times and scored only twice. A new edition of Ian Hamilton's marvellously entertaining essay-account of Gascoigne's career – *Gazza Italia* (the previous title had been *Gazza Agonistes*) – appeared in 'week nineteen of the Italian season '93–'94'. It ended on an upbeat note. Gazza had just played six games in a row and seemed to be playing well.

Disaster, however, was just around the corner. On 7 April, at 17.10 p.m., after flying into a needless tackle in training, Gazza crashed to the ground. He had come up against a young and unknown defender who would go on to greatness – Alessandro Nesta. Gazza, as usual, came off worse. His leg was broken, twice – the same leg that had gone in the FA Cup final, and in the night-club fight. It was a year before he played for Lazio again and by that time the management had finally lost patience. His career in Italy was over. Whilst he was injured, *La Repubblica* canvassed opinion from assorted players and critics concerning his return. They were not kind. For Paolo Rossi, 'he came to Italy on holiday'. His only legacy would be 'bottles of beer and bruises'.

Off the pitch, there had been problems from the very beginning. Following in the footsteps of Joe Baker and others, Gazza indulged in the traditional activities of the English player in Italy – missing training sessions and beating up annoying photographers. He became so frustrated with his bad press that he simply refused to give interviews – for four months – an eternity in Italy with its huge sports press. It was during this 'press silence' that Gazza emitted his famous burp. He also – according to his 'autobiography' – purchased nine Harley-Davidson motorbikes.[46]

Lazio were on the up at the time, on their way to becoming one of the biggest clubs in Europe, albeit for a brief period. Gazza was the first big-money buy of a big-money era at Lazio. The man behind the boom was Sergio Cragnotti, packaging and foodstuffs multi-millionaire and ambitious president. During his topsy-turvy years at Lazio, the club would win a league championship, the Italian Cup and a Cup-Winners cup. They would later come close to bankruptcy as Cragnotti's own company crashed, leading to the arrest of most of his family. Given his outlay, at first Cragnotti wanted Gazza to play. Manager Dino Zoff was less convinced. After his first game, Zoff complained that he had 'had to get him onto the pitch ... lots of people were waiting to see him'. This kind of pressure was put on Zoff throughout Gazza's time at the club.

It is now much easier to understand the behaviour of Gascoigne in Rome. Quite simply, he was an alcoholic masquerading as a professional athlete. This fact alone explains the ups and downs in his performances, and in his weight (five kilos overweight – 84 kilos in total – at the start of the 1993 season; a mere 72 kilos on his return in 1995 – his assistant Jane Nottage wrote at the time that he suffered from bulimia). His frequent mood changes were also expressed in a series of absurd changes to his look. Let's start with the hair. In August 1993 Gazza paid a hairdresser £275 to have his hair extended by 45 centimetres. The whole thing took six hours to complete. Gazza was not pleased with the result: 'I wanted to look like Mick Hucknall and now I seem like my mum in the 1940s'. For Hamilton, 'the effect was like Benny Hill in drag'.

After his broken leg, Gazza came back with a completely shaven head. When he arrived in Glasgow he had dipped into the peroxide. It is pop-psychology, but inside, the man was in deep pain, and nobody was there to help him. Only one journalist – Antonio Dipollina – understood the frequent cries for help, and wrote of the 'sixteen empty rooms' in Gazza's oft-robbed villa. And then there were the moments of hysteria, often in training (where nothing escapes the eagle eyes of Italy's reporters). In March 1994 Gazza walked out of a training session and was then seen to 'shout and cry' in the car park. Gazza was big news in Italy and even the quality, serious, non-sports press were interested in his every move. His burp made the front page of *The Sun* back in the UK. Gazza's body could not stand the strain it was under. He picked up numerous minor injuries during his time in Rome, driving the Lazio staff to distraction.

The press were merciless in their examination of the ups and downs of Gascoigne's relationship with Sheryl, and of his friendship with Jimmy Gardner – 'Five bellies', or *cinquepance* in the Italian translation – who got a job in a bar in Rome. They rejoiced in winding him up, and then reacted like spoilt children when he wouldn't speak to them. Like Maradona, he cracked, but unlike Maradona he didn't do enough on the field to merit forgiveness. Given what we now know about Gazza's life, it is something of a miracle that he ever took the field at all. When Gazza finally left, for Rangers, in 1995, few shed any tears. Italian journalist Gianni Mura was lapidary. 'Perhaps Paul Gascoigne has finally gone back home. He has been one of the worst buys since the war. We anxiously await the usual epilogue where he will criticize everyone and everything.' For many, Gazza deserved to be on the front of that *bidoni* video.

Apart from the Lazio fans, it was clear that many Italians had problems with the English in general, and especially with Gascoigne. Ian Hamilton argues that the roots of the antipathy lie in the 1960s, when a series of British players failed in Italy – taking refuge in drink, indiscipline and criticism of their adopted country. Some of this is certainly true. I would, however, also refer to two other moments. One was Heysel. Gazza's infantile boorishness fitted perfectly with the stereotype of the drunken and dangerous hooligan. He was not just mad, but potentially bad. A second moment was fascism. Mussolini actively promoted anti-English propaganda, calling the British 'the people of the five dinners'. Gazza looked as if he was part of a 'people of five dinners' – and his best friend had five bellies. This propaganda left its mark, as did the Allied bombing campaign that struck defence-less Italian cities in 1943–1944. Gazza was not funny for the Italians. He reminded them of tragedies – old and new.

## Other *Bidoni*. The 1980s and 1990s boom

The *bidoni* were not only from England, far from it. Slow relaxations of the rules in the 1980s and 1990s led to a veritable influx in *bidoni*, many of whom ended up in the reserves, or in the lower divisions. Some good players simply failed in Italy, for tactical or personal reasons – such as Dennis Bergkamp.[47] Others were probably overrated else-where, such as Darko Pancev, a celebrated *bidone* for Inter in the early 1990s who scored very few goals (three in nineteen games spread over three years) and sat out his huge contract in the stands. A few *bidoni* were simply terrible errors, recommended on the basis of video-tapes or greedy agents and brokers. Hugo Maradona was signed purely on the basis that his brother was called Diego, for example – and played just fifteen games for Ascoli. Occasionally, foreign players just could not be bothered: such as Socrates with Fiorentina. Other *bidoni* were not given enough time – they usually arrived with ridiculously high expectations. Edgar Davids was discarded by Milan after just one season and became a star at Juventus; Clarence Seedorf was sold on by Sampdoria and Inter before settling at Milan. Brazilian Juary failed miserably at Inter – who specialized in foreign *bidoni* – before scoring a winning goal in a European Cup final for Porto. Many became cult figures, ending up in fanzines, books and websites.

## Postscript. Pretending to be foreigners, pretending to be Italians. Passport and other scandals

The complicated restrictions on foreign players in Italy have led, over the years, to a series of fake-passport scandals. Players – or their hangers-on – have conjured up Italian grandparents, relatives who turned out not to exist at all. There were many such cases in the 1940s and 1950s, including the Brazilian winger Julinho – whose 'father' was said to be a Catholic priest. In the 1990s, a massive passport scandal exploded – which ended up in the courts and led to a number of bans. Big players were involved: Recoba – Inter's Uruguayan winger, Dida – Milan's Brazilian goalkeeper and above all Juan Sebastian Veron – Lazio's Argentinian midfielder. Veron's 'Italian' grandparents were fakes, and the case regarding the scandal (the player himself had nothing to do with what happened) is still dragging its way through the Italian courts. Those accused included Lazio's president Sergio Cragnotti, certain employees of a Buenos Aires 'agency' and a clerk from the small town of Orsomarso near Cosenza in the south of Italy, the 'invented' birthplace for the non-grandmother. The Veron case was made more controversial by the fact that the Argentinian had played, and won, a championship with Lazio using his fake passport.

However, the most bizarre case of all involved a Brazilian winger who played for Chievo Verona. In August 2002 the player whom everyone knew as Eriberto finally came clean. He was not 'Eriberto' at all, but Luciano Figuera de Oliviera. And he was not 23 years old, but 26. Eriberto/Luciano had got hold of a false passport in order to increase his chances of playing for the national team. After being blackmailed, and threatened, for years, he decided to come clean, after using fake documents since 1998. He received a ten-month ban, and returned to Chievo after an unhappy spell with Inter.

With the lifting of most restrictions on foreign players in the early twenty-first century, Italians became something of a rarity in Serie A.

The stock of young Italian players who worked their way through the elaborate youth system found it difficult to break into Serie A or even Serie B. For the first time, younger and even older Italians began to move abroad in significant numbers. Italian football was cosmopolitan and multi-racial, with players from all nations competing for places on the field and in the hearts of the fans. The all-Italian Juventus team of the 1970s, who won the UEFA Cup without a foreigner in the team, were a distant memory. *Calcio* was a globalized multinational business, with tentacles and interests that stretched far beyond the borders of the nation state, and there was no turning back.

# CHAPTER 15

# *Italia – La Nazionale.* The National Team

## Italia and *L'Italia*

When a number of intellectuals were asked, in the 1990s, what it was that held Italians together, a fair number cited the national football team. When Italy play in international tournaments, Italian flags – normally so rare – suddenly spring up on windowsills and on rooftops. In Naples in 2002 I witnessed an enormous Italian flag – which had been paid for by a door-to-door collection – being hung across a small urban street. Within days, Italy were out, and the flag came down. In a young and regionally divided nation, football has formed a powerful glue around which national identity has been able to form. *La Nazionale* – the national team – has always inspired classic nationalist sentiments, flag-waving, celebration and discussion. Italians are united when Italia is playing, at least in their support for the team itself.

The party that followed the 1982 World Cup victory is remembered as a joyous moment of collective celebration. That match still holds the record for an Italian TV transmission, with 32 million viewers, while seventeen million Italians watched the celebrated 1970 semi-final, a figure that almost doubled to 28 million for the final. This support has rarely been seen as a political issue, and has seldom divided Italians into left and right factions. It is quite normal for extreme left and extreme right-wing Italians to be united in their backing of *la nazionale*.

Not all Italians agree. At times, the national team has been booed, and anti-national feeling increased in the 1980s and 1990s with the rise of regionalism in the north. Italy were greeted with hostility when they played in Verona in the 1990s, and again in Florence in the same decade. Leaders of the regionalist Northern Leagues openly declared their hostility to the national team, saying that they would back any team against them. The reaction to this has sometimes been a festival of nationalism, as with the World Cup qualifier in Milan in November 1993 (when the Lega was at the height of its influence) replete with thousands of flags. 'For one night', wrote the centre-left *La Repubblica*, '*la nazionale* reunited Italy'.[1] With the right-wing domination of Italian stadiums in the 1990s, the singing of the national anthem by fans before or during league matches – sometimes complete with fascist salutes – became commonplace. Nationalism had made inroads into groups of the most fanatical spectators.

Unlike England Italy has never had travelling national team supporters. Italy play all over the country, as a matter of policy, and fans watch them when they come to town. At international tournaments, there have never been organized national fan groups (and consequently no hooligan problem). There were no national *ultrà*. In the early 1990s, however, a small organized group of right-wing fans began to follow *la nazionale* both abroad and within Italy, complete with extremist slogans and stiff-arm salutes. Their presence sometimes led to tension with other Italian fans, and clashes were seen in 1991 at Parma and in 2005 (during a match against Scotland) in Milan.[2]

The national sentiments of Italy's players have often been called into question. A long and frequently hilarious debate dragged on throughout the 1990s concerning the singing of the national anthem before games. Why were the players not belting out the anthem? One explanation was simple. They didn't know the words. In fact, many Italians don't – as the lyrics are so difficult.[3] Soon, the players began to get their act together, learning the whole thing from start to finish. Whether this made them more 'nationalist' is open to doubt. Once again, however, the question of national identity in Italy – as it had been so often throughout Italian history – was played out around symbols and superstructures. The core of Italian national sporting identity only really awoke – and then only very briefly – during World Cups: once every four years.

*      *      *

Italy's national team started slowly but by the late 1920s they had become world-beaters. In the 1930s – with the exception of England– Italy could lay a strong claim to being the strongest team in the world. This was a remarkable turnaround from a squad that had been soundly beaten by a weakened Reading FC side, from the Southern League, in 1913.

## The glorious 1930s and Vittorio Pozzo

Italian football has never been as successful as it was in the 1930s. From 1928 to 1938, Italy won two World Cups and the Olympic gold medal at the infamous Berlin games of 1936. In 1934 Italy organized the tournament at home, and milked the victory for all it was worth.[4] Very few national teams in world history – and certainly no managers – have come close to this kind of winning run, and it all came under the auspices of the world's first fascist regime. It would be naïve, however, to make a direct link between fascist ideology and practice and the winning of a lot of football matches. Fascism *was* very interested in sport, and did create the infrastructures that helped the game to grow – stadiums, above all – but Italian football was on the up before fascism, and its success outlived that of Il Duce. The propaganda power of football was not lost on the fascists, but then again the regime tried to make *everything* into propaganda – from harvests to childbirth.[5] The game was also modernized through the mass media, and nationalistic versions of sporting events were filtered through radio and the censored sporting press. In the 1930s 'localized supporting became a national passion'.[6]

A great effort was made for the 1934 World Cup. Ever since that tournament, stories have circulated about the 'help' given to Italy by referees. Gianni Brera later wrote that in the quarter-final against Spain 'the referee Baert behaved as if he was well aware where the game was taking place'.[7] Further controversy followed in the replay of the Spanish game where Meazza's winning goal might have been disallowed. Nonetheless, none of this was particularly strange, or 'fascist'. Home nations have always had help from referees. International football could work both ways, as it exposed fascism to censure abroad. This risk exploded in the 1938 World Cup, and in particular in the opening game in

Vittorio Pozzo with the World Cup and his winning team after the victory
in the final against Hungary, Paris, 19 June 1938.

Marseille, when anti-fascists staged a kind of demonstration before the
game during the Italian national anthem.

The glorious 1930s were superintended with some authority by an
extraordinary personality, Vittorio Pozzo.[8] Short, tubby, with black
glasses and a shock of bizarre white hair, Pozzo presided over *la nazionale* as a kind of dictator after the chaos of the initial period, with over
thirty different managers in the first fifteen or so years. After taking
charge of the 1912 Olympic campaign, Pozzo gained full control of the
national team in 1929. He was to remain in charge until 1948, when a
humiliating home defeat against England led to his resignation. Italy
played 88 times in that period, and their record read as follows: 60
wins, sixteen draws and a mere eleven defeats, with 227 goals scored
and 114 against.

Born in Turin, Pozzo fought in World War One (as an officer
with the highly patriotic mountain division). He was something of an
Anglophile, and had picked up information about modern techniques
during training sessions at Arsenal and in the north of England. Italy's
greatest manager adopted a semi-militaristic approach to the game and

he claimed that he 'never lost sight of my players, not even for a minute'. In Marseille in 1938, he ordered his team to hold their fascist salutes until the anti-fascists in the crowd had stopped whistling.[9] Many people associated Pozzo with fascism, and it was his supposed links to the regime that led to his isolation in the 1950s and 1960s and to the new stadium in Turin not being named after him in 1990. Yet, in that same decade, documents emerged which revealed that Pozzo had helped the anti-fascist resistance during the war. In the mountains around Biella he had taken food to partisans and aided the escape of Allied prisoners of war. This support was officially recognized by the partisan governing bodies. His son defined him as a Churchillian, a liberal-monarchist, but certainly not a fascist. Pozzo was an austere man. He was never paid during his nineteen years in charge of the national team and, after the war, he refused to buy a TV set. He also became a fine football journalist, writing regularly for the city's major newspaper, *La Stampa*, right up to his death in 1968, largely forgotten by the official football world.

Italy's two World Cup victories in the 1930s, and their Olympic gold medal in Berlin, have now entered into legend. In truth, however, very little is known about the games themselves. The victories were filtered down to the masses through a triumphant and censored press, where dissenting voices had no space, and via the highly patriotic radio transmissions and the voice of Niccolò Carosio. On the pitch, it is clear that without the 'help' of the *oriundi*, Italy would probably not have won any trophies at all, and the embarrassing Guaita and Orsi incident in 1935 cast something of a shadow over the 1934 victory. After all, Guaita scored in the semi-final and set up the winning goals in the final, and Orsi scored in the final itself. The fact that such key players had fled Italy to avoid fighting in an imperialist war was a major embarrassment for the regime, and their reaction was to gloss over the question.

The triumphant 1930s created a very strong identification between Italians and their national football team, based around a series of myths, heroes and stories that were retold time and again in the years to come. Nonetheless, the clear identification between aspects of the regime and footballing success also led to an embarrassed silence on behalf of many about those victories, that team and Pozzo himself.

Italy's relationship with the football of the 1930s, as in so many other areas, was a difficult one, bordering on schizophrenia.

## Italy and international tournaments. The record and the endless polemic

'Our champions are rubbish' MAURO DELLA PORTA RAFFO[10]

Italy's World Cup performances since 1945 have been extremely disappointing given the quality of the players available, with just one victory and two second-place finishes. Italian clubs dominated club football throughout the 1960s and then again in the 1990s, but the national team was a poor imitation of the hugely successful club sides of those years. Teams that could boast Sivori, Rivera, Riva, Baggio, Baresi, Maldini and Vialli should have been able to win more than one World Cup, and we must look for reasons as to why they did not. Italians have tended to concentrate *their* explanations in one area: team selection.

Every single Italian World Cup campaign has, since the 1950s at least, been accompanied by a series of 'polemics' – public debate and discussion – around certain repetitive themes. One key motive for discussion has been the presence of 'skill/flair' players in the team. It has been assumed that a winning team can only afford one flair player in midfield. Hence, the long-running debates over the *staffetta* – or relay – which reached a peak with 'Mazzola or Rivera?' in 1970. Later, the relay was transferred to front players – Vialli or Schillaci? (1990); Baggio or Signori? (1994); Baggio or Del Piero? (1998); Totti or Del Piero? (2002). The *staffetta* has always been a central part of World Cup folklore, and managers *have* often made the wrong choices. Relay-polemics have often been linked to rumours concerning divisions within the squad. Italian national teams also have a tradition of making terrible starts in World Cups. If they recover, they usually do well. If not, they go out in the early rounds.

## Love–Hate. Games with England

Italy's rapport with England – and English football – was a true love–hate relationship.[11] Despite winning two World Cups in the 1930s (England did not even *enter* the World Cup until 1950) Italy was unable to shake off its inferiority complex until the 1970s, when they started to beat us regularly.[12] The nirvana of victory against England obsessed managers and players for decades, and even led to defeats being presented as victories, as with the Lions of Highbury game in 1934. England were the best team in the world, the ultimate obstacle to footballing domination. Moreover, the British nation was seen as an enemy by Italian fascism from the mid-1930s onwards, and the regime pumped out negative propaganda depicting the English as imperialists and gluttons.

Defeats by England led to long post-mortems, elicited extensive interest in the press and amongst the public, and created a series of stories that were handed down from generation to generation. On the field, there is no doubt that England were the better team until the late 1960s, and this superiority led Italians to support almost any team against England. Journalist Enrico Deaglio recalls being surprised during the 1966 World Cup final at the massive support for West Germany in Italy.[13] Much of this anti-English feeling was filtered through the biased commentary of Niccolò Carosio – an almost fanatical Germanophile – who 'hated the English'.[14] Carosio commentated on every England–Italy match until the 1970s and one of the great disappointments of his career was that he was never able to report on an Italian victory.

Italy and England played each other for the first time in May 1933, in front of 50,000 spectators at the Fascist National Party stadium in Rome. The game finished 1–1, with Arsenal's Cliff Bastin equalizing after Italy had taken an early lead. On 14 November 1934 the world champions – Italy – played England in what was seen by everyone as a kind of playoff. The winner of the game would be declared – unofficially – as the best team on the planet. England, after all, had not even bothered to enter the competition, so sure were they of their superiority. The venue for the game was a muddy Highbury, and

England's manager obliged the local crowd by picking a record seven Arsenal players, as well as a young Stanley Matthews. The build-up to the game was fiery. Top Italian journalist Bruno Roghi called Highbury a 'theatre of international war' and an English paper published a racist photo of the Italian team bearing stereotyped moustaches. Italians 'watched' the match through the flowery rhetoric of Niccolò Carosio as crowds huddled around radios all over Italy,[15] waiting on his every word, whilst 61,000 fans packed into Highbury in the pouring rain.

The match itself lived up to its billing. After twelve minutes, England were 3–0 up, and had missed a penalty. It looked like a rout. To make matters worse, Italy's midfield 'director', Luisito Monti, was pushed out onto the wing with a broken foot after a tackle by Arsenal's Ted Drake. Violence marked the whole first half, and the final injury-list reads like a war-bulletin; as well as Monti, England's Eddie Hapgood suffered a broken nose, Barber a broken arm, Bowden injured his ankle and Barker his hand whilst Drake played on with a cut leg. No wonder that the game became known in both countries as the 'Battle of Highbury'. Italy, as the injuries show, refused to lie down and take defeat. True to their status as World Cup holders, they fought back. Giuseppe Meazza, their star forward, scored twice in four minutes in the second half and only the crossbar prevented a sensational hat-trick. In his old age, Meazza would often repeat that the failure of a team-mate to pass to him towards the end was the greatest regret of his life. England won, 3–2, but honours were, almost, even.

Back in Italy, defeat was translated into victory, both through Carosio's biased commentary – which one writer later called 'delirious rhetoric' – as well as via the press. Roghi's report claimed that Italy had 'played like a platoon of gladiators' and that the defeat was 'worth twice as much as victory'. The Italian team were nicknamed the 'Lions of Highbury' (a term which stuck to such an extent that it was applied to Inter after they beat Arsenal in the Champions League in 2003) – and the myth went unchallenged. Despite the gloss put on the match at home, the fact remained that England had beaten the World Cup winners. 'In short, Highbury was a lesson in football for Italy.'[16]

After Highbury, the two countries did not meet again for four and a half years, drawing 2–2 in Milan after Italy had been just thirteen minutes away from victory. That match was notorious for Silvio Piola's handballed goal, an incident censored from the press reports at the time. A further nine-year gap followed, during which the two countries had been at war for three years, and then allies for another two, whilst British troops occupied the peninsula as part of the Allied army. The 1948 game, played at the Comunale Stadium in Turin, was not Pozzo's last in charge of Italy, but it signalled the end of his dictatorial nineteen years at the helm. England – with Stanley Matthews, Billy Wright and Tom Finney – destroyed Italy 4–0. Stan Mortensen opened the scoring with a shot from near the by-line after just four minutes. Goals of that type have since been known as 'Mortensen-like' in Italy. Once again, however, Carosio's commentary was not objective. Brera later wrote that 'Carosio . . . led the Italians to believe that the guilty and corrupt party was the Spanish referee'.[17] More draws and English wins followed. That elusive Italy victory just would not come, and was becoming an obsession.

Jimmy Greaves and Gerry Hitchens inspired England to a 3–2 win in Rome in 1961, and both players were snapped up by Italian clubs. A twelve-year gap followed until the next game, played in June 1973 in Turin. By that time, Italy had won the European Championship and come second in the World Cup. At long last, Italy beat England, 2–0. Nearly forty years after their first encounter, the taboo had been broken, and it was no fluke. Wembley was *espugnato* (conquered) in November of the same year thanks to a Fabio Capello goal after a run and shot from Giorgio Chinaglia. England had attacked for most of the game and it was to be Alf Ramsey's penultimate match in charge of the national side. British journalists had indulged in some stereotyping before the match, with jokes about the '20,000 Italian waiters' who were to descend on Wembley. Since then, things have been very even. Italy have won the games which have mattered, knocking England out of the World Cup qualifiers in 1976 and winning in the European Championships in 1980. The fixture has lost much of its charm in recent years and in 2002 Sven Goran Eriksson made eleven substitutions as Italy won 2–1 with two late goals.

## Superga Psychosis? The disastrous 1950s

Italy's record in the World Cups of the 1950s was poor. This is usually put down to the after-effects of the Superga tragedy, which took away, in one night, ten of the eleven players who had turned out for Italy in 1947. In reality, although Superga was important, Italy was going through a deep technical crisis, from which it would only emerge in the early 1960s. In place of the Pozzo model, Italy adopted a strategy of management 'teams' – known as technical commissions – which could include up to six people. For years, the training of the team was separated from selection. This management by committee – a reaction to the almost-dictatorial power of Pozzo – was disastrous on the field. In the late 1950s the team went back to one or two managers, and then to one after 1967.

The 1950 fiasco can certainly be put down – albeit indirectly – to Superga. Torino's president Ferruccio Novo – who had only missed the Superga plane by chance – was in charge of the team and insisted that the squad travel to Brazil by boat. After two weeks on the oceans – where training was difficult – the team arrived in São Paolo and promptly lost to Sweden. Their victory against Paraguay was pointless as India, the other team in the group, didn't turn up. Italy were out – and the players were allowed to take a plane home. In 1954, Italy performed fairly well in Switzerland, but lost in a play off with the home team. Blame was laid at the door of the manager – Hungarian Lajos Czeizler – and a Brazilian referee. In 1958, the *azzurri* failed to qualify, for the first and only time, after defeats against Northern Ireland and Portugal. This footballing disaster was attributed to the use of four *oriundi* 'of whom two were clearly strangers to our blood'.[18] The crisis was a deep one: 'Italy stopped being part of the football aristocracy, and took up a place amongst the semiperipheral countries'.[19] The defeat in Northern Ireland had been controversial, and was preceded by a contentious 'non-game', which became known as the Battle of Belfast.

## The Battle of Belfast

This crucial qualifying match was originally scheduled for 4 December 1957. However, the Hungarian referee and his linesmen were unable to reach the stadium on time because of fog. A Northern Irish referee took over, and the game was re-designated as a 'friendly', although some journalists later claimed that the Italian players were unaware of this until the match had finished. Eddie Firmani, who was a reserve in that game, later wrote that 'the Italians were subjected to the worst beating and humiliation I've ever seen on the football grounds of the world'.[20] The fact that the event had been declared a 'non-match' enraged the 5,000-strong crowd, who proceeded to attack the Italians after booing their national anthem. The match itself was extremely dirty, and objects were thrown at the *azzurri* as they left the pitch at half-time. Fights broke out and the Italian Chiappella refused to leave after being sent off. After the game, a number of players were set upon before the police arrived. One of the victims of the violence – Rino Ferrario of Juventus, who was carried off unconscious – later earned the title of 'the Lion of Belfast' in homage to the 1934 Highbury Lions. While the Italian press wrote about 'an atmosphere of prejudice', the Protestant–Catholic question was never explicitly mentioned, although a nationalist MP apologized on behalf of his constituency which included a 'considerable number' of Italian emigrants. Rome's *Il Messaggero* called the Northern Irish fans 'barbarians from a primitive epoch' and *Il Popolo* claimed that Ferrario had narrowly escaped being lynched.

## The *Oriundi* and the National Team since 1945

After the successes of the 1930s, when many *oriundi* made it to the Italian national squad, a tentative pro-*oriundi* strategy was adopted in the late 1950s and early 1960s, following a new influx of foreign stars. Only the very best players were called up, and performed well in their few games for their adopted nation. However, the usual debates surrounded their selection and many journalists were hostile to them *a priori*. Huge controversy followed the use of *oriundi* in the 1962 World Cup in Chile. The weak performance of the national team in that tournament was blamed in part on the 'foreign' presence amongst the *azzurri*. Brera accused the *oriundi* of laziness.

For the *oriundi*, the choice to play for Italy was not a happy one. Striker José Altafini complained that it was 'the biggest mistake of his career'. Having won a World Cup with Brazil (in 1958) he opted for Italy in 1960.[21] However, FIFA then banned dual nationals, and Altafini was left in limbo as the *azzurri* stopped selecting *oriundi*. At the age of 24, his international career was over. For Brazil he was a mercenary, and the same accusation was made in Italy.[22] The origins of the turn against the *oriundi* lay in the debacle of the 1962 World Cup, in Chile.

## The 'Battle of Santiago'. Chile. 1962

'Good evening. The game you are about to see is the most stupid, appalling, disgusting and disgraceful exhibition of football, possibly in the history of the game'

DAVID COLEMAN, BBC TV, June, 1962

'The most scandalous game in the history of the World Cup' – *Dizionario del calcio italiano*

In the 1990s a poll was held to discover the top 100 fouls of all time. Only one game managed to get *two* fouls into the top fifteen; Chile–Italy, 2 June 1962: the 'Battle of Santiago', the most violent and controversial World Cup game of all time.

The usual story told by and to Italians concerning this game is the following. First, two journalists (Corrado Pizzinelli and Antonio Ghirelli), writing in the Florence daily *La Nazione* and the *Corriere della Sera*, Italy's most influential and authoritative daily paper, criticized Chilean living standards and organization and described the streets as packed with prostitutes. For Pizzinelli Chile was a country with 'malnutrition, illiteracy, alcoholism, poverty . . . these people are backward'. Ghirelli wrote that 'Chile is a small, proud and poor country: it has agreed to organize this World Cup in the same way as Mussolini agreed to send our airforce to bomb London (they didn't arrive). The capital city has 700 hotel beds. The phones don't work.

Taxis are as rare as faithful husbands. A cable to Europe costs an arm and a leg. A letter takes five days to turn up.' Gianni Brera wrote later that these articles were 'intolerable' and 'reminiscent of the way in which people used to talk about Italy'.[23] Ghirelli, in his marvellous history of Italian football, took some of the blame for what then happened.[24]

These pieces apparently irritated the Chileans no end, as did the selection of four *oriundi* for the Italian party – Altafini, Sivori, Maschio and Sormani. When Chile played Italy, the violent atmosphere plus the ineptitude and possible corruption of a British referee – Ken Aston – led to two Italians being sent off. Italy lost, and went out; Chile went through. Some of this was allegedly decided from on high. The referees were chosen 'by others' and 'the others were English' (Brera).[25] Aston had also, rather strangely, already refereed a game involving Chile (which they won) in the same World Cup. A further level to the conspiracy theory adds that information about the 'offensive' news-paper articles was spread by 'Germans' who 'controlled the press in Chile' and had an interest in knocking Italy out of the World Cup (they were in the same group).[26] Another urban myth claims that a Chilean painter in Florence sent on the *La Nazione* articles to his country's ambassador. As for the *Corriere* piece, it is said that Ghirelli was threatened with violence in a Rome restaurant.

In reality, things were somewhat different. The articles did appear in the Italian press, although it is unclear how much real impact they made on the World Cup or on this particular match. Aston was inept, and lost control of the game. However, given the violence and ridicu-lous play-acting of *both* teams, this loss of control was understandable, and if anyone turned a blind eye to events, it was the linesmen. More-over, Italy had been poor in the first match and selected the wrong team (with Rivera, Trapattoni and Maldini left out and two players making their national debuts) against Chile, and they certainly lost control of their tempers, albeit in the face of considerable provocation, in Santiago. It also appears that the Italian management opted for Aston ahead of a Spanish referee, who they feared would be biased towards the Chileans.

*        *        *

'I wasn't reffing a football match, I was acting as an umpire in
military manoeuvres'          KEN ASTON

As for the match itself, it reads more like the report of a bout than a
game of football. After four minutes, in an incident that went unre-
ported in the Italian press, Italy's Argentinian-born Humberto Dionisio
Maschio struck Chile's Lionel Sanchez, who fell to the ground. Ken
Aston, a tall, almost statuesque referee, didn't see the incident, as he
was surrounded by angry players at the time. Play continued. After six
minutes, and before most of the trouble had started, Giorgio Ferrini
reacted to a foul by kicking out. He was sent off – or, to be more
precise, led off the pitch by Aston and some policemen. In a mêlée
that followed, Sanchez punched Maschio, breaking the Italian player's
nose – in most versions Sanchez also shouted 'traitor [or rather
*traidor*]', referring to Maschio's South American origins. No action was
taken, while Ferrini attempted to come on again. The match had
already descended into chaos.

Later, after a tussle on the by-line, Sanchez punched Italian defender
Mario David right in front of the linesman. Aston, once again, was involved with some trouble elsewhere. The linesman spoke to Aston, who
took no action. Another fight followed, with the police on the pitch to
calm it down. After 47 minutes of a first half that lasted for 52, David
took his revenge. Flying through the air, he attempted to kick a ball
high above Sanchez's head: Brera later called the foul 'murderous'. It
certainly looked terrible on TV (and it later came second in the worst
100 fouls of all time) but Sanchez later said that David's boot had
missed him. Aston sent David off, again leading him to the side-lines:
it was his last game for Italy. Italy's management team contemplated
pulling the players off altogether at half-time. The *azzurri* held out –
rather heroically – for 76 minutes before falling to two late goals. Aston
could easily have sent off another couple of players on either side.
Italy's defeat meant that, more or less, they were out of the World Cup.

Most Italian journalists veered between hysteria and various conspiracy
theories. Aston was accused of a range of offences running from 'par-
tiality' to 'corruption'. He was 'gaunt and authoritarian', or simply 'an
idiot [and] the son of a good woman', a semi-polite way of calling him

Referee Ken Aston, with his back to the camera, sends off Mario David
(sitting on the ground) in the 47th minute of the first half. 'The Battle of
Santiago', Italy–Chile, World Cup, 2 June 1962.

a son of a bitch (Brera).[27] There was no truth to the allegations of
corruption, and Aston remained a respected referee elsewhere, but
Italian sports writers continued to repeat the story. The tabloids went
furthest at the time. The *Corriere dello Sport*'s headline was *Mondiale
Truffa* (World Cup Scandal) and the *Corriere Sportivo* led with this:
'Thanks to this referee [cue huge picture of Aston]: Robbery at Santiago. World Cup Scandal. Only through these methods could they
win.' *La Notte*, Milan's evening tabloid, claimed that the game had been
'one of the worst episodes in the history of sport'. Furious parliamentarians made official complaints in the House of Deputies. One Communist Deputy spoke of 'a referee who appeared to have been bribed'.
Another headline consisted of just one word: 'Shame'. In 2002 Italian
journalist Italo Cucci repeated the accusation of corruption against a
now-dead Aston. To complete their miserable day, stones were thrown
at the Italian team bus and crowds gathered outside the flying school
where the team were staying.

Other journalists, at least at the time, were more laid back. Italy had 'fallen into the Chilean trap'. Gianni Brera was highly critical of Ferrini's reaction which led to his sending-off and made similar accusations against David, asking whether he was 'clinically mad, or had been driven so by chemicals'? David threatened to sue as a result. Italy had 'proved once again that they were supercilious and incompetent'. 'We have reaped what we have sown', he concluded, but was critical of the 'disastrous' articles that supposedly had led to the violence. Later analyses have also been fairer, recognizing the violent nature of the match that would have been difficult for any referee to control. Gian Paolo Ormezzano wrote in the 1980s that Aston was, quite simply, 'not good enough for that match'.[28] Aston's reputation in Italy was ruined forever, but he went on to be a highly respected trainer of other officials and the inventor of the red and yellow cards.

The match was not shown live on Italian TV. Technology at the time dictated that the film was brought back physically to Italy by plane and an edited version was shown two days later, at 10 p.m. Sanchez's punches, with the linesman standing next to him, were given slow-motion replays and the Italian account originates from that televisual 'version' of the game.

Once the players had returned, there was a long post-mortem. Artemio Franchi – the nominal head of the World Cup party – spoke for over two hours to the football federation, and his intervention was followed by over five hours of discussion. Franchi blamed the hostile atmosphere that had been created towards Italy, a 'situation which prevented the players from freely expressing their full potential'. These excuses meant that nobody paid the price for the Chilean disaster apart from the *oriundi*. Players of the quality of Altafini, Maschio and Sivori had finished their brief experiences as Italian national players.

## 1966. Korea! Korea!

In Mario Tullio Giordano's six-hour political soap opera *La Meglio Gioventù* (*The Best of Youth*) three youngsters find themselves in a seaside town. It is 19 July 1966. All the people in a nearby bar are huddled around a small black and white TV as an important match is being played – at the World Cup in England – Italy–North Korea. Italy need just a draw to qualify for the next round, North Korea must win. Korea score – the TV shows the goal – and a man comes out of the bar in anguish – his head in his hands. The three *ragazzi*, meanwhile, are blissfully oblivious to the importance of the game. They laugh and even pretend to support Korea – *Korea, Korea*, they chant – a mantra that was to haunt the Italian players on their return to Italy after what was almost certainly the Greatest Shock in World Cup History.

In 2003, the story of *that* game was told for the first time from the other side – the Korean side, in a documentary film entitled *The Game of Their Lives*.[29] Two English film-makers were allowed unprecedented access to the players and a country that remains a mystery to most of us in the West. Many of the myths, legends and rumours surrounding that game and its aftermath were set straight for the first time. In fact, since 1966, very little has been heard of the unknown team that set the World Cup alight.[30] The film is extraordinary, not least for its fascinating insight into life inside North Korea. In 1966, the country was still recovering from the brutal civil war of the 1950s (in which US, British and Australian troops had been involved) which left four million dead and no peace treaty signed (a fact which remains true even today). No Western countries recognized North Korea (or the Democratic People's Republic of Korea – DPRK for short).

Qualification for the World Cup had actually been quite easy. A mere sixteen teams were to play in the tournament finals, and only *one* place was reserved for the whole of Africa, Asia and Oceania. In protest against this discriminatory policy almost every country from those continents pulled out of the competition entirely. Only two nations were left – North Korea and Australia. It was decided that a two-leg playoff would be staged. Since the two nations were still officially at war a neutral venue had to be found – and the authorities settled on Phnom Penh, in Cambodia. The Australian team – made up largely of seasoned English professionals – were destroyed by the fast, strong and well-organized North Korean team, who won 9–2 over two legs. The president of Cambodia had ordered, on grounds of fairness, that half the crowd would support Korea and half would support Australia. North Korea, amazingly, had qualified for the World Cup, in England.

Yet, the British were also 'still at war' with 'North' Korea, and frantic diplomatic negotiations took place to prepare for the arrival of a team from a country that, officially, did not exist. One option was to prevent entry altogether, but this was swiftly rejected. Another problem was the national anthems – how could a national anthem be played for a non-nation? A typical British compromise was reached – *no* national anthems at all would be played apart from before the final and the opening game. It was assumed that North Korea would not reach the final. However, on the issue of the flag, the authorities gave in – and North Korean flags flew in England with their red star. Finally, the British authorities ordered that the team would be referred to as North Korea, and never as the People's Democratic Republic of Korea.

Before leaving for England in July 1966, the team met Kim Il Sung – the dictator known as 'The Great Leader' – who asked them to win at least one game. North Korea's first game was in dour, grey, working-class Middlesbrough, against the mighty Russians. The average height of the North Koreans was only five feet five inches and they were outfought by the USSR squad – who won 3–0. The brutal tactics of the Russians seemed to turn the crowd around to the Korean side, and many became 'North Korean supporters' that night. The crowds were small, but noisy, and the World Cup had not yet become fully commercialized. You could turn up on the night, buy a ticket and walk in.

North Korea were close to elimination. They needed at least a point against Chile to survive. In the eighty-eighth minute, Pak Sung Jin scored with a stunning shot from the edge of the area to equalize. The crowd went wild, celebrating as if the Koreans had won the World Cup. In Middlesbrough, the North Korean players became stars – local boys asked for their autographs – many vowed to support them against the mighty Italian team.

Nineteenth of July 1966. Nobody gave the Koreans a chance. This was an Italian squad that would go on to win the European Championships in 1968 and reach the World Cup final in 1970.[31] In the game itself, the Italians missed a hatful of chances (three by winger Marino Perani in the first half alone) and then Giacomo Bulgarelli, the Italian captain, was forced to go off with an injury, after a terrible foul committed *by him* on a Korean player. There were no substitutes in those days. Then, the fateful forty-first minute came around. Pak Do Ik – who was not a dentist, as the Italians claimed for years, but a print-worker and professional footballer – blasted the ball past Albertosi. The photo of the goalkeeper's despairing dive is one of the most famous in football history. Middlesbrough went crazy again. The second half saw another series of chances and superb saves by the Korean goalkeeper Ri Chan Myong (who stood only five feet seven inches tall). Italy were out and North Korea were in the quarter-finals, against Portugal. The English commentator was ecstatic: 'good heavens, they've won, what is going on here, this is fantastic,' he cried. Many Italian players paid a heavy price for the disaster [*disfatta*] with Korea.[32] The only players to 'survive' Korea were Albertosi, Facchetti, Rivera and Mazzola. The mark of 'Korea' was a heavy one, which the players were to bear for the rest of their careers. *Korea! Korea!* was a much repeated chant at Italian grounds in the 1966–7 season. Manager Edmondo Fabbri was always known thereafter as 'a man called Korea'.

Pak Do Ik in Pyongyang during the shooting of the documentary
*The Game of their Lives* (2002).

The Koreans had nowhere to stay in Liverpool, so they took the Italians' hotel – which was now free. According to the players, they were scared by the religious symbols in their rooms, and could not sleep. The rumour that the team went out drinking and womanizing in Liverpool was denied by the players and the local pub owner claims that only water was ordered for the team. So to the quarter-final – this time in front of 51,000 people at Goodison Park – at least 3,000 English 'Korean' fans had travelled down from Middlesbrough – 150 miles –

many of them young boys. The first 22 minutes were quite stunning as Korea scored three times. The crowd began to shout 'easy, easy' and 'we want four'. But then the great Portuguese forward Eusebio came into the frame, scoring four in the next 28 minutes; Eusebio 4, North Korea 3. The game finished 5–3.

For the Italian team, meanwhile, the Korean nightmare has continued to return in successive World Cups. In 1986, Italy scraped past South Korea 3–2, and in 2002 (thanks in part to the infamous Ecuadorean referee Byron Moreno) Italy went out to the same nation at the last-sixteen stage. One of the commentators for the RAI that day was Giacomo Bulgarelli. A huge banner had been hung across one of the stands before the match – its message was simple, and effective. *Again 1966!* In North Korea, Pak Do Ik was watching on TV, cheering on the South. If the two Koreas were united, he says, they would win the World Cup.

## Tomatoes and drugs. Edmondo Fabbri and the Conspiracy Theory

For the Italians associated with the 1966 World Cup, the nightmare was far from over. First, the players had to endure rotten tomatoes and worse at Genoa airport on their return. From that moment on, the threat of 'tomatoes' hung over Italian World Cup squads. Journalists warned teams that they needed to win 'or else it will be time for tomatoes': *saranno pomodori*. The summer, meanwhile, was dominated by manager Edmondo Fabbri's extraordinary attempt to take refuge in conspiracy theories. For a time, his one-man campaign for retribution threatened to tear the football world apart. In the aftermath of defeat in England, Fabbri had taken the blame with some dignity – 'the responsibility is mine and mine alone', he said at a post-match press conference. However, once the team had returned to Italy, Fabbri began to prepare his defence. He visited a number of players, individually, on holiday all over Italy, and extracted statements from eleven of them. The similarity of the texts would later create suspicion that they had been written by Fabbri, and merely signed by the players. The accusations were made public by the magazine *Stadio* on 26 August, causing a nationwide scandal.

What did the players claim? Many wrote that they had been given medicine, which had made them play worse, not better: they had been *negatively doped*.[33] Bulgarelli said that he had received injections and taken pills during the tournament and Lodetti agreed, adding that he had 'experienced a sense of fear and insecurity which had not allowed me to perform as I would have liked to'. Facchetti also mentioned injections and a 'sense of insecurity and fear'. He accused Artemio Franchi (a major institutional figure in Italian football) of having ordered them 'not to overrate' North Korea in the dressing room before the game. Pascutti used slightly different terms – he had been 'tired and worn-down' and 'had not been able to react'. Janich also mentioned injections and 'a sense of loss and fear' while Mazzola talked of red, yellow and white pills, and of intensive saunas. Rosato, Fogli and Rivera also got involved, and repeated the accusations about Franchi's dressing-room speech. Many blamed the doctor for not ordering Bulgarelli to rest his injury. Whatever the truth of these allegations, they looked suspiciously like a combination of excuses and buck-passing. The similarity of the language pointed strongly towards Fabbri as the instigator. A power-struggle was now being played out publicly.

On the one side stood the players – and they were key players – and Fabbri. On the other, Franchi and the team doctor, Fini. The accusations were incredibly serious – elements within the national staff had conspired to produce a disaster. The 'conspiracy' was apparently aimed at getting rid of football federation president Giuseppe Pasquale. For journalist Ghirelli, Fabbri 'had clearly lost his head'.

When these letters hit the press (leaked by Fabbri himself) the storm they created terrified some of the players involved. A couple of them retracted their 'statements'. Facchetti said, 'I didn't want to make that statement', Mazzola stepped back from what he had signed and Albertosi reported that nothing strange had happened. Bulgarelli on the other hand confirmed everything and added that he was sick of the whole affair and did not want to play for Italy again (he did, but only twice more). Fogli and Pascutti also confirmed what they had said (and didn't play for Italy again). Rivera prevaricated. He agreed with Fabbri but said that the letters should have been kept secret. The national team doctor called the accusations 'stupid and absurd'. Fabbri maintained that he wanted the truth while Franchi counter-attacked, producing a report on the World Cup which blamed the manager, and accused him of cowardice (as in the claim that all the players were told to 'go home on their own' after Korea). Doctor Fini sued for libel.

After the defeat against North Korea, there was strong feeling against Edmondo Fabbri. 'Death to Fabbri', graffito, July 1966.

Fabbri, called up before a federation disciplinary board, moaned about 'bad luck' and argued that the players' declarations had been spontaneous. He was sacked, and banned for eleven months (ruining a possible contract with Milan). Later, Fabbri returned to football and achieved some respectable results with Torino and Bologna in the mid-to-late 1960s. Years later, he continued to repeat his accusations: 'if there is no justice on this earth, then Our Lord will sort things out ... I have had to go through my whole life with this burden of Korea, and who was to blame? Some people who wanted Italy to lose and, unfortunately, they helped us lose.' In 1967, Franchi became president of the football federation, a post he would hold for some time, with exceptional results.

## The Greatest Match of all Time? Italy–Germany 4–3. World Cup semi-final, 1970

'Riva, Riva, Riiiiivaaaa!'   NANDO MARTELLINI: commentary,
during extra time, on Riva's goal which made the score 3–2

Few football matches remain part of a nation's identity; have inspired books, films and innumerable newspaper articles; are told and re-told, in detail, by almost any fan you meet. Few games have a plaque dedicated to them because of the drama of the game itself.[34] One such match – *The Game* – was the 1970 World Cup semi-final between Italy and Germany in the Aztec stadium in Mexico City. In Italy, the kick-off was at 12.15 a.m., and millions watched the whole thing until way past two in the morning.

Yet for the first 90 minutes, the game had been rather dull. Italy took the lead in the eighth minute with a fierce shot from Roberto Boninsegna and then held on with old-fashioned *catenaccio* tactics. Fouls were frequent and the Italian players resorted to play-acting to waste time. The only real drama was provided by Franz Beckenbauer's decision to play on with a dislocated shoulder (held in a makeshift sling) and the referee's refusal to give two clear penalties to West Germany.[35]

Commentator Nando Martellini started counting the minutes: 'seventeen left'. After 85 minutes Martellini asked his audience 'to grit their teeth with me'. With only seconds to go, the Italian defence (led by the magnificent Burgnich and rescued by the acrobatic saves of Albertosi) was still holding out. Then, a cross from the left fell into the box and a tall, blond German thrust his left boot towards the ball. His shot from two yards out beat Albertosi easily. The German's name was Schnellinger – and he played for AC Milan. In five years with Milan, he had never scored (and his record in nine seasons with the club, 1965–1974, was to be 222 games, no goals). The Italians were furious. Some players went up to Schnellinger to insult him and one apparently told him that 'he would never return to Italy'. Extra-time beckoned and now another nightmare hung over Italy – the drawing of lots if the game ended in a draw, there being no penalty shoot-outs in 1970. Twice, Italian teams had had to draw, once in the 1960

Olympics (they lost) and once in the 1968 European Championships (they won).

The heat and the altitude made tactics pointless.[36] Unexpectedly, the two teams attacked each other with gusto. A different game emerged, full of drama, controversy, and spectacular end-to-end football. First the Germans went ahead after a dreadful error by the Italian substitute Poletti.[37] Of all people, it was Tarcisio Burgnich – 'The Rock', a great defender who had scored a mere five goals in eleven seasons – who equalized as Beckenbauer's injury began to take its toll. Gigi Riva then took centre stage. After a quiet tournament – so much had been expected of Riva, who had just inspired Cagliari to an extraordinary championship in Italy – the powerful centre-forward took the ball near to the edge of the German area, dribbled further to the left and crashed a shot low past Meier. The commentator simply cried *Riva, Riva, Riiiivvvaaaa!*.

But the drama was not over yet. Back the Germans came again with the master poacher – Gerd Müller. For some unknown reason, Gianni Rivera had come back to mark the left-hand post of the Italian goal. Müller's well-placed header seemed to be heading towards him; he simply watched it pass between his body and the post. He later claimed that he had never, ever, been in that position before in a game, and that he had no idea how to defend the ball.[38] Albertosi went crazy, threatening to strangle Rivera. All the debates over the 'Golden Boy's' supposed lack of backbone seemed to be confirmed by this incident. Popular mythology has it that Rivera was so terrified of Albertosi that he ran forward to the kick-off. Rivera himself claims that he wanted to dribble past the whole German team and score to make up for his error.

This plan, if it ever existed, was soon abandoned as Rivera pushed a pass out to the magnificent Boninsegna on the left wing. 'Bonimba' crashed past the whole German defence and to the by-line before sending over a low cross. Rivera arrived on the edge of the box, and was cool enough to side-foot the ball into the space left by Meier's desperate dive. The Germans had not touched the ball from the kick-off and less than 60 seconds had passed since Müller's goal. Rivera jumped up – arms aloft – and was then picked up by Riva. Millions of Italians poured onto the streets – forgetting the deep social and political

Gianni Rivera (second from left) scores the winning goal, Italy–West
Germany, World Cup semi-final, 17 June 1970.

tensions of the time – and partied into the early hours. It is said that
600,000 people partied and let off fireworks in Naples alone.

Nando Dalla Chiesa is a left-wing politician known for his struggle
against the mafia. His father – a *carabiniere* general – was killed by
*Cosa Nostra* in Palermo in 1982. He is also a brilliant football writer
and his analysis of the '4–3' is the richest so far produced in Italy.
Dalla Chiesa calls the 4–3 'the game of the century' and puts the match
firmly in political, social and cultural context. The celebrations after
the victory, with the presence of left and right, and the national flag,
were an atypical moment of unity during a period marked by political
violence and conspiracies. The 4–3 game was a rare example of collective identity, and it was radical.

Football was the most democratic game of all: 'the whole of Italy
had played football and her champions that night were able to represent
the entire country'.[39] Moreover, that Italian team – with its four Cagliari
players – was more 'national' than ever before. Above all, the 30
minutes of extra-time saw a new, revolutionary kind of game. In place
of traditional defensive tactics, which had so nearly worked, Italy went
for broke, on the attack, scoring three goals in 'an uncontrollable . . .

explosion of sentiments, passions, instincts . . . there were no more tactics, no more order, no more cynicism . . . the past was over . . . a defender who had never scored became a goalscorer . . . a stylish midfielder known for never helping out at the back found himself on his own goal line.' In extra-time the team behaved as if it was 'a collective movement', taking on a 'new identity'. 'They played with the spirit of 1968', leaving the past behind them, if only for half an hour.

Yet, the final was still to come, and Rivera's reward for his winning goal caused enormous controversy at home: he was dropped for the final against Brazil. The unity of the semi-final soon began to disintegrate, as Italy reverted to type. The World Cup final of 1970 contains some of the iconic images which have made modern football what it is today; Pelé's leap for the opener, his celebrations, his casual pass for Carlos Alberto's pile-driving fourth goal. *Italy are written out of this narrative.* Yet, the Italians have their own version of that final – with a very different set of images: 'Burgnich returned to the ground, subject to the inexorable laws of gravity. Pelé no. He obeyed his own laws of nature and stayed there, suspended in the air' (Nando Dalla Chiesa).[40] Later, Italy's version concentrates on the tiredness of the players, on the fact that Valcareggi brought back Mazzola, relegating Rivera to the bench, and on Boninsegna's lucky equalizer (born from Brazilian over-confidence). In fact, after an hour, the score was still at 1–1, and the referee had denied Brazil a certain goal by blowing for half-time almost as the ball entered the net. Hoping that this was to be his day, Valcareggi abandoned the relay. He left Mazzola on, hoping that his (slightly) superior defensive qualities could help Italy snatch a draw, or even a win.

One narrative of these events thus claims that Italy held its own for an hour with the greatest team of all time. Yet, the superiority of the Brazilians was obvious, and they ran riot in the last half-hour, scoring three beautiful goals and strolling all over the pitch, even resorting to an insulting series of keep-ball passes (known as *melina* in Italy). Valcareggi then made the most inexplicable and controversial decision of his career – Rivera was brought on, but only six minutes were left on the clock and Italy were 3–1 down. These were the most famous six minutes in Italian football history. Why did Valcareggi do it? Was he a masochist, or a sadist, or both? He later claimed to have misread the time. Others argue that Rivera had to be seen to be part of the team's defeat. In any case, many people in Italy saw the six minutes as an insult. Valcareggi was mocking Rivera (and Italy), and in a World Cup final.

The Italian squad were tired but happy to have performed beyond all expectations (and better than any Italian World Cup squad since 1938). They had knocked out the hosts, and beaten Germany in The Greatest Game of All Time. They expected, if not a hero's welcome, at least praise and support from fans and the general public at home.

This expectation was not fulfilled. On arrival at Fiumicino airport in Rome, 10,000 fans were there to greet the team – but most were not in a mood of celebration. Many had prepared hostile banners. Some cheered, but others were incandescent with rage and most of the comment centred on Rivera. There were no tomatoes, at least, but the threat of violence hung in the air and, in the end, the police had to step in to keep order and Italy's managerial team was forced to take refuge in an airport hangar. Throughout that summer, and ever since, debate has raged on concerning Rivera, *la staffetta* and the final. For many Italian fans, Gianni Rivera would be remembered for a game he *did not take part in* (he hardly touched the ball).[41] The joy of the semi-final had disappeared. Valcareggi was bitter, and was never allowed to forget the 'six minutes'. He apologized sarcastically for having only come second. If 1966's aftermath had been dominated by recriminations and conspiracy theories, 1970's post-mortem set the trend for individual controversies taking precedent over analysis of what had actually happened in the tournament.

## The World Cup of the 'Chinagliate'. 1974. West Germany

Italy went into the 1974 World Cup with a team still managed by Valcareggi and a plethora of ageing stars – Riva, Rivera, Facchetti, Burgnich and Mazzola. None of these great servants would be in the 1978 team. The team was deeply divided between the new and the old guard and between 'northern' and 'southern' players. Italy's tournament lasted just three games – with one win (against Haiti), one draw (Argentina) and one defeat (Poland) – and ended with Italian emigrants booing them off the field in Stuttgart. One man was made the scapegoat for this disaster – Giorgio Chinaglia. In 1974, the Italian-born and Welsh-raised striker was at the height of his powers. His aggressive centre-forward play had taken Lazio to a rare title victory and he had also played a key part in Italy's first victory at Wembley in 1973. Valcareggi saw Chinaglia as a vital part of his squad, but he had not reasoned with the explosion of Giorgio's 'difficult' character-traits.

Beginning the tournament as one of the favourites, Italy played poorly in the first game, against unknown Haiti. As if to erase the memories of Mexico, Valcareggi selected both Rivera and Mazzola. Many experts had underlined the need to avoid a 'second Korea', and the team was edgy. The worst fears of everyone in Italy seemed to be confirmed when Haiti took the lead in the second half, on the break. It had been something like 1,147 minutes and two years since Zoff last let in a goal when playing for Italy.[42] Brera later wrote that 'anyone who did not think back to Korea at that point was a well-bred man who was full of good-faith'. Brera also described Chinaglia's performance in that game as 'pitiful'.

Italy came back with two goals, the first by Rivera. Then came the moment everyone remembers. Chinaglia (who should have had a hat-trick) was substituted by another striker with twenty minutes to go and he lost it, on TV, in front of 350 million viewers. As he ran towards the dressing room there was a clear Italian 'fuck-off' plus hand gesture, towards his manager.[43] He later said that the applause from the bench for him was 'sarcastic'. Once in the dressing room versions differ as to exactly what happened. Chinaglia claims he smashed some empty bottles, others say they were full. Some say that a hair-dryer was also destroyed, others mention a smashed-up shower. One of Chinaglia's biographers, Mario Risoli, is adamant that 'eight empty mineral water bottles' were thrown 'against the wall'.[44] Lazio's manager Maestrelli had to be called in to calm him down. Again, versions differ here. Some – the story seems to have been started by Brera – claim that Maestrelli had taken a private jet, others argue that Chinaglia's father-figure was already in Germany.

Once again, Italy's campaign had been overwhelmed by non-footballing issues. Meanwhile, Anastasi, the substitute in question,

Giorgio Chinaglia gestures to the bench after being substituted, Italy–Haiti,
World Cup, 15 June 1974.

scored a third for Italy, making Chinaglia's hysterics look even worse.
'Long John' was dropped for the next match – although the official
line was that he was injured – but surprisingly not sent home. He came
back for the third game against Poland, who had destroyed Haiti 7–0.
They were no pushover, but Italy only needed a draw. Valcareggi left
out Rivera and Riva, both of whom never played for Italy again. This
time, nobody really complained as both great players were well past
their best. By half-time, it was all over, as Poland were 2–0 up and
Chinaglia was substituted, this time in the dressing room, to avoid
further trouble. Fabio Capello pulled one back near the end, but Italy
were out, if only on goal difference.

An elaborate mythology has evolved since the Poland game. The
Poles were already through, and only needed a draw to top the group.
After the cup was over, Polish staff first claimed that there had been
attempts to bribe their players at half-time, and then withdrew the
allegations. Later versions argue that the initial attempt to 'fix' the
game – as a draw – was made by the Poles. Nobody is really sure what
happened. What is clear is that any plans of that sort did not work
and Poland played to win.

*      *      *

A cycle – as the Italians call a winning period – was over. Valcareggi and the old guard moved on and a new squad had to be built. Most critics blamed 'out-of-date' tactics for the disaster – 'total football' was very much in fashion in 1974. Some took refuge in the age-old argument – Rivera or Mazzola, *but not both*. Once again, however, Rivera had been dropped from a key match, as in 1970. At last the endless debate over *this* particular *staffetta* was over. It was to turn up again, with other players, in subsequent tournaments.

As the Italian team bus moved away from the Stuttgart stadium, it was attacked by Italian emigrants, who had turned up in vast numbers. They were chanting 'Korea! Korea!' Albertosi, the substitute goalkeeper, came to blows with a fan. Giorgio Chinaglia was booed at every away game in Italy the following season, and mercilessly baited by the Florentine crowd in a friendly against Norway. In the same year, a sports journalist produced a book about the World Cup entitled *Il Mondiale delle Chinagliate*. Later, Piedmontese writer and sports journalist Giovanni Arpino published a marvellous novel based around his experiences in Germany in 1974 – *Azzurro tenebra* – *Blue Darkness*[45] – with its easily recognizable characters of *Il Golden* (Rivera), *Il Baffo* (Mazzola), *Grangiuáun* (Brera), *Giorgione* (Chinaglia), *Il Bomber* (Riva) and *Lo Zio* (Valcareggi).

## Argentina 1978. Third Place with the Generals

In the wake of the chaos of 1974, Enzo Bearzot, a solid, dependable ex-Torino player, was placed in charge of the team. Within eight years, he was to bring the World Cup back to Italy for the first time since 1938. Bearzot was lucky to have a great Juventus team (winners of the *scudetto* in 1977 and 1978) to draw from – with its spine of Zoff, Cabrini, Benetti, Cucureddu, Gentile, Causio, Scirea, Tardelli, Bettega and Rossi (who would soon move to Juve). Nine of the 22 called up for the 1978 squad were Juventus players and eight of those nine started most games in Argentina. Bearzot was also fortunate that foreigners were banned from Serie A in the 1970s, allowing space for the development of young Italian players. A new generation of defenders had come through in the early 1970s and many were modern players, very different from some of the brutal *stoppers* and markers of the past. Scirea in particular was a graceful and skilful sweeper. This young team had knocked out England on the way to qualification thanks to a fantastic goal from Bettega in Rome in 1976.

Italy's participation in the 1978 World Cup was controversial at home. In March 1976, a coup in Argentina had installed a military dictatorship that then carried out mass arrests, torture and murder of opposition militants, trade unionists and others. At least 7,000 people died under this regime and 20,000 'disappeared'. An unknown number were thrown into the sea, alive, from planes. Thousands of others were forced into exile. Italian emigrants were and are a huge part of Argentinian life and this repression was deeply felt in Italy. Many on the left argued that Italy should boycott the tournament and a number of books were published documenting the activities of the generals.[46] In 1976 there had been protests after Italy's Davis Cup tennis team had beaten Chile (still under the dictatorship of Pinochet) in the final after the USSR had withdrawn.

Moreover, for once, events elsewhere took precedence over *calcio*. In March 1978 the president of the governing Christian Democratic Party, Aldo Moro, was kidnapped in broad daylight in the centre of Rome by left-wing terrorist group the Red Brigades, who also murdered his five bodyguards. Moro was kept prisoner in the city for 55 days as the nation held its breath. After the state ostensibly refused to deal with the terrorists, Moro was executed and his body left in a car boot yards from his party's head office. Many aspects of this tragedy remain shrouded in mystery even today, and there are strong suspicions of an international conspiracy that used the Red Brigades in order to prevent Moro from forming an alliance with the Italian Communist Party.

Italy ended up in a qualification group with Argentina, France and Hungary and after 36 seconds of the tournament, they were 1–0 down to France. The Italians pulled back to win, 2–1, and went on to top the group, beating Argentina 1–0 with a superb strike from Bettega. This win led to the first set of debates back in Italy. Bearzot put out his best team in a game that counted for little or nothing, and journalists argued that vital energy had been 'wasted' against Argentina.

In the next group stage, Italy drew with Germany and beat Austria.

They needed to beat Holland to reach the final. After they had gone ahead in the first half through an own goal, Bearzot took off the excellent Causio, apparently to save him for the next match, and Italy lost to two fantastic long shots. Some journalists claimed that Zoff's international career was over (he was already in his mid-thirties) but they would be proved wrong in 1982. This time, there was general satisfaction at home and no tomatoes appeared, especially as Italy had beaten the eventual winners of the cup. Argentina's generals celebrated as their team won. They were to remain in power for another three years. It is unclear as to whether this murderous regime was prolonged by the World Cup victory, but it must have helped.

After finishing a dignified fourth in the European Championships held in Italy in 1980, which were notable more for the vicious crowd violence involving English fans than for the football, Italy moved on to the 1982 World Cup. In the meantime, *calcio* had been rocked by the *Totonero* betting scandal that saw Paolo Rossi, their best striker, banned for two years. Rossi only returned to first-team football towards the end of the 1981–2 season, playing in Juventus's last three games and scoring once. Bearzot, who had been accused of defensive tactics in the European Championships, as Italy scored only twice in four games, went into the tournament with more or less the same squad as in 1978. The new players, however, were to be crucial to the team's success. Up front, Bettega was injured and Bearzot could rely on the extravagant wing play of Bruno Conti. In midfield, the dirty work was done by Oriali, Inter's tireless ball-winner. Bearzot also called up a promising eighteen-year-old defender from Inter, Beppe Bergomi. The press had its usual field day with the players Bearzot *didn't* call up – Roma striker Pruzzo and Inter's creative midfielder Beccalossi.

In the group stages, Italy were dreadful. No censure was spared in the press as the *azzurri* struggled to put even a decent pass together against Poland (0–0), Peru (1–1) and Cameroon (1–1). Rossi was so out of form as to appear an ex-player. He later admitted that he had never played so badly. Nobody gave the team a hope of proceeding any further. Later, accusations were to emerge of match-fixing involving some Cameroon players, the sponsor Adidas and the Italian team. Suffice to say that Cameroon needed to win to go through, and appeared not to attack with great zeal despite their imminent elimination. Italy sneaked through not on goal difference, but only because they had scored more goals (2 as opposed to 1) than their closest challenger. Relations with the Italian press were so bad that the team was 'in' what is known as *silenzio-stampa* – refusing to talk to any journalists. Only Dino Zoff – laconic at the best of times, and a man of few words – was authorized to speak to the press.

Everything was transformed with the next group game against holders Argentina. Gentile cancelled out a young Maradona while Tardelli and Cabrini scored for Italy in a 2–1 victory. Yet, Italy still had to beat a multi-talented Brazil team to go through, and Brazil only needed a draw. *The Second Greatest Game of all Time* was about to take shape.

## Italy–Brazil. 3–2. 5.7.1982. Barcelona

Nobody who saw it can forget it. The incidents are burned on our memories, in the same way as Rivera's goal and Albertosi's anger remained in another generation's minds from 1970. Brazil were arrogant, and careless, and their goalkeeper was, well, dodgy. Italy didn't make a single mistake. After five minutes Rossi appeared like a ghost at the far post to nod in a fantastic swinging cross from Cabrini. Wicked rumours of a 'close relationship' between the two had been angrily denied; 1–0. Seven minutes later, Socrates – lazy rebel, revolutionary, intellectual – scored at the near post; 1–1. After 27 minutes, as the Brazilians languidly passed the ball across the defence, Rossi burst through and fired a shot close to the ageing keeper, Valdir Peres. He dived too late; 2–1. With 22 minutes left, Falção beat two men on the edge of the area before crashing home a shot; 2–2. Brazil were through, if the score remained the same. But, six minutes later, from a corner, the ball was knocked down and Rossi – always the great opportunist – swivelled and stroked it into the back of the net; 3–2. There was still time for two more dramatic moments – an Italian 'goal' by Antognoni wrongly disallowed for offside and a header from Oscar which Zoff caught, before dropping on the line, throwing up clouds of chalk. It was the eighty-ninth minute. The Israeli referee, Klein, refused to give a goal despite Brazilian protests. Italy were in the semi-final and their hero was the worst player from the first three games: Paolo Rossi.

Marco Tardelli's scream, after scoring the second goal for Italy in the World Cup final, 11 July 1982, Madrid. Italy–West Germany. The other player is Claudio Gentile.

Transformed, the team swept past Poland (who were without Boniek, their best player) with two more Rossi goals and were to face West Germany in their first World Cup final since 1970. Madrid: 11 July 1982, in Real's Bernabeu stadium – 30,000 Italian fans arrived for the game and the popular President of Italy, Sandro Pertini, was in the stands. A small, bespectacled Genoese socialist, Pertini had been one of the leaders of the anti-fascist Resistance. He had personally given the order from Milan in April 1945 that Benito Mussolini should be executed if caught. On his death in 1990, Pertini's coffin was draped with the Italian flag and the flag of the Resistance. In 1982, his personal press officer was Antonio Ghirelli, one of the great experts on Italian football and author of the first history of the game.

It was a dramatic final, in front of 90,000 fans in Spain and the biggest Italian TV audience with something like 95 per cent watching at home. Bergomi, just eighteen, had been chosen to shore up the defence while Antognoni was hurt – another misfortune in his extremely unlucky career. Just seven minutes in, Graziani was injured and

On their return from Madrid, President Sandro Pertini (with the glasses), manager Enzo Bearzot (with the pipe), goalkeeper and captain Dino Zoff and winger Franco Causio (hidden) play cards on the plane. The World Cup is in the foreground on the table.

Altobelli came on. After 25 minutes a doubtful penalty was awarded to Italy but Cabrini pushed it past the post. Thirty-two million Italians held their heads in their hands. On 57 minutes, Paolo Rossi, once again, gave Italy the lead with a diving header. He had scored six goals in 212 minutes of football. Nine minutes later came the defining moment of the final. After a long passing move, which saw two Italian defenders set up camp in the German area, Tardelli smashed in the ball from the edge of the box. At that point he set off, running, to nowhere in particular, his mouth open. This moment became known as 'Tardelli's scream'. It seemed to go on forever and has been repeated endlessly on television. Perhaps Tardelli would still be running now, if he hadn't been stopped. In the stands, Pertini stood up and raised his hands, overjoyed. Nine minutes from the end yet another cross came in from Bruno Conti, the outstanding player of the tournament. Altobelli, cool as ever, controlled the ball, waited for the goalie to move and slipped it past him: 3–0. Little Pertini was up again: '*Ormai non ci riprendono più*,' he said; 'That's it. Nobody can catch us now'. Breitner's late goal was a mere consolation. The referee ended the game by lifting the ball above his head and Zoff raised the cup at the age of 40. Commentator

Nando Martellini greeted the victory with a celebrated triple cry: *'Campioni del mondo, campioni del mondo, campioni del mondo'*. Pertini travelled back with the team to Italy on the plane. There is a celebrated photo of Bearzot, Zoff, Pertini and Causio sitting round an aeroplane table, playing cards (*scopa*, the most popular Italian card game). In the corner, on the table, there is the World Cup. Bearzot is smoking his famous pipe. Back in Italy, the party was only just beginning. *La Gazzetta dello Sport* sold nearly one and a half million copies the next day – a record – with its massive headline: *Campioni del mondo*.

## 1986. Decline of a Great Team

Bearzot later wrote that the 1982 victory had also been a kind of curse, as he had been forced to keep a team together which should have been broken up.[47] A disastrous European Championships qualifying campaign saw Italy lose to Romania and Sweden and draw with Cyprus. The hangover from 1982 meant that Italy failed to qualify at all. Italy went into the 1986 World Cup – as holders – with an ageing squad. Paolo Rossi was selected, but never played. The team started poorly – with the press savaging goalkeeper Giovanni Galli, dubbed 'Mr No-dive' – and got worse. Italy only won one game – against South Korea, and even then after they had been given a huge fright – and were comprehensively outclassed by Platini's France in the last-sixteen match. Bearzot resigned, but nobody back home was too angry, the 1982 honeymoon was still not over. A revolution would be needed to renew the national squad, especially since the next World Cup would be in Italy – *Italia '90*.

## 1990. Maradona's Revenge

In preparation for *Italia '90* a referendum was held to choose the name for the World Cup symbol, a small figure with a ball in Italian national colours. *'Ciao'* won, easily (and perhaps luckily) ahead of *'bimbo'* (child in Italian) and *'dribbly'* (someone who dribbles). Two completely new stadiums were built for the tournament: Bari's futuristic venue, designed by Renzo Piano (of Pompidou Centre fame), was beautiful but far too big (it has a 60,000 capacity) for such a minor club. Bari

was the home-town and political power-base of football administrator
Antonio Matarrese. In Turin costs spiralled out of control as Primo
Nebiolo, the all-powerful Italian athletics supremo, forced the architects
to include a running track in the project. The end result is a stadium
which nobody likes, where the crowd are too far away from the pitch
and which lies miles out of town. Both Turin clubs, and their fans,
hate the place. For some time, it appeared as if the whole thing would
be demolished. Genoa's stadium – almost entirely rebuilt for 1990 –
was perhaps the most successful compromise between a club venue
and an area conducive to international football. San Siro in Milan had
a whole new tier and roof put on, using enormous cranes, which
unfortunately did terrible things to the grass. The pitch has been laid
and re-laid umpteen times since at enormous cost.

The Italian state spent 3,500 billion lire in the cities which were to
host matches – and managed to lose money. A series of arrests in
1992–3 was linked to corruption in the reconstruction of various
stadiums and 24 workers died, and 678 were injured, during the work.
In Rome a new Tube line was constructed, just for the World Cup. The
line closed immediately after the competition, and remains closed
today. This flood of public money was into a corrupt system of institutionalized, politically-organized kickbacks which, after 1992, would
be exposed in one of the biggest judicial investigations of all time. The
name given to this system was to become *Tangentopoli* – Bribesville.[48]

Italy went into the tournament with a young, tight-knit and skilful
team, groomed by ex-under-21 manager Azeglio Vicini. The stars were
up front with Gianluca Vialli who had taken Sampdoria to their one
and only championship the year before, and in midfield, where 'the
Prince', Giancarlo Giannini – Roma's playmaker – ruled supreme –
alongside the skill of Donadoni and the muscle of De Napoli and
Ancelotti. The defence was Milanese – Baresi and Maldini (Milan) with
Ferri and Bergomi (Inter). In goal stood Walter Zenga – an eccentric
but brilliant keeper who would concede just one goal in the whole
tournament, and be crucified by the press for doing so. Thanks to an
excellent season with Juventus, a diminutive Sicilian striker, Salvatore
Schillaci, slipped into the squad. Almost everyone expected that his
main role would be to warm the bench.

Salvatore Schillaci was an extremely unlikely national hero. To explain his meteoric rise and fall from fame you need to be 'a witch-doctor and a sociologist'.[49] Twenty-six years old at the time of the tournament, he had been raised in the infamous mafia-ridden 1960s neighbourhood known as CEP (which stood roughly for Centre of Poor Expansion) in Palermo. A prolific striker (he once scored 75 goals in a junior team season, including eleven in one game) Schillaci passed most of his early career in serie D, C and B, with Messina, despite being a native of their hated rivals, Palermo. Throughout his career, Schillaci had 'always been an emigrant . . . a Palermitan at Messina, a Sicilian in the north, [and later] an Italian in Japan'.[50] A squat, rather ugly man, he was extremely quick and possessed a lethal right-foot shot. His big break came in 1989 when he was signed by Juventus after scoring 23 goals in a season for Messina in Serie B. Schillaci responded with fifteen goals in his first season as Juve won both the Italian Cup and the UEFA Cup. Still, a call-up to the national team seemed unlikely as Azeglio Vicini, the national coach, had been linked for years to two gifted players from Sampdoria, Vialli and Roberto Mancini, and his front two were confirmed as Vialli and Carnevale from Napoli. Schillaci began the first match, against Austria, on the bench.

Italy poured forward throughout the game, missing numerous chances. Vialli and Carnevale were particularly wasteful. With fifteen minutes left, and the score still, amazingly, 0–0, Vicini sent on Schillaci, for only his second appearance in the national team. As he was warming up, reserve goalkeeper and Juve player Stefano Tacconi told him to 'get ready, because you are soon going to go on and score . . . a header like John Charles'. Within four minutes, Vialli performed miracles on the by-line, crossed and there was Schillaci to head home. The stadium went wild, as did the whole of Italy, and Schillaci became a household name. Nonetheless, Vicini left him out for the next game, against the USA, and Italy scraped home with a Giannini goal, while Vialli missed a penalty. Schillaci came on again for Carnevale in the second half and on leaving the pitch the Napoli striker insulted Vicini with hand gesture and vocal accompaniment. It was a throwback to Chinaglia's similar hand signal in 1974. Bowing to popular pressure, Schillaci started the next game against Czechoslovakia. He responded with another goal, but was overshadowed by Roberto Baggio's brilliant second, a superb individual effort. The next round saw Italy come up against Uruguay. With 65 minutes gone, Schillaci received a pass thirty yards out. He swivelled and hit an instant, vicious swirling shot that swerved over the goalkeeper and into the net. The quarter-final against Ireland was also settled by Totò. By now, Schillaci was a permanent choice, Vialli was depressed and had fallen out with Vicini and Carnevale was side-lined, as punishment for his insubordination. Schillaci scored again in the semi-final, after a rebound from a Vialli shot, and his penalty against England in the third-place playoff secured his place as top scorer. Parties were held in Palermo in his honour after every game and he returned as a hero after the tournament. Schillaci's large, black eyes and his modest, almost naïve approach to the game made him the undisputed star of the competition.

After that unexpected triumph, Schillaci faded from view. He scored a mere eleven goals in two seasons with a weak Juventus side, and another eleven in a poor Inter squad in the two seasons that followed. The national team ignored him, after a few indifferent performances and injuries. From hero, Schillaci quickly became something of a vil-lain, and was the victim of racist taunts. He had been greeted with huge fake tyres when Juventus played Torino. The explanation for this bizarre insult (which had more than a touch of racism) was that his brother had been accused of stealing car tyres in Palermo. At Inter, he was booed by his own fans and insulted by graffiti around the ground (*Schillaci=terrone*, an offensive term used for southerners). Inter were going through something of a decline and Schillaci was marginalized and humiliated. He moved to the Japanese league in 1994, where he finished his career (scoring 60 goals in three seasons) before opening a football school in Sicily. His record with the national team was sixteen games, seven goals. In World Cup tournaments – or rather the one he played in – his record was seven games (two as sub), six goals. He latter dabbled in politics, being elected as a local councillor in Palermo in a centre-right coalition.

If the star – the hero – of *Italia '90* was undoubtedly Totò Schillaci, the villain of the piece was also crystal clear – Diego Armando

Maradona. Hated by many Italian football fans – especially in the north – he was adored only by Napoli supporters. Maradona had won two championships in three years with the Naples team – in 1987 and 1990 – and the latter *scudetto* had been marked by a bitter struggle with AC Milan. Naples was also the most southern of southern cities – a symbol of all that was seen as bad about the Mezzogiorno. Maradona, the symbol and leading light of the Naples team, quickly became the most unpopular player in northern Italy. Maradona *was* Napoli, he was anti-Milan (the club) and anti-Milano (the city), he was *the* south in a period when the regionalist Northern Leagues were at their peak.

As the camera panned across the Argentinian team in the opening match of the World Cup – in Milan, against Cameroon – the crowd remained relatively silent. When the frame stopped on Maradona, 80,000 people booed and whistled. They had found their hate figure. The crowd supported Cameroon throughout, as their racism was directed at a white Argentinian who played for a city in their own country, and not at a team of black men from Africa. Despite having two players sent off, Cameroon won, 1–0. Maradona would soon get his revenge, it would be in his beloved Napoli, and it would be sweet.

Before the World Cup the ever-outspoken Maradona had complained about the 'unfair' grouping of Argentina – who were the holders. He claimed that the tournament had been fixed in order for Italy to win. Maradona had his chance to prove himself wrong in Naples of all places, in 'his' San Paolo Stadium in the semi-final against the hosts, on 3 July. Italy had won all their matches without conceding a goal, whilst Argentina had scraped through to this stage thanks to a penalty shoot-out, the occasional genius of Maradona and good luck. Italy were firm favourites, but this was Naples. The build-up to the semi-final had been enlightening from the point of view of Italian nationalism. Whilst political leaders and sportsmen appealed to Naples fans to back their country (Italy) over their club (Maradona), Maradona himself made a crafty counter-appeal. 'For 364 days a year', he said, 'you are treated like dirt, and then they ask you to support them.' The Naples crowd responded with an ambiguous banner – 'Diego, we love you but at the end of the day we are Italians'. It is unclear quite how many Italians in the ground supported their national team that night. Some claim 'the majority' did, others are unsure. Most commentators argue that a significant minority of Italians backed Maradona, and therefore Argentina.

The game itself was dramatic. Vicini lost his nerve, and packed the team with defenders. Italy took the lead – through Schillaci again – and should have added more goals. Then Argentina suddenly began to play well, for the first time in the tournament. On 68 minutes, an innocuous-looking cross from the left tempted Zenga into an unwise attempt at a punch. Claudio Caniggia, his blond locks flowing, got there first, and backheaded the ball into the goal. The last time Zenga had seen the ball go past him for Italy had been in October 1989, 981 minutes and ten games earlier, against Brazil, before the World Cup had even begun. Italy poured forward, but couldn't score. The referee gave them a record nine minutes of extra-time to do so, but still they failed to breach the rugged Argentinian defence and the game went to penalties. Donadoni missed, and then Serena's shot almost wriggled under goalkeeper Sergio Goycochea, but stayed out. The key penalty was left to Maradona – the coolest head on the pitch. He strolled up and passed the ball into the net. The stadium went quiet: Italy were out. The recriminations went on for months, with specific heat being turned on the unlucky Zenga and Vialli – whose World Cup had been poor, with no goals, one missed penalty and reported 'depression'. Vicini survived the chop but soon lost his job after Italy failed to qualify for the 1992 European Championships.

*Italia '90* is fondly remembered in the UK for Pavarotti, Gazza's tears and Stuart Pearce's penalty miss, but it was probably the most boring World Cup of the post-war period (a title which would soon be taken by USA 1994). Argentina ruined the tournament, with their cynical tactics and brutal gamesmanship. The final was the worst in World Cup history, as the Germans dived to glory and Argentina reacted with hysteria. Italy's fans did not cover themselves in glory, booing the Argentinian national anthem before the final. As the camera stopped on an emotional Maradona, he mouthed an expletive easily interpreted by lip-readers across the world: *hijos de puta*; sons of bitches.

## 1994. 'God Exists!' Sacchi and Baggio

Many Italian commentators assumed that New York was packed with Italian-Americans, straining at the leash to support Italy in the USA World Cup. This cliché, based on ignorance, was spectacularly proved wrong when the *azzurri* took on Ireland in the sweltering heat on 18 June, for their opening match in the tournament. Only a few Italian-Americans were to be seen, and they were drowned out by magnificent Irish support. Italy lost and played appallingly, but, in terms of their World Cup chances, this was a good sign. Bad starts often lead to good tournaments, as 1994 was to prove, once again.

1994's Italian campaign was marked by the usual 'relay' debate – this time it was the choice between Baggio and Signori – and by a general dislike amongst Italian fans of the personality and tactics of Arrigo Sacchi. The manager's obsession with his 'module' over individual players verged on the ridiculous, and his tinkering was legendary. In 53 internationals he used 77 players, never fielding the same team twice. In 1994, he was to be saved by the quality of his defence and the genius of Roberto Baggio.

After one and a half games, Italy looked finished. They hadn't scored, had lost the opening game, and were down to ten men against Norway, having had goalkeeper Pagliuca sent off. Moreover, Sacchi had decided to take off Roberto Baggio, Italy's best and most famous player. On seeing his number come up, Baggio looked up, disgusted, and mouthed the words 'this man is mad!' He then proceeded to spit out an enormous quantity of water once he had arrived at the bench. Sacchi, however, had made a brave and correct decision. On his own up front, Signori ran and ran, while Paolo Maldini heroically hobbled on despite an injury and captain Franco Baresi hurt himself so badly that he needed an operation. Despite all this, Dino Baggio scored the all-important winner. Italy were still alive, just. They scraped through to the last sixteen as the worst of the qualifiers (as in 1982). Their opponents were to be Nigeria.

With five minutes left of the Nigeria game, patriotic commentator Bruno Pizzul made this comment: 'it looks like we are slipping out of the World Cup, without having left even a trace'. Few would have disagreed with him. The Africans were one up and Italy had done nothing. The heat was unbearable; Gianfranco Zola was sent on and then sent off after a mild foul by the preposterous Mexican referee. The eighty-ninth minute arrived and it was still 1–0. Suddenly, and with some considerable luck, defender Roberto Mussi broke on the right. He sent over a weak cross, which was met by Roberto Baggio's right foot. The shot was hardly a pile-driver, but it was accurate, passing between the legs of a Nigerian defender and rolling into the bottom left corner of the net. Against all the odds, Italy had equalized. Baggio ran towards the camera, screaming 'God exists, God exists'. From that moment on, 'the Divine Ponytail' was a changed player. In extra-time he chipped a delightful lobbed pass that earned a penalty, which he slotted away perfectly. There were no more relay debates, now. Italy beat Spain thanks to a last-minute Baggio breakaway and, in the semi-final, two brilliant Baggio goals took them through. Yet, at the moment of triumph, Italy's World Cup took a cruel twist of fate as Baggio was injured in the semi-final. Sacchi played him anyway in the final against Brazil, with a massive bandage around his right leg. Moreover, as if he was not taking enough risks, Sacchi threw Franco Baresi into the frame, only three weeks after a knee operation.

The final was both boring and fascinating. Italy, and especially Baresi and Maldini, defended superbly. Baggio hobbled around, but lasted the full 120 minutes. Neither team really looked like scoring and Uruguayan writer Eduardo Galeano wrote that 'if there had not been the penalties, it would have remained 0–0 for all eternity'. Penalties, Italy's *bête noire*, were inevitable. In the heat and sweat of Pasadena, Sacchi chose his penalty-takers. Baresi (who could hardly stand up); Albertini; Massaro; Evani; and finally Baggio, the player who had taken the most penalties in Italian football history.

An exhausted Baresi stepped up to take the first kick and smashed it miles over the bar, before bursting into tears: Brazil then had a penalty saved. In the sweltering heat of the Ligurian seaside town where I watched the match, the noise was deafening. But Massaro also missed, and Baggio – the fifth penalty taker – had to score to keep Italy in the World Cup. He looked as calm as ever, but scooped his shot over the bar, to the left. Brazilian goalkeeper Taffarel sank to his knees while Baggio just stood there, head in hands. The sequence is one of the most repeated images in televisual history. Later, both an Italian songwriter –

Roberto Baggio misses his penalty in the shoot-out, handing the World Cup to Brazil. World Cup Final, Pasadena, 17 July 1994.

Enzo Jannacci – and a sportswriter – Darwin Pastorin – were to write that the penalty had actually gone in.[51] 'Your shot was perfect', wrote Pastorin; 'in your mind, it was a goal', sang Jannacci. It was a tragic, poetic moment. The tournament's best player, the man who had single-handedly taken Italy to the final, was also the symbol of their defeat.

## Back to *catenaccio*? The Maldini reign. 1996–1998

After Sacchi's tinkering reached record levels in Euro '96 in England – leading to a defeat by the Czech Republic and a pointless draw with West Germany after Zola had missed a penalty – the Italians decided to return to the old school, to *catenaccio* and to a defensive maestro. Cesare Maldini, father of Paolo and mainstay of Milan in the 1960s, was appointed in 1996. 'Big Cesare' was an eccentric figure, who had taken the Italians to three consecutive European Under-21 titles through a combination of brutality, a siege mentality, technical skill, tactical awareness and luck. He was popular in Italy for his common touch and his farcically tinted hair. Comedian Teo Teocoli perfected a brilliant impersonation where Maldini was always calling for his son –

little Paolo ('Paolino') and appeared to be permanently drunk. Big Cesare complained about the impersonation, adding that he was on the wagon.

Maldini started brilliantly, beating England at Wembley thanks to a Zola goal, but their campaign stuttered after that and they were forced into a humiliating playoff with Russia after Glenn Hoddle's England topped the group. As the 1998 World Cup campaign began in France, the repetitive debates began – Baggio or Del Piero? (the relay) and 'attack or defence?' (tactics). Baggio, in excellent form, redeemed himself (for Pasadena) in the first game by scoring a penalty and making a goal for Vieri, as Italy scraped a draw with Chile. Victories over Austria, Cameroon and Norway saw the *azzurri* go through fairly comfortably. The crunch came on 3 July, against the host nation, France. Maldini opted for a wall-like defence, and Italy held the fort heroically, but Baggio was brought on far too late for Del Piero. In extra-time, an Albertini pass dropped over Baggio's shoulder. He volleyed, instinctively, and the ball shaved the far post. It would have been a golden goal, and France would have been out. As it was, the game went to penalties, and every Italian feared the worst. Henry and Trezeguet coolly slotted their kicks home, Italy missed through Luigi Di Biagio, who hit the bar, and then slumped back onto the turf. Italy were out, losing again on penalties, but the old-style tactics had very nearly paid off. Nobody gave France as hard a game in the whole tournament and the doubt remained that with a little bit more ambition, Maldini might have done a Bearzot. He certainly had the players to do so. Nonetheless, Big Cesare came in for heavy criticism at home, and was fired.

## Fifteen seconds from glory. Dino Zoff. 1998–2000

Italy turned to another man from the old school, and from the extreme north-east of Italy. A *Friuliano* like Bearzot and Maldini, Dino Zoff is a man of few words, who rarely smiles. Sacked by Juventus after winning a UEFA Cup and the Italian Cup in the same year in 1989–90, he had some success with Lazio in the 1990s (where he was forced to deal with the antics of Paul Gascoigne). With Italy, he was immediately accused of perpetuating *catenaccio* and of not exploiting the rich attacking potential of his team, with Totti, Vieri, Montella, Del Piero, and

Inzaghi all available. Zoff went into the 2000 European Championships amidst the usual hailstorm of criticism. He had not even taken Baggio this time – despite a massive press campaign in his favour – and Vieri was injured, as was goalkeeper Buffon. Mainly thanks to an inspired Totti, Italy made it through to the semi-finals, against hosts Holland, where they laid to rest the ghosts of the 1990s.

In a dramatic game, Holland managed to lose despite being awarded two penalties (both of which they missed) and having a one-man advantage for more than 90 minutes. Italy spent most of the game in their own half, and much of that on the edge of their own area. Once again, the game went to penalties. Here, Zoff pulled off a master stroke. He sent forward Di Biagio, who had missed the fatal spot kick in France in 1998. Twenty-five million Italians watching on TV shouted 'no'. Di Biagio smashed his penalty home (in Stuart Pearce fashion), whilst goalkeeper Toldo hypnotized the Dutch (they missed another two in the shoot-out, to add to the two in the game itself). Totti chipped his penalty into the middle of the goal – the first international outing for his trademark 'spoon' shot that he called *er cucchiaio*. Italy were in the final, against France.

True to their bizarre form, Italy surprised everyone by outplaying the World Cup-holders. Del Vecchio scored from a Pessotto cross after a Totti backheel, and Del Piero should have killed the game off, twice. With just fifteen seconds left of injury time, Cannavaro made his only mistake and the ball fell to Sylvain Wiltord, whose lucky scuffed shot bobbled over Toldo's left hand and into the net. In extra-time, and in shock, Italy fell to an inevitable golden goal after Pires danced down the left and crossed for Trezeguet to crash home.

The Italian team had exceeded all expectations, and returned in minor triumph, but Zoff's reign was soon to come to an end. Silvio Berlusconi – at that time leader of the opposition – 'let himself go' during a press conference (whose real subject has been lost in the mists of time). Berlusconi said that he 'had to get something off his chest'. He could not understand why Zoff had not man-marked Zidane and said that 'only an amateur' could have made such an error. Despite the fact that the whole sports press backed Zoff, and pointed out that Zidane had had a poor game, Dino was offended. He resigned and nobody made much effort to force him to change his mind. Zoff has been more or less ostracized from major football in Italy ever since, only returning briefly to manage an ailing Fiorentina side in 2005.

## Again 1966? Trapattoni and the Korean nightmare. 2000–2004

Within weeks, a new manager was appointed. Italy would be run by the most successful manager of modern times, and a man associated, once again, with defensive football. Giovanni Trapattoni – *Il Trap* – winner of a copious number of a titles with Juventus and Inter and of numerous trophies as a player with Milan, took over in 2000. The ever-popular Trap would lead Italy into the 2002 finals. The only problem was that *Il Trap* was clearly in decline. He had not had any major success at club level since the 1989 championship with Inter and a championship in Germany with Bayern Munich in the 1990s, and he still preached a type of football which appeared, to say the least, out of date.

After struggling through the qualifying stages, Italy, it seemed, had been drawn in an easy group. They destroyed Ecuador in the opening game – but the omens were not good: they had started too well. Trap's team proceeded to lose to Croatia and snatch a draw against Mexico – sneaking through to the last sixteen. However, the team, the manager and the press had an excuse for these poor performances – the referees. In their three games, *four* Italian goals had been wrongly disallowed for offside and one for a supposed foul on the goalkeeper. Trapattoni's behaviour became increasingly bizarre. He lashed out at anything he could find around him, screaming and shouting throughout each game.

The Italian players, managers and press went into the game against hosts South Korea convinced that a conspiracy was being organized against their team. The referee was a young and theatrical character from Ecuador, Byron Moreno. As the teams took the pitch, they noticed two huge banners: *Again 1966* and *Welcome to Azzuri's* [sic] *tomb*. The South Koreans were happy to remind Italy of their shock defeat at the hands of the North almost forty years earlier. The match itself was not a great advert for football. A legitimate penalty was awarded by Moreno to South Korea after just three minutes, but Buffon saved the kick. Vieri then scored with a header after sixteen minutes, and then Italy held on. They should then have scored a second to kill off the game, as Trapattoni became more and more frenzied on the bench, kicking over bottles, punching plastic windows and screeching at the fourth official. With time running out, South Korea equalized in the eighty-seventh minute. Extra-time, and the recurring nightmare of a golden goal or penalties, loomed over Italy again. There was still time for an exhausted Vieri to miss an open goal from a yard out. Then, Moreno sent off Totti for diving (and his decision was probably right).[52] The commentators did not agree. Summarizer Giacomo Bulgarelli said that 'Moreno could have stayed at home, we would not have missed him'. Yet another Italian goal was wrongly disallowed for offside. With three minutes of extra-time left, the only Korean player to ply his trade in Italy – Ahn – rose above Maldini to score. The Italian players proceeded to smash up the dressing room, but they were out.

Back home, the TV schedules were cleared for long and angry post-mortems. Perugia's president Luciano Gaucci said that Ahn would never play for his club again, and he kept his promise. Conspiracy theories, as ever, abounded. The editor of La Gazzetta dello Sport (Pietro Calabrese) wrote this in his editorial: 'we were knocked out in order to level out some old problems between us and the bosses of FIFA and UEFA . . . Italy has no weight . . . Shame on them . . . Shame on the World Cup'. Other journalists agreed: 'betrayal . . . this is not sport . . . they decided to eliminate us right from the start . . . they let us win against Ecuador . . . then a shameful series of thefts' (Italo Cucci). Other writers, however, laid the blame at the door of the manager and cautious tactics, symbolized by the substitution of Del Piero by Gattuso, a defensive midfielder, in the second half, a typical piece of Trapattonian circumspection. Xavier Jacobelli in Tuttosport spoke of 'inbred, maddening, bloody defensive tactics' while Gianni Mura argued that the team had played like 'a rich man who drives around a dangerous neighbourhood with a Rolex on his wrist, his arm hanging out of the window'. Moreno was 'a great big sheet which covers up errors, omissions, blame'. For Massimo Gramellini in La Stampa, 'a real team would have won even if the referee had been Korean . . . Moreno, with his face which looked like a depressed cow, has allowed Italy to hide behind an umbrella made by cry-babies'. Michele Serra wrote about 'a mad manager who swore, rolled his eyes, attacked people and objects ... the whole world witnessed his memorable fit of nerves'.

Trapattoni survived the chop, thanks to Moreno, while the suspicions of a fix were strengthened when Spain were the victims of some more terrible decisions against South Korea in the quarter-finals. Meanwhile, Italy had not finished with the Ecuadorean referee. A totally false story did the rounds in the press; that Moreno had purchased a new red Chevrolet after the tournament. Later, he was invited to appear on a state TV channel in a programme called *Stupido Hotel*, where he danced with ageing showgirls. Entire websites were dedicated to Moreno-abuse. The World Cup passed into folklore as another in a long line of 'thefts'.

## The Spit and the Scandinavian Fix. 2002–2004

The suspicion that Italy were simply not good enough was underlined when Trapattoni's team lost to Wales in their European Championship qualifying group, and only just recovered to qualify for Portugal. Once again, Baggio was left at home (despite another fine season) and Trap refused to take the brilliant young striker Alberto Gilardino, preferring to keep faith in a series of stars in evident decline – Del Piero and Vieri. In Portugal, the familiar tragicomedy was acted out. We had the relay debate (Cassano or Vieri?) and huge arguments with the media. Vieri gave an embarrassing press conference where he claimed to be 'more of a man' than the journalists present.

After a dreadful 0–0 draw in their first match, Francesco Totti was caught on video spitting at his Danish man-marker. The spit was shown on the world's television, umpteen times, and made the front page of the sports press.[53] It was even analysed using the *moviola*. Totti pleaded guilty, but claimed that he had been provoked and – through his top lawyer (a woman who had also defended seven-times prime minister and former mafia suspect Giulio Andreotti) he adopted a defence based on an original thesis. The spittle, she pointed out, had not actually struck the Dane in the face. UEFA were unimpressed and Totti was given a three-game ban – he would only return if Italy got to the semi-finals. Dark conspiracy theories were unearthed: Totti, it was claimed, had fallen into 'a trap' set for him by the Danes, who had set a camera on him for the whole match, waiting for something to happen. Totti had already made a fool of himself during the match. His expensive new boots, which he was paid a lot of money to sponsor, had given him huge blisters. The Roma star said that he felt like he was 'running on hot sand'. He had changed the boots halfway through the match, much to the dismay of his sponsor. Rival boot manufacturers made much of this public relations disaster, publishing a photo of 'their' players without blisters.

Italy played well in their next match against Sweden, but once again, they failed to score a second goal when well in control, and were punished by a lucky equalizer near the end. Qualification was now out of their hands. Under UEFA's inexplicable rules, if Sweden and Denmark were to draw 2–2 (or 3–3, or 4–4) Italy were out, whatever happened in their game against Bulgaria. A series of articles appeared warning against the dangers of a fixed game between the Scandinavians – what Italians call a *combine*. As the rain poured down, Italy gave their worst performance of all and went 1–0 down. Things improved in the second half, and Cassano managed to score a late winner but, by that time, the terrible news was coming through: the Scandinavians had indeed drawn 2–2. The Italians' worst fears had been confirmed and a series of moralistic articles appeared, although some journalists pointed out that Italy would have done exactly the same thing if they had been in the position of the Swedes or the Danes.

This time, Trap's reign was finally over. His record in the final stages of major competitions was a terrible one: played seven, won two, drawn two, lost three. Goals for: eight; goals against: eight. Despite their fantastic record at under-21 level, Italy's young players could not make the transition to the senior game. As the team returned home, complaining about plots and set-ups, there was talk of limiting the number of foreigners per team in Serie A. Italy's players were weighed down by the stress of their domestic league, with its crowd pressure and suffocating press presence.

Marcello Lippi took over from *Il Trap* in 2004, and appeared to be building a strong side from the rich stock of young players available to him in Serie A. After three *catenaccio*-inspired managers – Zoff, Maldini and Trapattoni – Lippi was at least in tune with the tactical requirements of the modern game. Italy had been starved of success since

1982, despite the quality of their league and their youth programme. They also had a monkey on their back. By 2004, Italy's list of last-gasp defeats in international tournaments had grown to rival that of England. In four semi-final and final games in major tournaments since 1982, Italy lost every time. In four penalty shoot-outs in major tournaments, Italy had been the victors on only one occasion, against possibly the only side in the world worse at taking penalties – Holland. Twice, key games, including a final, had been lost thanks to golden goals. A trophy had been snatched away just fifteen seconds from the end of a final. Italy's famous cynicism had simply disappeared. When the going got tough, they got weaker.

# CONCLUSION

# Money, Money, Money

## Cràc!

'There is a strong risk that we will be overcome by too much money, in our society materialism has won. This is the football of financiers' GIANNI RIVERA, 1998[1]

The Italians have a great word for bankruptcy – *Cràc*.[2] In the 1980s and 1990s, Italian football went *crack*. Financially, the whole system reached the edge of collapse and only a series of tricks, creative accounting and emergency laws prevented total breakdown. Two great teams – Fiorentina and Napoli – went bankrupt, and were relegated to lower divisions as a result. Others – Lazio, Roma – staggered on with enormous debts, or were bankrolled by presidents with bottomless pockets – Inter, Milan. Many lesser teams were left unprotected. In the lower leagues, bankruptcy and subsequent relegation were so common by the 1990s as hardly to merit comment. Big and small clubs like Bologna, Palermo, Ternana and Livorno all went bust, and had to suffer the humiliation of climbing up through the divisions. In 2004 eight clubs declared themselves bankrupt in July alone. However, going bust could actually help a club's finances, allowing them to clear their debts and move out over-expensive players. It was not a coincidence that three of the four above-mentioned teams were able to work their way right up to Serie A (the exception were Ternana, who came very close) after bankruptcy in the 1980s. Other (ex-) big clubs simply couldn't keep up, and refused to threaten their futures through insane spending. The consequence of this was austerity, and mediocrity on the pitch.

Yet this was at a time when there was more money and more interest in the game than ever before. Pay-TV had lavished huge sums on *calcio*, and the top players were continually in demand for advertising and interviews. This should have been a time of prosperity and profit. It was not. It was said by 2004 that if only those clubs who had actually paid their wages, taxes and insurance premiums were to be admitted to the championship, Serie A would consist of three clubs.[3]

## Administrative Doping

'The irregularity of accounts is a matter of opinion'
    FRANCO CARRARO (football administrator, attrib., 2002)

The euphoria of the Pay-TV age was not matched by the actual sums which had reached the clubs, and the money was distributed unevenly, with three or four big clubs taking most of the pot. Nor surprisingly, those three clubs were Juventus, Inter and Milan. Meanwhile, after Bosman, players' wage demands went through the roof and squads increased to unmanageable sizes. The Bosman ruling led to huge losses. Before Bosman, when a player was sold at the end of his contract the buying club had to pay a sum decided upon by the football federation. After Bosman such payments were illegal. Romano Prodi's centre-left government stepped in during the late 1990s with a special decree to make up the losses. Big players gained in bargaining power, but Bosman did not really help those minor stars – like Bosman himself – who had been imprisoned by their clubs. It was a gift to the stars and, above all, the agents. Smaller clubs found it more and more difficult to make ends meet by selling their players. Bosman was a 'financial time bomb'.[4]

Many teams lived on the verge of collapse, needing to qualify for Europe to survive. At the same time, corruption was rife, and controls over the system of football finance were similar to or worse than those in other sectors of the Italian economy – weak or non-existent. Finally, football was also part of a general economic decline. Big companies, which ran football teams as part of an umbrella of businesses, went under, taking their clubs with them. This happened to Cirio (and

Lazio) in the early twenty-first century and, spectacularly, to Parmalat (and Parma) in 2003–4. Both Sergio Cragnotti (Lazio/Cirio) and Calisto Tanzi (Parma/Parmalat) finished up in jail. Italian football was a big part of a sick financial system, where rules were optional and where it was relatively easy to hide the realities of debt and wheeler-dealing from the tax police, the shareholders and, of course, the fans.

The crisis manifested itself in other ways. Players went without pay for months, or even years. Nobody really cared about them, given the insane wages they were earning. By January 2004 Napoli had not paid its players for ten months. Transfer fees fell – especially after Bosman. Creative accounting reached unheard-of levels. The strangest example of this 'account-fixing' was the system of 'plus-valenze'.

## *Plus-valenze*. Added Value and Creative Accounting

How can we explain the crazy *plus-valenze* system? It is not easy, but let's try. One part is simple. A player is bought for 50 million and sold for 100 million. I have made a profit of 50 million. This profit is known as a *plus-valenza*. *Sales* are immediately entered into the accounts, whilst *purchases* are spread over the entire period of the contract. For most of football's history, the small clubs were those who gained such profits, as they invariably sold their discoveries to the big clubs. Then the big clubs discovered a trick. Why should *they* be left out? They decided to create some *plus-valenze* of their own, by swapping good players, or inflating the worth of not very good ones.

*Plus-valenze* became gold dust in a world built on debt and creative accounting. In 2002 nearly 70 per cent of footballing profits were made up of *plus-valenze*.[5] The most valuable trick of all was to exchange players for the same price, thus creating *plus-valenze* on both sides without any money actually changing hands. In 2004, a bizarre exchange of players took place between two top clubs, Inter and Juventus. Fabio Cannavaro, Italian national captain, was swapped with – *and valued at the same price as* – Juve's Uruguayan reserve goalkeeper Fabian Carini, who had barely played in the first team. Inter had given away one of their best players, and had created the 'mother and father of all *plus-valenza*' for Juventus. Why would Inter do such a thing?

Here we are in the realm of conspiracy and rumour, but it is clear that clubs did each other favours in order to boost *plus-valenze*. *Plus-valenze* – virtual or not – helped to balance the books. These favours were usually returned, sooner or later. Supposed rivals Milan and Inter swapped dozens of players in the 1990s. Not surprisingly, when top accounting firms were called in to look at the accounts of Italian clubs, they threw up their hands in horror. Nothing illegal had gone on here, but these deals were certainly not within the spirit of accounting law.

Players were valued in line with a hypothetical market value, and sold on at inflated prices. Accounts were therefore largely fictitious. Not surprisingly, the most bizarre series of these exchanges were between Parma and Lazio over the period when they were run by debt-ridden entrepreneurs. Hernan Crespo's move from Parma to Lazio for an exorbitant 110 billion lire has been described as a 'monument to *plus-valenze*'.[6] Often, the players exchanged for inflated sums were unknown youngsters, or over-the-hill veterans, who rarely played. Many players later realized that they had only been bought for budgetary reasons: 'I had become a *plus-valenza*', said one unemployed footballer in 2004. Gianmarco Fazza played just twice in Serie A, for Torino in 2002. However, he was very useful as a source of *plus-valenze*. He turned up in Inter's budget in 1999 as a sale to Chievo (*plus-valenza*? About 1.2 million pounds). Inter then brought Fazza back before he was loaned out, and then sold him to Roma for nearly three million pounds. Confused? Fazza must have been, and so were Inter, who even spelt his name wrong in their accounts. The player continued to turn up on other clubs' books, but rarely in their teams. This was an extreme case, but its grotesque nature showed how the foundation on which football was built was flimsy indeed.[7]

*Plus-valenze* kept budgets within limits for a while, but it was a short-term, crazy solution. It involved buying and selling worthless assets for huge amounts of money, and in the long run, led to chaos. Millions of pounds were spent on players nobody wanted, who were usually loaned out to the lower leagues straight away. Some clubs tried to hide their debts in other ways. Parma declared, for example, that they had spent (in one year) 30 billion lire for travel and scouting – some ten million pounds. Even in Italy, this situation could not last forever, and the whole championship almost came to a shuddering halt in 2003, with the real threat of bankruptcy hanging over three of the top six clubs in Italy (in terms of fans): Roma, Lazio and Napoli.

This was also a system with no limits. Ridiculous fees were paid for mediocre players who never took the field. Managers were sacked, but kept getting their wages. In 2004, Inter had three managers (Hector Cuper, Alberto Zaccheroni and Roberto Mancini) on its payroll, and their wages were not small. Ridiculous sums were paid to agents. When Hernan Crespo went to Inter in 2000 for 110 billion lire, his agent got eight billion lire (about £2.5 million) just for brokering the deal.

Footballers' wages were completely out of control by the 1990s. Rivaldo, who barely played for Milan in the 2002–3 season, was on €12 million a year (something like £9 million pounds – or £750,000 a month, or £23,000 a day, or £16 a minute). Milan's total wage bill in that season amounted to €111 million. Meanwhile, Empoli's whole team had a wage bill of €8.12 million. Even minor players were on absurd sums: Claudio Bellucci, a journeyman striker for Bologna, earned €3.2 million a year. Younger players sometimes started out on far less. Roma's teenage star De Rossi began on just €140,000 a year, but soon negotiated a better contract.[8]

Tax was also something of a problem. Clubs built up enormous tax debts, which they then were unable to pay off. In 2003–4 the government passed a special decree allowing clubs to pay off their debts over years – it was known as the *'debtspreading'* decree (which later became law, and was called 'legalized false accounting' by a former football administrator). This measure was later investigated by the European Commission as being in breach of EU competition laws as well as its budgetary regulations and the Italian government was forced to modify the legislation. Using the decree, Inter managed to save some €319 million and Milan, €242 million. Juventus noisily refused to use the measures in the decree and accused the other clubs of 'administrative doping'. In 2005 Lazio were only saved from collapse by a complicated deal with the taxman to spread their huge debts over a number of years.

A later 'emergency' decree was blocked after protests from within the government. FIAT manager Luca di Montezemolo called the decree 'the exact opposite of that which should be done in a serious country'. One other consequence of the comical *plus-valenze* system was the massive over-valuing of players, allowing these hypothetical 'values' to set off debts in the club budgets. Over-valued players were also loaned out cheaply to the lower leagues, meaning that their own club did not even pay their wages. Parma approved a budget in January 2004 that revealed a debt of €220 million. This was despite a series of big-money out-going transfers. By 2004, many clubs were close to collapse once again. No attempt had been made to clean up the system. The show had to go on, whatever the cost, and the people in charge were those who had presided over this disaster. Italian football was also part of the country's 'black economy'. Many players took money on the sly – in cash – in order to 'round up' their wages. Carlo Petrini freely admitted that most of the clubs he had played for in the 1960s and 1970s had done this, openly.

Various tricks have been used to falsify footballing accounts. In their budgets, for example, clubs have added such items as 'the rights over the next four years to the use of the photo and images of players'. This bizarre item is then written off against losses or tax. A whole series of other 'immaterial goods' were also added – such as investments in the youth scheme system, which supposedly would bring through players (but rarely did for the top clubs). All this made football into a financial world apart, a Disneyland of possible future benefits and airy-fairy items about which very little could be known. Some of these loopholes applied in the real world of businesses and industry, others were specific to football accounting.[9]

The rules applied to budgets are also, to say the least, flexible. Time and again, special circumstances have been cited which have allowed clubs to escape punishment. Nobody wanted to take the responsibility of relegating a really big club – such as Roma – for budgetary reasons. Fiorentina were an exception, as the club was declared bankrupt in the courts, leaving the federation with little option. Football finances in Italy are meant to be under the control of an organization known as *Covisoc*, which was set up in 1981. *Covisoc*'s powers were increased in the wake of the 1992–3 corruption scandals, but little really changed. When *Covisoc* threatened to come down hard on defaulting clubs, its president – Victor Uckmar – was quietly moved on.[10]

Going public in the stock market had not helped – on the contrary, it had exacerbated the crisis for many clubs. All the teams that had become public companies were in deep trouble, as share prices bounced around in line with results on the field. This was particularly true for Roma and Lazio. Lazio were the first club to go public in May 1998, and were soon followed by Bologna. The *La Repubblica* newspaper claimed that this step would guarantee that clubs would have to 'respect market rules and transmit with more openness the correct information concerning their business activities'.[11] The reality was the exact opposite of this. In order to allow Lazio to issue shares, the commission that controlled the Italian stock exchange relaxed the rule that only allowed in those companies that had been in profit for three successive years. In 1998, only six of the eighteen teams in Serie A declared a profit and, even before the crash of the late 1990s, the total losses of professional clubs stood at 1,000 billion lire.

Although much public attention concentrated on the plight of Roma, Lazio and Napoli, bankruptcies had been common in the lower leagues since the 1970s. It was unusual for the teams that were actually promoted or relegated on the pitch to be those that really went up or down. Many minor championships thus became something of a farce. In 1993, the year of Perugia's 'horse' scandal, *six* teams were excluded from Serie C1 alone due to financial irregularities. It was at this point that certain big businessmen were able to pick up clubs for next to nothing, whether or not they were interested in football. Luciano Gaucci was the most famous of these multiple presidents, but other similar personalities included Enrico Preziosi (who owned a toy company). All of these presidents also had difficult relationships with the football authorities, and frequently accused the referees of bias.

Clubs were exchanged in a bewildering series of deals. Franco Sensi had been president of both Roma and Palermo, and sold the latter to Maurizio Zamparini in July 2002. Zamparini himself had just sold Venezia and had tried to buy both Genoa and Verona. He took a large number of players from Venezia down to Palermo with him. Meanwhile, in stepped someone called Franco Dal Cin to buy Venezia. Dal Cin was a businessman who had strong links with Sensi. Palermo were promoted to Serie A in 2004, whilst Venezia languished in Serie B. Luciano Gaucci also sold and bought teams with alacrity. Enrico Preziosi dumped Como – about whom he had been so passionate – for Genoa. Como went bankrupt – not surprisingly as Preziosi took a whole set of players with him to Genoa for free, thereby asset-stripping his former club. Preziosi was elected vice-president of the league organization: he was clearly setting a good example to his peers.

Fiction led to further fiction. Here a further strange word needs explanation: *fideiussione* – financial guarantees. In 2001, former Roma president Franco Sensi – short and very angry – had led his club to only the third championship in its history, but had also taken them to a hair's breadth from bankruptcy. At the start of the 2003 season, in order to sign up legally for the championship, Roma and other clubs produced signed financial guarantees. The only problem was this: the certificates were forgeries. The club claimed they were the victims of fraud. Unbelievably, Roma were allowed to continue playing, as money was found from various sources – including *recapitalization* (where investors simply pay more cash). They were not forced to simply sell players *à la* Leeds United – although they should have been. Roma even purchased new players, but the money to pay for them did not come through for months. At the end of the season, Roma finally sold some of their stars. The whole credibility of the system was in tatters. Sensi himself, for example, had been involved in 'guaranteeing' other clubs in the 1990s. In 2005 Torino were also found to be using faked *fideiussione*.

Greed enveloped the world of football in the 1990s, leading to some very nasty side-effects. Promising youngsters were taken on at the age of seven and eight and tempted – along with their parents – with stories of vast wealth and false promises. Many young boys suffered at school, and physically, because of excessive training, stress and psychological pressure to perform. There were even cases of doping of ten- and eleven-year-olds. The competitive nature of the youth system – with money involved right from the start, crowds, pushy parents and agents – exacerbated these problems. For these kids, football was no longer a game, nor even a sport, but a business right from the start. Even a cursory glance at a boys' football game in Italy revealed that many young players were already copying the most unattractive features of the professional game – diving, play-acting, arguing with the referee, tactical fouling. If these players were the future, the future was bleak.

Football lived in a strange, illegal nether-world, where normal legal and financial rules did not apply, not even the weak laws used in Italy. Despite this, the signals coming from central government were not exactly encouraging. By 2004 Prime Minister Silvio Berlusconi had stood trial on numerous occasions for false accounting and tax evasion (including tax evasion on transfer fees) and one of his government's first acts on taking power in 2001 was to soften up the legal punishment for false accounting. The huge Parmalat food conglomerate was allowed to continue trading for years, and was even seen by many Italians as something of a model business, despite its enormous debts. Later, inspectors found that Parmalat had faked its bank records in a way similar to the illegal guarantees used by Roma. Life was imitating football, or was it the other way around?

The dramatic bankruptcy of Parmalat in 2004 nearly took Parma football club down with it, and led to the sale of most of the club's stars. A similar story was linked to the Cirio foodstuffs conglomerate (which also dealt in milk as well as tinned tomatoes) which also collapsed – *before* Parmalat hit the wall. Football was sick, but was only part of a warped financial-industrial system, built on power, corruption and evasion. The victims of these collapses were not the players – they all had their fat contracts paid off – or even the fans (both clubs continued to play in Serie A) but above all the small shareholders and employees, who saw their savings and/or their jobs disappear overnight.

Of the big clubs, only Fiorentina paid a heavy price on the field, being sent right down to C2 (three whole divisions) after going bankrupt, and losing their name and symbol, which had to be repurchased at public auction. Ironically, Florentina Viola, as they were known for their year in C2, went through something of a renaissance as a result. A number of overpaid players were off-loaded, and some good youngsters brought through alongside some excellent Italians from the lower leagues. Angelo Di Livio – a former Italian international – showed immense loyalty by deciding to stay with the club. He later wrote a book about his experiences called *Io resto qui: I am staying here.*[12] Diego Della Valle, a Florentine fashion entrepreneur, replaced the fake-tanned figure of Vittorio Cecchi Gori and finally brought sound management back to the club.[13] The fans seemed to revel in the return to 'real' football, going along in their thousands to home games and travelling to away games in obscure Tuscan towns. After one promotion – with just two to go until they reached Serie A again – the club were pushed straight into Serie B thanks to politics, being allowed in under the clause of 'sporting merit'. From there, after a bad start, Fiorentina – as they were now known again – sneaked into Serie A through the back door, via a playoff after having finished sixth. Their punishment had been relatively severe – much more so than the other clubs in similar financial trouble – but not excessively so. After all, Fiorentina would have been in Serie B anyway (they went down the year they went bankrupt) so the penance had really only amounted to one year in C2.

Since the end of the 1990s, Napoli also lurched from crisis to crisis. Art-auction millionaire Giorgio Corbelli took over in spring 2002 before he himself was arrested and charged with fraud. He cried conspiracy – the usual claim of those arrested in Italy. Corbelli left Napoli in a mess, from which it had by no means escaped by 2004. Napoli lived through that summer anxiously waiting to hear about the fate of their club, which had gone bankrupt. Eventually, Napoli were sent down just one division – to Serie C – despite fan protests. 'Napoli in C is the end of football as we know it. Let us hope in a miracle,' wrote one desperate fan.[14]

This whole disaster was presided over by two powerful men. Franco Carraro was European water-skiing champion when his father Luigi – president of Milan – died of a heart attack in 1967. Carraro took over his father's role with extraordinary results, at the age of just 27 – winning everything with Milan including the European Cup. He then began a long political and administrative career, mainly with the Italian Socialist Party, which, by the 1980s, was at the centre of a corrupt system of bribes and kickbacks that became known as Bribesville – *Tangentopoli*. Carraro rose to become Mayor of Rome for a time in the 1980s and briefly reached the giddy heights of Tourist Minister, but his main power-base was always in the world of sport. He was president of the football federation from 1976 to 1978 before heading up the potent Italian Olympic federation and then returning to football in 1986, where he presided over the 1990 World Cup. Even Italy's disastrous international performances in the 2002–2004 period, for which many fans held Carraro personally responsible, did not lead to his resignation. Or rather, they led to a kind of fake resignation popular in Italy, where a prestigious person offers to fall on his or her sword, and is then inevitably begged to return by their loyal subjects. Carraro was described as 'the incarnation of power' by Italy's authoritative *Dictionary of Football*.[15] Like the last leaders of the Soviet Union, football's ruling class were seemingly irremovable.

Antonio Matarrese's power-base was more political than Carraro's, and centred on Bari, the capital of the Apulia region in south-east Italy. Matarrese was a Christian Democrat politician who used his political weight to shift resources towards his home-town. In 1976 he was elected to Parliament for the first time with 61,000 preference votes and he proceeded to buy Bari. Triumphantly, the 1990 World Cup saw a post-modern Renzo Piano-designed stadium built, at enormous cost, in Bari. Unfortunately for Matarrese, Bari's team never really lived up to their post-modern stadium, and now languish in Serie B, with the terraces more empty than full. Both Carraro and Matarrese were at the helm during the chaotic preparations for the 1990 World Cup and they stayed firmly in their positions of power as football moved inexorably towards collapse. Matarrese and Carraro often cried wolf. In 1993, for example, the former had said that 'those who do not follow the rules should be chucked out'. In the real world, the politics and power of the big clubs was what really counted and, as Carraro said, accounting was 'a matter of opinion'.

## L'inferno (hell)

'Football is the last sacred representation of our time'

PIER PAOLO PASOLINI

'It would be incredibly boring if the best team always won'

GIANNI BRERA

By the time of the 2006 World Cup, Italian football was in disarray. Violence, fraud, scandal and intrigue were endemic. Two Serie B clubs had gone bust and two teams were excluded from Serie A due to excessive debts, and the same fate befell *fourteen* teams (two of which were officially penniless) in Serie C. Teams continued to play on despite bankruptcy, doping, arrests, and investigations. All this was surreal, and disturbing, but perhaps not all that surprising. After all, the president of the football federation was also a key figure in the running of Milan football club, whose president had been the prime minister of Italy for more than four years. In a country where the rules and laws are not only broken with impunity, but where those who do so are actually rewarded for their pains, and where judges are condemned as 'communists', it was unlikely that the most popular, the most important and the most wealthy sport would be a 'happy island' of legality, peace and tranquillity.

The excess, hysteria and waste of today's *calcio* are light-years away from those ragbag groups of foreigners and Italians who first decided to draw out a pitch, put up some goals and play something they called football. When Dr James Spensley of Stoke Newington, London stood in his makeshift goal in Genoa in the 1890s, he could never have dreamed that the game he helped to organize would take on such importance in people's lives. At times, working on this book, I wondered if the doctor should have concentrated on curing the sick. The dramatic events of the 2003–4 and 2004–5 seasons formed the backdrop to the writing of this book, and were marked by violence, scandals and catch-all conspiracy theories. Writing about football sometimes felt like descending into hell.

Yet, despite everything, millions of fans kept their faith. There were still moments of beauty, of loyalty, of drama and passion. The best team *didn't* always win, and the experts often got it wrong. Cristiano Lucarelli took a pay cut to play for his home-town club in Serie A, and scored 24 goals in an exceptional season. Gianfranco Zola turned down great riches to drag his local team back into the top division. *Calcio* was in deep trouble, but it still had the ability to anger and move people, to make them laugh, to unite and divide, to inspire like no other game. It was just as well, perhaps, that Dr Spensley had decided, more than a hundred years ago, to neglect his patients for a while.

# AFTERWORD

# The Great Italian Football Scandal and the World Cup Triumph. May–July 2006

PIERLUIGI PAIRETTO (REFEREE SELECTOR): Be careful ... have a good game, you know that there are always some ...
PAOLO DONDARINI (REFEREE): ... details ...
PAIRETTO: Absolutely, therefore keep fifty eyes well open ... to see also what is not there, sometimes. I know you will referee well.

'The King's stable-boy needs to know all the horse thieves'
GIANNI AGNELLI (attrib.) on Luciano Moggi

*Moggi, Moggi, quanti soldi rubi oggi?* [Moggi, Moggi, how much money are you stealing today?]      Torino chant circa 1993

Fixing a football match is a risky business. Players can be bribed, but things can easily go wrong under the gaze of a crowd and a TV audience. Alternatively, the referee can be offered a backhander. In Italy, there had traditionally been little need to resort to such crude methods. Ever since football became a mass sport in the 1930s, referees have naturally tended to assist the powerful clubs. In the 1960s this inclination was given a name: '*sudditanza psicologica*' – psychological slavery. The hegemony of powerful clubs was usually enough *on its own* to induce favouritism. By the 1990s, as TV money poured into the game and staying in the top rank became an economic necessity, the rich teams – and especially Juventus, the biggest and richest of them all – were no longer content to rely upon 'psychological slavery'. The system they constructed put referees, linesmen, journalists, the transfer market and agents under their control: in this way success was assured. In May 2006, this system was laid bare in what has been dubbed the biggest scandal in the history of sport. In comparison with 2006, those involved in the 1980 *Totonero* affair were mere 'chicken thieves'. This is the story of that scandal, which has become known as *calciopoli*.

Juventus are used to coming first. By 1994, the club had won the Italian football championship a record 22 times. Yet by their very high standards they were in something of a slump. One *scudetto* in nine seasons was not enough to satisfy the team's eleven million fans. Juventus, which was still run by the Agnelli family, owners of the FIAT car company, decided to turn to a man we have met before, whose methods were dubious, even by the standards of the dodgy world of Italian football. Luciano Moggi was the former deputy station master from a small Tuscan town, who had made himself a football power-broker. He was an unimpressive figure with no airs and graces (a bad fit with the aristocratic 'Juventus style') but the club needed to start winning again, and Moggi seemed the most likely man to bring success.

Moggi had begun his wheeler-dealing football career in 1973 as a scout for Juve. He then worked for Roma (twice), Lazio, Napoli and Torino. He could certainly spot talent – he discovered Paolo Rossi and Gianfranco Zola – but that wasn't his only appeal. After presiding over the scandal-packed Maradona years in Naples he moved to Torino, where he organized 'hostess' entertainment for international referees before matches. The Agnelli family could have been under no illusions when they hired him. Over the years, Moggi had frequently been caught hobnobbing with referees, usually adopting the time-worn defence of 'we met by chance'. He set up his son Alessandro as an agent, and formed relationships with other agents so that when the Bosman ruling opened up the transfer market in 1995, he was ready to take advantage. His political friends, especially in the Christian Democrat party (who governed Italy from 1945 to 1992), were many, and included Giuseppe Pisanu (DC deputy from 1972 to 1994 and Interior Minister from 2002 to 2006) and Clemente Mastella (Minister of Justice since 2006). Pisanu

A pre-scandal Luciano Moggi
dressed in his beloved Juventus shirt.

had known Moggi for forty years while Mastella said he wasn't ashamed to speak of their friendship and admitted that they had 'met many times'.

In 1994 Moggi became the Administrator and General Director of Juventus (the most powerful position in Italian club football after the President) alongside the chief executive and FIAT boss Antonio Giraudo and former player Roberto Bettega. Together they became known as the *triad* – a sinister term which was not intended as a compliment. Over the next twelve years, the *triad* led Juventus to a series of successes in keeping with their glorious history, including seven Italian championships and a Champions League trophy. Their domination was such that they led Serie A for a record 76 consecutive matches. In March 2006 the board of Juventus praised the *triad* for having 'fashioned a sober and above all a winning model of management'. *La Stampa* (controlled by FIAT) concluded that 'in an era of financial disaster, the *triad* is a model of virtue'. Less than six weeks later, the *triad* had resigned in disgrace, along with the whole Juventus board. The scandal focused on the club's sporting director, and many of the epithets used to describe what had taken place used his name: *Moggiopoli, Moggigate, Il sistema Moggi.*

Soon a squalid system of corruption was to be revealed, built upon 'a cupola of power marked by alliances between the managers of some big clubs, agents and referees', as the Neapolitan investigating magistrates put it. At the head of this sat Moggi, who had reached a position of absolute domination and control of the entire system of professional football thanks to blackmail, psychological violence and above all cohabitations of all kinds. According to *La Gazzetta dello Sport, Moggiopoli* worked like this: the championship was controlled step by step, from the transfer market to the goal disallowed at the last minute, from missed offsides to red cards given or not given according to the level of protection which each player enjoyed'.

On 5 May four referees were suspended. The following day Luciano Moggi and his son Alessandro were told that they were being investigated as part of a criminal inquiry relating to the 2004–5 season. They were joined by nine referees, eleven linesmen and twenty-one others, most of them football administrators of various kinds. It was suspected that more than twenty games had been 'adjusted'. Franco Carraro, President of the Football Federation, resigned on 8 May. Two days later, Innocenzo Mazzini, his vice-president, also went, to be followed by Tullio Lanese, President of the referees' association. Aldo Biscardi, presenter of the football chat show *Il processo del lunedì*, had been forced to stand down after it appeared that even slow-motion replays had been under Moggi's control.

Despite the revelations, when Juventus clinched their twenty-ninth championship on 14 May 2006 everything was in place for the usual polished celebrations: the open-top bus was booked and its route through the city mapped out. Thousands of fans had made the trip down to Bari to cheer on their team. In the stadium, everything went to plan. Juventus won easily, champagne corks popped in the dressing room, and the players threw their shirts into the crowd. Yet the headline in *La Gazzetta dello Sport* that morning had been unusual: 'They are playing, *sort of* ', it ran, and the next day's was equally strange: 'Juve win their twenty-ninth title ... *or not?*' In Piazza San Carlo in Turin only a few young and naive fans gathered to celebrate. The city was eerily quiet. No horns were honked, few flags were waved and the open-top bus was cancelled. That same day a tearful Moggi told the press he was leaving the world of football. It had become clear that the club's twenty-ninth *scudetto*, and perhaps their twenty-eighth as well (from the previous season), might well be taken away. The celebrations were a macabre ritual. Many *Juventini* were keeping their heads down. This was best summed up by the republication of a prescient article about Moggi from the 1990s by the well-known Juve supporter Beniamino Placido, who back then had written that 'Juventus fans will try and get by with a frown but they will feel endless shame'.

*Moggiopoli* dwarfs every other scandal in the scandalous history of Italian football. It involves not only Juventus but AC Milan, Fiorentina and Lazio. A whole system is on trial, including referees, the selectors of referees, journalists, slow-motion replay experts, policemen, agents, tax police, *carabinieri*, members of the Agnelli family and even the manager of the national team, Marcello Lippi. How was such an extensive system brought down so quickly?

As with Italian politics in the early 1990s, all attempts at reforming Italian football from the inside had failed. Only one body of people was powerful enough to take on Moggi and his cronies: the judiciary. The investigations which eventually unravelled *Moggiopoli* were intricate and geographically widespread. In 2004, an inquiry into the Neapolitan version of the mafia, the camorra, had uncovered an illegal betting ring involving players and referees, and investigating magistrates had ordered phone taps on Moggi's six or so mobile phones. For eight months, at least six transcribers typed out 100,000 conversations. This material was to provide the bulk of the evidence against all the accused at the subsequent series of sporting and criminal trials. The magistrates were also well informed about past footballing scandals. One confessed to having read 'all the books written by Carlo Petrini'.[1]

In Turin, the inquiry into the doping of Juventus players in the 1990s involved phone taps that revealed further disturbing aspects of the Moggi system. Much of this material had been passed on to the football authorities, who did absolutely nothing. They clearly hoped that the whole scandal would disappear. This time, they were wrong.

Investigators in Parma and Udine unearthed evidence of a gambling scam involving Serie A players. In Rome, meanwhile, magistrates were looking into GEA World, a firm of football agents staffed almost entirely by the sons and daughters of powerful people in the soccer world, including the son of the Italian team manager, as well as the children of important businessmen, politicians and bankers. GEA World had been formed in 2004 in Rome from the fusion of two agent organizations. In a short time, the organization managed to take control of a large sector of the football transfer market – as well as trainers and media interests. Many Juventus players were represented by Luciano Moggi's son Alessandro, an agent at GEA, who alone controlled an extraordinary 12.3 per cent of the entire agent football market in Italy (GEA had a share of nearly 20 per cent). Other agents who worked for GEA included Davide Lippi (son of Marcello), Chiara Geronzi (daughter of Cesare, boss of the powerful Capitalia Bank), Andrea Cragnotti (son of Sergio, former President of Lazio and now a bankrupt industrialist), Francesco Tanzi (son of the disgraced and bankrupt industrialist Calisto Tanzi) and last but not least Giuseppe De Mita, son of former Prime Minister and Christian Democrat politician Ciriaco. This grotesque monument to nepotism and patronage was a cancer within the game, with its huge costs and corrupt dealings. GEA dealings often led to ridiculous exchanges of players, or absurd prices being paid, or frequent movements for no apparent reason.[2] In July 2006 in the wake of the scandals, GEA World was effectively wound up and its staff laid off.

What did the phone taps and the other investigations reveal? Referees chatting with powerful club presidents, the same club presidents conversing with those who selected and disciplined the referees, the vice-president of the football federation joking with the same club presidents. *Everyone* was friendly with Moggi – as long as they did his bidding. Most worrying of all were the frequent conversations with the referees themselves. Some were worried, others were proud of 'their work'. Advice was frequently given as to *how* to referee. In this way, the whole nature of the referee's job was infected. As Tim Parks has written, 'the man's very profession is to be neutral'. In Italy, in 2004–5 (and probably before that, and since), referees were advised *not* to be neutral – and they seemed only too happy to oblige.

How do these revelations fit with that laid out in Chapter 2 of this book? Clearly, there is a need to draw a distinction between *calcio* and the transformation to what has been called *neo-calcio* in the 1990s. Something had gone very wrong in the last fifteen years. Football was not always fixed in this way, and it wasn't completely fixed under Moggi. Not all referees helped Juventus, and some tried to referee normally. The Moggi system was not omnipotent, but it had come close to being so, and it had extended its range of power beyond Juventus's backyard to the whole championship table.

Renewal was needed, and quickly. Professor Guido Rossi, a 75-year-old expert on company law and a well-respected 'super-manager',[3] was chosen as temporary President of the Football Federation and soon made a controversial appointment. On 23 May he asked 76-year-old Francesco Saverio Borelli, a retired judge, to take over the investigative wing of the football federation. Borelli had presided over the 'Clean Hands' anti-corruption investigations in Milan which had shaken Italy in the early 1990s. The reaction to Borelli divided Italy along political lines. Silvio Berlusconi claimed that the left had 'nominated its own referee': left-wing opinion was solidly behind the judge. *Calciopoli* had become part of the general tussle between the economic and political elites and the judiciary. Yet, there was a key difference here: sporting justice requires far less proof than normal justice. In the world of sport, intention is enough to implicate. You only need to discover if somebody *tried* to influence a match, not that it was actually manipulated. There were no juries, and a streamlined penal process. Sport had its own rules: it governed itself. Borelli moved with great speed, interviewing all the protagonists of the scandal except for Moggi, who refused to turn up. A succession of referees, players, journalists, policemen and judges passed through his offices. Meanwhile, the criminal investigations continued apace in Naples, Turin, Milan, Parma, Rome and Udine.

The effect of the phone-tap revelations was extraordinary, as they allowed every Italian to understand how power really worked. For once, the mask of arrogance and denial had been stripped away. However, most Italians were not shocked. The affair simply confirmed their suspicions about how the game worked. As one journalist put it, 'it is exactly how we imagined things to be'. *Moggiopoli* was a triumph for the conspiracy theorists. They had been proved absolutely right. Almost everything had been fixed: victories, defeats, relegation, slow-motion replays, bookings. A number of writers, journalists, analysts and football presidents had already identified the main features of the Moggi system in all their horrific detail – and had been ignored or laughed at for years by the authorities.[4] Many fans had long been convinced that the whole game was rotten. It was a farce, a sick joke. Now they had proof, pages and pages of it. Corruption had become a way of life. But not all fans necessarily disapproved of the way things had been organized. After all, Moggi was a winner and, as declared in the most terrifying and cynical banner displayed by Juventus fans after the scandal broke: 'The end justifies the means'.

It was also clear from the outset that this was not a one-club affair, despite Silvio Berlusconi's constant claims to the contrary and his attempts to paint Milan as a victim of Moggi's dealings. It turned out, for example, that AC Milan (Berlusconi's club) had employed a 'referee attaché': Leonardo Meani – an ex-Serie C official and restaurant owner – who would phone up officials before and after matches, and appeared able to influence the selection of linesmen for games involving Milan. Now Meani was no Moggi, but he did have a lot of 'friends' amongst the referee corps, and he had a hotline to Adriano Galliani, the President of Milan until 2006. Strong doubts also emerged concerning an end-of-season game between Milan and Udinese, and the transfer of an Udinese player to Milan. An alternative network of power seemed to emanate from Milan and its representatives.

There seemed little doubt that an employee of Milan had tried to influence the results of a series of games. Much less had been more than enough to relegate smaller clubs in the past. Berlusconi had also invited Moggi to his Rome residence in September 2005, well before the scandal erupted. Officially, the two had merely exchanged pleasantries. Unofficially, there were strong indications that Berlusconi had offered Moggi a job. Moggi himself said that 'he wanted me to go to Milan' and had replied that he would 'think about it'. Within weeks of their meeting, Berlusconi would accuse Moggi of 'stealing' two championships from Milan.

In the black-and-white world of *Moggiopoli* there was little room for dissent. Those chairmen who railed against the system were forced to grovel, or pay the consequences – relegation, bankruptcy, the application of the rules (but only for them). Sometimes these victims were genuinely trying to reform football, and were relatively honest. Usually, however, they were 'little Moggis' who merely wanted their piece of the action. Very few of these 'victims' were paragons of legality, and it was a fair bet that if they had been in charge, *Moggiopoli* would have continued unabated. Nobody in their right mind could argue that a renewal of the world of football could emerge via the sharks who had entered the game in the 1980s – Enrico Preziosi, Maurizio Zamparini, Luciano Gaucci, Franco Dal Cin. All of these personalities had been at the centre of their own scandals. All used Moggi-type methods, it was just that they were less powerful than the *triad*, and ended up squashed. However, these little Moggis certainly knew how the system worked, and if they were desperate, they were willing to speak out.

Diego Della Valle was a different case. A powerful businessman, he had sorted out Fiorentina's disastrous financial situation and taken the club back to Serie A, and he was a gentleman, as his own phone taps show. However, his campaign around the issue of TV rights infuriated those who ran the game – and they decided to teach him a lesson. The weapons were familiar ones. First, his club would pay, on the pitch. A series of 'unfortunate' refereeing decisions saw Fiorentina plummet down the table in the 2004–5 season. The culmination of this 'run of bad luck' came at Genoa against Sampdoria, where Fiorentina had two men sent off in the first eight minutes.

Della Valle was forced to grovel to the *triad*, who arrogantly promised him that they would 'save' Fiorentina from relegation. He was urged to phone referee boss Paolo Bergamo. The tone of this call – 'I didn't even realize that someone could pick up the phone and call you' – was very different from those between Moggi and Bergamo. A friendly lunch followed. Soon, things got better for Fiorentina on the pitch. A new sacrificial victim was identified – Bologna, whose President Gazzoni had made a point of criticizing those clubs whose financial irregularities gave them an advantage in the transfer market. Meanwhile Fiorentina were 'saved' and they were grateful. They had learnt their lesson and were happy to tone down their campaign for 'changes in the world of football'.

\*          \*          \*

Referee Massimo De Santis is another key figure in the affair. Opinion about him is divided. Massimo Cellino, the President of Cagliari, called him 'one of the worst bastards in the world'. On the other hand he had been asked to officiate in the World Cup (he was quickly removed from the list after the scandal broke). De Santis was identified as the referee at the centre of Moggi's system. An elegant, authoritarian official, he worked as a prison guard and had friends in the police force and the judiciary, including moles who were supposedly able to tip him off about inquests. His activities came as no surprise to most fans, players or club presidents: he had long been thought to favour Juventus, and he was willing to help Moggi out with other results. Phone-tap conversations revealed that De Santis was happy in his work: following a Livorno–Siena game in which he sent off a Livorno defender after just 17 minutes, a game Livorno would go on to lose 6–3, he was recorded crowing to Innocenzo Mazzini 'Did you see? Ready, go, *one off.*'

In some games, it seems, the players were irrelevant. They had become mere puppets in the hands of an all-powerful official. As Gino Corioni, President of Brescia, once claimed: 'the truth is that if a referee is clever he can direct a game in a certain direction, and you lose. And 99.9 per cent of the fans don't understand why.' In the wake of *calciopoli*, referees in Italy had reached a low point in their history. In truth, they had never been held in great esteem, but now things had reached a nadir. There was 'a real risk of a crisis of vocation' (Fulvio Bianchi).

Not all referees bowed to the system but those who didn't were punished for their impudence. Rebels were prevented from officiating in big matches, and as a result saw their careers suffer. Some would find their names dragged into the mud on TV or in the press. Others faced Moggi's wrath. Gianluca Paparesta was the most celebrated victim of all – locked in the dressing room by a furious Moggi after failing to award a penalty to Juventus in 2004. Rather absurdly, this alleged crime was investigated by magistrates as a case of kidnapping. But even Paparesta could not claim that he was squeaky clean, as phone taps showed him trying to obtain political favours through his contacts with Milan.

Soon, other branches of Italy's numerous law enforcement agencies got in on the act. It was open season. On 19 May, the tax police turned up at the house of Luciano Moggi in the centre of Turin at 7.30 in the morning. On that same day they also raided the private residences of Juve players Fabio Cannavaro – Juventus and Italy captain – and Zlatan Ibrahimovic, as well as the offices of Juve. The next day it was the turn of Milan and Inter. Turin magistrates were now looking into the accounts of 71 clubs, and 41 contracts. Having the tax police turn up on your doorstep is a very bad sign in Italy – for two main reasons. First, they always find *something*, and second, it means that your political protection has disappeared. Moggi was isolated, and vulnerable. He had lived and worked on the phone, but when the scandal broke, many of his former 'friends' abandoned him. *La Gazzetta dello Sport* described him as 'shut up inside his home, with his six silent mobiles which don't ring any more'.

Media interest was unprecedented. Despite rather important political news (the fallout from a dramatic general election in April, the swearing-in of a new President) *Moggiopoli* was the hot story. The first eleven pages of *La Repubblica* were dedicated to the scandal on 14 May. On one night that month three national chat shows were entirely given over to *calciopoli*. Commentators and journalists who had been sidelined or censored under Moggi's unofficial rule were suddenly (if briefly) back in vogue. Marco Travaglio, who had been the object of personal attacks from the *triad* and had co-written (anonymously) the best book about Moggi, appeared on national TV to confess that he was 'a Juventus fan in hibernation' who had stopped supporting his club when Moggi had taken over in 1994.[5] SkyItalia's split-screen news service had a permanent booth for *calciopoli*, while *La Gazzetta dello Sport*'s website contained a rolling news section entitled '*Tutta Moggiopoli minuto per minuto*': '*Moggiopoli* minute by minute', a play on the title of a popular radio football show.

Many commentators argued that the scandal showed how Italy really worked. Emanuele Gamba argued that Moggiopoli 'is very similar to the country in which we live'. Moggi's system was not just about football. He was a powerful man, and power in Italy allows you to procure favours, bypass rules, regulations and normal procedures, obtain free and unwarranted help and services. Thus, Moggi could help his friends jump the queue in public hospitals, or use state officials to look after his friends on shopping trips. When Juventus midfielder

Emerson lost his son's passport, Moggi simply phoned up his contacts at the airport to sort things out. The law meant nothing; everything dissolved in front of a simple phone call. As such, the phone taps (collected in two huge books running to some 700 pages in total) are a fascinating insight into the way Italy functions.[6] Power of this type always has two sides to it: those who exercise it, and those who bow to it. In Italy, large numbers of people were willing to do Moggi's bidding, and it was unlikely that the disappearance of one man would remove the culture which created the system. As Marco Revelli has written, 'the ethical and aesthetic catastrophe of the triad reflects the anthropological degeneration of contemporary Italy'.

The wheels of sporting justice moved forward with great speed in May and June 2006. They had no choice. UEFA needed to know who was going to be playing in its European competitions by 25 July. This echoed the political and economic pattern whereby Europe often acts as a restraint on Italy's economic and legal problems. The clubs who were not involved in European competitions (Siena, Messina, Reggina, Empoli and Arezzo) were divided from those who were (Juventus, Milan, Fiorentina and Lazio). Francesco Borelli quickly completed his preliminary investigation into the latter group of teams and passed the material on to the sporting public prosecutor, a man called Stefano Palazzi. The sporting trial of the century began in Rome in June, right in the middle of the World Cup. On 4 July, Italy beat Germany in a spectacular semi-final. That same day, in a dramatic twist worthy of Shakespeare, Palazzi laid out his charges to the court. Nobody had expected such a harsh set of possible penalties. Palazzi asked for *all four* clubs to be relegated, with points deductions. These were his requests to the court:

> Juventus: relegation to a division 'below Serie B' with six points deducted.
> Milan: relegation to Serie B and three points deducted.
> Lazio: relegation to Serie B and 15 points to be deducted.
> Fiorentina: relegation to Serie B and 15 points to be deducted.

Both the championships from 2004–5 and 2005–6 were to be taken away from Juventus. The former was not assigned, the winner of the latter would be left up to the president of the football federation,

Guido Rossi (an Inter fan). For the other personalities on trial, Palazzi generally asked for them to be banned for life (this was the case for most of the referees and other administrators) and fined. These were, it should be underlined, opening requests, not final verdicts. The shock from Rome was only tempered by the success of Italy in Germany. Over the next few days, the defence for all the parties made their pleas to the court, presided over by an 81-year-old ex-judge, Cesare Ruperto. No witnesses were allowed, and video evidence was not admitted. Everyone proclaimed their innocence, apart from Juventus, who – in the face of a possible Serie C meltdown – went into a form of plea bargaining. They would accept as 'fair punishment' relegation to Serie B. In the best-case scenario, the biggest club in Italian football, with its 11 million fans in Italy alone, would be playing outside of the top divison for the first time in its history, and with points deductions. Year zero indeed. The trial continued in parallel with events on the pitch, in Germany.

## The Agony and the Ecstasy.
## Germany 2006

As World Cup preparations go, Italy's was not ideal. While the team was gathering for pre-tournament training near Florence, *calciopoli* broke in the press. There were calls for Italy to be withdrawn from the competition altogether, and leading players had to make frequent trips to Rome, Milan and Naples to answer some tricky questions. Those interrogated included Fabio Cannavaro, the team captain. Meanwhile, the goalkeeper – Gigi Buffon – was trying to convince magistrates in Parma that he had not broken federation rules during his alleged Rooney-like excursions into a variety of sports-gambling websites. The team were subject to insults from fans who turned up to training. Press conferences were dominated by discussion of the scandal.

Massimo Lippi, the manager, was under the most pressure of all. Not only was he a Juventus man but his son, Davide, was officially under investigation for his links with GEA World. There were dark mutterings about favouritism for GEA players in national team selections in the past, and for the 2006 World Cup. Lippi was only confirmed as coach in the run-up to the team's departure for Germany thanks to the Federation president Guido Rossi turning up in an astonishing white suit to back him. Journalists called for Cannavaro to be stripped of the captaincy, especially after he claimed during a press conference that Moggi had 'worked well'. It was said that Cannavaro had been forced to hold a new press conference the next day, in which he 'corrected' his earlier statements. Injuries to Gennaro Gattuso and Giancarlo Zambrotta completed Lippi's misery. He kept faith with them, and was to be proved absolutely right.

Given the importance of this scandal, the start of the World Cup took second place to lengthy discussions of phone taps and sporting trials, and wild speculation. Moreover, terrestrial television only had a minority of games to show. Most matches were transmitted on Sky-Italia, which had only just taken off. Things seemed to be starting to change with the *azzurri*'s first game, an impressive victory over Ghana thanks to goals by Andrea Pirlo and Vincenzo Iaquinta. However, the team's second game against the US drifted into farce. Midfielder Daniele De Rossi was sent off for a violent elbow, defender Zaccardo scored an absurd own goal and the 10-men Italians could not beat an unfancied 9-man US team.

A fine victory over the Czech Republic – with a towering header from Marco Materazzi and a breakaway goal from Filippo Inzaghi – set up a last-sixteen match with Australia. It was after the Czech game, Marcello Lippi said later, that the Italians really started to believe they could win. The draw had been kind to them, and they could see a route through to the semi-final. Once again, however, a good performance was followed by a mediocre one in the second-round match against Australia, as Italy had a man sent off (Materazzi) and only won thanks to a 'generous' last-second penalty, won by left-back Fabio Grosso after a marauding run into the opposition area. Francesco Totti coolly crashed the spot-kick into the top corner, rejecting the chance to employ his risky trademark chip shot. Italy's defence had been immaculate throughout.

More to the point, the squad had formed itself into a group willing to fight for each other, not the collections of egomaniacs who had turned out for their country in 2002 and 2004. For many, it was this generation's last chance of international glory. Lippi employed direct attacking tactics rarely seen in recent tournaments, or from previous

Italy teams. Whereas Trapattoni, the previous manager, would always take off a forward when 1–0 up, Lippi was more likely to put on another attacking player. Midfield dynamo Gennaro Gattuso later described the team as 'working-class', and it was certainly true that the players worked hard for each other and accepted substitutions and team selection with grace. Gattuso came from a poor background in the south of Italy whilst midfielder Simone Perrotta was born (like Geoff Hurst) in Ashton-under-Lyme, where his father ran a wine business, before moving back to Italy at the age of six. Ten different players scored for Italy in the tournament, and every squad player took part at some point, apart from the two reserve goalkeepers. There wasn't even a real *staffetta* debate, a unique event for an Italian team during a World Cup.[7] After the Australia victory, the country was finally, but firmly, in the grip of World Cup fever. Flags – so rare in Italy – appeared everywhere. *Italia* T-shirts turned up in street markets. Pages and pages were dedicated to detailed tactical analyses. Three late-night chat shows discussed team selection late into the night, every night.

The team relaxed. On 27 June, Fabio Cannavaro was in the middle of a jokey press conference when tragic news came through via a mobile phone. He abandoned the room, clearly rattled. The news was astonishing. Gianluca Pessotto, Juventus right-back from 1995 to 2006, was in a serious condition in a Turin hospital. Pessotto had turned up for his new job as Juve team manager at 12.10 a.m. that day. He then proceeded to walk up to the roof of the Juventus building. After leaving his mobile phone and car keys on the wall, he threw himself off the roof, falling 15 metres onto the car of the club vice-president, Roberto Bettega. A Catholic, Pessotto had a rosary in his hand as he jumped. It was said that he had been suffering from depression. It was something of a miracle that Pessotto survived the fall – his injuries were terrible but he escaped paralysis. Three of his ex-team-mates (Del Piero, Zambrotta and Ciro Ferrara, who was working with the Italy team) obtained special permission to visit him in Turin from the German training camp where the team were based.

Once again, the football on the pitch appeared to be almost irrelevant. *Calciopoli* was also back on the front pages with a vengeance. On 29 June, in front of 200 journalists, the 'sporting trial' linked to the scandals opened in Rome. Four clubs (Juventus, Milan, Lazio and

Fiorentina), as well as a number of referees and administrators, were all 'on trial'. Many of the Italian-based players in Germany (including foreign stars such as Patrick Vieira and Davide Trezeguet) had no idea where they would be playing the following season, or if they would be taking part in the Champions League. This was the context in which Italy took the field against Ukraine for the quarter-final. In 1982, a scandal-hit team had been crucified by the press and given no chance in the run-up to the tournament. They went on to beat Argentina, Brazil, Poland and Germany to take the cup. The parallels were there, but there was a long way to go. Ukraine were overcome with some ease, thanks to goals from the superb Zambrotta (Pessotto's room-mate for years with Juventus) and two from Luca Toni. Once again, the team had kept a clean sheet. Buffon was unbeatable behind the best defence in the competition.

Dortmund, where Germany had never lost, was the setting for the most dramatic match of the whole World Cup – the semi-final. The build-up was marked by provocative tactics from the German gutter press (*Bild* ran this subtle headline: '*Arrivederci Pizza*') and the endless recall in Italy of two previous Italy–Germany matches – the 1970 4–3 classic and the 1982 final. Italian emigrants in Germany besieged the team's training sessions. Many had never been accepted by German society, a generation of Gastarbeiter subject to a series of stereotypes from the moment they had arrived in the country. Last time the World Cup was held in Germany, in 1974, the Italian team had let the emigrant community down badly. This time, they hoped, things would be different.

Fuel was added to the fire in the run-up to the game by the decision of FIFA to ban the German midfielder Thorsten Frings for a punch thrown in the fight which erupted after the Argentina–Germany quarter-final. Frings had been fingered by a SkyItalia football chat show, and there were dark mutterings of a set-up. Further spice was provided by the sad fate of a young mountain bear, known officially as JJ2 but renamed Bruno in the press. Bruno had gone walkabout from his natural habitat in the Trentino mountains in north-east Italy and had ended up in Germany, where he proceeded to slaughter various forms of livestock. Much to the dismay of the Italian authorities, Bruno was shot dead by German hunters near a lake in Bavaria in June.

Fabio Grosso sets off after his semi-final goal against Germany.

Trentino-based Italy supporters carried little toy bears on their way to watch the match in July. Bruno, it was said, had to be avenged.

The game itself was dominated by Italy, especially in the first half. Germany huffed and puffed, but produced very little to show for their effort. In extra time, Lippi went for broke. He sent on attacker after attacker, in a desperate attempt to avoid another penalty shoot-out. Substitute Alberto Gilardino hit the post in the second minute of extra time, and a minute later Gianluca Zambrotta smashed a shot against the bar. Still Italy kept coming forward. In the 119th minute, Andrea Pirlo coolly slipped a pass through the German defence and left-back Fabio Grosso, who only five years earlier had been playing in Serie C2 with lowly Chieti, curled a perfect first-time shot past Jens Lehmann. He set off on a mazy run to nowhere (while shouting 'Non ci credo' – 'I don't believe it') which was immediately compared to Tardelli's scream from 1982.

If they were being honest, few Italian fans even knew what Grosso looked like before the tournament began. Now he was a national hero. A minute later, Italy broke from defence through Cannavaro and Totti found Gilardino in space. Without even looking, Gilardino placed a perfect pass into the path of the onrushing Alessandro Del Piero, who clipped a shot into the far corner. It was a counter-attack of vertical beauty, in a tournament dominated by drab horizontal play. In 1995 Del Piero had announced himself to the world with a stunning curled shot in the same stadium in the Champions League. It was written in the stars that Alberto Gilardino would play a key part in the victory. He was born, after all, on the day Italy beat Brazil in the 1982 World Cup.

The game was over, but the celebrations had just begun. In the tiny mountain town of Calceranica al Lago, where I watched the match, cars drove around all night honking their horns. On that very day, the prosecutor in the *calciopoli* sporting trial in Rome had called for Juventus – Del Piero's club – to be relegated to Serie C. Only a game of this magnitude could have kept such news off the front pages. Grosso's goal went straight into the football history books – including this one. Germany had lost to Italy once again, and the Italians were crowing. One article carried the title: 'The revenge of the pizza'. Every footballing stereotype had been overturned. Famed for defensive football, the Italians had gone on the attack. The squad, united as rarely before, showed little sign of diving, or violence. Which team was fouled the most? Italy.

France were to be Italy's opponents in the final. Zinedine Zidane's team had been Italy's bogey team in recent years, knocking them out of the 1986 and 1998 World Cups (the latter on penalties) and sneaking the 2000 European Championship final through a last-second equalizer and a golden goal. Going into the final in Berlin, most Italian pundits were confident of victory, many claiming that Italy were 'superior' to France. The country's most sophisticated football journalist, Roberto Beccantini of *La Stampa*, predicted that Italy would win on penalties after a 1–1 draw in normal time, that the *azzurri* would score from a corner, and that Trezeguet would miss the decisive spot kick. Across the two teams eight Juventus players were to take part in the final. Of those, only Alessandro Del Piero, who had promised to stay no matter what the outcome of the investigations, was certain of being a Juventus player in the season to come.

As the final approached, I took a bike ride through the working-class neighbourhood of Quarto Oggiaro on the north-west periphery of Milan. Preparations were beginning in earnest for the game, and for the possible celebrations afterwards. Unhelmeted scooter riders raced through the streets with huge Italian flags in their hands, while every balcony sported a tricolore. Fireworks and horns were on sale on street corners. The party was ready, but would Italy deliver?

Things started badly for the *azzurri*. A charitable penalty was awarded to France after just six minutes and Zidane clipped it in off the crossbar, in a parody of Francesco Totti's trademark *cucchiaio*. Totti himself was more or less invisible as Italy hauled themselves back into the game through a towering Materazzi header from a corner – a carbon copy of his goal against the Czech Republic earlier in the tournament. Toni hit the bar from a similar position, and Italy ended the first half on top. From then on, it was all France. Thierry Henry spread panic in the defence – for the first and only time in the competition – with a couple of silky runs, but his team mates couldn't profit. Italy looked tired – and only broke sporadically to threaten the French goal. Once again, Buffon was magnificent, alongside everybody's (except for FIFA's) player of the tournament – Fabio Cannavaro. Zidane nearly sealed a fairy-tale end to his career with a late header, which Buffon turned over the bar.

Then things turned very sour and very strange. With 10 minutes left in extra time, Materazzi and Zidane had a conversation on the edge of the Italian box after the Italian defender appeared to tweak the French captain's nipple, lightly grabbing his shirt. It was a classic piece of mild provocation, common in Serie A where Zizou had played for five seasons. As the pair jogged back, Zidane told Materazzi that 'if you want my shirt, you can have it at the end of the game'. The response was a series of insults.

Zidane appeared to be returning to the game, before suddenly turning towards Materazzi and plunging a violent head-butt into his chest. Materazzi had rarely been the target of violence in his long career, and was known throughout Italy as a clumsy and at times brutal defender. He was an unlikely victim. Pandemonium followed. The referee had missed the incident, but someone else had not. Commentators claimed that TV evidence had been used, although FIFA denied that this was so. After two minutes of confusion, Zidane was sent off, and walked disconsolately past the World Cup to the dressing room. It was, of course, his last act on a football field. Usually a fair player, Zidane had been known to snap on occasion, as during the 1998 tournament when he was sent off for stamping, or with Juve in October 2000, when he was given a five-game ban for a violent head-butt. Some commentators interpreted the violence as a return to Zidane's roots: 'it was the gesture of a man from the periphery' (Davide Bidussa). *Guardian* journalist Simon Hattenstone saw it as a possible anti-imperialist act. 'Perhaps we'll never know what was said or what he was thinking,' he wrote. 'Perhaps the greatest riddle of all is that in destroying his legacy as a sporting hero, he might have immortalised himself as the man who stood up to bigots, real or imagined, no matter the price.'

Materazzi's words became the object of worldwide media speculation. Lip-readers were employed by various newspapers and TV stations to interpret the central defender's mumblings, but they couldn't agree. 'Terrorist' was the first version which emerged, but those who knew Materazzi thought this far too sophisticated an insult, and it was immediately denied. Some even thought Materazzi had labelled him an Algerian collaborator, a 'harki', again stretching belief in Materazzi's knowledge of colonial history. Materazzi also denied mentioning Zidane's mother. Another version was this Roman insult: '*Va a mori' ammazzato te e tutta la tu' famiglia*'. 'an ugly death to you and all your family'. Others spoke of Zidane's sister, who works in Turin. Zidane went on French TV to apologize for his head-butt, but not to Materazzi. 'Very hard words' had been said 'two or three times' about 'the women in his family'. He had tried to ignore them, but had not been able to. Italians felt that there was more than a little hypocrisy in this stance, and that of FIFA which immediately opened an investigation into the incident. When Francesco Totti had been provoked into spitting at Christian Poulsen of Denmark during the 2004 European Championships, nothing had been done about Poulsen's actions. The spit had cost Totti any further role in that competition. Materazzi was later given an unprecedented two-game ban by FIFA, while Zidane's head-butt cost him just a game more – irrelevant given his retirement

A disconsolate Zidane marches past
the World Cup on his way from the field.

from football. Both players confirmed that no racist comments had
been exchanged.

Without Zidane, the game drifted towards the final whistle. Penalties
would decide a World Cup final for the second time, and on both
occasions, Italy were involved. The *azzurri* – as against Holland in Euro
2000 – scored all theirs (including Materazzi with a perfect low shot)
and Trezeguet hit the bar. It was left to Fabio Grosso to smash in the
winning spot kick. Italy had won their fourth World Cup, the most of
any European side, and their first in 24 years. Only Brazil remained
ahead of them in the list of victories.

They had won it with a squad without stars, with four players from
Palermo, and where one of the team's top scorers was an ungainly
central defender who had started the competition on the bench. Above
all, they had conceded just one goal – an own goal – from open play.

It was appropriate that Fabio Cannavaro, in his hundredth game for Italy, should lift the cup. Cannavaro had been a ball-boy when Italy lost on penalties to Argentina in Naples during the 1990 World Cup. Before the game, Marcello Lippi had said that the winner would be the team which was 'hungrier' than the other. Italy was full of players who were unused to the big stage and for whom this was the chance of a lifetime. They took their opportunity. Throughout the tournament, for once, the referees had hardly been an issue. Italy had received favours and mistakes in almost equal measure – and the mistakes were seen as honest errors, not as part of a conspiracy.

Another party followed, well into the night, all over Italy. The game had achieved a 95 per cent share on television (88 per cent on state TV, 7 per cent on Sky). The *festa* contained the classic ingredients of such celebrations: bad driving, honking horns, dangerous fireworks and the inevitable tragedy (three deaths were officially put down to the partying). In a small Ligurian town, a woman called the *carabinieri* to stop her own son celebrating in the early hours of the morning. A prisoner escaped from jail in Alghero just as the penalty shoot-out began. In Turin, Gianluca Pessotto missed the match, but was 'delighted' at the news of the victory, and on their return his former team mates took the trophy to the hospital for him to see.

Although the celebrations were generally light-hearted and joyous – especially the million-strong *festa* in Rome's circus maximus – there were some disquieting aspects to the partying. In the capital, shops and signs in the former Jewish ghetto were daubed with swastikas and fascist slogans on the night when the cup returned to Italy. Anti-French feeling was whipped up by the players at various celebrations with chants of 'Who does not jump is French'. The most serious case of racism came from the regionalist ex-minister Roberto Calderoli, who had dismissed the chances of the Italian team during the tournament. The victory, said Calderoli, was a triumph of 'our' identity against a French team which contained 'blacks, Muslims and communists' and had 'sacrificed its own identity', echoing Jean-Marie Le Pen's famous comments about the French team. Journalist Mario Sconcerti was obsessed throughout the tournament with the black players in the French team. He wrote that 'Vieira is Senegalese, Makelele Congolese, Henry is Caribbean, Trezeguet is Argentinian, the other black players

are all sons of second-generation immigrants'. Nobody understood the
relevance of these points, quite apart from the fact that Henry and
Trezeguet were actually born in France. During the open-top tour of
Rome, goalkeeper Buffon waved a banner given to him by a fan. It
read 'Proud to be Italian' but carried a small neo-fascist symbol in the
corner. It may well be that Buffon did not notice the symbol, but his
previous flirtations with the language of the far right certainly created
some suspicions.

Other messages used irony: 'Give us back the Mona Lisa' read one
banner. Prime Minister Romano Prodi claimed that the victory had
'united Italy'. It was true that, for a brief moment, stars like Del Piero
and Totti were not seen as Juventus or Rome players, but Italians. On
11 July the Rolling Stones began their European tour in Milan's San
Siro stadium. Mick Jagger had famously foreseen Italy's victory in 1982,
when he danced on stage in Turin in an Italia shirt. This time his
prediction was slightly wrong (1–0 to Italy) and he refused to don a
blue top, yet the concert was Milan's answer to Rome's celebrations.
Del Piero and Materazzi paraded on stage and the penalties were shown
again on a huge screen, to crazy applause, just before the encore.

Italians generally have a light-hearted relationship with their
national symbols. It was appropriate that the song which became the
symbol of the victory was not the stuffy national anthem but this
refrain – *pooo-po-po-po-po-poo-poo* – taken from a White Stripes song
and picked up by Roma fans during the 2005–6 season. Silvio Berlusconi, the master of exploiting sport for political ends, was left fuming
as the brand-new centre-left government took all the credit. Many
Italians preferred the phrase '*Forza Azzurri*' to the traditional '*Forza
Italia*', now politicized by Berlusconi's party's name. Berlusconi's
spokesman even had the cheek to complain about the 'exploitation of
sport for political purposes'.

One outcome of the 2006 triumph was the final laying to rest of the
media obsession with the 1982 victory, which had again dominated
the World Cup coverage. It was not just the personalities involved –
Fulvio Collovati and Marco Tardelli on the RAI state channel, Paolo
Rossi on Sky – but also the 1982 *model*. Everything was compared to
the Spanish triumph – and there were calls for certain events from
1982 to be repeated, almost as if the Italians had only one way to win

a World Cup. Fabio Grosso's mad celebrations after his semi-final goal were immediately linked to 'Tardelli's scream'. After the final, the President of Italy Giorgio Napolitano was confronted with the ghost of Sandro Pertini and was even asked if he would play cards with the players on the plane home with the cup, as Pertini had done in 1982. TV commentators were concerned to copy those from the past, as was the press, unable to come up with anything more original than repetitions of 'Campioni del mondo' or 'E finita'. The front page of La Gazzetta dello Sport was more or less the same as in 1982 ('Tutto Vero. Campioni del Mondo'), while that of Tuttosport echoed Corriere dello Sport's 1982 'Eroici' ('Heroic') with an enormous 'Mitici' ('Legends'). La Gazzetta sold a record 2.3 million copies, over weeks of reprints, of its victory edition. Yet the celebrations were to be cut short very quickly, as the calciopoli trials sped on towards a conclusion in Rome.

'Without the scandal we would not have won'

GENNARO GATTUSO

'Football has experienced an institutional crisis . . . marked by a series of extremely serious and far-reaching cases of rule-breaking and cheating, involving the organizations which ran and controlled the game, some big clubs, their administrators and referees'

GUIDO ROSSI, speech to parliamentary committee, July 2006

In Italy, short revolutions have usually been followed by long periods of reaction. After the political scandals of the early 1990s, the counter-revolution was swift and brutal. Berlusconi took power, the judges were tamed and many investigations simply petered out. As recent scandals in the business world have shown – above all the collapse of the dairy company Parmalat in circumstances similar to the collapse of Enron – corrupt systems of clientelism and patronage remain untouched. In the case of calciopoli, the calls for restoration began even before the sporting trials had finished their work. Victory in the World Cup was used by many – politicians, fans, populists – to justify calls for a wholesale amnesty for the guilty parties.

Maurizio Paniz, an obscure Forza Italia parliamentarian and president of the Juventus Fan Club Montecitorio, had been the first politician to propose an amnesty for *calciopoli* if the *azzurri* managed to win the World Cup. Paniz was quickly silenced, but as the team progressed, bigger guns came into play. The most senior advocate of an amnesty for the wrongdoers was none other than Clemente Mastella, Italy's Minister for Justice, who promised that the government would not interfere although 'most fans' seemed to be asking for clemency. Mastella appealed to the emotions of those fans who had just celebrated victory. 'How could Cannavaro and Del Piero be forced to play in Serie C?' he asked. He also drew some historical comparisons: 'Should we imitate the British in 1945 who chucked out Churchill after he won the war?' Silvio Berlusconi called the sporting trials 'not serious' and argued that everything should continue as before. The individuals should pay, he claimed, but not the clubs or the fans. Large numbers of fans – especially those of the four teams involved in the scandal – agreed with him, but the majority of Italians wanted justice. As usual, Berlusconi claimed that the whole process had been part of a political conspiracy.

Italy's players had little time to enjoy their World Cup triumph. Immediately after his return from Germany, Marcello Lippi confirmed his decision to leave the national team. Roberto Donadoni, ex-Milan midfielder and Livorno manager, was appointed in his place. On a sweltering Friday evening in Rome – 14 July 2006 – the world's press gathered outside a luxury hotel to await the verdicts of the federation court. They were joined by 200 or so Lazio fans and a number of *carabinieri*. Cesare Ruperto read out the sentence to the assorted hacks after more than an hour's delay. Later, a 154-page document was issued to lawyers in order to prepare an appeal. The shock was great. Juventus had been stripped of two titles – which were not assigned to any club for 2004–5, with the decision left up to the federation for the 2005–6 *scudetto* – and were relegated to Serie B with a massive 30-point deduction. Lazio and Fiorentina were also sent down, with 7- and 12-point deductions respectively. Milan, meanwhile, had managed to remain in Serie A, but were to start the following season 15 points behind the others. They were also removed from all European competitions although they tried to re-enter the UEFA Cup through a loophole in the decision. As for the individuals involved, many of the referees were cleared and only Moggi and Giraudo from Juve were recommended for life bans.

Harsh with the clubs, the sporting authorities had been relatively lenient with administrators and officials. The fines imposed were a little incongruous, given the vast sums which the clubs were set to lose as a result of these measures. In their verdict, the judges disagreed with magistrates in Naples. There had not been a 'cupola' of power, or even a 'system', but rather a 'network' which worked outside of the rules in order to 'alter the impartiality of referees' and was 'a long way from the spirit of loyalty and correctness which should be at the foundation of all sport'. Corruption and cheating had perhaps not been the product of a system, but they had certainly been *systematic*, the judges concluded. Juventus were praised for their attempts at a new beginning. Unlike the other clubs involved in the scandal, Juve had actually got rid of the culprits and had promised a new 'ethical code' for its future business.

All the clubs involved announced that they would appeal. Some commentators wrote that the harsh sentences would be modified on appeal – especially the strong points deduction for Juventus, which effectively condemned the club to two years in Serie B and therefore a probable three years outside of European competition. Frantic calculations were carried out. If Juventus did as well as they had done last season in Serie A, they could still make the play-offs. Most fans felt that the sentences were extremely hard on Fiorentina and Lazio, and relatively soft on Juventus and Milan. In any case, all the clubs involved promised that they would go to the state administrative courts (and even the European court) for a final judgement. The whole process was likely to drag on for the whole summer, delaying the start of the next championship.

Meanwhile things were getting very nasty indeed in the press. After a long period of silence, Moggi began to send out a series of threatening messages in the media. In a long interview with *La Repubblica*, he promised that he was in a 'new phase of my life – an angry phase. I will return to the world of football as a ball-breaker. I will name all those false moralists who think that this world is clean merely because it has been freed of Luciano Moggi and Antonio Giraudo.' Moggi attacked Inter and Milan and assorted journalists, and claimed that his activities with Juve had been in the defence of the interests of the club.

On a sweltering hot day at the end of July, the appeal verdicts were announced, after a swift two-day 'trial'. As expected, all the clubs received better news. Lazio and Fiorentina were back in Serie A, with strong points deductions (–11 and –19 points respectively), although both lost their European spots they had gained from the 2005–6 season. Milan were more or less cleared of any wrongdoing: they were allowed into the Champions League and would start the next season with a mere 8-point deduction. The real losers remained Juventus, who would still start the next season in Serie B, but with their point deduction commuted from 30 to 17. They were also stripped of their last two *scudetti*. Inter were awarded the 2005–6 championship – a kind of consolation prize for all the trophies which had been 'stolen' from them in the past. Very few referees ended up paying any price at all. The appeal court decided that this was a system of corruption which largely involved Juventus, and had been controlled by Luciano Moggi and Antonio Giraudo. The other clubs were bit-part players, scrapping around for favours. Many commentators attacked the new verdict as a 'typically Italian' whitewash. *La Gazzetta dello Sport* agreed: after the first trial their headline had read 'Big Sting' ('*Stangatona*'), now it was 'Little Sting' ('*Stangatina!*').

The story was far from over, however, as a series of appeals to Italy's administrative tribunals were launched. These tribunals only had the power to order a new sporting trial, not to challenge any of the verdicts. It seemed like the protagonists of the scandal – especially Milan – had been let off lightly, but the richest and most successful club in Italy had been hit hard, and it would not be easy for Juventus to get back into the top flight. Italian football, whatever happened over the summer, would never be the same again.

In the wake of the scandal, the biggest transfer market of the century opened in earnest. Every Juventus player was up for grabs – except for club icons Alessandro Del Piero and Gigi Buffon, who had promised to stay with Juve. One key figure – Fabio Capello, the Juventus manager – had already jumped ship to Real Madrid in early July, and used the sale to recruit two of his former players, Cannavaro and Emerson, while Zambrotta and Thuram went to Barcelona. Fiorentina were also set to lose a number of their stars. With Torino in Serie A, Juventus in

Serie B and tiny Chievo Verona in the Champions League, the 2006–7 season would certainly be an interesting one. Juventus's pre-season training started badly, as rival *ultrà* fans (all of them Juve supporters) turned up not to back their team but to engage in vicious fighting, with knives. It was said that the conflict was over the control of the new stadium. The problems at the heart of the game – violence, racism, financial impropriety – were still ever-present.

Italy's stunning World Cup victory could not obscure a deep and structural crisis in the game. Italian football, and Italian society, are at a point of no return. It was difficult even to separate the success on the pitch from the scandals. Marcello Lippi had worked with Moggi for seven years at Juventus, winning five championships. That was a team which also contained Zinedine Zidane, Alessandro Del Piero and many other World Cup stars. Fabio Cannavaro had defended Moggi as the scandal broke, claiming that the Juve man had 'worked well' in his time at the club. There were also strong doubts about the background to the bizarre transfer of Cannavaro to Moggi's Juventus in 2003. Did the players know what had been going on, or were they simply puppets in an elaborate mise en scène? By 2006 Italian domestic football had become very similar to another very popular TV 'sport' – American professional wrestling: violent, over-the-top, ridiculous, hysterical and completely fake. In the past, the well-worn tactics of cover-up, delay and confusion have been employed in the face of scandal. This time there has to be a new beginning. It is quite possible, however, that there will be no long-term changes as a result of this affair.

Too much is at stake for a real revolution to take place. Moggi's system was not just about football. Power in Italy – as in many nations – allows you to procure favours, bypass rules, regulations and normal procedures and obtain undeserved help and services. Moggi could help his friends jump the queue in hospitals, or get state officials to look after his acquaintances on shopping trips. His power stretched way beyond the football field. Moggi was right in at least this one respect: the removal of one man, or one team, won't do away with the culture that created the system.

# NOTES

## Chapter 1

1 'Its re-inventors were English', *Storia critica del calcio italiano*, Baldini & Castoldi, Milan, 1975, p. 8.

2 The inscription reads: *Here lived the English Doctor James R. Spensley sportsman – a great friend of Italy – a football pioneer with the Genoa Cricket and Foot Ball Club, founder of Genoese scouting. Genoa Local Council and Genoa 1893, 1977.* For Genoa's origins see also Pietro Cheli, 'Genoa, e fu subito football', *Diario della settimana*, 29.8.2003, pp. 43–47.

3 Savage, according to the *Dizionario del calcio italiano*, also played for Juventus and imported the first real football from England, Volume 1, Baldini & Castoldi, Milan, 2000, p. 477.

4 *Storia del calcio in Italia*, Einaudi, Turin, 1990, p. 26.

5 Two years later, an Italian anarchist and emigrant – Gaetano Bresci – came back from the USA with a specific mission – to execute the King and avenge the victims of May 1898. He assassinated King Umberto I in a Monza street on 29 July 1900.

6 Goodley later officiated over Italy's first ever international fixture, in Milan in 1910.

7 Other versions of this same, semi-mythical event replace Notts County with Newcastle, and Goodley with the scorer of the first official goal in Italian football, John Savage.

8 Marco Cassardo, *Belli e dannati, Il popolo granata e l'arte della pazienza*, Limina, Arezzo, 2003, p. 5.

9 This is apparently the version of Richard Barnett, Professor of Religious History at Cambridge University and great-grandson of Charles Barnett, who was amongst the founders of Milan; see A. Papa and G. Panico, *Storia sociale del calcio in Italia*, Il Mulino, Bologna, 2002, p. 99.

10 Kilpin's success at Milan did not, however, herald a period of sustained dominance of the Italian game. Milan won nothing, apart from a minor cup competition, between 1907 and 1951.

11 *Lo Sport Illustrato*, 1.11.1916.

12 Inter adopted a stylized symbol designed, it is said, by Muggiani.

13 The details of this 'lost' tour have been reconstructed thanks to the painstaking work of Reading fan Ray Curry.

14 After 1914 some of Italy's English players and managers had left Italy to take part in the war – Spensley, as we have seen, died in Germany in 1915, Goodley fought at Flanders and it is sometimes said that Genoa's English manager William 'Willy' Garbutt – who had been in the army in his youth – fought on the Somme. However, no records to support this claim exist. Many other less famous players never made it back to Italy.

15 Papa and Panico, *Storia sociale del calcio in Italia*, p. 104.

16 *Storia del calcio in Italia*, Einaudi, Turin, 1990, p. 30.

17 *Storia del calcio*, p. 51.

18 *Storia del calcio*, p. 51.

19 Andreina Rastello and Lorenzina Opezzo, 'Vercelli: 1922–1927. Nascita e organizzazione del fascismo', *L'impegno*, I, April 1981.

20 James Walvin, *The People's Game. The History of Football Revisited*, Mainstream, Edinburgh, 2000, p. 84.

21 Gianni Brera puts Garbutt's income at 24,000 lire a year – this at a time when a worker in northern Italy would earn just 2–3 lire a day – but, as historian Pierre Lanfranchi points out, this is certainly an over-estimate; 'Mister Garbutt, il primo professionista', FIGC, *NewsLetter*, n. 4, June 2000, n. 9.

22 Aristodemo Santamaria and Enrico Sardi were the players involved.

23 Genoa were awarded this championship, posthumously, in 1919, despite the fact that they were still catchable by at least two clubs when the tournament was suspended.

24 The press mentioned 'scotch whisky he imported directly from England' (sic.).

25 Garbutt was the first manager in Italy to adopt the tactics of the 'system' in place of the old 'method'. See Simon Martin, *Football and Fascism. The National Game under Mussolini*, Berg, Oxford, 2004, pp. 200–204 for a discussion of early tactics.

26 There is some historical debate over the origins of the term. Football historians Papa and Panico claim that it was another English manager – Robert Spottiswood at Inter – who inspired the new term, which survived fascist attempts to Italianize football language; *Storia sociale del calcio*, p. 148 and p. 318.

27 Much of this account is based on the detailed research of Biagio Angrisani, *Mister. William Thomas Garbutt*, Edizioni La Campanella, Rome, 2004,

and Pierre Lanfranchi, '"Mister Garbutt": The First European Manager', *The Sports Historian*, 22 (1), May 2002, pp. 44–60.

28 'Mister Garbutt', p. 45.

29 They soon became blue, their colour to this day.

30 This record would stand for more than thirty years, until ten of the unbeatable Torino team of the 1940s turned out for Italy in April 1947.

31 Ex-Vercelli players still made significant contributions to Italy's 1934 and 1938 World Cup victories.

32 For this whole affair see also the account in Martin, *Football and Fascism*, pp. 52–5 and 72–3.

33 The star was introduced in 1958, just in time for Juve's tenth championship victory.

34 For a full and fascinating account of Arpinati's sporting career see Martin, *Football and Fascism*, pp. 109–140.

35 For more details on the strike see Martin, *Football and Fascism*, pp. 55–8.

36 The shift towards a working-class game had already taken place in England in the 1880s; Walvin, *The People's Game*, chapter 3.

37 The plaque reads: Working-class Bologna/honouring at the same time its heroic sons who fell during the twenty-year-long antifascist struggle with this stone consecrates/ANTEO ZAMBONI/who thanks to his audacious love of liberty/was here brutally killed on the 31.10.1926/young martyr/by the dictatorship's hired killers. See also Martin, *Football and Fascism*, pp. 130–132.

38 For the whole story see Brunella della Casa, *Attentato al duce. Le molte storie del caso Zamboni*, Il Mulino, Bologna, 2000.

39 Juventus and Milan were not alone. Later, the Cinzano family (as in the famous drink) helped to finance Torino, Juve's great rivals.

## Chapter 2

1 This usage dates from the 1970s: 'In political propaganda of the 1970s, and particularly graffiti, k. was often used instead of c. in order to indicate militarism and repressive violence (perhaps with reference to the frequent use of the letter k. in German, and the Nazi era)'; Garzanti, *Grandi dizionari, Italiano*, Milan, 2000, p. 1173.

2 Luca Cardinalini, *Cornuti e mazziati. La dura vita degli arbitri*, Collezione Biblioteca Umoristica Mondadori, Milan, 2001.

3 V. Foa and P. Ginsborg (eds), *Le virtù della Repubblica*, Il Saggiatore, Milan, 1994.

4 *Storia critica*, p. 46.

5 *Storia critica*, p. 46.

6 W. Gallie, the moral philosopher, first used this idea in 1956. Some of his examples were from the world of sport; 'Essentially Contested Concepts', in *Proceedings of the Aristotelian Society*, 56 (n.s.), 1956, pp. 167–220.

7 Paul Ginsborg, *Italy and its Discontents. Family, Civil Society, State, 1980–2001*, Penguin, London, p. 113.

8 He was wrong, by the way.

9 Giovanni Arpino and Alfio Caruso, *Area di rigore*, SEI, Turin, 1979.

10 One of the most eloquent expositions of this thesis was by Italo Calvino, 'Apologo sull'onestà nel paese dei corrotti', *La Repubblica*, 15.3.1980.

11 Jürgen Habermas, *Legitimation Crisis*, Polity, Cambridge, 1988, p. 46.

12 See, for example, http://www.fanofunny.com/mondiali2002/.

13 Bertotto was a 'designator', who were and are ex-referees who take part in the selection of individual referees for matches.

14 An exception to this rule was the brief period in the mid-1980s when Milan twice ended up in Serie B.

15 Simone Stenti, *Elogio del furto*, Gli speciali di Linea Bianca, 2004.

16 For *dietrologia* see Tobias Jones, *The Dark Heart of Italy: Travels Through Time and Space Across Italy*, Faber and Faber, 2003.

17 See chapter 1.

18 Examples include Pro Vercelli putting out their boys' team in protest in 1910, the Inter–Juve 1961 'pitch invasion' controversy, the 1964 doping debates. All of these cases are discussed elsewhere in this book.

19 For more details see chapter 9.

20 A similar technique is used for the Italian lottery – where numbered balls are drawn out of containers by blind or blindfolded children – although even this system was hit by corruption in the 1990s.

21 Moreover, individual referees could not preside over the same team for more than five games a season.

22 Vittorio Zambardino, 'Cara mamma, giù le mani dall'arbitro', *La Repubblica*, 17.2.1993.

23 Palumbo wrote that he wasn't sure if Lo Bello was 'proud of, or irritated by' these chants.

24 For a full explanation of the 'umbrella gesture' see the glossary.

25 For the concept of trust see the invaluable work of Diego Gambetta (ed.), *Trust: Making and Breaking Co-operative Relations*, Blackwell, Oxford, 1988.

26 The game was Juventus–Milan, 20.2.1972.

27 *Diario della Settimana* now at www.fondazionegiuseppelazzati.it.

28 Championships and other positions are not decided on goal difference in Italy. If two teams are level on points, a playoff (*spareggio*) is used to decide the winner.

29 Mario Sconcerti, 'Anche l'arbitro si inchina alla Juve' ('The referee also bows to Juve'), *La Repubblica*, 18.5.1982.

30 Leonardo Coen, Peter Gomez, Leo Sisti, *Piedi Puliti*, Garzanti, Milan, 1998.

31 There had been occasional precedents. In 1986 a group of Salernitana fans accused a referee of 'fraud' after a game in which he had sent off four

members of their team, disallowed a Salernitana goal and allowed a goal for their opponents which was probably offside. The fans requested that the investigating magistrate view the film of the game and the referee's report.

32 It appeared, in fact, in thirteen countries.

33 'Pierluigi Collina', *Observer Sports Monthly*, 20.6.2004; 'Io arbitro protagonista? No, solo uno che decide', *La Repubblica*, 9.6.2004.

34 *Le mie regole del gioco, Quello che il calcio mi ha insegnato della vita*, Mondadori, Milan, 2003, p. 125.

35 *Observer Sports Monthly*, 20.6.2004, and *La Repubblica*, 9.6.2004.

36 This optimism was misplaced. In 2005 Collina resigned after protests concerning his advertising work with Opel, also the sponsor of A. C. Milan.

## Chapter 3

1 Darwin Pastorin, 'Juve. Il gusto di vincere', *La Repubblica*, 6.5.2002.

2 Juventus won their first *scudetto* in 1905 and their second only in 1925–26. In the 72 seasons in which championships have been awarded since 1929, by 2005 Juventus had won 27 titles, as well as finishing second 15 times and third 8 times. They have never been close to Serie B. In more than two thirds of all league tables since 1926, Juve have been in the top three, in addition to winning numerous Italian cups and European competitions. This was despite a gap of fifteen years between 1935 and 1950, and another between 1952 and 1959. Five championships in a row went to Juventus between 1931 and 1936, and seven in ten years in the 1970s and early 1980s. By the start of the 2005–6 season, Milan had won 11 fewer championships, Inter 15 fewer.

3 *L'immigrazione meridionale a Torino*, Feltrinelli, Milan, 1975.

4 Papa and Panico, *Storia sociale del calcio*, p. 275.

5 Pastorin, 'Juve. Il gusto di vincere'.

6 See Massimo Raffaeli, 'Gli autogol dei dominati', *Il Manifesto*, 16.12.2003.

7 Gerhard Vinnai, *Il calcio come ideologia (Sport e alienazione nel mondo capitalista)*, Guaraldi, Rimini, 2003, cited in Raffaeli, 'Gli autogol dei dominati'. Football has also been seen by many historians – especially of the English game – as intrinsically linked to the rules, discipline and organization of modern industrial society.

8 Roberto Baggio had been called Raffaello by Agnelli, but that nickname failed to stick. More people remember Agnelli's criticism of Baggio after a poor performance in a rainy UEFA Cup match: *'coniglio bagnato'* (wet rabbit).

9 Club presidents are not always the club owners, although they can be the same person. The equivalent in the English game is the chairman.

10 Carlo Parola in 1976, Carlo Ancelotti in 2001.

11 Eighteen of the victims were players: Valerio Bacigalupo (25), goal-keeper; Aldo Ballarin (27), full-back; Dino Ballarin (23), goalkeeper; Emile Bongiorni (27), wing-back; Eusebio Castigliano (27), midfield; Rubens Fadini (21), midfield; Gugliemo Gabetto (33), centre-forward; Ruggero Grava (27), centre-forward; Giuseppe Grezar (30), midfield; Ezio Loik (29), wing-back; Virgilio Maroso (23), full-back; Danilo Martelli (25), midfield; Valentino Mazzola (30), wing-back; Romeo Menti (30), winger; Pierino Operto (22), full-back; Franco Ossola (27), winger; Mario Riga-monti (26), defender; Julius Schubert (26), wing-half. One player was not there – Sauro Tomà, who had been injured most of the season. Club president Ferruccio Novo had missed the trip due to illness. The other thirteen dead were made up of non-playing staff from the club: directors Rinaldo Agnisetta and Ippolito Civalleri; manager Egri Erbstein, the Hungarian who had masterminded Torino's success, English trainer Leslie Lievesley and masseur Ottavio Cortina. Three journalists were also on the plane – Renato Casalbore (*Tuttosport*), Luigi Cavallero (*La Stampa*) and Renato Tosatti (*La Gazzetta del Popolo*). Finally, there was the tour organizer – Andrea Bonaiuti – and the crew; pilots Pierluigi Meroni and Cesare Biancardi and flight engineers Antonio Pangrazi and Celestino D'Inca.

12 *Corriere Lombardo*, 5–6.5.1949.

13 In that time they won 132 out of 186 games, losing a mere 22 matches.

14 'Da Superga a Fiesole. La nuova lettura dell'art. 2043 C.C. da parte delle Sezioni Unite della Cassazione', *P. Q. M.*, III/99.

15 The fourth team in the group – India – failed to turn up and only one team went through from each group. Sweden already had three points (one win, one draw) by the time Italy played their last game. Italy were still the holders.

16 Of course, this kind of thing does not only happen in Italy. Munich 'songs' have taunted Manchester United fans for years.

17 Le Corbusier called the view 'the most beautiful in the world'. To the right, down in the valley, the vast expanse of the Fiat Mirafiori plant – which once employed 60,000 workers and now gives work to only a quarter of that number – can be clearly picked out.

18 On 2 September 1706, so the story goes, Prince Vittorio Amedeo II of the Savoy royal family climbed the hill at Superga to observe the positions of the Franco-Spanish armies which had been laying siege to Turin for four months. Again, according to legend, at that moment, he promised in the small church there to build a great temple on that spot if the French army was defeated. This promise, allegedly, came in front of a wooden statue of the Madonna now conserved in the basilica. The work was remarkable, involving amongst other things the lowering of the summit of the hill by over 40 metres to create space for the new church. Building began in

1717 and the basilica was not inaugurated until 1731 (when it was still unfinished).

19  This may now be about to change. One of the places visited by the Savoy dynasty on their return to Italy in 2003 was Superga, along with the tombs of many princes and kings which are housed here in a separate mausoleum.

20  See Illustration 13, p. 96.

21  The bibliography on the *Grande Torino* and Superga is huge. There is even an excellent volume in English dedicated to the tragedy. Alexandra Manna and Mike Gibbs, *The Day Italian Football Died. Torino and the Tragedy of Superga*, Breedon Books, Derby, 2000.

22  In terms of football history, some of this legendary status is exaggerated. Only five of those who died had actually won all five championships (Mazzola, Ossola, Gabetto, Loik and Grezar). Not all of the *Grande Torino* team died at Superga, as is often claimed. Four of the dead, Aldo Ballarin, Bacigalupo, Castigliano, Rigamonti and Maroso, had won four championships each, Menti and Martelli three, whilst Fadini, Grava, Operto, Bongiorni and Schubert were young players with only a handful of first-team games between them. The third-choice goalkeeper, Ballarin's brother (known as Ballarin II), had never turned out for the first team. Important *Grande Torino* players not involved in the Superga disaster included Pietro Ferraris II, who retired the year before the crash.

23  The oldest player to die was Gabetto, 33, followed by Grezar and Mazzola, 30, and Loik, 29.

24  One recent example was the feature film dedicated to the story, called *Ora e per sempre* (Director Vincenzo Verdecchi), released in 2005. Streets have also been named after various members of the team in Rome, Chioggia (near Venice) and many other Italian cities. Two stadiums carry the names of Superga victims: the Romeo Menti stadium in Vicenza and the Mario Rigamonti in Brescia. A mini-series transmitted on Italian TV in 2005 attracted record audiences.

25  The most famous sporting curse of all involves the Boston Red Sox. When Babe Ruth was sold by Boston to the New York Yankees in 1920 he allegedly told the Red Sox that they would never win the world series title again. This was known as the 'curse of the bambino'; see http://bambinoscurse.com/whatis/. The Red Sox finally 'lifted' the curse by winning the 2004 world series. The Chicago Cubs suffer from the 'curse of the Billy Goat'. This relates to a fan who was not allowed into a game with his goat in 1945, and responded angrily by saying that the team would never win a world series again. He has been right, so far.

26  Even when the cup was finally won, Torino did it the hard way. 3–0 up after the first leg, they went to Rome and lost 5–2. Midfielder Giuseppe Giannini scored three penalties for Roma and even hit the post near the end.

27  A new, violent and right-wing side to Torino support emerged. On the

night of 19 July 1997 a 21-year-old Moroccan man, Abdellah Doumi, drowned in the Po river in Turin's city centre. The man had been chased by at least ten young Italians and, whilst in the water, not only had they not come to his aid, but had pelted him with bottles, rocks, wooden boxes and even a vacuum-cleaner. Those responsible were arrested almost immediately – 24-year-old Piero Iavarone and three of his friends. At their first trial Iavarone and the other three were convicted of murder and sentenced to 22 years in prison. After a long campaign in their favour, this sentence was greatly reduced on appeal – to just nine years. Piero's brother, Paolo, a far-right activist and member of the *Granata Corps* group linked to the Torino football team, had originally been accused of the murder. *Corriere della Sera*, 20.7.1997.

28 Apart from the loss of their ground, this shift carried an extra humiliation. By a strange twist of fate, Juve's hard core had already made the end of the ground known as the 'Filadelfia *curva*' their own, leaving the 'Maratona *curva*' to the Torino faithful.

29 In 2006, a sparkling new stadium was due to open as part of the Winter Olympics rebuilding programmes.

## Chapter 4

1 This is common in big Italian cities, such as Turin (since 1963), Genoa (since 1946) and Rome (since the 1940s and then since the 1950s at the Olympic Stadium). San Siro was built for Milan by the Pirelli company in the late 1920s and expanded for the 1990 World Cup. For a long time, Inter played in the central Arena stadium.

2 Danilo Sarugia, *Grande Inter «Figlia di Dio». La leggendaria squadra di Moratti e Herrera*, Limina, Arezzo, 1996.

3 Guido Liguori and Antonio Smargiasse, *Calcio e neocalcio. Geopolitica e prospettive del football in Italia*, Il Manifesto, Rome, 2003, p. 25.

4 Beppe Severgnini, *Interismi. Il piacere di essere neroazzurri*, Rizzoli, Milan, 2002; *Altri interismi. Un nuovo viaggio nel favoloso labirinto neroazzurro*, Rizzoli, Milan, 2003. See also Fausto Bertolini, *La maledizione sotto porta. Un maleficio incombe sull'Inter?* Garassino, Milan, 2003.

5 *Basta perdere. Ventuno scrittori raccontano la loro insana passione per l'Inter*, Limina, Arezzo, 2002; Roberto Carli and Ronaldo Crespi, *Minimo Moratti. I disastri di un presidente*, Limina, Arezzo, 2003.

6 Sergio Scalpelli quoted in *La Repubblica*, 24.2.2001.

7 *Non vincete mai. Dedicato agli Inter-tristi*, New Editing Libri, Milan, 2003.

8 This chant has right-wing undertones. *Boia chi molla!* – death to those who give up – was a popular neo-fascist slogan in the 1970s.

9 Mussolini's reputation as a Lazio fan is rather undermined by these rumours, however.

10 The gesture was praised by Alessandra Mussolini, Benito's granddaughter,

as 'beautiful'. Di Canio angrily rebuked the right-wing politician and claimed that his 'celebrations' had 'nothing to do with politics'.. At first, Di Canio denied that he had done anything at all until photos were issued which were difficult to disprove. Later, Di Canio defended his 'gesture' in a book published in 2005 as 'instinctive . . . not premeditated or political . . . a moment of exaltation'; cited in Francesco Luti, 'Di Canio: "Io calciatore fascista"', *L'Unità*, 25.6.2005.

11  Liguori and Smargiasse, *Calcio e neocalcio*, p. 25.
12  Liguori and Smargiasse, *Calcio e neocalcio*.
13  Many thanks to Nick Dines for this information and for copies of the photos. Nick's seminal work on contemporary Naples will be published by Berghahn in 2006.
14  Amalia Signorelli, *Antropologia urbana. Introduzione alla ricerca in Italia*, Guerini, Milan, 1996, p. 181.
15  *La Repubblica*, 11.5.1987.
16  For the story of the DAMM see Nick Dines, 'Centri sociali: occupazioni autogestite a Napoli negli anni novanta', *Quaderni di sociologia*, 43, 1999, pp. 90–111.
17  *Storia sociale del calcio*, p. 374.
18  *The Life of Maradona*, Bloomsbury, 1996.
19  'In search of Dieguito', *The Guardian*, 1.10.2004.

## Chapter 5

1  For example Buffon, Toldo, Peruzzi, Rossi, Pagliuca, Marchegiani, Cudicini, Antonioli and Abbiati.
2  Its real meaning is closer to 'lock' – in reality the piece of metal used to close a door lock.
3  *The Miracle of Castel di Sangro*, Little, Brown and Company, Boston, 1999.
4  Papa and Panico, *Storia sociale*, p. 255.
5  The player in question was Alberto Piccinini, who went on to win two championships with Juventus.
6  But some astute analysts have noted signs of *defensivism* in the pre-war Inter of the late 1920s.
7  Some claim that Egri Erbstein's teams played a kind of total football, and the same claim is occasionally made for some of Fulvio Bernardini's teams in the 1950s and 1960s.
8  Gianni Brera had a difficult relationship with HH. He once wrote that he wouldn't even trust Herrera with managing his wine cellar, let alone a football club. But Brera admired the Inter team and even claimed that he personally had encouraged Herrera to move towards *catenaccio* after a defeat against Padova in 1961. See Gianni Brera, *Herrera*, Longanesi, 1966. Other good sources for Herrera are his autobiography, *My Life*, and Sarugia, *Grande Inter. 'Figlia di Dio'*.

9  The protest concerned a league decision after a pitch invasion during a crucial Juventus–Inter fixture.

10  For Picchi's life see the excellent Nando Della Chiesa, *Capitano, mio capitano. La leggenda di Armando Picchi, livornese nerazzurro*, Limina, Arezzo, 1999.

11  *Dizionario del calcio*, p. 419.

12  For once this epithet was not invented by Gianni Brera but by another journalist, Gualtiero Zanetti.

13  Picchi's death is often included amongst a series of suspicious deaths in some ways linked to widespread doping in the game in the 1960s.

14  One end of his ex-club's stadium was later named after him.

15  *Me Grand Turin*, Graphot editrice, Turin, 1998; *Vecchio cuore granata*, Graphot editrice, Turin, 1988.

16  *Me Grand Turin*, 1988, p. 126.

17  *Il più mancino dei tiri*, Il Mulino, Bologna, 1995, p. 101.

18  *Dizionario del Calcio*, edited by the Redazione della Gazzetta dello Sport, Rizzoli, Milan, 1990, p. 177.

## Chapter 6

1  *Regista* is also the Italian word for film or theatre director.

2  *Un tocco in più*, written with Oreste del Buono, Rizzoli, Milan, 1966.

3  Del Buono and Rivera, *Un tocco in più*, p. 138.

4  *Storia del calcio*, p. 311.

5  Gianni Brera, 'Rivera, rendimi il mio abatino' [Rivera, give me back my abatino], *La Repubblica*, 23.6.1985.

6  Above all *Ragazzi di Vita* (1955), *Accattone* (1960) and *Mamma Roma* (1962).

7  A full account of this fascinating tale can be found in Brian Glanville, *Champions of Europe*, pp. 105–6.

8  Valentino had 're-married' in 1949, just ten days before Superga, after obtaining a divorce in Romania. This option was something available only to rich Italians – divorce was illegal in Italy until 1974. The divorce, which had been contested by the Italian courts, attributed Sandro to the care of his father, whilst Ferruccio (the younger of the two) was to stay in Cassano d'Adda with his mother. In April 1948 Turin's appeal court validated the divorce, but the state appealed that decision, sending the case up to the high court in Rome. A final decision had still not been made before Superga intervened. In June (after Superga) the high court annulled the divorce, thereby making Mazzola's second marriage null and void. This bitter family split was raked over in the moralist press.

9  Ferruccio Mazzola, *Il terzo incomodo. Le pesanti verità di Ferruccio Mazzola. Una vita nel pallone fra intrighi e intrugli, colpi bassi e morti non chiarite*, Bradipolibri, 2004.

10 One headline summed up this idea: 'Mazzola? If he was called Pettirossi he would be playing for Pavia'.

11 The literal translation comes out as 'variety artist', so the term may have slightly negative origins.

12 This nickname was given to him by the Israeli team manager after a game against Italy in 1961.

13 Il Mulino, Bologna, 1995.

14 'He bent his left arm, with the hand closed in a fist, and he slapped his right palm on the inside of the elbow', Gianni Brera, *Storia critica*, p. 328.

15 Calimero was also black, as in the popular advertising slogan about him being 'little and black'.

16 The film was *La Riffa*, part of the episode movie *Boccaccio 70* (1962).

17 In 2004 Romero wrote about the accident for the first time, in a short piece for the magazine *L'Europeo*. Attilio Romero, 'Ho travolto il mio mito', *L'Europeo*, 2004, 1.

18 Nando Dalla Chiesa, *La farfalla granata. La meravigliosa e melanconica storia di Gigi Meroni, il calciatore artista*, Limina, Arezzo, 1995. This was the book that launched a new series of excellent football books in Italy, many of them published by the small publishing house Limina, based in Arezzo in Tuscany. Cesare Fiume has also written a lovely essay on Meroni, in his *Storie esemplari di piccoli eroi. Lo sport dell'Italia di ieri*, Feltrinelli, Milan, 1996.

19 Baggio also took four penalties after extra-time in his career, missing only one – the most famous of all – in the World Cup final in 1994.

20 Journalists dubbed their partnership *B2*, a play on words linked to *P2*, a Masonic lodge in the news at the time.

21 Roberto Baggio, *Una porta nel cielo. Un'autobiografia*, Limina, Arezzo, 2001, and *Il sogno dopo*, Limina, Arezzo, 2003.

22 Up to the end of the 2005 season.

23 Emilio Marrese, *Zola. Il ragazzo che faceva sorridere il pallone*, Limina, Arezzo, 2003, p. 177.

## Chapter 7

1 'A lightning fast dart beyond the full-backs, a brief sprint towards the goal . . . a light scornful flick into the corner just inside the post', *Storia critica*, p. 108.

2 '*La donzelletta vien dalla campagna leggendo* La Gazzetta dello Sport *e come ogni ragazza va pazza per Meazza che fa reti di fox-trot*'; 'The damsel comes from the countryside reading *La Gazzetta dello Sport* and like every girl she goes crazy for Meazza who scores goals with a fox-trot'.

3 The historical origins of the term lay in the name of the young hero of a 1746 revolt in Genoa against Austrian rule.

4 *Storia critica*, p. 104

5 Since Meazza, Silvio Piola and Nereo Rocco have also had stadiums named after them in their much smaller home-towns – Vercelli and Trieste respectively – and many other stadiums have taken the names of local players or presidents.

6 Ettore Brera, a journalist from Vercelli.

7 The six goals is a Serie A record held jointly with Omar Sivori, who scored his six against Inter in 1961.

8 *Tutto il calcio parola per parola*, Riuniti, Rome, 1997, p. 166.

9 Dario Piola, his son, called him this. It translates roughly as anti-star, and has been used for other similar figures in the entertainment and sporting worlds.

10 Emilio Violanti cited in Marco Barberis, *La leggenda di Silvio Piola*, Sugarco, Milan, 1986.

11 Eraldo Monzeglio was the honest defender. Monzeglio – who won two World Cups with Italy – also had the dubious honour of coaching Mussolini at tennis, a sport at which the dictator was notoriously terrible.

12 Maurizio Crosetti, 'Orfani di Piola, il signore del gol', *La Repubblica*, 5.10.1996.

13 Both Novara and Pro Vercelli named their small stadiums after him, making Piola the only player to have two stadiums – in the same region – carrying his name.

14 The playwright, actor and Nobel Prize winner Dario Fo was born just down the lake from Riva, and claims that he is distantly related to the player.

15 The nickname was first coined by Brera whilst he was assigning a mark to Riva in October 1970 in the *Guerin Sportivo* magazine.

16 One story that Riva tells is that after the 1966 defeat against North Korea at the World Cup (where Riva was in the squad but never played) a taxi driver in Milan refused to have him in his cab. There are a number of books on Riva, many of them dating from the 1970s; see, for example, Bruno Bernardi, *Rombo di tuono. Storia e leggenda di Gigi Riva*, Arnoldo Mondadori, Milan, 1977.

17 Riva had his own sex scandal to deal with, and it came at the worst possible time, during the 1970 World Cup. His affair with Gianna Tofanari, wife of a Sardinian businessman and mother of an eight-year-old boy, filled the pages of the popular Italian trash gossip press. Rumours spread, during the tournament, that Riva's 'disappointing' performances were due to his relationship with Tofanari. Years later, Riva had two sons with her.

18 *Dal Riva in + al 1/2 Rivera*, Editrice Japigia, Bari, 1970, p. 139.

19 Stefano Boldrini, *Professione gol. La straordinaria vita di Gigi Riva*, Limina, Arezzo, 1999, p. 135.

20 Including a play by Vito Biolchini, *Rombo di Tuono, scudetto e petrolio 25 anni fa* (1995).

21 Giampiero Boniperti later said that he had tried for four years to sign Riva for Juventus. 'Every time he played in the north of Italy I would ring him up.'

22 Maurizio Crosetti, 'Il miracolo di Riva', *La Repubblica*, 27.12.2003.

23 *Un tiro mancino. Riva, il Cagliari e uno scudetto che non finisce mai*, Fratelli Frilli Editori, Genoa, 2001, p. 85.

24 Riva has always refused to alienate some of his fans by going into politics. Silvio Berlusconi offered Gigi a candidature for his centre-right coalition in 2004. After thinking about it for some time, Riva turned the richest man in Italy down.

25 Paolo Rossi, *Ho fatto piangere il Brasile. Un'autobiografia* (with Antonio Finco), Limina, Arezzo, 2002.

26 Italian transfer rules at the time allowed two clubs to own the same player, a kind of contractually-based loan system.

27 Both goals came in one game: the derby, and they were his first for nine and a half months.

## Chapter 8

1 All managers have been men in the Italian professional game, with one exception. In June 1999 controversial football entrepreneur Luciano Gaucci appointed (and then sacked) the greatest Italian female football player of all time – Carolina Morace – as manager of one of his teams: Viterbese from Viterbo near Rome.

2 Managers in Italy are expected to be technically proficient. They are required to take an official training course to get a managing licence. Thus, there have hardly ever been player-managers in the Italian championship.

3 The owner is not always the president. Owners tended to be presidents in the 1960s, 1970s and 1980s. Since then the roles have sometimes separated. Silvio Berlusconi devolved this job to Galliani in the 1990s, Massimo Moratti later appointed Giacinto Facchetti as president of Inter.

4 Jimmy Greaves, *Greavsie. The Autobiography*, Time Warner, London, 2003, p. 133.

5 For these laws see John Foot, *Modern Italy*, Palgrave, 2003, chapter 2.

6 Fiora Gandolfi Herrera, *Tacalabala, Esercizi di magia di Helenio Herrera*, Tapiro, Venice, 2002. I would like to thank Fiora Gandolfi Herrera for her help with obtaining material on Herrera.

7 Brera, *Herrera*. Herrera was not fond of Brera, once calling him 'servile' and 'a drunken sclerotic'.

8 This was the story of Moratti's early years. In 1955 Inter began with Aldo Campatelli who was replaced by Giuseppe Meazza after 12 games. Inter finished third. In 1956 the club began the season with two managers: Annibale Frossi and Luigi Ferrero; but after 24 games it was back to Giuseppe Meazza. Inter ended up fifth. In 1957 Moratti called on an

English manager – Jesse Carver. The results were disastrous – ninth place. Carver was replaced by Alfredo Bigogno in 1958, who was sacked after 24 games (again), and Aldo Campatelli was brought back. Inter finished third. Moratti went back to dual managers in 1959, with Camillo Achilli and Aldo Campatelli. But then Achilli took over on his own and was later joined by Giulio Cappelli. Nothing much changed, as Inter ended up fourth. Read today, this seems eerily reminiscent of the Inter team of the 1990s under Moratti's son, Massimo.

9   Most commentators claim that the phrase was semi-Spanish but others argue that the slogan came from much closer to home. Two of Inter's players were from the Veneto region – Bedin and Corso. They called the ball 'la bala', and Herrera supposedly took up the phrase from them.

10  Phil Ball, *Morbo. The Story of Spanish Football*, WSC books, London, 2001, p. 144.

11  Some have blamed this death – which remains unexplained – on Herrera's insistence that Taccola play on through injury. For a recent account see Ferruccio Mazzola, *Il terzo incomodo*, pp. 109–113.

12  Gianni Brera, *Herrera*, p. 12.

13  In other versions of this exchange, the question was put by a journalist. Rocco, typically, replied in Triestian: *cio, speremo di no!*

14  Giovanni Arpino and Alfio Caruso, *Area di rigore*, SEI, Turin, 1979, p. 27.

15  In the 1930s a game for the national team gave you the right to become a manager. Later, strict controls were introduced on who could manage teams. Today, a coaching certificate is required. Sometimes, teams try to get around this rule by pretending a qualified coach is really the manager, if the real manager is not qualified. This happened with David Platt during his short period in charge of Sampdoria in the 1990s.

16  Trieste's new stadium is named after Rocco, and there is a bust of the former manager in the entrance hall.

17  G. Garanzini, *Nereo Rocco. La leggenda del paròn*, Baldini & Castoldi, Milan, 1999.

18  There is another stronger version of this quote: Kick everything that moves on the grass, even if it is the ball; 'a tuto quel che se movi su l'erba, daghe. Se xe'l balon, no importa'. Garanzini's book shows how many of the quotes attributed to Rocco were invented by journalists, or were misquotes.

19  *Champions of Europe*, Guinness, London, 1991, p. 120.

20  *Brilliant Orange. The neurotic genius of Dutch football*, Bloomsbury, London, p. 44.

21  *Champions of Europe*, p. 126. Ajax 'attacked cleverly and continuously, relentlessly and fluidly switching positions and appearing to overwhelm the ultra-defensive Italians intellectually and emotionally as well as physically and tactically', Winner, *Brilliant Orange*, p. 40.

22 *Dizionario del calcio italiano*, p. 2058.

23 Other systems were known as 'mixed-zones', and used a combination of man-marking and zonal defence. Later, some managers adopted a briefly fashionable 3–4–3 system. 3–4–3 is generally associated with national Belgium manager Guy Thys in the 1980s and the Dutch team in the 1990s. The most successful proponent of 3–4–3 was Alberto Zaccheroni with Udinese, Milan and Inter in the 1990s and early 21st century. 3–4–3 relied on wing-backs and a strong centre-forward – such as Bierhoff and Vieri – and left acres of space at the back for the counter-attack.

24 Ormezzano, *Tutto il calcio*, p. 196.

25 A whole issue of the football periodical *Linea Bianca* was dedicated to Sacchi in 2005.

26 Angelo Caroli, *Fischia il Trap. Vittorie e tormenti di un re della panchina*, Limina, Arezzo, 1996.

27 Here is an example of Trapattoni's German: 'Ein Trainer is nicht un idiot! Ein Trainer sehen, was passieren in Platz. In diese Spiel es waren zwei, drei oder vier Spieler, die waren schwach wie eine Flasche leer!' At this German website you can also download film and audio versions of the famous press conference, http://www.viaggio-in-germania.de/trap.html.

28 Giampiero Mughini, *Un sogno chiamato Juventus*, Mondadori, Milan, 2003, p. 154.

29 Myths and rumours surrounded Eriksson's private life in Italy, but neither the press nor the public at large were in the least bit interested.

## Chapter 9

1 *Storia critica*, p. 382.

2 Carlo Petrini, *Nel fango del dio pallone*, Kaos, Milan, 2000.

3 For a fascinating discussion of the Tuta case, see Filippo Benfante and Piero Brunello, *Lettere dalla Curva sud. Venezia 1998–2000*, Odradek, Rome, 2001, pp. 35–42. Another famous and similar case has recently spawned a book-length account; see Paolo Zillani, *Non si fanno queste cose a cinque minuti dalla fine! La vera storia del giallo Genoa–Inter*, Limina, Arezzo, 2005, for the story of a game where a late goal led to a full-scale investigation into match-fixing.

4 *A Season with Verona. Travels around Italy in search of illusion, national character and goals*, Secker and Warburg, 2002, p. 408 and p. 411.

5 Other occasions include a Milan derby in the 1950s when Inter striker Benito Lorenzi put a lemon under the ball. The crowd tried to tell the penalty-taker but he failed to notice and missed. In 2001, Torino midfielder Maspero put a piece of soil under the ball before a last-minute penalty in the Turin derby. Marcello Salas blasted the ball over the bar, leaving the score at 3–3.

6 For example in *Champions of Europe*, Guinness, London, 1991, pp. 82–113,

*Footballers Don't Cry. Selected Writings*, Virgin, 1999, pp. 91–140, *Football Memories*, Virgin, London, 1999.

7 For the documentation on the 1980 scandal I have used the press reports from the time and these volumes, Giovanni Arpino and Alfio Caruso, *Calcio nero: Fatti e misfatti dello sport più popolare d'Italia*, Milan, Feltrinelli, 1980; A. M. Perrino, *Tutto il calcio venduto per venduto: nomi, cifre, retroscena dei processi al calcio-scandalo*, Milano, Mondadori, 1980; A. Papa and G. Panico, *Storia sociale del calcio in Italia. Dai campionati del dopoguerra alla Champions League (1945–2000)*, Il Mulino, Bologna, 2000, pp. 124–126; Paolo Carbone, *Il pallone truccato. L'illecito nel calcio italiano*, Libri di Sport, Bologna, 2003, pp. 61–83; and Coen, Gomez and Sisti, *Piedi puliti*, pp. 50–52.

8 Rossi's side of the story can be found in his autobiography, *Ho fatto piangere il Brasile*, Limina, Arezzo, 2002, pp. 69–104.

9 1986's *Totonero* scandal was in some ways even worse. It involved nine clubs, although it made much less of a splash. The punishment handed down included relegation, 44 docked points and 45 bans for players (including Guido Magherini, again).

10 There is only one Serie B, but three Serie C divisions (C1, C2 and C3). Teams move from 3 to 2 to 1 and then to B. The mechanisms and forms of promotion and relegation have changed over time. In 1993 Serie C1 was divided into a north and south division (with Perugia, controversially, in the southern half).

11 Gaucci's other dream was to employ the first woman player in Serie A. Using spurious civil rights arguments (which sounded very strange coming from Gaucci), he tried to sign the best women players in the world but they all refused to come. It was another of his publicity-seeking bluffs. Gaddafi had been hanging around Italian football for years. He even trained with Paul Gascoigne at Lazio in the 1990s; *Gazza. My Story*, Paul Gascoigne with Hunter Davies, Headline, London, 2004, p. 177.

12 The technical term for the disease is '*sclerosi laterale amiotrofica*'.

13 Fabrizio Calzia and Massimiliano Castellani, *Palla avvelenata. Morti misteriose, doping e sospetti nel calcio italiano*, Bradipolibri, Turin, 2003.

14 And these are only the most well-known cases. For details on many others see Calzia and Castellani.

15 See also 'Non ci sono colpevoli per la morte di Curi', *Corriere della Sera*, 3.5.1979.

16 Or, as the federation put it, 'Amphetamines were discovered in their organic liquid'.

17 *Storia critica*, p. 342. The best – if most biased – account of the whole story is by Renzo Renzi, *Bologna carogna. Cronache della lotta contro la lega lombarda*, Alfa, Bologna, 1964 (republished in 2004).

18 'Una sola volta fu necessaria la "bella". Bologna-Inter la sfida che fece epoca', *La Gazzetta dello Sport*, 15.5.1982. See the chapter on the national team for the controversial accusations of 'inverse-doping' which surrounded Italy's defeat against Korea in the 1966 World Cup.

19 Another problem with Del Piero's increased physique, as Michel Platini later argued, was that the 'new' player seemed to have lost the grace and dribbling skill of the young player who so charmed Serie A and Europe in the late 1990s. For the Juventus trial see also *Processo alla Juventus per frode sportiva*, Kaos, Milan, 2004, and Carlo Petrini, *Scudetti dopati. La Juventus 1994–98: flebo e trofei*, Kaos, Milan, 2005.

20 Interestingly, the internal 'football' investigation opened up after Zeman's statements concluded that 'there is no doping in football'.

21 The full list as well as the trial documents can be found in Calzia and Castellani, *Palla avvelenata*, pp. 167–182.

22 For the concept of an organic crisis see David Forgacs (ed.), *An Antonio Gramsci Reader: Selected Writings, 1916–1935*, New York, Schocken Books, 1988.

## Chapter 10

1 Gabriele D'Annunzio (1863–1938) was a celebrated nationalist, poet, aesthete, painter and war hero.

2 There are now many collections of Brera's work; see, for example, Gianni Brera, *L'arcimatto, 1960–1966*, Baldini & Castoldi (edited by Andrea Maietti), Milan, 1993, and Gianni Brera, *63 partite da salvare*, Mondadori, Milan, 1978. On Brera and his life see Paolo Brera and Claudio Rinaldi, *Gioannfucarlo. La vita e gli scritti inediti di Gianni Brera*, Edizione Selecta, Pavia, 2001, and Andrea Maietti, *Com'era bello con Gianni Brera*, Limina, Arezzo, 2002.

3 *Tutto il calcio parola per parola*, Riuniti, Rome, 1997, p. 58.

4 This is a quote from Gianni Mura, one of Brera's heirs, who were known collectively as the *withoutBreras*.

5 Umberto Eco called Brera 'Gadda made simple for the people'. Gadda was a novelist who liked to play with local dialects.

6 Maurizio Mosca.

7 Claudio Rinaldi, 'Dall'addio alla Gazzetta al ritorno a San Zenone' in *Gioannfucarlo*, p. 240.

8 Rinaldi, 'Dall'addio . . .', p. 266. Brera was also involved in a long court case with the Pozzo family, who sued him for libel for some comments he made about Vittorio Pozzo.

9 *L'arcimatto, 1960–1966*, Baldini & Castoldi (Andrea Maietti, ed.), Milan, 1993.

10 *Storia del calcio in Italia*, Einaudi, Turin, 1990 (new edition).

11 Giorgio Lauro, Marco Ardemagni and Sergio Ferrentino, *Caro Bar Sport*.

*Pebbacco o Devimorire. 15 anni di lettere alla più parziale e tifosa delle redazioni sportive*, Comix, Milan, 1998, p. 8.

12 An interesting sports pundit and writer was Beppe Viola, who worked for the RAI but used the weapons of irony and satire in his reports on games. One of the many guests on *Mai Dire Gol* was the comic Paolo Rossi. A fanatical Inter fan, Rossi dedicated a hilarious monologue to his childhood hero, midfielder Evaristo Beccalossi. The piece is based around a real incident – two missed penalties in the same game in the 1980s, by the same player.

13 Juventus even played a 'home' UEFA Cup semi-final leg in Milan in the 1990s, selling out San Siro.

14 Aldo Grasso, 'Processini del lunedì', *La Gazzetta dello Sport*, 9.9.2004.

15 See 'La domenica sportiva', *Enciclopedia della Televisione*, Garzanti, Milan, 1996, pp. 218–220 and *Dizionario del calcio Italiano*, Volume 2, pp. 1963–1984.

16 For an account of the success of this programme see '90° minuto', *Enciclopedia della Televisione*, pp. 498–9.

17 For an analysis of sport and football on television see 'Calcio in TV' and 'Sport in TV' in Aldo Grasso (ed.), *Enciclopedia della Televisione*, pp. 97–99 and pp. 719–721.

18 Much of this section is based on the excellent book by Valerio Piccioni, *Quando giocava Pasolini. Calci, corse e parole di un poeta*, Limina, Arezzo, 1996.

19 Papa and Panico, *Storia sociale*, p. 323.

20 Einaudi, Turin, 1977. For a series of studies on the literature of sport, and not just in Italy, see Istituto Universitario di Scienza Motorie, *Letteratura e sport*, edited by Nicola Bottiglieri, Limina, Arezzo, 2003.

21 *Footballers Don't Cry. Selected Writings*, Virgin, London, 1999, p. 247.

22 See for Milan, Mauro Raimondi, *Invasione di campo. Una vita in rossonero*, Limina, Arezzo, 2003, and for Napoli, Davide Morgera, *Volevo essere Sergio Clerici*, Limina, Arezzo, 2003.

23 Cristiano Militello, *Giulietta è 'na zoccola. Gli striscioni più esiliranti degli stadi italiani*, Kowalski, Milan, 2004.

24 Francesco Caremani (on the Heysel massacre), *La verità sull'Heysel*, Libri di sport, Bologna, 2003; Calzia and Castellani (on doping), *Palla avvelenata;* Vittorio Malagutti (on financial scandals), *I conti truccati del calcio. Perché il mondo del Pallone è sull'orlo del fallimento*, Carocci, Rome, 2002; Guido Liguori and Antonio Smargiasse (on the politics of football), *Calcio e neocalcio. Geopolitica e prospettive del football in Italia*, Il Manifesto, Rome, 2003; Paolo Carbone (on scandals), *Il Pallone truccato. L'illecito nel calcio italiano*, Libri di sport, Bologna, 2003.

25 Kaos, Milan, 2003 (first edition 2000).

26 Kaos, Milan, 2003.

27 Tim Parks often visits the Verona 'muro' in his *A Season with Verona*.

# Chapter 11

1 Papa and Panico, *Storia sociale*, p. 120.

2 It was used also as a noun; supporting was '*il tifo*'. Only in 1935 did *tifosi* turn up in dictionaries and encyclopaedias.

3 Papa and Panico, *Storia sociale*, p. 121.

4 English fans were often seen as epitomizing fair play in the way they followed the game (and other sports).

5 For a discussion of these themes see Rocco de Biasi and Pierre Lanfranchi, 'The Importance of Difference: Football Identities in Italy' in Gary Armstrong and Richard Giulianotti (eds), *Entering the Field. New perspectives on world football*, Berg, Oxford, 1997, pp. 92–94.

6 Benfante and Brunello, *Lettere dalla Curva Sud*, p. 119.

7 The material on the *ultrà* is vast, and includes some excellent sociological and anthropological work; see, for example, Antonio Roversi, *Calcio, tifo e violenza. Il teppismo calcistico in Italia*, Bologna: Il Mulino, 1992, Alessandro Dal Lago, *Descrizione di una battaglia*, Il Mulino, Bologna, 1990, Alessandro Dal Lago and Roberto Moscati, *Regalateci un sogno*, Bompiani, Milano, 1992, Giorgio Triani, *Mal di stadio. Storia del tifo e della passione per il calcio*, Edizioni Associate, Roma, 1990, Carlo Podaliri and Carlo Balestri, 'The *Ultras*, racism and football culture in Italy', pp. 88–101 in Adam Brown, ed., *FANATICS! Power, identity and fandom in football*, Routledge, London, 1998, Dario Colombo and Daniele De Luca, *Fanatics. Voci, documenti e materiali dal movimento ultrà*, Castelvecchi, Rome, 1996. Other materials range from novels (Nanni Balestrini, *I Furiosi*, Bompiani, Milan, 1994) to fan-produced material of differing quality: Collettivo Autonomo Curva Nord Ancona, *1987–1997, Un guerriero non si ferma mai*, Ancona, 1997, C.U.C.S.: *Commando Ultrà*, Multimedia, Rome, 1988. Huge quantities of stuff – much of it of a very low quality – can be found on the web. There are also two interesting documentaries about Juve *ultrà*, made by Daniele Segre, *Il Potere deve essere bianconero*, 1978, and *Ragazzi di stadio*, 1980.

8 Antonio Roversi and Carlo Balestri, 'Gli Ultras oggi. Declino o cambiamento?', *POLIS*, 3, 1999. However, Roversi and Balestri use a rather outdated concept of British hooliganism as a working-class phenomenon.

9 For example, many Torino supporters' clubs were formed across Italy in the 1940s, following the success of the *Grande Torino*.

10 The *fossa* hard-core fans can still be found at level 17 in the central part of the San Siro *curva*.

11 It is often said that Helenio Herrera encouraged Inter president Angelo Moratti to organize away fan travel for his team in the early 1960s. Although this did lead to organized away support for Inter on a larger scale than before, these fans should not be confused with the *ultrà* movement (which was spontaneous) of the 1960s, 1970s and 1980s.

12 For example, the small, sleepy, seaside town of Sapri to the south of Salerno had an *ultrà* group named after an Italian nationalist hero, Carlo Pisacane. Pisacane gave the town a brief moment of national fame in 1857 when he landed on the beach with 300 ex-convicts in an unlikely, and disastrous, attempt to foment a revolt in the south that would unite Italy. The ex-convicts were massacred before they got beyond the beach.

13 The issue of the special trains came to a head with the Salernitana train disaster of 1999, when four young fans died (in a train fire) after a nightmarish 20-hour round trip to Piacenza in the north.

14 Lazio fans created a market for their own material. Songs were invented by the *curva*, sung at matches and then sold on CDs that could sometimes shift up to 20,000 copies. Marco Benvenuto, 'Le ragioni del cuore', *Calcio 2000*, October 2003.

15 A survey of the 128 professional teams in Italy in 2003 found that 28 *curve* were controlled by the right, 15 by the left and 7 had strong groups from both extremes.

16 For Filippo Benfante, 'many people go to the stadium not only to watch a match, but also to demonstrate opinions and sentiments about the places in which we live', *Lettere*, p. 2.

17 Some analysts have described the role of the police within stadiums as a 'militarization'. This should be seen within the context of a general move amongst Italy's police towards military-type activity, something seen most terrifyingly in the face of the G8 protests in Genoa in July 2001. In 1997 a diplomatic incident was created after the wanton batoning of England fans by Italian police in Rome.

18 Tim Parks's book on Verona is quite brilliant when it limits itself to a description of the *ultrà* way of life, as with the study of a horrific coach trip to an away game in Bari; *A Season with Verona*, pp. 1–55.

19 I made these points in an article in *La Gazzetta dello Sport*.

20 A week later, Torino's fans replied with a joke – *Onore a Gatto Silvestro*. Silvestro the cat is a well-known cartoon character.

21 See also Parks, *A Season with Verona*, pp. 72–3.

22 But see also my review for a critique of Parks's provocative account; *TLS*, 2002 (n.5174), pp. 32–34.

23 *Paolo Di Canio. The Autobiography*, p. 258.

24 For Juventus and Torino see Patrick Hazard and David Gould, 'Three confrontations and a coda: Juventus of Turin and Italy', in Gary Armstrong and Richard Giulianotti, *Fear and Loathing in World Football*, Berg, Oxford, 2001, pp. 199–219.

25 Pietro Cheli, 'Genoa, e fu subito football', *Diario della settimana*, 29.8.2003, p. 46.

26 *Giulietta è 'na zoccola. Gli striscioni più esiliranti degli stadi italiani*, Kowalski, Milan, 2003.

27  A phrase such as 'To kill a hunchback is not a crime' summed up the
    more violent side of anti-Juventus 'againstism'.

28  For a brilliant analysis of football songs, see Piero Brunello in Benfante
    and Brunello, *Lettere*, pp. 109–118, and Brunello, *Storia e canzone in Italia:
    il Novecento, Itinerari educativi*, Comune di Venezia, 2000, pp. 399–401.

29  *Paolo Di Canio. The Autobiography*, Collins, London, 2000, p. 257, and see
    also pp. 255–258. Strangely, very little was made of this in England where
    Di Canio's lovable, cuddly image remained intact despite his long ban for
    pushing a referee over. Yet, there were signs that the issue was a sensitive
    one. When he did an advert that demanded that he appear naked, Di
    Canio's *Dux* tattoo was quietly airbrushed out.

30  See the comments by left-wing Lazio fans and journalists Guido Liguori
    and Antonio Smargiasse, *Calcio e neocalcio. Geopolitica e prospettive del
    football in Italia*, Il Manifesto, Rome, 2003. Di Canio also became a highly
    popular TV pundit in Italy in the late 1990s and was a regular presence
    on Sunday night programmes after his return in 2004.

31  Alessandro Dal Lago has described football games as 'an occasion in which
    different conceptions of justice and sporting legitimacy meet and compete';
    *Descrizione di una battaglia. I rituali del calcio*, Il Mulino, Bologna, 1990,
    cited in Benfante and Brunello, *Lettere*, p. 38. Fans go to games not just
    to watch the match, but also to interpret and express their opinions –
    loudly – on what is happening in front of them.

32  Inter fans left '*Chiuso per dignità*' behind in 1998 and the eloquent '30
    Years 3 Championships . . . bloody bastards' in 2001.

33  In the 1990s Florence fans displayed a banner that read *Game over, insert
    coin*, calling on club president Cecchi Gori to spend money.

34  Benfante and Brunello, *Lettere*.

35  Benfante and Brunello, *Lettere*, p. 155.

36  And beyond . . . in Rome it is now common practice to leave football
    scarves, shirts, newspaper covers and symbols on the graves of ex-fans;
    see Alberto Crespi, 'Una sciarpa per sempre', *Diario della settimana*,
    16.2.2002, pp. 43–7. Other tombs had footballing symbols carved into the
    tombstone itself.

## Chapter 12

1  *Storia del calcio*, p. 33.

2  Edmondo Berselli, 'Ultràs. Fenomenologia dell'ossessione da stadio', *La
   Repubblica*, 24.3.2004. In the 1990s sociologist Alessandro Dal Lago published an outstanding study of football violence entitled *Descrizione di una
   battaglia. I rituali del calcio*, Il Mulino, Bologna, 2001 (Description of a
   Battle: the rituals of *calcio*).

3  There have also been numerous cases of players being hit by flares, coins
   or small makeshift bombs, or bottles, over the years. A bottle hit Milan

defender Mario David at Venice in 1963. Milan were awarded the game, 2–0. Roma goalkeeper Tancredi was hit in the head by a flare thrown by Milan fans in December 1987, leading to a 'table' victory for Roma. A small bomb was thrown during a Fiorentina UEFA Cup match in Salerno (where Fiorentina were playing after their own ground had been banned) in November 1997, after which the Florence club were thrown out of the competition. The throwing of flares onto the pitch by Roma fans in May 2004 marred the game during which Milan clinched the championship that year, and this is a only a small selection of cases. The most famous throwing case of all remains the 'tin-can' incident involving Inter and Borussia Dortmund in the 1971–2 European Cup. Inter lost the away leg 7–1 after striker Boninsegna was allegedly struck by a Coke can. After an appeal, the game was replayed (in Berlin) and Inter went through. Doubts remain about the real damage done to Boninsegna that night.

4 The story is sometimes repeated on the internet. Other reports confirmed the stabbing but said that the Liverpool fan survived. The *Gazzetta* report ('Morto anche l'inglese che era stato accoltellato' – 'The Englishman who was stabbed has died', *La Gazzetta dello Sport*, 31.5.1985) was full of detail.

5 *These are the names of the victims:* Rocco Acerra, 29, was a southern migrant (from Francavilla near Chieti in the Abruzzo) and worked for the post office; Bruno Balli, 50, was from Prato in Tuscany; Giancarlo Bruschera, 34, was from Taino near Varese; Giovanni Casula, 44, a Communist Party militant from Cagliari in Sardinia, 44, died with his son Andrea, 11, the youngest victim; Nino Cerullo, 24, was also from Francavilla near Chieti in the south of Italy; Giuseppina Conti, 16, was from Arezzo in Tuscany; Dionisio Fabbro, 51, was from Avilla di Bula near Udine, and was a worker; Eugenio Gagliano, 35, was from Catania in Sicily; Francesco Galli, 25, from a place called Calcio near Bergamo, was the youngest of eleven children. He was a carpenter; Giancarlo Gonnelli, 46, was a school caretaker from Pisa; Alberto Guarini, 21, was from a small town near Brindisi in the south of Italy; Giovacchino Landini, 50, was from Turin. He left two children; Roberto Lorentini, 31, was a doctor from Arezzo in Tuscany. Roberto stopped to give the kiss of life to a boy, before being crushed by the crowd. He was later awarded a medal for his bravery; Barbara Lusci, 58, Genoa; Franco Martelli, 46, Todi in central Italy; Loris Messore, 23, Turin; Gianni Mastroiaco was in his twenties and came from the Abruzzo region in the south; Sergio Mazzino, 38, was from Cogorno near Genoa and left a 12-year-old daughter; Luciano Papaluca, 38, was a southern immigrant who worked in Milan's Linate airport; Benito Pistolato, 50, was a shopkeeper from Bari; Domenico Ragazzi, 43, was a builder from a small town, Roccastrada, near Brescia. He had seven sisters and two brothers; Antonio Ragnanese, 29, lived in Brugherio near Milan but was a southern migrant and worked in a dentist's surgery. He left a

wife and a six-year-old son; Mario Ronchi, 43, Bassano del Grappa; Domenico Russo, 26, was an electrician from Moncalieri near Turin. He left his wife Tiziana, who was seven months pregnant; Tarcisio Salvi, 45, from Brescia left four children; Gianfranco Sarto, 47, was from Donada near Rovigo in the Veneto region; Giuseppe Spalaore, 55, Bassano del Grappa; Mario Spanu, 41, was a cook from Novara who worked in a motorway service station; Tarcisio Venturin, 23, from Pero near Milan, was a worker; Claudio Zavarone, 29, Reggio Emilia; Luigi Pidone, 31, from Nicosia; a 39th victim died after 66 days in a coma in a Brussels hospital. *Non-Italians:* Alfons Bons, 35, Belgium; Willy Chielens, 41, Belgium; Dirk Daenecky, 27, Belgium; Jean Michael Walla, 32, Belgium; Jacques François, 45, France; Claude Robert, France; Patrick Radcliffe, 37, from Northern Ireland, was the only British victim. He was an archivist who worked for the European Commission in Brussels. Presumably, he had somehow picked up a ticket for the game in Sector Z.

6 Paolo Rossi, *Ho fatto piangere il Brasile. Un'autobiografia*, Limina, Arezzo, 2002, pp. 209–219. The book is ghost-written by Antonio Finco and includes an interview with a survivor from Heysel.

7 Antonio Cabrini, *Io, Antonio*, Sonzogno, Milan, 1988, pp. 133–137. See also the comments of Marco Tardelli on the twentieth anniversary of the tragedy, 'Tardelli chiede scusa: "un errore giocare all'Heysel"', *Il Manifesto*, 21.5.2005. 'I never felt that that European Cup was a victory . . . we should not have celebrated with the fans . . . I want to say sorry'.

8 For the record, this was a position taken up by Prime Minister Bettino Craxi (who accused UEFA of cynicism) and Minister Gianni De Michelis, who was at the game.

9 This is what the statement said: 'Juventus, despite the dramatic situation which has emerged and which is clearly nothing to do with the club or its fans, and which has led to the deaths of tens of Italian nationals, has accepted, with our hearts full of sorrow, UEFA's decision to play the game for "public order reasons"', Giampiero Boniperti.

10 See also the analysis of Baudrillard, 'This phantom football match should obviously be seen in conjunction with the Heysel Stadium game, when the real event, football, was once again eclipsed – on this occasion by a much more dramatic form of violence. There is always the danger that this kind of transition may occur, that spectators may cease to be spectators and slip into the role of victims or murderers, that sport may cease to be sport and be transformed into terrorism: that the only event occurring is strictly televisual in nature. Every real referent event may become acceptable on television's mental screen'; Jean Baudrillard, *The Transparency of Evil: Essays in Extreme Phenomena*. London: Verso Books, 1993, p. 80.

11 *La verità sull'Heysel. Cronaca di una strage annunciata*, Libri di sport, Bologna, 2003.

12  Glanville, *Champions of Europe*, p. 154.

13  Other plaques were put up locally, such as in Arezzo, home-town of two dead fans. In Noto, in Sicily, a plaque was unveiled which read: 'In memory of the fallen who were brutally murdered in Brussels. Noto's sportsmen and women. 29.5.1985'.

14  For information on this new monument see the site www.290585.com/.

15  The Liverpool–Juventus game led to a series of newspaper features concerning Heysel, ahead of the anniversary. The *Liverpool Echo* produced a special issue with the names of the victims and a simple headline – *Sorry*. Some Juventus *ultrà* were not amused, literally turning their backs on the attempts to remember the tragedy at Anfield. The Juventus authorities used the game as a belated opportunity to remember Heysel, with a simple ceremony in Turin. In the 1980s, Heysel also led to a boom in studies of football and football fans. As Benfante and Brunello have written, 'Italian sociology entered the stadiums after the massacre of Heysel'; *Lettere*, p. 76.

16  *Fever Pitch*, p. 157.

17  The reconstruction of events in this section is largely based upon the research of Luca Vincenti, *Diari di una domenica ultrà! Ventinove gennaio. Claudio Vincenzo Spagnolo*, Franco Angeli, Milan, 2000.

18  The Italians were not always the victims, however. In March 2002 a Roma–Galatasaray Champions League match in Italy ended in a huge fight, which continued in the dressing room. At one point, the Italian police started beating up the Galatasary players.

19  Corrado Sannucci, 'Quella battaglia con l'Estudiantes tra sputi, botte e Combin in manette', *La Repubblica*, 12.12.2003.

## Chapter 13

1  *Declaration of war*, 10 June 1940. The irony of the quote was lost on the Inter fans. Italy's war effort was not distinguished by victory.

2  Giuliano Sadar, *Una lunga giornata di bora. Trieste e la Triestina, storie di calcio attraverso terre di confine*, Limina, Arezzo, 2003.

3  Other versions have his real name as Colausig; *Dizionario del calcio italiano*, I, p. 156.

4  When Paul Gascoigne unveiled his own stepover in the 1990s, the name of Colaussi was immediately invoked.

5  After a long career with Trieste (he made his debut at just 17, and played for 12 years), Colaussi was transferred to Juventus for big money in 1940. His career interrupted by the war, and having lost most of his money, Colaussi was forced to manage a series of minor teams all over Italy (and even in Libya) to get by. His situation was such that the Italian football federation helped him out with a subsidy 'awarded for sporting merit' in the 1980s and 1990s.

6 Like Colaussi, Pasinati also came back to Trieste after the war and was often to be seen in the stands with his former team-mate in the 1980s and 1990s.

7 Similar atrocities had also been extended to other zones of Friuli in 1943. The best accounts of the *Foibe* events are Raoul Pupo and Roberto Spazzali, *Foibe*, Bruno Mondadori, Milan, 2003, Giampaolo Valdevit, ed., *Foibe il peso del passato: Venezia Giulia 1943–1945*, Marsilio, Venice, 1997, and Raoul Pupo, *Il lungo esodo. Istria: le persecuzioni, le foibe, l'esilio*, Rizzoli, Milan, 2005.

8 See Map.

9 Jan Morris, *Trieste and the Meaning of Nowhere*, Faber & Faber, 2002.

10 Giuliano Sadar, *Una lunga giornata*, p. 60.

11 'L'Inghilterra in 20 anni ha sconfitto la violenza', *La Gazzetta dello Sport*, 22.4.2005.

12 'Il Napoli è in serie A ma Lauro in serie B', *Il Giorno*, 13.6.1962.

13 See Percy Allum, 'Laurismo e gavismo a Napoli', in M. Donzelli, ed., *Economia politica ed istituzioni della Campania*, Teti, 1978.

14 Guy Chiappaventi, *Pistole e palloni. Gli anni Settanta nel racconto della Lazio campione d'Italia*, Limina, Arezzo, p. 170.

15 See Mario Risoli, *Arrivederci Swansea. The Giorgio Chinaglia Story*, Mainstream Publishing, Edinburgh, 2000.

16 Chiappaventi, *Pistole e palloni*, p. 129.

17 Giovanni Arpino, Alfio Caruso, *Calcio nero. Fatti e misfatti dello sport più popolare d'Italia*, Feltrinelli, Milan, 1980, p. 34.

18 Many Roma fans were also left-wing, or professed to be so, in the 1970s and 1980s. Other extremist fans exalted terrorist groups such as the Red Brigades or protest movements such as the Autonomists.

19 Whilst still a player he graduated in law with an undergraduate thesis entitled: 'The Relationship between Ordinary and Sporting Law'. This was rather strange, as it was precisely the lack of any real laws concerning 'sporting fraud' which was to save Wilson in 1980, when he was banned for three years for match-fixing but absolved by the criminal courts.

20 Mario Pennacchia, *Football Force One. La biografia ufficiale di Giorgio Chinaglia*, Limina, Arezzo, 2001, p. 73.

21 For Re Cecconi see above all Carlo D'Amicis, *Ho visto un re. Luciano Re Cecconi, l'eroe biancoazzurro che giocava alla morte ed è morto per gioco*, Limina, Arezzo, 1999.

22 Giacomo Papi, 'Il ragazzo che portava il pallone', *Diario della settimana*, 9.4.2004, pp. 20–26.

23 Ginsborg, *Italy and its Discontents*, n. 104, p. 399.

24 G. Triani, *Bar Sport Italia. Quando la politica va nel pallone*, Elèuthera, Milan, 1994.

25 G. Ferrari, *Il padrone del diavolo: la storia di Silvio Berlusconi*, Camunia,

Milan, 1990, p. 136. For Berlusconi and Milan see also my *Milan since the Miracle. City, Culture and Identity*, Berg, Oxford, 2001, chapter 5.

26 Christian Bromberger, *La partita di calcio. Etnologia di una passione*, Riuniti, Rome, 1999, pp. 10–11.

27 Massimo Novelli, *Bruno Neri. Il calciatore partigiano*, Graphot editrice, Turin, 2002.

28 Novelli, *Bruno Neri*, p. 121.

29 The SICP is also known as the AIC.

30 Specifically with law 91 in 1981.

31 'In campo a sinistra', interview with Corrado Sannucci, *Zapruder*, 4, 2004, pp. 110–117.

32 He described himself in this way: 'I don't know how to trap the ball but generally I'm OK. I run a lot. I score a few goals. I help the team. I even enjoy it.'

33 *Dizionario del calcio italiano*, p. 502.

34 Paolo Sollier, *Calci e sputi e colpi di testa. Riflessioni autobiografiche di un calciatore per caso*, Gammalibri, Milan, 1976.

35 Fernando Acitelli, *La solitudine dell'ala destra. Storia poetica del calcio mondiale*, Einaudi, Turin, 1998.

36 *Storia sociale*, p. 349.

37 Lucarelli had also lived, for a time, in another working-class neighbourhood of the city made famous by Livorno-born film director Paolo Virzi's popular comedy, *Ovosodo* (1997).

38 Protti also made no secret of his left-wing political views; 'Ciao compagno Protti', *Il Manifesto*, 7.6.2003.

39 He also has a tattoo of the BAL's symbol on his left arm. Lucarelli dramatically fell out with club president Spinelli during the season over the issue of the banning of many members of the BAL from Livorno's ground.

40 Carlo Pallavicino, *Tenetevi il miliardo. La sfida di Lucarelli che portò Livorno in serie A*, Baldini and Castoldi, Milan, 2004. A new expanded edition of the book was published in 2005 with a new subtitle, *Lucarelli e Livorno, storia d'amore in 53 gol* – Lucarelli and Livorno a love story in 53 goals (the number he had scored in two seasons).

41 Lucarelli's 'return' to his home team was also part of a long-term strategy, which led to a number of Livorno-born players turning out for the squad, including Cristiano's brother, Alessandro. Fellow-striker Igor Protti began his career in Livorno, despite being born in Rimini. The plan was hatched by president Spinelli and stretched right down to the youth and junior teams, and seemed to work, at last, in the period after 1999.

42 A play on the title of a (terrible) popular film from the Italy of the 1980s: 'Under her clothes, nothing' (*Sotto il vestito, niente*).

## Chapter 14

1 For the history of La Boca see Vicente Osvaldo Cutolo, *Historia de los barrios de Buenos Aires*, Editorial ELCHE, Buenos Aires, 1988, pp. 198–242, and Jason Wilson, *Buenos Aires*, Signal Books, Oxford, 1999, pp. 185–91 and 206–9. For the club see 'Arrivò una nave e nacque il Boca', *Sportsweek*, 6, 24, 25.6.2005, pp. 60–66, and 'Nel nome del Boca', *Ventiquattro*, 7, 5.6.2004, pp. 61–3.

2 1934 World Cup winner Luisito Monti also played for Boca Juniors, as did 1950s Inter star Antonio Angelillo and Gabriel Batistuta.

3 The full set of rules and the ways in which they developed can be found in the Appendix below.

4 Monti remains the only player to have played two World Cup finals with two different countries (he had lost the 1930 final with Argentina).

5 'E' Orsi cittadino italiano?' in *La Gazzetta dello sport*, 5.10.1928.

6 But Orsi earned twice that sum, according to Pierre Lanfranchi, 'Orsi e i suoi fratelli', *FIGC NewsLetter* n. 6, 30/1/2001.

7 The phrase was actually coined by a journalist, Eugenio Danese.

8 He was instrumental in bringing over one of the most popular post-war *oriundi* – Omar Sivori – in 1957 when he became manager of Juventus, winning a championship in 1959–60. For Cesarini see Lanfranchi, 'Orsi e i suoi fratelli'.

9 Gian Paolo Ormezzano also used the same terms, later on: 'those players were without doubt Italians by blood'; *Storia del calcio*, p. 148.

10 It is not strictly correct, therefore, to argue that the *oriundi*-status constituted a kind of 'loophole' in the Viareggio Charter, as both Ghirelli (*Storia del calcio*, p. 133, and R. Gordon and J. London, 'Italy 1934: Football and Fascism', in Alan Tomlinson and Chris Young (eds), *National Identity and Global Sports Events. Culture, Politics, and Spectacle in the Olympics and the Football World Cup*, Suny Press, Albany, 2005) claim. The separate category of *oriundi* – created by the football federation – was not in line with Italian law, but conceded that these players were not really 100% Italians – they were *different* in some way – by placing restrictions on their numbers.

11 Vittorio Pozzo, *Campioni del mondo. Quarant'anni di storia del calcio italiano*, Centro Editoriale Nazionale, Rome, 1960, p. 396.

12 Sacerdoti became president of Roma again in 1951.

13 *Storia critica*, p. 143.

14 The fascists later invented a song about the three 'deserters':
'Roma der core/squadra divina/tu porti er vanto/sei 'na squadra che cammina/si abbandonatte so' stati tre/de' giallorossi centomila so' co' te!' The song was sung to the music of the fascist song 'Faccetta nera' (Little black face), 1935. Rome of our heart/divine team/you are the cause of great pride/you are a team which moves forward/If the three abandoned you/100,000 redandyellows stay by your side.

15 *Storia del calcio*, p. 150.

16 By far the most popular countries for foreigners have always been those with strong footballing traditions linked to Italian emigration: Argentina, Brazil and Uruguay. In Europe, the most important imports have been from Hungary (largely in the 1940s), Sweden, Denmark, France and Switzerland. See *Dizionario del calcio italiano*, II, pp. 1815–1845, FIGC, 'Gli stranieri in Italia dal 1929 ad oggi', *FIGC NewsLetter* n. 8, 11.7.2001.

17 Sarugia, *Grande Inter 'Figlia di Dio'*, p. 38

18 Schiaffino played for Milan and then with Angelillo at Roma.

19 Sarugia, *Grande Inter*, p. 39.

20 Brera, *Herrera*, p. 76.

21 *Il Giorno*, 4.12.1960.

22 *Alias*, December 2003/January 2004.

23 He managed the following teams: Santa Maria degli Angeli (Assisi), Montevarchi, Chieti, Campobasso, Rimini, Brescia, Reggio Calabria, Pescara (A and B), Arezzo, Avellino, Palermo and Mantova. Angelillo then went to coach in Morocco, for two years, before returning to Italy, in C2 with the Sardinian team Torres.

24 He also played eighteen times for Argentina.

25 John Charles, *The Gentle Giant*, Stanley Paul, London, 1962, p. 9. With 'the giant' in defence, Juve lost 5–1 to Milan, a game which launched Rocco's team towards the 1962 title. It is not clear if Charles and Sivori fell out in the same way as Boniperti and Sivori. Certainly, the Argentinian does not play a huge part in Charles's ghosted autobiography. Practically the only mention of Sivori in the text (aside from a few photographs) claims that he tended to 'overdo his trickery' at times.

26 Brian Glanville calls him 'a hopeless businessman' in his excellent obituary of Charles, *The Guardian*, 23.2.2004.

27 Later, Elland Road's west stand – partly paid for from Charles's 1957 transfer fee – was renamed the John Charles Stand.

28 Time Warner, London, 2003, p. 130.

29 Greavsie's memory, meanwhile, is no better about this game. He has it down as a 2–2 draw in his autobiography.

30 In June 2003 Joe Baker died on a golf course of a heart attack at the age of 63.

31 Joe Jordan was already 29 when he was signed by Milan in 1981, by the same president who later paid a million pounds for Luther Blissett. His first year with Milan was a complete disaster. Joe scored 2 goals in 22 games and Milan were relegated. Milan persisted with him, and he became a folk hero in Serie B, as the club's fans took masochistic pleasure in their club's decline. His ten goals in B took Milan back up (where they were to stay) and made '*lo squalo*' (the shark) extremely popular at the San Siro. After a mediocre few games with Verona, Joe went back

to Southampton, Bristol City, management and Channel 4 commentary.

32 *No Milan. Guida teorica e pratica all'antimilanismo (per interisti e non solo)*, Limina, Arezzo, 2001, p. 27.

33 The book (ghosted in diary form) is almost unreadable. Mark Hateley, *Home and Away* (with Tony Francis), Stanley Paul, London, 1986, p. 37.

34 The Attila nickname came about in part because they couldn't pronounce his name. They tended to call him 'Ateley', which merged into Attila. Hateley had been over-optimistic about Berlusconi's arrival, ending his book with 'I am far more confident now that my future will be in Italy'; *Home and Away*, p. 180.

35 'Entry' for 22 August 1988, p. 130.

36 Lee Honeyball, '"It was like living in a foreign country". Ian Rush rebuts his Italian myth', *The Observer*, 6.2.2005.

37 The official by-line is that the *Daily Star* journalist 'helped Ian Rush compile this diary'.

38 See John Williams, 'Ian Rush: From Flint to Turin – and Back', in *Welsh Football Greats*, Peter Stead and Huw Richards (eds), University of Wales Press, Cardiff, 2000. I would like to thank John Williams for sending me this article.

39 1995–7; 54 games, 10 goals.

40 Or Frank Ratcliffe, who went from Aldershot to Alessandria for one season in the late 1940s, and Carlo Sartori (Italian-born, but Manchester-raised), who played a few games in the 1970s. Paddy Sloan went from Sheffield United to Milan in 1948 and went on to play for Udinese and Brescia.

41 Eddie Firmani, *Football with the Millionaires*, The Sportsmans Book Club, London, 1960.

42 The source is Gazza himself, *Gazza. My Story*, Paul Gascoigne with Hunter Davies, Headline, London, 2004, p. 169. Judging by some of the unlikely stories in this particular book, everything there should be taken with a pinch of salt.

43 See the hilarious web site http://www.clarence.com/contents/sport/speciali/020312bidoni/.

44 *Gazza*, p. 3.

45 Gascoigne's recollection of the burp is somewhat different; see *Gazza*, pp. 168–9. Unfortunately, the whole thing was captured by the cameras.

46 *Gazza*, p. 194.

47 Bergkamp had arrived amidst huge pomp and ceremony ('Inter, I will lead you', *La Gazzetta dello Sport*, 11.6.1993) and the expectations were too much. He attracted a damaging nickname ('Cold Turkey') and in his second season scored just three goals as Inter flirted with relegation, although he did help Inter to a UEFA Cup victory.

## Chapter 15

1 'Milano tricolore', *La Repubblica*, 18.11.1993.
2 See http://www.ultrainside.it/vikingitalia/.
3 Here, for example, is the first verse:

Fratelli d'Italia
L'Italia s'è desta,
Dell'elmo di Scipio
S'è cinta la testa.
Dov'è la Vittoria?
Le porga la chioma,
Ché schiava di Roma
Iddio la creò.
Stringiamci a coorte
Siam pronti alla morte
L'Italia chiamò.

4 Gordon and London, 'Italy 1934: Football and Fascism', Martin, *Football and Fascism*. At club level, Italian teams dominated the new European competitions. Bologna were known locally (and very rhetorically) as 'the team who shook the world', and won the Central European Cup in 1932 and 1934.
5 Much of this was pretty over-the-top rhetoric. This is what *L'Illustrazione Italiana* wrote after the 1938 victory: 'the whistlers of Marseilles can no longer let off steam; they have a fat lip after the blow they have received to the face. The fascist athletes led by Vittorio Pozzo, passionate and magic anima of Italian football, have their hands on the world cup and they are celebrating because an even bigger prize awaits them: they will be received by il Duce'.
6 Antonio Papa has written, 'the feeling of a footballing nation was born and local fandom became a national passion'; 'Il campionato di calcio', in M. Isenghi, ed., *I luoghi della memoria. Personaggi e date dell'Italia unita*, Laterza, Bari, 1997, p. 394.
7 *Storia critica*, p. 132.
8 There is only one biography of Pozzo: Mauro Grimaldi, *Vittorio Pozzo. Storia di un italiano*, Società stampa sportiva, Rome, 2002. His own version of events can be found in his Vittorio Pozzo, *Campioni del mondo. Quarant' anni di storia del calcio italiano*, Centro Editoriale Nazionale, Rome, 1960.
9 For other examples of links between fascist ideology and Pozzo's national team see Gordon and London, 'Italy 1934: Football and Fascism', and Martin, *Football and Fascism*.
10 'I nostri campioni sono dei brocchi', *La Gazzetta dello Sport*, 20.8.2004.
11 The other great Italian footballing rivalry was with the (West) Germans, and was in part linked to the difficult relationship with Germany during

the war – when Italy was invaded by Nazi troops who proceeded to carry out hundreds of massacres, above all in Tuscany and Emilia-Romagna. Nando Dalla Chiesa has written of 'the anti-German spirit hidden deep within Italian national popular culture' (*La partita del secolo. Storia di Italia-Germania 4–3*, Rizzoli, Milan, 2001, p. 33 and the whole of chapter 2). In the bar where Dalla Chiesa watched the game one friend screamed 'send them all to concentration camps' after the last-minute equalizer. See also Alessandro Portelli, 'Memory and globalization in the Terni general strike of 2004' (unpublished paper given at the IOHA conference in Rome, June 2004), pp. 7–9.

12 Although there is also no doubt that Italy had great players – especially in 1938 when both Meazza and Piola were at their peak – and that Pozzo was a master tactician and motivator, it is difficult to classify the two 1930s World Cups on the same level as those from the 1950s onwards, when all the world's nations took part.

13 'I watched the final in a working-class bar in Liguria in a left-wing town, where the anti-fascist resistance had been very strong. I was surprised by the fact that everyone was supporting Germany, and everyone really hated England – because they thought that England were arrogant and helped by the referees'; cited in Francesco Caremani, *Il calcio sopra le barricate. 1968 e dintorni: L'Italia campione d'Europa*, Limina, Arezzo, 2004, p. 91.

14 Paolo Ferretti, *Dizionario del calcio italiano*, II, p. 1955.

15 The impact of radio was central in those years. For the Highbury match 'the whole of Rome was listening'; cited in Papa and Panico, *Storia sociale*, p. 199. Brera wrote of 'delirious rhetoric' with relation to the game, *Storia critica*, p. 139, and that he himself had 'been exalted' after listening to Carosio's commentary, ibid., p. 141.

16 Ghirelli, *Storia del calcio*, p. 143. See also Peter Beck, 'For World Footballing Honours: England versus Italy, 1933, 1934 and 1939', in *Europe, Sport, World: Shaping Global Societies*, edited by J. A. Mangan, Frank Cass, 2001, Martin, *Football and Fascism*, and David Winner, *These Feet: A Sensual History of English Football*, Bloomsbury, 2005, pp. 202–206.

17 *Storia critica*, p. 208.

18 *Storia critica*, p. 284. Even Ghirelli blamed the defeat on the use of the *oriundi*: 'where we should have been fighting to the death, with the national flag between our teeth, against the bold patriotism of the British (sic), we chose foreign professionals who, without being reduced to the level of mercenaries, were naturally less attached to the pull of the blue shirt'; *Storia del calcio*, p. 242.

19 Papa and Panico, *Storia sociale*, p. 64.

20 *Football with the millionaires*, The Sportsmans Book Club, London, 1960, p. 113.

21 In 1958 Argentina decided not to pick those players who were playing abroad, depriving themselves of some talented star players.

22 From 1926 to 2003, something like 44 *oriundi* 'opted' to play for Italy, most in the 1930s and late 1950s; after that, good Argentinian and Brazilian players played for their home countries, and Italy abandoned the *oriundi* road to success, only picking the occasional player for the occasional game. The *Dizionario del calcio italiano* lists only 33 *oriundi*: clearly they are using different definitions.

23 *Storia critica*, p. 317.

24 *Storia del calcio*, p. 264.

25 *Storia critica*, p. 318.

26 Andrea Bacci, *Dal Cile alla seconda Corea: le undici partite della Nazionale da giocare un'altra volta*, Libri di sport, Bologna, 2003, p. 13.

27 *Storia critica*, p. 317.

28 *Storia del calcio*, p. 133.

29 For more information on the film see the web site: www.thegameoftheir lives.com and Verymuchsoproductions, *The game of the their lives. The greatest shock in world cup history. The book of the film*, Sheffield, 2002; see also Mario Gismondi, . . . *E fu subito Corea*, Dedalo libri, 1967, Gianni Brera, *Storia critica del calcio italiano*, Baldini & Castoldi, 1998, Bacci, *Dal Cile alla seconda Corea. Dizionario del calcio italiano*, Baldini & Castoldi, 2002 (two volumes), Gabriele Romagnoli, 'Lunga vita a Pak Doo Ik', *Diario* (special edition), 31.5.2002, pp. 28–34, Gian Paolo Ormezzano, 'Ma era dentista, il killer?', *Diario* (special edition), 31.5.2002, pp. 28–34.

30 Although the North Koreans played in the 1976 Olympics; with Pak Do Ik – the goalscorer against Italy – as coach.

31 Rivera, Mazzola, Albertosi, Burgnich, Facchetti and Riva (who didn't play in 1966) were all part of the 1966 squad and of the 1968 European Championship-winning team.

32 Barison, Janich and the scapegoat Perani never played for Italy again. Fogli played one more game, against Cyprus. Spartaco Landini made just two more appearances for the national team. Even the talented Bulgarelli played only twice more – ending his career with the national team at the age of 26 – while Guarneri played only nine more games.

33 Bacci , *Dal Cile*, p. 36.

34 The plaque reads: 'The Aztec stadium renders homage to the teams of Italy (4) and Germany (3), protagonists during the 1970 world cup of the "MATCH OF THE CENTURY", 17 June 1970'; for a photo of the plaque see *Diario della Settimana*, front page, 11–17.6.1997.

35 For the German side of the story see Ulrich Hesse-Lichtenberger, *Tor! The Story of German Football*, WSC, London, 2002, pp. 233–5.

36 As they say in Italy – the '*schemi sono saltati*'.

37 Poletti had been with Gigi Meroni when he was run over and killed in 1967.

38 Dalla Chiesa *La partita del secolo*, p. 123.

39 ibid., p. 150.

40 ibid., p. 141.

41 Right from the start, the 1970 campaign had been dominated by controversy, whipped up by the press. Rivera's team-mate Lodetti was unexpectedly sent home and replaced by another striker, then Rivera attacked the management team during a press conference and threatened to leave altogether. Pelé wound up the Italians by asking them to 'give us Rivera if you don't need him'. Gianni Brera wrote a ferocious article in *Il Giorno* on 29 May. Riva was also in the news thanks to a scandal involving his private life.

42 Although one source – the *Dizionario del calcio italiano* – gives this figure as 1,144 minutes, whilst Andrea Bacci cites the figure of 1,143; *Dal Cile*, p. 59.

43 In the Italian version this was '*vaffanculo*' – go and take it up the arse – plus an open hand raised towards the manager.

44 Mario Risoli, *Arrivederci Swansea. The Giorgio Chinaglia Story*, Mainstream Publishing, Edinburgh, 2000, p. 145.

45 Einaudi, 1977.

46 See also the story told by Gian Paolo Ormezzano of his experiences in Buenos Aires in 1978; *Poveri campioni. La tribù degli assi alla lente di rimpicciolimento*, I libri de La Stampa, Turin, 1995, pp. 25–32.

47 Gigi Garanzini, *Il romanzo del vecio. Enzo Bearzot, un vita in contropiede*, Baldini & Castoldi, Milan, 1997, pp. 113–14.

48 John Foot, *Milan since the Miracle. City, Culture, Identity*, Berg, Oxford, 2001.

49 *Dizionario del calcio italiano*, vol. 1, p. 483.

50 Gianni Mura, in Benvenuto Caminiti, *Ragazzi di latta. Totò Schillaci si racconta*, Limina, Arezzo, 2003, p. 2.

51 Darwin Pastorin, *Ti ricordi, Baggio, quel rigore? Memoria e sogno dei mondiali di calcio*, Donzelli, Rome, 1998.

52 See Bacci, *Dal Cile alla seconda Corea*, p. 144, for an excellent and fair re-analysis of the game. Bacci's book is based around the very simple but, in Italy, revolutionary premise of re-watching all the key games of Italy's World Cup campaigns with something like an open mind.

53 'Follia Totti' (front page of *La Gazzetta dello Sport* with an enormous photo of the spit in question), 17.6.2004. The first *eight* pages of the daily were dedicated to the various aspects of the affair.

## Conclusion

1 'Calcio travolto dal denaro', *La Repubblica*, 16.12.1998.

2 See for example 'Calcio crac', *La Repubblica*, 14.1.2004.

3 See for example Carlo Bonini and Giuseppe D'avanzo, 'Il calcio delle cifre fasulli ecco i trucchi delle società. Giocatori, vivai e cessioni: nascosti 1,3 miliardi di debiti', *La Repubblica*, 13.4.2004.

4 Vittorio Malagutti, *I conti truccati del calcio. Perché il mondo del pallone è sull'orlo del fallimento*, Carocci, Rome, 2002, p. 25.

5 The best explanation of this system is by Antonio Maglie, *Il calcio truccato*, Linea Bianca, 1, Limina, Arezzo, 2004.

6 Vittorio Malagutti, *Buconero SpA; dentro il crac Parmalat*, Laterza, Bari, 2004, p. 124. Juan Sebastian Veron also moved from Parma to Lazio.

7 Salvatore Napolitano and Marco Liguori, *Il pallone nel burrone. Come i maggiori imprenditori italiani hanno portato il calcio al crac*, Riuniti, Roma, 2004.

8 All figures from *Il Giorno*, 11.11.2003.

9 A full explanation can be found in Carlo Bonini and Giuseppe D'Avanzo, 'Ecco i conti truccati del calcio', *La Repubblica*, 13.4.2004.

10 For Uckmar and the *Covisoc* see Malagutti, *I conti*, pp. 27–32 and pp. 38–51.

11 Rinaldo Gianola, 'Il calcio approda a Piazza Affari', *La Repubblica*, 18.4.1998.

12 Prisma, 2003.

13 Cecchi Gori's case was clear, but it was also clear that Fiorentina were a scapegoat for the sins of others. The fact that the police later raided Cecchi Gori's Rome apartment was an obvious sign – in the Byzantine world of Italian politics – that the over-bronzed film-maker had 'too little political protection' for his own good.

14 *Il Mattino*, 2.8.2004.

15 *Dizionario del calcio italiano*, p. 619.

## Afterword

1 Carlo Petrini was the most important whistle-blower in Italian football. An ex-player, he had published a series of volumes exposing corruption, match-fixing and doping in the game.

2 Examples of such transfers can be found in Chapter 15.

3 Rossi was also an Inter fan and ex-member of the Inter board, as well as a former parliamentarian as an independent left candidate in the late 1980s. He had 'always been interested in rules': see his *Il gioco delle regole*, Adelphi, Milan, 2006.

4 For example, Marco Travaglio, Peter Gomez, Andrea Malaguti, Oliviero Beha. See also for a clear description of the whole system, Alessandro Leogrande, 'Introduzione' and especially Andrea De Caro, 'Le regole del

palazzo' in A. Leogrande (ed.), *Il pallone è tondo*, L'Ancora del Mediterraneo, Napoli, 2005. See also Simone Stenti, *Moggi Bianco & Noir. Indagine su un cittadino dietro ogni sospetto*, Limina, Arezzo, 2006.

5 The book was *Lucky Luciano. Intrighi, maneggi e scandali del padrone del calcio Luciano Moggi*, Kaos, Milan, (2nd edition) 2003.

6 *Il libro nero del calcio*, L'Espresso, 2006; *Il libro nero del calcio 2*, L'Espresso, 2006.

7 For *staffetta* debates in the past see Chapter 15.

## Glossary

1 The glossary has been put together from a combination of sources, my own memory and the following books: Marco Sappino (ed.), *Dizionario del calcio italiano*, Baldini & Castoldi, Milan, 2002, Carlo Chiesa (ed.), *Dizionario internazionale illustrato del calcio*, 2004, Guido Guerrasio, *Dizionario filosofico satirico polemico del gioco del calcio*, ediz. Carcano, Milan, 1967, Gian Paolo Ormezzano, *Tutto il calcio parola per parola*, Riuniti, Rome, 1997, and Andrea Maietti, *Com'era bello con Gianni Brera*, Limina, Arezzo, 2002.

# GLOSSARY

## A brief guide to some key Italian football terms, usages and personalities[1]

*Abatino/abatini*

Literally, a young priest. In football jargon, a (rather insulting) term invented by Gianni Brera for skilful midfield players who didn't try very hard and weren't interested in tackling or running.

*Bidone*

A rubbish bin. Term often applied to rubbish (and usually to foreign) players. Also *super-bidone*.

*Brera, Gianni*

The most famous Italian football journalist of all time. Author of the 'War and Peace' of Italian football books – his *Storia critica del calcio italiano* (1975). A great polemicist and linguistic innovator, he invented a whole new language for talking about football, much of which is still in use today. Inspired the debate over the *abatini* (q.v.).

*calcio, il*

Italian for football, but also for *kick* and for an ancient ball game called *calcio fiorentino*.

*catenaccio, il*

Defensive tactical system usually ascribed to Italian teams from the 1960s. Also applied to the supposed Italian psychological approach to football.

*Cesarini*

As in *Zona Cesarini*, the Cesarini Zone, meaning the last few minutes of any match. This term came into use after some games in the 1930s – and in particular a fixture against Hungary in December 1931 – when Renato Cesarini scored a late goal to win the game.

**classifica, la**

The championship table. Also used in other phrases – 'getting points on the board' – *muovere la classifica* – or in clichés – *non guardiamo la classifica*; 'we don't care about the table'.

**coglione (i) (palle, le)**

Testicles, balls. Symbol of courage, hard work, To have or get out your *coglioni* (metaphorically) is to show courage and the fact that you are ready to fight. Strangely, *un coglione* – a testicle – is an insult applied to an idiot. However, when a player is said to 'have testicles' – *avere le palle* – that is to be taken as a compliment, whilst the phrase *che palle!* (what balls!) signifies something very boring.

**crisi, la** (crisis)

In Italy a team is defined as *in crisi* (in crisis) at various moments. Crisis can set in after only one defeat. After a few defeats the crisis becomes 'official'. Managers often deny that their teams are 'in crisis'. One or two victories are usually enough for teams to 'exit' from their crisis. Classic headlines include: 'Juve lose. It's a crisis'; 'Juve win. The crisis is squashed/overcome'.

**curva, la**

The Italian 'end' (literally the curve of the stadium – usually *south* or *north* depending on geography) where the most fanatical *ultrà* fans stand. In grounds shared by city clubs (Turin, Milan, Rome, Genoa) different *curve* are assigned to different clubs (south for Roma, north for Lazio, for example) and are sometimes given specific names (of players, or streets). Some grounds have more than two *curve*.

**distruggitore del gioco**

Literally 'destroyer of the game'. There is a long Italian tradition of tackling midfielders more interested in breaking up the opposition game – and a few legs – than construction of play. Their main task was usually to pass the ball to the *regista*, once they got it back. Also known as *mediano*.

**English terms or words with English origins**

These abound. For example, penalty; derby; corner; etc., etc.

### Gazzetta dello Sport, La

The first and the greatest daily Italian sports paper. Pink since the 1890s, it is also still the most read daily paper in Italy, in part because most bars have a copy lying around. The Monday edition is still the most important.

### media inglese, la

A strange Italian statistic, known as the 'English average' which (before three points for a win) was used to calculate, supposedly, the perfect score needed to win a championship: winning your home games and drawing away.

### melina

Term applied to the practice of passing the ball around meaninglessly at the back, which could imply an attempt to insult the opposition, or simply a means of using up time, or a lack of ideas.

### il mister

Manager. A term usually attributed to certain English managers in the early years of Italian football. Still widely used, as in *Decide il mister* (the manager decides).

### oriundo/oriundi

When the Italian football federation banned foreign players in 1926, they still allowed for foreigners 'of Italian origin'. These players – as long as they had an Italian grandmother or grandfather (at least) – were known as *oriundi*. For a time many *oriundi* also played for the Italian national team. Rule changes at various times changed the position of the *oriundi*.

### La pagella/i voti

Marks out of ten for individual players, managers and referees, awarded by journalists after each match and averaged out over whole seasons. In Italy there is a deep-rooted culture of numerical 'marks' (which originates in the school system) that tends to universalize the meaning of marks given to players.

Some aspects of the marking system need further explanation.

s.v. – *senza voti* – no votes. Usually given to substitutes who have not had enough time to – as the Italians put it – get into the game (or pick up the pace in English football jargon). Also given to goalkeepers with a hint of irony if they have not had a save to make.

Occasionally a whole team is given *s.v.* – especially in end-of-season matches where a draw suits both teams or where teams have – how shall we put this – 'not tried as hard as they might have done'.

Individual marks:

1, 2. Never given.

3. Very rarely given. Unbelievably bad.

4. Occasionally awarded. There are a number of possible cases here. First, a truly terrible performance, contributing personally to a team's defeat. Second, being sent off, idiotically. Third, a 4 is sometimes given for 'moral' reasons – for a bad foul, a dive, an insult, a pathetic show of petulance.

5. Often given. This is a classic mark of 'non-sufficiency' – not good enough. Usually given, simply, for a mediocre performance. Below average.

5.5. As above but slightly better. Just less than good enough.

6. Sufficient. A good, normal, performance. Sometimes journalists will use scholastic variations on the '6' theme as in 6 *meno* – 6 minus – somewhere between 5.5 and 6.

6.5. Good. This is a very good mark, which most players would be very happy with. The average of the very *best* players at the end of a long season usually oscillates around the 6.8 mark.

7. Excellent. Close to outstanding. A fairly rare mark.

8. Very rare. Decisive for a victory – perhaps in an important game – a hat-trick, a penalty save, etc., etc.

9. Extremely rare. Bordering on the historic.

10. Never given.

### *pretattica, la* (pre-tactics)

Word used to encompass the psychological games that go on before matches – fake injuries, pretend formations, attempts to psych-out the opposition.

*regista, il*

Literally director, as in *regista di film*, film director. Central midfielder who directs the play. Dying breed in the 1980s and 1990s, after the pressing game became all-powerful.

*salvezza, la*

Staying up, literally *salvation*. Being saved from relegation. The only ambition of probably the majority of Serie A teams at the beginning of each season.

*scudetto, lo*

Shield-shaped emblem which signifies that a team has won the Serie A championship (see below). Introduced in 1924, in the early years the symbol consisted of a patch which was literally pinned or sewn on to the winning team's shirts for the whole season in which they were champions. Teams win the *scudetto*. Juventus have won 28 *scudetti* (up to 2005).

*Serie A*

Italy's top football league, made national in 1929. The second division is Serie B. There then follow various other divisions: C1, C2, etc.

*staffetta, la*

Literally, relay or relay baton, this term was used to refer to two players who could not play at one time for the same team, usually because they were both *abatini*. The first great debate over a *staffetta* was that concerning Mazzola and Rivera during the 1970 World Cup. Relay debates have re-occurred at every international tournament since.

*stopper*

Central defender whose job it was to stop the opposition centreforward, at all costs.

*sudditanza psicologica*

Pyschological conditioning. Term first used in the 1970s by a Venetian referee to refer to a kind of conditioning which led referees to favour big clubs over smaller clubs. Used above all with reference to the power of Juventus since then.

*Totocalcio (la schedina)*

The Italian sports betting system, run entirely by the state, which asks punters to predict if thirteen (now fourteen) matches will end in a home win, draw or away win: 1, X or 2. Betters mark their predictions with a pen on small pieces of paper compiled in bars – the *schedina*. The total takings are divided between the winners, minus tax. In the 1950s, an eleven was enough to win. Now fourteen, thirteen and twelve win. Weird sets of results mean big jackpots. Predictable results lead to small payouts – the 'democratic *schedina*'. Incredibly popular in the 1950s, *Totocalcio* has had to re-invent itself to keep pace with the times.

*ultrà*

Term applied to groups of semi-fanatical and organized fans. The first *ultrà* groups appeared in the late 1960s and by the 1980s every team had various sets of *ultrà*. *Ultrà* control the *curva* and have become increasingly politicized. Violence is associated with some *ultrà* groups. Dictionary definition: 'fanatic fan – often inclined to intimidation and violence against fans from other teams'.

*Umbrella gesture (Il gesto dell'ombrello)*

This consists of slapping one's right palm onto one's left arm, or literally 'hooking' one's right hand over the left arm. The meaning of the gesture is simple – up yours! It is often accompanied by a sound such as 'teh'. In 1969 Brazilian striker José Altafini was prosecuted and fined after his 'umbrella gesture' appeared to provoke Palermo fans into a full-scale riot.

*vaffanculo – Fuck off!*

Can be purely verbal, or accompanied by a waving open hand moved from below and aimed at the person in question. It can also be purely non-verbal.

*Veneziano/Venezia*

Literally: Venetian/Venice. Greedy player who won't pass. Nobody really knows where this term comes from.

# APPENDIX

## Rules regarding foreign players in Italian football

**1946**  Only two foreigners for each team (plus three *oriundi*).

**1949**  The category of *oriundi* was abolished (in theory: in fact it remained). Each team could play three foreigners. A new category of *fuori quota* was introduced to cover those who had played for five years in Italy, who counted as Italians.

**1952**  Back to two foreigners per team.

**1953**  The *fuori quota* category was abolished for new players. Each team could only have five 'foreigners' including the *fuori quota*.

**1953**  21 May (after Italy's 3–0 home defeat against Hungary on 17 May). The *Andreotti veto* (after the then minister Giulio Andreotti) was a normal administrative order banning all foreign players from the Italian league. Only the *oriundi* could play. This decision was softened in June with a phasing-out of foreigners.

**1955**  One foreigner per team allowed. *Oriundi* status was awarded only to those who had played for Italy.

**1956**  Each team can play one *oriundo* and one foreigner. Later the *oriundi* were limited to those who had played at least three games for Italy.

**1957**  More restrictions were introduced. No more new foreigners could be signed.

**1958**  Further restrictions were introduced for the *oriundi*. They had to be under 25 and be given a contract of at least three years. In the same year the FIGC allowed the free transfer of foreigners already in Italy. Every team could now have one foreigner, one *oriundo*, one *fuori quota*.

The only foreigner in Serie A in the 1958–9 season was José Altafini.

**1963** Each team could have three foreigners on their books, of whom only two could play at any one time. A tax had to be paid to the federation for each foreigner.

**1965** About-turn again. All foreigners including foreign managers were banned. The block was confirmed in 1966. The Italian-only period began, which lasted for fifteen years, during which the Italian team enjoyed a fair amount of success.

**1980** The borders were re-opened. Each team could sign one foreigner. The *oriundo* category was abolished (this time for real).

**1982** The foreigner limit was raised to two.

**1985–6** A new foreigner block was introduced.

**1987** Two foreigners were allowed again, per club.

**1988** The limit was raised to three.

**1992** Free movement for European players (within complicated limits). Only two non-European Union players per club.

**1995** *The Bosman Ruling*. All European Union citizens could move and work freely within the European Union – all 1992's limits were abolished. This led to a rash of European passports and Italian grandparents. A number of fake passports were produced around this time.

**May 2001** All restrictions on foreigners were removed (with some games still to play in the season).

**2004** Discussions begin on ways to limit the number of foreigners on the field, after Italy's failure in the 2004 European Championships.

# PICTURE CREDITS

1, 2, 3, 5, 8, 10, 11, 12, 16, 19, 20, 21, 22, 23, 26, 27, 28, 30, 32, 33, 34, 36, 38, 39, 42, 43, 44, 45, 46, 47, 48, 49, 50, 51, 52, 53, 55, 56, 57, 58, 59, 60, 61, 62, 63: Olycom, Milan.
4: Toni Furio.
6, 14, 15, 24, 40: John Foot.
7: Photo taken from a now-defunct site dedicated to spoof Moreno photos, 18.6.2002.
9: Copyright unknown.
13: Postcard. Gogito, Torino, Via Barbaroux, 26.
17: Nick Dines.
25: www.interfc.it/gallery/Meazza.asp.
29: Copyright unknown.
31: Copyright unknown.
35: Fondo Pasolini (www.pasolini.net).
37: www.solointer.3x.ro/.
41: www.sslazio2000.net.
54: Copyright *The Game of their Lives*. For information about the film see www.thegameoftheirlives.com and for merchandise www.astateofmind.co.uk.

# INDEX

Entries in **bold** indicate illustrations.